Corporate Finance Theory

Corporate
Finance
Theory

William L. Megginson
University of Georgia

ADDISON-WESLEY

An imprint of Addison Wesley Longman, Inc.

Reading, Massachusetts • Menlo Park, California • New York • Harlow, England
Don Mills, Ontario • Sydney • Mexico City • Madrid • Amsterdam

Acquisitions Editor: Joan Cannon
Developmental Editor: Elaine Silverstein
Project Coordination and Text Design: Interactive Composition Corporation
Cover Design: Kay Petronio
Art Studio: Interactive Composition Corporation
Electronic Production Manager: Eric Jorgensen
Manufacturing Manager: Hilda Koparanian
Electronic Page Makeup: Interactive Composition Corporation
Printer and Binder: RR Donnelley & Sons Company
Cover/Jacket Printer: Phoenix Color Corp.

For permission to use copyrighted material, grateful acknowledgment is made to the
copyright holders on pp. 532-534, which are hereby made part of this copyright page.

Library of Congress Cataloging-in-Publication Data

Megginson, William L.
    Corporate finance theory / William L. Megginson.
    p. cm.
    Includes bibliographical references and index.
    ISBN 0-673-99765-0
    1. Corporations—Finance. I. Title.
HG4011.M44 1996
658.15—dc20   95-54009
                                                CIP

Copyright © 1997 by Addison-Wesley Educational Publishers Inc.

0–673–99765–0

12345678910–DOC–99989796

Author Index

to accompany

Corporate Finance Theory

by William L. Megginson

Author Index

This book is dedicated to the memory of

Jason M. Verbrugge

(1967–1995)
Banker, son, brother, friend.

BRIEF CONTENTS

CONTENTS

PREFACE

A ny scientific discipline can be viewed as a collection of ideas that time has hallowed into facts. Ideas which seem to explain a given piece of objective reality will be subjected to empirical investigation, and those which pass these intellectual market tests become part of a discipline's core theory. Although financial economics is one of the youngest of the modern scientific disciplines—most people date its birth to the year 1958—its contribution to our economic understanding of the world has already been massive. Financial researchers have, as examples, (1) formalized the concept of informationally efficient capital markets, (2) explained the pricing of options and other derivative instruments, (3) described a modern theory of corporate governance, (4) showed how corporate debt and equity securities are valued in frictionless markets, (5) quantified investment risk, and (6) explained economically pervasive agency relationships in terms of predictable human behavior. Not bad for a thirty-something discipline!

The objective of this book is to survey the most important theoretical concepts in the field of corporate finance, and then to examine whether these theories have been supported by empirical research. This is designed to be primarily a conceptual book, and the focus will be on synthesizing the key empirical and theoretical literature. In fact, many readers will be surprised by the relative lack of equations and derivations, as compared to other upper-level finance texts. Further, there are few direct applications of the concepts discussed in the text to specific business cases. Instead, we concentrate on describing the key pieces of financial theory, and discuss how this body of knowledge has developed over time. This focus on core theory also explains why there are only nine (albeit often long) chapters in this text.

There are three principal target markets for this book. First, it is designed to be useful to business professionals (especially in investment or commercial banking) who have had advanced academic training in finance, but who wish to refresh their knowledge and/or "come up to speed" on current research. Second, the book is designed to be used in upper-level MBA corporate finance readings courses, or as the theory textbook for a case course. Finally, the book should prove useful as a reference source for finance, economics, and accounting doctoral students (and hopefully professors as well). While the book is designed for a reader who has had at least two corporate finance courses, we have tried to keep the writing nontechnical enough that a general reader will be able to at least follow the main threads of the discussion. Finally, this text is designed to be a general reference book for anyone wishing to find a listing of important citations for a given topic, so we have included multiple citations for almost all of the topics covered.

Several basic policies were followed in the writing of this manuscript to ensure consistency (and to keep the project manageable enough to be completed). These are listed and briefly discussed below.

1. Since the first person singular pronoun "I" and all its variants (me, my, mine) can be quite jarring when seen in print, the royal "we" (and its cousins us, our, ours) is used throughout the text, even though it is single-authored. Since a coauthored variant of this book (with Larry Gitman), aimed at an undergraduate audience, will be forthcoming within a year this artifice will become honest in due course.

2. We limit citations almost exclusively to published journal articles, rather than working papers or books. There are two justifications for this, the first being temporal self-defense. The number of working papers in wide distribution at any one time is truly enormous, and no mortal (certainly not this author) could hope to both stay completely current in this field and simultaneously write a literature review. The second reason for relying primarily on published journal articles is that these manuscripts have passed a very important market test—the blind reviewing process—and this cannot be said for either working papers or books.

3. In deciding which articles to select for citation or discussion in the body of the text, we relied on the following general rules. First, older (pre–1990) articles were selected primarily on the basis of their impact on subsequent research, roughly measured as the frequency with which they were cited in later studies. In selecting more recent articles for citation, we relied primarily on academic darwinism and concentrated on papers published in the more prestigious journals.

One further point requires explicit mention. The canny observer will soon notice a propensity towards self-citation in this text. This is not due to an inflated assessment of importance, but is merely a convenient way for an author to point to articles where a given point is described in greater detail or a particular argument is presented at greater length than can be justified in a survey text.

Anyone writing a new book for an established field attempts to differentiate, and we feel the following features of this text are unique:

1. The first chapter organizes our presentation of material the same way that financial economics has grown as a discipline—chronologically. We present the key building blocks of modern finance theory in the order they were presented in the literature, and we then show how each concept was developed and strengthened after the seminal papers were published.

2. Our second chapter—Ownership, Control, and Compensation—is unique among finance texts, and is presented as the first substantive chapter to stress how important corporate governance has become in modern business. This chapter also presents three models of corporate organizational structure (the open corporate form, the closed corporate form, and the industrial grouping model) that mirror actual patterns observed in, respectively, Great Britain and the United States, western Europe (especially Germany), and Japan and Korea.

3. We include a survey of the most important empirical and theoretical research on asset pricing models in our third chapter. This chapter also summarizes the literature on market efficiency—including discussions of variance bounds tests, the

noise trading literature, and recent research that suggests our received asset pricing models actually explain very little.

4. We adopt a "comparative corporate finance" perspective throughout this text, and incorporate discussions of international financial topics in all major areas. There is no separate "International Finance" chapter in the text, just as there is no longer any meaningful distinction between domestic and international finance in practice.

5. Our Chapter 4—Bond and Stock Valuation—includes several topics not usually covered in corporate finance texts, including debt maturity structure choice, bond covenants, the relationship between stock prices and corporate earnings numbers, and the impact of liquidity and taxes on security valuation. We also present a detailed analysis of the market microstructure literature.

6. We present a separate chapter (5) on option valuation and also incorporate option pricing concepts into our discussion of capital budgeting procedures in Chapter 6. Our discussion of capital budgeting also incorporates recent research documenting the value of these timing, flexibility, and production capability options.

7. Our chapters on capital structure, dividend policy, and financial markets all begin with a summary of "stylized facts," or patterns observed in actual corporate policies around the world. We find, for example, that there are significant industrial patterns in the leverage and dividend payout policies observed in all countries, even though these countries have widely varying average leverage and dividend levels.

Any new book is an experiment, and this is certainly true here. We welcome feedback on this manuscript from any and all sources, but are especially keen to receive the following information: (1) any factual errors in citation, attribution, or interpretation, (2) recommendations concerning topics to include or delete in any future editions that might evolve from this work, (3) feedback on how the book can best be used in academic or professional training courses, and (4) any tables, figures, equations or derivations which should be included in subsequent editions.

Finally, I wish to thank several people for their help in the development of this manuscript, beginning with my long-suffering family. This author is eager to once again become a husband and a father. Larry Gitman's role in this project has also been pivotal, as has Kirstin Sandberg's. I cannot thank either of them enough. Additionally, the staff at HarperCollins College Publishers—especially Joan Cannon—and the development editor for this book, Elaine Silverstein, have provided extremely valuable support. Finally, I wish to thank my University of Georgia colleagues for their support, encouragement, and understanding while I was writing this book. In particular, Marc Lipson and Steve Jones read and commented on (but cannot be held responsible for) large segments of the text when it was in a very rough form. Their assistance was crucial. All remaining errors are, of course, mine alone.

William L. Megginson
Athens, Georgia USA

August 1, 1995
w.megginson@cbacc.cba.uga.edu

ABOUT THE AUTHOR

William L. Megginson

Bill Megginson is an associate professor of banking and finance in the Terry College of Business at the University of Georgia, where he teaches entrepreneurial finance and international finance at the undergraduate and masters degree level. He also teaches a doctoral corporate finance theory course, and has served as the departmental graduate coordinator for seven years. During that time, he has chaired eight dissertations and twelve masters theses—most of which have examined corporate or international finance issues.

— · —

Professor Megginson's research interests include corporate governance, the impact of taxation on corporate financial policies, venture capital, and international finance—particularly share issue privatizations, project finance, and international syndicated bank lending. He has published ten refereed articles in several top academic journals, including the *Journal of Finance,* the *Journal of Financial and Quantitative Analysis,* and the *Journal of Money, Credit, and Banking.* His recent co-authored study documenting significant performance improvements in recently privatized companies won a Smith Breeden Distinguished Paper Award as one of the outstanding papers published in the *Journal of Finance* during 1994.

— · —

Dr. Megginson earned a B.S. degree in chemistry from Mississippi College in 1976. Following that, he worked for two years as plant chemist (and acting environmental chemist) at Cosden Oil and Chemical Company's styrene monomer plant in Carville, Louisiana. He then served for three years as analytical group leader at GHR Energy Corporation's Good Hope Refinery near New Orleans, Louisiana. During this time, he earned an MBA from Louisiana State University, graduating in August 1982. He then earned a Ph.D. in finance from Florida State University before joining the faculty at the University of Georgia in June 1986.

— · —

Professor Megginson has traveled extensively outside the United States, both personally and professionally. He has visited forty-one countries during his lifetime, and has lived in Spain and Pakistan. More recently, he has presented papers at academic conferences in Paris, Copenhagen, Milan, and Santiago.

The Role of Financial Theory and Evidence

For the third time today, you ask yourself, "why did I take this job?" As the newly-appointed Chief Financial Officer (CFO) of the Information Technology Development Corporation (ITDC), you have been charged with imposing orderly financial management on an inherently chaotic business system. Although relatively small by multinational corporate standards, with sales of $4 billion per year, ITDC operates manufacturing facilities in five countries, sells products and services in a dozen more, and routinely invests almost 10 percent of gross sales into research and development in laboratories on three continents. Perhaps the most challenging feature of ITDC, however, is the fact that the company's sales and assets have been growing at a compound annual rate of over 20 percent for the past five years, and this growth is likely to continue. Now you must learn to ride, and manage, this financial tiger or risk burnout at a very early age (just like your predecessor). Among the specific issues and challenges you have been asked to make a decision on are the following:

• Whether to immediately increase manufacturing capacity at the company's Silicon Valley production facility, at a cost of almost $100 million, or to delay building a new unit and run the existing facilities on an overtime basis for another year to see if demand for the plant's output remains strong or to see if interest rates might fall.

• Whether to adopt a risk management/hedging strategy to lock in (1) the price of raw material inputs for the company's production process, (2) the dollar value of the firm's foreign currency-denominated accounts receivables, and/or (3) the cost of borrowing money needed to fund the company's day-to-day operations.

• How best to secure financing for the aggressive capital investment spending program the company plans to execute over the next three years.

Internally-generated funds will be woefully inadequate, but ITDC's investment bankers have assured you that almost any type of debt or equity security the company might choose to issue would be favorably received by investors. You must weigh the dilution cost of issuing new equity against the additional burden that the interest payments on new debt would place on the firm's already-stretched cash flows from operations. You are also acutely aware that ITDC's current debt-to-equity ratio is already considered high by industry standards.

- You have been asked by ITDC's board of directors to recommend whether the company should adopt a new deferred compensation plan for the company's senior executives. Members of the board's Management Compensation Committee have recommended that the current plan—which relies almost exclusively on short-term stock options, along with salary and yearly bonuses—be augmented to include a deferred compensation plan that managers cannot receive unless they meet specific performance targets and remain with the company for several years. The clear intent of this new plan is to retain (and motivate) key employees, but some board members fear it might prove exceedingly costly.

- Several large institutional shareholders are pressing the company to increase the small cash dividend payout on the firm's common stock. Some are even recommending that the company begin repurchasing its own shares in order to increase the value of those which remain outstanding. The board has asked you to examine whether the company's expected earnings will be able to support a higher dividend payout and, if so, to recommend what the new dividend level should be. Before deciding on a share repurchase program, the board has asked you to determine whether the firm's stockholders have been earning a fair, risk-adjusted return on their investment, and then to predict what effect a share repurchase program would have on stock price and required return.

- Finally, as if all the above issues were not difficult enough, the board has confidentially informed you that a large American telecommunications company has approached ITDC's Chief Executive Officer with a merger proposal. This company seeks a friendly merger with ITDC, but has made it clear that a hostile takeover bid will probably follow if ITDC rejects its merger offer. You have been asked to determine whether the merger proposal is in the shareholders' best interests and, if not, to determine what steps ITDC can legally take to defend itself against these unwanted advances. You have also been asked to assess the likely reaction of ITDC's foreign joint venture partners—many of which are headquartered in countries where takeovers (particularly hostile ones) are rare—to an acquisition of ITDC by an American firm against which several of your partners compete ferociously.

Feeling lost and completely alone, you wonder whether modern corporate finance theory and empirical research can provide you with any practical guidance for overcoming the challenges you face. As we hope to show below, the answer to your question is an emphatic yes! We will draw on the major theoretical advances that have been made in recent years to present finance as both a practical business skill and a rigorous theoretical discipline. In many ways, finance is to business and economics what engineering is to basic science—the financial "engineer" draws upon his or her theoretical training to design practical solutions to real world business problems. The financial manager tries to obtain adequate funding for the company at the lowest possible cost, while the investment manager (or individual investor) attempts to achieve the highest possible financial return at the lowest risk. The competition of companies for funds and of investors for return ensures that, in well-functioning financial markets, capital will flow to firms with the most valuable investment opportunities and individual savers can achieve a competitive return for any given level of risk they want.

We can draw a further analogy between finance's relationship to business and economics and engineering's relationship to basic science. To develop their theoretical models, financial researchers typically assume an economic world without "frictions" such as taxes and transactions costs, just as scientists and engineers sometimes assume a natural world without frictions such as gravity, pressure, and energy losses. Specifically, most finance theories assume a world of **perfect capital markets** characterized by: (1) a large number of fully-informed buyers and sellers, no one of whom has the power to influence market prices; (2) the absence of market frictions such as taxes, fees, information-acquisition or other transactions costs; (3) unanimity of opinion concerning the future value of asset prices, interest rates, and other relevant economic factors (this assumption is often called "homogeneous expectations"); (4) perfectly competitive product and factor markets that are always in equilibrium; and (5) costless and instantaneous market access for all potential buyers and sellers. Theorists begin their work by assuming perfect capital markets, not because they believe real markets are frictionless, but because they are able to derive fundamental results in such idealized environments. The test of the principles so attained is how well they explain real financial markets, where taxes, transactions costs, bankruptcy costs, and vastly different information sets between market traders are all too real.

While modern finance theory was developed largely in the United States and Great Britain, the principles are applicable in any market economy, and in recent years a truly global system of financial markets has emerged. Today an American corporation may fund its working capital needs by borrowing from a French bank operating in the United States; and that same American company may finance a new plant being built in Indonesia with capital obtained by selling dollar-denominated Eurobonds to institutional investors in Asia, the Middle East and Western Europe. Similarly, a Japanese company setting up shop in the U.S. may issue revenue bonds to American investors and then employ a British investment banking firm to swap the dollar cash flows the firm receives for a yen-denominated payment stream. At the same time, investors are increasingly able to safely and quickly move their money anywhere in the world in search of the highest possible risk-adjusted return. Furthermore, this process of internationalizing finance seems certain to continue, and may well intensify. The collapse of communism in eastern Europe and the former Soviet Union, the embrace of market-oriented economic policies in Latin America, southeast Asia, and even China, and the spread of large-scale privatization programs in Europe (and elsewhere) clearly signals that the role of financial markets and financially-trained managers is likely to increase dramatically during the working career of anyone reading this book.

Our objective as authors is to present the most important financial concepts that underlie current practice in a clear, yet systematic, manner and to explain how these concepts are applied to solve business problems both in the United States and in international markets. Our basic approach throughout this book will be to first present these theoretical models and then to describe how actual financial practice has evolved to meet specific business needs. We will generally introduce a topic conceptually, then discuss the academic research that has been directed toward examining the topic, and finally conclude by linking the conceptual issue to a real corporate finance application with a "real world" example or with a specific policy prescription.

1.1   BUILDING BLOCKS OF MODERN FINANCE THEORY

In this section we will describe twelve major building blocks of modern finance theory. As mentioned above, financial practitioners use these conceptual building blocks to first analyze, and then design, practical means to address real business challenges. As is true for most good theoretical models, these building blocks are both easy to understand and intuitively appealing—they make sense and they provide a powerful tool for explaining objective reality. We will present these building blocks in the chronological order in which they were developed in the academic literature. Experience has taught us that the best way to describe how finance has developed as a profession is to describe how each major new theoretical advance grew out of, and provided reinforcement for, existing knowledge. These building blocks have stood the test of time and, while they will surely be revised and refined in the future as new research and feedback from actual practice becomes available, they will almost surely not be discarded or rendered obsolete.

1.1.1 Savings and Investment in Perfect Capital Markets

In the early decades of this century, the famous American economist Irving Fisher developed the basic principles of investment and consumption in a world with and without well-functioning capital markets. Fisher (1930) shows how capital markets increase the utility both of economic agents with surplus wealth (savers) and of agents with investment opportunities that exceed their own wealth (borrowers) by providing each party with a low-cost means of achieving their goals. Savers can earn a higher return by lending on the capital market than they could by seeking out individual borrowers, and borrowers can obtain inexpensive financing without incurring search costs. The net result is that savers choose to save more than they otherwise would without capital markets and borrowers can obtain more, lower-cost, financing than they could if forced to search for funding on their own. Total saving and total investment in an economy is therefore greater than it would be without capital markets, and this is achieved without making any individual agent less satisfied, even as several agents can significantly increase their utility.

Fisher's work provided yet another extremely important result that later researchers were able to build on. The **Fisher Separation Theorem** demonstrates that capital markets yield a single interest rate that both borrowers and lenders can use in making consumption and investment decisions, and this in turn allows a separation between investment and financing decisions. Businesses and individuals with access to productive investment opportunities should accept all projects whose return is greater than or equal to the market interest rate, and they should then turn to the capital market for any funding they cannot provide internally. Borrowers do not have to consider the consumption preferences of individual investors—they merely have to earn the market interest rate. Savers likewise do not have to search out borrowers making investments of a particular type (with a preferred maturity date or cash flow pattern). Instead they can invest in any of several projects via the capital market and obtain any desired pattern of consumption over time simply by redeeming their stakes in these projects or selling them to other investors.[1]

Without this separation of investment and financing decisions result, firms would have to tailor their investment decisions to the preferences of individual investors, and the large, modern corporation with its own legal identity and infinite time horizon could never have come into existence. In fact, as we will see later, one of the most significant problems confronting small businesses around the world is that they usually cannot make this separation. Instead, they are almost invariably viewed as mere extensions of their entrepreneur/founders, and are thus unable either to raise capital in their own right or to establish an existence separate from their individual owners. Partly for this reason, business life around the world is dominated by a relative handful of large, professionally-managed, limited liability companies, that have many widely dispersed shareholder/owners and which can tap a variety of financing sources. The most successful of these **open corporations** have also devised solutions to the set of problems that typically accompany size and dispersed ownership (see agency costs below).

The basic Fisherian principles of investment and consumption were refined into effective analytical tools for investment and corporate financial decision-making by several authors.[2] In particular, an essential tool of modern financial analysis is the discounted cash flow (DCF) method of assigning current dollar valuations to one or a stream of cash flows to be received in the future. This is the principal method investors use for valuing stocks and bonds, and it is also the basic procedure used in capital budgeting decision-making within a corporation. Without DCF analysis, modern finance could not exist.

1.1.2 Portfolio Theory

The next major advance in finance theory occurred when Professor Harry Markowitz (1952) published his famous article laying out the basic principles of portfolio theory. Although this paper is primarily a statistical analysis, the essence of rational portfolio allocation is captured in the phrase "don't put all your eggs in one basket." Markowitz shows that as you add assets to an investment portfolio the total risk of that portfolio—as measured by the variance (or standard deviation) of total return—declines continuously, but the expected return of the portfolio is a weighted average of the expected returns of the individual assets. In other words, by investing in portfolios rather than in

---

1. For an excellent discussion of Fisher's results, and of their relevance to real investment and financial decision-making today, see chapters 1 and 2 of Copeland and Weston (1988). We will also discuss the theory of real investments in much greater depth in the capital budgeting and investments chapter.

2. Fisher's work was extended into the field of security analysis first by John Burr Williams (1938) and then later Durand (1952) and other authors. Fisherian principles were applied to corporate decision-making by several researchers, including Hirshleifer (1958) and Rubinstein (1973).

individual assets, investors could lower the total risk of investing without sacrificing return. This principle is demonstrated graphically in Figure 1.1.

As often occurs once an important article is published, Markowitz's results seemed to have the ring of truth—in fact, they seemed intuitively obvious, though he was the first person to present portfolio theory in a structured and consistent manner.[3] His primary theoretical contribution was to prove that the unique, individual variability in an asset's return (unsystematic risk) shrinks to insignificance as that asset's weight in a portfolio declines, and in a well-diversified portfolio the only risk that remains is that which is common to all assets (systematic risk). It is this covariance risk remaining after diversification has washed out the effects of individual asset risks that an investor must bear and be compensated for, because there is no effective method of eliminating it. Similarly, it is only the covariance of each asset's return with the return of other assets that is important to investors, who would be willing to pay a higher price for assets with a low covariance with other assets (a negative covariance would be even better) than for high-covariance assets. Therefore, the Markowitz portfolio selection rule is to pick stocks with the highest return to risk (covariance) ratios, and combine these stocks into **efficient portfolios**—where risk is minimized for any given level of expected return or, conversely, where return is maximized for any given level of risk.

Markowitz also presented the basic techniques for measuring and describing correlation, covariance, standard deviation and total variance in a portfolio setting. In fact, the terms and symbols he used are the same ones used today. As important as this article was, however, it did not in and of itself constitute a useful positive economic theory describing how capital markets quantify and price financial risk. That achievement would come a decade later, when Sharpe (1964) would add two critical pieces to the Markowitz efficient portfolio to develop (with Lintner (1965) and Mossin (1966)) the Capital Asset Pricing Model, or CAPM. This is described in section 1.1.5 below.

1.1.3 Capital Structure Theory

As upper-level finance students or professionals, you have surely studied the Modigliani and Miller (M&M) capital structure irrelevance propositions. Like most people, your first reaction was probably to consider these models to be working definitions of "esoteric research"—true in a world of perfect theory but useless in the practical world of real business decision-making. In fact, the article by Modigliani and Miller (1958) remains a surprisingly robust and vibrant description of financial market equilibrium almost fifty years after first being presented. Like the ideal gas laws of physics, the M&M model describes how a system will work without frictions, such as gravity in physics and transactions costs (brokerage fees, taxes) in finance. While this idealized world clearly does not reflect objective reality, it is possible to add elements of the "real world" one by one and see how the theory's predictions will change until a working model of reality emerges. With this in mind, let's examine the basic M&M model and then see how well it adapts to more realistic assumptions.

The central point of the M&M model is that the economic value of the bundle of assets owned by a firm derives solely from the stream of operating cash flows those assets produce. It is the stream of operating cash flows (profits) expected to be generated by

---

3. In fact, the work was important enough to make him one of the first finance professors (along with Merton Miller and William Sharpe) to be awarded the Nobel Prize in Economics in 1990.

FIGURE 1.1

THE IMPACT OF DIVERSIFICATION ON PORTFOLIO RISK

As more assets are added to a portfolio, the total variance of portfolio return declines—precipitously at first, then more slowly as the number of assets in the portfolio reaches double digits. Inclusion of international assets causes portfolio variance to decline even more. In both cases, portfolio expected return is a weighted average of individual asset expected returns. If enough assets are added to the portfolio, its return variance will approach σ_m^2, the variance of return on the market portfolio.

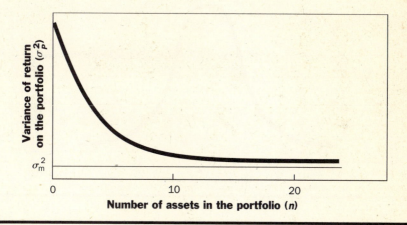

those assets that creates value—market participants will forecast the average level of these flows and then compute a present value based on the perceived riskiness of the cash flows. So what, you ask? These seemingly noncontroversial statements of how financial markets generate valuations say absolutely nothing about how those cash flows are split between equity and debt security-holders, and this is no oversight. Value comes strictly from the stream of economic profits—that core value cannot be increased or destroyed by repackaging into different investor income streams. This principle is demonstrated in Figure 1.2. The bell-shaped curve represents the stream of economic earnings, with a mean value of μ and standard deviation of σ, that results from the business activities of a firm. How this stream of earnings is repackaged by corporate executives into debt payments and equity payments cannot change the fundamental value of the earnings stream.

This **Law of Conservation of Value** is what underlies M&M's Proposition I, which says that "the market value of any firm is independent of its capital structure and is given by capitalizing its expected return at the rate ρ appropriate to its risk class." And if you buy Proposition I, Proposition II follows automatically. If the expected return on the firm's assets is the constant ρ, then the required return on levered equity must increase directly and linearly as risk-free debt is added to the firm's capital structure. Taken together, these two propositions establish that capital structure is irrelevant in a perfect capital market and the required return on a given firm's equity is computed directly from its debt-to-equity ratio and the required return for firms of its risk class. Or, to turn these propositions around, *if* capital structure affects firm value or *if* the firm's

FIGURE 1.2

HOW VALUE IS CREATED IN THE MODIGLIANI-MILLER CAPITOL STRUCTURE MODEL

According to Modigliani and Miller (1958), the economic value of a firm is based solely on the expected value of the firm's stream of operating profits (with value μ) and the standard deviation (σ) of the probability distribution describing those returns. How this stream of expected returns is allocated among different investor classes (equity and debt) cannot change the fundamental value of the firm's cash flows.

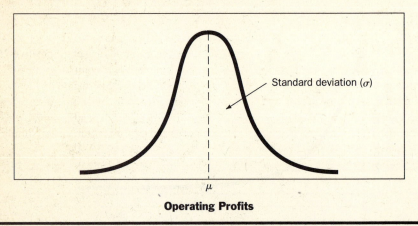

μ

Operating Profits

overall cost of capital (risk-adjusted required return) changes as debt is substituted for equity in the firm's capital structure, then it must be because one or more of the assumptions of the Modigliani & Miller model has been violated.

Since 1958, finance theorists (including M&M themselves) have examined how relaxing first one and then another assumption affects the capital structure irrelevance result.[4] The model held up surprisingly well until corporate taxes, personal taxes, and deadweight bankruptcy costs were included—these all change the model's implications, but do so in predictable ways.[5] The development of agency cost and asymmetric information models in the 1970s also led to a modification of the basic M&M model, but even today—after almost five decades of intensive theoretical and empirical re-

4. Interestingly, in their original 1958 article Modigliani and Miller provided an extension of their model to incorporate corporate income taxes, still obtaining a capital structure irrelevance result. It soon became obvious that this treatment was incorrect, however, and in M&M (1963) they published a "corrected" model of capital structure assuming corporate profits are taxed and interest on corporate borrowings is tax deductible. This model yielded the rather embarassing result that 100% debt financing was optimal (though the authors never quite admitted that implication of their paper), since this would minimize the government's tax claim on corporate profits and put more of these profits in private hands.

5. In addition to the M&M (1963) paper mentioned above, important extensions of the basic M&M model were provided by Hamada (1969) and Stiglitz (1974). Miller (1977) was also able to reestablish the original capital structure irrelevance result (at the individual firm level) in his insightful presidential address.

search—we can offer no simple, unambiguous answer to the question, "does capital structure matter?" Perhaps, in time, you can.

1.1.4 Dividend Policy

Not being content with revolutionizing capital structure theory, in Miller and Modigliani (1961) they addressed dividend policy—and came up with another irrelevance result. They show that, holding a firm's investment policy fixed, the payment of cash dividends cannot affect firm value in a frictionless market because whatever the firm pays out in dividends it must make up by selling new equity. This result is really fairly obvious when you think about it. If you assume that a firm is going to accept all positive-NPV investments projects whether it pays dividends or not, then it is committed to spending an amount *INV*, whatever its operating profits are in the coming period. Based on the actual level of operating profits for the year, *PROF*, the firm will either have a cash deficit, a cash surplus, or a zero cash balance at the end of the year depending upon whether profits are less than, greater than or equal to investment expenditures. For simplicity, let's assume that profits equal investment expenditures ($PROF - INV = 0$), and the firm has neither a cash surplus nor deficit at year-end. It can still pay any level of cash dividends it wants—but to make the cash flow identity hold, whatever cash the firm distributes as dividends must be replenished with the proceeds from an identically valued share offering!

It is this **cash flow identity**, which merely says total cash inflows (from operating profits and external financings) must equal total cash outflows (for investments and dividends), that drives the M&M dividend irrelevance model. If a firm's investment expenditures equal or exceed its operating profits, then the firm clearly has to issue new equity if it wants to pay dividends. And, in a world of frictionless capital markets, the firm is able quickly and costlessly to issue shares whenever necessary; and investors are indifferent between receiving a cash dividend, thereby causing the value of their shares to decline by an identical amount, and not receiving dividends. The logic also holds if the firm's profits exceed its investments. It can still pay any dividend desired and total market valuation will be unaffected, but the model's assumption of a fixed investment policy will be violated if the firm retains any of the surplus cash (in excess of investment) generated, because this actually results in additional investment (the firm's level of assets would increase). One must be very careful to hold investment fixed, but if this is done the M&M dividend irrelevance result is easy to understand.

Right now you are probably thinking, "OK, but the real world does not have frictionless capital markets." Fair enough, but it turns out that most "real" market frictions work against the payment of dividends. In fact, it is much easier to show why firms should not pay dividends than it is to show why they should! As examples, consider what happens to the irrelevance model if you assume that: (1) rather than being able to issue new equity without cost, firms must pay substantial fees to investment bankers to float a new share issue; (2) investors must pay income taxes at their top marginal rate on all cash dividends received, but can defer taxes on share price gains for many years; and (3) the stock market response to the announcement of new equity issues is almost always negative (the announcing firm's stock price falls). All three assumptions are in fact true in the U.S. financial system, yet each year American corporations pay out roughly half of their earnings as cash dividends. Why, then, do almost all large American (and European and other non-U.S.) companies pay dividends when theory suggests they should not?

There are two answers to this question. The quick, but honest, answer is that we are not entirely sure either why firms begin paying dividends or why there is such a pronounced regularity to dividend payments both within an industry and within a country. The second answer is that the simple M&M dividend model did not allow either for agency problems between corporate managers and shareholders or asymmetric information between those same two groups. Once these two elements of reality are incorporated into the perfect capital markets model of M&M, much more of the actual pattern of dividend payments becomes explainable. Incorporating positive costs to issuing new equity into the model also provides a rationale for rapidly-growing firms to choose to retain most of their earnings, while mature companies with fewer investment opportunities might choose to have a higher dividend payout. We can therefore conclude that the state of dividend policy theory is in flux—we can explain much of what we see in the financial world around us, but important basic questions remain unanswered.

1.1.5 Asset Pricing Models

It can be said that finance became a full-fledged, scientific discipline in 1964, when Sharpe published his paper deriving the **Capital Asset Pricing Model** (CAPM).[6] This model was revolutionary in that, for the first time, financial economists could describe and quantify what "risk" was in a capital market and specify how it was **priced** (what extra return would investors expect to receive for bearing this risk). In scientific terms, theorists could rigorously describe what constitutes capital market **equilibrium** (where there is a balance between supply and demand, and there is no tendency for prices to change) and this, coupled with the M&M dividend and capital structure models, meant that finance had robust theories for both the capital markets and the corporate finance sides of the field.

As mentioned in section 1.1.2 above, the CAPM assumes that investors hold well-diversified portfolios within which the **unsystematic risk** (asset-specific risk that can be diversified away) of individual assets is unimportant. Only the systematic risk of individual assets is important, and the systematic risk of the portfolio is a weighted average of the risks of the assets in the portfolio. As the name implies, **systematic risk** refers to an asset's (or portfolio's) sensitivity to economy-wide factors such as interest and exchange rates, inflation, and business cycle fluctuations. Since these factors influence all financial assets (to varying degrees), portfolio diversification will not eliminate or even reduce systematic risk, and investors will therefore demand a premium—in the form of a higher expected return—for holding risky assets. Obviously, the greater an asset's systematic risk, the higher will be its required rate of return.

So far, we have said nothing that would have been considered either new or surprising to a pre–1964 audience. Sharpe's main contribution was to uniquely define systematic risk and to specify exactly how investors can trade off risk and return. He did this by assuming investors can either invest in risky assets, such as common stocks, or in a risk-free asset, such as a treasury bill. Rational portfolio selection means that investors

---

6. Similar financial models were also developed almost simultaneously by Lintner (1965) and Mossin (1966).

will choose to invest only in efficient portfolios—those where risk is minimized for any given level of return or, conversely, return is maximized for any given level of risk. Sharpe then pointed out that, since investors can invest in either the risk-free asset or in risky asset portfolios, there is one unique risky asset portfolio that dominates (is superior in either risk or return, or both) all others, and he labeled this the **market portfolio**, M.

This leads to a fundamental result—all investors will allocate their wealth into some combination of the risk-free asset and the market portfolio, and the slope of the line measuring this trade-off between risk and return is called the **capital market line** (CML). This relationship is demonstrated in Figure 1.3. Highly risk-averse investors will allocate most of their wealth into the risk-free asset, and will thus lie on the bottom left side of the CML; while less-risk-averse investors will allocate most of their wealth to the market portfolio and will therefore lie higher up and to the right in risk/return space on the CML. Truly risk-tolerant investors can even borrow money at the risk-free rate and invest more than their total wealth in the market portfolio, thus taking them far up and to the right on the CML. In other words, investors can attain any desired level of risk, and still earn a competitive return, simply by allocating their wealth between the risk-free asset and the market portfolio.

Sharpe's final contribution was to point out that, in equilibrium, every asset must offer an expected return that is linearly related to the covariance of its return with expected return on the market portfolio, R_m . He defined this covariance as beta, β, and the beta of an individual asset j as β_j.[7] To be included in the market portfolio, every individual stock j will sell at a price that yields investors the appropriate expected return, $E(R_j)$, implied by its level of systematic risk and the current return on a risk-free asset, R_f. Mathematically, the CAPM can be expressed as in Equation 1.1 below:

$$E(R_j) = R_f + \beta_j(R_m - R_f) \tag{1.1}$$

In this formula, the quantity $R_m - R_f$ is called the **market risk premium**, and represents the additional expected return investors require to be willing to hold a broadly-diversified equity portfolio rather than simply holding the risk-free asset. Therefore, in words, the CAPM says that an individual asset's expected return is equal to the risk-free rate plus the product of the asset's beta and the market risk premium.

Sharpe's work touched off a torrent of academic research aimed at testing whether the CAPM accurately described objective market reality. This work also led to Sharpe being awarded, along with Harry Markowitz and Merton Miller, the Nobel Prize in Economics in 1990. And the early verdict on the CAPM was quite positive, although basic problems of measuring systematic risk and computing expected returns based on actual historical returns quickly became apparent (and these problems still bedevil researchers). Various studies documented a trade-off between an individual stock's systematic risk and its required return, though the trade-off was not quite linear and the return on the **zero-beta asset** (the asset with zero systematic risk) seemed too high.[8] As these and other "anomalies" came up, researchers modified the basic CAPM to try to account for inconsistencies. As examples, Black (1972) developed a CAPM that did

---

7. The CAPM will be derived more rigorously in Chapter 3: Risk, Return, and Market Efficiency.

8. For a survey of early CAPM research, see Jensen (1972). An excellent specific example of this early research can be found in Fama and MacBeth (1973).

FIGURE 1.3

THE CAPITAL MARKET LINE (CML) WITH A RISK-FREE ASSET

This figure graphically demonstrates investor choice when faced with a risk-free asset yielding return, R_f. While a rational investor might otherwise pick any efficient portfolio on the curve BMD (for which return is maximized for any given level of risk), the presence of a risk-free asset means that all investors will instead seek to hold some combination of the risk-free asset and the market portfolio of risky assets, M, and will thus plot somewhere on the ray R_fM. Their exact positions on this ray will be determined by personal risk preferences.

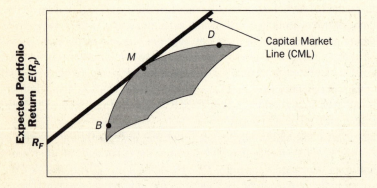

Standard Deviation of Returns $\sigma(R_p)$

not assume the availability of a risk-free asset, Brennan (1970) incorporated personal income taxes into the model to create an **after-tax CAPM**, and Merton (1973) extended the single-period CAPM into a continuous time, multi-period setting with his **intertemporal CAPM**.

By the early 1980s, however, many people were convinced that the CAPM was not an adequate model to describe equilibrium in a modern capital market. To them it was clear that more than one "factor" had a pervasive influence on financial asset prices, and so the search for a multi-factor asset pricing model began in earnest.[9] This search culminated with Ross's (1976) **Arbitrage Pricing Theory** (APT), which holds that the expected return on a given asset is based on that asset's sensitivity to one or more systematic factors, rather than being based solely on the asset's covariance with the return on the market portfolio—as in the CAPM. The sensitivities of an asset's return to each factor's realization (how much the asset's return would change given a one percent increase in a factor) were called **factor loadings**, and preliminary research suggested that most common stocks were significantly influenced by between three and five factors.

---

9. A very strong theoretical challenge to the CAPM, at least to its testability, was delivered by Roll (1977). This was followed five years later by an empirical test of the CAPM which used a new methodology and concluded that the economic validity of this model could be rejected at any reasonable level of significance (see Gibbons 1982).

A major problem with the APT, which is still not solved, is that there is no prior specification of exactly what economic variables the factors represent. In other words, no one can say that the "first" factor represents changes in the level of interest rates, while the next factor represents changes in the level of industrial production, and so on. Instead, the factors and factor loadings are statistical values that come from subjecting large samples of security returns to an analytical technique called **factor analysis**, where systematic factors are extracted from return data based on statistical commonalties. Although several researchers have attempted to empirically tie APT factors to individual economic variables, these attempts have been only partially successful.[10] Therefore, asset pricing theory is currently in an unsatisfactory state: the CAPM, which is both self-contained and easily understandable, has been shown to have far less power to explain observed security returns than does the APT, but the newer multi-factor model cannot (at least cannot yet) be expressed in economically meaningful terms. And we, as textbook authors, are in something of a quandary because we must integrate discussions of "risk" throughout this corporate finance text, but the existing literature offers no clear-cut indication of how best to do this. As you will see, we adopt the attitude (as do most textbook writers) that "you can't beat someone with no one," and will continue to use the CAPM as our principal model for determining financial risk until a challenger is unambiguously crowned as the new champion.

1.1.6 Efficient Capital Market Theory

One of the most important papers in economic history was published by Fama in 1970. Fama presents both a statistical and a conceptual definition of an **efficient capital market**, where efficiency is defined in terms of the speed and completeness with which capital markets incorporate relevant information into security prices. In an informationally efficient market, security prices incorporate all publicly-available information about a company's products, profits, management quality and prospects, and if important new information about the company is publicly announced, prices will instantaneously change to fully reflect the impact of this new data. It bears repeating that, in Fama's model, efficiency is defined in terms of how well financial markets process information rather than how well they allocate capital in an economy or how economically they produce outputs from inputs. While this definition is awkward at first for most finance students, it won't be long before your mind will have to "translate" when it hears efficiency used in any other context.

Fama actually provides three definitions of efficiency—or, more accurately, three degrees of efficiency. In a **weak form** efficient market, security prices incorporate all relevant historical information. In other words, there is nothing to be gained by studying past trends in security prices because there is no prediction that can be drawn from them about the future course of price changes. Research has unambiguously supported weak form efficiency in almost all major U.S. financial markets, and this modest definition is alone sufficient to suggest that the various forms of "technical analysis" being purveyed by Wall Street financial analysts are complete nonsense. In a **semi-strong-**

---

10. The most important of these attempts was that by Chen, Roll, and Ross (1986). For examples of empirical tests supporting and rejecting the APT, see, respectively, Roll and Ross (1980) and Dhrymes, Friend, and Gultekin (1984).

form efficient market, security prices reflect all relevant, *publicly-available* information. This is stronger than weak form efficiency, in that it predicts that security prices will always reflect relevant historical information, and will react fully and instantaneously whenever new information is revealed in a public medium such as television, newspapers, government documents, or a wire service report. Academic research has also largely supported semi-strong form efficiency for most of the important U.S. financial markets, and perhaps the most dramatic practical demonstrations of this efficiency are seen during takeover battles, which have occurred with great frequency during the last ten years.[11] To nail down the intuition behind the efficient market hypothesis, let's digress briefly to examine how these dramatic contests reflect market efficiency principles.

What generally happens in, say, a **hostile takeover** contest is that one company, the bidder, makes a public offer to buy a controlling fraction of the shares of a second company (the target) for a fixed price, which has in recent years usually been 30–50% higher than the current price of the target's shares. The amount by which the offer price exceeds the pre-bid stock market price is called the **tender offer premium**.[12] This offer—which is made directly to the target firm's shareholders, effectively bypassing the target's managers and directors—establishes a firm price that any shareholder can sell his or her shares for, if the bid is successful. And what happens to the target's stock price during this period? It immediately jumps from the preannouncement level to a price very close to the bid price (if the bidder makes an offer to purchase all shares tendered) or to the weighted average of the bid price and the expected post-acquisition price of the remaining target firm shares if a partial bid (say, for 51% of the target's shares) is announced. The actual price set will be a function of the fraction of the target firm's shares the bidder wants to obtain, and will also be influenced by traders' expectations concerning the likelihood of a higher, competing bid being offered (in which case the post-announcement share price can be even higher than the bid price) or that the target firm's managers will be able to somehow block the bid from being consummated (in which case the target firm shares might not increase much, if at all). The key point is that the market price of the target firm's shares changes immediately after a takeover bid is announced, the actual price change embodies an informed forecast of the end result of the contest, and the post-announcement price does not then change further until new information is announced.

Fama's third level of market efficiency is called **strong-form** efficiency, and this is a degree of market omniscience which is indeed difficult to imagine. In a strong form efficient market, security prices incorporate all relevant information—public *and* private.

---

11. We should not leave the impression that support for the efficient markets hypothesis is even close to unanimous in academic circles, for it is not. This hypothesis is one of the most extensively tested propositions in all of economics, and during the past two decades an increasing number of unexplained phenomena have been documented. For examples of theoretical and/or empirical challenges to the efficient markets hypothesis, see Rozeff and Kinney (1976), Basu (1977), French (1980), Grossman and Stiglitz (1980), Banz (1981), Shiller (1981), Keim (1983), DeBondt and Thaler (1985), Lo and MacKinlay (1988), and DeLong, Shleifer, Summers and Waldmann (1990). Not surprisingly, at least as many articles supporting the efficient markets hypothesis could be cited. Rather than do this, we will simply refer the interested reader to Fama's (1991) survey article.

12. For an excellent empirical study that neatly lays out both the mechanics of takeover bids and the combined bidder and target stock returns over a twenty-year period, see Bradley, Desai, and Kim (1988).

In such a market, the shares of the target firm described above would change in value as soon as the bidding firm's managers decided to make the takeover bid, rather than immediately after it was publicly announced. As another example, in a strong form efficient market a company that experienced an unexpected drop in quarterly profits would see its share price decline as soon as the earnings change was discovered by the firm's own accountants, rather than after it was publicly announced. Both research and common sense indicate that strong form efficiency usually does not hold in real world financial markets. The clearest evidence we have of this is the finding that corporate **insiders** (officers and directors) can and sometimes do earn excess profits from trading on information about unexpected changes in corporate earnings, dividends and investment policies before these are publicly announced. Outside investors who try to mimic insider trades after these are publicly announced earn only normal returns.[13]

In spite of the fact that strong form efficiency does not generally hold, Fama's **Efficient Market Hypothesis** has revolutionized our view of how financial markets work. Because competition among traders ensures that security prices accurately reflect all relevant information, market prices can be "trusted." Investors can rely on efficient markets to ensure that they will not be taken advantage of by better-informed traders, corporations can assume that they will be able to issue new securities without having to fear that these will be "irrationally" priced, and government policy-makers can (but often don't) rely on financial markets to allocate investment capital to its highest and best use. In many ways, this hypothesis has provided the theoretical underpinnings for the worldwide shift towards greater reliance on market-oriented economic policies and on capital market financing (as opposed to government direction of investment flows) that has occurred in recent years and which, if anything, seems to be accelerating.

1.1.7 Option Pricing Theory

As will become clear in the following sections, finance theory made greater strides during the decade of the 1970s than during any comparable period, before or since. Within three years of the publication of Fama's efficient markets paper, Black and Scholes (1973) published an article describing the model for pricing stock options that still bears their names.[14] The **Black-Scholes Option Pricing Model** (OPM) was a genuine breakthrough because it provided a closed-form solution for pricing put and call options that relies solely on five observable (or at least readily calculable) variables: the exercise price of the option, the current price of the firm's stock, the time to maturity of the option, the variance of the stock's return, and the risk-free rate of interest. All prior models had required a specification of either the *average* investor's utility function or the *expected* return on the market portfolio, or both. Since publication of the OPM coincided with the 1973 opening of the Chicago Board of Options Exchanges (CBOE), it was immediately put to—and quickly passed—an important market test. Options trading proved wildly popular; and within a decade of its founding, the volume of stock options trading on the CBOE regularly exceeded cash market trading volumes in the underlying stocks themselves.

---

13. See especially the series of articles by Seyhun (1986, 1988a, 1988b, 1990).

14. Almost simultaneously, Merton (1973a) published a theoretical article establishing basic dominance rules for the pricing of different types of options.

This is not to say that the OPM worked perfectly. Very quickly it was discovered that a variety of systematic biases were present in the pricing model, particularly when it was used to price deep **in-the-money** and **out-of-the-money** options (where the current stock price was, respectively, much greater than or much less than the exercise price of the option).[15] Furthermore, the basic OPM assumes that stocks do not pay dividends, and can yield significant pricing errors if applied to stocks making large nominal dividend payments. In addition, the OPM was developed for **European options**—which can only be exercised on the day the option expires—but virtually all real options traded are **American options** that can be exercised at any time prior to and including the expiration date. In spite of these difficulties, the OPM (and its later derivatives) has proven itself to be an amazingly robust and accurate model for pricing options on all types of financial assets.

Option pricing theory has also dramatically impacted financial practices outside of the narrow field of pricing stock options. For example, the opportunity to make high net present value investments in such things as research and development or in commercializing a hot new technology can be viewed as a **growth option**.[16] Since these options will often be immensely valuable to any company that can generate them, traditional capital budgeting techniques have had to be modified to account for the strategic necessity of seeking out and exploiting growth options. The logic of option pricing theory has also dramatically impacted the entire field of management compensation. Today, virtually all large American companies have performance-related incentive compensation contracts (that rely heavily on stock options) for their top executives that directly tie the net pay of corporate managers to the wealth changes experienced by company shareholders.[17]

Finally, option pricing theory has proven to be a useful tool for analyzing any situation where a corporation or individual wants to ensure against the risk of an adverse price change without giving up the opportunity to profit if prices change in your favor. Since an option gives the owner the right, but not the obligation, to exercise a trade, it is an ideal tool to use for many **hedging activities** (protecting company costs or revenues from adverse price movements). For example, an American exporter who has a German mark-denominated accounts receivable that will be paid in sixty days is exposed to the risk that the dollar will appreciate in value relative to the mark (DM, for Deutsche Mark) over that period. If this were to occur, the DM-denominated payment could be exchanged for fewer dollars than expected, and the exporter would suffer a loss. On the other hand, if the mark were to appreciate relative to the dollar, the DM receivable would increase in dollar value and the exporter would enjoy a windfall dollar profit. The exporter can ensure against the risk of a dollar appreciation, and still keep open the opportunity to profit from a dollar depreciation, by purchasing a DM put option today with a 60-day maturity. If, by the payment and expiration date the dollar has increased

---

15. Some of these pricing relationships were pointed out by Black and Scholes (1972) themselves. For additional references on early option research, see the Smith (1976) survey.

16. The first author to use the phrase "growth options" in a corporate investment context was Myers (1977). Option pricing was more fully integrated into capital budgeting decision models by Brennan and Schwartz (1985), Majd and Pindyck (1987), and Ingersoll and Ross (1992).

17. For example, Walkling and Long (1984) show that the value of executives' stock and option holdings often exceeds their annual salaries and bonuses by ten times or more.

in value, the exporter will exercise the put option and will sell the DM received for dollars at the option exercise price. If, on the other hand, the dollar has depreciated, the exporter will allow the option to expire unexercised and will instead sell the DM received at the higher, open market price.

1.1.8 Agency Theory

Prior to 1976, finance theorists generally used the standard **economic model of the firm** to describe corporate behavior. This model viewed the firm as a "black box" that processed inputs into usable outputs and that responded rationally to economic incentives.[18] Little thought was given to the motivations of the managers who ran the firm—in fact, it was usually assumed that the company was controlled and operated by a single, wealth-maximizing entrepreneur/owner whose incentives were identical with those of the firm and any outside shareholders. While some theorists had tried to expand this model of the firm to account for the fact that most corporate activity was undertaken by large companies with professional managers (rather than entrepreneur/owners) and numerous, widely-dispersed shareholders, even these models generally assumed that managers would always act in the best interests of the shareholders.

The fundamental contribution of the **agency cost model of the firm** put forth by Jensen and Meckling (1976) is that it incorporates human nature into a cohesive model of corporate behavior.[19] In the Jensen and Meckling model, the "firm" is a legal fiction that serves merely as a **nexus of contracts** for agreements between managers, shareholders, suppliers, customers and other parties (including employees). All the parties are consenting adults who act in their own self-interest, and fully expect all other parties to act in theirs. In other words, it is a model that relies on rational behavior by self-interested economic agents who understand the incentives of all the other contracting parties, and who take steps to protect themselves from predictable exploitation by these parties. The agency cost model often strikes the new finance student as being rather cold-blooded, and idealists will always find it difficult to accept, but even the most casual observer of modern corporate life (or student of human history) will recognize that the model provides an objective, scientific description of how investors actually allocate capital and how corporate managers actually make decisions.

Jensen and Meckling begin their analysis by asking what happens when an entrepreneur/owner decides to sell a fraction α of the ownership of the firm to outside investors. Initially, the entrepreneur owns 100% of the stock in the company and bears all the consequences (or reaps all the rewards) of his or her actions. If the entrepreneur spends corporate funds on **perquisites** such as lavish office furnishings, corporate jets, or extended vacations, these costs are borne solely by the entrepreneur. But as soon as the entrepreneur sells a fraction α of the firm's stock to outside investors, he or she no longer bears the full cost of perquisite consumption but rather only $1 - \alpha$ of the cost. Since perquisite consumption is pleasurable and hard work generally is not, a decline in the cost of the former and a decline in the personal benefit from the latter will cause the

---

18. For one of the most readable and tightly reasoned examples of this literature, see Alchian and Demsetz (1972).

19. Since its publication, this has become one of the most widely-cited recent articles in all of economics.

rational entrepreneur to work less and consume more perquisites as his or her stake in the firm is reduced.

Unfortunately for the entrepreneur, outside investors are perfectly aware of these incentives and will only offer to buy shares from the entrepreneur at a price that reflects the induced decline in the value of the shares after the entrepreneur's stake is reduced. This means that the entrepreneur will bear all of the **agency costs** that arise when a sale of equity leads to a separation of corporate ownership and control. In the new situation, the entrepreneur becomes an *agent* of the shareholder-owners, and should theoretically work solely to further the owners' best interests, but both parties understand that there is an inherent conflict of interests in this or any other agency relationship. Furthermore, since the entrepreneur will bear all of the agency costs of the new relationship (in the form of a discount on the price that shares can be sold), he or she also has an incentive to minimize these costs.

This can be done in one of two ways. First, the entrepreneur can take various steps to credibly *bond* his or her behavior after shares are sold. For example, the entrepreneur can retain a larger-than-desired stake in the firm after an equity issue, or can sell outside investors shares with voting rights—thereby providing investors with a means to remove the entrepreneur from office if performance is unsatisfactory. The dollar values of all these steps taken by the entrepreneur are referred to as **bonding expenditures**. Second, the entrepreneur can promise to make (or allow outside investors to make) **monitoring expenditures** such as paying outside auditors to inspect the company's accounts, buying insurance for the firm's assets, or paying ratings agencies to rate the firm's bonds. The dollar value of the total agency costs remaining after these monitoring and bonding expenditures is referred to as the **residual loss**, which is the irreducible cost of separating ownership and control in large modern corporations. Since these very same companies have generally prospered relative to 100% owner-operated firms, the agency cost model realistically describes both the costs and benefits of modern corporate life.

Jensen and Meckling further fleshed out their model by demonstrating both how issuing outside debt can help overcome the agency costs of issuing equity, and how the presence of too much debt can generate an entirely different set of agency problems. This helped convert their work into a full-fledged model of corporate capital structure, as well as one of corporate governance; and this theory also helps explain why investors demand—and corporations are willing to pay—regular cash dividends. Perhaps the most important application of the agency cost model, however, is in explaining the corporate control contests that burst on the scene so dramatically during the 1980s. By viewing the takeover battles of this period as contests between rival management teams for control of corporate resources, it is easy to understand (1) why firms might be undervalued in the first place (because they are controlled by inefficient but entrenched managers); (2) why potential acquirers might be willing and able to pay such a high price for the target's shares (investors value the target to reflect the poor performance of incumbent management and would value the firm more positively with a more competent management team in place); and (3) why target firm managers often resist takeover bids so vehemently (since they stand to lose both the financial and personal benefits that come with controlling a large corporation). As we will see later, several aspects of the takeover battles of the 1980s, especially the frequency with which target firm managers and directors adopted value-reducing defenses such as "poison pills" and other "shark repellents," can only be explained with an agency cost model that explicitly recognizes the conflict of interest between corporate managers and shareholders.[20]

Another very important vein of academic research concerning agency costs has examined the potential of **compensation policy** to overcome agency problems between corporate investors and managers. This literature—which began in earnest with Murphy (1985) and Brickley, Lease, and Smith (1988) and includes Jensen and Murphy (1990) and Smith and Watts (1992)—describes how a properly-structured package of fixed (salary) and contingent (bonus and option-related) compensation can help align the incentives of managers and shareholders. The classic problem in this area is that managers—who have most of their human capital at risk with their current employers—typically will prefer a far less risky investment strategy than will investors, who can costlessly diversify their wealth among many financial assets. A pay scheme that ties the payoffs to managers to the payoff received by shareholders can partially overcome this problem, and stock-option-based executive compensation packages have indeed become almost universal in large American corporations (though these are far less common in European and Asian companies). Many other compensation innovations have also been developed during the past fifteen years to align managerial and shareholder interests, including the incorporation of **golden parachutes** into executive contracts, which compensate the executive with a cash payment in the event of a change of control that costs the executive his or her job or diminishes the executive's responsibilities (see Lambert and Larcker 1985).

1.1.9 Signaling Theory

Signaling theory was developed in both the economics and finance literature to explicitly account for the fact that corporate insiders (officers and directors) generally are much better informed about the current workings and future prospects of a firm than are outside investors. In the presence of this asymmetry of information, it is very difficult for investors to objectively discriminate between high-quality and low-quality firms. Statements by corporate managers convey no useful information. Both "good" and "bad" firm managers will claim to have excellent growth and profitability prospects and, since only the passage of time will prove who was correct, low-quality firm insiders could profit by making false claims if these claims were believed by investors. Because of this asymmetric information problem, however, investors will assign a low average quality valuation to the shares of all firms. In the language of signaling theory, this is referred to as a **pooling equilibrium** since both high and low quality firms are relegated to the same valuation "pool".

Obviously, high-quality firm managers have an incentive to somehow convince investors that their firm should be assigned a higher valuation based on what the managers know to be superior prospects for the company. How do these managers convey this information to investors in a way that cannot be duplicated, or *mimicked*, by the

---

20. The literature in this area is truly vast, so we will only cite a few key articles here. See Fama (1980), Fama and Jensen (1983), Jensen (1986), and Jensen and Warner (1988).

managers of low-quality firms? One method would be for high-quality firm managers to employ a **signal** that would be costly, but affordable, for their firms but which would be prohibitively expensive for low-quality firms to mimic. One example of a potentially useful signal would be the payment of large cash dividends. This strategy would be expensive for the high-quality firm, because it would have to reduce its planned level of capital expenditures below what would be optimal in order to pay the dividend; but the firm would remain sufficiently profitable to both finance a high level of investment and pay out cash to investors. On the other hand, this signal would be prohibitively costly for the weaker firm to duplicate because the cost of paying the dividend would be too high in terms of the investment that would have to be foregone. Since investors understand these incentives, they would assign high values to firms that paid high dividends and would assign low valuations to firms that either paid low dividends or paid none at all. This result is referred to as a **separating equilibrium** because investors are able to assign separate, and economically rational, valuations to high- and low-quality firms. It is also a stable equilibrium, in spite of its deadweight cost in terms of foregone investment, because high-quality firms are able to achieve the higher valuations they desire and deserve, low-quality firms receive the valuations they deserve (but do not desire), and investors are able to confidently invest in firms with the most promising prospects.[21]

As you might have guessed from the discussion above, a signal must meet two tests to be useful in a market characterized by asymmetric information. First, it must be costly to the signaling firm in the sense that the company would not otherwise choose to adopt it except to convey information to investors (the signal itself must be a negative-NPV project that simply "burns money"). Second, the signal must be more costly for weaker firms to adopt than for stronger firms (ideally, it would be prohibitively expensive for weaker firms). Besides dividend payments, several other corporate or managerial actions have been modeled as signals. For example, in the first major financial application of signaling theory, Leland and Pyle (1977) demonstrate how entrepreneurs seeking external funding for an investment project could signal that the project had a high intrinsic value by retaining more of the project themselves than individual portfolio considerations would suggest as optimal.[22] Ever since this paper was published, theorists have employed insider shareholdings as a credible signal of insider beliefs in a variety of signaling models.[23] The same is true for the use of debt in a firm's capital structure—by employing more debt financing, insiders in highly profitable companies are signaling that their firms are relatively less vulnerable to bankruptcy or other forms of financial distress than are less profitable companies (See Ross 1977).

Signaling models are intuitively appealing because their predictions tend to make sense even to the casual observer (the same cannot be said for the original academic papers themselves, however, because they tend to be almost impenetrably mathematical

---

21. See Miller and Rock (1985) and Ambarish, John, and Williams (1987) for theoretical models where dividends serve as information signals.

22. The original economics papers on signalling were Akerlof (1970) and Spence (1973).

23. See, as examples, Downes and Heinkel (1982) and Grinblatt and Hwang (1989).

in nature). Unfortunately for fans of these models, however, they have not fared well in empirical testing because they typically predict exactly the opposite of what is actually observed corporate behavior.[24] For example, signaling models typically predict that the most profitable and the most promising (in terms of growth prospects) firms will also pay the highest dividends and will have the highest debt-to-equity ratios. In actual practice, however, rapidly-growing technology companies tend not to pay any dividends at all while mature companies in stable industries usually pay out most of their earnings as dividends. The same is true for capital structures—observed debt ratios tend to be *inversely* related to both profitability and industry growth rates. In spite of these problems, signaling models remain valuable tools in finance theory, both because the early models have been modified to more accurately reflect reality and because the predictions of these models in areas outside of dividend policy and capital structure have proven to be much more robust.

1.1.10   The Modern Theory of Corporate Control

Even as the 1980s will surely be remembered as the decade of mergers and acquisitions (M&A) in the business world, they were also a decade that witnessed the creation and development of the modern theory of corporate control in academic life. And these two developments were not independent events. Academic research provided a logical explanation of, and justification for, the wave of M&A activity, and the rapid pace of innovation and takeover activity provided academic researchers with a wealth of data and practical examples of theoretical concepts. The first major exposition of a truly modern theory of corporate control was presented by Bradley (1980), who studies the stock price performance of companies that are the targets of takeover bids. Bradley documents that these shares increase in value by approximately 30% immediately after a **tender offer** (a publicly announced offer to buy shares at a fixed price from anyone who "tenders" their shares) is announced, and then stays at about that same level until the acquisition is either completed or canceled. While these results were neither new nor particularly surprising, his third major finding was. He documents that those shares which are not purchased in a successful takeover, as will always occur if a bidder only purchases, say, 51% of the target's shares, drop in price back towards their initial value immediately after the takeover is completed.

So what, you ask? The reason this result is so important is because of what it says about the motivations of the managers of the bidding firm when they launch a takeover bid. Prior to Bradley's work, most observers assumed that bidding firms acquired majority stakes in target firms either to loot the assets of the target company or to profit from an appreciation of the target firm's shares after the takeover is announced. Bradley's results are inconsistent with either of these explanations. Since unpurchased shares remain above their pre-bid price even after a takeover is completed, it is clear that successful bidders are not looting their acquired companies because this would

---

24. For a good direct comparison between signalling and agency cost models of observed corporate behavior, see Smith and Watts (1992).

have caused the price of unpurchased shares to fall far below their pre-bid price. On the other hand, since the price of unpurchased shares falls below the tender offer price once the takeover is completed, it is obvious that bidders are suffering a capital *loss* on the shares they purchased rather than a gain.

It is in providing an explanation for his results that Bradley makes his greatest contribution. His theoretical model assumes that bidding firm managers will launch a tender offer primarily in order to gain control over the assets and operations of a target firm that is currently being run in a sub-optimal manner. Once the bidder gains control of the target, a new, higher valued operating strategy will be implemented and the bidding firm will earn a profit from operating the target more effectively. While this theory may not seem revolutionary, its implications are in fact profound both because of what it says about the economic benefits of an unrestricted takeover market and because it explains observed behavior in this market so well (at least in the United States). In Bradley's model, rival management teams compete for the right to control corporate assets. Inefficient teams are replaced by more capable ones, and the control of corporate resources naturally flows towards those people able to put the resources to their highest and best use. Therefore, a vibrant takeover market is good for the economy because it weeds out inefficiencies and concentrates corporate control in the most capable hands. Shareholders also benefit because they are the impartial referees who have the right to choose between competing offers for the shares they own. This competition means that rival management teams have to offer target firm shareholders most of the profit that is expected to accrue from improved post-acquisition performance in the form of a high tender offer premium. It is little surprise then that shareholders did so well during the 1980s, because the vibrant M&A market contributed to a tripling in the value of common stock from 1982 to 1990.

In the wake of the Bradley article, as well as an equally-influential survey article by Jensen and Ruback (1983), research into corporate control during the 1980s exploded along with the M&A market itself.[25] Theoretical articles explored numerous topics, such as the economic function of common stock voting rights, the proper role of corporate boards of directors, and the value of concentrated-versus-dispersed ownership structures. Empirical articles investigated a staggering variety of topics, such as examining the combined wealth effects of takeovers for both bidders and targets (positive), the stock price responses to various "takeover defenses" adopted by target firm managers (negative), the value of dual-share-class companies where one share class has vastly greater voting power (ambiguous), and the benefits to shareholders resulting from corporate adoptions of various stock-based incentive compensation plans for company managers (usually positive). Based on this body of literature, we in finance can confidently claim to have a sophisticated and remarkably accurate model of how corporate control and corporate governance actually works in the "real world," both in the U.S. and abroad.

---

25. A readable and informative survey of the takeover literature is provided in Jarrell, Brickley, and Netter (1988). Takeover defenses and poison pills have been studied by Jarrell and Poulsen (1987) and Ryngaert (1988), among others.

1.1.11 The Theory of Financial Intermediation

Americans have long prided ourselves on the size and efficiency of our national capital markets, and these indeed dwarf those of most other developed countries. For example, of the $1.502 trillion worth of securities issued on capital markets around the world in 1993, over two-thirds of this total ($1.048 trillion) was issued by American corporations and the vast majority of this was issued in the United States. Furthermore, American investment banking firms such as Salomon Brothers, Goldman Sachs, Morgan Stanley and Merrill Lynch tend to dominate the high-value-added areas of securities trading around the world even though they are no longer the largest in absolute size (Japan's Nomura Securities is several times larger than the largest U.S. securities firm). Academic finance has also mirrored this American emphasis on capital market financing of corporate activity, as virtually all our theoretical models assume that companies can issue securities on perfect (or at least informationally efficient) capital markets.

Within the past decade, however, it has become clear that capital market financing is often a much more costly and economically wasteful method of funding routine corporate activities than is financing via banks and other financial intermediaries. Commercial banks, in particular, seem to have a clear competitive advantage over capital markets for all but the very largest types of corporate fundings, and even here the development of syndicated lending techniques has allowed banks to raise vast sums of money quickly and quietly (see Megginson, Poulsen, and Sinkey 1995).

If you stop to think about it, the superiority of banks for most corporate financings is obvious. They are naturally equipped to raise investment capital cheaply and on a routine basis (by accepting deposits); they are staffed with trained professionals who understand both the techniques of credit analysis and the financial needs of specific markets; and they can offer business a full range of financial services beyond credit extension, including cash management, payroll services, data processing, factoring, leasing and even trust services for family-owned businesses. Most importantly, by establishing an ongoing relationship with corporate managers, bankers are able to become true corporate insiders who are able to assess and meet the financing needs of a growing corporation without having to disclose sensitive information to competitors and without having to overcome the informational asymmetries inherent in security issues on public capital markets. Largely because of these competitive advantages, commercial banks tend to dominate corporate finance in almost all developed and developing countries of the world except the United States.

The reason for this odd state of affairs is clear—bad public policy. The McFadden Act, passed by the U.S. Congress in 1927, prohibited interstate banking and effectively limited banks to operating within a single state (many state governments went even further and restricted branching within the state itself). Even though Congress finally passed legislation allowing interstate branch banking in 1994, the historical damage of the McFadden Act has been done and the U.S. has produced no banks with a nationwide reach comparable to that of Germany's Deutsche Bank, Japan's Dai-Ichi-Kangyo Bank (the world's largest in terms of assets), Britain's National Westminster or the other top European, Canadian, or Japanese banks. The Glass-Steagall Act, passed by Congress in 1934, also contributed to the neutering of American banks by legally separating commercial and investment banks. This meant that commercial banks operating in the U.S. were prohibited from owning the common stock of other corporations, underwriting the public sale of corporate securities, or engaging in brokerage services, while investment banks were prohibited from accepting deposits or making commercial loans. While this act promoted the growth of very strong American investment banks, U.S. commercial banks were put at a serious competitive disadvantage (which became particularly telling as corporate finance became more globalized during the post-World War II era). American corporations were also deprived of access to the same types of strong "merchant banking" firms their international competitors were able to tap for both investment and commercial banking services.

In academic circles, an early description of the informational advantages of financial intermediation (obtaining funding through an intermediary, such as a bank, rather than directly via capital markets) was provided in the same 1977 article by Leland and Pyle mentioned above. Several other articles that document large, negative returns to shareholders following the announcement of new security issues (particularly equity issues) by corporations reinforce the idea that capital market financing is inherently costly and disruptive.[26] James (1987) provides an important contribution to this literature by documenting positive returns to corporate shareholders following the announcement that a firm has obtained a loan from a commercial bank. Since all other corporate financing announcements are associated with negative or insignificant returns, this represents striking evidence of the uniqueness of bank lending. Since a bank presumably has direct access to a company's accounts and intimate contact with a company's executives, stock market participants clearly interpret the announcement that a bank will grant a firm credit as an important vote of confidence in that firm's prospects by an informed party.

James' work has since been extended by other researchers, who show both where financial intermediation is superior to capital market financing and, conversely, where various types of security market transactions—including the **securitization** (the repackaging and sale of bank loan products to public investors) of traditional bank loan products such as mortgages and car loans—will enjoy competitive advantages. It also seems safe to say that, over time, the American corporate financing scene will begin to look more like that of other developed countries—with banks assuming a greater role in funding routine corporate activities—even as these countries come to rely more on American-style capital market financing. In fact, the immense popularity of **privatization** programs around the world, wherein the national government sells shares of state-owned firms to private investors, has already propelled the growth of large stock markets in both developed and developing countries, and these programs seem on the verge of accelerating even more in the years to come.

1.1.12 Market Microstructure Theory

During the past fifteen years, and particularly since 1985, a startling amount of scholarly research has been focused on examining the internal structure and workings of different securities markets. This academic interest in **market microstructure** (the study of how securities markets set prices, compensate market makers, and incorporate pri-

---

26. See especially the excellent survey article by Smith (1986).

vate information into equilibrium price levels) in many ways only mirrors the importance that financial practitioners have always assigned to the costs of operating real capital markets. Unlike professors, securities dealers and investors cannot simply assume away the financial and opportunity costs of trading and the dangers of transacting with a potentially better-informed partner—they must establish workable trading mechanisms that allow for trading to take place in a manner that is equitable to (and protects the property rights of) all parties. Once academics brought the tools of economic analysis to bear on microstructure issues, it became clear that they had much to offer investment professionals in the way of explaining observed market realities.

Microstructure research can be classified into two separable, though related, streams of analysis. First, **market structure/spread models** study the relative merits of different market structures (monopoly specialist versus multiple dealer markets, electronic order book versus human dealer markets, etc.), and examine the determinants of the size of the bid-ask spread that dealers earn in different markets. Second, **price formation models** analyze how private information is incorporated into securities prices, and study—among other things—how trade size, aggregate trading volume, and price levels are related.

Although the first truly modern market structure/spread study was Ho and Stoll (1981), earlier works by Demsetz (1968) and Tinic (1972) describe the role that dealers play in providing liquidity to market participants, and Branch and Freed (1977) document bid-ask spreads on the two major exchanges. Ho and Stoll's innovation was to develop a model of an individual dealer operating under return and transactions uncertainty, and to document theoretically that part of the bid-ask spread charged by the dealer represented compensation for moving the dealer away from his or her preferred inventory level as a result of trading. This **inventory cost component** of the spread reflects the return required to compensate dealers for accumulating unwanted inventory, and represents a second component of the bid-ask spread—the first being the **order cost component**, encompassing the liquidity services dealers provide and the costs they incur in processing client buy and sell orders. Later, Ho and Stoll (1983) extend their single-dealer model into a multiple-dealer framework.

The next major market structure/spread model innovation occurred when Copeland and Galai (1983) demonstrate that dealers (market makers) must usually be compensated, in the form of a higher bid-ask spread, for the risk of dealing with a trader who has relevant, non-public information. This **adverse selection component** of the spread will increase whenever the risk of such trading increases, and a dealer who believes that the last trade he or she made was with an informed trader will increase bid and offer prices if the informed trader bought shares, and decrease prices if the trader sold. Glosten and Milgrom (1985) present a similar model and reach similar conclusions, while Glosten and Harris (1988) and Stoll (1989) examine bid-ask spreads empirically. Stoll finds that the average *realized* bid-ask spread is equal to only 57 percent ($0.57S$) of the *quoted* spread, S, and he further decomposes the quoted spread into its individual components: adverse information costs ($0.43S$), order processing costs ($0.47S$), and inventory holding costs ($0.10S$). Later studies have refined the methodology of decomposing bid-ask spreads into their constituent parts and inferring the pattern of trades from the observed pattern of spread revisions.

A second vein of the market structure/spread literature has examined the relative merits of different organizational structures for securities markets—particularly whether a monopoly specialist market such as the New York Stock Exchange (NYSE), where one dealer is charged with managing trading in a given stock) is operationally superior or inferior to a multiple dealer market such as National Association of Securities Dealers Automated Quotations (NASDAQ), and whether a physical exchange is required for efficient trading or whether a computerized (screen-based) market is optimal.[27] Although the weight of evidence seemed to be falling in favor of multiple dealer, screen-based systems, two papers by Christie and Schultz (1994) and Christie, Harris, and Schultz (1994) appear to document systematic collusion between NASDAQ market makers to keep spreads artificially high, thus casting doubt on a central premise of multiple dealer systems—that competition for order flow will result in minimum trading costs. On the other hand, Glosten (1994) makes a strong theoretical case that an electronic limit order book—where dealers publicly post their bid and offer prices and amounts—may be inevitable, and is in any case at least as efficient (usually more so) as any competing human dealer-based trading system.

The price formation literature grew out of the need to solve an apparent theoretical dilemma. Grossman and Stiglitz (1980) show that informationally efficient securities markets cannot exist, because there is no incentive for anyone to invest in information acquisition if relevant information is always costlessly available to all parties. Yet if no one has the incentive to acquire information, how will it become imbedded in securities prices? Kyle (1985) was the first author to present a viable model explaining how a trader with private information will profit by trading strategically in a multi-period setting. In the Kyle model, there are three types of traders—a single risk-neutral insider, random (uninformed) noise traders, and competitive risk-neutral market makers. Kyle shows that the insider will profit by making numerous small trades over time, hiding his or her trades in with the more common noise trader transactions, rather than by trying to make one big trade—which would naturally be viewed with suspicion by market makers and noise traders alike. Kyle thus presents a realistic, continuous time trading regime that incorporates all private information into prices by the end of trading, and which provides a rationale for the empirically observed negative relationship between trade size and trade price.[28] Later authors, such as Easley and O'Hara (1987), also show that trade size introduces an adverse selection problem into securities trading because, given that they wish to trade, informed traders prefer to trade larger amounts at any given price. Therefore, market makers will protect themselves by executing large trades only at less favorable prices.

A further extension of the price formation models is in explaining various intraday trading regularities that numerous researchers have documented, including a tendency for both trading volume and return variance to bunch at the open and close of trading (see Wood, McInish, and Ord (1985)). Admati and Pfleiderer (1988) present a model of intraday volume and price variability, where the U-shaped pattern of intraday trading volume arises endogenously as a result of the strategic behavior of liquidity traders and

---

27. Yet another, related stream of research has decomposed "liquidity" into at least three components—tightness (the cost of turning around a position in a short period of time), depth (the size of an order flow innovation required to change prices a given amount), and resiliency (the ability to rebound from informationless trades). See Kyle (1985) for a summary of this research and an in-depth description of these components.

28. For these and other reasons, Kyle (1985) has become the most widely-cited of all the market microstrucure papers.

informed traders. Their major theoretical innovation is to introduce discretionary liquidity traders who, like informed traders, can time their trades and also prefer to trade when market volume is greatest. This model provides an information-based rationale for the observed pattern of concentrated volume and volatility at the open and close. Later papers dealing with intraday trading patterns include Foster and Viswanathan (1990) and Brock and Kleidon (1992).

Taken as the sum of its parts, the market microstructure literature fits neatly into the evolving corpus of corporate finance theory.[29] It is based on rational, wealth-maximizing activity by informed agents; it assumes financial markets operate efficiently; and it explains an important real-world phenomenon in a rigorous, internally-consistent manner that provides guidance both to practicing managers and aficionados of the most esoteric academic research.

1.2   USING THE BUILDING BLOCKS TO SOLVE REAL BUSINESS PROBLEMS

A popular book of the 1980s was entitled **The Revolution in Corporate Finance** (Stern and Chew 1986), and it was an apt description of how the practical world of corporate financing had been (and continues to be) transformed by the modern, scientific principles outlined above. In the chapters immediately following we will explore how these theories have impacted the state of the practical financial art in the areas of capital market equilibrium (investments); bond, stock and option valuation; capital structure; dividend policy; and capital budgeting. We will also examine how practitioners use these basic theoretical building blocks to analyze and solve real business problems. To conclude this introductory chapter, we will now simply try to distill a few basic principles that the reader should keep in mind as he or she works through this book, and then sallies forth to begin a career in the challenging and demanding world of finance.

> **In pricing financial assets, only systematic risk matters.** Although the current state of asset pricing theory does not allow us to state definitively which economic factors are priced in financial markets, or even to specify how many factors are relevant, one thing is clear—only systematic, economy-wide factors that have a pervasive impact on all financial assets are important. Portfolio diversification works, and any risk that can be diversified away by investors will be. For the practicing finance professional, this is important both in corporate finance contexts—such as in capital budgeting—and in investment management decisions, such as in portfolio selection. In capital budgeting, the professional need only determine a candidate asset's systematic risk to compute an appropriate discount rate for use in an NPV investment analysis. Likewise, the professional charged with selecting various stocks for an investment portfolio can ignore the total variance of a stock's return and focus instead only on that asset's contribution to the total variability of the portfolio's return.

> **Trust market prices.** While only the most cosmic form of market efficiency would predict that all financial market prices accurately reflect fundamental economic

---

29. For surveys of the market microstructure literature, see the special issues of the **Review of Financial Studies** (1991, no. 3) and **Financial Management** (Winter 1992).

value all of the time, common sense, finance theory, and academic research all suggest that market prices embody an unbiased (and therefore accurate, on average) assessment of a company's current value and future prospects. Financial managers should view financial markets in general, and stock markets in particular, as expert consultants who provide advice free of charge. A financial market is a giant information processor that continuously evaluates corporate prospects, and expresses opinions by revising prices for corporate securities. This means that, if a company announces a new product or a new policy and is greeted by a sharp drop in its stock price, it would probably be wise to reconsider the policy before proceeding. Conversely, a favorable stock price change should help allay fears about the wisdom of a potentially risky new venture.

Furthermore, finance professionals should not take seriously the innumerable comments in the popular press that financial markets impart a "short-term bias" to corporate executives. This idea is similar to the proverbial "lie with a thousand lives," although there undeniably is a seductive plausibility to the notion that corporate managers who have to report earnings quarterly and answer to "greedy, myopic" shareholders will forego making long-term investments that might depress earnings in the short term. Fortunately, this argument can be refuted on both conceptual and empirical grounds. Conceptually, it is hard to see why common stockholders would ever have a short-term bias since they hold the corporate security with the longest term to maturity (infinity). If anyone should have a short-term bias, it should be creditors in general, and bankers in particular. Empirically, academic research has conclusively shown that stock prices rise when a company announces increased capital investment plans, as well as when increased research and development spending plans are announced. Markets aren't perfect, but investors play with real money and thus tend to be more objective than most commentators and less politicized than most government officials.

Emphasize investment rather than financing. Given the competitiveness of modern capital markets, the opportunities to create wealth through clever financing strategies are strictly limited. Although successful financial innovations do occur, these represent a minuscule fraction of the total volume of all corporate financings, and profit opportunities are competed away very quickly. Corporate executives should concentrate on creating and exploiting profitable investment opportunities rather than on finding ways to "beat the market." A company's long-term competitive advantage must ultimately be based on the quality of its assets and the creativity and competence of its employees, not on financial maneuverings.

On the other hand, company managers should be ready to exploit any profitable financing opportunities that do arise, even though these are likely to be fairly minor and quick to disappear. Real examples of such opportunities have been documented. For example, Kim and Stulz (1988) document that American multinational corporations that could issue dollar-denominated debt to European investors in the early 1980s were able to borrow at a lower interest rate than the federal government had to pay, simply because the companies were in position to meet an unexpected surge in European demand for unregistered, dollar-denominated debt at a time when the dollar was rising sharply against European currencies. More recently,

Walt Disney and several other large U.S. corporations issued 100-year maturity bonds that were eagerly bought by investors hoping to lock in a fixed yield. By being the first to market, these companies were able to borrow long-term capital at very attractive rates.

Emphasize cash flows rather than accounting profits. The life blood of any business is cash flow. This is what companies use to pay their debts, finance their investments, and pay dividends to their shareholders. By now, this single-minded focus on cash flow rather than earnings in finance probably seems a bit maniacal to you, but there are good reasons for it. Corporate profits are computed by applying an ever-changing set of accepted accounting rules to a company's accounts, and the profit figures generated will often change dramatically if different depreciation, income realization, or other rules are applied. Cash flow, on the other hand, can usually be computed easily and unambiguously. Furthermore, using earnings instead of cash flow in capital budgeting problems will sometimes yield "incorrect" answers, particularly in multi-period problems, whereas using cash flow always yields the correct solutions. The finance emphasis on incremental cash flows in capital budgeting problems also helps focus the analyst's attention on what is truly relevant.

Remember that finance is now a global game. In the early 1960s, the United States accounted for over half the world's total output of goods and services. Today the U.S. accounts for less than one fourth of total world output, even though the American economy has more than doubled in real terms over the last three decades. Furthermore, this trend seems certain to continue, since many developing countries are experiencing growth rates several times higher than that of the U.S. or any other developed country. What this means for the apprentice American business professional is that he or she can no longer afford to concentrate solely on business practices in one country and ignore the rest of the world.[30] Finance, in particular, is now a global industry and is becoming more so by the day. For example, the total value of all currencies traded on the world's foreign exchange markets currently exceeds $1 trillion *per day*, and will probably double by the end of this decade. This international flavor makes finance an exciting and challenging field, but it also dramatically raises the cost of ignorance about non-U.S. business practices.

Remember that finance is a quantitative discipline. At all academic levels, finance tends to attract the mathematically-inclined. It is easy to understand why this is so—by its nature, our field deals with numbers, equations, and the value of wealth today compared with its value in the future. The quantitative skills required to compete effectively are high now, and will surely be even higher in the years ahead. Not only math and statistical skills are required. Solid computer skills are already an absolute prerequisite for success in modern finance and, with no less than 40 million personal computers being sold each year (mostly to businesses), the finance professional of the twenty-first century will have to be as comfortable with information technology as he or she is with the management of money.

---

30. This has, of course, always been the case for European students, since their countries depend so heavily on international trade for their economic health.

—SUMMARY—

This chapter has traced the development of corporate finance theory from its birth with Markowitz's portfolio theory in the early 1950s; through the capital structure and dividend irrelevance propositions of Modigliani and Miller in the late 1950s and early 1960s; the asset pricing theories of Sharpe and Ross in the 1960s and 1970s; the Black-Scholes option pricing theory, intermediation theory, and Jensen and Meckling's agency theory in the 1970s; culminating with the development of market microstructure theory and the modern theory of corporate control in the 1980s. All of these theories are based on the principles of informationally efficient capital markets populated by rational, utility-of-wealth-maximizing investors who can costlessly diversify unsystematic risk and are thus concerned only with pervasive, economy-wide forces. These, plus the other theoretical models described here, constitute the core of modern corporate finance theory, which practitioners around the world have used to create and manage immense wealth. In four decades, finance has been transformed from an academic and theoretical backwater into a dynamic, internally-consistent methodology for explaining the objective realities observed in modern financial markets and institutions. This chapter traces the development of these models, demonstrates their usefulness in analyzing modern business problems, and provides a brief summary of principles finance practitioners should keep in mind. In later chapters we will examine each of the modern theories of corporate finance in much greater depth and provide a synthesis of both the classic and most recent academic research on each topic.

—QUESTIONS—

1. How do capital markets increase the economic welfare of both savers and borrowers?

2. What is the Fisher Separation Theorem, and what does it imply for optimal corporate investment and financing policies?

3. In the language of Markowitz's portfolio theory, what is an efficient portfolio? What information would an investor need to construct such a portfolio?

4. What is the Law of Conservation of Value, and what role does this law play in the Modigliani and Miller capital structure irrelevance propositions?

5. Briefly describe why dividend policy is irrelevant in perfect capital markets. Which market frictions discourage cash dividends and which frictions encourage dividend payments?

6. Why is it easier to show theoretically that dividends should not exist than it is to demonstrate why they should be observed?

7. What does it mean to say that a certain factor (or influence) will be "priced" by investors in an asset pricing model?

8. What role does the risk-free asset play in the development of the CAPM?

9. How are "factors" defined in the APT? What are "factor loadings," and why are they important in the APT?

10. Briefly compare and contrast the APT and the CAPM.

11. Define and compare the three forms of market efficiency. Which of these three forms has not been empirically supported?

12. What is the typical stock market response to the announcement that a firm is the target of a takeover attempt? How does the stock price level typically evolve as a takeover contest proceeds?

13. What five variables influence the price of an option? Why was the Black-Scholes specification of option valuation in terms of these five factors such a breakthrough in finance theory?

14. Briefly discuss how option pricing theory has impacted capital budgeting and other financial areas besides the explicit pricing of stock and bond options.

15. How might an American *importer* use options to hedge foreign exchange risk?

16. Compare and contrast the "economic model" of the firm derived from microeconomic theory with Jensen and Meckling's "nexus of contracts" model of the firm.

17. Why do Jensen and Meckling conclude that entrepreneurs, rather than investors, will bear all of the agency costs of their perquisite consumption? How can entrepreneurs partially overcome these costs?

18. What is the difference between a "pooling" and a "separating" equilibrium in signaling theory?

19. What is the economic definition of a "signal?" What prerequisites must be met for signaling to be effective and maintainable?

20. Briefly describe Bradley's view of the economic function of corporate control contests. How does it contrast with prior models of the motivations of those involved in takeover contests?

21. What competitive advantages do you think financial intermediaries (in particular, commercial banks) have over capital markets in financing corporate activities? What advantages do capital markets have?

22. Why has the United States not developed commercial banks as large, and as nationally-dominant, as those in other industrialized countries?

23. What are the three costs that impact the size of the bid-ask spread in dealer markets? Which are related to information asymmetries between dealers and informed investors?

24. How might you refute the claim that stockholders impart a "short-term bias" to corporate decision-making?

—REFERENCES—

Admati, Anat R. and Paul Pfleiderer, "A Theory of Intraday Volume and Price Variability," **Review of Financial Studies** 1 (Spring 1988), pp. 3–40.

Akerlof, George, "The Market for 'Lemons,' Qualitative Uncertainty and the Market Mechanism," **Quarterly Journal of Economics** 84 (August 1970), pp. 488–500.

Alchian, Armen and Harold Demsetz, "Production, Information Costs and Economic Organization," **American Economic Review** 62 (December 1972), pp. 777–795.

Ambarish, Ramasastry, Kose John, and Joseph Williams, "Efficient Signaling With Dividends and Investments," **Journal of Finance** 42 (June 1987), pp. 321–343.

Banz, Rolf W., "The Relationship Between Return and Market Value of Common Stocks," **Journal of Financial Economics** 9 (March 1981), pp. 3–18.

Basu, Sanjoy, "The Investment Performance of Common Stocks in Relation to Their Price-Earnings Ratios: A Test of the Efficient Markets Hypothesis," **Journal of Finance** 32 (June 1977), pp. 663–682.

Bhagat, Sanjai, James A. Brickley, and Ronald C. Lease, "Incentive Effects of Stock Purchase Plans," **Journal of Financial Economics** 14 (June 1985), pp. 195–215.

Black, Fischer, "Capital Market Equilibrium With Restricted Borrowing," **Journal of Business** 45 (July 1972), pp. 444–455.

Black, Fischer and Myron Scholes, "The Valuation of Options Contracts and a Test of Market Efficiency," **Journal of Finance** 27 (May 1972), pp. 399–418.

————"The Pricing of Options and Corporate Liabilities," **Journal of Political Economy** 81 (May/June 1973), pp. 637–654.

Bradley, Michael, "Interfirm Tender Offers and the Market for Corporate Control," **Journal of Business** 53 (October 1980), pp. 345–376.

Bradley, Michael, Anand Desai, and E. Han Kim, "Synergistic Gains From Corporate Acquisitions and Their Division Between the Stockholders of Target and Acquiring Firms," **Journal of Financial Economics** 21 (May 1988), pp. 3–40.

Branch, Ben and Walter Freed, "Bid-Asked Spreads on the AMEX and the Big Board," **Journal of Finance** 32 (March 1977), pp. 159–163.

Brennan, Michael J., "Taxes, Market Valuation and Corporate Financial Policy," **National Tax Journal** 23 (December 1970), pp. 417–427.

Brennan, Michael J. and Edwardo Schwartz, "Evaluating Natural Resource Investments," **Journal of Business** 58 (April 1985), pp. 135–157.

Brickley, James A., Ronald C. Lease, and Clifford W. Smith, Jr., "Ownership Structure and Voting on Antitakeover Amendments," **Journal of Financial Economics** 20 (January/March 1988), pp. 267–291.

Brock, William A. and Allan W. Kleidon, "Periodic Market Closure and Trading Volume," **Journal of Economic Dynamics and Control** 16 (1992), pp. 451–489.

Chen, Nai-Fu, Richard Roll, and Stephen A. Ross, "Economic Forces and the Stock Market: Testing the APT and Alternative Asset Pricing Theories," **Journal of Business** 59 (July 1986), pp. 383–403.

Christie, William G., Jeffrey H. Harris, and Paul H. Schultz, "Why Did NASDAQ Market Makers Stop Avoiding Odd-Eighth Quotes?," **Journal of Finance** 49 (December 1994), pp. 1841–1860.

Christie, William G. and Paul H. Schultz, "Why do NASDAQ Market Makers Avoid Odd-Eighth Quotes?," **Journal of Finance** 49 (December 1994), pp. 1813–1840.

Copeland, Thomas E. and Dan Galai, "Information Effects on the Bid-Ask Spread," **Journal of Finance** 38 (December 1983), pp. 1457–1469.

Copeland, Thomas E. and J. Fred Weston, **Financial Theory and Corporate Policy**, Third Edition (New York: Addison-Wesley Publishing Company, 1988).

Debondt, Werner F. and Richard H. Thaler, "Does the Stock Market Overreact?," **Journal of Finance** 40 (July 1985), pp. 793–805.

Delong, J. Bradford, Andrei Shleifer, Lawrence Summers, and Robert J. Waldmann, "Noise Trader Risk in Financial Markets," **Journal of Political Economy** 98 (1990), pp. 703–738.

Demsetz, Harold, "The Cost of Transacting," **Quarterly Journal of Economics** 82 (February 1968), pp. 33–53.

Dhrymes, Phoebus J., Irwin Friend, and N. Bulent Gultekin, "A Critical Reexamination of the Empirical Evidence on the Arbitrage Pricing Theory," **Journal of Finance** 39 (June 1984), pp. 323–346.

Downes, David H. and Robert Heinkel, "Signaling and the Value of Unseasoned New Issues," **Journal of Finance** 37 (March 1982), pp. 1–10.

Durand, David, "Cost of Debt and Equity Funds for Business: Trends and Problems of Measurement," in **Conference on Research in Business Finance** (New York, NY: National Bureau of Economic Research, 1952).

Easley, David and Maureen O'Hara, "Price, Trade Size, and Information in Securities Markets," **Journal of Financial Economics** 19 (September 1987), pp. 69–90.

Fama, Eugene F., "Efficient Capital Markets: A Review of Theory and Empirical Work," **Journal of Finance** 25 (May 1970), pp. 383–417.

———"Agency Problems and the Theory of the Firm," **Journal of Political Economy** 88 (April 1980), pp. 288–298.

———"Efficient Capital Markets II," **Journal of Finance** 46 (December 1991), pp. 1575–1614.

Fama, Eugene F. and James D. MacBeth, "Risk, Return and Equilibrium: Empirical Tests," **Journal of Political Economy** 81 (May 1973), pp. 607–636.

Fama, Eugene F. and Michael C. Jensen, "Agency Problems and Residual Claims," **Journal of Law and Economics** 26 (June 1983a), pp. 327–349.

———"Separation of Ownership and Control," **Journal of Law and Economics** 26 (June 1983b), pp. 301–325.

Fisher, Irving, **The Theory of Interest** (New York: Macmillan, 1930).

Foster, F. Douglas and S. Viswanathan, "A Theory of the Interday Variations in Volume, Variance, and Trading Costs in Securities Markets," **Review of Financial Studies** 3 (1990), pp. 593–624.

French, Kenneth R., "Stock Returns and The Weekend Effect," **Journal of Financial Economics** 8 (March 1980), pp. 55–69.

Gibbons, Michael R., "Multivariate Tests of Financial Models," **Journal of Financial Economics** 10 (March 1982), pp. 3–27.

Glosten, Lawrence R., "Is the Electronic Open Limit Order Book Inevitable?," **Journal of Finance** 49 (September 1994), pp. 1127–1161.

Glosten, Lawrence R. and Lawrence E. Harris, "Estimating the Components of the Bid / Ask Spread," **Journal of Financial Economics** 21 (May 1988), pp. 123–142.

Glosten, Lawrence R. and Paul R. Milgrom, "Bid, Ask, and Transactions Prices in a Specialist Market With Heterogeneously Informed Traders," **Journal of Financial Economics** 14 (March 1985), pp. 71–100.

Grinblatt, Mark and Chuan Yang Hwang, "Signaling and the Pricing of New Issues," **Journal of Finance** 44 (June 1989), pp. 393–420.

Grossman, Sanford and Joseph E. Stiglitz, "On the Impossibility of Informationally Efficient Markets," **American Economic Review** 70 (June 1980), pp. 393–408.

Hamada, Robert, "Portfolio Analysis, Market Equilibrium, and Corporation Finance," **Journal of Finance** 24 (March 1969), pp. 435–452.

Hirshleifer, Jack, "On the Theory of Optimal Investment Decision," **Journal of Political Economy** 66 (August 1958), pp. 329–352.

Ho, Thomas and Hans R. Stoll, "Optimal Dealer Pricing Under Transactions and Return Uncertainty," **Journal of Financial Economics** 9 (March 1981), pp. 47–73.

———"The Dynamics of Dealer Markets Under Competition," **Journal of Finance** 38 (September 1983), pp. 1053–1074.

Ingersoll, Jr., Jonathan E. and Stephen A. Ross, "Waiting to Invest: Investment and Uncertainty," **Journal of Business** 65 (March 1992), pp. 1–29.

James, Christopher, "Some Evidence on the Uniqueness of Bank Loans," **Journal of Financial Economics** 19 (December 1987), pp. 217–236.

Jarrell, Gregg A., James Brickley, and Jeffrey Netter, "The Market for Corporate Control: The Empirical Evidence Since 1980," **Journal of Economic Perspectives** 2 (Winter 1988), pp. 49–68.

Jarrell, Gregg A. and Annette B. Poulsen, "Shark Repellents and Stock Prices: The Effects of Antitakeover Amendments Since 1980," **Journal of Financial Economics** 19 (September 1987), pp. 127–168.

Jensen, Michael C., "Capital Markets: Theory and Evidence," **Bell Journal of Economics and Management Science** 3 (Autumn 1972), pp. 357–398.

———"Agency Costs of Free Cash Flow, Corporate Finance and Takeovers," **American Economic Review** 76 (May 1986), pp. 323–329.

Jensen, Michael C. and William Meckling, "Theory of the Firm: Managerial Behavior, Agency Costs and Ownership Structure," **Journal of Financial Economics** 3 (October 1976), pp. 305–360.

Jensen, Michael C. and Kevin Murphy, "Performance Pay and Top Management Incentives," **Journal of Political Economy** 98 (April 1990), pp. 225–264.

Jensen, Michael C. and Richard Ruback, "The Market for Corporate Control: The Scientific Evidence," **Journal of Financial Economics** 11 (April 1983), pp. 5–50.

Jensen, Michael C. and Jerold B. Warner, "The Distribution of Power Among Corporate Managers, Shareholders, and Directors," **Journal of Financial Economics** 20 (January/March 1988), pp. 3–24.

Keim, Donald B., "Size-Related Anomalies and Stock Return Seasonality: Further Empirical Evidence," **Journal of Financial Economics** 12 (June 1983), pp. 13–32.

Kim, Yong Choel and René M. Stulz, "The Eurobond Market and Corporate Financial Policy: A Test of the Clientele Hypothesis," **Journal of Financial Economics** 22 (December 1988), pp. 189–205.

Kyle, Albert S., "Continuous Auctions and Insider Trading," **Econometrica** 53 (November 1985), pp. 1315–1335.

Lambert, Richard A. and David F. Larcker, "Golden Parachutes, Executive Decision-Making and Shareholder Wealth," **Journal of Accounting and Economics** 7 (April 1985), pp. 179–203.

Leland, Hayne, and David Pyle, "Information Asymmetries, Financial Structure, and Financial Intermediation," **Journal of Finance** 32 (May 1977), pp. 371–387.

Lintner, John, "The Valuation of Risk Assets and the Selection of Risky Investments in Stock Portfolios and Capital Budgets," **Review of Economics and Statistics** 47 (February 1965), pp. 13–37.

Lo, Andrew W. and A. Craig MacKinlay, "Stock Market Prices do not Follow Random Walks: Evidence From a Simple Specification Test," **Review of Financial Studies** 1 (Spring 1988), pp. 41–66.

Majd, Saman and Robert S. Pindyck, "Time to Build, Option Value, and Investment Decisions," **Journal of Financial Economics** 18 (March 1987), pp. 7–28.

Markowitz, Harry, "Portfolio Selection," **Journal of Finance** 7 (March 1952), pp. 77–91.

Megginson, William L., Annette B. Poulsen, and Joseph F. Sinkey, Jr., "Syndicated Loan Announcements and the Market Value of the Banking Firm," **Journal of Money, Credit, and Banking** (May 1995).

Merton, Robert C., "An Intertemporal Capital Asset Pricing Model," **Econometrica** 41 (September 1973a), pp. 867–888.

————"Theory of Rational Option Pricing," **Bell Journal of Economics and Management Science** 4 (Spring 1973b), pp. 141–183.

Miller, Merton, "Debt and Taxes," **Journal of Finance** 32 (May 1977), pp. 261–275.

Miller, Merton and Franco Modigliani, "Dividend Policy, Growth and the Valuation of Shares," **Journal of Business** 34 (October 1961), pp. 411–433.

Miller, Merton H. and Kevin Rock, "Dividend Policy Under Asymmetric Information," **Journal of Finance** 40 (September 1985), pp. 1053–1070.

Modigliani, Franco and Merton Miller, "The Cost of Capital, Corporation Finance, and the Theory of Investment," **American Economic Review** 48 (June 1958), pp. 261–297.

————"Corporate Income Taxes and the Cost of Capital: A Correction," **American Economic Review** 53 (June 1963), pp. 433–443.

Mossin, Jan, "Equilibrium in a Capital Asset Market," **Econometrica** 34 (October 1966), pp. 768–783.

Murphy, Kevin J., "Corporate Performance and Managerial Remuneration: An Empirical Analysis," **Journal of Accounting and Economics** 7 (April 1985), pp. 11–42.

Myers, Stewart C., "The Determinants of Corporate Borrowing," **Journal of Financial Economics** 5 (November 1977), pp. 147–176.

Roll, Richard, "A Critique of the Assets Pricing Theory's Tests; Part I: On Past and Potential Testability of the Theory," **Journal of Financial Economics** 4 (March 1977), pp. 129–176.

Roll, Richard and Stephen A. Ross, "An Empirical Investigation of the Arbitrage Pricing Theory," **Journal of Finance** 35 (December 1980), pp. 1073–1103.

Ross, Stephen A., "The Arbitrage Theory of Capital Asset Pricing," **Journal of Economic Theory** 13 (December 1976), pp. 341–360.

————"The Determination of Financial Structure: The Incentive-Signaling Approach," **Bell Journal of Economics and Management Science** 8 (Spring 1977), pp. 23–40.

Rozeff, Michael and William Kinney, "Capital Market Seasonality: The Case of Stock Returns," **Journal of Financial Economics** 3 (October 1976), pp. 379–402.

Rubinstein, Mark, "A Mean-Variance Synthesis of Corporate Financial Theory," **Journal of Finance** 28 (March 1973), pp. 167–182.

Ryngaert, Michael, "The Effects of Poison Pills on the Wealth of Target Shareholders," **Journal of Financial Economics** 20 (January/March 1988), pp. 377–417.

Seyhun, H. Nejat, "Insiders' Profits, Costs of Trading, and Market Efficiency," **Journal of Financial Economics** 16 (June 1986), pp. 189–212.

————"The Information Content of Aggregate Insider Trading," **Journal of Business** 61 (January 1988), pp. 1–24.

————"Overreaction or Fundamentals: Some Lessons From Insiders' Response to the Market Crash of 1987," **Journal of Finance** 45 (December 1990), pp. 1363–1388.

Sharpe, William F., "Capital Asset Prices: A Theory of Market Equilibrium Under Conditions of Risk," **Journal of Finance** 19 (September 1964), pp. 425–442.

Shiller, Robert J., "Do Stock Prices Move Too Much to be Justified by Subsequent Changes in Dividends," **American Economic Review** 71 (June 1981), pp. 421–435.

Smith, Clifford W., "Option Pricing: A Review," **Journal of Financial Economics** 3 (January–March 1976), pp. 3–51.

———"Investment Banking and the Capital Acquisition Process," **Journal of Financial Economics** 15 (January/February 1986), pp. 3–29.

Smith, Clifford W. Jr. and Ross L. Watts, "The Investment Opportunity Set and Corporate Financing, Dividend and Compensation Policies," **Journal of Financial Economics** 32 (October 1992), pp. 263–292.

Spence, Michael, "Job Market Signaling," **Quarterly Journal of Economics** 87 (August 1973), pp. 355–374.

Stern, Joel M. and Donald H. Chew, Jr., eds., **The Revolution in Corporate Finance** (New York, NY: Basil Blackwell, 1986).

Stiglitz, Joseph E., "On the Irrelevance of Corporate Financial Policy," **American Economic Review** 64 (December 1974), pp. 851–866.

Stoll, Hans R., "Inferring the Components of the Bid-Ask Spread: Theory and Empirical Tests," **Journal of Finance** 44 (March 1989), pp. 115–134.

Tinic, Seha, "The Economics of Liquidity Services," **Quarterly Journal of Economics** 86 (February 1972), pp. 79–93.

Walkling, Ralph A. and Michael S. Long, "Agency Theory, Managerial Warfare and Takeover Bid Resistance," **Rand Journal of Economics** 1 (Spring 1984), pp. 54–68.

Williams, John Burr, **The Theory of Investment Value** (Cambridge: Harvard University Press, 1938).

Wood, Robert A., Thomas H. McInish, and J. Keith Ord, "An Investigation of Transactions Data for NYSE Stocks," **Journal of Finance** 40 (July 1985), pp. 723–741.

CHAPTER
2

Ownership, Control, and Compensation

2.1 INTRODUCTION

Modern corporate finance theory has largely been built using the assumptions of perfect capital markets, and implicit in most of the path-breaking papers is an assumption that finance either occurs in an Anglo-American legal and institutional framework, or that the theoretical models will hold regardless of the institutional setting. As finance's world view has broadened in recent years to include the study both of successful economic systems outside the United States and of the vibrant entrepreneurial sector of the U.S. economy, it has become clear that a country's legal, cultural, and historical environment dramatically impacts how that nation's companies organize their financial affairs. When one first compares the corporate finance systems of, say, Germany, Japan, and the United States, one is immediately struck by how fundamentally different these systems appear from each other. Yet all three nations have capitalist economies based on private property and free enterprise, all three are representative democracies, and all three must be considered historical successes by any economic or political standard.[1] How can this be? How can these three countries, which collectively account for over forty percent of total world output, all succeed with such apparently dissimilar corporate financial systems?[2] What factors

---

a 1. Three highly readable summaries of the strengths and weaknesses of the United States, Japan, and western Europe (particularly Germany) are provided in the July/August 1992 edition of the **Harvard Business Review**. See Prowse (1992), Cutts (1992), and Hentzler (1992). A rather alarmist, late–1980s view of the Japanese challenge to American capitalism is provided in Murphy (1989), while a more upbeat assessment of America's enduring economic strength is provided in Ohmae (1991).

2. Yet another indication of just how strong these economies are is provided in the 1994 World Competitiveness Report, issued by the Swiss-based International Institute for Management Development and cited in a **Financial Times** article by Williams (1994). The United States ranks as the most competitive economy in the world, with Japan and Germany grabbing ranks three and five (Singapore and Hong Kong are second and fourth, respectively).

are common to these three systems, and to the other successful economic models observed in both developed and developing countries? This chapter will attempt to answer these questions.

To be successful, any economic system must strike a series of effective balances between conflicting objectives. It must promote keen competition between individuals and between companies to ensure that resources are used efficiently and that new ideas and processes are rapidly incorporated, while simultaneously maintaining a sense of common purpose and preventing healthy competition from degenerating into economic conflict. A society must develop a government powerful enough to maintain a stable legal and regulatory environment, without allowing that government to become so intrusive and bureaucratic that initiative and entrepreneurship are stifled. Finally, an economic system must provide a method for individuals to pool their talents and resources into companies that are able to produce goods and services efficiently, but the system must then develop an effective means to monitor and control these companies and the professional managers hired to run them.[3]

In this chapter, we focus on this monitoring and disciplining objective, and begin by examining how Americans have chosen to organize and control business activity. We then contrast the U.S. corporate control and corporate governance models with those of other societies in order both to determine what features are common to all successful economic systems and to explore how the American system might be improved by learning from others. Finally, we examine management compensation policies commonly employed by American corporations, and we evaluate how effectively these policies overcome the agency problems inherent in the relationship between shareholders and managers.

2.2   LEGAL FORMS OF BUSINESS ORGANIZATION IN THE UNITED STATES

There are three basic forms of business organization in the United States: the sole proprietorship, the partnership, and the corporation. These forms differ from each other primarily in terms of the number of people who own the business, the degree to which individual owners are legally responsible for the activities of other group members, and the tax treatment of business income. Furthermore, experience has fostered the evolution of several hybrid organizational forms that combine features of one or more of the main forms. This group includes limited partnerships, S corporations, personal

---

3. This is hardly an abstract issue, since numerous governments around the world are attempting to create (or recreate) market-oriented economic systems that provide incentives for producers, without trampling on the rights of consumers—and many governments are trying to do this with new (and often exuberant) democratic political systems. One of the most important such transformations being attempted is in Russia, and the special "challenges" encountered there are described by Kvint (1994) and Galuszka, Kranz, and Reed (1994). Johnson and Loveman (1995) provide a somewhat more upbeat assessment of the progress of economic reform in post-communist Poland.

service corporations, and limited liability companies.[4] While each of the main and hybrid forms seems to occupy a distinct competitive niche in the American economy, the vast bulk of total business income is earned by regular corporations, and—in almost all fields outside of life insurance, investment banking and professional services—the corporate form becomes virtually mandatory for all businesses once they pass a threshold size (that varies by industry) in terms of revenues, assets, or employees. We will examine each organizational form in turn, and examine each form's strengths and weaknesses.

2.2.1 The Sole Proprietorship Form

As the name implies, a **sole proprietorship** is a business with a single owner. In fact, there is no distinction between the business and the owner. The business is the owner's personal property, it exists only as long as the owner lives and chooses to operate it, and all business assets belong to the owner personally. Furthermore, the owner/entrepreneur is personally liable for all debts of the company (including monies owed a plaintiff who has successfully sued the company), and business profits are taxed as ordinary income of the entrepreneur. As Table 2.1, which provides a breakdown of the distribution of business income by organizational form, clearly shows, sole proprietorships are by far the most common type of business in the United States—accounting for over 74 percent of all business tax returns filed each year—but they receive less than 6 percent of business income and employ less than ten percent of the work force.

The principal benefits of the proprietorship form are the ease with which it can be established and the tax treatment of its business income. Technically, if you have ever sold magazine subscriptions or earned money mowing yards, you have operated a sole proprietorship. Even for more permanent business activities, proprietorships are extremely easy to create and to wind down. For many activities, all you need to begin operating a for-profit enterprise is a business license, and this "company" can be shut down simply by ceasing operations. Record-keeping is also much easier for proprietorships than for other business forms—there are no other owners to answer to and the business tax form that must be filed is simply an addendum to the entrepreneur's personal tax form. Furthermore, sole proprietorships enjoy the same tax benefits from operating a business that other entrepreneurs do. They can deduct legitimate business expenses (including, in some cases, items such as cars, computers, health insurance premiums, and pension contributions) from their personal income. On top of everything else, a successful sole

---

4. We choose not to examine one common form of business organization, the mutual form, in this chapter primarily because it is a not-for-profit, "mutual benefit" business association. Anyone interested in this form should refer to Mayers and Smith (1986), Masulis (1987), or Lamm-Tennant and Starks (1993). We also choose not to examine franchising in this chapter, in spite of the fact that franchised outlets account for over one-third of all retail sales in the U.S. This hybrid business form is described and analyzed in Brickley and Dark (1987), and by Brickley, Dark, and Weisbach (1991). More generally, the issues to be addressed in choosing the proper legal form for a new business to adopt are discussed in Peat Marwick Main & Company (1988) and Rexer and Sheehan (1994).

TABLE 2.1

DISTRIBUTION OF BUSINESSES BY ORGANIZATIONAL FORM IN THE UNITED STATES, 1992

This table shows the number of returns filed, the total dollar amount of business receipts, and total net income of nonfarm sole proprietorships, partnerships, and corporations in the United States for calendar year 1992. Dollar amounts are in millions, and the numbers in parentheses are percentages of the total for all organizational forms.

Organizational Form	Number of Returns	Business Receipts	Net Income
Sole Proprietorships	15,495,419 (74.3%)	$737,082 (5.7%)	$153,960 (25.7%)
Partnerships	1,484,752 (7.1%)	$595,855 (4.6%)	$ 42,917 (7.2%)
Corporations	3,868,004 (18.6%)	$11,712,540 (89.8%)	$402,658 (67.1%)
Total	**20,848,175**	**$13,045,470**	**$599,535**

SOURCE: STATISTICS ON INCOME, U.S. INTERNAL REVENUE SERVICE (FALL 1994).

proprietor does not have to answer to anyone else—she can be her own boss. So, with all of these advantages, why don't proprietorships dominate the business landscape?

There are actually two answers to that question. First, in many industries—where the optimal firm size is small, and capital requirements are minimal—sole proprietorships do in fact dominate due to their low costs and great flexibility. The second, and more important, answer is that proprietorships also have serious competitive disadvantages, and these tend to increase exponentially as firm size increases. The three most critical disadvantages are limited life, limited access to capital, and unlimited personal liability. By definition, a proprietorship ceases to exist when the founder dies or retires. While the entrepreneur can pass the assets of the business on to her children (or sell them to a third party), the company itself cannot be transferred, and most changes in ownership of successful companies will trigger potentially devastating estate tax liabilities. Also, by definition, a proprietorship cannot obtain equity capital either by taking on one or more partners or by selling common or preferred stock to outside investors. It can obtain operating capital from only two sources—reinvested profits and personal borrowings by the entrepreneur—and both of these sources are easily exhausted in the real world. Finally, only the bravest entrepreneur will be willing to continue accepting the risk of unlimited personal liability once she is successful enough to have something to lose. The United States is the most litigious society in history (each year over 20 *million* lawsuits are filed in state courts alone), and a single jury verdict can destroy a lifetime's accomplishments and impoverish the most successful business family.

2.2.2 The Partnership Form

A (general) **partnership** is essentially a proprietorship with two or more owners who have joined together their skills and personal wealth. As before, there is no legal distinction between the business and the business' owners, each of whom can execute contracts binding on all of the others, and each of whom is personally liable for all of the debts of the partnership. There is no legal requirement that the owners must formalize the terms of their partnership in a written partnership agreement, but this is highly recommended since in its absence the business is dissolved whenever any one of the partners dies or retires. Furthermore, unless there is a partnership agreement specifying otherwise, each partner shares equally in business income and each has equal management authority. As with a proprietorship, partnership income is taxed only once—at the personal level.

The principal benefit of the partnership form versus the sole proprietorship is that the partnership allows a large number of people—often professionals such as accountants, engineers, and investment bankers—to pool their capital and expertise to form an enterprise of competitive size. Fama and Jensen (1983a,b) suggest that partnerships will be competitive in those industries where it is optimal for the firm's **control rights** (supervisory and oversight prerogatives) to be concentrated in the hands of technically-skilled managers who already have **decision rights** (operating management rights). In other words, partnerships will be most competitive in those industries where the separation of ownership and control would be sub-optimal.[5] This distinction helps explain why, for example, partnerships such as Goldman Sachs can be internationally competitive in the investment banking industry (where ongoing personal relationships, combined with access to large amounts of capital, are key ingredients to success), but all large commercial banks are corporations. Partnerships are also competitive in knowledge-intensive service businesses that need little financial capital, such as advertising, public relations, and the legal profession.[6]

The principal benefit of the partnership form, as with the proprietorship, is that business income is taxed only once, at the personal level of the individual partners. Furthermore, partnerships are more flexible than proprietorships in that the capital of many different partners can be pooled, and the business need not automatically terminate following the death or retirement of one partner, provided a well-crafted partnership agreement has been drawn up. On the other hand, the drawbacks of the partnership form are also similar to those of the proprietorship organizational form: (1) limited life, particularly if only a few partners are involved, as well as problems resulting from the instability inherent in long-term, multiperson business associations; (2) limited access to capital (the firm is still limited to retained profits and personal borrowings); and (3) unlimited personal liability, made all the worse by the fact that the partners are subject to joint and several liability, since any partner can contract for the firm and each partner is completely liable for all the firm's debts.

2.2.3 The Corporate Form

In American law, a **corporation** is a separate legal entity with all the rights and responsibilities enjoyed by human citizens. A corporation can sue and be sued, it can own

---

5. In addition to Fama and Jensen, Demsetz (1983) and Wruck and Jensen (1994) also analyze control and decision rights.

6. For a description of the investment problems that arise in partnerships, see Fama and Jensen (1985). A more general examination of the operating and investment problems that arise in owner-managed companies is provided in Jensen and Meckling (1979), while Weisbach (1995) surveys and tests agency-cost-based theories of corporate investment.

property and execute contracts in its own name, and it can be tried and convicted for crimes committed by its employees. In other words, a corporation is a person in the eyes of the law, with one critical difference: once created, a corporation will have a perpetual life unless it is explicitly terminated.

BENEFITS   The fact that a corporation is an entity separate from its owners also means that liability for corporate activity stops at the corporation itself. The firm's shareholders have **limited liability**, meaning that they can lose their equity investment in the corporation, but successful plaintiffs (or the tax authorities) cannot look to the shareholders personally for satisfaction of their claims. This limited liability feature is an immense advantage of the corporate form and, coupled with the perpetual life feature, implies that corporations that prosper can operate for many generations without having to reincorporate. Furthermore, as separate economic entities, corporations can contract individually with managers, suppliers, customers, and ordinary employees— and each individual contract can be renegotiated, modified, or terminated without affecting other stakeholders.[7] It is this feature of the corporate form that prompts Jensen and Meckling (1976) to view corporations as legal fictions, providing a "nexus" for contracting among various parties.

As a vehicle for conducting ongoing business activities, corporations also have the very valuable ability to issue a variety of different types of securities to investors in exchange for cash that can be used to acquire fixed assets or to meet the firm's working capital needs. The company itself (rather than its owners) can borrow money from creditors, and it can also issue various class of preferred and common stock to equity investors.[8] Furthermore, the ownership claims themselves—individual shares of common stock—can be freely traded among investors without obtaining the permission of other investors if the corporation is a **public company**, meaning that its shares are listed for trading on a public security market.[9] This provides the company with both immense flexibility and stability. The company's ownership structure can be continuously changed without imposing any recontracting costs on the company and without disrupting the stability of its control structure.

A corporation may be a legal person but, unlike humans, it is the property of the shareholders who own its common stock. Shares of stock have voting rights, and whichever investor (or group of investors) can assemble a majority of votes recorded in a corporate election is able to select the board of directors, who collectively hire and fire managers,

---

7. This fundamental point was first elaborated by Alchian and Demsetz (1972), and later by Fama (1980).

8. The practical importance of corporate (versus personal) borrowings is questionable for small companies, however, because banks almost invariably demand personal guarantees of corporate loans for all but their largest and most established business borrowers.

9. We should point out that legal restrictions are placed on share trading by corporate insiders (managers, directors, and owners of 5 percent or more of the company's shares) immediately after an initial public offering and during takeover contests. Furthermore, insiders must always report their trades to the Securities and Exchange Commission (SEC), which are then disclosed publicly with a lag. Not surprisingly, studies have found that insiders tend to earn abnormal returns on their trades, presumably because they are privy to information not yet impounded in security prices, see Seyhun (1986, 1988, 1990). In addition, Meulbroek (1992) documents that insiders earn significant profits on *illegal* insider trades, and that the market impounds the fact of such trades into stock prices.

and set overall corporate policy.[10] The rules governing voting rights and other parameters of corporate governance are spelled out in the firm's corporate charter (provided they conform to state law), and can only be changed by the shareholders themselves (not by the directors) with a vote at a shareholders meeting.[11] It is interesting to note that, in the United States, corporate charters are granted by the fifty individual states—not by the federal government—and most applicable corporate law is based on state, not federal, legislation.[12] On the other hand, federal laws and regulations govern corporate activities in the critical areas of interstate commerce, employment regulation, securities law, and mergers and acquisitions involving publicly-traded firms, as well as other areas of business activity.[13] Furthermore, all domestic corporations are subject to federal taxation of business income both at the corporate level (corporate profits are taxed when earned) and at the personal level, when profits are distributed to individual shareholders as dividends.

TAX AND COST DISADVANTAGES   The fact that corporate income is taxed at both the company and the personal levels represents the single greatest disadvantage of the corporate form in the United States (but not in other countries)—the infamous **double taxation of dividends**.[14] To demonstrate the importance of this tax rule, we will compare how $100,000 of operating income would be taxed for a corporation and for an otherwise-equivalent company organized as a partnership. Assume the corporate income tax rate is 35 percent, and that both the corporation's shareholders and the partnership's owners face personal tax rates of 40 percent on ordinary income received (this is how both partnership profits and dividend income are taxed). As Table 2.2 makes clear, the $100,000 in partnership profits is taxed once, at the personal level, and the partners then have $100,000 $(1 - 0.4) = $60,000$ in disposable, after-tax income. On the other hand, the corporation's operating income is first taxed at the corporate level, where federal taxes take a $100,000 $(0.35) = $35,000$ bite, and then again when the remaining $65,000 is distributed to shareholders in the form of cash dividends, which are taxed at

---

10. An excellent survey of the state and federal laws governing voting rights, and an analysis of the economic function of voting rights in corporate governance, is provided in Easterbrook and Fischel (1983). Theoretical evaluations of the optimal allocations of corporate voting rights are provided in Grossman (1988) and in Harris and Raviv (1988, 1989).

11. The wealth effects associated with the announcement of proposals to change shareholder voting rights are described in Bhagat and Brickley (1984), and in the series of papers during the 1980s that examined firms with two classes of common stock with differential voting rights (usually called simply dual-class firms). This series, which amounts almost to a cottage industry in its volume, began with Levy (1983) and Lease, McConnell, and Mikkelson (1983). The series included Partch (1987), Jarrell and Poulsen (1988), Megginson (1990), Lehn, Netter, and Poulsen (1990), Bergstrom and Rydqvist (1992), Zingales (1994), and several others.

12. For an economic analysis of the importance of state-versus-federal chartering of corporations, see Easterbrook and Fischel (1983) or Dodd and Leftwich (1980).

13. For discussions of the sometimes conflicting nature of state and federal regulation of business, and of how government can sometimes be enlisted to protect (or exploit) managerial interests, see Jarrell and Bradley (1980), Fields, Ghosh, Kidwell, and Klein (1990), and Szewczyk and Tsetsekos (1992).

14. Descriptions, and economic analyses, of tax systems in Canada, Japan, Germany, Sweden, the U.K., and other western economies are provided in Bailey (1988), Hammer (1975), King and Fullerton (1984), and Poterba and Summers (1984).

TABLE 2.2

TAXATION OF BUSINESS INCOME FOR CORPORATIONS AND PARTNERSHIPS

	Corporation	Partnership
Operating Income	$100,000	$100,000
Corporate profits tax ($\tau_c = 0.35$)	($135,000)	0
Net Income	$65,000	$100,000
Cash Dividends or Distributions	$65,000	$100,000
Personal Tax on Owner Income ($\tau_p = 0.40$)	($26,000)	($140,000)
After-Tax Disposable Income	**$39,000**	**$60,000**

SOURCE: STATISTICS ON INCOME, U.S. INTERNAL REVENUE SERVICE (FALL 1994).

the full marginal tax rate of 40 percent, leaving only $65,000 $(1 - 0.4) = \$39,000$ in disposable, after-tax income (we ignore state taxes in our example, but they simply make the comparison more onerous for corporations). In other words, if a given business activity can be conducted through a partnership, rather than through a corporation, the firm's owners can save 21 cents in taxes on every dollar earned. Even given the massive, non-tax benefits of the corporate form for most business activities, this tax "wedge" is a very heavy burden for American companies to shoulder, and it is one which other countries try to lighten for their limited liability corporations.

Corporations also suffer from other competitive disadvantages relative to proprietorships and partnerships. Some of these disadvantages relate to transaction costs of setting up and running a corporation, and some are more fundamental in that they relate to problems of monitoring and disciplining corporate executives. First, corporations are relatively expensive to create—particularly for small businesses that are just starting operations—and, once created, most states levy annual corporate charter taxes on active corporations. Publicly-listed corporations also face non-trivial annual listing fees from most securities exchanges. Furthermore, the printing, mailing, legal, auditing and other reporting expenses involved in complying with Securities and Exchange Commission (SEC) regulations covering public companies can run to several million dollars per year for large corporations—and these costs skyrocket whenever the corporation becomes involved in a control contest (such as a merger or a proxy contest), or if the firm needs to register a new security issue for public sale. Physically interacting with stockholders can also be surprisingly expensive, particularly for large firms that may have 500,000 or more individual shareholders—each of whom must receive an annual report (printed in full color on glossy paper, of course), a proxy statement, and any other legal documentation the corporation may have to distribute each year. Add to this the expenses involved with maintaining a professionally-staffed Shareholder Relations Department (as many companies do), and it becomes clear that simply maintaining the good name and legal existence of a large, public corporation is a multi-million dollar per year undertaking.

GOVERNANCE PROBLEMS   In spite of these significant out-of-pocket costs, it has become clear in recent years that the most important economic problems associated with corporate law in the U.S. revolve around the separation of ownership and control inherent in the corporate form, and these are exacerbated by the institutional rules promulgated by American courts, legislators, and regulators.[15] In theory, well-informed shareholders will vote for a board of directors, who will then hire, monitor, and set the compensation of the company's managers. This supreme board is also supposed to supervise the affairs of the corporation and ensure that it is being run in the shareholders' best interests.[16] Since shareholders are **residual claimants**, who can only earn a return on their investment after the claims of creditors, employees, and other senior claimants have been satisfied in full, vesting control of the corporation firmly in their hands is both economically optimal and morally defensible. As shareholders are also presumed to be well-diversified, and thus less risk-averse concerning a single company's prospects than managers or other stakeholders, they should also be willing to select and fund the risky, long-term investment projects that represent the future for all modern economies, (see Fama and Jensen 1985).

Unfortunately, this comforting model of corporate governance fails to work properly for far too many publicly-traded American companies. To see why, consider the company with over half a million shareholders discussed above. Such a company probably has a market value of at least $10 billion dollars, so it is unlikely that any one shareholder owns as much as one percent of the outstanding stock—since such a stake would be worth $100 million. Clearly, with this many atomistic shareholders, no single "owner" has the incentive to closely monitor corporate management, nor can that shareholder act unilaterally even if he or she is convinced that action is called for. This is a classic **collective action** problem. It is in the group's best interest for action to be taken (to monitor and discipline management), but it is in no individual group member's rational self-interest to precipitate action since he or she bears all of the cost of taking action, but the benefits are dispersed among the group.[17] In other words, all group members hope that someone (other than themselves) will take action to improve corporate performance so that they can **free-ride** on the activist's efforts.

In such an environment it is all too easy for corporate executives to seize effective control of the corporation, and then to run it in their own interests—rather than for the benefit of shareholders. Since managers control the director nominating machinery, and because the corporate governance rules discourage institutional investors (who may well own several million dollars worth of a given firm's stock) from banding together

---

15. For descriptions of these rules, and of the governance problems they cause, see Roe (1990, 1993), Grundfest (1990), Black (1992), Jensen (1993), and Bhide (1993).

16. The rights, responsibilities, and effectiveness of American corporate boards are discussed at length in three articles in the **Journal of Financial Economics** 20 (January/March 1988). See Jensen and Warner (1988), Weisbach (1988), and Warner, Watts, and Wruck (1988). Other articles dealing with these issues include Furtado and Rozeff (1987), Morck, Shleifer, and Vishny (1989), Holderness and Sheehan (1991), Byrd and Hickman (1992), Shivdasani (1993), Brook and Rao (1994), and Pound (1995). Finally, three articles in the Winter 1994 **Journal of Applied Corporate Finance** assess the effectiveness of the American system of corporate governance in comparison to that of Japan and other countries. See Bernstein (1994), Miller (1994), and Prahalad (1994).

17. A classic exposition of the free-rider problem in a corporate control setting is provided in Grossman and Hart (1980). Harrington and Prokop (1993) provide a more recent example of these problems in takeover contests.

to challenge management, the only effective means of disciplining or replacing entrenched managers are through a hostile takeover bid or through a **proxy fight** (wherein a challenger solicits proxies from shareholders, giving the challenger the right of
voting their shares at the stockholders meeting).[18] Both of these steps are extremely expensive, and recent legislation—coupled with defensive innovations such as **poison
pills** (conditional, discounted voting security purchase rights that accrue to existing
stockholders when a hostile bidder makes a tender offer)—have also lowered the probability that either step will be successful.[19] We will discuss these corporate control
problems more fully later in this chapter, but now we need to complete our discussion
of organizational forms by examining several specialized, or hybrid, forms.

2.2.4 The Limited Partnership Form

In many ways, a **limited partnership** combines the best features of the (general)
partnership and the corporate organizational forms, in that most of the participants in
the partnership (the limited partners) have the limited liability of corporate shareholders, but their share of the profits from the business is taxed as partnership income.[20] In any limited partnership (LP), there must be one or more general partners,
each of whom has unlimited personal liability. The general partners operate the business, and because of this and the fact that they alone are legally exposed, the general
partners usually receive a greater-than-proportional (based on their capital contribution) share of partnership income. The limited partners, on the other hand, must be
totally passive. They contribute capital to the partnership, but they cannot have their
names associated with the business, and they cannot take any active role in the operation of the business (even as employees). In return for this passivity, the limited
partners are not held personally liable for the debts of the business, and thus have the
liability protection of shareholders; but they are able to share proportionally in partnership income, and that income is taxed only once, as ordinary personal income for
the partners.

---

18. Proxy contests are described and examined in Dodd and Warner (1983), Pound (1988), DeAngelo and
    DeAngelo (1989), and Ikenberry and Lakonishok (1993).

19. Poison pills are studied and described in Malatesta and Walkling (1988) and Ryngaert (1988). Both of
    these papers document significant, negative abnormal stock returns for shareholders following the
    announcement of these plans, suggesting they are intended primarily to entrench and enrich corporate
    insiders at shareholder expense. An intriguing counter-argument is presented in Comment and Schwert
    (1995). These authors show that poison pills actually benefit shareholders by raising acquisition bid
    premiums, and suggest that the takeover boom of the 1980s died of natural causes—principally a
    sickening economy—rather than because of the effectiveness of takeover defenses. Brickley, Coles, and
    Terry (1994) show that the stock market reaction to poison pill adoptions is positive when a firm's
    board has a majority of outside (non-officer) directors, and negative when it does not. Finally, Cook and
    Easterwood (1994) document negative stock price—and positive bond price—reactions to a firm's
    decision to issue poison put debt (bonds which make hostile takeovers prohibitively costly). Clearly the
    net market reaction to "poison" security issues depends upon whether the firm's managers are perceived
    as attempting to merely entrench themselves or to protect shareholders by maximizing the premium an
    acquirer will have to pay in an acquisition.

20. Valuation effects of forming limited partnerships are examined in Moore, Christensen, and Roenfeldt
    (1989) and Denning and Shastri (1993).

Table 2.3 provides a breakdown of total partnership activity between limited and general partnerships for the 1992 tax year, and reveals that while only 18.2 percent of all partnerships filing returns are LPs, there are over 11.3 million limited partners (71.9 percent) versus only 4.4 million (28.1 percent) general partners. Clearly, LPs are characterized by large numbers of passive investors, while general partnerships are composed of relatively few, active principals—who often have considerable wealth at stake.

As you might expect, limited partnerships are ideal vehicles for funding long-term investments that generate large non-cash operating losses in the early years of the business, because these losses are able to "flow through" directly to the limited partners, who can then use the tax losses to offset taxable income from other sources. Two of the most common uses of this vehicle are in financing commercial real estate ventures and in funding research and development limited partnerships (RDLPs). In both cases the attractions of this format are the same for investors—tax losses in the early years, followed by regular cash payments in later periods. The industry breakdown provided in Table 2.3 dramatically underscores this point. Over 60 percent of all LPs are in the real estate business, and these LPs generated $17.2 billion in net *losses* in 1992. The aggregate figures for the less capital-intensive manufacturing-oriented RDLPs are much smaller, but the targeted nature of their impact belies their small numbers. While Congress significantly reduced the tax benefits of "passive" income from limited partnerships in the Tax Reform Act of 1986, they remain popular for these and other specialized tasks.

The principal disadvantages of LPs are their relatively long lives and illiquidity, plus the fact that they are costly to establish and it is often difficult to effectively monitor or discipline the general partner(s). Furthermore, many investors believe that having limited partnership income listed on their personal tax forms is a "red flag" for the IRS, that dramatically increases the likelihood that the investor will be audited. Whether or not this is true, the illiquidity problem with LPs can sometimes be solved by registering the partnership with the SEC, thereby allowing limited secondary market trading of partnership interests.

2.2.5 The S Corporation Form

In contrast to a regular corporation, an **S corporation** (previously called a Subchapter S corporation) allows shareholders to be taxed as partners, while still retaining their limited liability status as corporate stockholders. This type of company is an ordinary corporation (or C corporation), where the stockholders have elected to be treated as S corporation shareholders. To be eligible for S status, a firm must have 35 or fewer shareholders, the shareholders must be individuals or certain types of trusts (not corporations), and the S corporation cannot be a holding company (it cannot hold a controlling fraction of the stock in another company). Furthermore, an S corporation can have only a single class of equity security outstanding, which can be very restrictive for companies seeking venture capital financing—because these investors typically invest in portfolio companies using convertible preferred stock.[21]

---

21. For an excellent discussion of how venture capitalists evaluate and structure their investments in entrepreneurial growth companies, see Sahlman (1988, 1990).

TABLE 2.3

LIMITED AND GENERAL PARTNERSHIPS IN THE UNITED STATES, 1992 VERSUS 1991

This table shows the number of returns (number of active partnerships), the number of partners, and the net income of limited and general partnership for calendar years 1992 and 1991. The table also provides a breakdown of this data by industry.

Tax year, industrial group	Limited partnerships			General partnerships		
	Number of returns	Number of partners	Net income (less deficit)	Number of returns	Number of partners	Net income (less deficit)
	(1)	(2)	(3)	(4)	(5)	(6)
1992						
All industries[1]	270,748	11,313,483	−3,277,692	1,214,004	4,421,208	46,194,340
Agriculture, forestry, and fishing	8,576	172,616	−43,585	115,988	331,701	2,270,624
Mining	15,145	1,196,978	2,040,028	21,254	191,629	−1,031,403
Oil and gas extraction	14,025	1,170,310	1,990,619	17,794	173,556	−1,270,691
Construction	2,478	28,772	−150,226	56,933	129,162	2,056,012
Manufacturing	1,631	170,319	411,136	22,443	54,581	1,458,677
Transportation and public utilities	4,103	448,268	−240,277	19,433	79,082	1,293,876
Wholesale and retail trade	12,649	84,962	765,383	149,823	340,419	1,787,408
Finance, insurance, and real estate	203,587	7,762,898	−6,289,429	593,736	2,565,224	5,537,572
Real estate	167,424	5,470,951	−17,186,165	490,381	1,815,715	1,825,763
Operators and lessors of buildings	133,369	4,890,273	−13,579,304	400,344	1,452,535	3,445,910
Services	22,576	1,448,645	217,371	229,941	717,999	32,786,982

(continued)

TABLE 2.3 (CONTINUED)

Tax year, industrial group	Limited partnerships						General partnerships		
	Number of returns	Number of partners	Net income (less deficit)	Number of returns	Number of partners	Net income (less deficit)
	(1)	(2)	(3)	(4)	(5)	(6)
1991						
All industries[1]	270,681	11,265,537	−16,702,278	1,244,665	4,535,511	38,108,885
Agriculture, forestry, and fishing	9,780	219,931	−242,252	117,293	331,784	1,981,930
Mining	16,295	1,198,240	1,790,279	22,728	216,247	−1,010,792
Oil and gas extraction	15,149	1,162,041	1,840,527	19,031	197,487	−1,201,381
Construction	1,406	28,003	−312,608	55,789	123,689	1,806,380
Manufacturing	1,946	126,447	−614,965	22,028	48,710	1,519,294
Transportation and public utilities	3,797	439,268	−2,177,849	22,309	79,874	746,509
Wholesale and retail trade	13,640	96,779	378,997	157,342	351,055	2,249,053
Finance, insurance, and real estate	201,502	7,674,167	−13,769,218	602,335	2,642,348	982,822
Real estate	162,890	5,218,011	−22,224,989	506,077	1,883,482	−3,395,851
Operators and lessors of buildings	134,481	4,736,783	−17,978,664	410,722	1,489,667	−619,368
Services	22,232	1,481,958	−1,754,293	238,217	724,531	29,790,360

NOTE: [1]TOTAL INCLUDES PARTNERSHIPS WHOSE PRINCIPAL BUSINESS ACTIVITY COULD NOT BE DETERMINED.
SOURCE: STATISTICS ON INCOME, U.S INTERNAL REVENUE SERVICE (FALL 1994).

If, however, a corporation can meet these requirements, then election of S corporation status allows the company's operating income to escape separate taxation at the corporate level.[22] Instead, each shareholder claims a proportionate fraction of total company profits as personal income and pays tax on this profit at his or her marginal tax rate. As with a limited partnership, S corporation status yields the limited liability benefit of the corporate form along with the favorable taxation of the partnership form. In addition, an S corporation can easily switch back to being a C corporation whenever company growth causes it to outgrow the 35 shareholder ceiling, or if it needs to issue multiple classes of equity securities. Changing status may well be impossible for a limited partnership, and in any case will be costly and difficult. Given its inherent flexibility, it is quite common for successful companies to begin life as S corporations and to retain S status until they decide to go public and are forced to become regular corporations.

2.2.6 Organizational Choices Confronting U.S. Business Owners

As we have shown, American entrepreneurs have a virtual smorgasbord of organizational forms to choose from when they launch a new business. These forms differ from each other primarily regarding ease of formation, length of existence, access to capital, liability of equity investors, and the tax treatment of business income. Once a firm seeks a listing for its stock on a public security market, it must fulfill all the disclosure and registration requirements mandated by the U.S. Securities and Exchange Commission in order for its stock to be sold to outside investors through an **initial public offering** (IPO).[23] After the IPO, the firm is usually listed on one of the three major U.S. stock markets—the New York Stock Exchange (NYSE), the American Stock Exchange (AMEX), or the National Association of Securities Dealers Automated Quotations (NASDAQ) system—and is thereafter referred to as a **public company**.[24] As a public company, it has extensive, ongoing disclosure requirements that it must meet, and it must hold general stockholders meetings, with shareholder elections, at least annually.

Privately-held American companies are not required (and rarely volunteer) to report much information publicly—not even basic data such as sales revenue or number of employees, much less more sensitive information like corporate profits, executive compensation, or the identities of major shareholders (all of which public companies must report). It may therefore seem surprising that, in spite of discriminatory tax treat-

---

22. In 1992, over 46 percent (1.784 million of 3.868 million) of all corporations filing tax returns were S corporations, which indicates both the popularity of this organizational form and the relatively small *average* size of U.S. businesses.

23. The financial prerequisites and legal requirements for a firm to execute an initial public offering are discussed in Peat Marwick Main & Company (1987), and in Jones, Cohen, and Coppola (1992). A very useful summary of the empirical evidence on IPO pricing and valuation is provided in Ibbotson, Sindelar, and Ritter (1988, 1994), while Ritter (1991) examines the three-year, market-adjusted return earned by IPO investors. More recently, the Spring 1993 issue of **Financial Management** and the October 1993 issue of the **Journal of Financial Economics** both examine U.S. and international new (stock) issue markets, while Loughran, Ritter, and Palepu (1994) summarize the empirical evidence on non-U.S. IPOs.

24. This is not to be confused with becoming a publicly-owned company, as in a state-owned or nationalized firm. Instead, the company continues to be the property of private investors, who can now trade their ownership shares on a public capital market. A firm making an IPO is thus also said to be **going public**, since it will hereafter be publicly traded.

ment of business income, virtually all major U.S. corporations are organized as regular, or C corporations, rather than as S corporations, limited or general partnerships, or sole proprietorships. It seems that the capital raising requirements of almost all large companies—plus the need to achieve liquidity for founding equity stakes—eventually force all but the most intransigent family-owned firms to go public, and public listing virtually mandates C corporation status.[25]

Finally, in recent years it has become painfully obvious that many large American corporations suffer from the agency problems between managers and shareholders that result from the separation of corporate ownership and control. We will now briefly examine the forms of business organization available to non-U.S. companies, and we will then examine whether investors in other countries are better equipped to deal with monitoring large, powerful business entities than are American investors.

2.3 FORMS OF BUSINESS ORGANIZATION USED BY NON-U.S. COMPANIES

While a comprehensive survey of international forms of business organization is beyond the scope of this chapter, we will begin this section by examining basic organizational patterns that are commonly observed in all advanced, non-communist economies. We will then highlight differences among these forms and between them and comparable American models.

2.3.1 Worldwide Patterns

Even the most cursory glance at non-U.S. systems shows striking universal patterns. In almost all capitalist economies, some form of joint-stock, limited liability business structure—with freely tradeable equity claims—is allowed, and in most societies these companies dominate economic life. They may go by different names in different countries. In Britain they are called public limited companies (plc); in Germany they are referred to as *Aktiengesellschaft* (AG); in France, *Société Generale*; and in Spain, Mexico and elsewhere in Latin America these companies are called *Sociedad Anónima* (SA). While details vary, all of these structures are similar to the publicly-traded corporations Americans know and love.[26] Key differences between international and U.S. companies revolve around tax treatment of business income—which is typically, though not always, more punitive in the United States than abroad—and the amount of information that publicly-traded companies are required to disclose, which is invariably greater for U.S. versus non-U.S. companies.

Many countries also make a distinction between limited liability companies that are meant to be publicly traded and those which are meant to be privately held. In Germany,

---

25. This is true even if the company remains privately-held (it does not have an IPO) but sells equity directly to investors in the same state or to "sophisticated" investors, such as insurance companies, pension funds, or wealthy individuals. See Arnold (1985) or especially Zeune (1992) for a description of the rules governing private placements of equity securities.

26. A very good survey of governance systems in Japan and Germany is provided in Kester (1992), while a direct comparison between of informational asymmetries in the Japanese and U.S. stock markets is provided in Jacobson and Aaker (1993). Finally, Templeton (1995) cites evidence that Germans may be growing disillusioned with their bank-centered corporate finance and governance system.

Gesellschaft mit beschränkten Haftung (GmbH) are privately-owned and unlisted limit-ed liability stock companies, while in France these are called *Société à Responsibilité Limitée* (SARL). As we will see later in this chapter, private companies—particularly family-owned firms—form the backbone of most developing countries, and of many in-dustrialized countries as well. For example, the German postwar "economic miracle" was not propelled by giant companies but rather by mid-size, export-oriented companies that pursued niche market strategies at home and abroad—and these *Mittelstand* (middle market) firms still account for almost 80 percent of (West) German economic activity. A similar set of relatively small, entrepreneurial companies has helped propel Taiwan, Hong Kong and other Asian nations to growth rates that are consistently multiples of those achieved in the West.[27]

2.3.2 State-Owned Enterprises and Privatization

By far the biggest difference between the corporate organizational system of the United States and those of other countries is the almost total absence of **state-owned enter-prises** (SOEs) in the American economy. SOEs are companies owned and operated by the government (usually, but not always, the national government) that conduct busi-ness activities in areas outside of what Americans would consider purely governmental affairs. As examples, in many European countries (and throughout most of the develop-ing world) the state has historically owned and operated the telephone, television, elec-tric utility, airline, and railroad companies—and it has typically allowed little or no pri-vate sector competition. Outside of the U.S., virtually all national oil companies have been state-owned, and the same is true to a lesser degree for other "strategic" industries such as steel, aluminum, aerospace, heavy engineering, and even chemicals.[28] Even fi-nancial institutions such as commercial and investment banks, insurance companies, and savings banks have been state-owned in whole or in part. Of course, in the newly-non-communist countries of Eastern Europe and the former Soviet Union the state held (and will continue to hold) massive sway over all sectors of the economy.[29]

---

27. Interestingly, a key feature of the corporate governance systems adopted by most of the dynamic Asian capitalist economies—including Japan, Korea, Taiwan, and Thailand—during their take-off phase was an explicit restriction on foreign (particularly American) ownership in key industries. Development of these sectors was considered to be so important that it could not be left in the hands of potential competitors, and the very high national savings rates and native entrepreneurial talent of these countries' citizens allowed this policy of excluding foreign direct investment to be successful. On the other hand, Singapore and Hong Kong took exactly the opposite tack—welcoming foreign investment—and achieved equally impressive growth rates, without the distortions inherent in a nationalistic investment and corporate ownership strategy. As Bailey and Jagtiani (1994) document, restrictions on foreign share ownership can lead to perverse equity valuation patterns.

28. For analyses of the relative efficiency of state-owned versus privately-owned firms, see Peltzman (1971), Caves and Christensen (1980), Pryke (1982), Atkinson and Halvorsen (1986), Boardman, Freedman, and Eckel (1986), Eckel and Vermaelen (1986), and Boardman and Vining (1989).

29. The special problems that must be addressed by policy-makers in these countries are discussed in Nellis and Kikeri (1989), Shirley and Nellis (1991), and in Boycko, Shleifer, and Vishny (1993, 1994). An early and passionate (but tightly reasoned) indictment of socialism's social cost is presented in Kornai (1988).

We have used the past tense advisedly in our discussion of SOEs above, because the role of the state in economies around the world is being transformed by the spread of **privatization** programs, wherein the state sells off all or part of its holdings in SOEs to private companies or to individual private investors.[30] While the first major privatization program of the modern era was initiated by the West German government of Conrad Adenaeur in the early 1960s, it was the Conservative government of Britain's Margaret Thatcher that really launched the current popularity of privatizations—which were called "denationalizations" until she gave them the more user-friendly name. When the Thatcher government came to power in 1979, the state owned more than 10 percent of British industry and its SOEs directly employed more than 1.5 million people.[31] After a gingerly start, the Conservatives privatized all or part of the aerospace, telecommunications, automobile, airline, steel, oil and gas, electric and water utility, and air and seaport operating industries, raising over $60 billion in the process and transforming the role of the state in the British economy in little more than a decade.

Prompted by the British success, conservative governments in France, Canada, Japan, Germany, Chile, New Zealand and the Netherlands launched privatization programs of varying degrees of ambitiousness during the 1980s, and even socialist governments in Austria, Spain, Sweden and Denmark embraced limited divestment programs during this period. The privatization wave has turned into a flood during the 1990s, however, as it has now spread throughout most of Latin America and South Asia, and has been reinforced in continental Europe with changes in governments in France, Italy, and—of course—the former Soviet bloc. Privatization programs are expected to raise between $30 billion and $50 billion per year in Europe alone for at least the next decade (see Palmer 1993 and Middelmann 1995). If these programs continue to catch on elsewhere in the world—and particularly if the People's Republic of China fully embraces this technique as part of its modernization drive—the cumulative value of privatized assets should exceed $1 trillion by the early 21st century.

2.4   OWNERSHIP STRUCTURE AND CORPORATE POLICY

So far we have examined legal forms of business organization in the U.S. and abroad, and have examined the changing role of the state in economic life around the world. We will now focus not on legal *forms* of organization but on observed international *patterns of corporate ownership* in order to determine how different systems address the problems of monitoring and controlling powerful corporate entities. We examine three basic

---

30. Privatization programs are discussed and/or analyzed in Austin, Wortzel, and Coburn (1986), Kay and Thompson (1986), Yarrow (1986), Candoy-Sekse and Palmer (1988), Vuylsteke (1988), Bishop and Kay (1989), Caves (1990), Baldwin and Bhattacharya (1991), Galal, Jones, Tandon, and Vogelsang (1992), Goodman and Loveman (1992), Guney and Perotti (1993), Boycko, Shleifer, and Vishny (1994), Megginson, Nash, and van Randenborgh (1994), North (1994), and Jones, Megginson, Nash, and Netter (1995).

31. See Moore (1992) for an insider's view of how the Thatcher privatization program evolved over time (Moore was a key member of Ms. Thatcher's economic team during the 1980s).

ownership structure "models" that are observed in a variety of settings throughout the non-communist world. These are (1) the **open corporate model** most frequently associated with large, publicly-traded American corporations; (2) the **closed, or entrepreneurial, corporate model** most frequently associated with large private companies in western Europe and east Asia, and increasingly important in the entrepreneurial sector of the U.S. economy; and (3) the large **industrial group model**, made famous by the *Keiretsu* in Japan and the *Chaebol* in South Korea. Other commentators, observing the same phenomena we describe, refer instead to **capital-market-based**, **financial-intermediary-based**, and **industrial-group-based** *systems of corporate finance*. While there are a few minor differences between our terminology and theirs, the categorizations are similar enough that we will use both labels in our discussion below, with the system terminology in brackets.[32] Our focus in the text will be the theoretical differences between firm types, based on the ownership structure of the individual company. However, our table summaries (Tables 2.4 through 2.6) will describe the three main systems of corporate finance observed around the world, since such a tabulation provides a ready reference for comparing international patterns of financial behavior. The characteristics, strengths and weaknesses of each of the three ownership structure forms (corporate finance systems) are analyzed below.

2.4.1 The Open Corporate Model

An open corporation can be defined as a limited liability company with freely alienable (transferable) claims that can be traded on public capital markets, staffed by professional managers, and enjoying access to a wide variety of financing sources.[33] These corporations are typically not part of any larger industrial grouping, but rather belong solely to their stockholders—who may number in the hundreds of thousands. They are thus referred to as capital-market-based corporate finance systems. Though relatively few in number, these companies dominate business life in the United States, Canada, and Great Britain, and important examples of this type of firm can be found in all advanced economies.[34] The key financial characteristics of these firms are that (1) they rely on public capital markets for external financing (but can meet most fi-

---

32. Other international financial commentators use yet a third terminology to refer to these three models. In particular, the **Economist** magazine—with its European roots and global business perspective—frequently describes and compares the Anglo-American, European (or German), and Japanese models of corporate finance and governance. These correspond closely enough to our open corporate, closed corporate, and industrial group models—as well as to the capital-market-based, commercial-bank-based, and industrial-group-based systems of corporate finance—that the terms can be used interchangeably (see also Michael Prowse 1992) for most purposes.

33. Much of the basic terminology used to describe open and closed corporations is presented in Fama and Jensen (1983a,b).

34. To understand both the relative rarity of these corporations and their disproportionate macroeconomic impact, consider that the firms in the 1994 **Business Week** 1000 account for less than 0.01 percent of the 2 million-plus businesses operating in the United States, but these same companies had combined revenues of $4.49 trillion and a combined market valuation of $4.34 trillion—equal to over one-third and one-half of the respective national totals, see Bongiorno (1995).

nancing needs with internally-generated cash flow); (2) their shares are diffusely held by many atomistic shareholders, none of whom owns more than a small percentage of the total outstanding shares; and (3) the countries where these firms are most apparent tend to rely more on formal legal contracting, government regulation, and private litigation for controlling corporate behavior and resolving business conflicts than is true in other countries.[35] The characteristics, strengths, and weaknesses of the capital-market-based system of corporate finance (populated by open corporations) are detailed in Table 2.4.

Open corporations can be colossal in scale and in their financing needs. For example, American issuers raised $688 billion in capital from security market transactions in 1994 alone (and an incredible $1.017 *trillion* in 1993), and the vast bulk of that was raised by open corporations with household names such as Exxon, General Motors, Caterpillar, AT&T and IBM.[36] These companies tend to dominate their industries at home, and also frequently operate in dozens of countries worldwide—thereby earning the title of **multinational companies** (MNCs). In fact, their primary competition in international markets comes from successful non-U.S. open corporations that have also become MNCs.

WEAKNESSES   As you might expect, there is much to admire about these companies, and they only reached their lofty status by being historical successes. But success can also breed arrogance, insularity, and managerial entrenchment. Once the founding entrepreneurs of these companies die or retire, professional managers who may or may not be responsive to outside shareholders usually take over.[37] Since managers control the corporate voting machinery in the U.S., they may opt to select directors who owe their loyalty to the managers rather than the shareholders, and who will then support management in attempts to effectively disenfranchise outside stockholders by erecting defenses against hostile takeovers—which in many cases are the only method of removing an entrenched group of insiders. While capital markets might provide a brake on the ambitions of managers who have to raise capital through public security sales, this will be an ineffective tool for disciplining managers of companies with enough **free cash flow** (uncommitted cash flow from

---

35. As Kester (1992) makes clear, the contrast between the importance of contracts in the U.S. and Japan could hardly be more striking. An economic and historical analysis of the role of contracts in Anglo-American company law is provided in Cooter and Ulen (1988), while the theoretical role of contracts in aligning managerial and shareholder incentives is described in Chang (1993).

36. A survey of security market issues around the world is published in a late-January edition of the **Investment Dealers Digest** each year. This survey details new issues volume by type of security and by whether an issuer is a U.S. or non-U.S. institution, but its primary objective is to "keep score"—to document which investment banking firms underwrote the largest volumes of new issues.

37. The passing of the founder does not necessarily mean that founding family involvement in a company's affairs ceases. Many public companies have sizeable share blocs that are owned by the founder's estate, and these and other non-family **blocholders** often play an important role in American corporate governance. Papers that have examined the importance of blocholders include Demsetz and Lehn (1985), Shleifer and Vishny (1986), Wruck (1989), and Admati, Pfleiderer, and Zechner (1994).

TABLE 2.4

CHARACTERISTICS, STRENGTHS, AND WEAKNESSES OF THE CAPITAL-MARKET-BASED SYSTEM OF CORPORATE FINANCE

This table details the key financial, managerial, and operational characteristics of the open corporations that are typical of the capital-market-based corporate finance systems commonly associated with the United States, Canada, and the United Kingdom. The strengths and weaknesses of this system are also detailed.

A. Characteristics of the Capital-Market-Based Corporate Finance System

1. Many large, independent, publicly-traded corporations, each with several thousand relatively small shareholders—few of whom own more than 1–5 percent of a company's shares.

2. Much greater reliance on public capital markets—rather than on financial intermediaries—for external financing. Commercial banks play specialist financing roles, and have virtually no corporate governance functions.

3. Very large, liquid, and informationally-efficient stock and bond markets, and well-established procedures for listing new equity and debt securities. Although equity issues are common, most net external funding comes from bond issues.

4. Small stockholders are the focus of the corporate governance system, with regulations and strong legal rules designed to protect their interests over those of large shareholders. A great deal of corporate information disclosure is mandated.

5. Almost all large companies are controlled by professional (non-founding-family) managers, who have great influence over the firm's board of directors and great discretion in setting corporate policies.

6. Great reliance on equity-based compensation for managers and employees, who often own 10 percent or more of the firm's stock—directly or through their pension plans.

7. Very active market for corporate control, including hostile takeovers and leveraged buyouts.

B. Strengths of the Capital-Market-Based Corporate Finance System

1. Able to raise enormous sums to finance corporate investments, and able to spread economy's financial risk to well-diversified individual investors.

2. Transparency—financing activities are visible to all, information is readily available, and investors can easily analyze corporate performance. Promotes political support for market-oriented policies in a modern democracy.

3. Allocational efficiency—active M&A market ensures corporate resources will be controlled by management teams able to use them most efficiently.

4. Allows for specialization of labor—separate markets exist for managers and for wealthy risk-bearers (investors), so corporate power need not be inherited to be attained.

5. Liquid capital markets promote the development of pension funds and privately-financed pension systems (rather than purely government-run systems).

6. Risk-tolerant equity markets seem to have significant comparative advantage in financing and nurturing entrepreneurial growth firms, and the venture capital funds that help identify and develop growth companies.

7. Technology seems to favor capital markets over financial intermediaries because it dramatically lowers information acquisition, monitoring, and trading costs.

(continued)

TABLE 2.4 (CONTINUED)

C. Weaknesses of the Capital-Market-Based Corporate Finance System

1. Separation of ownership and control—significant agency and collective action problems result when those who own corporate assets (shareholders) are totally removed from active management, and instead hire professional agents (managers) to operate these assets.

2. Entrenchment incentives—since they are professional managers who can be dismissed at the shareholders' pleasure, managers have a strong incentive to invest in protecting their tenure in office (entrenchment), rather than concentrating solely on creating value.

3. Lack of powerful, informed monitors makes it very difficult to prevent corporate managers from over-investing in negative-NPV projects, or under-investing in positive-NPV projects with long-maturity payoffs.

4. Excessive, mandated information disclosure lowers the value of proprietary product or strategic information to corporations, since it may have to be disclosed to competitors.

operations over and above that needed to fund all positive NPV projects), and unless a manager owns a large block of company stock, she is unlikely to be directly penalized by her actions.[38]

The problems caused by the separation of ownership and control could theoretically be ameliorated by allowing institutional investors—who now own over 53 percent of all the equity of publicly listed companies in the U.S. and control assets worth $8.3 trillion—to take an active role in monitoring and disciplining corporate managers.[39] These large investors have both the expertise and the proper incentives to act as monitors, but American security laws, regulations, and court rulings severely

---

38. The disciplinary role that capital markets can play for firms that need external financing is discussed, in a slightly different context, in Easterbrook (1984), while the disciplinary role of leverage itself is assessed in recent papers by Maloney, McCormick, and Mitchell (1993), Denis (1994), Wruck (1994), and Phillips (1995). The importance of managerial shareholdings in aligning the interests of managers and stockholders is addressed theoretically in Jensen and Meckling (1976), Leland and Pyle (1977), and Stulz (1988), among others. The significance of insider shareholdings in explaining several observed corporate finance and corporate control phenomena is documented in numerous empirical studies, including Walkling and Long (1984), Lewellen, Loderer, and Rosenfeld (1985), Mikkelson and Partch (1989), McConnell and Servaes (1990), Chang and Mayers (1992), Song and Walkling (1993), Barclay, Holderness, and Pontiff (1993), Bagnani, Milonas, Saunders, and Travlos (1994), Cotter and Zenner (1994), and Fields and Mais (1994).

39. The data on institutional share ownership is reported in Weis (1995), while the $8.3 trillion figure for institutional asset holdings ($4.4 trillion of which is controlled by pension funds) is reported in **Business Week** (October 17, 1994, pg. 8). The first systematic analysis of the role that institutional investors can and should play in corporate governance is provided in Brickley, Lease, and Smith (1988). Several other papers have included measures of institutional shareholdings as key explanatory variables in empirical studies. These include Agrawal and Mandelker (1990), Stulz, Walkling, and Song (1990), Prowse (1990), Ambrose and Megginson (1992), and Gordon and Pound (1993). Many other studies have given institutional shareholdings less prominent roles as explanatory variables, particularly in corporate control and capital structure studies.

restrict their ability to play an active role in corporate governance.[40] This leaves the takeover market as the "court of last resort" for removing incompetent or ineffective management teams, and both the U.S. and the U.K. experienced massive merger and acquisition (M&A) booms during the 1980s.[41] The fact that bidders were able to offer takeover premiums averaging more than 30 percent throughout the decade suggests just how far the incumbent management teams had allowed firm market values to slip. That other countries did not witness significant M&A waves (particularly of hostile bids) during the 1980s also suggests that a key flaw in the open corporate form is their tendency towards managerial entrenchment and self-enrichment at shareholder expense.[42]

STRENGTHS   On the other hand, the open corporate form cannot easily be dismissed as a doomed relic, especially given that Britain, Canada and the U.S. experienced faster economic growth than most other Western countries (except Japan) throughout the 1980s, and many of the open companies headquartered in these countries are the largest and most profitable in their industry anywhere in the world. One answer to this riddle is that corporations are disciplined both by their internal governance systems and by competition in product and factor markets. While we have focused on the governance problems of these firms, we have so far overlooked both the governance problems competing firms must struggle with and the natural competitive advantages that open corporations seem to enjoy—which are numerous. First, in many industries, size is still a competitive advantage, and no other class of firm can attain either the scale of operation or access to financing that large open corporations can achieve. Furthermore, the very lack of a tight ownership structure in these firms also means that they are less prone to paralyzing conflicts of interest among members of their control coalitions than are closed corporations or industrial group companies. Second, publicly-traded also means publicly-mentioned, and open corporations tend to have much greater "brand awareness" among potential suppli-

40. Empirical support for the idea that institutions may well be beneficial monitors and owners is provided by Kiefer (1992), and a persuasive legal and financial argument in favor of enhancing the monitoring role of these investors is provided in Black (1992).

41. The research into this merger wave has been voluminous, and we will delay even a partial listing of references until section 2.4. Instead, let us say that the first truly "modern" empirical study of the takeover market—that modeled takeovers as corporate control contests—is Bradley (1980), and an early (but still informative) survey article was Jensen and Ruback (1983). Excellent later American studies include Travlos (1987), Bradley, Desai, and Kim (1988), Jarrell and Poulsen (1989), and Healy, Palepu, and Ruback (1992). An empirical analysis of managerial motivations in takeovers is provided in Berkovitch and Narayanan (1993).

42. International comparisons should not, however, be pushed too far, since there are important regulatory, cultural, and industrial structure differences between modern economies that clearly affect the incentives to engage in takeovers. Furthermore, many European markets did witness numerous corporate combinations (albeit friendly ones) in the run-up to the market opening labeled Europe 1992. The British takeover experience (through the mid–1980s) is detailed in Franks and Harris (1989). A form of "takeover" in the French capital markets—the nationalization of several major companies by the socialist Mitterand government of the early 1980s—is studied in Langohr and Viallet (1986). Finally, the importance of foreign buyers in the U.S. takeover market is addressed in Harris and Ravenscraft (1991), Manzon, Sharp, and Travlos (1994), and Dewenter (1995).

ers, customers, employees, and competitors than do similar-sized companies that are more tightly controlled.

Widely dispersed share ownership can also translate into widespread political support in participatory democracies, where investors typically constitute an important interest group in policy-making decisions. Furthermore, having publicly-traded shares allows corporate boards to craft very effective incentive stock option and stock purchase programs, and to target these either narrowly (on a few key executives) or broadly (on most or all permanent employees), depending upon corporate needs.[43] The responsiveness of modern stock markets also helps focus employees on value-maximizing activities, which cause the firm's stock price to rise; and to discourage them from value-decreasing activities, which cause the stock price to fall with equal speed. Finally, the transparency of the financial and ownership structures of open corporations serves to lessen mistrust of their intentions on the part of regulators, customers, and potential business partners. To summarize, in business as in biology, an entity that has survived in direct competition with other forms must be presumed to have survival value, but that it has not eliminated its competition suggests that they too have important strengths to balance their areas of weakness.

2.4.2 The Closed, (Entrepreneurial) Corporate Form

At first glance, the closed corporation may simply appear to be a younger, not-yet-mature open corporation, and in some cases that is true. However, recent research suggests that these companies represent a separate business form that has clear competitive advantages versus competing models. While some of these companies will "graduate" to open corporation status through an IPO and subsequent growth, and some will inevitably go bankrupt, many more will remain prosperously small and private. A closed corporation is characterized by non-alienable (not tradeable) shares, a very tight ownership structure consisting of a relative handful of major shareholders, and less-than-perfect access to public capital markets. These companies tend to be smaller than open corporations in the same industry, and many are still controlled by their entrepreneur/founders, or by the founders' families. The characteristics, strengths, and weaknesses of the financial-intermediary-based system of corporate finance (populated primarily by closed corporations) are detailed in Table 2.5.

GEOGRAPHIC DISTRIBUTION On a macroeconomic level, closed corporations are relatively most important outside the United States—particularly in Europe and east Asia—at least partly because the optimal company size in those countries is typically smaller than in the U.S. To see this, consider the case of western Europe. While visionaries proclaim a "one world, fully globalized" economy, the fact remains that most real industries are dominated by national (or regional) firms, for a variety of reasons. And since the largest economy in Europe, Germany's, is less than one third the size of the United States', it follows that even very competent German, French, Italian, or Spanish

---

43. A Towers Perrin Company survey of 1,575 firms quoted in Gleckman (1994) documents that over 35 percent of responding companies offered incentive payments to non-executives in 1994 (up from just 30 percent in 1992), and the average payout as a percentage of base pay was 7.3 percent (compared to 6.2 percent in 1992).

TABLE 2.5

CHARACTERISTICS, STRENGTHS, AND WEAKNESSES OF THE FINANCIAL-INTERMEDIARY-BASED SYSTEM OF CORPORATE FINANCE

This table details the key financial, managerial, and operational characteristics of the closed corporations that are typical of the financial-intermediary-based corporate finance systems commonly associated with continental Europe (particularly Germany) and most developing countries. The strengths and weaknesses of this system are also detailed.

A. Characteristics of the Financial-Intermediary-Based Corporate Finance System

1. Relatively few large, independent, publicly-traded companies. European economies typically dominated by a large number of mid-sized, closely-held companies that are either private or have infrequently-traded shares listed. Many companies remain family-owned or controlled. Even the largest European companies tend to be smaller than American or Japanese firms from the same industry.

2. A small number of very strong commercial banks dominate corporate financing, and also play key corporate governance roles. Banks and client companies have close, enduring financial ties, and bankers frequently serve on company boards.

3. Commercial banks have investment banking powers as well, and serve as universal financiers for client firms—providing bank loans for working capital and long-term financing, and underwriting (or purchasing) stock when equity financing is required.

4. Capital markets play small, but growing, roles in corporate finance—with public equity financing being fairly rare for private companies (but commonly used for privatizations of state-owned enterprises). Bond markets very small and illiquid—often reserved exclusively for government bond issues.

5. Very little (by U.S. standards) mandated information disclosure, and therefore little transparency in corporate finance or governance. Less reliance on formal regulation and legal contracting than in U.S. system, and greater reliance on long-term and informal business relationships.

6. Far less reliance on professional managers (particularly MBA-trained) in most European companies than in competing U.S. firms, and far less reliance on stock-based compensation for either managers or employees.

7. Relatively inactive market for corporate control, with hostile takeovers being particularly rare. Formal and informal protection of national firms from hostile foreign acquisition, or even competition. Often very close relationship between leading companies and the national government.

B. Strengths of the Financial-Intermediary-Based Corporate Finance System

1. Intermediaries are natural corporate monitors, and usually have the internal clout to discipline poorly-performing management teams. European bankruptcy laws also tend to favor creditors over shareholders and managers—effectively increasing the corporate governance power of bank monitors.

2. Commercial banks enjoy natural comparative advantages (established branch networks, connections to the national payments system, etc.) in raising and allocating investment capital, compared to public capital markets. Able to provide full line of financial services for client firms.

(continued)

TABLE 2.5 (CONTINUED)

3. Intermediaries are especially capable of building long-term relationships with client firm management teams (becoming insiders). This close relationship allows direct, low cost transfer of information between banker and client.

4. Intermediary-based systems appear better able to handle borrower financial distress than capital-market-based systems. Negotiating workout terms is much easier in a private, high-information setting than in a public forum with a large number of bondholders.

5. Intermediaries seem able to fund multi-year investment programs of their client firms more effectively than capital markets—which are geared to single, large, infrequent financings.

C. Weaknesses of the Financial-Intermediary-Based Corporate Finance System

1. Inherent conflict of interest for bankers simultaneously acting as creditors and shareholders—particularly when bankers sit on client firm boards.

2. Very little transparency in corporate financing and corporate governance systems. High potential for abuse and self-dealing when key corporate decisions are made secretly—without fear of ever having to face public disclosure or accounting.

3. Channeling even large scale financings through intermediaries can result in higher costs than if large projects were funded on capital markets. Higher financing costs for business an especially severe problem if nation's banking system is not sufficiently competitive.

4. Information processing technology is weakening the value of bank franchises—and strengthening the competitive advantages of capital markets—around the world. Simultaneously, deregulation is reducing bank access to low-cost funding.

(not to mention Dutch, Belgian, Greek, or Swedish) companies are likely to be far smaller than their North American counterparts. History and political philosophy also influence the preference for the open corporate form in the U.S. and for the closed form elsewhere. Few other countries have taken as extreme steps as Americans have to limit the growth of concentrated economic power within families or to restrict the growth of financial intermediaries to limited geographic areas.[44] Therefore, European and Asian companies have often viewed their governments as allies and protectors (rather than as adversaries), and the fact that they could rely on strong "universal" banks for interme-diated debt and equity financing meant that successful family businesses were not forced to sell shares publicly in order to finance continued growth.

All of this is not to suggest that European and Asian economies are populated only by small "cottage industries"—far from it. All of these countries have their share of large, globally-competitive companies (although many of the larger companies either are or were SOEs); and all have stock markets. The fact remains that publicly-traded companies account for a much smaller fraction of total economic activity in continental

---

44. The flaws in America's corporate governance system are analyzed in detail in Grundfest (1990), Roe (1990), and Porter (1992).

Europe, east Asia (outside of Japan), and Latin America than in the U.S., Canada, and Great Britain. And even in the U.S., closed corporations play a far greater role in economic life than is commonly realized, because most of the companies in the vibrant entrepreneurial sector of the economy are either privately held or have retained very tight ownership structures even after becoming publicly-listed. Since companies with fewer than 500 employees have generated most of the more than 25 million new jobs created in the U.S. during the last fifteen years (since 1979, employment at Fortune 500 companies has declined by a third, to 12 million), the competitiveness of the entreprenurial form seems well established.

STRENGTHS   What, then, are the competitive advantages of the closed corporate form? Principally focus, flexibility, and unity of will. Since the ownership structures of these firms are so tight, important decisions on corporate policy can be made quickly, and then can be executed by people with a significant ownership stake in the business.[45] In a related vein, since managers and shareholders tend to be the same people (or very close associates), there are few agency problems resulting from the separation of ownership and control. Furthermore, as relatively small companies, closed corporations almost have to specialize and adopt a niche market strategy—and are thus likely to develop a contestable expertise in their industry. An important recent stream of academic research has documented that publicly-traded companies which pursue one or a very few lines of business in which they enjoy a core competency are rewarded with a higher market valuation than are firms with many lines of business. If corporate **focus** is positively related to market valuation for publicly-traded U.S. corporations, it is likely to be an even more decisive competitive advantage for smaller private companies.[46]

WEAKNESSES   On the other hand, we should not glamorize closed corporations, because they also suffer from inherent competitive disadvantages. The fact that corporate shareholders have non-saleable ownership claims, and are often also corporate managers, has several unsatisfactory implications. For one thing, illiquid claims imply an inability for current stockholders either to diversify their personal wealth or to attract and compensate non-family, professional managers, since new owner/managers must be able to buy out existing owners.[47] Basic principles of labor economics suggests that

---

45. A sense of the flexibility that capable private firm managers enjoy can be found in Cornell and Shapiro (1988) and Finegan (1991). However, the challenges are also great. To understand the creativity (and sense of humor) required to finance a growing young company, see Posner (1992).

46. With the exception of Lang and Stulz (1994), the most influential articles in the focus literature—including work by Berger and Ofek (1995), Lang, Poulsen, and Stulz (1995), John and Ofek (1995), and the paper which gave the literature its name, Comment and Jarrell (1995)—appear in the January 1995 issue of the **Journal of Financial Economics**.

47. A related problem that bedevils many private (or closely held) firms is the inability to separate the financial preferences of the managers from those of the other owners. This usually causes the firm to have less-than-optimal debt levels, because of the manager's fear that high debt levels will lead to financial distress—which would harm poorly-diversified managers far more than other shareholders. For documentation of this point, see Friend and Lang (1988). In a similar vein, Saunders, Strock, and Travlos (1990) document that stockholder controlled banks are willing to take greater risks than are managerially controlled banks.

artificially restricting the pool of available executive talent to those people with existing (usually inherited) wealth is sub-optimal, and is likely to leave a firm at a competitive disadvantage relative to companies that can hire the best and the brightest, regardless of their wealth endowments. Furthermore, if current owners cannot sell their shares to outsiders, they can become trapped in a hostile control coalition, made all the more ugly because no one can escape.[48] One need only reflect on painful family memories to understand some of the strains that can occur in closely-held firms.

Closed corporations are also prone to being financially constrained, especially when they must compete with publicly-traded companies.[49] Since it is very expensive and difficult, if not impossible, to raise new equity capital through private equity sales, closed corporations are typically limited to retained earnings or private debt issues.[50] This reliance on intermediated financing can be a severe competitive disadvantage for private companies, particularly in rapidly growing industries and in international trade—where orders tend to be quite large, and where the lag between ordering, producing, delivering, and then receiving payment for specialized products can stretch for six months or more, putting great strain on firms with inadequate levels of working capital. Finally, privately-held companies reap none of the brand promotion benefits that inevitably comes from having actively-traded stock, and must therefore rely on (purchased) advertising for market penetration.

2.4.3 Large Industrial Groupings

It has only been recently that finance researchers have begun to seriously examine industrial groups, since they have played virtually no role in the American economy since the early 1900s. The key features of the large industrial groupings—which are most prominent in Asia—are (1) a close alliance of large manufacturing, marketing, and banking companies that seek to control all aspects of sourcing, production, and retail distribution; (2) the group is held together by a series of cross-shareholdings, joint ventures, and product-development agreements; and (3) there is typically a commercial bank at the center of the grouping, providing for the financial needs of group companies, and often exercising direct managerial control, particularly if the company encounters operating or financial difficulties.[51] In most cases, some or all of the group

---

48. As Karpoff and Rice (1989) make clear, restrictions on share tradeability can lead to degenerate control contests and generally poor corporate performance.

49. For documentation that smaller companies are in fact more financially constrained than larger ones, in that small firms have lower levels of liquidity and higher debt ratios than do larger firms, see Dwyer and Lynn (1989). The economic significance of being financially constrained has been demonstrated by Hoshi, Kashyap, and Scharfstein (1990), and Whited (1992). Both of these papers document that financial stress (particularly illiquidity) can lead to reduced levels of corporate investment. Clark and Ofek (1994) discuss how being financially distressed changes the likelihood that a firm will be acquired. They also document the disheartening fact that mergers rarely cure financial distress—which is not surprising, since Hotchkiss (1995) demonstrates that even Chapter 11 restructuring leaves most distressed firms financially weak.

50. As Timmons and Sandler (1989), among others, make clear, few private companies can issue bonds on public capital markets.

51. The role of banks in Japanese industrial groupings is discussed in Aoki (1990), Hoshi, Kashyap, and Scharfstein (1990, 1991), Stephen Prowse (1990, 1992), Frankel (1991), and Berglof and Perotti (1994).

companies have publicly-traded shares—and for most Japanese groupings, other group firms typically own less than half of the outstanding shares of any one company—but public shareholders generally are powerless to control, or even influence, group policy. Power is tightly held by the lead company of the group, which frequently coordinates managerial training and transfers within group companies.[52] The characteristics, strengths, and weaknesses of the industrial-group system of corporate finance are detailed in Table 2.6.

The most successful examples of large industrial groupings can be seen in Japan and South Korea, two countries which industrialized only within the last century and which also had to recover from massively destructive wars and foreign conquest within the past six decades. As might be expected, this historical need to play industrial "catch up"—and to do so without surrendering control of their development to western companies—explains why these societies have been willing to tolerate these truly colossal companies that wield a degree of economic power that would be considered intolerable in the West. In fact, the "trusts" and industrial families assembled by John D. Rockefeller, J. P. Morgan, and other American business leaders around the turn of the twentieth century closely resemble the modern Asian groups (except the latter tend to cover far more industries than did the American groups). The U.S. groupings were long ago broken up by government action, and any reemergence of these groups in America or Europe has been rendered impossible by a combination of social pressure and regulatory policy—particularly antitrust legislation.[53] On the other hand, the undoubted industrial success of these groups in two non-Western nations has prompted many developing countries in Asia, Africa, and Latin America to attempt to develop their own versions of the Japanese *Keiretsu* or the Korean *Chaebol*.

HISTORICAL EVOLUTION   In order to understand how these groups function, lets briefly examine how these groups developed in Japan, and consider how they function today. We then examine the strengths and weaknesses of this organizational form, which encompasses such household names as Hitachi, Toshiba, Mitsubishi, and Toyota. When Commodore Perry first forced Japan to open itself to international trade in 1853, the country was stuck in a 250-year time warp and was hopelessly behind the West technologically and militarily. Since this was the heyday of western imperialism, it soon became obvious to Japanese leaders that a crash industrialization program would have to be adopted for the country to retain its independence. Following the Meiji Restoration in 1868—which brought the emperor and a group of forward-looking aristocrats to power—Japan began to industrialize at a phenomenal rate. This economic transformation was spearheaded by several large, family-controlled corporate groups

---

52. While most *Keiretsu* companies began as family businesses, many are several hundred years old and no residual family influence exists in any of the major groups. These companies are effectively controlled by incumbent management, in spite of the fact that managers typically own very little of their own firms' stock. Kaplan and Minton (1994) describe the determinants of corporate board appointments and discuss the implications of outside director appointments for corporate managers.

53. Not everyone is convinced that this Western hostility to powerful financial groupings is warranted. In particular, Jensen (1989) describes the workings of the 1920s-era Morgan group of companies in very favorable terms.

TABLE 2.6

CHARACTERISTICS, STRENGTHS, AND WEAKNESSES OF THE INDUSTRIAL GROUP SYSTEM OF CORPORATE FINANCE

This table details the key financial, managerial, and operational characteristics of the interlocking corporations that are typical of the industrial group corporate finance systems commonly associated with Japan (*Keiretsu*) and Korea (*Chaebol*). The strengths and weaknesses of this system are also detailed.

A. Characteristics of the Industrial Group Corporate Finance System

1. National economies are dominated by a small number of immensely large and powerful industrial groups, who compete with each other in a broad range of industries.

2. The industrial groups include numerous large manufacturing, distribution, and assembly companies, with a lead company (usually a major commercial bank) at the center coordinating group activities. Group companies own sizeable blocs of each other's shares, and there are frequently interlocking directorships.

3. The lead company, which is typically a bank, exercises control over the group either through direct majority shareholdings (*Chaebol*) in group companies, or through heirarchical personal and managerial authority—supplemented by sizeable, but not majority, shareholdings—exercised by the lead company's management team (*Keiretsu*).

4. In addition to being dominant in their home markets, the groups are also their countries' leading exporters. Most enjoy close relationships with the national government, which supports and protects the groups from foreign competition. Foreign ownership of group company shares is limited or non-existent.

5. The two main types of industrial groups differ regarding the extent of founding family involvement. Founding families still effectively control Korea's *Chaebol*, but Japan's *Keiretsu*—being centuries old, in some cases—all are run by professional managers.

6. Capital markets in general, and equity markets in particular, play very small roles in the corporate finance and governance systems of countries with industrial groups. Even where group company shares are publicly-traded (Japan), individual shareholders have almost no real power, and the stock market is not truly a market for corporate control. Takeovers are rare, and hostile takeovers are nonexistent.

7. Except for *Chaebol* founding-family members, significant share ownership is rare for managers of group companies, and stock-based compensation is almost never observed for employees or managers.

B. Strengths of the Industrial Group Corporate Finance System

1. The group system appears to be an effective way to achieve rapid economic development—without reliance on foreign investment, and without excessive government involvement in the private sector—provided that government policy assures competition between the groups.

2. Competition between groups, and non-exclusive intra-group purchasing policies, allow the groups to build networks of strong, inter-related companies that rival small national economies in their size and in the breadth of their industrial capabilities. This ability to manage coordinated technological *systems* makes the groups potent competitors—particularly in international markets—and discourages foreign entry into the domestic market.

(continued)

TABLE 2.6 (CONTINUED)

3. Strong intra-group links allow efficient financial contracting. Group members can rely on the lead bank for financing of both routine business activities and long-term investment programs, and banks are able to monitor and discipline group managers more easily. Group system is particularly effective at managing financial distress.

4. Centralized managerial control allows rapid dissemination of market information, manufacturing expertise, and technological innovations throughout group companies. Most groups are technological leaders in several different industries, so this cross-pollination can be very beneficial.

C. Weaknesses of the Industrial Group Corporate Finance System

1. Unless all group members grow at similar rates, the group will become inherently unstable—as strong companies are "taxed" to provide subsidies for weaker companies. Also a tendency for strongest, most internationalized companies to "graduate" out of group control by tapping international capital markets for financing.

2. Groups must fight a natural tendency to purchase inputs exclusively from group members, even if competitors offer lower cost or higher quality. Put differently, it is very hard to inject market discipline into group contracting, while still capturing internal synergies and the benefits of economies of scale and scope.

3. National reliance on industrial groups (who control distribution channels) imposes immense costs on consumers, who are invariably precluded from purchasing lower cost foreign products—or domestic products produced by non-group companies.

4. There is little evidence that industrial group system can be effectively transplanted outside of Japan and Korea. Similar groupings—U.S. conglomerates, multi-national European industrial syndicates, and state-owned enterprises in developing countries and in command economies—in other countries have been dismal failures.

called *Zaibatsu*, which held massive sway over the economy and provided the where-withal for Japan's military to fight two great wars against Western powers—successfully against Czarist Russia in 1905 and then catastrophically against the United States in 1941–1945. During the American occupation of Japan after World War II, the *Zaibatsu* were broken up and shares in the companies were sold to public shareholders. However, once the American occupation ended in 1955, these corporate groups reemerged in more benign form as the *Keiretsu,* and these groups once again led Japan from total defeat to world prominence, and made Japanese products synonymous with quality and technological prowess the world over.

CHARACTERISTICS   Companies within modern Japanese *Keiretsu* typically own 20–25 percent of each other's shares, and the groups are typically organized heirar-chically—with supplier companies producing intermediate goods for companies at the top of the pyramid, which then market products domestically through retailers they effectively control and internationally through huge trading companies. Mutual shareholdings help cement these long-term business relationships (the supplier firms are typically *not* subsidiaries of the lead company), and group strategy is often controlled by the lead bank. These groups seem to have developed a very effective balance between the production efficiencies resulting from horizontal and vertical integration and the competitive benefits of arms-length contracting with more than one supplier.

While Korea did not explicitly set out to copy a Japanese model, the policies adopted by the government after the end of the Korean War in 1953 led to the creation of huge, family-owned corporate groups (the best known of which is Hyundai) that resemble the *Keiretsu*, except that the lead companies usually have even tighter control of group companies. These *Chaebol* control a much larger fraction of total economic activity in Korea than the *Keiretsu* do in Japan—so much that the new democratic government in Korea is attempting to rein in their power (see Nakarmi 1995).

As successful as these Japanese and Korean groups have been, the model has not proven to be particularly portable, as few countries have been able to develop successful imitators.[54] American conglomerates, pan-European industrial syndicates, and state-owned development companies throughout the Third World are all examples of large corporate groupings that have failed abysmally. It is also clear that reliance on such immensely powerful corporations has real social costs, which are principally borne by consumers in the form of high-priced products and limited choices and by employees, who suffer from severely restricted alternative career opportunities (see Kester 1991). Dominance by giant firms also tends to restrict entrepreneurial opportunities, which is a tremendous problem for countries trying to develop without relying on foreign companies for capital or technology. Furthermore, both Korea and (especially) Japan are encountering severe friction with their trading partners in the West, at least partly because these groups play such dominant roles in the national production and distribution systems, and they make it very difficult for foreign companies to successfully enter the domestic markets—even if the foreign companies offer high-quality, competitively-priced goods.[55] Finally, experience has shown that when managers of conglomerate firms are able to rely completely on internally-generated cash flows for investment—as happens when manufacturing firms become profitable enough to no longer need bank financing—they almost inevitably squander these profits through diversification attempts or by trying to prop up existing businesses from which the firm should actually exit.[56] When the state plays a leading role in large industrial groups, as it frequently does in the developing world, these problems of high-cost products, restrictions on market entry by competitors, and unwise investment spending become even worse.

---

54. While there are clearly no simple rules that will guarantee international business success in the 1990s, useful guides to assessing opportunities and formulating strategies are provided in Pavel and McElravey (1990), Hirtle (1991), and Lessard (1991).

55. Cutts (1992) has an especially good description of how the Japanese distribution system works to keep foreign goods out of the domestic market.

56. A classic example of this problem is provided in Cooper and Richards (1988), where they document that Standard Oil of Ohio (SOHIO) essentially squandered the immense cash flows received from their Alaskan North Slope investments. Jensen (1993) also describes the immense difficulties involved with the need to exit a declining industry, though Dial and Murphy (1995) provide a case study example (General Dynamics) of how a properly-executed exit strategy can be value-creating.

2.5   HOW CORPORATE CONTROL IS EXERCISED

As we said earlier, one of the most important and pervasive problems any modern economy must solve is how to properly structure the incentives of managers who run large corporations, and then ensure that these companies are run in the best interests of society in general, and shareholders in particular. We focus in this section on how the **corporate governance system** operates for large, open corporations in the United States, but we also conclude by briefly comparing this system of governance with that of non-U.S. companies and of American closed corporations. When we speak of the corporate governance *system*, we will be including both the internal (boards of directors, shareholders meetings, proxy contests) and the external mechanisms that shareholders can employ to influence the behavior of corporate managers. When we speak more specifically about how corporate managers are disciplined through external transactions (mergers and acquisitions, leveraged buyouts, shareholder lawsuits), we will discuss the workings of the **market for corporate control**.

2.5.1   Internal Corporate Governance Mechanisms in the United States

Publicly-traded U.S. companies are required (either by law or by exchange regulations, or both) to annually disclose a great deal of information about corporate revenues, expenses, and profits, as well as about executive compensation and the ownership of the company's voting securities.[57] These firms are also required to hold an annual shareholders' meeting, which is open to all owners of even a single share of common stock. In announcing these meetings, corporations send every shareholder a **proxy statement** that describes the meeting agenda, spells out precisely which issues are to be voted on by shareholders, and provides a form for the shareholders to use either to vote personally at the meeting or to assign the right to vote the shares they own to someone else—which is what "giving someone your proxy" means. While common law gives one vote to each shareholder, modern corporate law assigns one vote to each share held, so a single shareholder owning 50 percent-plus-one-share can win every election and generally is able to set corporate policy. The most important votes taken by shareholders occur when they select the company's **board of directors**, since this board is the primary vehicle of internal corporate governance in the United States (as well as in all other modern capitalist systems).

Most corporate elections are usually staid affairs where shareholders are asked to vote for or against a single slate of company directors—who have been nominated by a committee of the current board of directors—and the results of these elections are almost always foreordained. However, these elections can become quite exciting if the current management team (and the board of directors supporting it) is being challenged by a rival group in a "proxy fight". In these contests, shareholders of the firm are solicited by both the current managers and the rival group, and individual stockholders are asked to assign their proxies to one group or the other. Whichever group can garner the most votes wins the election, elects its slate of directors, and then sets corporate policy. Shareholder votes

---

57. A summary of the disclosure requirements for exchange-listed companies is provided in chapter 6, "How Public is Public?", of Peat Marwick Main & Company (1987).

are also required to approve corporate mergers, to authorize major asset sales, to amend the firm's corporate charter, and to authorize the issuance of new equity securities.

RIGHTS AND RESPONSIBILITIES OF CORPORATE BOARDS   Once elected, the firm's board of directors is responsible for hiring, firing, monitoring, and setting the compensation of the firm's managers—the most important of which is the Chief Executive Officer (CEO). The board has broad discretion to direct the affairs of the company, and is supposed to ensure that the firm is managed in the best interest of shareholders. In other words, both the board of directors and the firm's managers are supposed to act as "agents" of the shareholders, but there is no guarantee they will do so, and—practically speaking—there is very little that shareholders can do to discipline or replace a group of managers and directors that begins to confuse the corporate good with its own.[58] This is primarily because of the **collective action problems** that arise from having a large number of atomistic shareholders rather than having ownership concentrated in the hands of a few, powerful stockholders. While it might collectively be in the shareholders' best interests for someone to monitor and discipline corporate managers, it is in no one individual shareholder's best interest to do so, because he or she would bear all the cost of this action but would have to share the bulk of the benefits with other stockholders.

The net result of these improperly aligned incentives is that many corporations can become effectively "hijacked" by entrenched corporate managers. Frequently, a company controlled by such an incompetent or predatory management team will begin to lose ground in product or factor markets to more efficient and energetic competitors, which eventually causes the firm to experience financial distress—or even bankruptcy. Alternatively, a poorly-performing company can become the target of a takeover attempt.

2.5.2 The U.S. Market for Corporate Control

Corporate combinations in the United States fall into one of two categories, depending upon whether the target firm is purchased by the bidder in an **acquisition**, or whether the two firms are combined as equals in a **merger** that creates a third, new company. These combinations differ from each other in terms of.

1. *Accounting treatment.* Acquisitions are generally subject to the **purchase method of accounting**—where the transaction is accounted for as if the acquirer simply purchased assets with the market value of the target firm—while mergers are usually subject to **pooling of interest** treatment, where the resulting firm is essentially accounted for as a linear combination of the accounts of the merging companies.[59]

---

58. Though some boards become cheering sections for incompetent but domineering managers, many others do not. In fact, there is considerable evidence that most company boards will (eventually) replace poorly performing managers, and that the stock market will reward them with a stock price increase. Papers that examine the factors that precipitate top management turnover, the wealth effects of company-initiated management changes, or operating changes following management changes include Furtado and Rozeff (1987), Warner, Watts, and Wruck (1988), Weisbach (1988), Gilson (1989), Gilson and Vetsuypens (1993), Murphy and Zimmerman (1993), and Weisbach (1995).

59. The tax and accounting treatment accorded different types of mergers is described in Hayn (1989), while Jarrell and Bradley (1980), Bittlingmayer (1992), and Malatesta and Thompson (1993) describe the effect of the various laws that regulate takeover activity in the United States.

2. *Method of payment.* Acquisitions usually involve cash payments made by the bidder to target firm shareholders, while mergers usually involve an exchange of stock.[60]

3. *Role of the target firm's board of directors and both firms' shareholders.* Mergers are almost invariably negotiated between the boards of the two companies and must then be approved by the shareholders of both companies, while an acquirer can bypass the target firm's board by making a **tender offer** to buy shares directly from target firm shareholders.[61]

Takeover attempts that are supported by the target firm's board of directors are called **friendly offers**, while those bids that are opposed by the target's board are called **hostile offers**. A summary of merger and acquisition activity in the United States over the period 1969–1993 is provided in Table 2.7.

Because tender offers can be made directly to target firm shareholders, even if these bids are opposed by the target's board of directors, many "disciplinary" takeovers are effected through tender offers. Given that they stand to be replaced, entrenched insider groups frequently fight these bids using legal tactics, share repurchases, poison pills, and other **defensive strategies** designed to discourage the bidder from pursuing the target further. They frequently succeed in fending off takeover bids even when they would yield target firm shareholders very large share premiums.[62]

PATTERNS   While a detailed description of the empirical regularities that have been documented by scholars researching the American corporate control market is beyond the scope of this chapter, it is worthwhile to list a few of the most important facts that have been documented during the past dozen years. These are listed below:[63]

---

60. For analyses of how the method of payment affects shareholder returns, see Travlos (1987) and Huang and Walkling (1987).

61. See Huang and Walkling (1987) and Jennings and Mazzeo (1993) for documentation of the importance of target firm resistance.

62. Takeover defenses can be grouped into two main categories, those which must be voted on beforehand by the firm's shareholders and those which can be adopted unilaterally by the firm's board of directors. The former are generally referred to as "antitakeover charter amendments" (ACAs), because they are actually revisions of a firm's corporate charter and are usually designed to force a bidder to either pay a higher price for a firm's shares or to offer the same terms to all shareholders, rather than to a fraction of shareholders in a "two-tiered" offer. ACAs are studied in Jarrell and Poulsen (1987), McWilliams (1990), and Comment and Schwert (1995). Unilaterally-adopted takeover defenses include poison pills, legal challenges to bidders, and targeted share repurchases—at a premium over market value—of firm shares held by potential hostile bidders. This practice is called "greenmail", and is studied in Bradley and Wakeman (1983) and Klein and Rosenfeld (1988). Legal challenges are examined in Jarrell (1985). The ability of non-targeted share repurchases to serve as takeover deterrents is examined in Persons (1994).

63. These summary points are drawn from an enormous number of academic articles. Rather than attempt to document each point with its own citations, we will refer the interested reader to a handful of the most important and widely-cited corporate control empirical papers and literature reviews. These include Jensen and Ruback (1983), DeAngelo, DeAngelo, and Rice (1984), Dennis and McConnell (1986), Palepu (1986), Huang and Walkling (1987), Travlos (1987), Bradley, Desai, and Kim (1988), Jarrell, Brickley, and Netter (1988), Kaplan (1989a), Marais, Schipper, and Smith (1989), Mikkelson and Partch (1989), Kaplan and Stein (1990), McConnell and Servaes (1990), Muscarella and Vetsuypens (1990), Stulz, Walkling, and Song (1990), Ambrose and Megginson (1992), Healy, Palepu, and Ruback (1992), Song and Walkling (1993), Vijh (1994), Cotter and Zenner (1994), Wruck (1994), Denis (1994), and Denis and Denis (1995).

TABLE 2.7

STATISTICAL OVERVIEW OF U.S. CORPORATE CONTROL MARKET, 1969–1993

This table provides annual summaries of the number of merger and acquisition (M&A) announcements, the total value of these announced deals, the method of payment, the number of divestitures, the average price-earnings (P/E) ratio offered, and the average premium offered in M&A deals for the period 1969 to 1993.

Year	Number of M&A Announcements	Total Dollar Value Offered ($ billions)	Method of Payment			Number of Divestitures	Average P/E Offered	Average Prem. Offered
			Cash	Stock	Comb.			
1969	6,107	$23.7	32%	57%	11%	801	21.0	25.7%
1970	5,152	16.4	29	52	16	1,401	23.1	33.4
1971	4,608	12.6	32	49	17	1,920	24.3	33.1
1972	4,801	16.7	34	51	14	1,770	21.4	33.8
1973	4,040	16.7	41	44	14	1,557	18.9	44.5
1974	2,861	12.5	48	33	16	1,331	13.5	50.1
1975	2,297	11.8	48	27	23	1,236	13.3	41.4
1976	2,276	20.0	52	26	20	1,204	15.1	40.4
1977	2,224	21.9	54	26	18	1,002	13.8	40.9
1978	2,106	34.2	46	30	23	820	14.3	46.2
1979	2,128	43.5	53	26	20	752	14.3	49.9
1980	1,889	44.3	47	31	21	666	15.2	49.9
1981	2,395	82.6	42	34	23	830	15.6	48.0
1982	2,346	53.8	38	29	31	875	13.9	47.4
1983	2,533	73.1	32	35	33	932	16.7	37.7
1984	2,543	122.2	43	26	30	900	17.2	37.9
1985	3,001	179.8	51	23	26	1,218	18.0	37.1
1986	3,336	173.1	42	32	26	1,259	22.2	38.2
1987	2,302	163.7	41	34	24	807	23.3	38.3
1988	2,258	246.9	56	21	22	894	21.6	41.9
1989	2,366	221.1	46	30	23	1,055	20.9	41.0
1990	2,074	108.2	40	31	28	940	20.1	42.0
1991	1,877	71.2	34	34	31	849	20.0	35.1
1992	2,574	96.7	22	40	37	1,026	22.7	41.0
1993	2,663	176.4	25	40	35	1,134	24.4	38.7

SOURCE: MERGERSTAT ® REVIEW 1993 (MERRILL LYNCH BUSINESS ADVISORY SERVICES: SCHAUMBERG, IL, 1994).

1. There appear to be distinct takeover waves in the U.S. corporate control market. Both the number and dollar values of friendly and hostile takeovers surged during the 1890s, the 1920s, the late 1960s, the mid-to-late 1980s, and the mid 1990s. While there are important differences in the degree to which these takeover waves increased corporate concentration, and in the preferred method of payment, all of these periods were times of technological change and economic expansion, and all coincide with sharp increases in overall equity valuations.

2. Most corporate control transactions that yield significant ownership changes—including successful mergers and acquisitions, **divestitures** (the sale or spinning off of corporate divisions), **leveraged buyouts** (wherein incumbent managers and LBO specialists buy out public shareholders with borrowed money), and **leveraged recapitalizations** (buying out some, but not all, public shareholders with newly-issued debt while remaining publicly-traded)—also yield **net synergistic gains** for the security-holders of the firms involved (the combined value of outstanding securities increases after the transaction). These gains—plus microeconomic analyses suggesting that transformed firms maintain or increase value-creating financial investments (capital expenditures and R&D spending), as well as employment levels—contradict the negative public image that takeovers have acquired, and instead suggest that these transactions transfer ownership of corporate resources into more economically capable hands.

3. There are distinct, systematic patterns to the returns various security-holder classes earn during corporate control transactions. The strongest and most consistent regularity is that target firm shareholders earn large, positive abnormal returns in virtually all types of transactions. Target shareholder returns are larger (1) for LBOs than for external takeovers; (2) for cash transactions than for stock transactions; (3) in contested bids than in single-bidder transactions; and (4) in recent years than during the 1960s. Bidding firm shareholder returns are more mixed, in that (1) bidder shareholders earned significantly positive abnormal returns during the 1960s, but these have decreased over time; (2) bidding firm shareholders on average break even in those takeovers where cash is used, but lose when stock is the the form of payment; and (3) invariably lose when their firm acts as a **white knight** (enters an ongoing takeover battle to rescue the target firm from an unwanted suitor). Finally, bondholders tend to break even in mergers and acquisitions, but typically lose out in LBOs.

4. The likelihood that a takeover bid will be launched, the likelihood that the bid will be opposed by target firm management, the likelihood that the bid will ultimately be successful, and the division of total security-holder wealth gains are all related to target and bidder firm insider and institutional shareholdings. In general, insider shareholdings tend to increase equity values for all firms (whether involved in corporate control contests or not), and they serve to increase the share of total gains target firm shareholders will reap in a takeover contest—though they lessen the likelihood of a bid being launched. Institutional shareholdings have a more ambiguous (and less generally positive) impact on equilibrium valuation, the likelihood of a takeover bid being launched, and the division of total gains if a bid is successful. Finally, though takeover targets cannot be predicted in advance, they

do tend to be smaller, less profitable, and less popular with institutional investors than other firms in their industry.

5. At the federal government level, there has been a pronounced relaxation of antitrust enforcement since the Reagan Administration came to power in 1981, and this has resulted in many **horizontal** (within industry) mergers and acquisitions that would have been unthinkable during the 1960s or 1970s. Furthermore, many of the technology-driven corporate combinations (particularly those involving the "information superhighway") of the early 1990s were actively supported by federal regulators. On the other hand, state governments have become increasingly willing to intervene in—or to discourage the launching of—corporate control contests that target companies headquartered in their state. Finally, at both the state and federal levels, the primary legal venue for regulating or adjudicating corporate control contests has shifted from the regulatory agencies to the courts.

ALTERNATIVE MEANS OF EXERCISING CORPORATE CONTROL   Even when disciplinary takeovers work as planned, hostile acquisitions must be considered very crude (though effective) methods of exercising corporate control. Given the high costs associated with relying on takeovers to correct corporate governance problems, and given the ineffectiveness of other disciplinary methods—such as proxy contests and individual shareholder activism—academics and policy-makers have begun to explore alternative methods of ensuring that public companies will become and will remain responsive to the legitimate desires of corporate shareholders. One important development of the early 1990s has been the rise in the power and the assertiveness of institutional investors, who collectively control over 50 percent of the publicly-traded stock of Corporate America. The largest single bloc of equity is controlled by pension funds, and these—particularly the public funds, such as the California Public Employees Retirement System (CALPERS) fund—have been in the vanguard of opposing management-sponsored takeover defense initiatives, challenging "unwarranted" grants of stock options and other executive perks, and demanding performance from poorly-performing management teams. These newly-energized large shareholders were instrumental in effecting a series of major boardroom "coups" that toppled the CEOs of IBM, General Motors and American Express (among others) in the early 1990s, and increased institutional investor activism probably offers the single best (practical) hope for effectively improving the American corporate governance system in the years ahead.

2.5.3 Non-U.S. Corporate Governance Systems

While most other countries did not experience a takeover boom comparable to that experienced in the U.S. (and the U.K.) during the 1980s, we should not jump to the conclusion that the corporate governance systems of any of these countries works flawlessly. Few nations seem to have as much trouble monitoring and controlling large companies as Americans do, but that is partly because there are generally fewer large companies outside of the U.S., and where they do exist the corporate governance systems often make trade-offs Americans would consider unacceptable. In Japan, for example, *Keiretsu* companies are firmly controlled and monitored by the lead company of the group—thereby ensuring efficiency and loyalty to group objectives—but individual shareholders are effectively powerless in corporate affairs and corporate dividend pay-outs are meagerly. European companies, on the other hand, are monitored and disciplined by banks to a much greater degree than are American companies, but they too are generally unresponsive to shareholder demands (especially in Germany, where **codetermination** laws give workers the right to elect one-third of the board of large companies) and are also frequently hobbled by protectionist government policies and mandated spending for employee benefits.

2.5.4 Governance Systems Employed by U.S. Venture Capitalists

Perhaps the single most efficient corporate governance model anywhere in the world is that observed in venture-capital-backed firms in the United States. Venture capital investment agreements typically strike a remarkably precise balance between shifting business risk onto the entrepreneur and giving him or her the incentives to accomplish mutually-agreed upon objectives and to maximize overall firm value.[64] Unfortunately, this governance model is strictly limited in its general applicability and is usually considered unduly restrictive by all but the most confident of managers.[65] In summary, all real corporate governance systems have both strengths and weaknesses, and the overall effectiveness of a given firm's control system usually depends on the competence, integrity, and inter-personal skills of the owners and managers involved.

2.6   COMPENSATION AND INCENTIVES: THEORY AND EVIDENCE

In addition to sparking research on takeovers, voting arrangements, and other corporate control issues, the importance of the agency costs inherent in the shareholder/manager relationship in large firms has also prompted increased interest in how these problems might be addressed through the design of a firm's compensation policies.[66] While most people are aware that American executives tend to be much better paid than their counterparts in other countries, and most have heard "horror stories" about executives re-

---

64. The workings of institutional venture capital firms are described in Sahlman (1988, 1990). In addition, Lerner (1994) examines how venture capitalists decide whether or not a firm is ready to go public, while Lerner (1995) discusses how venture capitalists provide ongoing monitoring for firms that have already gone public.

65. Another example of an organizational hybrid form that has demonstrated remarkable effectiveness is the previously-public company that has become privately-held following a leveraged buyout (LBO). While LBOs have been much maligned in the popular press, academic research has found them to be very effective at resolving corporate governance agency problems and at creating value while privately held. See Kaplan (1989a,b), Lehn, Netter, Poulsen (1990), Muscarella and Vetsuypens (1990), and Ofek (1994).

66. As with corporate control, this "modern" theory of management compensation only came of age during the 1980s, and its development was also driven primarily by a handful of core theoretical and empirical articles. These include Miller and Scholes (1982), Smith and Watts (1982), Murphy (1985), Baker, Jensen, and Murphy (1988), Jensen and Murphy (1990), Smith and Watts (1992), Garen (1994), and Haubrich (1994).

ceiving multi-million dollar stock option grants even as they exhort workers to show pay "restraint", relatively few business observers understand just how complex and sophisticated modern executive compensation programs can be or how precisely they can structure (for better or worse) the incentives facing the firm's key decision-makers.[67] In this section, we will describe the principal building blocks of these packages, and then we will discuss how they can be used (and abused) to resolve manager/stockholder agency problems. We will conclude this section, and this chapter, with a brief survey of the academic research measuring the effectiveness of real compensation policies adopted by modern American open corporations.

2.6.1 Components of Standard Compensation Packages in U.S. Firms

Entry-level professional and managerial employees at most corporations have very simple compensation packages, consisting of a base annual salary plus a package of benefits that typically includes health insurance, life insurance, and a pension plan.[68] As a person moves up the corporate ladder into middle management, and finally into an executive-level position, his or her compensation package typically becomes steadily more sophisticated, and a far greater fraction of the total compensation will generally be **performance-based compensation**.[69] This means that its total value is not fixed but instead depends upon the financial performance of the business unit the person is responsible for, or upon the corporation's stock price performance, or both.

At the very top corporate levels, a manager's compensation package usually has four basic components: (1) a base salary that will be received regardless of performance; (2) a cash bonus the executive can receive as a reward if business-unit performance exceeds a certain level during a quarter or a year (bonuses are usually granted based upon recent, historical performance); (3) stock options that give the executive the right to purchase stock at a fixed price, for a given number of years into the future, but which will expire valueless unless the firm's stock price rises high enough during the option period to make exercise worthwhile; and (4) deferred cash or stock

---

67. Interestingly, it is no longer true that American executives are the highest paid in the world. A Wyatt Company study, cited in Koretz (1995), shows that in 1994 Japanese managers of large companies were the world's highest paid, and executives from Mexico, Argentina, and Hong Kong all earned more than did managers of large U.S. companies, whose cash compensation (salary and bonus) averaged slightly less than $200,000. These results, however, were largely driven by the recent appreciation of the yen against the dollar, and by the fact that U.S. managers were far more likely to receive stock options than were managers from other countries.

68. Many companies have, however, experimented with incentive compensation programs that cover most or all of a firm's employees, rather than just top management, but the empirical support for the effectiveness of these plans is hardly overwhelming. See Bhagat, Brickley, and Lease (1985), Conte and Kruse (1991), and Kohn (1993).

69. For descriptions of the components of executive compensation packages used by large corporations, see the Murphy (1985) and Jensen and Murphy (1990) articles cited above, plus Antle and Smith (1985). That shareholders approve of these plans is documented in Brickley, Bhagat, and Lease (1985) and Tehranian and Wagelein (1985). Compensation packages used in entrepreneurial companies are discussed in Tibbetts and Donovan (1989), and in the annual compensation surveys published in **Inc.** magazine.

payments that the executive can only receive if he or she remains with the company for, say, three years.

As you have probably already deduced, each of the components listed above is designed to achieve a different objective by focusing the executive's incentives on a different managerial dimension. Base salary is generally set to match industry patterns, and its economic function is to provide the manager with a fixed level of income each period that is high enough to reduce his or her fear that a few bad quarters could lead to financial ruin (as could happen if compensation was totally performance-based).[70] Bonuses are usually paid when the financial performance—measured in accounting terms such as growth in sales revenue or operating profit—of the business unit (division, subsidiary, group, etc.) an executive is responsible for exceeds a previously-agreed-upon target level.[71] Bonuses are designed to (conspicuously) reward exceptional short-term performance, and have the benefit of being targetable to business decisions and business units the executive can directly control. This is not true for stock-based compensation, since few people below the CEO level directly and materially influence the corporation's stock price.

Where bonuses focus on the individual business unit, stock option grants are designed to ensure that all executives also focus on the common corporate good, since options will only become valuable if the firm's stock price increases substantially during their managerial tenures.[72] Economists tend to love options, both because these help align the interests of managers and shareholders, and because options give managers the incentive to stress long-term corporate needs over short-term accounting profits.[73] Finally, deferred compensation packages are designed to be **golden handcuffs** that give managers the incentive to remain with the company for several years by making it very costly (in terms of compensation they would forfeit) for them to leave prior to the time these benefits **vest** (are the executive's to keep).[74] These deferred payments also effectively raise the price a competitor would have to pay to entice away one of a firm's best employees.

---

70. Baker, Jensen, and Murphy (1988) discuss salary-based compensation, and also analyze why incentive systems used in business frequently rely more on promotions and other non-cash benefits than on explicit cash payments. The importance of promotion in rewarding superior performance is documented in Blackwell, Brickley, and Weisbach (1994).

71. Reasons for using accounting earnings, rather than stock price performance, as a basis for short-term bonuses are discussed in three papers surveyed by Lambert (1993). More generally, Skinner (1993) describes how a firm's investment opportunity set affects its accounting, leverage, and compensation policies.

72. The incentive effects of stock options are discussed in Murphy (1985) and in Hemmer (1993), while Agrawal and Walkling (1994) document that takeovers are more frequent in industries where CEOs are "over-payed" (have positive abnormal compensation). The tax consequences of using options are discussed in Hite and Long (1982), Smith and Watts (1982), and Stevenson and Turner (1992). Valuation issues in the pricing (and repricing) of stock options are discussed in Huddart (1994) and Saly (1994).

73. One of the most controversial issues in the debate over compensation policies in the United States is the extent to which these policies cause managers to emphasize long-term investment over short-term earnings increases. This issue is addressed in Larcker (1983), Gibbons and Murphy (1992a), and Gaver and Gaver (1993).

74. The incentive-alignment effects of various compensation schemes are discussed in Narayanan (1985), Gibbons and Murphy (1992b), and John and John (1993).

2.6.2 Specialized Compensation Techniques and Instruments

In addition to these "standard" compensation components, there are a great many specialized current and deferred compensation schemes that can be used to achieve specific objectives. One well-publicized example is a **golden parachute**, which is a cash payment made to an executive if she loses her job (or finds her responsibilities and authority reduced) after a takeover or other change of control. This is designed to minimize key executives' opposition to takeovers that will be beneficial to shareholders but harmful to the personal interests of the management team.[75] Another specialized tool is the **stock-appreciation right**, or **phantom stock** scheme, which is designed to give managers cash payments that mirror those received by shareholders, but to do so without actually giving managers title to the underlying shares themselves. This technique is particularly useful in companies that want to minimize stock ownership dilution, but also want managers to act in shareholders' best interests. Finally, companies sometimes reward a top executive with an outright gift of a large bloc of stock, or allow the executive to purchase the bloc at a very low price. This practice is usually only observed when a new person becomes CEO, and is justified on the grounds that the firm's CEO must own a large bloc of shares—that would be prohibitively costly for an individual to purchase—to faithfully act in the shareholders' interests.[76]

—SUMMARY—

The modern corporation is an amazingly efficient and effective tool for organizing economic activity and creating wealth. So competitive is this form of business organization, that virtually every country in the world allows the legal formation of some kind of limited liability company with a separate existence from its owners, and with the right to have ownership shares traded on public capital markets. Indeed, this type of company dominates business activity throughout the developed world. However, the patterns of ownership of these limited liability companies, and the methods used to control corporations, differs fundamentally between the United States, continental Europe, and the principal economies of east Asia. This chapter describes and analyzes these differing methods of corporate control and corporate governance, compares the corporate form to other forms of business organization (proprietorships and partnerships), and then concludes with a discussion of how American corporations compensate—and provide performance incentives for—their managerial employees. Research over the past two decades has clearly indicated that corporate governance issues—the form of organization, the legal rules dictating how corporate control will be exercised and how ownership shares will be traded, whether an active takeover market is allowed to function, and how corporate managers are attracted and compensated—critically impact an individual company's success or failure and, in the aggregate, significantly influence how dynamic and productive a nation's economic system will be.

---

75. Many people are surprised to learn that stockholders seem to welcome the adoption of these plans (stock prices increase upon their announcement), presumably because of their incentive-alignment effect. See Lambert and Larcker (1985).

76. The critical role that compensation policies play in attracting, monitoring, and disciplining CEOs is described in Gilson and Vetsuypens (1993), Murphy and Zimmerman (1993), Parrino (1993), and Weisbach (1995).

—QUESTIONS—

1. Citing statistics as necessary, comment on the following statement: "In spite of being the most numerous form of business, sole proprietorships are almost irrelevant to the macroeconomic performance of the United States."

2. Discuss the strengths and weaknesses of the following forms of business organization: (*a*) sole proprietorship; (*b*) partnership; and (*c*) corporation.

3. According to Fama and Jensen (1983a), in which fields are partnerships most likely to be competitive? Why? In which fields (industries) are they likely to be at a competitive disadvantage?

4. Jensen and Meckling (1976) view corporations as "legal fictions that provide a nexus for contracting among various firm stakeholders." What does this mean, and why is such a view different from the traditional "economic" view that business is conducted primarily by profit-maximizing human entrepreneurs?

5. Which has legal primacy in regulating U.S. corporate activity—the states or the federal government? [Hint: trick question]. Why might this ambiguity be perplexing to a non-U.S. businessperson?

6. Provide a numerical example of the "tax wedge" in U.S. tax law that penalizes the corporate form relative to the sole proprietorship and partnership forms. What non-tax costs are also more onerous for corporations than for other forms?

7. Briefly describe the corporate governance problems that result from the near total separation of ownership and control that characterizes large U.S. corporations.

8. What is a poison pill? Why is it considered a defensive innovation, as the word "defensive" is used in discussing corporate control issues?

9. Discuss the key differences between the following: (*a*) limited partnerships and regular partnerships; (*b*) limited partnerships and regular C corporations; (*c*) S corporations and regular C corporations.

10. What is an IPO? Why is it considered to be a transforming event for companies experiencing it?

11. Discuss the key similarities observed between U.S. and non-U.S. forms of business organization. Why do you think these universal patterns of corporate governance are observed?

12. Describe the role that state-owned enterprises (SOEs) have played in European, Asian, and developing country economies. How have "privatization" programs been changing that role?

13. Discuss the defining characteristics of the following three ownership structure models: (*a*) the open corporate form; (*b*) the closed, or entrepreneurial, corporate form; and (*c*) the industrial group model.

14. Discuss the strengths and weaknesses of the ownership structure models listed in question number 13 (above).

15. What is "free cash flow," and how can its presence shield corporate managers from market discipline?

16. Comment on the following statement: "American entrepreneurial firms are more similar—in terms of governance structure and financing opportunities—to European companies than they are to large, publicly-traded U.S. firms."

17. What historical events have shaped the development of industrial groups in Japan (*Keiretsu*) and Korea (*Chaebol*)? Why do you think the industrial group model has proven so difficult to transplant outside of these two societies?

18. What is a proxy statement? Describe its role in the corporate governance of U.S. companies.

19. What are "collective action problems?" Which such problems are most troublesome for publicly-traded U.S. corporations?

20. Which groups of security-holders typically "win" when corporate mergers and acquisitions are announced? Which security-holders typically "lose?"

21. How do "mergers" and "acquisitions" differ from each other in the U.S. market for corporate control? Which of the two types of combination is most likely to be "friendly?" Why?

22. Discuss the current role that institutional investors play in the U.S. corporate governance system. How might this role be increased in the future?

23. What are some of the important corporate governance problems non-U.S. companies typically face?

24. What are the components of the "standard" compensation package mid-level managers of American firms typically receive? How does this package change when a person is promoted into the ranks of top management—particularly if he or she becomes the firm's chief executive officer (CEO)?

25. What are stock options designed to achieve? More generally, what is the theoretical justification for the spreading use of "performance-based compensation" programs in the United States?

26. Define the following terms: (*a*) golden handcuffs; (*b*) vesting; (*c*) golden parachute; (*d*) stock-appreciation rights.

—REFERENCES—

Admati, Anat R., Paul Pfleiderer, and Josef Zechner, "Large Shareholder Activism, Risk Sharing, and Financial Market Equilibrium," **Journal of Political Economy** 102 (December 1994), pp. 1097–1132.

Agrawal, Anup and Gershon Mandelker, "Large Shareholders and the Monitoring of Managers: The Case of Antitakeover Charter Amendments," **Journal of Financial and Quantitative Analysis** 25 (June 1990), pp. 143–161.

Agrawal, Anup and Ralph A. Walkling, "Executive Careers and Compensation Surrounding Takeover Bids," **Journal of Finance** 49 (July 1994), pp. 985–1014.

Alchian, Armen A. and Harold Demsetz, "Production, Information Costs, and Economic Organization," **American Economic Review** 62 (December 1972), pp. 777–795.

Ambrose, Brent W. and William L. Megginson, "The Role of Asset Structure, Ownership Structure, and Takeover Defenses in Determining Acquisition Likelihood," **Journal of Financial and Quantitative Analysis** 27 (December 1992), pp. 575–589.

Antle, Rick and Abbie Smith, "Measuring Executive Compensation: Methods and an Application," **Journal of Accounting Research** 23 (Spring 1985), pp. 296–325.

Aoki, Masahiko, "Toward an Economic Model of the Japanese Firm," **Journal of Economic Literature** 28 (1990), pp. 1–27.

Arnold, Jerry L., "Exempt Offerings: Going Public Privately," **Harvard Business Review** (January/February 1985), pp. 16–30.

Atkinson, Scott and Robert Halvorsen, "The Relative Efficiency of Public and Private Firms in a Regulated Environment: The Case of U.S. Electric Utilities," **Journal of Public Economics** 29 (1986), pp. 281–294.

Austin, James E., Lawrence H. Wortzel, and John F. Coburn, "Privatizing State-Owned Enterprises: Hopes and Realities," **Columbia Journal of World Business** 21 (1986), pp. 51–60.

Bagnani, Elizabeth Strock, Nikolaos T. Milonas, Anthony Saunders, and Nickolaos G. Travlos, "Managers, Owners, and the Pricing of Risky Debt: An Empirical Analysis," **Journal of Finance** 49 (June 1994), pp. 453–477.

Bailey, Warren, "Canada's Dual Class Shares: Further Evidence on the Market Value of Cash Dividends," **Journal of Finance** 43 (December 1988), pp. 1143–1160.

Bailey, Warren and Julapa Jagtiani, "Foreign Ownership Restrictions and Stock Prices in the Thai Capital Market," **Journal of Financial Economics** 36 (August 1994), pp. 57–87.

Baker, George P., Michael C. Jensen, and Kevin J. Murphy, "Compensation and Incentives: Practice vs. Theory," **Journal of Finance** 43 (July 1988), pp. 593–616.

Baldwin, Carliss Y. and Sugato Bhattacharyya, "Choosing the Method of Sale: A Clinical Study of Conrail," **Journal of Financial Economics** 30 (November 1991), pp. 69–98.

Barclay, Michael J., Clifford G. Holderness, and Jeffrey Pontiff, "Private Benefits From Block Ownership and Discounts on Closed-End Funds," **Journal of Financial Economics** 33 (June 1993), pp. 263–291.

Berger, Philip G. and Eli Ofek, "Diversification's Effect on Firm Value," **Journal of Financial Economics** 37 (January 1995), pp. 39–65.

Berglof, Eric and Enrico Perotti, "The Governance Structure of the Japanese Financial Keiretsu," **Journal of Financial Economics** 36 (October 1994), pp. 259–284.

Bergstrom, C. and K. Rydqvist, "Differentiated Bids for Voting and Restricted Voting Shares in Public Tender Offers," **Journal of Banking & Finance** 16 (February 1992), pp. 97–114.

Berkovitch, Elazar and M. P. Narayanan, "Motives for Takeovers: An Empirical Investigation," **Journal of Financial and Quantitative Analysis** 28 (September 1993), pp. 347–362.

Bernstein, Peter L., "Is the Dazzle of Our Markets Blinding or Enlightening?," **Journal of Applied Corporate Finance** 6 (Winter 1994), pp. 70–74.

Bhagat, Sanjai and James A. Brickley, "Cumulative Voting: The Value of Minority Shareholder Voting Rights," **Journal of Law and Economics** 27 (October 1984), pp. 339–365.

Bhagat, Sanjai, James A. Brickley, and Ronald C. Lease, "Incentive Effects of Stock Purchase Plans," **Journal of Financial Economics** 14 (June 1985), pp. 195–215.

Bhide, Amar, "The Hidden Costs of Stock Market Liquidity," **Journal of Financial Economics** 34 (August 1993), pp. 31–51.

Bishop, Matthew R. and John A. Kay, "Privatization in the United Kingdom: Lessons From Experience," **World Development** (1989), pp. 643–657.

Bittlingmayer, George, "Stock Returns, Real Activity, and the Trust Question," **Journal of Finance** 47 (December 1992), pp. 1701–1730.

Black, Bernard S., "Institutional Investors and Corporate Governance: The Case for Institutional Voice," **Journal of Applied Corporate Finance** 5 (Fall 1992), pp. 19–32.

Blackwell, David W., James A. Brickley, and Michael S. Weisbach, "Accounting Information and Internal Performance Evaluation: Evidence from Texas Banks," **Journal of Accounting and Economics** (May 1994), pp. 331–358.

Boardman, Anthony, Ruth Freedman, and Catherine Eckel, "The Price of Government Ownership: A Study of Domtar Takeover," **Journal of Public Economics** 31 (1986), pp. 269–285.

Boardman, Anthony and Aidan R. Vining, "Ownership and Performance in Competitive Environments: A Comparison of Private, Mixed, and State-Owned Enterprises," **Journal of Law and Economics** 32 (1989), pp. 1–33.

Bongiorno, Lori, "The Business Week 1000," **Business Week** (March 27, 1995), pp. 88–165.

Boycko, Maxim, Andrei Shleifer, and Robert W. Vishny, "A Theory of Privatization," Working paper (Harvard University, Cambridge, MA), 1993.

———"Voucher Privatization," **Journal of Financial Economics** 35 (1994), pp. 249–266.

Bradley, Michael, "Interfirm Tender Offers and the Market for Corporate Control," **Journal of Business** 53 (October 1980), pp. 345–376.

Bradley, Michael, Anand Desai, and E. Han Kim, "Synergistic Gains From Corporate Acquisitions and Their Division Between the Stockholders of Target and Acquiring Firms," **Journal of Financial Economics** 21 (May 1988), pp. 3–40.

Bradley, Michael, and L. MacDonald Wakeman, "The Wealth Effects of Targeted Share Repurchases," **Journal of Financial Economics** 11 (April 1983), pp. 301–328.

Brickley, James A., Sanjai Bhagat, and Ronald C. Lease, "The Impact of Long-Range Managerial Compensation Plans on Shareholder Wealth," **Journal of Accounting and Economics** 7 (April 1985), pp. 115–129.

Brickley, James A., Jeffrey L. Coles, and Rory L. Terry, "Outside Directors and the Adoption of Poison Pills," **Journal of Financial Economics** 35 (June 1994), pp. 371–390.

Brickley, James A. and Frederick H. Dark, "The Choice of Organizational Form: The Case of Franchising," **Journal of Financial Economics** 18 (June 1987), pp. 401–420.

Brickley, James A., Frederick H. Dark, and Michael S. Weisbach, "An Agency Perspective on Franchising," **Financial Management** 20 (Spring 1991), pp. 27–35.

Brickley, James A., Ronald C. Lease, and Clifford W. Smith, Jr., "Ownership Structure and Voting on Antitakeover Amendments," **Journal of Financial Economics** 20 (January/March 1988), pp. 267–291.

Brook, Yaron and Ramesh K. S. Rao, "Shareholder Wealth Effects of Directors' Liability Limitation Provisions," **Journal of Financial and Quantitative Analysis** 29 (September 1994), pp. 481–497.

Byrd, John W. and Kent A. Hickman, "Do Outside Directors Monitor Managers? Evidence From Tender Offer Bids," **Journal of Financial Economics** 32 (October 1992), pp. 195–221.

Candoy-Sekse, Rebecca and Anne Ruig Palmer, **Techniques of Privatization of State-Owned Enterprises: Inventory of Country Experience and Reference Materials** (The World Bank, Washington, D.C.), 1988.

Caves, Richard E., Lessons From Privatization in Britain: State Enterprise Behavior, Public Choice, and Corporate Governance, **Journal of Economic Behavior and Organization** 13 (March 1990), pp. 145–169.

Caves, Richard E. and Laurits R. Christensen, "The Relative Efficiency of Public and Private Firms in a Competitive Environment: The Case of Canadian Railroads," **Journal of Political Economy** 88 (October 1980), pp. 958–976.

Chan, Chang, "Payout Policy, Capital Structure, and Compensation Contracts When Managers Value Control," **Review of Financial Studies** 6 (1993), pp. 911–933.

Chang, Saeyoung and David Mayers, "Managerial Vote Ownership and Shareholder Wealth: Evidence From Employee Stock Ownership Plans," **Journal of Financial Economics** 32 (August 1992), pp. 103–131.

Clark, Kent and Eli Ofek, "Mergers as a Means of Restructuring Distressed Firms: An Empirical Investigation," **Journal of Financial and Quantitative Analysis** 29 (December 1994), pp. 541–565.

Comment, Robert and Gregg A. Jarrell, "Corporate Focus and Stock Returns," **Journal of Financial Economics** 37 (January 1995), pp. 67–87.

Comment, Robert and G. William Schwert, "Poison or Placebo? Evidence on the Deterrent and Wealth Effects of Modern Antitakeover Measures," **Journal of Financial Economics** 39 (September 1995), pp. 3–43.

Conte, Michael A. and Douglas Kruse, "ESOP's and Profit Sharing Plans: Do They Link Employee Pay to Company Performance?," **Financial Management** 20 (Winter 1991), pp. 91–100.

Cook, O. Douglas and John C. Easterwood, "Poison Put Bonds: An Analysis of Their Economic Role," **Journal of Finance** 49 (December 1994), pp. 1905–1920.

Cooper, Kerry and R. Malcolm Richards, "Investing the Alaskan Project Cash Flows: The Sohio Experience," **Financial Management** 17 (Summer 1988), pp. 58–70.

Cooter, Robert and Thomas Ulen, **Law and Economics** (Scott Foresman: Glenview, Illinois, 1988).

Cornell, Bradford and Alan Shapiro, "Financing Corporate Growth," **Journal of Applied Corporate Finance** 1 (Summer 1988), pp. 6–22.

Cotter, James F. and Marc Zenner, "How Managerial Wealth Affects the Tender Offer Process," **Journal of Financial Economics** 35 (February 1994), pp. 63–97.

Cutts, Robert L., "Capitalism in Japan: Cartels and Keiretsu," **Harvard Business Review** (July/August 1992), pp. 48–55.

Dann, Larry Y. and Harry DeAngelo, "Standstill Agreements, Privately Negotiated Stock Repurchases, and the Market for Corporate Control," **Journal of Financial Economics** 11 (April 1983), pp. 275–300.

DeAngelo, Harry and Linda DeAngelo, "Proxy Contests and the Governance of Publicly Held Corporations," **Journal of Financial Economics** 23 (June 1989), pp. 29–59.

DeAngelo, Harry, Linda DeAngelo, and Edward M. Rice, "Going Private: Minority Freezeouts and Stockholder Wealth," **Journal of Law and Economics** 27 (October 1984), pp. 367–401.

Demsetz, Harold, "The Structure of Ownership and the Theory of the Firm," **Journal of Law and Economics** 26 (June 1983), pp. 375–390.

Demsetz, Harold and Kenneth Lehn, "The Structure of Corporate Ownership: Cases and Consequences," **Journal of Political Economy** 93 (December 1985), pp. 1155–1177.

Denis, David J., "Organizational Form and the Consequences of Leveraged Transactions: Kroger's Recapitalization and Safeway's LBO," **Journal of Financial Economics** 36 (October 1994), pp. 193–224.

Denis, David J. and Diane K. Denis, "Causes of Financial Distress Following Leveraged Recapitalizations," **Journal of Financial Economics** 37 (February 1995), pp. 129–157.

Denning, Karen C. and Kuldeep Shastri, "Changes in Organizational Structure and Shareholder Wealth: The Case of Limited Partnerships," **Journal of Financial and Quantitative Analysis** 28 (December 1993), pp. 553–564.

Dennis, Debra K. and John J. McConnell, "Corporate Mergers and Security Returns," **Journal of Financial Economics** 16 (June 1986), pp. 143–187.

Dewenter, Kathryn L., "Does the Market React Differently to Domestic and Foreign Takeover Announcements? Evidence From the U.S. Chemical and Retail Industries," **Journal of Financial Economics** 37 (March 1995), pp. 421–441.

Dial, Jay and Kevin J. Murphy, "Incentives, Downsizing, and Value Creation at General Dynamics," **Journal of Financial Economics** 37 (March 1995), pp. 261–314.

Dodd, Peter and Richard Leftwich, "The Market for Corporate Charters: 'Unhealthy Competition' Versus Federal Regulation," **Journal of Business** 53 (July 1980), pp. 259–283.

Dodd, Peter and Jerold B. Warner, "On Corporate Governance: A Study of Proxy Contests," **Journal of Financial Economics** 11 (April 1983), pp. 401–438.

Dwyer, Hubert J. and Richard Lynn, "Small Capitalization Companies: What Does Financial Analysis Tell Us About Them?," **Financial Review** 24 (August 1989), pp. 397–415.

Easterbrook, Frank H., "Two Agency-Cost Explanations of Dividends," **American Economic Review** 74 (September 1984), pp. 650–659.

Easterbrook, Frank H. and Daniel R. Fischel, "Voting in Corporate Law," **Journal of Law and Economics** 26 (June 1983), pp. 395–427.

Eckel, Catherine C. and Theo Vermaelen, "Internal Regulation: The Effect of Government Ownership on the Value of the Firm," **Journal of Law and Economics** 29 (October 1986), pp. 381–403.

Fama, Eugene F., "Agency Problems and the Theory of the Firm," **Journal of Political Economy** 88 (April 1980), pp. 288–298.

Fama, Eugene F. and Michael C. Jensen, "Separation of Ownership and Control," **Journal of Law and Economics** 26 (June 1983a), pp. 301–325.

———"Agency Problems and Residual Claims," **Journal of Law and Economics** 26 (June 1983b), pp. 327–349.

———"Organizational Forms and Investment Decisions," **Journal of Financial Economics** 14 (March 1985), pp. 101–119.

Fields, Joseph, Chinmoy Ghosh, David Kidwell, and Linda Klein, "Wealth Effects of Regulatory Reform: The Reaction to California's Proposition 103," **Journal of Financial Economics** 28 (November/December 1990), pp. 233–250.

Fields, L. Paige and Eric L. Mais, "Managerial Voting Rights and Seasoned Public Equity Issues," **Journal of Financial and Quantitative Analysis** 29 (September 1994), pp. 445–457.

Finegan, Patrick T., "Maximizing Shareholder Value at the Private Company," **Journal of Applied Corporate Finance** 4 (Spring 1991), pp. 30–45.

Frankel, Jeffrey A., "The Japanese Cost of Finance: A Survey," **Financial Management** 20 (Spring 1991), pp. 95–127.

Franks, Julian R. and Robert S. Harris, "Shareholder Wealth Effects of Corporate Takeovers: The U.K. Experience 1955–1985," **Journal of Financial Economics** 23 (August 1989), pp. 225–249.

Friend, Irwin and Larry H. P. Lang, "An Empirical Test of the Impact of Managerial Self-Interest on Corporate Capital Structure," **Journal of Finance** 43 (June 1988), pp. 271–281.

Furtado, Eugene P. H. and Michael S. Rozeff, "The Wealth Effects of Company Initiated Management Changes," **Journal of Financial Economics** 18 (March 1987), pp. 147–160.

Galal, Ahmed, Leroy Jones, Pankaj Tandon, and Ingo Vogelsang, **Welfare Consequences of Selling Public Enterprises** (The World Bank: Washington, D.C., 1992).

Galuszka, Peter, Patricia Kranz, and Stanley Reed, "Special Report: Russia's New Capitalism," **Business Week** (October 10, 1994), pp. 68–80.

Garen, John E., "Executive Compensation and Principal-Agent Theory," **Journal of Political Economy** 102 (December 1994), pp. 1175–1199.

Gaver, Jennifer J. and Kenneth M. Gaver, "Additional Evidence on the Association Between the Opportunity Set and Corporate Financing, Dividend, and Compensation Policies," **Journal of Accounting and Economics** 16 (January/April/July/ 1993), pp. 125–160.

Gibbons, Robert and Kevin J. Murphy, "Does Executive Compensation Affect Investment," **Journal of Applied Corporate Finance** 5 (Summer 1992a), pp. 99–109.

————"Optimal Incentive Contract in the Presence of Career Concerns: Theory and Evidence," **Journal of Political Economy** 100 (June 1992b), pp.468–505.

Gilson, Stuart, "Management Turnover and Financial Distress," **Journal of Financial Economics** 25 (December 1989), 241–262.

Gilson, Stuart C. and Michael R. Vetsuypens, "CEO Compensation in Financially Distressed Firms: An Empirical Analysis," **Journal of Finance** 48 (June 1993), pp. 425–458.

Gleckman, Howard, "Bonus Pay: Buzzword or Bonanza?," **Business Week** (November 14, 1994), pp. 62–64.

Goodman, John B. and Gary W. Loveman, "Does Privatization Serve the Public Interest?," **Harvard Business Review** (November-December 1992), pp. 26–38.

Gordon, Lilli A. and John Pound, "Information, Ownership Structure, and Shareholder Voting: Evidence From Shareholder-Sponsored Corporate Governance Proposals," **Journal of Finance** 48 (June 1993), pp. 697–718.

Grossman, Sanford J., "One Share-One Vote and the Market for Corporate Control," **Journal of Financial Economics** 20 (January/March 1988), pp. 175–202.

Grossman, Sanford J. and Oliver D. Hart, "Takeover Bids, the Free-Rider Problem, and the Theory of the Corporation," **Bell Journal of Economics** 11 (Spring 1980), pp. 42–64.

Grossman, Sanford and Oliver Hart, "The Costs and Benefits of Ownership: A Theory of Vertical and Lateral Integration," **Journal of Political Economy** 94 (1986), pp. 691–719.

Grundfest, Joseph A., "Subordination of American Capital," **Journal of Financial Economics** 27 (September 1990), pp. 89–114.

Guney, Serhat and Enrico Perotti, "Successful Privatization Plans: Enhanced Credibility Through Timing and Pricing of Sales," **Financial Management** 22 (1993), pp. 84–98.

Hammer, Richard M., "The Taxation of Income From Corporate Shareholders: Review of Present Systems in Canada, France, Germany, Japan, and the U.K.," **National Tax Journal** 28 (1975).

Harrington, Joseph E., Jr. and Jacob Prokop, "The Dynamics of the Free-Rider Problem in Takeovers," **Review of Financial Studies** 6 (Winter 1993), pp. 851–882.

Harris, Milton and Artur Raviv, "Corporate Governance: Voting Rights and Majority Rules," **Journal of Financial Economics** 20 (January/March 1988), pp. 203–235.

————"The Design of Securities," **Journal of Financial Economics** 24 (October 1989), pp. 255–287.

Harris, Robert S. and David Ravenscraft, "The Role of Acquisitions in Foreign Direct Investment: Evidence From the U.S. Stock Market," **Journal of Finance** 46 (July 1991), pp. 825–844.

Haubrich, Joseph G., "Risk Aversion, Performance Pay, and the Principal-Agent Problem," **Journal of Political Economy** 102 (April 1994), pp. 258–276.

Hayn, Carla, "Tax Attributes as Determinants of Shareholder Gains in Corporate Acquisitions," **Journal of Financial Economics** 23 (June 1989), pp. 121–153.

Healy, Paul M., Krishna G. Palepu, and Richard S. Ruback, "Does Corporate Performance Improve After Mergers?," **Journal of Financial Economics** 31 (April 1992), pp. 135–175.

Hemmer, Thomas, "Risk-Free Incentive Contracts: Eliminating Agency Cost Using Compensation Schemes," **Journal of Accounting and Economics** 16 (October 1993), pp. 447–473.

Hentzler, Herbert A., "The New Era of Eurocapitalism," **Harvard Business Review** (July/August 1992), pp. 57–68.

Hirtle, Beverly, "Factors Affecting the Competitiveness of Internationally Active Financial Institutions," Federal Reserve Bank of New York **Quarterly Review** (Spring 1991), pp. 38–51.

Hite, Gailen L. and Michael S. Long, "Taxes and Executive Stock Options," **Journal of Accounting and Economics** 4 (July 1982), pp. 3–14.

Hodak, Marc, "How EVA™ Can Help Turn Mid-Sized Firms Into Large Companies," **Journal of Applied Corporate Finance** 7 (Spring 1994), pp. 98–102.

Holderness, Clifford G. and Dennis P. Sheehan, "Monitoring an Owner: The Case of Turner Broadcasting," **Journal of Financial Economics** 30 (December 1991), pp. 325–346.

Hoshi, Takeo, Anil Kashyap, and David Scharfstein, "The Role of Banks in Reducing the Costs of Financial Distress in Japan," **Journal of Financial Economics** 27 (September 1990), pp. 67–88.

————"Corporate Structure, Liquidity, and Investment: Evidence From Japanese Industrial Groups," **Quarterly Journal of Economics** 106 (1991), pp. 33–60.

Hotchkiss, Edith Shwalb, "Postbankruptcy Performance and Management Turnover," **Journal of Finance** 50 (March 1995), pp. 3–21.

Huang, Yen-Sheng, and Ralph A. Walkling, "Target Abnormal Returns Associated with Acquisition Announcements: Payment, Acquisition Form, and Managerial Resistance," **Journal of Financial Economics** 19 (December 1987), pp. 329–350.

Huddart, Steven, "Employee Stock Options," **Journal of Accounting and Economics** 18 (September 1994), pp. 207–231.

Ibbotson, Roger C., Jody L. Sindelar, and Jay R. Ritter, "Initial Public Offerings," **Journal of Applied Corporate Finance** 1 (Summer 1988), pp. 37–45.

————"Initial Public Offerings," **Journal of Applied Corporate Finance** 7 (1994), pp. 6–14.

Ikenberry, David and Josef Lakonishok, "Corporate Governance Through the Proxy Contest: Evidence and Implications," **Journal of Business** 66 (July 1993), pp. 405–435.

Jacobson, Robert and David Aaker, "Myopic Management Behavior With Efficient, But Imperfect, Financial Markets," **Journal of Accounting and Economics** 16 (October 1993), pp. 383–405.

Jarrell, Gregg A., "The Wealth Effects of Litigation by Targets: Do Interests Diverge in a Merge?," **Journal of Law and Economics** 28 (April 1985), pp. 151–177.

Jarrell, Gregg A. and Michael Bradley, "The Economic Effects of Federal and State Regulations of Cash Tender Offers," **Journal of Law and Economics** 23 (October 1980), pp. 371–407.

Jarrell, Gregg A., James A. Brickley, and Jeffry M. Netter, "The Market for Corporate Control: The Empirical Evidence Since 1980," **Journal of Economic Perspectives** 2 (Winter 1988), pp. 49–68.

Jarrell, Gregg A. and Annette B. Poulsen, "Shark Repellents and Stock Prices: The Effects of Antitakeover Amendments Since 1980," **Journal of Financial Economics** 19 (September 1987), pp. 127–168.

————"Dual-Class Recapitalizations as Antitakeover Mechanisms: The Recent Evidence," **Journal of Financial Economics** 20 (January/March 1988), pp. 129–152.

————"Returns to Acquiring Firms in Tender Offers: Evidence from Three Decades," **Financial Management** 18 (Autumn 1989), pp. 12–19.

Jennings, Robert H. and Michael A. Mazzeo, "Competing Bids, Target Management Resistance, and Structure of Takeover Bids," **Review of Financial Studies** 6 (Winter 1993), pp. 883–909.

Jensen, Michael C., "Eclipse of the Public Corporation," **Harvard Business Review** (September/October 1989), pp. 61–74.

————"The Modern Industrial Revolution, Exit, and the Failure of Internal Control Systems," **Journal of Finance** 48 (July 1993), pp. 831–880.

Jensen, Michael C. and William H. Meckling, "Theory of the Firm: Managerial Behavior, Agency Costs, and Ownership Structure," **Journal of Financial Economics** 3 (October 1976), pp. 305–360.

————"Rights and Production Functions: An Application to Labor-Managed Firms and Codetermination," **Journal of Business** 52 (October 1979), pp. 469–506.

Jensen, Michael C. and Kevin J. Murphy, "Performance Pay and Top-Management Incentives," **Journal of Political Economy** 98 (April 1990), pp. 225–264.

Jensen, Michael C. and Richard S. Ruback, "The Market for Corporate Control: The Scientific Evidence," **Journal of Financial Economics** 11 (April 1983), pp. 5–50.

Jensen, Michael C. and Jerold B. Warner, "The Distribution of Power Among Corporate Managers, Shareholders, and Directors," **Journal of Financial Economics** 20 (January/March 1988), pp. 3–24.

John, Teresa A. and Kose John, "Top Management Compensation and Capital Structure," **Journal of Finance** 48 (July 1993), pp. 949–974.

John, Kose and Eli Ofek, "Asset Sales and Increase in Focus," **Journal of Financial Economics** 37 (January 1995), pp. 105–126.

Johnson, Simon and Gary Loveman, "Starting Over: Poland After Communism," **Harvard Business Review** (March-April 1995), pp. 44–57.

Jones, Seymour, M. Bruce Cohen, and Victor V. Coppola, "Going Public," in **Guide to Growing Your Business** (Coopers & Lybrand), reprinted in William A. Sahlman and Howard Stevenson, **The Entrepreneurial Venture** (Harvard Business School Publications: Boston, Massachusetts, 1992), pp. 394–416.

Jones, Steven L., William L. Megginson, Robert C. Nash, and Jeffry M. Netter, "Share Issue Privatization as Financial Means to Political and Economic Ends," Working paper (University of Georgia, Athens, GA), October 1995.

Kaplan, Stephen, "Management Buyouts: Evidence on Taxes as a Source of Value," **Journal of Finance** 44 (July 1989a), pp. 611–632.

————"The Effects of Management Buyouts on Operating Performance and Value," **Journal of Financial Economics** 24 (October 1989b), pp. 217–254.

Kaplan, Steven N., "Top Executive Rewards and Firm Performance: A Comparison of Japan and the United States," **Journal of Political Economy** 102 (June 1994), pp. 510–546.

Kaplan, Steven N. and Bernadette A. Minton, "Appointments of Outsiders to Japanese Boards: Determinants and Implications For Managers," **Journal of Financial Economics** 36 (October 1994), pp. 225–258.

Kaplan, Steven N. and Jeremy C. Stein, "How Risky is the Debt in Highly Leveraged Transactions?," **Journal of Financial Economics** 27 (September 1990), pp. 215–245.

Karpoff, Jonathan M. and Edward M. Rice, "Organizational Form, Share Transferability, and Firm Performance: Evidence From the ANCSA Corporations," **Journal of Financial Economics** 24 (September 1989), pp. 69–105.

Kay, J. A. and D. J. Thompson, "Privatization: A Policy in Search of a Rationale," **Economic Journal** 96 (March 1986), pp. 18–38.

Kester, W. Carl, "The Hidden Cost of Japanese Success," **Journal of Applied Corporate Finance** 3 (Summer 1991), pp. 90–97.

————"Governance, Contracting, and Investment Horizons: A Look at Japan and Germany," **Journal of Applied Corporate Finance** 5 (Summer, 1992), pp. 83–98.

Kiefer, Donald W., "Are Pension Funds Short-Term Investors?" (Congressional Research Service: Washington, D.C., 1992).

Khon, Alfie, "Why Incentive Plans Cannot Work," **Harvard Business Review** (September/October 1993), pp. 54–63.

Kikeri, Sunita, John Nellis, and Mary Shirley, **Privatization: The Lesson of Experience** (The World Bank: Washington, D.C., 1992).

King, Mervyn A. and Donald Fullerton, eds., **The Taxation of Income From Capital: A Comparative Study of the United States, The United Kingdom, Sweden, and West Germany** (The University of Chicago Press: Chicago, 1984).

Klein, April and James Rosenfeld, "Targeted Share Repurchases and Top Management Changes," **Journal of Financial Economics** 20 (January/March 1988), pp. 493–506.

Koretz, Gene, "Losing Ground at the Top," **Business Week** (February 27, 1995), pp. 34.

Kornai, Janos, "Individual Freedom and the Reform of the Socialist Economy," **European Economic Review** 32 (1988), pp. 233–267.

Kvint, Vladimir, "Don't Give Up On Russia," **Harvard Business Review** (March-April 1994), pp. 62–74.

Lambert, Richard A., "The Use of Accounting and Security Price Measures of Performance in Managerial Compensation Contracts," **Journal of Accounting and Economics** 16 (January/April/July 1993), pp. 101–123.

Lambert, Richard A. and David F. Larcker, "Golden Parachutes, Executive Decision-Making and Shareholder Wealth," **Journal of Accounting and Economics** 7 (April 1985), pp. 179–203.

Lamm-Tennant, Joan and Laura T. Starks, "Stock Versus Mutual Ownership Structures: The Risk Implications," **Journal of Business** 66 (January 1993), pp. 29–46.

Lang, Larry, Annette Poulsen, and René Stulz, "Asset Sales, Firm Performance, and the Agency Costs of Managerial Discretion," **Journal of Financial Economics** 37 (January 1995), pp. 3–37.

Lang, Larry H. P. and René M. Stulz, "Tobin's q, Corporate Diversification, and Firm Performance," **Journal of Political Economy** 102 (December 1994), pp. 1248–1280.

Langhor, Herwig M. and Claude J. Viallet, "Compensation and Wealth Transfers in the French Nationalizations, 1981–1982," **Journal of Financial Economics** 17 (December 1986), pp. 273–312.

Larcker, David F., "The Association Between Performance Plan Adoption and Corporate Capital Investment," **Journal of Accounting and Economics** 5 (April 1983), pp. 3–30.

Lease, Ronald C., John J. McConnell, and Wayne H. Mikkelson, "The Market Value of Control in Publicly-Traded Corporations," **Journal of Financial Economics** 11 (April 1983), pp. 361–399.

Lehn, Kenneth, Jeffrey Netter, and Annette Poulsen, "Consolidating Corporate Control: Dual Class Recapitalizations Versus Leveraged Buyouts," **Journal of Financial Economics** 27 (October 1990), pp. 557–580.

Leland, Hayne and David Pyle, "Information Assymetries, Financial Structure, and Financial Intermediation," **Journal of Finance** 32 (May 1977), pp. 371–387.

Lerner, Joshua, "Venture Capitalists and the Decision to go Public," **Journal of Financial Economics** 35 (June 1994), pp. 293–316.

———"Venture Capitalists and the Oversight of Private Firms," **Journal of Finance** 50 (March 1995), pp. 301–318.

Lessard, Donald R., "Global Competition and Corporate Finance in the 1990s," **Journal of Applied Corporate Finance** 3 (Summer 1991), pp. 59–72.

Levy, Haim, "Economic Evaluation of Voting Power of Common Stock," **Journal of Finance** 38 (March 1983), pp. 79–93.

Lewellen, Wilbur, Claudio Loderer, and Ahron Rosenfeld, "Merger Decisions and Executive Stock Ownership in Acquiring Firms," **Journal of Accounting and Economics** 7 (April 1985), pp. 209–231.

Loughran, Tim, Jay R. Ritter, and Krishna Palepu, "Initial Public Offerings: International Insights," **Pacific-Basin Finance Journal** 2 (1994), 165–199.

Malatesta, Paul H. and Rex Thompson, "Government Regulation and Structural Change in the Corporate Acquisitions Market: The Impact of the Williams Act," **Journal of Financial and Quantitative Analysis** 28 (December 1993), pp. 363–379.

Malatesta, Paul H. and Ralph A. Walkling, "Poison Pill Securities: Stockholder Wealth, Profitability, and Ownership Structure," **Journal of Financial Economics** 20 (January/March 1988), pp. 347–376.

Maloney, Michael T., Robert E. McCormick, and Mark Mitchell, "Managerial Decision Making and Capital Structure," **Journal of Business** 66 (April 1993), pp. 189–217.

Manzon, Gil B., Jr., David J. Sharp, and Nickolaos G. Travlos, "An Empirical Study of the Consequences of U.S. Tax Rules for U.S. Firms," **Journal of Finance** 49 (December 1994), pp. 1893–1904.

Marais, Laurentius, Katherine Schipper, and Abbie Smith, "Wealth Effects of Going Private for Senior Securities," **Journal of Financial Economics** 23 (June 1989), pp. 155–191.

Masulis, Ronald W., "Changes in Ownership Structure: Conversions of Mutual Savings and Loans to Stock Charter," **Journal of Financial Economics** 18 (March 1987), pp. 29–59.

Mayers, David and Clifford Smith, Jr., "Ownership Structure and Control: Mutualization of Stock Life Insurance Companies," **Journal of Financial Economics** 16 (May 1986), pp. 73–99.

McConnell, John J. and Henri Servaes, "Additional Evidence on Equity Ownership and Corporate Value," **Journal of Financial Economics** 27 (October 1990), pp. 595–612.

McWilliams, Victoria B., "Managerial Share Ownership and the Stock Price Effects of Antitakeover Amendment Proposals," **Journal of Finance** 45 (December 1990), pp. 1627–1640.

Megginson, William L., "Restricted Voting Stock, Acquisition Premiums, and the Market Value of Corporate Control," **Financial Review** 25 (May 1990), pp. 175–198.

Megginson, William L., Robert C. Nash, and Matthias van Randenborgh, "The Financial and Operating Performance of Newly-Privatized Firms: An International Empirical Analysis," **Journal of Finance** 49 (June 1994), pp. 403–452.

Merrill Lynch Business Advisory Services, **Mergerstat Review 1993** (Schaumberg, IL, 1994).

Meulbroek, Lisa K., "An Empirical Analysis of Illegal Insider Trading," **Journal of Finance** 47 (December 1992), pp. 1661–1699.

Middelmann, Conner, "OECD Warns on Scale of Privatization Programmes," **Financial Times** (March 6, 1995), pg. 17.

Mikkelson, Wayne H. and M. Megan Partch, "Managers' Voting Rights and Corporate Control," **Journal of Financial Economics** 25 (December 1989), pp. 263–290.

Miller, Merton H., "Is American Corporate Governance Fatally Flawed?," **Journal of Applied Corporate Finance** 6 (Winter 1994), pp. 32–39.

Miller, Merton H. and Myron S. Scholes, "Executive Compensation, Taxes, and Incentives," in William F. Sharpe and Cathryn M. Cootner, eds., **Financial Economics: Essays in Honor of Paul Cootner** (Prentice-Hall, Englewood Cliffs, NJ, 1982), pp. 139–157.

Moore, John, "British Privatization—Taking Capitalism to the People," **Harvard Business Review** (January/February 1992), pp. 115–124.

Moore, William T., Donald G. Christensen, and Rodney L. Roenfeldt, "Equity Valuation Effects of Forming Master Limited Partnerships," **Journal of Financial Economics** 24 (September 1989), pp. 107–124.

Morck, Randall, Andrei Shleifer, and Robert W. Vishny, "Alternative Mechanisms for Corporate Control," **American Economic Review** 79 (September 1989), pp. 842–852.

Murphy, Kevin J., "Corporate Performance and Managerial Remuneration: An Empirical Analysis," **Journal of Accounting And Economics** 7 (April 1985), pp. 11–42.

Murphy, Kevin J. and Jerold L. Zimmerman, "Financial Performance Surrounding CEO Turnover," **Journal of Accounting and Economics** 16 (January/April/July 1993), pp. 273–315.

Murphy, Robert T., "Power Without Purpose: The Crisis of Japan's Global Financial Dominance," **Harvard Business Review** (March/April 1989), pp. 71–83.

Muscarella, Chris J. and Michael R. Vetsuypens, "Efficiency and Organizational Structure: A Study of Reverse LBOs," **Journal of Finance** 45 (December 1990), pp. 1389–1413.

Nakarmi, Laxmi, "A Flying Leap Towards the 21st Century?," **Business Week** (March 20, 1995), pp. 78–80.

Narayanan, M. P., "Managerial Incentives for Short-Term Results," **Journal of Finance** 40 (December 1985), pp. 1469–1484.

Nellis, John and Sunita Kikeri, "Public Enterprise Reform: Privatization and the World Bank," **World Development** (1989), pp. 659–672.

North, Douglass C., "Privatization, Incentives, and Economic Performance," Working paper (Washington University: St. Louis, 1994).

Ofek, Eli, "Efficiency Gains in Unsuccessful Management Buyouts," **Journal of Finance** 49 (June 1994), pp. 637–654.

Ohmae, Kenichi, "Lies, Damned Lies, and Statistics: Why the Trade Deficit Doesn't Matter in a Borderless World," **Journal of Applied Corporate Finance** 3 (Summer 1991), pp. 98–106.

Palepu, Krishna G., "Predicting Takeover Targets: A Methodological and Empirical Analysis," **Journal of Accounting and Economics** 8 (March 1986), pp. 3–35.

Palmer, Jay, "Europe on the Block: But Should U.S. Investors Buy Into the the Old World?," **Barron's** (June 14, 1993), pp. 16–27.

Parrino, Robert, "CEO Turnover and Outside Succession: A Cross-Sectional Analysis," working paper (University of Texas: Austin, 1993).

Partch, M. Megan, "The Creation of a Class of Limited Voting Common Stock and Shareholder Wealth," **Journal of Financial Economics** 18 (June 1987), pp. 313–339.

Pavel, Christine and John N. McElravey, "Globalization in the Financial Services Industry," Federal Reserve Bank of Chicago **Economic Perspectives** (May/June 1990), pp. 3–18.

Peat Marwick Main & Company, "How Public is Public?," in **Going Public: What the High Technology CEO Needs to Know** (1987).

Peat Marwick Main & Company, **Building the High Technology Business: Positioning for Growth, Profitability, and Success** (1988).

Peltzman, Sam, "Pricing in Public and Private Enterprises: Electric Utilities in the United States," **Journal of Law and Economics** 14 (April 1971), pp. 109–147.

Persons, John C., "Signaling and Takeover Deterrence With Stock Repurchases: Dutch Auctions Versus Fixed Price Tender Offers," **Journal of Finance** 49 (September 1994), pp. 1373–1402.

Phillips, Gordon M., "Increased Debt and Industry Product Markets: An Empirical Analysis," **Journal of Financial Economics** 37 (February 1995), pp. 189–238.

Porter, Michael, "Capital Disadvantage: America's Failing Capital Investment System," **Harvard Business Review** (September-October 1992), pp. 65–83.

Posner, Bruce G. "How to Finance Anything," **Inc.** (April 1992), pp. 61–62.

Poterba, James and Lawrence Summers, "New Evidence That Taxes Affect the Valuation of Dividends," **Journal of Finance** 39 (December 1984), pp. 1397–1415.

Pound, John, "Proxy Contests and the Efficiency of Shareholder Oversight," **Journal of Financial Economics** 20 (January/March 1988), pp. 237–265.

———"The Promise of the Governed Corporation," **Harvard Business Review** (March-April 1995), pp. 89–98.

Prahalad, C. K., "Corporate Governance or Corporate Value Added?: Rethinking the Primacy of Shareholder Value," **Journal of Applied Corporate Finance** 6 (Winter 1994), pp. 40–50.

Prowse, Michael, "Is America in Decline?," **Harvard Business Review** (July/August 1992), pp. 34–45.

Prowse, Stephen D., "Institutional Investment Patterns and Corporate Financial Behavior in the United States and Japan," **Journal of Financial Economics** 27 (September 1990), pp. 43–66.

———"The Structure of Corporate Ownership in Japan," **Journal of Finance** 47 (July 1992), pp. 1121–1140.

Pryke, Richard, "The Comparative Performance of Public and Private Enterprises," **Fiscal Studies** 3 (July 1982), pp. 68–81.

Rexer, Christian and Timothy J. Sheehan, "Organizing The Firm: Choosing the Right Business Entity," **Journal of Applied Corporate Finance** 7 (Spring 1994), pp. 59–65.

Ritter, Jay R., "The Long Run Performance of Initial Public Offerings," **Journal of Finance** 46 (March 1991), pp. 3–28.

Roe, Mark J., "Political and Legal Restraints on Ownership and Control of Public Companies," **Journal of Financial Economics** 27 (September 1990), pp. 7–41.

———"Mutual Funds in the Boardroom," **Journal of Applied Corporate Finance** 5 (Winter 1993), pp. 56–61.

Ryngaert, Michael, "The Effect of Poison Pill Securities on Shareholder Wealth," **Journal of Financial Economics** 20 (January/March 1988), pp. 377–417.

Sahlman, William A., "Aspects of Financial Contracting in Venture Capital," **Journal of Applied Corporate Finance** (Summer 1988), pp. 23–36.

———"The Structure and Governance of Venture-Capital Organizations," **Journal of Financial Economics** 27 (October 1990), pp. 473–522.

Saly, P. Jane, "Repricing Executive Stock Options in a Down Market," **Journal of Accounting and Economics** 18 (November 1994), pp. 325–356.

Saunders, Anthony, Elizabeth Strock, and Nickolaos G. Travlos, "Ownership Structure, Deregulation, and Bank Risk Taking," **Journal of Finance** 45 (June 1990), pp. 643–654.

Seyhun, H. Nejat, "Insiders' Profits, Costs of Trading, and Market Efficiency," **Journal of Financial Economics** 16 (June 1986), pp. 189–212.

———"The Information Content of Aggregate Insider Trading," **Journal of Business** 61 (January 1988), pp. 1–24.

———"Overreaction or Fundamentals: Some Lessons From Insiders' Response to the Market Crash of 1987," **Journal of Finance** 45 (December 1990), pp. 1363–1388.

Shirley, Mary and John Nellis, **Public Enterprise Reform: The Lessons of Experience** (The World Bank: Washington, D.C., 1991).

Shivdasani, Anil, "Board Composition, Ownership Structure, and Hostile Takeovers," **Journal of Accounting and Economics** 16 (January/April/July 1993), pp. 167–198.

Shleifer, Andrei and Robert W. Vishny, "Large Shareholders and Corporate Control," **Journal of Political Economy** 94 (June 1986), pp. 461–488.

Skinner, Douglas J., "The Investment Opportunity Set and Accounting Procedure Choice," **Journal of Accounting and Economics** 16 (October 1993), pp. 407–445.

Smith, Clifford W. Jr., and Ross L. Watts, "Incentive and Tax Effects of Executive Compensation Plans," **Australian Journal of Management** 7 (December 1982), pp. 139–157.

———"The Investment Opportunity Set and Corporate Financing, Dividend and Compensation Policies," **Journal of Financial Economics** 32 (December 1992), pp. 263–292.

Song, Moon H. and Ralph A. Walkling, "The Impact of Managerial Ownership on Acquisition Attempts and Target Shareholder Wealth," **Journal of Financial and Quantitative Analysis** 28 (December 1993), pp. 439–457.

Stevenson, Howard H. and James Z. Turner, "Compensation Planning for Entrepreneurs," in William A. Sahlman and Howard Stevenson, **The Entrepreneurial Venture** (Harvard Business School Publications: Boston, 1992).

Stulz, René M., "Managerial Control of Voting Rights: Financing Policies and the Market for Corporate Control," **Journal of Financial Economics** 20 (January/March 1988), pp. 25–54.

Stulz, René M., Ralph A. Walkling, and Moon H. Song, "The Distribution of Target Ownership and the Division of Gains in Successful Takeovers," **Journal of Finance** 45 (July 1990), pp. 817–833.

Szewczyk, Samuel and George T. Tsetsekos, "State Intervention in the Market for Corporate Control: The Case of Pennsylvania State Bill 1310," **Journal of Financial Economics** 31 (March 1992), pp. 3–22.

Tehranian, Hassan and James F. Wagelein, "Market Reaction to Short-Term Executive Compensation Plan Adoption," **Journal of Accounting and Economics** 7 (April 1985), pp. 131–144.

Templeton, John, "Suddenly, Germans Love to Hate Their Banks," **Business Week** (February 20, 1995), pg. 56.

Tibbetts, Joseph S. Jr. and Edmund T. Donovan, "Compensation and Benefits for Startup Companies," **Harvard Business Review** (January/February 1989), pp. 140–147.

Timmons, Jeffrey A. and Dale A. Sandler, "Everything You [Didn't] Want to Know About Raising Capital," **Harvard Business Review** (November/December 1989), pp. 70–73.

Travlos, Nickolas G., "Corporate Takeover Bids, Method of Payment, and Bidding Firms' Stock Returns," **Journal of Finance** 42 (September 1987), pp. 943–963.

Vijh, Anand M., "The Spinoff and Merger Ex-Date Effects," **Journal of Finance** 49 (June 1994), pp. 581–609.

Vuylsteke, Charles, **Techniques of Privatization of State-Owned Enterprises** (The World Bank: Washington, D.C., 1988).

Walkling, Ralph A. and Michael S. Long, "Agency Theory, Managerial Warfare and Takeover Bid Resistance," **Rand Journal of Economics** 1 (Spring 1984), pp. 54–68.

Warner, Jerold B., Ross L. Watts, and Karen H. Wruck, "Stock Prices and Top Management Changes," **Journal of Financial Economics** 20 (January/March 1988), pp. 461–492.

Weis, C. Edward, Jr., "Trading Patterns of Institutional Investors: Implications for the Production of Information," Unpublished dissertation (University of Georgia: Athens, 1995).

Weisbach, Michael S., "Outside Directors and CEO Turnover," **Journal of Financial Economics** 20 (January/March 1988), pp. 431–460.

———"CEO Turnover and the Firm's Investment Decisions," **Journal of Financial Economics** 37 (February 1995), pp. 159–188.

Whited, Toni M., "Debt, Liquidity Constraints, and Corporate Investment: Evidence From Panel Data," **Journal of Finance** 47 (September 1992), pp. 1425–1460.

Williams, Frances, "The Art of Staying Ahead is Adaptation," **Financial Times** (September 30, 1994), World Economy and Finance Special Supplement, pg. 8.

Wruck, Karen H., "Equity Ownership Concentration and Firm Value: Evidence From Private Equity Financings," **Journal of Financial Economics** 23 (June 1989), pp. 3–28.

Wruck, Karen Hopper, "Financial Policy, Internal Control, and Performance: Sealed Air Corporation's Leveraged Special Dividends," **Journal of Financial Economics** 36 (October 1994), pp. 157–192.

Wruck, Karen Hopper and Michael C. Jensen, "Science, Specific Knowledge, and Total Quality Management," **Journal of Accounting and Economics** 18 (November 1994), pp. 247–287.

Yarrow, George, "Privatization in Theory and Practice," **Economic Policy** 2 (1986), pp. 324–364.

Zeune, Gary D., "Accessing the Capital Markets," Chapter 31 in Richard Bort, ed., **Corporate Cash Management Handbook** (Warren Gorham Lamont: Boston, 1992).

Zingales, Luigi, "The Value of the Voting Right: A Study of the Milan Stock Exchange Experience," **Review of Financial Studies** 7 (Spring 1994), pp. 125–148.

CHAPTER
3

Risk, Return, and Market Efficiency

3.1 INTRODUCTION

Financial research and instruction is often classified into one of two broad categories. The first category, **investments** (also known as capital market theory), examines how financial markets price securities by studying how individual investors select among financial assets, based on perceived risks and returns. The primary theoretical objective of research in this field is to develop robust, practical, yet theoretically consistent asset pricing techniques that model the required return on all investments as a function of a relative handful of observable factors. The second category, and the focus of this textbook, is **corporate finance**, the study of how business enterprises raise and then invest capital to produce the goods and services desired by society. We corporate finance types often view ourselves as creative artists, concerned with generating and nurturing society's entrepreneurial gems. Therefore, an interesting (if arrogant) question can be asked in this part of a corporate finance textbook: What do we need from investments research?

As it turns out, we in corporate finance need precisely the same information as our investments colleagues—we need to know how financial risk is defined and measured, and we need to understand how risk is "priced" by the capital markets. At the simplest level, **risk** is defined as the chance of financial loss, usually measured in terms of probabilities that various outcomes will occur, ranging from very good (the asset doubles in value in a year) to very bad (the assets become worthless). The price of risk is the extra increment of expected return that investors require to be willing to buy and hold a financial asset that is riskier than, say, a default-free Treasury bill issued by the U.S. government.

This idea, that there will be a direct (hopefully linear) tradeoff between risk and required return, represents the very core of modern investments theory; and we in corporate finance should understand this relationship for three principal reasons. First, since corporate managers should operate the firm to maximize shareholder wealth, they must understand how share prices are determined before they can adopt strategies aimed at value maximization. Second, the financial manager of a corporation that needs to sell securities to raise operating capital must understand how financial assets are priced in order to select the least costly security type to issue. Finally, and perhaps most importantly, corporate managers must be able to determine the rate of return investors expect the firm to earn on its investments in order to develop a risk-adjusted discount rate for use in capital budgeting decisions.

Having addressed why corporate finance types need to understand risk and return, the rest of this chapter will discuss the theoretical and empirical legacy that capital markets researchers have left us. Our focus will always be on the need for financial managers to assess accurately the risk-adjusted return that investors must earn to be willing to buy and hold their firms' common stock. While the ability to manage a firm in the shareholders' interest is important to managers throughout the world, it is especially critical to American managers, given the central role that capital markets play in the U.S. corporate finance system. In Section 3.2, we provide algebraic definitions of risk and return, first for a single asset and then for a portfolio of assets. Section 3.3 then shows how diversification minimizes the risk of an asset portfolio by reducing return variability to the absolute minimum amount that is explained by pervasive, economy-wide influences. This section finally examines the important role that the normal distribution plays in modern asset pricing theory.

After discussing basic portfolio theory, we examine how a handful of insightful academic researchers turned this simple set of statistical relationships into workable equilibrium models of financial risk and required return. We begin in Section 3.4 with the basic, one-period capital asset pricing model (CAPM) developed by Sharpe (1964), Lintner (1965), and Mossin (1966), and then examine the theoretical extensions of this model that result from weakening one or more of the model's underlying assumptions. Our next task is to briefly (but hopefully rigorously) describe the results of empirical testing of the CAPM and its extensions. Similarly, Section 3.5 examines the theoretical development and subsequent empirical testing of the CAPM's primary asset pricing rival, the arbitrage pricing theory (APT), developed initially by Ross (1976, 1977) at least partly to overcome several limitations of the original CAPM. As we will see, neither model has received unambiguous empirical support, although current thinking clearly favors the APT (though without much enthusiasm). We conclude the asset pricing sections of this chapter by summarizing and analyzing the current state of investments theory. Unfortunately, from a corporate finance perspective, we will be forced to the conclusion that asset pricing theory is currently a mess, offering us very few clear guidelines on assessing and pricing risk in modern financial markets, and no viable equilibrium asset pricing model that a consensus of researchers will support. Faced with this disarray, we are forced to keep doing what we've always done—assume that the CAPM is at least theoretically correct but qualify it with even more than the usual caveats and hedged phrases.

Section 3.6 of this chapter examines the theoretical development and subsequent extensions of Fama's (1970) Efficient Markets Hypothesis (EMH), and then discusses how well this hypothesis has stood up to empirical testing. As we will see, early empirical studies strongly (in some cases, almost reverentially) supported the EMH, but more recent work has been more ambiguous. While most researchers probably still believe that the EMH reasonably and accurately describes how markets process information, the theory is clearly under fire, and recent research has identified several "anomalies" that seemingly conflict with the idea that capital markets rationally and instantaneously incorporate all relevant information into security prices.

3.2   RISK AND RETURN FUNDAMENTALS

Before diving into a full-blown discussion of portfolio and asset pricing theory, we must define, conceptually and algebraically, the basic terminology of investments. We begin with definitions of risk and return for a single asset, and then extend these concepts to include portfolios of assets. It is important to understand that the issues we examine in this section are generally applicable to all investments, and are not tied to any one particular theoretical asset pricing model. Instead, both of the major equilibrium models (CAPM and APT) presume that investors are risk-averse agents, who prefer more wealth to less, and who hold well-diversified asset portfolios.

3.2.1 Risk Defined

As mentioned in the introduction, **risk** can be defined as the chance of financial loss.[1] Assets with greater chances of loss are viewed as more risky than those with lesser chance of loss. More formally, the term *risk* is used interchangeably with *uncertainty* to refer to *the variability of returns associated with a given asset*. For instance, a U.S. government bond that guarantees its holder $100 interest after 30 days has no (default) risk, since there is no variability associated with the return.[2] An equivalent investment in a firm's common stock that may earn over the same period anywhere from $0 to $200 is very risky due to the high variability of return—even if the expected payoff in 30 days was the same $100 promised by the government bond. A certain payment is generally preferable to a risky payment of the same size, and if a typical investor must choose between two risky assets, the one with the lowest variability is generally preferred to the more variable asset.

3.2.2 Return Defined

The **return** on an investment is measured as the total gain or loss experienced on behalf of its owner over a given period of time. It is commonly stated as the change in the asset's value (capital gain or loss) plus any cash distributions (dividends or interest payments), expressed as a percentage of the beginning-of-period investment value. The

---

1. The sophisticates among you are probably rolling your eyes and groaning at this simplistic definition of risk. As we will see shortly, an accurate professional definition of risk must incorporate the covariability of an asset's return with that of other risky assets. This is the definition of risk implied by both of the asset pricing models we will examine, as well as by simple portfolio theory. For now, we will use a layperson's definition of risk to nail down key concepts—then proceed up the intellectual food chain.

2. A sovereign government's debt, *denominated in its own currency,* can usually be considered free of default risk, since the government can always print more money to pay off the debt at maturity even if the treasury's tax coffers are empty. However, sovereign debt will not be free of *inflation risk* (it will not guarantee a real rate of return), unless the government has issued floating-interest-rate debt indexed to the period's realized inflation rate—and few governments have been willing to so match their inflation fighting "commitments" with actual security issues.

expression for calculating the rate of return actually realized on any asset i, over period t, is defined as:

$$R_{it} = \left[\frac{P_{it} - P_{it-1} + C_{it}}{P_{it-1}} \right] \tag{3.1}$$

where P_{it} = price (value) of asset i at the end of period t
$\quad P_{it-1}$ = price (value) of asset i at the end of period $t - 1$
$\quad\quad C_{it}$ = cash (flow) received from asset i during period t.

As can be seen, the return reflects the combined effects of changes in value, $P_t - P_{t-1}$, and cash flow, C_t, realized over the period.

The equation presented above is an after-the-fact, or **ex-post**, definition of return that assumes nothing about the distribution of possible outcomes or about what return was actually expected on that asset. In discussing asset pricing and portfolio theory, we will often want to incorporate uncertainty into the very fabric of our discussion. One way to do this is to formally acknowledge, before-the-fact (**ex-ante**), that period t prices, cash flows, and returns will be realizations from an underlying probability distribution of possible outcomes. Another way to phrase this is to say that prices, cash flows, and returns are **random variables** that can take on any of several (perhaps an infinite number of) possible outcomes during period t, and the actual values they will take on cannot be predicted *with certainty*. The proper statistical method of expressing a random variable is to place a *tilde* (˜) over each variable that is not deterministic (known in advance). Therefore, our basic return formula can be restated to incorporate ex-ante uncertainty as follows:

$$\tilde{R}_{it} = \left[\frac{\tilde{P}_{it} - \tilde{P}_{it-1} + \tilde{C}_{it}}{\tilde{P}_{it-1}} \right] \tag{3.2}$$

where all variables are as before, except they are explicitly modeled as random variables whose values are not known in advance. While most of the return variables presented in the remainder of this chapter properly should be expressed as random variables, we will express them in the standard R_t format in the interest of simplicity, and because our primary purpose is exposition of the basic risk/return relationships.

So far our discussion of return has embodied no expectation about what the return on asset i will be during period t. We can, however, develop an **expected return**—defined as $E(R_{it})$—whenever we are provided with a description of all possible investment outcomes, along with the associated probability of each outcome being realized. Alternatively, if we employ one of the major asset pricing models such as the CAPM we can generate a **conditional expected return**. This means that we can predict what the asset's return will be conditional on the return realized by another variable—in the case of the CAPM the return on the market portfolio of risky assets, R_{mt}. Finally, we can tie together expected and realized return by expressing actual return as the expected return plus a random error term (residual)—noted ϵ_{it} for random error of asset i at end of period t—as follows:

$$R_{it} = E(R_{it}) + \epsilon_{it} \tag{3.3}$$

We will explore the concept of expected return more fully, both when we discuss probability distributions and later when we discuss the CAPM and APT.

3.2.3 Basic Risk Concepts: A Single Asset

Although the risk of a single asset is measured in much the same way as the risk of an entire portfolio of assets, it is important to differentiate between these two entities, since certain benefits accrue to holders of portfolios. Furthermore, our discussion in the next section will make clear that modern asset pricing theory is based upon an asset's risk/return performance within a portfolio, rather than as a stand-alone investment. Nonetheless, we first examine the risk of an individual asset, beginning with a discussion of probabilities and probability distributions. The **probability** of a given outcome is its relative likelihood of occurring, and is usually expressed as a percentage value between 0 and 100, or a fractional value between 0 and 1.

A **probability distribution** is a mathematical or graphical expression of the range of possible outcomes, weighted by the probability that each will occur. As an example, assume an investor is trying do decide which of two assets, A or B, to invest in. Each requires an initial investment of $10,000, and in each case there is a 25 percent probability that the most pessimistic outcome will occur, a 25 percent probability that the most optimistic outcome will occur, and a 50 percent probability that a middle (most likely) outcome will occur. We can compute the expected return for assets A and B using the generic formula for the **expected value of a return** for asset i, $E(R_i)$, presented below as equation 3.4. For simplicity in exposition, we drop the time period subscripts from this formula.

$$E(R_i) = \sum_{j=1}^{n} (R_j \times Pr_j) \tag{3.4}$$

where R_j = return for the jth outcome
Pr_j = probability of occurrence of the jth outcome
n = number of outcomes considered

Using this formula, we can determine that the expected value for each asset's return is 15 percent, as follows:

$$E(R_A) = [(13\% \times 0.25) + (15\% \times 0.50) + (17\% \times 0.25)] = 15\%$$

$$E(R_B) = [(7\% \times 0.25) + (15\% \times 0.50) + (16\% \times 0.25)] = 15\%$$

From this point forward, we will frequently express this return in its fractional form, 0.15, rather than 15 percent, since it will often be used in combination with other fractional values. If we knew all the possible outcomes and associated probabilities, we could develop a **continuous probability distribution**. Figure 3.1 presents continuous probability distributions for assets C and D, which have the same expected values as assets A and B.

3.2.4 Standard Deviation

The most common statistical indicator of an asset i's risk is the **standard deviation** of that asset's expected return, $\sigma(R_i)$, which measures the dispersion around its expected value. This can be calculated using equation 3.5 below:

$$\sigma(R_i) = \sqrt{\sum_{j=1}^{n} [R_j - E(R_i)]^2 \times Pr_j} \tag{3.5}$$

FIGURE 3.1

CONTINUOUS PROBABILITY DISTRIBUTIONS FOR ASSET C'S AND ASSET D'S RETURN

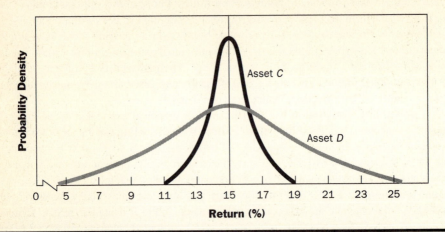

SOURCE: GITMAN, LAWRENCE J., PRINCIPLES OF MANAGERIAL FINANCE, 7TH EDITION, (HARPERCOLLINS PUBLISHERS; NEW YORK, 1994).

where all the variables are as defined before. In general, the higher the standard deviation, the greater the risk.[3] Table 3.1 presents the calculation of standard deviations of assets A and B, based on the data presented earlier. The standard deviation of asset A is 1.41 percent, and the standard deviation of asset B is 5.66 percent. It is often preferable to measure dispersion as an asset's **variance**, Var(R_i), which is simply the squared standard deviation, as defined in equation 3.6 below:

$$\text{Var}(R_i) = \sigma^2(R_i) = \sum_{j=1}^{n} [R_j - E(R_i)]^2 \times Pr_j \qquad (3.6)$$

As with standard deviation, the higher an asset's variance, the greater the (total) risk.

A **normal probability distribution**, depicted in Figure 3.2, is one that always resembles a "bell-shaped" curve. It is symmetrical: From the peak of the graph, the curve's extensions are mirror images of each other. The symmetry of the curve means that half the curve's area lies to the left of the peak and half to the right. Therefore, half the probability is associated with values to the left of the peak and half with values to the right. As is noted in the figure, for normal probability distributions, 68 percent of the possible outcomes will lie between ±1 standard deviation from the expected value, 95 percent of all

---

3. Once again, we are using the term risk here somewhat loosely. Our current measure should properly be labeled *total risk*, since it includes both variability that can be eliminated by investors by forming portfolios (diversifiable, or unsystematic risk) and variability that cannot be diversified away (nondiversifiable, or systematic risk). As long as we are discussing the risk of a single asset we will use the term risk in the interest of simplicity.

outcomes will lie between ±2 standard deviations from the expected value, and 99 per-cent of all outcomes will lie between ±3 standard deviations from the expected value.

In addition to being the most widely studied and well-understood probability distribu-tion in statistics, the normal distribution has the very desirable feature that it can be com-pletely described by specifying only two parameters—mean (average) and variance. In-vestments researchers have been able to exploit this feature to build full-scale asset pricing models, most particularly the CAPM, without having to make implausible assumptions about investor behavior or imposing extreme restrictions on allowable security return dis-tributions. Investors simply must be risk-averse and select between investment portfolios based solely on expected return (mean) and the variance (or standard deviation) of returns. Then as long as security returns are normally distributed—which, to a first approximation, they seem to be—one can describe the important interactions between any two or more se-curities simply by specifying their covariances (the extent to which returns move together). Since other parameters of the joint distributions of security returns are unimportant, one can construct an equilibrium asset pricing model that implies that all investors will hold some combination of a risk-free asset and a single "market portfolio" of risky assets, re-gardless of the investor's individual risk preferences. This two-fund separation principle

TABLE 3.1

CALCULATION OF EXPECTED VALUES AND STANDARD DEVIATIONS FOR ASSETS A AND B

Expected Values of Returns for Assets A and B

Possible Outcomes	Probability (1)	Returns (%) (2)	Weighted Value (%) [(1) × (2)] (3)
Asset A			
Pessimistic	.25	13	3.25
Most likely	.50	15	7.50
Optimistic	.25	17	4.25
Total	1.00	Expected return	15.00
Asset B			
Pessimistic	.25	7	1.75
Most likely	.50	15	7.50
Optimistic	.25	23	5.75
Total	1.00	Expected return	15.00

(Continued)

| | | | TABLE 3.1 (CONTINUED) | | | |

The Calculation of the Standard Deviation of the Returns
for Assets A and B[a]

Asset A

i	k_i	$\bar{k}$	$k_i - \bar{k}$	$(k_i - \bar{k})^2$	Pr_i	$(k_i - \bar{k})^2 \times Pr_i$
1	13%	15%	-2%	4%	.25	1%
2	15	15	0	0	.50	0
3	17	15	2	4	.25	$\underline{1}$

$$\sum_{i=1}^{3}(k_i - \bar{k})^2 \times Pr_i = 2\%$$

$$\sigma k_A = \sqrt{\sum_{i=1}^{3}(k_i = \bar{k})^2 \times Pr_i} = \sqrt{2\%} = \underline{1.41\%}$$

Asset B

i	k_i	$\bar{k}$	$k_i - \bar{k}$	$(k_i - \bar{k})^2$	Pr_i	$(k_i - \bar{k})^2 \times Pr_i$
1	7%	15%	-8%	64%	.25	16%
2	15	15	0	0	.50	0
3	23	15	8	64	.25	$\underline{16}$

$$\sum_{i=1}^{3}(k_i - \bar{k})^2 \times Pr_i = 32\%$$

$$\sigma k_B = \sqrt{\sum_{i=1}^{3}(k_i = \bar{k})^2 \times Pr_i} = \sqrt{32\%} = \underline{5.66\%}$$

[a]CALCULATIONS IN THIS TABLE ARE MADE IN PERCENTAGE FORM RATHER THAN DECIMAL FORM, E.G., 13% RATHER THAN .13. AS A RESULT, SOME OF THE INTERMEDIATE COMPUTATIONS MAY APPEAR TO BE INCONSISTENT WITH THOSE THAT WOULD RESULT FROM USING DECIMAL FORM. REGARDLESS, THE RESULTING STANDARD DEVIATIONS ARE CORRECT AND IDENTICAL TO THOSE THAT WOULD RESULT FROM USING DECIMAL RATHER THAN PERCENTAGE FORM.

SOURCE: GITMAN, LAWRENCE J., *PRINCIPLES OF MANAGERIAL FINANCE*, SEVENTH EDITION (NEW YORK: HARPERCOLLINS PUBLISHERS, 1994).

(defined more fully in Section 3.3) is extremely important because it leads to a pricing model that assigns a unique, market-determined required rate of return to all risky assets. Furthermore, normally distributed returns yield an asset pricing model that is empirically testable (at least theoretically) using fairly simple regression methodology, since the residuals (the difference between actual and expected returns) from different estimations will be uncorrelated.

Several concepts and terms in the paragraph above are probably unclear at this point. Hopefully, they will be made more understandable later when we work through the CAPM. The key point now is to develop an intuitive feel for the importance of the normal distribution in investments theory and practice. There was, however, one concept raised

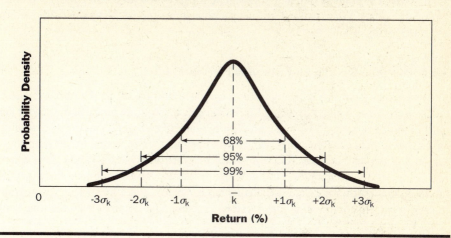

FIGURE 3.2

NORMAL PROBABILITY DISTRIBUTION, WITH RANGES

which we should address immediately—the concept of risk preferences or risk aversion. Simply put, a **risk-averse** investor is an individual who, when given a choice between two investments with equal expected returns, will always choose the investment with the lowest variance. An investor who is indifferent between two investments having equal returns but different variances is said to be **risk neutral**. A **risk-seeking** investor is one who will actually choose the riskier of two investments offering the same expected payoff. Individual risk preferences are ultimately based on a person's **utility function**—defined as the tradeoff an investor chooses to make between current and future wealth, and between current consumption opportunities and the financial security that comes from an investment portfolio, in order to maximize his or her level of personal satisfaction. Most finance theorists and practitioners assume that investors are trying to maximize utility by maximizing their wealth, which is practically achieved by maximizing the value of their investment portfolio. Furthermore, it is commonly assumed that most investors are risk-averse. While it is possible to define utility functions mathematically, and to compare investment outcomes that have different risks *and* different expected returns, for our purposes an intuitive understanding of risk preferences and utility functions is sufficient.[4]

3.3   PORTFOLIO RISK AND RETURN

The risk of any single asset investment should not be viewed independent from other assets. Investments must be considered in light of their impact on the risk and return of the investor's portfolio of assets. An investor's goal is to create an **efficient portfolio**,

---

4. Utility theory has a long and distinguished history in economic thought, beginning with Friedman and Savage (1948). The strengths and weaknesses of utility theory are discussed—and the relevant literature is summarized—in Schoemaker (1982), while Copeland and Weston (1988, chapter 4) discuss its role in the development of finance theory.

one that maximizes return for a given level of risk, or minimizes risk for a given level of returns. The statistical concept of correlation underlies the process of diversification that is used to develop an efficient portfolio of assets. Before discussing these and other aspects of portfolio risk, we will look at the procedures for calculating portfolio return and standard deviation.

3.3.1 Portfolio Return and Standard Deviation

The return on a portfolio is calculated as a weighted average of the returns on the individual assets from which it is formed. The concepts of portfolio return and variance are most easily demonstrated with the simplest two-asset case, so let's begin by assuming we can select between two assets, i and j. Let w_i equal the proportion of our portfolio's total dollar (or yen, or franc, or peso) value represented by asset i and let w_j, where $w_j = (1 - w_i)$, equal the proportion invested in asset j. We can compute the expected return on this portfolio, $E(R_p)$, using equation 3.7 below. Note that we are expressing returns in our equations as random variables, and we have again deleted the time subscript for simplicity.

$$E(R_p) = w_i E(R_i) + w_j E(R_j) \tag{3.7}$$

In words, *portfolio return is a weighted average of the expected returns of individual assets*, and this is true for portfolios of all sizes (not just two-asset combinations). This linearity feature is not observed for portfolio variance, however, with fantastically important implications.

The variance of a portfolio's return, Var (R_p), is defined as follows:

$$\text{Var}(R_p) = E[R_p - E(R_p)]^2$$

$$\text{Var}(R_p) = w_i^2 \, \text{Var} \, (R_i) + w_j^2 \, \text{Var} \, (R_j) + 2w_i w_j E\{[(R_i - E(R_i)][R_j - E(R_j)]\}$$

$$\text{Cov}(R_i, R_j) = E\{[R_i - E(R_i)][R_j - E(R_j)]\}$$

$$\text{Var}(R_p) = w_i^2 \, \text{Var}(R_i) + w_i^2 \, \text{Var}(R_j) + 2w_i w_j \, \text{Cov}(R_i, R_j) \tag{3.8}$$

Note that portfolio variance is not simply a weighted sum of the individual asset variances, but rather includes these terms plus a third term that incorporates a weighted measure of the covariance between the returns of asset i and asset j, $\text{Cov}(R_i, R_j)$. **Covariance**, in turn, is a statistical expression of the tendency of two random variables to move together. Two variables which have positive covariance move together in the same direction, while variables with negative covariances move together in opposite directions.

In order to compare covariation of various combinations of assets, we scale the covariance term to a value between -1 and $+1$ by converting it into a correlation coefficient. The **correlation coefficient**, ρ, between two variables is obtained by dividing the covariance by the product of the standard deviations. Therefore, we can convert Cov (R_i, R_j) into the correlation coefficient ρ_{ij} using the formula below:

$$\rho_{ij} = \frac{\text{Cov} \, (R_i, R_j)}{\sigma_i \sigma_j}$$

A correlation coefficient of -1 implies that two variables are **perfectly negatively correlated** (they move together, in equal amounts, but in opposite directions), while a correlation coefficient of $+1$ indicates that two variables are **perfectly positively correlated**—they move together, in equal amounts, in the same direction. Variables with a correlation coefficient of 0 are said to be **uncorrelated**, meaning they do not move together at all.

By incorporating correlation into our definition of portfolio variance, we are able to obtain our final, easily understood expression of portfolio return variance, equation 3.9:

$$\text{Var}(R_p) = w_i^2 \, \text{Var}(R_i) + w_j^2 \, \text{Var}(R_j) + 2w_i w_j \rho_{ij} \sigma_i \sigma_j \tag{3.9}$$

The fundamental importance of this equation becomes clear when it is generalized to include many assets in a portfolio. As the number of assets increases the equation becomes increasingly complex, since each new asset's covariance with every other asset must be accounted for. This causes the number of covariance terms to increase, quite literally, exponentially. However, the contribution of individual asset variances to total portfolio variance declines rapidly. To see this, consider the two-asset case where $w_i = w_j = 0.5$. In this case, the portfolio's variance includes only 25 percent of asset i's variance $[w_i^2 \, \text{Var}(R_i) = (0.5)^2 \, \text{Var}(R_i) = 0.25 \, \text{Var}(R_i)]$, plus an equal amount of asset j's variance. If, however, a portfolio is constructed with equal fractions of ten assets, then each asset's weight equals 10 percent ($w_i = w_j = w_n = 0.1$), and portfolio variance includes *only one percent* of each asset's individual return variance $[(0.1)^2 \, \text{Var}(R_i) = 0.01 \, \text{Var}(R_i)]$. Even collectively, the contribution of all individual asset variances to total portfolio variance is small, and becomes infinitesimal as the number of assets in a portfolio increases past a few dozen.

3.3.2 Diversifiable and Nondiversifiable Risk

As individual asset variances shrink in importance, the covariance terms become increasingly dominant. Furthermore, these terms become dominant in a very specific and important way. As an asset is added to a broadly **diversified** portfolio—one with many randomly selected components—that asset's covariance with any other single asset, like its own variance, contributes very little to portfolio variance. It is only that asset's covariance *with all other assets* that has a measureable impact on the variance of portfolio return, and an investor contemplating adding this asset to his or her portfolio will only be concerned about that asset's covariance *with the market portfolio of risky assets*. This observation allows us to draw a distinction between an asset's **diversifiable risk**, defined as that part of an asset's total variance which is uncorrelated with the return on all other assets, and **nondiversifiable risk**—that fraction of an asset's return variance which is attributable to market forces that affect all firms, and which cannot be diversified away.

Diversifiable risk, which is also called **unique risk** or **unsystematic risk**, is attributable to investor reaction to firm-specific events, such as strikes, lawsuits, regulatory action, or loss of a key account. Nondiversifiable risk, which is also called **systematic risk**, is related to a firm's sensitivity to macroeconomic and political forces that affect all firms and all financial assets. To summarize, we can say that the **total risk** of a security can be viewed as consisting of two parts:

$$\textit{Total risk} = \textit{diversifiable risk} + \textit{nondiversifiable risk} \qquad (3.10)$$

The relationship between diversifiable and nondiversifiable risk can also be presented graphically. Using the standard deviation of portfolio return, $\sigma(R_p)$, to measure total portfolio risk, Figure 3.3 depicts the behavior of diversifiable, nondiversifiable, and total risk (y-axis) as more securities are added (x-axis) to one's portfolio. With the addition of securities, the total portfolio risk declines due to diversification, until it approaches a limit—where all unsystematic risk has been removed—leaving only the portfolio's sensitivity to systematic risk. Research has shown that most of the benefits of diversification can be gained by forming portfolios containing 15 to 20 randomly selected securities. As you might expect, if one includes foreign securities, portfolio risk can be reduced even further while achieving the same or even a higher expected return.[5]

What does the analysis above tell us about the way assets will be priced in a well-functioning capital market? Specifically, when evaluating whether an asset should or should not be included in a portfolio, how does an investor assess whether an asset offers a return that is attractive enough to compensate him or her for the risk associated with purchasing that asset? While we are not (quite) yet ready to quantify the required return an asset must offer—that requires a specific asset pricing model—we can conclude that the investor will require a higher expected return for an asset that covaries positively with other assets, and will be willing to accept a lower expected return for an asset that was relatively insensitive to systematic risk factors. The ideal asset, in fact, is one whose return is negatively correlated with the returns on other assets, since by combining negatively correlated assets, the overall variability of portfolio returns can be reduced. A portfolio containing the negatively correlated assets F and G, both having the same expected return $E(R_i)$, also has the expected return $E(R_i) = E(R_p)$, but has less risk (variability) than either of the individual assets. On the other hand, the creation of a portfolio by combining two assets having perfectly positively correlated returns cannot reduce the portfolio's overall risk below the risk of the least risky asset.

3.3.3 The "Efficient Frontier" of Risky Portfolios

The process of constructing a portfolio of assets that minimizes return variability for any given level of expected return is referred to as creating the **minimum variance portfolio**. These portfolios are **mean-variance efficient portfolios** that offer investors the best achievable combination of risk and return. Of course, a very small subset of all possible investment portfolios will be efficient. Figure 3.4 displays how the population of achievable portfolios would be represented in a graph of expected portfolio return (y-axis) versus standard deviation of portfolio return (x-axis). Any portfolio on, below, or to the right of the boundary BCDE is attainable by investors, but a rational investor

---

5. See, for example, Agmon and Lessard (1977) for a discussion of the benefits of international diversification, and of the role of corporations in helping investors achieve these benefits indirectly by purchasing the stock of internationally active firms.

FIGURE 3.3

PORTFOLIO RISK AND DIVERSIFICATION

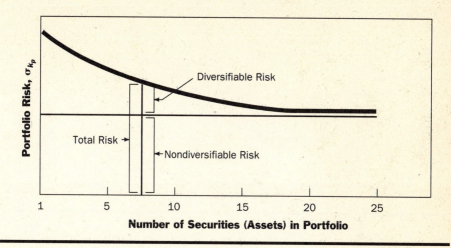

would only select from those portfolios that actually plot on this boundary. This boundary is called the **efficient frontier**, and investors can maximize return for any level of portfolio risk they are comfortable with simply by selecting a portfolio on this frontier. Very risk-averse investors would choose portfolio B, while investors willing to tolerate more risk might choose portfolio D, or even E.

To see why the portfolios on boundary BCDE dominate all others, consider portfolio F. No rational investor would select this portfolio, because he or she could attain a higher level of expected return with no additional risk by choosing portfolio D. Alternatively, the investor could achieve the same expected return as with portfolio F, but be forced to assume far less risk, simply by selecting portfolio C. The same logic applies for portfolio A, which superficially appears to be on the efficient frontier. It is not, however, because an investor could achieve a higher return, at lower risk, by choosing portfolio B. In equilibrium, all available assets would be combined into a portfolio that lay on the boundary BCDE, though one cannot predict which individual portfolio—since an infinite number of efficient portfolio combinations are attainable.

We are now ready to take the final step in the development of what is often called **Efficient Portfolio Theory**.[6] Assume that investors who face the investment opportunity

---

6. The basic principles of portfolio theory were finrst systematically presented by Markowitz (1952), in one of the most important papers of modern finance (indeed, the *first* paper of modern finance). His work was to be rewarded almost forty years later with the awarding of the Nobel Prize in Economics. Markowitz's principles were further refined by Tobin (1958), and then incorporated into the CAPM by Sharpe (1964). Both Tobin and Sharpe are also Nobel Laureates.

FIGURE 3.4

PORTFOLIO RETURNS AND STANDARD DEVIATIONS

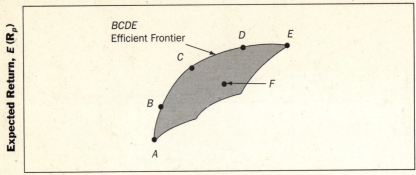

Standard Deviation of Returns $\sigma(R_p)$

set described in Figure 3.4 are also given the opportunity to invest in a risk-free ($\sigma(R_f) = 0$) asset offering a certain return R_f, as shown in Figure 3.5. Such an opportunity funda-mentally expands the attainable investment opportunity set for market participants even as it simplifies the choices they need to make. To see why this is so, we draw a line con-necting R_f with portfolio C, which represents the tangency of the line between R_f and the efficient frontier. The line segment R_fC represents a portfolio combining nonnegative fractions of portfolio C and the risk-free asset, while the ray extending up and away from point C represents additional investment in portfolio C financed by borrowing money at the risk-free rate.

The line from R_f through point C is referred to as the **Capital Market Line**, and in-vestors are able to achieve better risk-return combinations on this boundary than is at-tainable by investing in risky asset portfolios alone. To demonstrate this, consider a risk-averse investor who would previously have selected portfolio B. That investor can now attain a higher expected return, for the same risk, by selecting portfolio B′ on the CML. Alternatively, he or she can choose portfolio B″ rather than portfolio B and re-ceive the same return at lower risk. Similar logic applies to an investor with greater tolerance for risk, who might before have selected portfolio D. He or she can now choose either portfolio D′, achieving a higher return for the same risk, or portfolio D″, achieving the same return for lower risk. Clearly, portfolios on ray R_fC dominate all other attainable portfolios, and the insight that all investors will choose some combi-nation of the risk-free asset and the tangency portfolio is referred to as the **separation theorem** or, in an operational sense, as **two-fund separation**.

If this chapter were a movie, now would be an ideal time for a drum roll of anticipa-tion, for we are very close to developing a workable model for pricing individual risky assets. All that remains is the specification of a mathematical definition of financial risk, and a formula for determining the required return for individual assets. Before proceeding, however, it is worth summarizing just how much we can say about risk and

FIGURE 3.5

THE CAPITAL MARKET LINE WITH A RISK-FREE ASSET

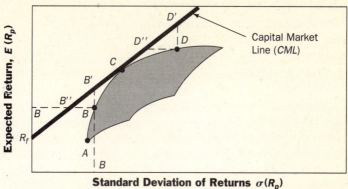

return simply by drawing basic lessons from portfolio theory. We know that it is an asset's covariance with the population of other risky assets—formed into a portfolio—that is important to an investor, not the asset's own variance or its covariance with any other single asset. We know that rational, risk-averse investors will choose portfolios that offer the maximum return for any given level of risk, and vice versa. We know that investors, who are limited to selecting risky portfolios, will choose only from portfolios that lie on the efficient frontier, and the specific portfolios they choose will depend upon their personal risk preferences. Finally, we know that when investors have the opportunity to purchase a risk-free asset as well as risky asset portfolios they will choose some combination of the risk-free asset and a specific tangency portfolio. What we now must do is specify how individual assets are priced in relation to the market of all risky assets, and to each other.

3.4   THE CAPITAL ASSET PRICING MODEL (CAPM)

Although our discussion of portfolio theory in the previous section was phrased in conversational (hopefully intuitive) terms, even that simple explanation was actually based on several quite specific assumptions about investor preferences and perceptions, the technical efficiency of the market for risky assets, and the distribution of security returns. Since we now want to develop a true equilibrium asset pricing model, rigor must substitute for intuition, and we must make clear that efficient portfolio theory and the Capital Asset Pricing Model (CAPM) both require the following assumptions to be made:

1. All investors are single period, risk-averse, utility-of-terminal-wealth maximizers who choose among portfolios solely on the basis of the mean and variance of expected returns.

2. There are no taxes, transactions costs, or other market imperfections. There are a large number of perfectly divisible assets, all of which are marketable. There are also numerous fully-informed buyers and sellers, all of whom are price takers (they lack the market power to influence prices with their trades).

3. All investors have homogeneous expectations regarding the probability distribution of security returns.

4. A risk-free asset exists, and all investors can borrow and lend unlimited amounts at a given, riskless rate of interest.

In addition to these assumptions, one must assume either that security returns are normally distributed or that investors have quadratic utility functions in order to ensure that investors select portfolios based solely on mean and variance (assumption 1). Since quadratic utility functions have several implausible features (the worst being declining marginal utility of wealth past a certain point), our final assumption will specify allowable security return distributions.

5. All asset returns are described by a joint normal probability distribution, so that all portfolios can be described by specifying their means and variances.

Obviously, these are very restrictive assumptions that are not fully met in any real capital market. Nevertheless, as we will see later, the basic predictions of the CAPM are surprisingly robust to minor violations of most (but not all) of these assumptions. In any case, the true test of a theory is how well it explains objective reality and how strongly it is supported by empirical testing—not how believable its assumptions are. We now turn to a brief description of the CAPM model itself and a listing of its principal empirical predictions.

3.4.1 Development of the CAPM

The basic CAPM was developed almost simultaneously by Sharpe (1964), Lintner (1965), and Mossin (1966), and was immediately embraced by the academic community. Practitioners took somewhat longer to accept the model, but it was ultimately hailed almost universally as a simple and powerful tool for anyone interested in investments or in the workings of capital markets. The reason for this enthusiasm is not hard to find: For the first time, researchers and practitioners alike had a model that generated testable predictions about the risk and return characteristics of individual assets by specifying how they would covary with the market portfolio of all risky assets.

To understand how the Sharpe-Lintner-Mossin CAPM was developed, refer back to Figure 3.5 where the capital market line connected the risk-free asset with a tangency portfolio. The CAPM's contribution was to show that this cannot represent an **equilibrium result**—a state of affairs in the capital market where there is no tendency for asset prices to change, and where investors are satisfied with their current asset holdings. As investors seek to purchase the assets in portfolio C their prices will be bid up, while the prices of assets in all other portfolios will decline. But by how much will each asset decline or increase in price? The insightful answer offered was that each asset will change in price until it offers an expected return that is commensurate with its risk, and which places it on the capital market line.

An asset's risk, in turn, is based solely on how it impacts the variability of returns of a well-diversified portfolio if an investor chooses to purchase the asset for inclusion in his or her portfolio. Since an asset's unique risk can be diversified away, it is only the asset's **systematic risk**—defined as the asset's return covariance with the market portfolio of risky assets—that matters to an investor. Investors will only be willing to purchase assets with high systematic risks if they offer high expected returns. But investors will be willing to accept low expected returns if they purchase assets with low systematic risk—since inclusion of these assets will lower the systematic risk of the entire portfolio. The specific measure of systematic risk used in the CAPM is called an asset's **beta**, β_i, and is defined as the correlation of the asset's return with the return on the market portfolio, R_m, as specified in equation 3.11 below:

$$\beta_i = \frac{\text{Cov}(R_i, R_m)}{\text{Var}(R_m)} \tag{3.11}$$

This is a direct, linear estimate of the degree of co-movement between an asset's return and the return on the market portfolio. In fact, the more statistically-oriented of you will have noticed that the beta for any individual asset can be readily estimated by regressing the return on that asset with the return on the market portfolio during the same period. In this case, beta is interpreted (almost) directly as the regression coefficient from that equation. To make the final step to the CAPM we must incorporate the option of investing in the risk-free asset, as well as investing in the market portfolio of risky assets.

To understand the importance of a risk-free asset to the CAPM, refer again to Figure 3.5. Equilibrium requires that portfolio C be the minimum variance market portfolio, where all risky assets are held according to their actual market value weights. Since investors can choose combinations of this portfolio and the risk-free asset, we can specify the capital asset pricing model's predicted return for any risky asset as equation 3.12:

$$E(R_i) = R_f + \beta_i [E(R_m) - R_f] \tag{3.12}$$

where the $[E(R_m) - R_f]$ term is called the **market risk premium** (or equity risk premium), since it is the additional return required by investors in order to hold the market portfolio instead of the risk-free asset.

The CAPM is presented graphically in Figure 3.6, where expected return is again on the y-axis, but now beta (rather than standard deviation) is on the x-axis. The ray extending up and to the right from R_f is referred to as the **Security Market Line**, because all assets will plot along this line in expected return-beta space. We therefore have an equilibrium asset pricing model which yields a required return for all risky assets based solely on a linear relationship between that asset's correlation with the market risk premium, beta, and its expected return. Before moving on to empirical tests and extensions of the CAPM, let us transform equation 3.12 so that we can express an asset's required return in risk premium form as equation 3.13:

$$E(R_i) - R_f = \beta_i [E(R_m) - R_f] \tag{3.13}$$

This says that the risk premium (over the risk-free rate) required for an individual asset is equal to its beta times the market risk premium. While this formulation is often useful,

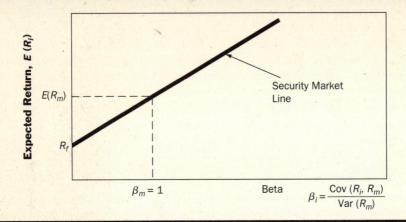

FIGURE 3.6

THE CAPITAL ASSET PRICING MODEL PRESENTED GRAPHICALLY

most empirical tests attempt to verify whether the basic CAPM formula given in equation 3.12 is an accurate reflection of realized security returns.

3.4.2 Early Empirical Tests of the CAPM

Although the CAPM is quite easy to understand intuitively, empirical testing of the model is far from simple, for several reasons. First, by definition the CAPM generates *expected* returns, but tests of the model must use *realized* (historical) returns. In order to test an ex ante model using ex post returns, researchers must make a somewhat heroic **rational expectations** assumption that investors will make unbiased estimations of expected returns that, over time and in the average, will equal realized returns. Second, the CAPM is a one-period model that must be tested using returns from several months, or even years. An unavoidable implication of this dilemma is that empirical tests of the CAPM are likely to be very sensitive to the particular time periods selected as starting and ending points, and that test periods which encompass large fluctuations in risk-free interest rates or major macroeconomic disruptions are likely to generate very "noisy" results—of dubious economic significance. A third, related, problem involves the **stationarity** assumptions that must be made in order to test a single period model using multi-period data. To test such a model, one must assume not only that the risk-free rate is **non-stochastic** (it does not change over time), one must also assume that the market risk premium and the asset's beta coefficient remain constant throughout the test period. Finally, one must use a proxy for the market portfolio to compute the market return, since the "true" market portfolio is unobservable.[7]

In spite of these difficulties, several very careful tests of the CAPM were performed in the years immediately after it was publicly unveiled. Most early studies model ex-

---

7. Commonly used proxies for the market portfolio include the S&P 500 Stock Index or the equally-weighed Center for Research in Security Prices (CRSP) datafile of companies listed on the New York Stock Exchange (NYSE) and the American Stock Exchange (AMEX).

pected returns using some variant of the following **excess return**, or equity premium, version of the basic CAPM equation, where the expected excess return on asset i, $E(R'_i)$, is expressed as the expected return minus the risk-free rate. The excess return on the market portfolio, $E(R'_m)$, is similarly defined as the expected return minus the risk-free rate, as shown in equation 3.14:

$$E(R'_i) = E(R'_m)\beta_i \qquad (3.14)$$

where $E(R'_i) = E(R_i) - R_f$
$E(R'_m) = E(R_m) - R_f$

The actual empirical tests involved estimating the cross-sectional model presented in equation 3.14, where R'_i, the mean excess return over a time interval for a set of securities, was regressed on estimates of the systematic risks, β_i, of each of the securities.

$$R'_i = \gamma_0 + \gamma_1\beta_i + \epsilon_i \qquad (3.15)$$

where γ_0, γ_1 = regression coefficients, and
ϵ_i = a residual, assumed to be independent and normally distributed.

Expressed in this way, we can easily specify the results that the basic CAPM predicts, both mathematically and intuitively. The CAPM predicts:

1. The mean realized return on a security should be positively *and linearly* related to the security's estimated systematic risk, β_i. Therefore, γ_1 in equation 3.15 should be positive and significantly different from zero. In fact, γ_1 should be equal to $(R_m - R_f)$, the market risk premium.

2. The intercept term, γ_0 in equation 3.15, should not be significantly different from zero. This is equivalent to testing whether the risk-free rate is truly the base upon which equity risk premiums are priced. In graphical terms, this would be testing whether the empirical Security Market Line of Figure 3.6 actually intercepts the y-axis at point R_f, or somewhere above or below this point.

3. Realized returns should not be systematically related to anything except beta. Variables such as dividend yield, residual variance, beta squared, or any other variable should not be significantly related to security returns.

4. The parameters of equation 3.15 should be stable from one period to the next. In other words, an asset's beta should not change over time and the model should yield the same conditional returns (actual returns conditional on the market's return) each period.

Early empirical studies offered qualified support for the CAPM, in that there appeared to be a linear trade-off between beta and realized return, and nonlinear variables such as residual variance and beta squared were not consistently related to returns. Empirical support was far from unambiguous, however. One important early study, by Black, Jensen, and Scholes (1972), finds that returns are positively related to beta, but that high-beta securities have significantly negative intercepts ($\gamma_0 < 0$), while low-beta securities have significantly positive intercepts ($\gamma_0 > 0$). This implies that the slope of the estimated security market line is lower than predicted by the theoretical model $[\gamma_1 < (R_m - R_f)]$, meaning that beta risk is priced too low.

A possible explanation for these results is offered by Black (1972). He derives an extended CAPM based on the assumption that investors can lend, but cannot borrow, at the risk-free rate of interest (they can buy, but cannot issue, Treasury bills). Without access to a risk-free asset, investors instead use a portfolio of securities that is uncorrelated with other efficient portfolios. Market equilibrium occurs when all investors choose combinations of this zero-beta portfolio and the efficient portfolio that yields the best attainable tradeoff between risk and return. As it happens, this **zero-beta CAPM** yields a lower γ_1 than the original CAPM, and exactly the same pattern of intercept terms for high and low betas that Black, Jensen, and Scholes document. Fama and MacBeth (1973) find that the zero-beta model explains observed returns better than does the standard CAPM. These researchers also document that a squared beta term is not consistently or significantly related to observed returns. Shortly thereafter, Black and Scholes (1974) document that dividend yield also is not significantly related to returns in a CAPM estimation model.

The Fama and MacBeth study does, however, document one particularly disquieting empirical regularity. While risk is, on average, related to return, the relationship is far from stable. Their study examines subsequent five-year estimation periods, and all parameters of the regression equation change dramatically from one period to the next—but not in a way that can be interpreted as an evolving trend. (For example, the beta regression coefficients fluctuate randomly rather than becoming consistently more positive over time.) Nonetheless, since no other asset pricing model was being supported by empirical tests, by the mid-1970s most researchers were confident that the CAPM was at least an acceptable model of how financial risk is priced in modern capital markets.

3.4.3 Theoretical Extensions of the CAPM

Concurrent with empirical testing of the CAPM, several authors examined how weakening the assumptions used to derive the original model affected the CAPM's theoretical validity and/or empirical predictions. In general, the early news was surprisingly good. As mentioned earlier, Black's (1972) study shows that the lack of a risk-free asset can readily be incorporated into a linear pricing model, and in fact even explains the observed results better than does the standard model. In addition, Mayers (1972) examines the impact of nonmarketable assets, such as human capital, on the CAPM and finds that the basic linear tradeoff between beta and expected return remains intact—but that the relationship is less precise than if all assets were marketable. Even the assumption of homogeneous expectations concerning the probability distribution of security returns is shown to be less than critical to the theoretical validity of the CAPM, as Williams (1977) demonstrates. The CAPM is also coupled with other areas of finance theory by Hamada (1972), who shows how a firm's capital structure influences the systematic risk of its common stock, and by Rubinstein (1973), who integrates the CAPM with the firm's capital budgeting decisions.

Several other authors present important theoretical extensions of the CAPM that are less easily reconciled with the received model and existing empirical tests. Brennan (1970) develops an **after-tax CAPM** that accounts for the fact that investors have to pay higher taxes on high-dividend-yield stocks than on low-yield stocks if dividends are taxed at a higher marginal rate than capital gains (as is true in the U.S. tax system, and in many others). The principal empirical prediction of this is that high-yield stock must offer higher nominal (actual, pre-tax) returns than is required of low-yield stocks to compensate investors for the higher personal taxes they have to pay on dividends. Merton's (1973) **intertemporal CAPM** extends the one-period model into a multi-period framework—indeed into continuous time. While this model does not yield easily-interpretable empirical predictions, it does show that the simple CAPM is unlikely to hold in a multi-period setting. Sharpe (1977) himself modifies the basic asset pricing model to account for more than one systematic risk factor in his **multi-beta CAPM**. Breeden's (1979) **consumption CAPM** predicts that investors will be more concerned with protecting their consumption opportunities during economic contractions than with protecting the market value of their wealth, per se. The principal empirical prediction of this model is that security returns will be closely correlated with aggregate economic output, as proxied by gross national product or personal income expenditures. Finally, Adler and Dumas (1983) present an **international asset pricing model (IAPM)** in their survey of the international investment and corporate finance literature. Their IAPM presents the conditions that have to be met for capital markets to be in equilibrium and to be fully **integrated**—where all assets offer the same risk-adjusted, real expected return worldwide.

3.4.4 Roll's Critique

In 1977 Roll presented a major intellectual challenge to the CAPM in his classic paper, the contents of which have come to be known as **Roll's Critique**. Roll asserts that the CAPM is not testable, even in theory, unless the *exact* composition of the *true* market portfolio is known with certainty, and this portfolio is used in all empirical tests. Roll also makes clear that the CAPM, as usually presented, is actually a tautology (a statement that is true by definition), since the "implications" of the model flow logically and directly from the mean-variance efficiency assumptions used to construct the model. He shows that the one and only testable hypothesis associated with either of the standard CAPMs (the original SLM model or the Black zero-beta model) is that the market portfolio is mean-variance efficient. As if that wasn't damaging enough, Roll goes on to show that using proxies for the true market portfolio cannot possibly overcome this problem, since any number of ex post efficient portfolios can be found for any sample of data, and thus finding that a proxy is efficient says nothing about the efficiency of the true market portfolio. On the other hand, the same will be true if a study rejects the efficiency of the proxy being used—this obviously implies nothing meaningful about the efficiency of the market portfolio itself.

As you can imagine, Roll's Critique was greeted with all the enthusiasm usually accorded to leprosy, and several authors presented models that purported to show that his analysis was inaccurate, or incomplete, or less damaging than it appeared to be, or (best of all) simply a misreading of the original Greek.[8] Alas, within a few short years, the awful truth dawned that Roll's Critique was probably correct, meaning that the finance profession would have to make do with an asset pricing model that is probably untestable—or develop an entirely new model. One result of this realization was the

---

8. Articles in this debate include Mayers and Rice (1979), Cornell (1979), Roll (1979), and Verrechia (1980).

development and ready (perhaps too ready) acceptance of the arbitrage pricing theory (APT) model as a competitor of the CAPM (we will discuss the APT in detail in the next section). Other authors attempted to modify, or to use various econometric techniques to test, the CAPM in ways that accounted for Roll's Critique. We now briefly describe and assess this stream of literature.

3.4.5 Recent Empirical Tests and Theoretical Extensions

After 1977, research on the CAPM generally followed one or more of eight basic paths: (1) *mainstream* empirical tests (and theoretical extensions) retained the model's basic structure and used existing test methodology, but changed estimation periods or employed new data sets for testing; (2) *multivariate* tests of the model's pricing implications tested the CAPM indirectly by econometrically examining whether logical restrictions on returns data implied by the model were in fact observed; (3) tests of the *consumption CAPM*; (4) empirical and theoretical tests of the CAPM that allowed for *time-varying betas and market risk premiums*; (5) tests for *nonnormality of returns* data and the relationship between conditional variance and expected return; (6) empirical documentation and assessment of various *seasonal and size "anomalies"* documented in returns series that could not be explained by the basic asset pricing model; (7) tests of the *after-tax CAPM*, and; (8) empirical tests of the *international asset pricing* model and tests of the degree of international capital market integration. The key recent articles in each of these areas are cited and briefly discussed below, but a full scale review of this literature is far being the scope of this chapter. Our objective is simply to list important articles, and then to summarize critical findings.

MAINSTREAM EMPIRICAL TESTS AND THEORETICAL EXTENSIONS   Most of the researchers who test the CAPM in a way that accounts for Roll's Critique, while still using previously-employed estimation techniques or test methodologies, are able to reject the model's validity with depressing regularity. Using Fama and MacBeth's (1973) own procedures, Tinic and West (1986) reject the two-parameter, zero-beta CAPM in favor of a four-factor model that includes beta-squared (β^2) and residual standard deviation (σ). Kandel and Stambaugh (1987) present a framework for examining the mean-variance efficiency of an unobservable portfolio (the market portfolio of Roll's analysis) based on its correlation with an observable proxy portfolio. They show that the market portfolio implied by the CAPM would not be the mean-variance efficient tangent portfolio, even if it were observable, and Shanken (1987) reaches a similar conclusion. Campbell and Mei (1993) try to estimate the relative importance of various economic influences on an asset's measured beta, and then use this information to test the CAPM. They find no evidence of the expected strong covariance of asset excess returns with market returns which the model implies. Even the theorists were able to shoot holes in the CAPM. Dybvig and Ingersoll (1982) show that the model holds in **complete capital markets** (where investors can purchase financial claims that pay off in any given state of nature) only if all investors have implausible utility functions (quadratic), and only if arbitrage opportunities are left unexploited.

The most damaging blows to the CAPM did not, however, come from theoretical assaults, but rather from two major empirical papers. First, in his American Finance Association Presidential Address, Richard Roll (1988) demonstrates that less than 40 percent of the cross-sectional variation in stock returns can be explained by systematic economic influences, *even with hindsight* (after the fact). As an ex ante pricing model, the CAPM cannot be expected to predict next period returns with great accuracy, but Roll shows that the CAPM cannot even explain *historical* returns—even after all dates with firm-specific information releases are deleted. Since he reaches the same conclusions for the APT, Roll's findings are bad news for both of finance's assets pricing models. This is also true for Fama and French's (1992) article on the cross-section of expected stock returns. Although Fama and French only examine the CAPM, their finding that (1) firm size and (2) book-to-market value of equity (BE/ME) are the only significant factors in explaining stock returns is damaging both to the CAPM and the APT. Once size and BE/ME are accounted for, *beta has no significant explanatory power*, and the relation between market beta and average return is flat—even when beta is the only explanatory variable.

The mainstream assessment of the CAPM is not, however, completely bleak. Handa, Kothari, and Wasley (1989) show that estimated beta is very sensitive to the return interval used in its calculation (daily, weekly, monthly, or annual). As the return interval increases to one year, the CAPM cannot be rejected using annual betas—and this result is not solely due to the smaller number of estimation periods used to calculate standard errors for the test statistics. Finally, Bailey and Chan (1993) show that the **basis** in futures contracts (the spread between commodity spot [cash] and futures prices) reflects the macroeconomic risks common to all asset markets. While this study examines futures rather than common stocks, it at least documents the importance of systematic factors in pricing financial assets.

MULTIVARIATE TESTS   Several authors have sought to finesse the unobservability of the true market portfolio discussed by Roll by using econometric procedures to test the CAPM indirectly. The basic objective in most of these papers has been to ask, "what restrictions would a mean-variance efficient market portfolio impose on the pattern of realized security returns?" In other words, if we cannot use a known market portfolio to test whether observed security returns are priced according to the CAPM, perhaps we can use observed returns to determine whether they could have been priced relative to an unobserved market portfolio using a single-factor, mean-variance-efficient asset pricing model. While most of these papers are econometrically challenging, they at least offer an objective method of testing the CAPM. Unfortunately, at least two multivariate analyses reject the CAPM with little difficulty. Gibbons (1982, page 3) concludes that, "with no additional variable besides ß, the substantive content of the CAPM is rejected for the period 1926–1975 with a significance level less than 0.001." Further, Shanken (1985b) finds that the stock index most commonly used in empirical tests, the CRSP equally-weighted index, is mean-variance inefficient. Other authors are less conclusive in their assessment, though they offer various econometric warnings about how carefully multivariate tests must be performed and interpreted.[9]

---

9. This group includes Amsler and Schmidt (1985), MacKinlay (1987), Wheatley (1989), Kandel and Stambaugh (1989), and Shanken (1992a,b).

Multivariate tests have not been invariably hostile to the CAPM, however. In an important article, Stambaugh (1982) uses four market proxies—two of which include real estate and other nonfinancial assets as well as securities—in a simulation analysis and critique of the multivariate methodology used by Gibbons. Using the correction he proposes, Stambaugh is unable to reject the zero-beta CAPM, and this result is duplicated using another multivariate technique in Jobson and Korkie (1982). Given these conflicting results, and the lack of more recent analyses, we must conclude that multivariate tests are unable to either conclusively support or reject the CAPM.

TESTS OF THE CONSUMPTION CAPM   As mentioned previously, Breeden's (1979) consumption CAPM assumes that investors will use securities to transfer consumption opportunities from periods when they are plentiful (economic expansions) to periods when they are scarce (economic recessions). Since this is, almost by definition, a multi-period (or intertemporal) pricing model, a key objective of researchers examining the consumption CAPM has been to econometrically estimate the representative investor's **intertemporal marginal rate of substitution** (IMRS) regarding consumption. The IMRS of consumption can be viewed as the cost, in terms of foregone current utility, of transferring consumption possibilities through time. Another key objective of researchers has been to reconcile macroeconomic income and production data—which is published monthly (or even quarterly) and generated for purposes of assessing national economic performance—with stock return data, which is generated continuously.[10] An advanced econometric procedure called **generalized method of moments** (GMM) estimation has been used both in estimating investor utility functions and in analyzing the return and macroeconomic time series.[11]

The most comprehensive empirical test of the consumption CAPM (CCAPM) to date is presented in Breeden, Gibbons, and Litzenberger (1989). These researchers identify, and then adjust for, several biases in reported macroeconomic production and consumption time series. They then use these indices in tests of the model itself. While the CCAPM by no means perfectly fits the data, the regression coefficient on their consumption variable is significantly positive. Furthermore, while the linearity of the return/risk trade-off implied by the CCAPM is rejected for the entire 1929–1982 study period, this is mostly due to the 1929–1939 Depression era. In summary, the consumption version of the basic CAPM has been partly supported by empirical testing, but the economic relationship predicted by this model is almost surely not the

---

10. See Hansen and Singleton (1982, 1983), and Ferson and Merrick (1987) for analyses of the time-series behavior of consumption and asset returns. Restoy and Rockinger (1994) provide a theoretical reconciliation of firm-level investment policies and stock market returns, while investor utility functions are examined by Ferson and Constantinides (1991) and Epstein and Zin (1991).

11. The first widely-cited uses of GMM estimation are in Hansen (1982) and Hansen and Singleton (1982), while a good description of the properties of this procedure in empirical testing is provided in Ferson and Foerster (1994). In point of fact, GMM is actually a very general class of estimation techniques—which includes ordinary, generalized, and weighted least squares, as well as other maximum likelihood techniques—but is most commonly used in estimating time series parameters for data that exhibit non-constant variance and other violations of the ordinary least squares (OLS) assumptions.

only (or even the primary) explanation of the observed cross-sectional variation in stock returns.[12]

TESTS ALLOWING FOR TIME-VARYING BETAS AND RISK PREMIUMS   Given the poor performance of empirical tests of the single-period, fixed-parameter CAPM with multi-period data, several researchers have attempted to test asset pricing models that allow changes in the market beta, the equity risk premium, or both. These are often called tests of the **conditional CAPM**, because the next period expected return (and/or variance) is regularly updated *conditional* on the actual return achieved during the most recent period. The intuition behind such models is unassailable. Clearly equity risk premiums are likely to be higher during economic recessions than during expansions, and the covariance between a stock's return and the return on the market portfolio (however defined) surely changes over time as a company alters its leverage level, its dividend policy, its product mix, or pursues divestitures and acquisitions. The cost of such flexibility, unfortunately, is that it eviscerates an asset pricing model's predictive ability. If asset betas and risk premiums can change over the coming holding period, how does an investor determine a stock's required return? As we will see, most researchers in this field have sought ways of generating expected returns other than by making them strictly proportional to realized market returns.

Gibbons and Ferson (1985) test asset pricing models with time-varying risk premiums and an unobservable market portfolio. Expected returns are generated simply by making the last period's actual return the next period's expected return [$E(R_{it}) = R_{it-1}$]. Using this methodology, they are unable to reject the single-factor CAPM. Bollerslev, Engle, and Wooldridge (1988) develop and test a variant of the intertemporal CAPM allowing for time-varying conditional (expected, next period) covariance between individual asset and overall market returns. They assume that investors update their estimates of an asset's return covariance based on the current period's realized covariance, and this feeds back into their computation of required return. Obviously, such a procedure implies significant autocorrelation in excess returns from one period to the next, and the authors account for this by modeling the conditional covariances as **generalized autoregressive conditional heteroscedastic** (GARCH) processes.[13] Their model

---

12. One important byproduct of CCAPM research has been an awakened interest among finance professionals in the inexplicable large equity risk premium documented by Mehra and Prescott (1985), and examined subsequently by Mankiw and Seldes (1991), Ferson and Constantinides (1991), and Siegel (1992). The long-term, inflation-adjusted excess return for investing in stocks, rather than fixed-income corporate or government securities, has increased from less than one percent during the subperiod 1802–1870 to almost six percent during the most recent subperiod of 1926–1990 (Siegel [1992]). This equity premium is far higher than can be accounted for by any plausible level of investor risk aversion, nor can it be explained by macroeconomic forces. Given the importance of this **equity risk premium puzzle** to finance theory, it will certainly attract a great deal of research in coming years.

13. This process, and the more restrictive autoregressive conditional heteroscedastic (ARCH) model, is widely used in this branch of literature to account for autocorrelated covariances and variances. The original paper that presented ARCH in an economic setting is by Engle (1982), while GARCH was first presented in Bollerslev (1986). However, the most intuitive explanations of these processes we have found are in Connolly (1989) and Lamoureux and Lastrapes (1990), who succinctly state (page 222) that "the GARCH model … restricts the conditional variance of a time series to depend upon past squared residuals of the process."

fits the observed data quite well, which suggests that a properly-specified CAPM is consistent with actual stock returns—but the systematic risk/expected return relationship is complex and time-varying.

Harvey (1989) proposes a way of testing the CAPM and multi-factor asset pricing models that allow for both time varying expected return and conditional covariances (betas), and concludes that the CAPM is unable to capture the dynamic nature of actual security returns. On the other hand, Ferson and Foerster (1994) test several conditional (time-varying) asset pricing models, and conclude that the conditional CAPM with time-varying betas explains more of the cross-sectional variation in security returns than does either a single-premium or fixed-beta, two-premium model.[14] Taken as a whole, the conditional CAPM literature offers limited empirical support for a version of this model that allows for time-varying parameters in the expected return generating process. At present, however, the practical utility of such a model in an ex ante pricing sense is rather questionable.

Partly in response to the difficulties encountered in empirical tests of the CAPM with time-varying parameters, another very important stream of asset pricing literature has emerged that generates expected returns for individual assets *without* an explicit asset pricing model. This **predictable returns** literature models expected returns as a function of ex ante observable asset price or macroeconomic variables. Keim and Stambaugh (1986) examine the predictability of returns to bonds and stocks based on two asset price level variables derived from stock price indices, and on one risk premium variable derived from the yield spread between risky and riskless debt securities. They find that the expected risk premiums on individual assets change over time in a manner that is at least partially predictable using these variables. These results are echoed by Fama and French (1989), who find that expected returns on common stocks and long-term bonds contain a term or maturity premium that has a clear business-cycle pattern, as well as risk premiums that are related to longer-term aspects of business conditions. The general message of their study is that expected returns are lower when economic conditions are strong, and higher when economic conditions are weak. Finally, Ferson and Harvey (1993) investigate the risk and predictability of international equity returns, and show how to estimate the fraction of the predictable excess return that is captured by a one- or multiple-factor asset pricing model. In their models, the conditional betas of the national equity markets depend on local information, but the global equity risk premium is based on global factors. Their models are able to account for a substantial fraction of the predictability of international stock returns. As you probably have surmised, the predictable returns literature offers something of a challenge to the idea that capital markets are informationally efficient, but the overall importance of this literature—either as a test of market efficiency or as a practical tool for generating expected returns—remains unclear.

NONNORMALITY OF SECURITY RETURNS AND THE RELATIONSHIP BETWEEN CONDITIONAL VARIANCE AND EXPECTED RETURN   As we discussed earlier, the theoretical development of the CAPM presumes that security returns are normally dis-

---

14. Mark (1988) examines time-varying betas and risk premiums in the pricing of foreign exchange forward contracts, and also strongly rejects beta stationarity. His pricing model, however, is quite robust, and he concludes that forward contracts are priced with reference to essentially the same systematic risk factors as are other financial assets.

tributed. It also happens that one aggressive form of the efficient market hypothesis, the **random walk hypothesis**, implies that stock returns must be independent over time and characterized by identical (normal) distributions. Given the weight of this theoretical load, it is not surprising that numerous authors have empirically examined actual security return distributions. Most of the early work was strongly (but not completely) supportive of the normality assumption. Fama (1965) shows that security returns are best characterized by the **stable Paretian distribution**—which is similar to the normal distribution, but has "fatter" tails and less probability mass in the center, peaked region. Blattberg and Gonedes (1974) conclude that security returns are best characterized by a **Student distribution**, which is also a stable, symmetrical distribution with fat tails and compressed peak. Finally, Kon (1984) surmises that a mixture of normal distributions is a better explanation of observed return distributions than any single distribution model alone. The key point in all three studies is that security returns are approximately normally distributed, and the deviations from normality are all of a specific type (fat tails, compressed peak).

Later authors have reexamined return distributions in light of new evidence that they are **heteroscedastic** (for an individual security, this means that variance changes over time), and that there may be a relationship between current period variance and expected return. French, Schwert, and Stambaugh (1987) show that the volatility of monthly returns on the S&P composite portfolio was almost twice as high during the 1928–1952 period (especially during the Depression era, 1929–1939) as during the 1953–1984 period, and they also document a positive relationship between conditional (expected) variance and expected excess return. Several authors have examined time-varying volatility using Engle's (1982) ARCH or Bollerslev's (1986) GARCH methodologies, since both allow updates of expected volatility based on current period volatility "surprises" (higher or lower than expected variance). Using a modified GARCH model, Glosten, Jagannathan, and Runkle (1993) document a significant *negative* relationship between conditional expected monthly return and conditional variance, and also find that volatility shocks are not as persistent over time as was believed. Further, these authors find that positive unanticipated returns apparently cause a downward revision in conditional volatility, while negative unanticipated returns result in an upward revision in expected variance.

Several other researchers have examined heteroskedasticity in stock returns in other contexts. Lamoureux and Lastrapes (1990) show that much of the observed heteroskedasticity in returns is due to changes in the flow of information about a stock to market participants. When trading volume is included in their analysis as a proxy for information flow, much of the **autocorrelation** (the tendency for positive or negative "surprises" to persist over time) of conditional variance disappears. Schwert and Seguin (1990) present—and provide empirical evidence supporting—a single factor model of heteroskedasticity of individual security returns, where the market return variance is the single factor. Their model implies time-varying betas, and increases empirical support for the small firm effect—the hypothesis that small firms earn higher risk-adjusted returns than large firms (this effect is discussed more fully below). Finally, Zhou (1993) shows that the mean-variance efficiency of the CRSP value-weighted stock index can easily be rejected under the assumption that security returns are normal, but the efficiency of the index cannot be rejected under a plausible alternative assumption that returns are characterized by an elliptical distribution. He also shows that tests of the

CAPM that ignore this distributional possibility will reject the validity of the pricing model too frequently. The overall impact of this provocative finding is not yet evident.

SEASONAL AND SIZE ANOMALIES   A key feature of any equilibrium asset pricing model, including the CAPM, is exclusivity. If the asset pricing model is correct, then no other factor should significantly and systematically impact security valuation. Unfortunately for the CAPM, at least three major, and several minor, unexplainable anomalies have been identified in historical stock returns. The three principal anomalies—(1) the day of the week, or Monday effect, (2) the small firm effect, and (3) the January effect—are discussed briefly below.

Nineteen-eighty-one turned out to be a vintage year for anomalies, since the original papers identifying both the **Monday effect** (Gibbons and Hess) and the small firm effect (Banz, Reinganum) were published that year. Gibbons and Hess (1981) document significantly negative abnormal returns for stocks, and below average positive returns for treasury bills, on Mondays. Subsequent papers by Harris (1986) and Smirlock and Starks (1986) examine how the Monday effect differs between small and large firms, and how it has evolved from being a phenomenon that occurs during trading hours on Monday to one that results from price drops from Friday's close to Monday's open (a weekend effect). A more recent study by Connolly (1989), however, casts serious doubt on the idea that the Monday effect was ever economically significant, and shows in any case that the effect had disappeared entirely by 1975.[15]

The **small firm effect** identified by Banz (1981) and Reinganum (1981b) is not so easily disposed of. These and subsequent authors document that NYSE firms in the bottom size quintile (ranked by the market value of equity) earn significantly positive risk-adjusted excess returns. Based on this finding, Reinganum concludes that the CAPM is mis-specified as a model of security returns, and debate has raged ever since as to whether his conclusion is correct. Several papers in a special issue of the **Journal of Financial Economics** (summarized by Schwert 1983) examine the small firm effect from various perspectives, and conclude that it is economically and statistically significant, and cannot be explained solely by higher transactions costs for trading in small firms. Keim (1983) offers the intriguing evidence that roughly half of the return differential identified by Reinganum occurs in the month of January, and half of this premium occurs in the first five trading days of the year.

Tinic and West (1984) go one step further, and document that stocks (small and large) earn risk premiums *only* in January. In other words, the expected relationship between beta and expected return is significant in January but is insignificantly different from zero in the other eleven months. Maloney and Rogalski (1989) offer indirect support for the importance of the January effect in security prices by showing that the ef-

---

15. Connolly makes two other very important cautionary points about examining stock returns for the presence of anomalies. First, given the size of the databases available to finance researchers, it is very important to adjust the significance levels of classical test statistics (which were developed for relatively small samples) downwards to avoid accepting spurious events as being statistically significant. When a researcher examines several million individual daily returns for any particular anomaly, as frequently occurs with CRSP data, he or she is likely to end up with extremely small standard errors for use in significance tests. Second, Connolly documents significant deviations from normality in stock returns, and warns against using test statistics that assume the data meet OLS distributional properties.

fect is reflected in call option premiums around the turn of the year. Earlier, in a very readable survey paper, Keim (1983) notes that a **January effect** shows up in most of the other documented anomalies. He also concludes that the size effect literature indicates that small firms with the highest abnormal returns are those that have recently become small, that either don't pay dividends or have high dividend yields, and that have low prices and low price-to-earnings (P/E) ratios.

After the mid–1980s, most empirical papers conclude that the January and small firm effects are related, though another strand of the January effect literature (to be discussed in the market efficiency section below) examines whether it is in fact primarily a tax effect. By far the strongest empirical support for the importance of firm size is presented in Fama and French (1992). As discussed earlier, they conclude that stock returns are related *only* to size and book-to-market equity (BE/ME) value. Beta has no explanatory power, even when it is the only variable in the cross-sectional regressions. They find security returns to be inversely related to size, and directly related to BE/ME. All other variables and previously-reported anomalies are subsumed by the effect of these two variables (though they do find significant January seasonals in several equations.)

As persuasive as Fama and French are, however, the size effect is by no means unanimously accepted by finance researchers. Chan, Chen, and Hsieh (1985) investigate the effect using a multi-factor pricing model, and conclude that the higher returns earned by smaller firms are justified by their higher systematic risk. Their risk adjustments cause the unexplained return differential between the top and bottom five percent of NYSE firms to drop from about 12 percent per year to 1–2 percent per year. Furthermore, Handa, Kothari, and Wasley (1989) document that the size effect is sensitive to the length of the return interval used in estimating beta. The size effect becomes statistically insignificant when risk is measured by betas estimated using annual data. Finally, Black (1993) suggests that most of the "anomalies" identified by researchers are really the result of conscious or unconscious data-mining. Since everyone is using the same basic data sources, and most authors are aware of prior research, it is probably inevitable that someone will notice an artifact that appears unexplainable. Black also makes the telling point that the January effect has disappeared since it was first identified in 1981—so even if it once existed, it was quickly arbitraged away by rational traders.[16] All in all, the anomaly literature offers a serious challenge to the CAPM's position as a complete asset pricing model, but does not (at least not yet) by itself constitute a refutation of the model's basic validity.

TESTS OF THE AFTER-TAX CAPM   Several authors have attempted to test the empirical validity of Brennan's (1970) after-tax CAPM. The principal testable prediction of this model is that investors should demand a higher nominal (pre-personal-tax) return for holding high dividend yield stocks than for holding low yield stocks in order to be compensated for the higher personal taxes they would pay on dividend versus capital gains income. Virtually all studies test this proposition by inserting a dividend yield variable into a regression equation with returns as the dependent variable and beta as

---

16. Fama (1991) also presents empirical evidence that the January effect has largely disappeared since first being identified.

the other independent variable. If the after-tax CAPM is correct, the coefficient on the dividend yield variable should be significantly positive. Sounds simple, doesn't it?

Somewhat surprisingly, researchers have arrived at completely different conclusions even though all employ the same basic data and similar economic models (the econometric procedures employed differ vastly, however). Black and Scholes (1974) and Miller and Scholes (1982) find that there is no significant dividend yield premium (they reject the after-tax CAPM), while Litzenberger and Ramaswamy (1979, 1982), Blume (1980), and Ang and Peterson (1985) all document positive dividend yield coefficients, and conclude that the after-tax CAPM is supported by their results. In our opinion, the weight of empirical evidence supports the after-tax model, but logic weighs in favor of the model's critics. The critics make the disarmingly simple point that an extra return premium for high-yield stock is inconsistent either with market equilibrium or with rational managerial behavior, since any manager of a company paying cash dividends could lower the firm's cost of capital (lower the required return on the firm's stock) simply by cutting the dividend payout. Since positive cash dividend payments are a worldwide phenomenon, something is clearly wrong with the after-tax model's predictions.

TESTS OF INTERNATIONAL ASSET PRICING MODELS AND THE DEGREE OF MARKET INTEGRATION   One important theoretical point left unaddressed by early developers of the CAPM, but subsequently examined as the model was fleshed out, concerned whether all financial assets should yield the same currency- and risk-adjusted expected returns to investors the world over. In other words, is there a single, global equity risk premium or are there different risk premiums for each national market? If the basic parity conditions of international finance are met (no barriers to trade or to financial flows), then all markets will be fully **integrated** and a single risk premium will result. If, however, there are barriers to capital flows, then capital markets can be **segmented** from each other and may well demonstrate substantially different risk/return trade-offs, volatility, and P/E valuations. Since the evidence on parity conditions is mixed, we cannot predict a priori whether capital markets will be integrated, and must therefore rely on empirical tests.[17]

The original exposition of an international asset pricing model (as well as a discussion of segmented versus integrated capital markets) is presented in Stulz (1981). This model is generalized and incorporated into other areas of the international finance literature in an influential survey article by Adler and Dumas (1983). Subsequent empirical tests of international asset pricing models have examined whether there is one or several equity risk premiums worldwide and/or whether international capital markets are integrated. Using a simple consumption CAPM, Wheatley (1988) finds little evidence against the joint hypothesis that equity markets are integrated internationally and that the

---

17. Recent evidence supporting the idea that **purchasing power parity** (the same basket of goods should sell for the same currency-adjusted price worldwide) holds in the long-term, but not necessarily in the short-term, is presented by Abuaf and Jorion (1990). Studies which examine interest rate parity, and other relationships based on debt securities, document very few economically meaningful deviations from equilibrium. However, the evidence on stock market integration is far less conclusive. The five principal parity conditions in international finance are presented, and empirical studies on these conditions are discussed, in chapter 7 of Shapiro (1992).

asset pricing model (with a single global risk premium) holds.[18] In Wheatley's model, the representative investor of a country measures an asset's risk by the covariance of its real return with the growth of his or her real consumption. In a somewhat similar vein, Ferson and Harvey (1993) investigate the predictability of international equity returns using a model in which conditional betas of the national equity markets depend on local information variables, while global risk premia depend on global variables (implying a single risk premium). They find that most of the substantial return predictability they document is due to variations in this global risk premium. Glen and Jorion (1993) document that hedging international portfolio risks with forward contracts significantly improves the risk/return profiles of global investments. They also show that if one exploits the predictable component of security returns, the hedging strategy pays off even more.

Several authors have documented that international equity markets demonstrate surprisingly low levels of return correlation (usually less than 25 percent), and that volatility levels remain systematically higher in some markets than in others. These papers are summarized by Roll (1992), who then examines possible causes of this apparent segmentation. He empirically documents three separate, primarily technical, influences: (1) some national indices are more diversified than others; (2) each country's industrial structure has a major impact on stock price behavior; and (3) for most countries, a portion of the seemingly anomalous return behavior is an exchange rate effect. Heston and Rouwenhorst (1994) reexamine the influence of industrial structure on international equity market return correlation and volatility, and reach a somewhat different conclusion than Roll did. They conclude that the low correlation between country indices is due to country-specific sources of return variation, rather than technical characteristics of the indices themselves. Heston and Rouwenhorst's study suggests that capital markets are less than perfectly integrated, and they also document a clear benefit to international diversification of investment portfolios.

We now turn our attention to examining the CAPM's main rival as an asset pricing model, the APT. At the end of the next section we will provide a summary of the literature on both models, and evaluate the state of asset pricing theory at the dawn of the twenty-first century.

3.5   THE ARBITRAGE PRICING THEORY

The primary theoretical alternative to the CAPM as a model for pricing financial assets is the arbitrage pricing theory (APT), developed by Stephen Ross (1976, 1977). This model was initially greeted with great enthusiasm by the finance profession because it overcame many of the theoretical problems associated with the CAPM, and also seemed able to address many of that model's nagging empirical anomalies. As with the CAPM, however, early enthusiasm cooled as the APT demonstrated its own peculiar foibles. Nonetheless, the APT is the closest thing we have to a viable model for pricing risk in competitive financial markets, and most of the model's remaining theoretical and methodological problems seem cureable. Since some variant of this theory seems

---

18. In an examination of Eurocurrency deposit market integration, which also employs an intertemporal consumption CAPM, Lewis (1990) reaches a somewhat different conclusion. She rejects the constant beta form of this model, but finds that this result is very sensitive to the holding period employed. As the maturity horizon increases, the model is rejected less frequently.

likely to remain part of the core of modern finance theory for the foreseeable future, we will both examine the theoretical justification for the APT and summarize the empirical tests of the model's predictions.

3.5.1 Development of the Basic Pricing Model

The APT is based on five principal assumptions.[19] First, capital markets are presumed to be perfectly competitive and frictionless. Second, investors have homogeneous expectations about the process generating expected returns for individual securities. Third, those expected returns are produced by a (linear) k-factor generating model of the form:

$$R_i = E(R_i) + b_{i1}\delta_1 + \cdots + b_{in}\delta_n + \epsilon_i$$

$$i = 1, \cdots, n \tag{3.16}$$

where R_i = the random return on asset i
$E(R_i)$ = the expected return on asset i
δ_j = the mean zero j^{th} factor common to all assets under consideration
b_{ij} = a measure of the sensitivity of asset i's return to movements in the jth factor.

The APT's fourth assumption is that the common factors capture all of the systematic risk to which assets are exposed, so the error terms (ϵ_i) are uncorrelated with each other cross-sectionally, and over time. As we will see, this is critically important, because this means the error terms will effectively disappear as large numbers of assets are added to a portfolio. The fifth and final assumption is that the number of systematic factors, k, is far smaller than the number of assets, n.

The actual arbitrage process in the APT exploits the fact that an investor can use money obtained by shorting (selling) some securities to purchase others, and can therefore construct an **arbitrage portfolio** requiring no commitment of wealth, and exposing the investor to no systematic or unsystematic risk. An investor can construct such a portfolio by combining a group of assets so that the dollar values of his or her investments in individual assets, w_i, sum to zero:

$$\sum w_i = 0$$

If this portfolio is constructed using many assets, its idiosyncratic risk will be very close to zero, and if the portfolio is also constructed such that all systematic risk is eliminated ($b_{ij} = 0$ for all factors) it will be riskless. Such a portfolio cannot earn a positive return in a competitive market, yet investors could construct a positive return portfolio using this technique if any asset offered too high or too low an expected return. Furthermore, since it is a (riskless) arbitrage process that will force assets to offer the correct return, no assumptions need be made regarding a representative investor's utility function, other than nonsatiation (more wealth is always preferred to less).

---

19. Throughout this section, we will follow closely the logic and terminology used by Roll and Ross (1980) in their development of the APT model, as this is perhaps the clearest exposition available in journal form. A more detailed, but equally readable, development of the basic theory is presented in Copeland and Weston (1988, pages 219–228).

A necessary condition for the residuals in equation 3.16 to be uncorrelated is that the systematic factors also be uncorrelated with each other. As mentioned above, this is important economically, because it ensures that residual variance will disappear as the number of assets in the economy increases. Uncorrelated factors are also important econometrically, because most tests or applications of the APT use a statistical technique called **factor analysis** both to determine how many factors significantly impact security returns and to estimate the sensitivity of individual asset returns to factor movements. In econometric terms, factors that are completely uncorrelated with each other are referred to as being **orthogonal**, and the number of factors extracted from data depends on how many statistically significant orthogonal influences are discovered.

If the assumptions of the APT are met, the original return equation 3.16 can be converted into the ex ante, expected return equation 3.17, where expected returns are expressed as a function of an asset's sensitivites, b_{ij}, and factor risk premiums, λ_j:

$$E(R_i) = \lambda_0 + \lambda_1 \beta_{i1} + \cdots + \lambda_k \beta_{ik} \qquad (3.17)$$

Furthermore, if there is a riskless asset with return, $E(R_0)$, then $b_{0j} = 0$ and $E(R_0) = \lambda_0$. We can therefore rewrite equation 3.17 in risk premium form as:

$$E(R_i) - E(R_0) = \lambda_1 \beta_{i1} + \cdots + \lambda_k \beta_{ik}$$

How do we intuitively grasp what a factor risk premium is, and what it measures? Perhaps the best way to do this is to consider what an asset's return will be if it has unit systematic risk on factor j ($b_{ij} = 1$) and zero exposure ($b_{ik} = 0$) to all other factors. Such an asset will have an expected excess return of:

$$E(R_j) - E(R_0) = \lambda_j$$

For example, if a one unit positive movement in factor j is associated with a 5 percent risk premium, and the risk free rate is 4 percent, asset i should earn 9 percent.

AN APT PRICING EXAMPLE USING THE ECU   A useful illustration of how the APT's return generating process presumably works for stocks and bonds can be made by comparing it with the pricing formula for the **European Currency Unit** (ECU). The ECU is a weighted average of the twelve (soon to be fifteen) national currencies of the countries that are members of the European Union, and each currency's weighting in the ECU is set by agreement among the member governments. Although the ECU does not (yet) circulate as money, it is used to denominate many financial assets (particularly bonds) and so a U.S. dollar price for the ECU itself is continuously being generated. Since all of the underlying currencies also trade separately against the dollar, there is a clear, if implicit, arbitrage bound around how much the ECU or any of the underlying currencies can fluctuate in price versus the dollar, and against each other. To express this in the language of the APT, the underlying risk factors (λ_j) of the ECU are the individual currency values versus the dollar, the weights used in constructing the ECU from the underlying currencies are the factor loadings (b_{ij}), and the dollar price of the ECU is the end result of the underlying return generating process—expressed as a price rather than an expected return. The arbitrage process that will force the ECU to have a specific dollar value is analogous to the arbitrage portfolio technique we discussed earlier for the APT. If the ECU is priced too high versus the dollar, an arbitrageur can construct new

ECUs from the underlying currencies and sell them in the ECU market for a profit. Similarly, if the ECU is priced too low, arbitrageurs can buy maturing ECU securities cheaply and then profit from selling the underlying currencies for dollars in local currency markets. Either way, the ECU will be forced into a single dollar price that is a function of the underlying "risk factors" and "factor loadings."

3.5.2 Benefits and Drawbacks of the APT

Now that we have a model that expresses expected returns as a linear combination of factor risk premiums and individual asset sensitivities to those premiums, we can test the APT's ability to explain actual security returns. First, however, we should examine the theoretical benefits and drawbacks of using this model rather than our trusty standby, the CAPM. The APT's relative strengths are numerous and important, and include the following:

1. The APT requires no assumption about the underlying distribution of security returns.

2. Other than nonsatiation, no specification of a representative investor's utility function—not even risk aversion—is required to derive the APT.

3. There is no special role either for the market portfolio or for a risk-free asset in the APT, and therefore no apparent need to identify the exact composition of the "true" market portfolio or to worry if riskless borrowing and lending rates exist or are equal. Furthermore, the APT can be estimated using a subset of assets, rather than requiring the universe of risky assets to be used as a benchmark.

4. The APT allows multiple factors to influence security returns.

5. The APT can easily be expressed in a multi-period setting.

Given this list of attractive qualities, it is not surprising that the APT has attracted many true believers. Unfortunately, the APT also has three identifiable weaknesses, which are listed below in order of increasing criticality:

1. In its original arbitrage framework, the APT holds only approximately, and there is no guarantee that it will accurately price individual assets. A derivative "equilibrium APT" (discussed in the next section) allows more exact pricing, but only at the cost of more restrictive assumptions.

2. The APT assumes that the true factor structure generating returns is known with certainty. If this is not true (and it of course is not), economic and econometric difficulties arise, as we will discuss later.

3. Since the APT does not specify what the systematic risk factors represent (what macroeconomic risks are priced), it is virtually impossible to operationalize the model in a corporate finance setting.

In our opinion, the third point is an extremely serious problem for the APT. For all its flaws, the CAPM is at least able to tell managers and investors alike that an asset's required return is a function of the correlation of its return with that of the market portfolio. The APT cannot (at least not yet) make such a precise economic statement.

We now examine the empirical tests (and theoretical extensions) of the APT that have appeared in major journals since the theory was initially developed. We begin with the early tests, and then briefly discuss the more recent literature. We conclude with a summary of the current state of the APT, and of asset pricing generally.

3.5.3 Early Tests of the APT

Any major new economic theory inevitably generates a great deal of theoretical and empirical interest, and this was particularly true of the APT—since it offered the prospect of an entirely new and quite general method for assessing financial risk. The first major empirical study, by Roll and Ross (1980) supports the APT's predictions and documents perhaps as many as four priced factors. Brown and Weinstein (1983) and Chen (1983) identify a similar number of factors, and also interpret their results as supporting the APT. Brown and Weinstein present an indirect test of the APT that is similar in spirit to multivariate tests of the CAPM in that it specifies characteristics of the return-generating process that must be met if the APT is the correct pricing model.[20] Chen is the first of several authors to examine whether the APT can explain anomalies identified by the CAPM. He finds that firm size and (an asset's own) residual variance have no explanatory power after the factor loadings are used to adjust for risk.

Other early empirical tests do not support the APT. Reinganum (1981a) examines whether it can explain the size effect, and concludes that it cannot. Perhaps even more disturbing to APT adherents is the finding by Dhrymes, Friend, and Gultekin (1984) that the factor analysis methodology universally employed by early researchers is a fundamentally flawed tool for testing the new theory's validity. These authors document that the number of factors extracted from large sample portfolios is systematically greater than the number extracted from small portfolios, and that the number of significant factors identified increases monotonically with sample portfolio size. This suggests that as computer technology progresses, and larger sample sizes can be factor analyzed, the number of priced factors will increase without bound and without any underlying economic rationale.

Other early papers examine the theoretical underpinnings of the APT. Huberman (1982) clarifies the precise nature of the model's arbitrage condition that will allow unsystematic risk to be eliminated by diversification. Chamberlain and Rothschild (1983) prove the APT can hold if returns conform to an approximate, rather than an exact, factor structure. They also lay the econometric groundwork for using a methodology called principal components analysis in estimating APT factors and testing the model's validity. This methodology is used extensively by later researchers (discussed below). Another major theoretical contribution is made by Grinblatt and Titman (1983), who derive an **Equilibrium APT** by placing restrictions (primarily risk aversion) on the utility functions of representative investors. The principal benefit of the equilibrium APT versus the arbitrage-based APT is that the former allows more exact

---

20. Brown and Weinstein actually reject the APT in several of the subperiods they study, but they make an argument similar to that made later by Connolly (1989) about statistical inference with large sample sizes. When using huge data sets (several thousand observations), one should adjust significance levels downwards to prevent spurious rejections of hypotheses. After making this adjustment, Brown and Weinstein are unable to reject the APT's predictions.

pricing of individual assets, since an equilibrium model is derived based on the requirement that all assets yield their correct risk-adjusted return and are held by rational, well-informed agents.[21]

Mirroring the history of the CAPM, an early theoretical and econometric debate arose concerning whether the APT was even testable. Shanken (1982) asserts that the APT must identify the true factor structure generating returns before the model can be independently tested, and we have no idea what that structure is. This, of course, is very similar in spirit to Roll's critique of the CAPM. Dybvig and Ross (1985) take issue with Shanken's view that the APT is not testable, but Shanken (1985a) answers with the observation that most researchers confuse the arbitrage and equilibrium APTs—keeping the very unrestrictive assumptions of the original arbitrage model while also testing predictions based on the more concrete equilibrium model.[22] While this debate may never be fully resolved, it seems clear that the principal flaws in the APT are econometric rather than theoretical, and most studies of the APT from the mid-1980s onward have focused on empirical testing of the theory.

3.5.4 Recent Empirical Tests of the APT

During the past decade, the primary story in APT research has been the employment of increasingly sophisticated econometric procedures to test the model's validity, and to determine how many factors are priced. Lehmann and Modest (1988) perform factor analysis on very large stock portfolios, and find that the APT is able to explain the expected returns of portfolios formed based on dividend yields and own variance (anomalies unexplained by the CAPM), but is unable to explain the firm size effect. After noting that the size effect is concentrated in the very largest and smallest firms, they conclude that the APT prices most listed equities with little error.

Connor and Korajczyk (1986, 1988) employ **principal components analysis** (PCA) to identify and estimate the pervasive factors influencing equity returns. PCA is similar to factor analysis in that it extracts (but does not identify) pervasively influential factors from return data, but imposes less restrictive assumptions on the distribution of returns than does factor analysis. Connor and Korajczyk are able to explain the January seasonal effect in stock returns with the APT, but not the more general size effect. They conclude that their five-factor APT explains the cross-sectional variation in stock returns better than the CAPM. Later, Connor and Korajczyk (1993) develop a

---

21. To the uninitiated, such esoteric discussions of theoretical assumptions may seem as relevant as the medieval debates about how many angels can dance on the head of a pin. Certainly, the true test of an economic theory must be how well it explains objective reality and predicts the future—regardless of the validity of the assumptions used in its development. However, valid theoretical assumptions are more important to the APT than they are to most economic models, because the APT does not yield predictions that are readily interpretable based on observable values.

22. This debate was picked up again much later, when Shanken (1992a) suggested that researchers focus on approximate arbitrage relationships that are more robust than the exact formulations generally employed. Shanken was actually discussing results presented in Reisman (1992a), who shows that almost any set of variables correlated with the true factor structure of returns can serve as a benchmark in an APT framework, provided certain assumptions are met. Reisman (1992b) also shows under what conditions the APT will hold in an intertemporal setting.

test statistic for determining the number of factors in an approximate (and very general) APT factor model.[23] They find evidence of between one and six priced factors in security returns, with the influence of factors beyond the first being particularly strong in January. In non-January months, only one or two factors are significant.

Shukla and Trzcinka (1990) test the APT assuming very long term (up to twenty years) stability in mean returns, variances, and covariances. They also compare empirical pricing errors using factor analysis, PCA, and CAPM beta estimates. They find that a five-factor APT explains a great deal (up to 40 percent) of the cross-sectional variation of returns—with the best results coming from the longest sample period tests—and conclude that the APT offers better empirical results than the CAPM primarily because the former allows more sources of variation.

Mei (1993a) develops a semiautoregressive test methodology to test for the number of factors in the APT. This technique allows the researcher to directly estimate the severity of measurement errors involved in estimating factors, a problem that has plagued all previous studies.[24] Mei finds that the APT explains observed asset returns slightly better than the CAPM does, and he clearly demonstrates that factor risk premiums vary over time in response to changes in the business cycle. This supports evidence presented earlier by Fama and French (1988a,b, 1989, 1992) and others that stock returns are at least partly predictable. In another paper, Mei (1993b) uses an autoregressive approach to test a multi-factor APT model that explicitly allows for time-varying risk premiums.[25] He finds that at least five factors significantly influence security returns, and he is able to explain the firm size effect—but not the book-to-market effect identified by Fama and French (1992) or the earnings yield effect identified by Reinganum (1981b). Furthermore, he concludes that a constant-beta multi-factor APT model is unable to satisfactorily explain the cross-sectional variation in security returns, though a moving-beta model might.

THE OBSERVABLE VARIABLES APPROACH   One final avenue of empirical research has attempted to develop an APT model with observable variables by first determining which macroeconomic variables significantly influence security prices. The foremost study adopting this approach is by Chen, Roll, and Ross (1986), who test whether innovations in various macroeconomic variables are risks that are priced in the stock market. They find that security prices are significantly related to (1) changes in industrial production, (2) the yield spread between long- and short-term interest rates (interpreted as a business cycle proxy), (3) the yield spread between low- and high-grade bonds (interpreted as a proxy for overall business risk in the economy), and (4) changes in expected and unexpected inflation—though this is highly significant only during periods of pronounced inflation volatility. Perhaps most intriguing are the variables that the

---

23. Their model allows the diversifiable components of returns to be correlated across assets, and is estimated as before using principal components analysis.

24. This paper also provides a very good description of the strengths and weaknesses of factor analysis and PCA as used in most tests of the APT.

25. As the methodology's name implies, this technique uses past returns to generate estimates of systematic risk for the coming period. This eliminates unobservable betas from the pricing equation. The substitution of lagged returns for unobservable betas is similar to the "mimicking portfolio" approach described in Huberman, Kandel, and Stambaugh (1987) and Burmeister and McElroy (1988).

authors find are not significant. After accounting for the macroeconomic factors, the return on the overall stock market itself is not significant, and there is no significant relationship between stock returns and aggregate consumption (which is bad news for the consumption CAPM). Finally, oil prices are not significantly related to stock returns.

3.5.5 The Current State of Asset Pricing Theory

So, what is the state of asset pricing theory in the mid–1990s? Rather confused, unfortunately, but at least there are several conclusions we can draw based on our extended pilgrimage through the CAPM and APT literature. First, it seems clear that the single-factor, constant-risk-premium CAPM is almost useless as a model either to explain observed returns or to generate expectations concerning future returns. Second, few other variants of the CAPM appear to offer much hope of emerging as the standard asset pricing model of the future.[26] Third, a three- to five-factor APT appears to explain more of the cross-sectional variation in stock returns than any other single model, although the lack of observable variables in this model makes it a purely statistical construct that is maddeningly difficult to understand or explain economically. Fourth, the empirical evidence linking firm size to positive abnormal returns is unambiguous, but very strange, and *must* be explained before real progress can be made in asset pricing. Clearly, size must be proxying for some other risk factor, but what? Fifth, it seems clear that the actual return generating process for stocks has multiple factors and the parameters of the process vary through time. Furthermore, at least part of this variation in risk premiums is predictable based on macroeconomic, business cycle-related data.

What are the most pressing issues that need to be addressed in order to develop a viable asset pricing model that a consensus of the profession can support? In our opinion, the most vital task is to determine how many factors are systematically priced, *and conclusively document what those factors are*. The work of Chen, Roll, and Ross (1986) represents an important first step in this direction, and it is somewhat surprising that few major papers on this topic have subsequently been published. A second important objective should be to definitively establish whether capital markets are indeed integrated around the world. In other words, we should determine if there is a single, global, currency- and risk-adjusted required return for holding financial assets, and, if there is, in which national market is this hurdle rate set? As Richard Roll (1988, page 541) observed in his presidential address, "the immaturity of our science is illustrated by the conspicuous lack of predictive content about some of its most intensely interesting phenomena, particularly *changes* in asset prices." We still have far to go before we catch up with the predictive ability of the physical sciences, but at least we are closer than we were before Harry Markowitz explained portfolio theory to us.

3.6   MARKET EFFICIENCY

The distinguishing characteristic of a revolutionary scientific theory is that it changes the world-views of educated people once the theory is explained to (and accepted by) them. Prior to the publication of *De revolutionibus orbium coelestium* by Nicholas

---

26. If, however, someone is able to develop a variant of the CAPM that accounts for time-varying risk premiums, yet still provides a closed form pricing equation based on observable variables, such a model would likely prove very popular—especially if empirical testing showed it to be competitive with other asset pricing models.

Copernicus in 1543, western scholars viewed the world as the center of the universe around which planets, moons, stars, and angels danced for the glory of mankind. After the Copernican heliocentric (sun-centered) theory of planetary motion was presented, it explained objective reality so well that it soon completely replaced the Ptolemaic system in the minds (at least in the open minds) of European intellectuals. After Copernicus, the geocentric model of the universe seemed quaint and absurd.

While it is far too early to predict that the **Efficient Markets Hypothesis** (EMH), as formally presented by Eugene Fama (1970), will have an impact on human history comparable to that of the Copernican model, it is clear that the EMH has already revolutionized financial economics.[27] The EMH asserts, with beguiling simplicity, that financial asset prices fully reflect all available, relevant information. Implicit in this assertion is the idea that financial asset prices reflect all relevant *historical* and *current* information, and that they incorporate every piece of forecastable information into unbiased forecasts of *future* prices. In its most extreme form, the EMH asserts that prices reflect all information—including "private" information that only corporate insiders are privy to—but most modern finance scholars and professionals are more comfortable with a version that only requires prices to reflect publicly-available information.

This section examines the impact that the efficient markets hypothesis has had on modern finance. We begin with a brief, formal description of the three forms of market efficiency originally presented by Fama (1970). We then adopt the system of categorizing empirical tests of market efficiency that Fama presented in his later (1991) survey article to assess whether the research of the past quarter-century has supported the EMH's central predictions. This section then concludes with a summary of the current state of the theory of efficient financial markets.

3.6.1 The Three Forms of Market Efficiency

Financial academics are not known for flowery prose, and Fama's (1970) designation of the forms of market efficiency is strictly utilitarian. He presents three increasingly stringent degrees of information processing efficiency, based on how much of the available public and private information market prices are expected to reflect.[28] In markets characterized by **weak-form efficiency,** asset prices incorporate all historical information. While a seemingly innocuous proposition, this form of efficiency implies that trading strategies based on analyses of historical pricing trends or relationships cannot

---

27. Furthermore, the model's soul mate in economic thought, the rational expectations hypothesis, has transformed the way people view macroeconomic policy-making, and the worldwide adoption of market-oriented economic policies during the past fifteen years is almost surely based on an intellectual acceptance of the idea that markets efficiently process all available information and then allocate resources to their highest and best use.

28. It should be stressed that the EMH deals specifically with the information-processing efficiency of financial markets, not necessarily with other notions of efficiency that most people carry in their minds. For example, a financial market can be *operationally efficient*—in that it produces outputs (security trades, loan approvals, debt renegotiations, etc.) at the minimum possible cost in labor and overhead expense—without being informationally efficient, and vice versa. The distinction between the informational and *allocational efficiency* of a financial market is less clear-cut. While a market must be informationally efficient to allocate capital to its highest and best (most profitable) use, the converse does not necessarily apply. The securities of a monopolist producer can be priced quite rationally in a financial market, offering investors only a normal return on their investments, even if the monopolist is earning unjustifiably large economic profits.

consistently yield excess returns to investors.[29] Since prices are "memoryless," they are unforecastable, and will only change in response to the arrival of new information.[30] This in turn implies that asset prices follow a **random walk**, meaning that there is (on average) no correlation between subsequent price changes, and the asset price fluctuates randomly and unpredictably.

In markets characterized by **semi-strong-form efficiency**, asset prices incorporate all publicly-available information. One implication of this is that the *level* of asset prices should reflect all pertinent historical, current, and forecastable (future) information that can be obtained from public sources. A second implication of this form of efficiency is that asset prices should *change* fully and instantaneously in response to the arrival of relevant new information. There is thus both a "stock" and a "flow" aspect to the information processing capabilities of semi-strong-form efficient markets. The key point about this form of efficiency is that it only requires information that can be gleaned from *public* sources (newspapers, press releases, computer databases) to be reflected in asset prices.

In markets characterized by **strong-form efficiency**, asset prices reflect *all* information—public and private. As is probably obvious to you, this is an extreme form of market efficiency, because it implies that important company-specific information (a pending takeover bid, a dividend increase) will be fully incorporated in asset prices with the very first trade after the information is generated (immediately after the board of directors vote for a dividend increase), and before it is publicly announced. In strong-form efficient markets, most insider trading would be unprofitable, and there would be no benefit whatsoever to ferreting out information on publicly-traded companies, since any data morsel so obtained would already be reflected in stock and bond prices. As with semi-strong-form efficiency, this form also implies that there is both a stock and flow aspect to a market's information processing capabilities.

In another repeat of the experience with the introductions of the CAPM and the APT, the EMH was initially received with great enthusiasm by finance professionals, but this early acceptance soon gave way to gnawing doubts as (at least seemingly) contradictory evidence began to trickle in. Rather than discuss this stream of research chronologically, as we were forced to do with the asset pricing theories, we exploit the fact that Fama surveyed this literature himself in 1991. Instead of relying on the original "forms" of market efficiency, Fama classified empirical tests of market efficiency into three categories: (1) tests for return predictability; (2) event studies (or tests for rapid price adjustment); and (3) tests for private information. We use these three classifications as a framework for discussing the evidence on market efficiency, and concentrate on papers which he either did not survey or which have been published since 1991. We also discuss a fourth category, (4) tests for rational fundamental valuation, that Fama did not explicitly examine in depth in his survey—probably because many of the key articles in this area have been published only recently. Each of these four categories is discussed in turn below, beginning with the evidence on return predictability.

---

29. Professional financial analysts have long been reluctant to accept the efficient markets hypothesis, and the reason is easy to see. If it is correct, much of what many analysts do—particularly those who practice the art of technical analysis—is of no economic value to their clients.

30. In one of the pivotal early papers in this field, Samuelson (1965) proves that asset prices in efficient markets will fluctuate randomly, and only in response to the arrival of new information.

3.6.2 Tests for Return Predictability

Somewhat surprisingly, the vast bulk of the research on market efficiency that has been published since 1970 has examined the validity of the weak-form efficiency prediction that asset prices reflect all historical information. Since most of these studies examine whether asset price changes can be predicted using historical or contemporaneously-available information, Fama refers to these as tests for return predictability, and we adopt the same phrasing. We further classify these tests into three categories: (1) tests of simple trading rules based on very recent stock returns, the day of the week, or the month of the year; (2) tests for short-horizon (weekly or monthly) return predictability based on the observed positive correlation in short-term returns; and (3) tests for long-horizon return predictability based on the negative correlation observed over longer (2–3 year) return horizons.

SIMPLE TRADING RULE TESTS   Prior to the 1950s, it was widely believed that perceptive investors could easily identify patterns in stock price movements that could be exploited through the adoption of a trading strategy. It therefore came as quite a surprise when first Kendall (1953), then Roberts (1959) and Fama (1965) all documented that subsequent stock price changes were essentially uncorrelated with each other (prices followed a random walk). This lack of persistence in price trends means that a strategy of buying recent winners and shorting recent losers would not be profitable.[31] Fama and Blume (1966) test a number of more sophisticated **filter rules**—such as, "buy a stock after it has increased by x percent, and don't sell it until it has dcreased by y percent"— and find that none of these strategies yields significant profits, particularly after trading costs are accounted for. Since the mid–1960s, it has generally been accepted that trading rules based on such simple recent return information are not worth pursuing.

If not filter tests, what about other mechanistic trading strategies? As we discussed earlier in this chapter, numerous asset pricing "anomalies" have been identified in stock return data. These include the day-of-the-week (Monday) effect identified by Gibbons and Hess (1981), the small-firm effect identified by Banz (1981), and the January effect identified by Keim (1983). In all three cases, expected returns are shown to vary in a systematic way that seems ideally suited to exploitation by a trading strategy. For example, if returns are, on average, lower on Mondays than during the rest of the week, wouldn't it pay an investor (or a mutual fund) to short stocks on Friday afternoons and then repurchase them at a lower price on Tuesday mornings? Likewise, the very large abnormal returns identified for small stocks in early January seem to be exploitable by a trading strategy that buys small stocks—particularly those which have declined in price and are thus likely candidates for tax-loss selling—in late December and then resells them at the end of January.

Perhaps surprisingly, there has been little published research that explicitly examines the profitability of such a trading strategy, and the consensus within the profession

---

31. Fama's examination of daily price changes was easily the most extensive of any performed prior to the preparation of the CRSP daily return databases during the 1970s. He documented very small positive serial correlations in stock returns that could not be exploited by an investor facing positive transactions costs. He also performed "runs tests," as suggested by Roberts, to examine whether returns showed any tendency to persist in one direction (a series of two or more price increases or decreases constitutes a run). No such tendency was observed.

seems to be that such trading strategies do not yield excess profits. There are three reasons for this. First, transactions costs would likely eat up most or all of the potential profits that would accrue to someone adopting such a trading strategy—especially one involving the purchase of thousands of shares of thinly-traded small company stocks. Second, almost all tests of asset pricing models and/or market efficiency are subject to a serious **joint hypothesis problem**. This means that a finding of, for example, "excess" returns for small company stocks in January may be caused by an inefficient capital market improperly pricing securities one month of every year; *or* it may be simply the result of using an incorrect (improperly-specified) asset pricing model; *or* it may be the result of both an inefficient market *and* an incorrect pricing model. Without divine guidance as to the one true model of equilibrium asset pricing, one cannot be sure that an apparently exploitable anomaly even exists. Finally, both Ritter and Chopra (1989) and Fama (1991, Table I) document that the magnitude (even the existence) of the January effect is very sensitive to the stock index used for comparison, and Fama shows that the effect—however measured—has shrunk dramatically since attention was first focused on it in 1983.

TESTS FOR SHORT-HORIZON RETURN PREDICTABILITY To a "classically" trained finance person who has not visited the efficiency literature in several years, it comes as quite a shock to learn that researchers have identified significant predictability in both short- and long-horizon stock returns. While the question of whether this predictability in and of itself refutes the Efficient Markets Hypothesis remains in doubt, the existence of substantial autocorrelation in stock returns is now well established. This predictability is of two types. First, researchers have documented consistent autocorrelation patterns in security returns (usually tested with size-grouped portfolios of stocks), finding significant positive autocorrelation in short-horizon (weekly and monthly) returns and negative serial correlation in longer-horizon (2–3 year) returns. Second, a number of studies have demonstrated that next-period returns for stock and bond portfolios can be predicted based on currently observable variables that proxy for the level of asset prices, the overall level of business risk, and the term structure of interest rates. This evidence of "derived predictability" offers a potential explanation of how predictable returns can be compatible with an efficient capital market that is free of riskless arbitrage opportunities. We first examine the evidence on short-term return predictability, and then turn to long-horizon predictability and derived predictability later in this section.

Most of the published research on short-horizon predictable returns has appeared within the past ten years, and tends to fall into one of two categories. First, several papers test whether stock prices follow a random walk, and then examine the underlying causes of the deviations documented. A second group of studies mount a much more open and aggressive attack on the Efficient Markets Hypothesis by explicitly testing the ability of investors to profit from the perceived tendency of stock prices to "overreact" to news or events, and then to revert back to equilibrium price levels over several months' time. These studies are often called **tests of mean reversion**. We examine each group of studies briefly in turn, beginning with the random walk studies.

Lo and MacKinlay (1988) develop a unique and innovative method of testing for serial correlation in stock returns by exploiting the fact that the variance of uncorrelated stock returns should increase in direct proportion to the sampling interval (monthly variances should be four times larger than weekly variances). They find strong evidence that weekly stock returns are positively correlated, and thus reject the random walk hypothesis. In fact, Lo and MacKinlay compute the weekly first-order autocorrelation (correlation with the immediately preceding week) coefficient of the equally-weighted CRSP returns index to be a strikingly high 30 percent! Finally, they conclude that the patterns of autocorrelation they document are not consistent with the stationary mean-reverting models of Summers (1986), Poterba and Summers (1988), and Fama and French (1988b) [discussed below]. In a later paper, Lo and MacKinlay (1990) show that less than 50 percent of the profits from a **contrarian investment strategy** (buying recent losers and shorting recent winners) is due to overreaction. Most of the profit is due to cross-autocorrelation between stock returns—specifically to the tendency of large stock portfolio returns to lead those of small stock portfolios.

In a series of papers, Conrad and Kaul (1988, 1989) and Conrad, Kaul, and Nimalendran (1991) examine the positive autocorrelation patterns in weekly and monthly stock returns. In the first article, they document that expected weekly stock returns vary through time and are well-characterized by a stationary first-order autoregressive process. They also find that the expected returns they extract explain up to 26 percent of the return variance of the smallest stock portfolio, but this proportion drops systematically to only one percent for the largest stock portfolio.[32] Conrad and Kaul extend their original methodology to monthly stock returns in their second study, where they find that the mean reversion in weekly expected returns explains a significant fraction (over 25 percent for small firm portfolios) of the monthly stock return variance. Finally, Conrad, Kaul, and Nimalendran document that up to 24 percent of the variation in weekly security returns can be explained by positively autocorrelated expected returns, a negatively autocorrelated component induced by bid-ask spread errors, and a white noise (random variation) component.

OVERREACTION TESTS   In all of the studies discussed above, the authors felt (or at least hoped) that their results were compatible with market efficiency. Several other researchers who document short-horizon return predictability make no such claim—indeed most document seemingly enormous arbitrage possibilities from exploiting the positive autocorrelation in security returns. One of the most important early tests of market overreaction is by DeBondt and Thaler (1985). They draw on research in experimental psychology suggesting that most people overreact to unexpected and dramatic events, and ask whether the same thing occurs in the stock market. Their results indicate that portfolios of prior extreme "losers" dramatically outperform prior extreme "winners", even though the latter are more risky. The effect cumulates to the point that, 36 months after portfolio formation, the prior period losing stocks have earned 25 percent more than the winners. Finally, DeBondt and Thaler show that the overreaction

---

32. This is a pattern that is documented in virtually all tests of return predictability specifically, or tests of market efficiency generally. Small firm stocks are shown to have fundamentally different return dynamics than large firm stocks, and the degree of return predictability is usually several times higher for small than for large companies. While small firm "anomalies" have been the focus of an immense body of research, Fama (1991, page 1589) quite correctly points out that the macroeconomic significance of these studies is probably negligible since the bottom quintile of stocks on the three major U.S. stock markets represent only 1.5 percent of their total market value. In contrast, the largest quintile of stocks represent 77.2 percent of the combined market valuation of all listed stocks.

return is strongest in January, and they conclude that the frequently-documented January effect is actually a "losing firm" effect rather than a tax-loss selling effect.

Fama and French (1988b) and Poterba and Summers (1988) both document that short-horizon returns are positively autocorrelated and longer-horizon returns are negatively autocorrelated, but they differ in their interpretation of these results. Fama and French believe their results are caused by a slowly-decaying stationary component, such as a large stock price increase or decrease caused by the arrival of unexpected news, that affects measured returns over an extended period. They are agnostic about whether their results are caused by market inefficiency or by time-varying expected returns that result from rational investor behavior. Poterba and Summers attribute their results to transitory (and presumably ephemeral) components in stock prices that account for more than half of the monthly return variance. They suggest that **noise trading** (trades made by uninformed investors reacting to preceived valuation errors that are really simply "noise" in the return data) provides a plausible explanation for the transitory component in stock prices.

Two other studies explicitly test trading strategies based on stock price overreaction, and document seemingly massive profit opportunities. Jegadeesh (1990) documents significantly *negative* first-order autocorrelation in monthly stock returns, but significantly positive higher-order (two or more months previous) autocorrelations. After forming portfolios based on these correlation patterns, he finds that the difference between the abnormal returns on the highest and lowest decile portfolios is 2.49 percent *per month* (34.3 percent per year). Later, Jegadeesh and Titman (1993) document that momentum strategies which buy stocks that have recently performed well and sell stocks that have performed poorly generate significant positive abnormal returns over 3- to 12-month intervals. Their most closely examined strategy yields an excess return of 12.01 percent per year on average, although these returns dissipate over multi-year holding periods.

What are we to make of these studies showing large predictable components (and, implicitly, large trading strategy profits) in short-horizon returns? While their importance cannot be dismissed out of hand, their negative impact on the Efficient Markets Hypothesis is not likely to be great (or lasting), for two principal reasons. First, more recent empirical papers cast doubt on the empirical significance of the predictability studies. Richardson and Smith (1994) show that many of the test statistics for serial correlation are themselves highly correlated under a null hypothesis that stock prices follow a random walk. Once these biases are corrected for, the new test statistics are consistent with the random walk model of stock returns—and with the EMH. Furthermore, studies by McQueen (1992) and Jones (1993) show that the mean reversion documented by DeBondt and Thaler (1985) is caused almost entirely by the Depression and World War II period, and largely disappears in the postwar era.[33] Second, the potential profits identified by Jegadeesh (1990) and Jegadeesh and Titman (1993) are

---

33. Fama and French (1988b) also document that their autocorrelation results are stronger in the 1926–1940 period than afterwards. Further doubt on the validity of DeBondt and Thaler's overreaction hypothesis is cast by Cox and Peterson (1994), who show that much of the daily "bounce back" in stock prices following large (10 percent or more) one-day price declines is caused by liquidity and bid-ask spread effects, not by market irrationality. They also document that even this pattern of "overreaction" has disappeared since 1987.

simply too large to be credible.[34] If real, such simple trading strategies should have been adopted by at least a few mutual fund managers, and thus have left a discernible trace in the empirical literature, but no evidence of this exists. Finally, Roll (1994) argues persuasively (from personal experience as a multi-billion-dollar mutual fund manager) that real trading strategies based on these and other anomalies do not yield excess returns.

LONG-HORIZON RETURN PREDICTABILITY   Numerous studies, several of which have already been cited, document two features about long-horizon returns. First, there is significant negative autocorrelation in return intervals of between two and five years. Second, the predictable component in the total variation of returns increases with the return interval. These patterns are documented by DeBondt and Thaler (1985), Poterba and Summers (1988), and Fama and French (1988a), while Reichenstein and Rich (1994) discuss how investors can attempt to exploit this predictability in their own investment portfolios. Fama and French's results are typical of this literature. They document negative autocorrelation in returns beginning at about a two-year lag, with the minimum coefficient values being reached for 3–5 year horizons, before moving back towards zero for longer horizons. The size of these negative coefficients suggests substantial predictability in returns—estimated to be about 40 percent of total return variance for small firms for the 3–5 year horizon, and about 25 percent for larger firms.

On the other hand, McQueen (1992) casts doubt on the significance, even the existence, of long-horizon return predictability. He documents that the use of OLS regression techniques in previous studies implicitly (but dramatically) over-weight the Depression and World War II eras, both of which have large error variances and stronger mean-reverting tendencies. Using generalized least squares (GLS) tests for the 1926–1987 period, McQueen cannot reject the hypothesis that monthly stock returns follow a random walk, and are thus not forecastable.[35] Ball and Kothari (1989) also cast doubt on the anomalous nature of negative serial correlation in long-horizon returns. They find this negative autocorrelation is due almost entirely to variation in relative risks, and thus expected returns, through time. In other words, their results support market efficiency, in that the expected returns on riskier stocks should increase after firms have experienced negative stock returns and decrease after firms have enjoyed positive returns. Such a rational pricing response would, in fact, induce negative serial correlation in measured stock returns.

To see more clearly how time-varying expected returns might impart seeming predictability to long-horizon returns, consider a company that has just enjoyed a banner two year period of increasing profits and a rapidly rising stock price. The increase in share value has lowered the firm's (market value) leverage, thereby decreasing the stock's risk and required return. Furthermore, assume the good times are expected to

---

34. Fama (1991, page 1582) suggests that these results might be caused by CRSP pricing errors, which would tend to show up as price reversals.

35. Nelson and Kim (1993) also suggest that biases in the econometric procedures commonly used to test for long-horizon return autocorrelations may indicate predictability even if none is present. Nonetheless, they find that return predictability is highly significant in the post-1947 period, even after accounting for these biases.

continue for this firm, further lowering the perceived risk and increasing the share price. Consider what the returns are expected to be for this firm over the next 2–3 years. It is now selling at a very high price-earnings ratio, and its risk has declined—so it should earn, at best, normal returns over the coming period. But a researcher examining this stock's return pattern after the fact would see an extremely high realized return (during the two fat years of rising profits), followed by much lower returns during the subsequent two years, which the researcher might easily conclude was evidence of negative long-horizon autocorrelation in returns. This logic would work in reverse for a company that has just weathered a harrowing period of poor earnings and falling stock prices. The required return on this company's stock would increase, its share price would fall, but it would be expected to enjoy extremely high returns over the next 2–3 years (if it survives at all). Once again, this pattern of falling stock prices (negative returns) followed by very high (required) realized return would manifest itself as "predictable" negative correlation in long-horizon returns, even though it actually resulted from rational pricing behavior by investors in an informationally-efficient capital market.

"DERIVED PREDICTABILITY" TESTS   One of the most intriguing streams of research in finance recently has been that which attempts to model changing (conditional) expected returns on stocks and bonds as a function of currently-observable macroeconomic and financial variables. We refer to this as "derived predictability," because the predictability of returns is computed (derived) largely from data external to the firm—rather than from an analysis of the firm's own return history. There is thus much less concern about whether this type of return predictability violates the weak form of the efficient market hypothesis, since security pricing is based on contemporaneous, rather than historical, information.

This stream of literature was kicked off by Keim and Stambaugh (1986), who show that ex post risk premiums for stocks *and* bonds can reliably be predicted based on three ex ante variables—one derived from the bond market and two derived from the stock market. The bond variable is the spread between yields on low-grade corporate bonds and one-month treasury bills, and thus represents both a default risk proxy and a yield curve proxy. The first stock market proxy is an expression of the current level of the real S&P index relative to its historical average, and thus measures whether the recent trend of asset prices has been up or down. The final variable is a measure of the average share price of the smallest quintile of NYSE firms, implying another measure for asset prices as well as a small firm proxy. Keim and Stambaugh document that all three variables are negatively related to current asset prices and positively related to expected returns. In other words, when asset prices are low, expected next-period returns are high, and vice versa.

The second major derived predictability paper, by Fama and French (1988a), differs from the others in that it presents evidence that the expected return on *individual* stocks can be predicted from that stock's own dividend yield (dividend per share divided by stock price). Several previous authors had noted that high yield stocks tended to outperform low yield stocks; Fama and French's contribution is to show that the predictive power of dividend yield increases with the return horizon. This time variation in expected returns accounts for less than 5 percent of the variance in monthly or quarterly returns, but more than 25 percent of 2–4 year returns.

As Goetzmann and Jorion (1993) point out, this is a troubling finding since it suggests that a simple trading rule would offer easy abnormal profits. An investor would only need to concentrate his or her capital in high-yield firms to beat the market indices over time.[36] They show that the predictive ability of dividend yields is almost surely over-stated because, with relatively unchanging nominal dividend payments, stock price changes themselves will account for virtually all of the intermediate term variation in dividend yields. With a fixed dividend payment, finding that dividend yields predict future stock returns is tantamount to finding evidence of mean-reverting returns (expected returns increase after a period of poor stock performance, and vice versa). When Goetzmann and Jorion model stock returns under the null hypothesis of no forecast ability, they find only marginal statistical evidence against the idea that returns follow a random walk.[37]

Finally, Fama and French (1989) document that the expected returns on stocks and long-term bonds are systematically related to business conditions. They model business conditions with three variables: (1) the default-risk spread between low-risk (AAA rated) corporate bonds and the market portfolio of corporate bonds, which is a measure of overall business risk; (2) the dividend yield on the value-weighted portfolio of NYSE stocks, also a proxy for overall business risk; and (3) the yield spread (a term structure measure) between short-term and long-term corporate bonds, which is a short-term proxy for the stage of the business cycle. Generally, expected returns are lower when business conditions are strong and higher when business conditions are weak. This becomes a very logical result when one considers that investors are likely to be relatively flush with cash (and content with life) during business cycle expansions, but they are likely to be relatively poor (and worried) during recessions. Investors would thus be willing to accept a lower expected return during business expansions than during recessions. Balvers, Cosimano, and McDonald (1990) provide theoretical and empirical support for this linkage between expected returns and production levels in the real economy, and further documenting this relationship should be one of the ongoing fields of academic research.

3.6.3 Tests for Rapid Price Adjustment

As mentioned earlier, Fama (1991) suggested that tests of the semi-strong form of the EMH be categorized as tests of the rapid adjustment of prices to new information. He suggested the title of event studies for these tests, since these were the focus of the work he cited. Since our desired coverage of material is somewhat broader than Fama's, and since several important articles have been published since then, we classify tests of the semi-strong form of the EMH as tests for rapid price adjustment. We specifically group studies into two main categories. First, we follow Fama in reviewing

---

36. An investor could even achieve essentially complete diversification by purchasing the highest yielding stocks in several different industry groups. The inability to achieve adequate diversification is a serious, though usually unrecognized, flaw in many highly-touted trading rules that seem to offer excess returns.

37. It should also be noted that Fama and French themselves later (1992) show that the predictive power of dividend yields is subsumed when the variables (1) size and (2) book-to-market value of equity are included in a model of expected returns.

event studies, which examine whether stock prices instantaneously and fully incorporate new information into asset prices (usually, but not always, stock prices). Second, we examine a rather amorphous group of studies that examine whether (and how) financial markets rationally process all available information. Included in this group are tests of how markets process rumors, unexpected announcements with uncertain outcomes, and news about additions and deletions of shares from major stock indices, as well as other topics.

EVENT STUDIES   Almost certainly, event studies have emerged as the single most important tool of empirical finance research due to their ease of use, clarity of purpose, flexibility, and absence of confounding influences. The logic of an event study is really quite simple. To determine the average stock market response to a particular type of announcement, one simply lines individual stocks up in event time (rather than calendar time) and then examines the average stock price change accompanying the announcement. For example, in order to assess the average impact of dividend initiation announcements on the stocks of U.S. companies adopting such a policy, one would do the following.[38] First, collect a sample of NYSE or AMEX firms that have initiated cash dividend payments since July 2, 1962 by examining the relevant sections of each annual **Wall Street Journal Index** (or other nationally-distributed news source) for the last three decades.[39] The researcher would record the date the dividend initiation was announced (not when it was actually paid), along with other relevant information such as the dividend amount and the reason given by management for the change in policy. Second, the researcher would define the announcement date as *event day zero* ($t = 0$), and define time intervals relative to that day (rather than relative to, say, February 27, 1985). Third, the researcher would regress returns on this stock with returns on the overall stock market during the *estimation period*, often defined as the period from six months to one month before the announcement date (day -150 to day -20 [or t = $-150, -20$] in event time). The purpose of this exercise is to generate expected returns during the *event period* (the days immediately before and after the announcement date, including the date itself) by determining what the return on the stock would normally be if the overall stock market increased by, say, 0.5 percent.[40] Fourth, the actual return of the stock during each day of the event period is then computed and compared with

---

38. Such a study is presented in Asquith and Mullins (1983). This was also the first empirical study to subject the abnormal returns created by the event study to regression analysis to determine whether stock responses to initiation announcements were related to firm-specific financial variables.

39. Event studies can be performed using either daily or monthly stock returns, although the precision of daily event studies is far greater. The principal databases used in event studies are stock price and return files maintained by the Center for Research in Security Prices (CRSP) at the University of Chicago. The monthly file contains end-of-month stock prices and returns for NYSE-listed stocks beginning in January 1926. The daily file contains daily closing prices and returns for NYSE- and AMEX-listed stocks beginning on July 2, 1962. There are also several other files containing similar data for Canadian, NASDAQ, and other groups of stocks. All of the files are updated annually, and are available to (quite literally) thousands of researchers in academia, business, and government.

40. For example, if the estimated beta on a stock is 2.0, and its alpha (intercept term) is 0.0002, or 0.02 percent per day, the expected return on this stock given that the stock market increases that day by 0.5 percent will be $0.02 + 2.0 (0.5) = 1.02$ percent. If instead the stock market declines by 1.0 percent that day, the stock's expected return will be $0.02 + 2.0 (-1.0) = -1.98$ percent.

that stock's expected return—the return predicted conditional on the overall market's performance. The difference between the actual return and the predicted return is referred to as an **abnormal return** (AR), and when several days' abnormal returns are summed the result is referred to as a **cumulative abnormal return** (CAR).[41] Most researchers focus attention on a very narrow event window surrounding the day the announcement is published in the **Wall Street Journal,** in order to determine what the immediate reaction to the announcement is. The final step in an event study is to aggregate all of the announcements being examined (often several hundred or more), compute an average abnormal return for the event, and determine whether the AR or CAR is statistically different from zero.

Event studies have several major strengths. First, by averaging out random noise over many different observations, a researcher is able to gain an unbiased assessment of how stock prices react to a given event. Additionally, by determining the number of positive and negative ARs that went into the overall average, the researcher is able to determine if the average values are being driven by a small number of large abnormal returns or if most stocks are reacting in the same way. Second, and perhaps most important, the joint hypothesis problem is effectively finessed by the event study methodology, since the method for computing expected returns typically has very little impact on the actual AR computed.[42] Essentially, all one is doing is computing the average stock response to a given type of announcement, and as such, event studies are very "clean" tests that yield unambiguous results. Third, event studies provide a direct test of semi-strong-form market efficiency, since they allow one to determine if information is incorporated fully and instantaneously into stock prices.

Event studies have been used most frequently in corporate finance empirical studies, and they have dramatically advanced our understanding of how stockholders view dividend payments, security issues, takeover bids, and myriad other internal and external financial events.[43] Survey articles by Jensen and Ruback (1983), Jensen and Warner (1988), and Smith (1986) provide a feel for the impact that event studies have had on mainstream corporate finance. For our purposes here, the key point of this research is that, almost without exception, event studies have strongly supported market efficiency.[44] Prices react virtually instantaneously, and in an unbiased way, to firm-specific news announcements.

---

41. Abnormal returns are sometimes also called *excess returns* (ER) or *prediction errors* (PE), and the latter term is actually the most accurate. We will stick with abnormal returns in our discussion, however, since it is by far the most commonly used term.

42. The vagaries of event study methodology have been explored at length in numerous studies. See, for example, Scholes and Williams (1977), Dimson (1979), Ball and Torous (1988), Corrado (1989), Eckbo, Maksimovic, and Williams (1990), Boehmer, Musumeci, and Poulsen (1991), Salinger (1992) and, especially, Brown and Warner (1980, 1985).

43. The very first event study, by Fama, Fisher, Jensen, and Roll (1969), examined the stock market response to stock splits. Most of the basic technologies used today were either employed or foreshadowed in that paper. Ironically, Fama (1991) reveals that this study was designed primarily as a marketing tool to show the usefulness of the newly-created CRSP data files. None of the four authors expected to change the world of finance (at least not with that paper).

44. Jensen (1978) surveys several papers that present evidence seemingly anomalous with market efficiency, but most of the articles he cited employed monthly rather than daily data (daily return files only became available in the late 1970s). Very few recent event studies have documented comparable inefficiencies.

TESTS OF RATIONAL INFORMATION PROCESSING   In addition to event studies, numerous researchers have examined whether financial markets process current information in a rational and rapid manner. Taken together, these studies provide indirect evidence largely supportive of semi-strong-form market efficiency. First, French and Roll (1986) provide a striking commentary on how markets process information during trading versus non-trading periods. They document that the per-hour variance of stock returns during a normal trading day is 72 times that of a normal weekend. They find that only 4 to 12 percent of the daily return variance is possibly due to mispricing (hurray for market efficiency), and also document that little of the difference in variance is the result of the arrival of more public information during business hours than over weekends. French and Roll instead determine that the higher variance during periods when the exchange is open is caused by private information being revealed in stock prices through the trades of informed investors. Although Jones, Kaul, and Lipson (1994) find that more of the return variance difference results from public information arrival than French and Roll do, they also document that noise-trading-induced mispricing has little impact on stock price changes.[45]

Brown, Harlow, and Tinic (1988) develop and test an uncertain information hypothesis to determine whether stock prices respond efficiently to the arrival of unanticipated information. Their theory predicts that following news of a dramatic financial event, both the risk and expected return of the affected company's stock will increase systematically, and that prices will react more strongly to bad than to good news. This pattern will appear to be an overreaction to bad news and an underreaction to good news, but the authors show that this is how rational, risk-averse investors should act. Their empirical results, drawn from an investigation of over 9000 marketwide and firm-specific events, support the uncertain information hypothesis and also semi-strong-form market efficiency.

Pound and Zeckhauser (1990) examine whether stock market participants rationally respond to rumors about potentially important events. They study the response to takeover rumors published in the "Heard on the Street" column of the **Wall Street Journal**, and find that the market responds efficiently—a simple trading rule based on buying rumored takeover targets yields no excess returns. They also document that these rumors are usually incorrect—only 18 of the 42 sample companies receive takeover bids within one year, and only two receive bids within 50 days.

Dhillon and Johnson (1991) examine whether the previously-documented positive stock price response for a company when it is chosen for inclusion in the S&P 500 list is compatible with market efficiency. As had earlier researchers, they document a positive stock price effect upon inclusion announcement. But unlike prior authors, Dhillon and Johnson find no evidence that this price increase dissipates in the months after inclusion, as predicted by the price-pressure hypothesis of Harris and Gurel (1984). Their findings that option prices respond as expected and that bond prices also increase on

---

45. Several other researchers also examine the relationship between stock returns and stock price variance. One of the most important of these studies, by French, Schwert, and Stambaugh (1987), documents that expected market risk premiums are positively related to the predictable volatility of stock returns. These authors also find that unexpected stock returns are negatively related to the unexpected change in the volatility of stock returns. LeBaron (1992) finds that daily and weekly serial correlations are inversely related to the conditional (expected) volatility of the indices he examines. He also documents that serial correlations are lower during periods of increased return volatility.

the inclusion announcement generally support the notion that inclusion of a firm by S&P in its premier index reveals positive new information about a company to market participants. These findings are, however, incompatible with the predictions of the imperfect substitutes hypothesis presented by Shleifer (1986). Dhillon and Johnson also show that the market became more informationally efficient after the introduction of S&P 500 index futures and options in 1983.

Finally, Ederington and Lee (1993) examine the impact of scheduled macroeconomic news announcements on interest rate and foreign exchange futures contract prices. They examine futures markets because they open for trading ten minutes prior to the 8:30 AM time when these announcements are made, whereas stock markets do not open for another hour. In addition to documenting that several types of macroeconomic announcements significantly impact interest rate and foreign exchange contracts (an important contribution in itself), these authors document that the bulk of the price adjustment to a major announcement occurs within the first minute of trading, although volatility remains substantially higher than normal for at least fifteen minutes after announcement. Remarkably, other than these announcements, volatility is flat across the trading day and across the trading week.

The evidence discussed above, coupled with the earlier event study results, suggests that financial markets respond very rapidly and completely to new information. Whatever else might be said, these markets clearly exhibit semi-strong-form informational efficiency.

3.6.4 Tests for Private Information

In place of tests of strong form market efficiency, Fama (1991) suggested the phrase tests for private information. Implied in this is an examination of whether someone— such as a corporate insider or a particularly perceptive mutual fund manager—could earn excess returns by trading on private (non-public) information. While a logical extension of the EMH, most people intuitively assume that it is a straw man which can easily be rejected. As we will see, however, even this form of market efficiency can only consistently be rejected for trades made by corporate insiders. The evidence that any group of outside analysts can consistently "beat" the market is tenuous at best. We begin our discussion with a very brief discussion of the early tests for private information by Sharpe (1966) and Jensen (1968), which had such an immense impact on the collective consciousness of finance professionals. Next, we examine the results of two major studies on the profitability of insider trading—and of the trades by those outside investors who mimic insider actions. We then examine the evidence on mutual fund performance, beginning with a brief discussion of the "Value Line Enigma." This discussion is broken into surveys of those tests that show superior mutual fund stock picking ability (which contradicts market efficiency), and those which show no such superior ability. Finally, we examine two recent studies that assess the performance of pension fund managers. Since U.S. pension funds control over $4 trillion in assets, their relative investment performance is a matter of some import.

EARLY TESTS OF PRIVATE INFORMATION   Even before the theory of informationally efficient capital markets had been presented by Fama (1970), Sharpe (1966) and Jensen (1968) had published studies showing negative net returns (gross returns minus fund operating costs) for the majority of mutual fund managers. Jensen's study was particularly important because he presented a model for assessing mutual fund performance that has been used by many subsequent researchers. This model measures the excess return (nominal return minus the risk-free rate) on a managed portfolio, R_{pt}, as a function of the beta of the portfolio, β_p, the excess return on the market portfolio, R_{mt}, an intercept term, α_p, and an error term, u_{pt}, as follows:

$$R_{pt} = (\alpha_p + \beta_p) \times (R_{mt} + u_{pt}) \tag{3.18}$$

In this framework, testing for superior investment performance reduces to a test of whether the intercept term, α_p, is significantly different from zero. To this day, even casual discussions of a mutual fund's performance will often be couched as, "what is the fund's alpha?" Jensen found that the funds in his sample had negative alphas—meaning that they were not even breaking even as managers, and their shareholders were doing even worse. Since Sharpe documented a similar result, the received wisdom within the profession (at least within academia) was that mutual fund managers could not beat the stock market. As we will see later, several subsequent papers took issue with this conclusion, but their impact was far less pervasive than the two original articles.

TESTS OF THE PROFITABILITY OF INSIDER TRADING   By far the most extreme test of strong form market efficiency is a test of whether corporate insiders who trade in their own firms' securities can earn abnormal profits. As you surely suspect, both Jaffe (1974) and Seyhun (1986) conclusively document that insiders do earn supernormal returns on their trades, and their results thus reject strong form market efficiency. The tests differ, however, on the critical issue of whether outside investors can earn excess profits by mimicking insider trades after they are publicly disclosed. Jaffe reports that outsiders can profit from mimicking trades, which constitutes a rejection of semi-strong form efficiency. However, Seyhun argues persuasively that this apparently profitable trading strategy is actually due to Jaffe's assumption that outside investors gain access to news of insider trades sooner than they actually do, and are thus able to trade on this news earlier than they really can. Using data that provides actual information release dates, Seyhun shows that outside investors cannot profit from mimicking the announced trades of corporate insiders. These two studies thus represent a rejection of strong form market efficiency, but at least the more recent study supports semi-strong form efficiency.

THE VALUE LINE ENIGMA   A series of articles during the 1970s and early 1980s seemed to indicate that an investor who followed the recommendations of the Value Line Investment Service could earn excess, risk-adjusted returns. Two recent studies have re-examined this issue. Holloway (1981) finds that when realistic trading costs are used, active trading based on Value Line (VL) recommendations is not profitable. For a buy-and-hold strategy, however, VL recommendations do earn excess returns. Even this conclusion is challenged by Huberman and Kandel (1990). They find that the purported abnormal returns of positions based on VL recommendations are merely reflections of the systematic risks associated with these positions. Once these risks are accounted for, VL recommendations earn normal returns and the EMH emerges unscathed.

MUTUAL FUND STUDIES DOCUMENTING SUPERIOR INVESTMENT PERFOR-MANCE   Since the early Sharpe and Jensen studies were published in the 1960s, a veritable cottage industry has sprung up to assess the investment performance of mutual fund managers. Before diving into a survey of the most recent of these papers, we should point out that most studies separate managerial investment performance into two components: **selectivity** (stock-picking ability) and **timing**—the ability to time market turns, getting in before upturns and getting out before crashes. Another characteristic of most performance studies is that they are very sensitive to three variables: (1) the specific benchmark (stock index or relative performance of other managers) used for comparison purposes; (2) the specific methodology used to assess portfolio risk and compute managerial investment performance, and (3) the specific time periods examined in the studies.

With these caveats in mind, let us briefly examine several important recent studies that claim to document superior mutual fund performance, beginning with Bjerring, Lakonishok, and Vermaelen (1983). These authors demonstrate that an investor following the recommendations of an unnamed Canadian brokerage house would have achieved superior returns. Cumby and Modest (1987) examine the market-timing ability of a group of seven technical analysts in the foreign exchange market using both a standard performance measure and an improved measure they present. Based on their measure, these advisers demonstrate superior market timing ability, although this is not the case with the standard performance measure. Cumby and Modest's results are somewhat weakened by the fact that when the investment advisers are evaluated over a consistent sample period, the evidence of market timing is much weaker.

Lee and Rahman (1990) examine the market timing and selectivity performance of a sample of mutual fund managers. They present a simple model of performance assessment that requires as inputs only the return earned by the fund and that earned by the market portfolio. They document some evidence of superior micro- and macro-forecasting ability at the individual mutual fund level, though not for the entire sample of funds. Hendricks, Patel, and Zeckhauser (1993) examine fund performance from a somewhat different perspective. They evaluate whether there is short-run persistence in either superior or inferior mutual fund performance. They find that the relative performance of no-load, growth-oriented mutual funds persists in the near term, with the strongest evidence being found for a one-year evaluation horizon. They also present provocative findings that an investor who pursues an investment strategy of buying the funds managed by "hot hands", and avoiding funds managed by "icy hands" (the evil twin of hot hands), will earn risk-adjusted abnormal returns as high as 6 percent per year. Goetzmann and Ibbotson (1994) also present evidence that winning mutual fund managers tend to repeat their performance in subsequent periods.

Probably the single most important recent study supporting the idea that mutual fund managers at least earn their keep is by Ippolito (1989).[46] He does not reject the EMH; rather he incorporates the Grossman and Stiglitz (1980) idea that there must be an economic return to information gathering or else asset prices could not reflect all

---

46. Ippolito (1993) later discusses this study, as well as several others, in an excellent survey article that also presents a very useful summary of mutual fund studies through 1989 (Table II).

available information. Ippolito finds empirical support for his modified EMH, in that he documents for his sample of mutual funds an average positive alpha of about 200 basis points (2 percent of asset value) per year, which almost exactly offsets the average expense ratio of all mutual funds. He later (1993) reperforms Jensen's (1968) study using a sample free of survivor bias, and finds an average alpha of $+81$ basis points rather than the alpha of -111 basis points originally documented by Jensen. Before moving on, we should note that Elton, Gruber, Das, and Hlavka (EGDH, 1993) take issue with Ippolito's results, charging that he does not properly account for the performance of non-S&P assets in computing mutual fund returns. Once these assets are properly accounted for, EGDH find that mutual funds do not earn returns that justify their information acquisition costs (their alphas are significantly negative). They also document that funds with higher fees and turnover underperform those with lower fees and turnover.

TESTS SHOWING NO SUPERIOR PERFORMANCE EGDH are by no means the only researchers who find that mutual fund managers do not earn investment returns that exceed (or even cover) their operating expenses. Jagannathan and Korajczyk (1986) show theoretically and empirically that it is possible to construct portfolios that show artificial timing ability when no true ability exists. In particular, investing in options or in levered equities will show spurious market timing, but only at the expense of measured selectivity. They suggest two ways of avoiding these biases in performance evaluation studies.

Grinblatt and Titman (1989) examine mutual fund performance using a sample of quarterly holdings that is free of survivor bias. They make the important point that a mutual fund manager with superior stock picking ability does not have to earn positive net excess returns for outside investors, he or she merely has to earn gross returns sufficient to cover fund operating expenses (earn an alpha of about 200 basis points per year) to remain in business over time. In other words, it is highly likely that talented mutual fund managers will be able to capture most of the benefits of any superior investing ability in the form of higher fees and expenses. Alas, Grinblatt and Titman find little evidence of managers even being able to earn superior gross returns, and no consistent evidence of positive net returns.[47]

Hartzmark (1991) goes even farther—he demonstrates that the fortunes of futures traders are determined purely by luck, not by forecast ability. Specifically, he shows that there are fewer superior forecasters, and more forecasters exhibiting no skill at all, than would be the case if market participants trade randomly. He also shows that there is no tendency for superior performance to be followed by more superior performance—which is exactly what you would expect if actual performance was based on luck rather than skill.

PENSION FUND MANAGER INVESTMENT PERFORMANCE Before concluding this section, we will briefly discuss the results of two recent studies examining whether pension fund managers are able to earn superior investment returns. Somewhat surprisingly, the investment performance of pension funds has attracted far less attention than

---

47. The moral of this story for ambitious young stock pickers is thus obvious—it is far better to be a vendor of mutual fund investment advice than to be a consumer.

have mutual funds, in spite of the fact that total pension fund assets have historically been far larger and pension fund managers outnumber mutual fund managers by a ratio of approximately ten to one (see Coggin, Fabozzi, and Rahman 1993). Brinson, Hood, and Beebower (1986) demonstrate that investment policy (percentage allocation of funds to different asset classes) is far more important than investment strategy in explaining the cross-sectional variation in fund returns, since policy explains 93.6 percent of total variance. They also document that active management yields an average total return 1.10 percent per year *less* than that achievable with a passive strategy of buying the market index. On the other hand, Coggin, Fabozzi, and Rahman (1993) find that the best pension fund managers produce risk-adjusted excess returns 6 percent higher than those achieved by the poorest fund managers.

In summary, there is no clear answer to the question whether mutual fund (or pension fund) managers are able to achieve investment returns high enough to cover information acquisition costs. Even this lack of conclusive evidence, however, amounts to damning these managers with faint praise, because there is no evidence that they can achieve significantly positive *net* returns for fund shareholders. The mutual fund performance studies therefore do no violence to the semi-strong form of the efficient market hypothesis.

3.6.5 Tests for Rational Fundamental Valuation

While the weight of evidence clearly seems to indicate that financial markets *react* efficiently to new information, this does not necessarily mean that financial asset prices always fully reflect "true" fundamental values. For example, a company's stock price may instantly and fully incorporate news of a dividend increase, yet still be over- or under-valued by a significant amount. Rational valuation is obviously a much more difficult concept to define and operationalize than informational efficiency, but it is perhaps no less important—since it reflects on the very legitimacy of the capitalist economic system. Furthermore, several respected economists have begun seriously questioning whether capital markets (in particular, American capital markets) provide rational valuations.

This assault on rational efficiency has taken one of two tracks, which we will briefly discuss in turn—along with the response of efficiency's defenders. First, the "variance bounds" literature asserts that stock and bond prices are too volatile—based on actual ex post fluctuations in dividends and interest payments—to have been generated by a rational valuation process. Second, the "noise trader" literature suggests that capital markets generate irrational valuations because of the activity of noise traders—uninformed investors who believe they *are* informed, and who trade on random information as though it were news. These investors presumably are very active in financial markets, and the very irrationality of their trading activity imparts so much risk to the markets that truly informed traders fear to trade against them.

VARIANCE BOUNDS TESTS Shiller (1979) launched the variance bounds literature with his observation that long-term interest rates vary far more than they should, given the actual ex post fluctuations in short-term interest rates. In later studies, Shiller (1981) and Grossman and Shiller (1981) develop tests to determine whether the observed variance in real stock prices can be explained by ex post variations either in the real dividend series or in the discount rates used by investors to compute the present value of the dividend series. These authors visually and statistically compare the time series of observed prices with the series of "perfect foresight" prices (p_t^*)—defined as the time t discounted value of (actual) future period real dividends. When the variance of actual stock prices exceeds the maximum rational variation (the variance bound) in perfect foresight prices, these authors conclude that stock prices are too volatile to have been produced by rational investors.

These studies were immediately attacked on both theoretical and econometric grounds. One of the most influential critiques is presented by Kleidon (1986), who argues that the tests of the perfect foresight model used by most early researchers are incorrectly specified. He shows that a properly specified variance bound is unable to reject the hypothesis that, over the long term, stock prices follow a random walk. Furthermore, he notes that stock prices may be nonstationary—they may experience large, discontinuous leaps or crashes—a possibility which the early variance bounds tests (which assumed stationarity of prices, dividends, and discount rates) are unable to handle.

Although the Kleidon article makes several telling points, the fans of variance bounds tests are able to counter many of his criticisms and still show excess volatility. In particular, the newer tests allow dividends and discount rates to vary, and also do not impose stationarity on the return generating process. These "second generation" variance bounds tests are surveyed in Gilles and LeRoy (1991)—who conclude that stock price series unquestionably display greater than expected volatility—but they are nonetheless agnostic about the enduring importance of this stream of research.[48] Campbell and Ammer (1993) attempt to answer several lingering questions about the source of this volatility by decomposing stock and bond returns into components based on changes to future expected cash flows and discount rates. Although they are able to attribute a large fraction of observed variability to rationally changing expectations, Campbell and Ammer conclude that the postwar U.S. stock market displays "excess volatility"—since returns have a standard deviation two or three times higher than the standard deviation of news about future dividend growth.

The most recent critique of the variance bounds literature may be the most telling yet, because it questions *whether* (rather than why) stock price variability is too large to be explained by dividend payments. Using Canadian data, Ackert and Smith (1993) show that when the definition of "dividends" is expanded to include stock repurchases and cash takeover payments made to shareholders, the measured total of corporate cash distributions to shareholders roughly doubles during the postwar period, and variance bounds tests no longer reject market efficiency.

In our minds, the central hypothesis of the variance bounds literature—that excess price variability implies market inefficiency—remains unproven. In addition to theoretical and econometric problems, there is a rather surreal aspect to the proposition that estimates of future cash flows and stock prices *can* be too variable. At face value, this literature seems to imply that investors in, say, early 1933 should have been able to foresee the eventual triumph of democratic capitalism over depression, fascism, and

---

48. Although Gilles and LeRoy present a very readable survey article, they readily acknowledge that almost all of the papers in this field require an extreme degree of econometric sophistication to truly understand. This is clearly no area for the statistically challenged.

communism—and thus should never have allowed stock prices to decline by 86 percent from their 1929 peak. Likewise, investors in 1974 should presumably have been able to foresee that the West would recover from the quadrupling of oil prices caused by the Arab oil embargo, even though this increase in the price of industrialized society's core commodity seemed at the time to presage a fundamental shift in the balance of world economic power. The uncertainty of the present is always clarified by time.

THE NOISE TRADER APPROACH TO FINANCE   Since the proponents of the noise trader approach to finance provide a complete, internally-consistent model of financial equilibrium—which nonetheless is characterized by pervasive mispricing of financial assets—their work represents a potentially serious attack on the orthodox notion that markets provide rational fundamental valuations. Summers (1986) kicked off this stream of research by noting that the very fact that asset mispricing is so hard to document statistically also suggests that pricing errors will be hard to identify and correct. In other words, the same noise which confounds statistical tests makes exploiting valuation errors risky. Furthermore, if risk is rewarded by higher expected returns, noise traders who plunge heedlessly into riskier-than-desired stocks may well come to dominate the market.

Shleifer and Summers (1990) develop a more formal model of asset mispricing by suggesting that markets are populated by two types of investors: (1) rational arbitrageurs, who accurately assess the true risks and expected returns offered by all securities; and (2) uninformed **noise** (or liquidity) **traders** who trade based on beliefs or sentiments that are not fully justified by fundamental news. The activities of noise traders cause prices to diverge from fundamental valuations, but the rational traders are unwilling to attempt to arbitrage prices because they face two types of risk. The first is fundamental risk, or the chance that the overall market may go up or down during the coming period. The second risk is the unpredictability of the future resale price—even if an asset is overpriced today, it may become even more overpriced next period.

DeLong, Shleifer, Summers, and Waldman (DSSW 1990) present a model of how extended deviations of prices from fundamental values can result from **positive-feedback trading strategies**—buying when prices rise and selling when prices fall. The initial price increases, which are caused by the trades of rational speculators seeking to exploit pricing, attract noise traders—who then jump on the bandwagon and push prices even farther away from fundamental values. DSSW also present a model of a financial market in which noise traders affect prices, thereby directly increasing the risk of rational speculators who might otherwise be tempted to trade against them. In DSSW (1991), noise traders do not affect prices, but they still earn higher expected returns than rational traders with similar risk aversion, because the noise traders' very irrationality causes them to purchase riskier securities than they believe they are buying. The assumptions underlying the DSSW (1990) paper allow noise traders to survive in financial markets, while the assumptions in DSSW (1991) allow them to dominate these markets.

THE EFFICIENT MARKETS REBUTTAL   Though clever and tightly-reasoned, the noise trader hypothesis is still only accepted by a small minority of finance professionals—at least in its current form. This is partly due to fondness for a theory (the EMH) that has been proven robust in virtually all other settings, and has certainly not yet been disproven by noise trading studies. There is also substantial empirical support for the notion that price changes are not driven by irrational bandwagon effects or speculative bubbles. Fama (1990), for example, documents that fully 58 percent of total stock return variability is caused by time-varying expected returns or shocks to cash flows or shocks to expected return, and this result is verified by Schwert (1990) for a full century of American history. Kothari and Shanken (1992) are able to explain even more (up to 70 percent) of the observed variation in annual returns. Furthermore, Fama and French's (1989) finding that both stocks and bonds are influenced by similar business condition variables is evidence against the importance of bubbles or fads in asset price histories—since these would tend to influence only one type of security. Finally, proponents of any important pricing anomaly must explain how it has remained stable in the face of the explosive growth in the size, sophistication, liquidity, and technical efficiency of financial markets during the past two decades. When billions of dollars are committed to arbitraging bond pricing errors as small as a few basis points, it seems inconceivable that deviations from fundamenatal valuation as gross as those implied by the noise trader literature could long endure.

—SUMMARY—

One of the holy grails of modern finance has been to develop robust, internally-consistent, and quantifiable measures of financial risk. At the simplest level, risk is defined as the uncertainty surrounding the payoff for a single asset held in isolation. The most important thrust of financial research, however, has been to develop theoretically sound asset pricing models that value assets based on their risk and return when held in a well-diversified portfolio. The two leading asset pricing models, the Capital Asset Pricing Model (CAPM) and the Arbitrage Pricing Theory (APT) methodology, have been subjected to rigorous empirical testing for thirty and twenty years, respectively. In spite of the fact that both have major operational or theoretical flaws, both remain popular because they express the expected return required on an asset as a function of one or more pervasive risk factors that systematically impact all financial assets. The CAPM has the benefit of being readily understandable—asset returns are directly related to the asset's return correlation with the market portfolio—but seems far too simple to ever serve as a complete equilibrium model of expected returns. The APT allows multiple factors to influence security returns, and has received significant empirical support as a statistical model of ex post security returns, but it suffers from the maddening inability to specify—in economically understandable terms—precisely what these factors are.

Although asset pricing theory remains rather muddled, investments research has given economic thought a true jewel in the theory of informationally efficient capital markets. Market efficiency is such a deceptively simple concept—that capital markets will fully and instantaneously incorporate all relevant public information into security prices—that it is easy to underestimate the impact this theoretical construct (plus the empirical tests supporting it) has had on capital market operations, regulation, and research. Indeed, the worldwide trend towards greater reliance on market forces to organize output and allocate rewards is at least implicitly based on the idea that markets are able to process information more effectively, and with less bias, than can any group of mortal policy-makers. While empirical tests of capital market efficiency do not provide completely unqualified support for the most extreme versions of efficiency, there remains little doubt that modern capital markets are immensely fast, accurate, and impartial processors of information.

—QUESTIONS—

1. Why is it important that finance professionals, particularly managers, understand the relationship between risk and return?

2. Compare and contrast ex ante and ex post measures of financial return. What assumptions must be made in order to test the accuracy of expected (ex ante) return predictions using historical (ex post) returns?

3. [Numerical problem] Compute the expected return and standard deviation of expected return for an asset with the following pattern of probability-weighted returns.

Return	Probability	Return	Probability
8%	5%	14%	30%
10%	15%	16%	15%
12%	30%	18%	5%

4. Describe the key features of a normal distribution, and discuss the role it plays in modern asset pricing theory.

5. [Essay question] Discuss how portfolio expected return is computed as a function of the expected returns of the underlying assets. Then compare this with the method of calculating the standard deviation of portfolio expected return. Why are these contrasting computations so important to modern portfolio theory?

6. Define the following terms: (a) diversifiable risk; (b) systematic risk; (c) total risk; (d) efficient portfolio; (e) efficient frontier; (f) minimum variance portfolio.

7. What is two-fund separation and the separation theorem? Why are these concepts so important to modern portfolio theory?

8. List and briefly discuss the assumptions underlying the CAPM.

9. [Essay question] Using formulas and text, efficiently describe the development of the CAPM. Why was the development of this model such an important breakthrough in asset pricing theory and practice?

10. What have been the chief difficulties encountered in empirically testing the CAPM? How have researchers sought to overcome these difficulties?

11. Using text and formulas, describe the key empirical predictions of the (basic) CAPM.

12. [Essay question] Discuss the key theoretical and/or empirical predictions of the following CAPM extensions: (a) the zero-beta CAPM; (b) the consumption CAPM; (c) the after-tax CAPM; (d) the international asset pricing model (IAPM).

13. Briefly describe the essential elements of Roll's Critique. Why does Roll believe the CAPM is untestable, even in theory?

14. [Essay question] Have empirical tests of the CAPM supported or rejected the model's economic validity? Which versions of the CAPM have held up the best to empirical testing, and which have fared the worst?

15. What is the random walk hypothesis? What are its key predictions? Has it been supported or rejected by empirical testing?

16. List and briefly describe three of the return "anomalies" that have been identified by researchers testing the CAPM.

17. [Essay question] Using text and formulas, efficiently discuss the development of the APT? What are the key empirical predictions of this model?

18. Discuss the theoretical and empirical strengths and weaknesses of the APT compared with the CAPM.

19. What are the key findings to result from empirical tests of the APT?

20. List and briefly describe the predictions of the three forms of market efficiency defined by Fama (1970). What are the three new categories of empirical tests of market efficiency defined by Fama (1991)?

21. [Essay question] What are the three categories of tests for return predictability? What have been the findings that have resulted from these tests?

22. Briefly describe the logic and mechanics of an event study. Have event studies generally supported or rejected market efficiency?

23. Briefly discuss the key findings that have resulted from tests for private information.

24. At a cocktail party, you—as an acknowledged financial theorist—are asked whether mutual fund managers and/or investment advisers can consistently "beat" the market. How do you respond?

25. What are variance bounds tests of market efficiency? Have these conclusively supported or rejected market efficiency?

26. What is the noise trader model of financial market equilibrium? How have efficient market supporters responded to the intellectual challenge posed by this model?

—REFERENCES—

Abuaf, Niso and Philippe Jorion, "Purchasing Power Parity in the Long Run," **Journal of Finance** 45 (March 1990), pp. 157–174.

Ackert, Lucy F. and Brian F. Smith, "Stock Price Volatility, Ordinary Dividends, and Cash Flows to Shareholders," **Journal of Finance** 48 (September 1993), pp. 1147–1160.

Adler, Michael and Bernard Dumas, "International Portfolio Choice and Corporation Finance: A Synthesis," **Journal of Finance** 38 (July 1983), pp. 925–984.

Agmon, Tamir and Donald R. Lessard, "Investor Recognition of Corporate International Diversification," **Journal of Finance** 32 (September 1977), pp. 1049–1055.

Amsler, Christine E. and Peter Schmidt, "A Monte Carlo Investigation of the Accuracy of Multivariate CAPM Tests," **Journal of Financial Economics** 14 (September 1985), pp. 359–375.

Ang, James S. and David R. Peterson, "Return, Risk and Yield: Evidence From Ex Ante Data," **Journal of Finance** 40 (March 1985), pp. 537–548.

Asquith, Paul and David W. Mullins, Jr., "The Impact of Initiating Dividend Payments on Shareholders' Wealth," **Journal of Business** 56 (January 1983), pp. 77–96.

Bailey, Warren and K. C. Chan, "Macroeconomic Influences and the Variability of the Commodity Futures Basis," **Journal of Finance** 48 (June 1993), pp. 555–573.

Ball, Clifford A. and Walter N. Torous, "Investigating Security-Price Performance in the Presence of Event-Date Uncertainty," **Journal of Financial Economics** 22 (October 1988), pp. 123–153.

Ball, Ray and S.P. Kothari, "Nonstationary Expected Returns: Implications for Tests of Market Efficiency and Serial Correlation in Returns," **Journal of Financial Economics** 25 (November 1989), pp. 51–74.

Balvers, Ronald J., Thomas F. Cosimano, and Bill McDonald, "Predicting Stock Returns in an Efficient Market," **Journal of Finance** 45 (September 1990), pp. 1109–1128.

Banz, Rolf W., "The Relationship Between Return and Market Value of Common Stocks," **Journal of Financial Economics** 9 (March 1981), pp. 3–18.

Beneish, Messod D., "Stock Prices and the Dissemination of Analysts' Recommendations," **Journal of Business** 64 (July 1991), pp. 393–416.

Bhide, Amar, "Return to Judgement," **Journal of Portfolio Management** 20 (Winter 1994), pp. 19–25.

Bjerring, James H., Josef Lakonishok, and Theo Vermaelen, "Stock Prices and Financial Analysts' Recommendations," **Journal of Finance** 38 (March 1983), pp. 187–204.

Black, Fischer, "Capital Market Equilibrium With Restricted Borrowing," **Journal of Business** 45 (July 1972), pp. 444–455.

——— "Noise," **Journal of Finance** 41 (July 1986), pp. 529–543.

——— "Beta and Return," **Journal of Portfolio Management** 20 (Fall 1993), pp. 8–18.

Black, Fischer, Michael C. Jensen, and Myron Scholes, "The Capital Asset Pricing Model: Some Empirical Tests," in Michael C. Jensen, ed., **Studies in the Theory of Capital Markets** (Praeger: New York, 1972).

Black, Fischer and Myron S. Scholes, "The Effects of Dividend Yield and Dividend Policy on Common Stock Prices and Returns," **Journal of Financial Economics** 1 (May 1974), pp. 1–22.

Blattberg, Robert C. and Nicholas J. Gonedes, "A Comparison of the Stable and Student Distributions as Statistical Models for Stock Prices," **Journal of Business** 47 (April 1974), pp. 244–280.

Blume, Marshall E., "Stock Returns and Dividend Yields: Some More Evidence," **Review of Economics and Statistics** 62 (November 1980), pp. 567–577.

Boehmer, Ekkehart, Jim Musumeci, and Annette B. Poulsen, "Event-Study Methodology Under Conditions of Event-Induced Variance," **Journal of Financial Economics** 30 (December 1991), pp. 253–272.

Bollerslev, Tim, "Generalized Autoregressive Conditional Heteroskedasticity," **Journal of Econometrics** 31 (1986), pp. 307–327.

Bollerslev, Tim, Robert F. Engle, and Jeffrey M. Wooldridge, "A Capital Asset Pricing Model With Time-Varying Covariances," **Journal of Political Economy** 96 (February 1988), pp. 116–131.

Breeden, Douglas T., "An Intertemporal Asset Pricing Model With Stochastic Consumption and Investment Opportunities," **Journal of Financial Economics** 7 (1979), pp. 265–296.

Breeden, Douglas T., Michael R. Gibbons, and Robert H. Litzenberger, "Empirical Tests of the Consumption-Oriented CAPM," **Journal of Finance** 44 (June 1989), pp. 231–262.

Brennan, Michael J., "Taxes, Market Valuation and Corporate Financial Policy," **National Tax Journal** 23 (December 1970), pp. 417–427.

Brennan, Michael J., Narasimhan Jegadeesh, and Bhaskaran Swaminathan, "Investment Analysis and the Adjustment of Stock Prices to Common Information," **Review of Financial Studies** 6 (1993), pp. 799–824.

Brinson, Gary P., L. Randolph Hood, and Gilbert L. Beebower, "Determinants of Portfolio Performance," **Financial Analysts Journal** 50 (July/August 1986), pp. 39–44.

Brown, Keith C., W. V. Harlow, and Seha M. Tinic, "Risk Aversion, Uncertain Information, and Market Efficiency," **Journal of Financial Economics** 22 (December 1988), pp. 355–385.

Brown, Stephen J. and Jerold B. Warner, "Measuring Security Price Performance," **Journal of Financial Economics** 8 (September 1980), pp. 205–258.

————"Using Daily Stock Returns in the Case of Event Studies," **Journal of Financial Economics** 14 (March 1985), pp. 205–258.

Brown, Stephen J. and Mark I. Weinstein, "A New Approach to Testing Asset Pricing Models: The Bilinear Paradigm," **Journal of Finance** 38 (June 1983), pp. 711–743.

Burmeister, Edwin and Marjorie B. McElroy, "Joint Estimation of Factor Sensitivities and Risk Premia for the Arbitrage Pricing Theory," **Journal of Finance** 43 (July 1988), pp. 721–733.

Campbell, John Y. and John Ammer, "What Moves the Stock and Bond Markets? A Variance Decomposition for Long-Term Asset Returns," **Journal of Finance** 48 (March 1993), pp. 3–37.

Campbell, John Y. and Jianping Mei, "Where do Betas Come From? Asset Price Dynamics and the Source of Systematic Risk," **Review of Financial Studies** 6 (1993), pp. 567–592.

Carroll, Carolyn and K. C. John Wei, "Risk, Return, and Equilibrium: An Extension," **Journal of Business** 61 (October 1988), pp. 485–499.

Chamberlain, Gary and Michael Rothschild, "Arbitrage, Factor Structure, and Mean-Variance Analysis of Large Asset Markets," **Econometrica** 51 (September 1983), pp. 1281–1323.

Chan, K. C., Nai-Fu Chen, and David A. Hsieh, "An Exploratory Investigation of the Firm Size Effect," **Journal of Financial Economics** 14 (September 1985), pp. 451–471.

Chen, Nai-Fu, "Some Empirical Tests of the Theory of Arbitrage Pricing," **Journal of Finance** 38 (December 1983), pp. 1393–1414.

Chen, Nai-Fu, Richard Roll, and Stephen A. Ross, "Economic Forces and the Stock Market," **Journal of Business** 59 (July 1986), pp. 383–403.

Coggin, T. Daniel, Frank J. Fabozzi, and Shafiqur Rahman, "The Investment Performance of U.S. Equity Pension Fund Managers: An Empirical Investigation," **Journal of Finance** 48 (July 1993), pp. 1039–1055.

Connolly, Robert A., "An Examination of the Robustness of the Weekend Effect," **Journal of Financial and Quantitative Analysis** 24 (June 1989), pp. 133–169.

Connor, Gregory and Robert A. Korajczyk, "Performance Measurement With the Arbitrage Pricing Theory: A New Framework for Analysis," **Journal of Financial Economics** 15 (January/February 1986), pp. 373–394.

Connor, Gregory and Robert A. Korajczyk, "Risk and Return in an Equilibrium APT: Applications of a New Test Methodology," **Journal of Financial Economics** 21 (September 1988), pp. 255–289.

————"A Test for the Number of Factors in an Approximate Factor Model," **Journal of Finance** 48 (September 1993), pp. 1263–1291.

Conrad, Jennifer and Gautam Kaul, "Time Variation in Expected Returns," **Journal of Business** 61 (October 1988), pp. 409–425.

————"Mean Reversion in Short-Horizon Expected Returns," **Review of Financial Studies** 2 (1989), pp. 225–240.

Conrad, Jennifer, Gautam Kaul, and M. Nimalendran, "Components of Short-Horizon Individual Security Returns," **Journal of Financial Economics** 29 (October 1991), pp. 365–384.

Constantinides, George M., "Capital Market Equilibrium With Personal Tax," **Econometrica** 51 (May 1983), pp. 611–636.

Copeland, Thomas E. and J. Fred Weston, **Financial Theory and Corporate Policy,** Third Edition (Addison-Wesley Publishing Company: Reading, Massachusetts, 1988).

Cornell, Bradford, "Asymmetric Information and Portfolio Performance Measurement," **Journal of Financial Economics** 7 (1979), pp. 381–390.

Corrado, Charles J., "A Nonparametric Test for Abnormal Security-Price Performance in Event Studies," **Journal of Financial Economics** 23 (August 1989), pp. 385–395.

Cox, Don R. and David R. Peterson, "Stock Returns Following Large One-Day Declines: Evidence on Short-Term Reversals and Longer-Term Performance," **Journal of Finance** 49 (March 1994), pp. 255–267.

Cumby, Robert E. and David M. Modest, "Testing for Market Timing Ability: A Framework for Market Forecast Evaluation," **Journal of Financial Economics** 19 (September 1987), pp. 169–189.

DeBondt, Werner and Richard Thaler, "Does the Stock Market Overreact?" **Journal of Finance** 40 (July 1985), pp. 793–805.

DeLong, Bradford, Andrei Shleifer, Lawrence H. Summers, and Robert J. Waldmann, "Positive Feedback Investment Strategies and Destabilizing Rational Speculation," **Journal of Finance** 45 (June 1990), pp. 379–395.

——— "The Survival of Noise Traders in Financial Markets," **Journal of Business** 64 (January 1991), pp. 1–19.

Dhillon, Upinder and Herb Johnson, "Changes in the Standard & Poor's List," **Journal of Business** 64 (January 1991), pp. 75–85.

Dhrymes, Phoebus J., Irwin Friend, and N. Bulent Gultekin, "A Critical Reexamination of the Empirical Evidence on the Arbitrage Pricing Theory," **Journal of Finance** 39 (June 1984), pp. 323–350.

Diamond, Douglas W. and Robert E. Verrechia, "Information Aggregation in Noisy Rational Expectations Economy," **Journal of Financial Economics** 9 (1981), pp. 221–235.

Dimson, Elroy, "Risk Measurement When Shares are Subject to Infrequent Trading," **Journal of Financial Economics** 7 (1979), pp. 197–226.

Dybvig, Philip H. and Jonathan E. Ingersoll, Jr., "Mean-Variance Theory in Complete Markets," **Journal of Business** 55 (1982), pp. 233–251.

Dybvig, Philip H. and Stephen A. Ross, "Yes, The APT is Testable," **Journal of Finance** 40 (September 1985), pp. 1173–1188.

Eckbo, B. Espen, Vojislav Maksimovic, and Joseph Williams, "Consistent Estimation of Cross-Sectional Models in Event Studies," **Review of Financial Studies** 3 (1990), pp. 345–365.

Ederington, Louis H. and Jae ha Lee, "How Markets Process Information: News Releases and Volatility," **Journal of Finance** 48 (September 1993), pp. 1161–1191.

Elton, Edwin J., Martin J. Gruber, Sanjiv Das, and Matthew Hlavka, "Efficiency With Costly Information: A Reinterpretation of Evidence From Managed Portfolios," **Review of Financial Studies** 6 (1993), pp. 1–22.

Engle, Robert E., "Autoregressive Conditional Heteroskedasticity With Estimates of the Variance of United Kingdom Inflation," **Econometrica** 50 (1982), pp. 987–1007.

Epstein, Larry G. and Stanley E. Zin, "Substitution, Risk Aversion, and the Temporal Behavior of Consumption and Asset Returns: An Empirical Analysis," **Journal of Political Economy** 99 (April 1991), pp. 263–286.

Fama, Eugene F., "The Behavior of Stock Market Prices," **Journal of Business** 38 (January 1965), pp. 34–105.

——— "Efficient Capital Markets: A Review of Theory and Empirical Work," **Journal of Finance** 25 (May 1970), pp. 383–417.

——— "Stock Returns, Expected Returns, and Real Activity," **Journal of Finance** 45 (September 1990), pp. 1089–1108.

—————— "Efficient Capital Markets: II," **Journal of Finance** 46 (December 1991), pp. 1575–1617.

Fama, Eugene F. and Marshall E. Blume, "Filter Rules and Stock-Market Trading," **Journal of Business** 39 (January 1966), pp. 226–241.

Fama, Eugene F., Lawrence Fisher, Michael C. Jensen, and Richard Roll, "The Adjustment of Stock Prices to New Information," **International Economic Review** 10 (February 1969), pp. 1–21.

Fama, Eugene F. and Kenneth R. French, "Dividend Yields and Expected Stock Returns," **Journal of Financial Economics** 22 (October 1988a), pp. 3–25.

—————— "Permanent and Temporary Components of Stock Prices," **Journal of Political Economy** 96 (April 1988b), pp. 246–273.

—————— "Business Conditions and Expected Returns on Stocks and Bonds," **Journal of Financial Economics** 25 (November 1989), pp. 23–49.

—————— "The Cross-Section of Expected Returns," **Journal of Finance** 47 (June 1992), pp. 427–465.

—————— "Common Risk Factors in the Returns on Stocks and Bonds," **Journal of Financial Economics** 33 (1993), pp. 3–56.

Fama, Eugene F. and James D. MacBeth, "Risk, Return, and Equilibrium: Empirical Tests," **Journal of Political Economy** 81 (May/June 1973), pp. 607–636.

Ferson, Wayne E. and George M. Constantinides, "Habit Persistence and Durability in Aggregate Consumption," **Journal of Financial Economics** 29 (October 1991), pp. 199–240.

Ferson, Wayne E. and Stephen R. Foerster, "Finite Sample Properties of the Generalized Method of Moments in Tests of Conditional Asset Pricing Models," **Journal of Financial Economics** 36 (August 1994), pp. 29–55.

Ferson, Wayne E. and Campbell R. Harvey, "The Risk and Predictability of International Equity Returns," **Review of Financial Studies** 6 (1993), pp. 527–566.

Ferson, Wayne E. and John J. Merrick, Jr., "Non-Stationarity and Stage-of-the-Business-Cycle Effects in Consumption-Based Asset Pricing Relations," **Journal of Financial Economics** 18 (March 1987), pp. 127–146.

French, Kenneth R. and Richard Roll, "Stock Return Variances: The Arrival of Information and the Reaction of Traders," **Journal of Financial Economics** 17 (September 1986), pp. 5–26.

French, Kenneth R., G. William Schwert, and Robert F. Stambaugh, "Expected Stock Returns and Volatility," **Journal of Financial Economics** 19 (September 1987), pp. 3–29.

Friedman, Milton and Leonard J. Savage, "The Utility Analysis of Choices Involving Risk," **Journal of Political Economy** 56 (August 1948), pp. 279–304.

Gibbons, Michael R., "Multivariate Tests of Financial Models: A New Approach," **Journal of Financial Economics** 10 (1982), pp. 3–27.

Gibbons, Michael R. and Wayne Ferson, "Testing Asset Pricing Models With Changing Expectations and an Unobservable Market Portfolio," **Journal of Financial Economics** 14 (June 1985), pp. 217–236.

Gibbons, Michael R. and Patrick Hess, "Day of the Week Effects and Asset Returns," **Journal of Business** 54 (October 1981), pp. 579–596.

Gibbons and Murphy, *Journal of Political Economy* 100 (June 1992), pp 468–505.

Gilles, Christian and Stephen F. LeRoy, "Econometric Aspects of the Variance-Bounds Tests: A Survey," **Review of Financial Studies** 4 (1991), pp. 753–791.

Giovannini, Alberto and Philippe Jorion, "The Time Variation of Risk and Return in the Foreign Exchange and Stock Markets," **Journal of Finance** 44 (June 1989), pp. 307–325.

Gitman, Lawrence J., **Principles of Managerial Finance,** Seventh Edition (HarperCollins: New York, 1994).

Glen, Jack and Philippe Jorion, "Currency Hedging for International Portfolios," **Journal of Finance** 48 (December 1993), pp. 1865–1886.

Glosten, Lawrence R., Ravi Jagannathan, and David E. Runkle, "On the Relation Between the Expected Value and the Volatility of the Nominal Excess Return on Stocks," **Journal of Finance** 48 (December 1993), pp. 1779–1801.

Goetzmann, William N. and Roger G. Ibbotson, "Do Winners Repeat?," **Journal of Portfolio Management** 20 (Winter 1994), pp. 9–18.

Goetzmann, William N. and Philippe Jorion, "Testing the Predictive Power of Dividend Yields," **Journal of Finance** 48 (June 1993), pp. 663–679.

Grinblatt, Mark and Sheridan Titman, "Factor Pricing in a Finite Economy," **Journal of Financial Economics** 12 (December 1983), pp. 497–507.

——— "Mutual Fund Performance: An Analysis of Quarterly Portfolio Holdings," **Journal of Business** 62 (July 1989), pp. 393–416.

Grossman, Sanford J. and Robert J. Shiller, "The Determinants of the Variability of Stock Market Prices," **American Economic Review** 71 (May 1981), pp. 222–227.

Grossman, Sanford J. and Joseph E. Stiglitz, "On the Impossibility of Informationally Efficient Markets," **American Economic Review** 70 (June 1980), pp. 393–408.

Hamada, Robert S., "The Effects of the Firm's Capital Structure on the Systematic Risk of Common Stock," **Journal of Finance** 27 (May 1972), pp. 435–452.

Handa, Puneet, S. P. Kothari, and Charles Wasley, "The Relation Between the Return Interval and Betas: Implications for the Size Effect," **Journal of Financial Economics** 23 (June 1989), pp. 79–100.

Hansen, Lars Peter, "Large Sample Properties of Generalized Method of Moments Estimators," **Econometrica** 50 (July 1982), pp. 1029–1054.

Hansen, Lars Peter and Ravi Jagannathan, "Implications of Security Market Data for Models of Dynamic Economies," **Journal of Political Economy** 99 (April 1991), pp. 225–261.

Hansen, Lars Peter and Kenneth J. Singleton, "Generalized Instrumental Variables Estimation of Nonlinear Rational Expectations Models," **Econometrica** 50 (September 1982), pp. 1269–1286.

——— "Stochastic Consumption, Risk Aversion, and the Temporal Behavior of Asset Returns," **Journal of Political Economy** 91 (1983), pp. 249–265.

Harris, Lawrence, "A Transaction Data Study of Weekly and Intradaily Patterns in Stock Returns," **Journal of Financial Economics** 16 (May 1986), pp. 99–117.

Harris, Lawrence and Eitan Gurel, "Price and Volume Effects Associated With Changes in the S&P 500 List: New Evidence for the Existence of Price Pressures," **Journal of Finance** 41 (September 1984), pp. 815–830.

Hartzmark, Michael L., "Luck Versus Forecast Ability: Determinants of Trader Performance in Futures Markets," **Journal of Business** 64 (January 1991), pp. 49–74.

Harvey, Campbell R., "Time-Varying Conditional Covariances in Tests of Asset Pricing Models," **Journal of Financial Economics** 24 (October 1989), pp 289–317.

——— "The World Price of Covariance Risk," **Journal of Finance** 46 (March 1991), pp. 111–157.

Haugen, Robert A., "The New Finance: The Case *Against* Efficient Markets," unpublished working paper (University of California: Irvine, September 1993).

Hendricks, Darryll, Jayendu Patel, and Richard Zeckhauser, "Hot Hands in Mutual Funds: Short-Run Persistence of Relative Performance, 1974–1988," **Journal of Finance** 48 (March 1993), pp. 93–130.

Heston, Steven L. and K. Geert Rouwenhorst, "Does Industrial Structure Explain the Benefits of International Diversification?," **Journal of Financial Economics** 36 (August 1994), pp. 3–24.

Holloway, Clark, "A Note on Testing an Aggressive Investment Strategy Using Value Line Ranks," **Journal of Finance** 36 (June 1981), pp. 711–719.

Huberman, Gur, "A Simple Approach to Arbitrage Pricing Theory," **Journal of Economic Theory** 28 (1982), pp. 183–191.

Huberman, Gur and Shmuel Kandel, "Market Efficiency and Value Line Record," **Journal of Business** 63 (April 1990), pp. 187–216.

Huberman, Gur, Shmuel Kandel, and Robert F. Stambaugh, "Mimicking Portfolios and Exact Arbitrage Pricing," **Journal of Finance** 42 (March 1987), pp. 1–9.

Ippolito, Richard A., "Efficiency With Costly Information: A Study of Mutual Fund Performance, 1965–1984," **Quarterly Journal of Economics** 104 (February 1989), pp. 1–23.

——— "On Studies of Mutual Fund Performance, 1962–1991," **Financial Analysts Journal** 49 (January-February 1993), pp. 42–49.

Jaffe, Jeffrey F., "Special Information and Insider Trading," **Journal of Business** 47 (1974), pp. 410–428.

Jagannathan, Ravi and Robert A. Korajczyk, "Assessing the Market Impact of Managed Portfolios," **Journal of Business** 59 (April 1986), pp. 217–235.

Jegadeesh, Narasimhan, "Evidence of the Predictable Behavior of Security Returns," **Journal of Finance** 45 (July 1990), pp. 881–898.

Jegadeesh, Narasimhan and Sheridan Titman, "Returns to Buying Winners and Selling Losers: Implications for Stock Market Efficiency," **Journal of Finance** 48 (March 1993), pp. 65–91.

Jensen, Michael C., "The Performance of Mutual Funds in the Period 1945–1964," **Journal of Finance** 23 (May 1968), pp. 389–416.

——— "Some Anomalous Evidence Regarding Market Efficiency," **Journal of Financial Economics** 6 (June-September 1978), pp. 95–101.

Jensen, Michael C. and Richard S. Ruback, "The Market for Corporate Control: The Scientific Evidence," **Journal of Financial Economics** 11 (April 1983), pp. 5–50.

Jensen, Michael C. and Jerold B. Warner, "The Distribution of Power Among Corporate Managers, Shareholders, and Directors," **Journal of Financial Economics** 20 (January/March 1988), pp. 3–24.

Jobson, J. D. and Bob Korkie, "Potential Performance and Tests of Portfolio Efficiency," **Journal of Financial Economics** 10 (December 1982), pp. 433–466.

Jones, Charles M., Gautam Kaul, and Marc Lipson, "Information, Trading, and Volatility," **Journal of Financial Economics** 36 (August 1994), pp. 127–154.

Jones, Steven L., "Another Look at Time-Varying Risk and Return in a Long-Horizon Contrarian Strategy," **Journal of Financial Economics** 33 (1993), pp. 119–144.

Jorion, Philippe and Eduardo Schwartz, "Integration vs. Segmentation in the Canadian Stock Market," **Journal of Finance** 41 (July 1986), pp. 603–614.

Kandel, Shmuel and Robert F. Stambaugh, "On Correlation and Inferences About Mean-Variance Efficiency," **Journal of Financial Economics** 18 (March 1987), pp. 61–90.

———— "A Mean-Variance Framework for Tests of Asset Pricing Models," **Review of Financial Studies** 2 (1989), pp. 125–156.

Keim, Donald B., "Size-Related Anomalies and Stock Return Seasonality: Further Empirical Evidence," **Journal of Financial Economics** 12 (June 1983), pp. 13–32.

———— "The CAPM and Equity Return Regularities," **Financial Analysts Journal** 42 (May/June 1986), pp. 19–34.

Keim, Donald B. and Robert F. Stambaugh, "Predicting Returns in the Stock and Bond Markets," **Journal of Financial Economics** 17 (December 1986), pp. 357–390.

Kendall, Maurice G., "The Analysis of Economic Time Series," **Journal of the Royal Statistical Society,** Series A, Vol. 96 (1953), pp. 11–25.

King, Benjamin, "Market and Industry Factors in Stock Price Behavior," **Journal of Business** 39 (January 1966), pp. 139–190.

Kleidon, Allan W., "Variance Bounds Tests and Stock Price Valuation Models," **Journal of Political Economy** 94 (October 1986), pp. 953–1001.

Kon, Stanley J., "Models of Stock Returns—A Comparison," **Journal of Finance** 39 (March 1984), pp. 147–165.

Kothari, S. P. and Jay Shanken, "Stock Return Variation and Expected Dividends," **Journal of Financial Economics** 31 (April 1992), pp. 177–210.

———— "Fundamentals Largely Explain Stock Price Volatility," **Journal of Applied Corporate Finance** 6 (Summer 1993), pp. 81–87.

Lai, Tsong-Yue, "An Equilibrium Model of Asset Pricing With Progressive Personal Taxes," **Journal of Financial and Quantitative Analysis** 24 (March 1989), pp. 117–127.

Lamoureux, Christopher G. and William D. Lastrapes, "Heteroskedasticity in Stock Returns Data: Volume versus GARCH Effects," **Journal of Finance** 45 (March 1990), pp. 221–229.

LeBaron, Blake, "Some Relations Between Volatility and Serial Correlations in Stock Market Returns," **Journal of Business** 65 (April 1992), pp. 199–219.

Lee, Cheng-Few and Shafiqur Rahman, "Market Timing, Selectivity, and Mutual Fund Performance: An Empirical Analysis," **Journal of Business** 63 (April 1990), pp. 261–278.

Lehmann, Bruce N. and David M. Modest, "The Empirical Foundations of the Arbitrage Pricing Theory," **Journal of Financial Economics** 21 (September 1988), pp. 213–254.

Lewis, Karen K., "The Behavior of Eurocurrency Returns Across Different Holding Periods and Monetary Regimes," **Journal of Finance** 45 (September 1990), pp. 1211–1236.

Lintner, John, "The Valuation of Risk Assets and the Selection of Risky Investments in Stock Portfolios and Capital Budgets," **Review of Economics and Statistics** 47 (February 1965), pp. 13–37.

Litzenberger, Robert H. and Krishna Ramaswamy, "The Effect of Personal Taxes and Dividends on Capital Asset Prices: Theory and Empirical Evidence," **Journal of Financial Economics** 7 (June 1979) pp. 163–195.

Litzenberger, Robert H. and Krishna Ramaswamy, "The Effects of Dividends on Common Stock Prices: Tax Effects or Information Effects?," **Journal of Finance** 37 (May 1982), pp. 429–443.

Lo, Andrew W. and A. Craig MacKinlay, "Stock Market Prices do not Follow Random Walks: Evidence From a Simple Specification Test," **Review of Financial Studies** 1 (Spring 1988), pp. 41–66.

———— "Data-Snooping Biases in Tests of Financial Asset Pricing Models," **Review of Financial Studies** 3 (1990a), pp. 431–467.

———— "When are Contrarian Profits Due to Stock Market Overreaction?," **Review of Financial Studies** 3 (1990b), pp. 175–205.

MacKinlay, A. Craig, "On Multivariate Tests of the CAPM," **Journal of Financial Economics** 18 (June 1987), pp. 341–371.

Maloney, Kevin J. and Richard J. Rogalski, "Call-Option Pricing and the Turn of the Year," **Journal of Business** 62 (October 1989), pp. 539–552.

Mankiw, N. Gregory and Stephen P. Zeldes, "The Consumption of Stockholders and Nonstockholders," **Journal of Financial Economics** 29 (March 1991), pp. 97–112.

Mark, Nelson C., "Time-Varying Betas and Risk Premia in the Pricing of Forward Foreign Exchange Contracts," **Journal of Financial Economics** 22 (December 1988), pp. 335–354.

Markowitz, Harry, "Portfolio Selection," **Journal of Finance** 7 (March 1952), pp. 77–91.

Mayers, David, "Non-Marketable Assets and the Determination of Capital Market Equilibrium Under Uncertainty," in Michael Jensen, ed., **Studies in the Theory of Capital Markets** (Praeger: New York, 1972).

Mayers, David and Edward M. Rice, "Measuring Portfolio Performance and the Empirical Content of Asset Pricing Models," **Journal of Financial Economics** 7 (March 1979), pp. 3–28.

McQueen, Grant, "Long-Horizon Mean-Reverting Stock Prices Revisited," **Journal of Financial and Quantitative Analysis** 27 (March 1992), pp. 1–18.

Mehra, Rajnish and Edward Prescott, "The Equity Premium: A Puzzle," **Journal of Monetary Economics** 15 (1985), pp. 145–161.

Mei, Jianping, "A Semiautoregression Approach to the Arbitrage Pricing Theory," **Journal of Finance** 48 (June 1993a), pp. 599–620.

——— "Explaining the Cross-Section of Returns via a Multi-Factor APT Model," **Journal of Financial and Quantitative Analysis** 28 (September 1993b), pp. 331–345.

Merton, Robert C., "An Intertemporal Capital Asset Pricing Model," **Econometrica** 41 (September 1973), pp. 867–887.

——— "On the Current State of the Stock Market Rationality Hypothesis," in Rudiger Dornbusch, Stanley Fischer, and John Bossons, eds., **Macroeconomics and Finance: Essays in Honor of Franco Modigliani** (MIT Press: Cambridge, MA, 1987), pp. 93–124.

Miller, Merton H. and Myron Scholes, "Dividends and Taxes: Some Empirical Tests," **Journal of Political Economy** 90 (December 1982), pp. 1118–1141.

Mossin, Jan, "Equilibrium in a Capital Asset Market," **Econometrica** 24 (October 1966), pp. 768–783.

Muller, Frederick L., "Equity Securities Analysis in the U.S.," **Financial Analysts Journal** 50 (January-February 1994), pp. 6–9.

Nelson, Charles R. and Myung J. Kim, "Predictable Stock Returns: The Role of Small Sample Bias," **Journal of Finance** 48 (June 1993), pp. 641–661.

Pfleiderer, Paul, "A Short Note on the Similarities and the Differences Between the Capital Asset Pricing Model (CAPM) and the Arbitrage Pricing Theory (APT)," unpublished working paper (Stanford University: Palo Alto, CA, November 1983).

Poterba, James M. and Lawrence H. Summers, "Mean Reversion in Stock Prices: Evidence and Implications," **Journal of Financial Economics** 22 (October 1988), pp. 27–59.

Pound, John and Richard Zeckhauser, "Clearly Heard on the Street: The Effects of Takeover Rumors on Stock Prices," **Journal of Business** 63 (July 1990), pp. 291–308.

Reichenstein, William and Steven P. Rich, "Predicting Long-Horizon Stock Returns: Evidence and Implications," **Financial Analysts Journal** 50 (January-February 1994), pp. 73–76.

Reinganum, Marc R., "The Arbitrage Pricing Theory: Some Empirical Results," **Journal of Finance** 36 (May 1981a), pp. 313–321.

———— "Misspecification of Capital Asset Pricing: Empirical Anomalies Based on Earnings' Yields and Market Values," **Journal of Financial Economics** 9 (March 1981b), pp. 19–46.

Reisman, Haim, "Reference Variables, Factor Structure, and the Approximate Multibeta Representation," **Journal of Finance** 47 (September 1992a), pp. 1303–1314.

———— "Intertemporal Arbitrage Pricing Theory," **Review of Financial Studies** 5 (1992b), pp. 105–122.

Restoy, Fernando and G. Michael Rockinger, "On Stock Market Returns and Returns on Investment," **Journal of Finance** 49 (June 1994), pp. 543–556.

Richardson, Matthew and Tom Smith, "A Unified Approach to Testing for Serial Correlation in Stock Returns," **Journal of Business** 67 (July 1994), pp. 371–399.

Ritter, Jay and Navin Chopra, "Portfolio Rebalancing and the Turn-of-the-Year Effect," **Journal of Finance** 44 (March 1989), pp. 149–16.

Roberts, Harry V., "Stock Market "Patterns" and Financial Analysis: Methodological Suggestions," **Journal of Finance** 14 (March 1959), pp. 1–10.

Roll, Richard, "A Critique of the Asset Pricing Theory's Tests; Part I: On Past and Potential Testability of the Theory," **Journal of Financial Economics** 4 (1977), pp. 129–176.

———— "Measuring Portfolio Performance and the Empirical Content of Asset Pricing Models: A Reply," **Journal of Financial Economics** 7 (1979), pp. 391–400.

———— "R-Squared," **Journal of Finance** 43 (July 1988), pp. 541–566.

———— "Industrial Structure and the Comparative Behavior of International Stock Market Indices," **Journal of Finance** 47 (March 1992), pp. 3–41.

———— "What Every CEO Should Know About Scientific Progress in Economics: What is Known and What Remains to be Resolved," **Financial Management** 23 (Summer 1994), pp. 69–75.

Roll, Richard and Stephen A. Ross, "An Empirical Investigation of the Arbitrage Pricing Theory," **Journal of Finance** 35 (December 1980), pp. 1073–1103.

———— "On the Cross-Sectional Relation Between Expected Returns and Betas," **Journal of Finance** 49 (March 1994), pp. 101–121.

Ross, Stephen A., "The Arbitrage Theory of Capital Asset Pricing," **Journal of Economic Theory** (December 1976), pp. 341–360.

———— "Risk, Return, and Arbitrage," in Irwin Friend and James L. Bicksler, eds., **Risk and Return in Finance** I (Ballinger: Cambridge, MA, 1977), pp. 189–218.

Rubinstein, Mark E., "A Mean-Variance Synthesis of Corporate Financial Policy," **Journal of Finance** 28 (March 1973), pp. 165–167.

Salinger, Michael, "Standard Errors in Event Studies," **Journal of Financial and Quantitative Analysis** 27 (March 1992), pp. 39–53.

Samuelson, Paul A., "Proof That Properly Anticipated Prices Fluctuate Randomly," **Industrial Management Review** 6 (Spring 1965), pp. 41–49.

Schlarbaum, Gary G., Wilbur G. Lewellen, and Ronald C. Lease, "The Common-Stock-Portfolio Performance Record of Individual Investors: 1964–1970," **Journal of Finance** 33 (May 1978), pp. 429–441.

Scholes, Myron and Joseph T. Williams, "Estimating Betas From Nonsynchronous Data," **Journal of Financial Economics** 5 (December 1977), pp. 155–183.

Schoemaker, Paul J. H., "The Expected Utility Model: Its Variants, Purposes, Evidence and Limitations," **Journal of Economic Literature** 20 (June 1982), pp. 529–563.

Schwert, G. William, "Size and Stock Returns, and Other Empirical Regularities," **Journal of Financial Economies** 12 (June 1983), pp. 3–12.

——— "Stock Returns and Real Activity: A Century of Evidence," **Journal of Finance** 45 (September 1990), pp. 1237–1257.

Schwert, G. William and Paul J. Seguin, "Heteroskedasticity in Stock Returns," **Journal of Finance** 45 (September 1990), pp. 1129–1155.

Seyhun, H. Nejat, "Insiders' Profits, Cost of Trading, and Market Efficiency," **Journal of Financial Economics** 16 (June 1986), pp. 189–212.

Shanken, Jay, "The Arbitrage Pricing Theory: Is it Testable?," **Journal of Finance** 37 (December 1982), pp. 1129–1140.

——— "Multi-Beta CAPM or Equilibrium-APT?: A Reply," **Journal of Finance** 40 (September 1985a), pp. 1189–1196.

——— "Multivariate Tests of the Zero-Beta CAPM," **Journal of Financial Economics** 14 (September 1985b), pp. 327–348.

——— "Multivariate Proxies and Asset Pricing Relations: Living With the Roll Critique," **Journal of Financial Economics** 18 (March 1987), pp. 91–110.

——— "The Current State of the Arbitrage Pricing Theory," **Journal of Finance** 47 (September 1992a), pp. 1569–1574.

——— "On the Estimation of Beta-Pricing Models," **Review of Financial Studies** 5 (1992b), pp. 1–33.

Shapiro, Alan C., **Multinational Financial Management,** Fourth Edition (Allyn and Bacon: Needham Heights, MA, 1992).

Sharpe, William F., "Capital Asset Prices: A Theory of Market Equilibrium Under Conditions of Risk," **Journal of Finance** 19 (September 1964), pp. 425–442.

——— "Mutual Fund Performance," **Journal of Business** 39 (January 1966), pp. 119–138.

——— "The Capital Asset Pricing Model: A 'Multi-Beta' Interpretation," in Haim Levy and Marshall Sarnat, eds., **Financial Decision Making Under Uncertainty** (Academic Press: New York, 1977).

Shefrin, Hersh and Meir Statman, "Ethics, Fairness and Efficiency in Financial Markets," **Financial Analysts Journal** 49 (November-December 1993), pp. 21–29.

Shiller, Robert J., "The Volatility of Long-Term Interest Rates and Expectations Models of the Term Structure," **Journal of Political Economy** 87 (December 1979), pp. 1190–1219.

——— "Do Stock Prices Move Too Much to be Justified by Subsequent Changes in Dividends?" **American Economic Review** 71 (June 1981), pp. 421–436.

Shleifer, Andrei, "Do Demand Curves for Stocks Slope Down?," **Journal of Finance** 41 (July 1986), pp. 579–590.

Shleifer, Andrei and Lawrence H. Summers, "The Noise Trader Approach to Finance," **Journal of Economic Perspectives** 4 (Spring 1990), pp. 19–33.

Shukla, Ravi and Charles Trzcinka, "Sequential Tests of the Arbitrage Pricing Theory: A Comparison of Principal Components and Maximum Likelihood Factors," **Journal of Finance** 45 (December 1990), pp. 1541–1564.

Siegel, Jeremy J., "The Equity Premium: Stock and Bond Returns Since 1802," **Financial Analysts Journal** 48 (January-February 1992), pp. 28–38.

Skinner, Douglas J., "Options and Stock Return Volatility," **Journal of Financial Economics** 23 (June 1989), pp. 61–78.

Smirlock, Michael and Laura Starks, "Day-of-the-Week and Intraday Effects in Stock Returns," **Journal of Financial Economics** 17 (September 1986), pp. 197–210.

Smith, Clifford W., Jr., "Investment Banking and the Capital Acquisition Process," **Journal of Financial Economics** 15 (January/February 1986), pp. 3–29.

Stambaugh, Robert F., "On the Exclusion of Assets From Tests of the Two-Parameter Model: A Sensitivity Analysis," **Journal of Financial Economics** 10 (November 1982), pp. 237–268.

Stiglitz, Joseph E., "Pareto Optimality and Competition," **Journal of Finance** 36 (May 1981), pp. 235–251.

Stulz, René M., "A Model of International Asset Pricing," **Journal of Financial Economics** 9 (1981), pp. 383–406.

Summers, Lawrence, "Does the Stock Market Rationally Reflect Fundamental Values?," **Journal of Finance** 41 (July 1986), pp. 591–601.

Tinic, Seha M. and Richard R. West, "Risk and Return: January Versus the Rest of the Year," **Journal of Financial Economics** 13 (December 1984), pp. 561–574.

———— "Risk, Return, and Equilibrium: A Revisit," **Journal of Political Economy** 94 (1986), pp. 126–147.

Tobin, James, "Liquidity Preference as a Behavior Toward Risk," **Review of Economic Studies** 25 (February 1958), pp. 65–86.

Verrechia, Robert E., "The Mayers-Rice Conjecture: A Counterexample," **Journal of Financial Economics** 8 (1980), pp. 87–100.

Wheatley, Simon, M., "Some Tests of International Equity Integration," **Journal of Financial Economics** 21 (September 1988), pp. 177–212.

Wheatley, Simon M., "A Critique of Latent Variable Tests of Asset Pricing Models," **Journal of Financial Economics** 23 (August 1989), pp. 325–338.

Williams, Joseph T., "Capital Asset Prices With Heterogeneous Beliefs," **Journal of Financial Economics** 5 (November 1977), pp. 219–239.

Zhou, Guofu, "Asset-Pricing Tests Under Alternative Distributions," **Journal of Finance** 48 (December 1993), pp. 1927–1942.

CHAPTER
4

Bond and Stock Valuation

4.1 INTRODUCTION

In the popular imagination, "finance" is closely associated with markets for stocks, bonds, and other securities. Americans in particular grow up with daily references to closing levels of the Dow Jones Industrial Average, and most come to understand that this number can have a profound—if often indirect—influence on their personal and professional lives. As more and more countries adopt market-oriented economic policies, the number of people whose lives will be touched by security market valuations will reach into the billions. However, relatively few people understand exactly how security prices are determined, or how fluctuations in market interest rates impact valuations on virtually all debt, equity, and derivative instruments. Fortunately, this lack of understanding can be readily addressed, because security valuation is in essence a simple process. Regardless of the security in question, valuation always involves determining the present value of a stream of cash flows that are expected to accrue to the holder of the security over its life using an appropriate, risk-adjusted discount rate that is related to the economy's riskless rate of interest.

Our primary objective in this chapter is to describe the most important theoretical models commonly used to value bonds, stocks, and options, and then to discuss the empirical research that has been presented to date in support of (or contradictory to) each model. We begin with the simplest discounted cash flow model of bond pricing, and then move on to more advanced valuation issues such as the term structure of interest rates, duration and immunization, liquidity and tax effects in bond valuation, and the valuation of floating rate and mortgage-backed debt instruments. In a similar vein, our discussion of stock valuation begins with the simplest DCF pricing models before progressing into a description of more advanced earnings-based stock pricing models and a discussion of the empirical research relating to the impact of inflation, liquidity, and personal taxes on equity values. Our stock valuation section concludes with an overview of the increasingly important issue of market microstructure.

4.2   VALUATION FUNDAMENTALS

The value of any asset is the present value of all its future cash flows. For bonds, this is the present value of promised interest and principal payments over the life of the security. In the particular case of common stock, value can be computed as the present value of all future earnings available to common stockholders, or as the discounted value of all future cash dividends that will be paid out to stockholders. Valuation is also the process that links risk and return to determine the worth of an asset. The key inputs to the valuation process include cash flows (returns), timing, and the required return (risk).

The value of any asset depends on the cash flow(s) it is expected to provide over the ownership period. To have value, an asset does not have to provide an annual cash flow; it can provide an intermittent cash flow or even a single cash flow over the period. We will limit our analysis in this chapter to the valuation of debt and equity securities, though the same basic process can be applied to the valuation of real estate, copyrights and patents, employment contracts, franchises, or even art collections. All that is required is that one be able to estimate the magnitude, timing, and riskiness of cash flows that will accrue to the owner of an asset over its economic life.

4.2.1 Required Return (Risk)

For a single asset, risk describes the chance that an expected outcome will not be realized. In general, the greater the risk of (or the less certain) a cash flow, the lower its value. In terms of present value, greater risk can be incorporated into an analysis by using a higher required return or discount rate. Recall that in the capital asset pricing model (CAPM) presented in chapter 3, the greater the risk of an asset as measured by beta, β, the higher the required return, k. In the valuation process, too, the required return is used to incorporate risk into the analysis. The higher the risk, the greater the required return (discount rate), and the lower the risk, the less the required return.

4.2.2 The Basic Valuation Model

Simply stated, the value of any asset is the present value of all future cash flows it is expected to provide over its economic life.[1] The value of an asset is therefore determined by discounting the expected cash flows back to their present value, using the required return commensurate with the asset's risk as the appropriate discount rate.

---

1. While it might at first seem that an individual investor's desired holding period should influence the valuation model, this is not the case. Even if you are planning to hold, say, a share of stock for only one year, and are thus only interested in projecting the market value of the share in twelve months, this does not finesse the long-term valuation problem. The reason, of course, is that the market value of that stock in one year will be the discounted value of all its future cash flows.

Utilizing basic present-value techniques, we can express the value of any asset at time zero, V_0, as

$$V_0 = \frac{CF_1}{(1+k)^1} + \frac{CF_2}{(1+k)^2} + \ldots + \frac{CF_n}{(1+k)^n} \qquad (4.1)$$

where V_0 = value of the asset at time zero

      CF_t = cash flow expected at the end of year t

      k = appropriate required return (discount rate)

      n = relevant time period[2]

Using present-value interest factor notation, $PVIF_{k,n}$ from Table A.3, Equation 4.1 can be rewritten as:

$$V_0 = [CF_1 \times (PVIF_{k,1})] + [CF_2 \times (PVIF_{k,2})] + \ldots + [CF_n \times (PVIF_{k,n})] \quad (4.2)$$

Substituting the expected cash flows, CF_t, over the relevant time period, n, and the appropriate required return, k, into Equation 4.2, we can determine the value of any asset.

4.3 BOND VALUATION

The basic valuation equation can be customized for use in valuing specified securities—bonds, preferred stock, and common stock. Bonds and preferred stock are similar, since they have stated contractual interest and dividend cash flows. Bonds provide their holders with fixed, contractual cash flows at prespecified points in time, while preferred stocks provide fixed, but not contractual, cash flows to their holders at set times. The dividends on common stock, on the other hand, are not known in advance. Bond valuation is described in this section, while common and preferred stock valuation is discussed in the following section.

4.3.1 Bond Fundamentals

Bonds are long-term debt instruments used by business and government to raise large sums of money, typically from a diverse group of lenders. Most corporate bonds pay interest semiannually (every six months) at a stated coupon interest rate, have an initial maturity of 10 to 30 years, and have a **par value** (also called face or principal value) of $1,000 that must be repaid at maturity. An example will illustrate the point. The Mars Company, a large aerospace company, on January 1, 1997, issues a 10 percent coupon interest rate, 10-year bond with a $1,000 par value that pays interest semiannually. Investors who buy this bond receive the contractual right to (1) $100 annual interest (10 percent coupon interest rate x $1,000 par value) distributed as $50 (1/2 x $100) at the end of each six months and (2) the $1,000 par value at the end of the tenth year. Using data presented for Mars Company's new issue, we look now at basic bond valuation and other issues.

---

2. The stock and bond valuation formulas used in this chapter are derived (with permission) from those used in chapter 7 of Gitman (1994).

4.3.2 Basic Bond Valuation

The value of a bond is the present value of the contractual payments its issuer is obligated to make from the current time until it matures. The appropriate discount rate would be the required return, k_d, which depends on prevailing interest rates and risk. The basic equation for the value, B_0, of a bond that pays annual interest of I dollars, that has n years to maturity, that has an M dollar par value, and for which the required return is k_d is given by Equation 4.3:

$$B_0 = I \times \left[\sum_{t=1}^{n} \frac{1}{(1+k_d)^t} \right] + M \times \left[\frac{1}{(1+k_d)^n} \right] \tag{4.3}$$

$$= I \times (\text{PVIFA}_{k_d,n}) + M \times (\text{PVIF}_{k_d,n}) \tag{4.3a}$$

Equation 4.3a along with the appropriate financial tables (A.3 and A.4) can be used to calculate bond value. Using the Mars Company data for the January 1, 1997, new issue and assuming that interest is paid annually and that the required return is equal to the bond's coupon interest rate $(I = \$100, k_d = 10$ percent, $M = \$1,000,$ and $n = 10$ years), the bond's value is computed as follows:

$$B_0 = \$100 \times (\text{PVIFA}_{10\%,10\text{yrs}}) + \$1,000 \times (\text{PVIF}_{10\%,10\text{yrs}})$$

$$= \$100 \times (6.145) + \$1,000 \times (0.386)$$

$$= \$614.50 + \$386.00 = \$1,000.50$$

The bond therefore has a value of approximately $1,000.

4.3.3 Bond Value Behavior

The value of a bond in the marketplace is rarely constant over its life. A variety of forces in the economy as well as the mere passage of time tend to affect value. Whenever the required return on a bond differs from the bond's coupon interest rate, the bond's value will differ from its par, or face, value. The required return on the bond is likely to differ from the coupon interest rate because either (1) economic conditions have changed, causing a shift in the basic cost of long-term funds, or (2) the firm's risk has changed. Increases in the basic cost of long-term funds or in risk will raise the required return, and decreases in the basic cost or risk will lower the required return.[3]

Regardless of the exact cause, the important point is that when the required return is greater than the coupon interest rate, the bond value, B_0, will be less than its par value, M. In this case the bond is said to sell at a **discount**, which will equal $(M - B_0)$. On the other hand, when the required rate of return falls below the coupon interest rate, the bond value will be greater than par. In this situation the bond is said to sell at a **premium**, which will equal $(B_0 - M)$. An example will illustrate this point using Equation 4.3a along with financial tables. In the preceding example we saw that when the required return equaled the coupon interest rate, the bond's value equaled its $1,000 par

---

3. In addition to the overall demand for credit in an economy, probably the most important determinants of the overall level of interest rates are the policy objectives of the central bank. The real and perceived interest rate targets of the Federal Reserve clearly seem to have a massive impact on American bond markets, and thus indirectly on debt markets around the world.

value. If for the same bond the required return were to rise to 12 percent, its value would be found as follows:

$$B_0 = \$100 \times (\text{PVIFA}_{12\%, 10\text{yrs}}) + \$1,000 \times (\text{PVIF}_{12\%, 10\text{yrs}})$$

$$= \$100 \times (5.650) + \$1,000 \times (0.322) = \$887.00$$

The bond would therefore sell at a discount of $113.00 ($1,000 par value − $887.00 market value). If, on the other hand, the required return fell to, say, 8 percent, the bond's value would be found as follows:

$$B_0 = \$100 \times (\text{PVIFA}_{8\%, 10\text{yrs}}) + \$1,000 \times (\text{PVIF}_{8\%, 10\text{yrs}})$$

$$= \$100 \times (6.710) + \$1,000 \times (.463) = \$1,134.00$$

The bond would therefore sell for a premium of about $134 ($1,134.00 value − $1,000 par value). The results of this and earlier calculations for the Mars Company's bond values are graphically depicted in Figure 4.1.

4.3.4 Time to Maturity and Bond Values

Whenever the required return is different from the coupon interest rate, the amount of time to maturity affects bond value, even if the required return remains constant until maturity. Two important relationships exist among time to maturity, required return, and bond value. They are concerned with constant required returns and changing required returns. When the required return is different from the coupon interest rate and is assumed to be constant until maturity, the value of the bond will approach its par value as the passage of time moves the bond's value closer to maturity. Of course, when the required return equals the coupon interest rate, the bond's value will remain at par until it matures.

Figure 4.2 depicts the behavior of the bond values calculated earlier for Mars Company's 10 percent coupon interest rate bond paying annual interest and having 10 years to maturity. Each of the three required returns—12 percent, 10 percent, and 8 percent—is assumed to remain constant over the 10 years to the bond's maturity. The bond's value in each case approaches and ultimately equals the bond's $1,000 par value at its maturity. At the 12 percent required return, the bond's discount declines with the passage of time as the bond's value increases from $887 to $1,000. When the 10 percent required return equals the bond's coupon interest rate, its value remains unchanged at $1,000 over its maturity. Finally, at the 8 percent required return, the bond's premium will decline as its value drops from $1,134 to $1,000 at maturity. With the required return assumed to be constant to maturity, the bond's value approaches its $1,000 par or maturity value as the time to maturity declines.

CHANGING REQUIRED RETURNS   The shorter the amount of time until a bond's maturity, the less responsive is its market value to a given change in the required return. In other words, short maturities have less **interest rate risk** than do long maturities when all other features—coupon interest rate, par value, and interest payment frequency—are the same. The effect of changing required returns on bonds of differing maturity can be illustrated by using Mars Company's bond and Figure 4.2. If, as denoted by the dashed line at eight years to maturity, the required return declines from 10 to 8 percent, the bond's value rises from $1,000 to $1,114.70—an 11.47 per-

FIGURE 4.1

Bond value and required return (Mars Company's 10 percent coupon interest rate, 10-year maturity, $1,000 par, January 1, 1997, issue paying annual interest)

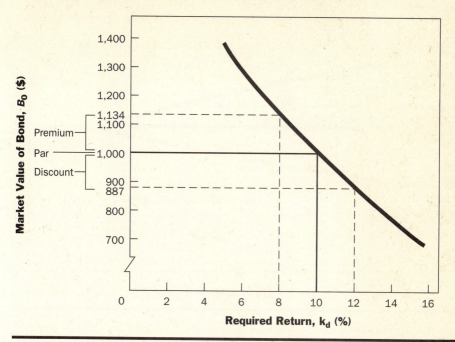

cent increase. If the same change in required return had occurred with only three years to maturity, as denoted by the dashed line, the bond's value would have risen to just $1,051.70—only a 5.17 percent increase. Similar types of responses can be seen in terms of the change in bond value associated with increases in required returns. The shorter the time to maturity, the smaller the impact on bond value caused by a given change in the required return.

4.3.5 Yield to Maturity (YTM)

When investors evaluate and trade bonds, they commonly consider yield to maturity (YTM), which is the rate of return investors earn if they buy the bond at a specific price, B_0, and hold it until maturity. The measure assumes, of course, that the issuer makes all scheduled interest and principal payments as promised. The yield to maturity on a bond with a current price equal to its par, or face, value (i.e., $B_0 = M$) will always equal the coupon interest rate. When the bond value differs from par, the yield to maturity will differ from the coupon interest rate. Assuming that interest is paid annually, the yield to maturity on a bond can be found by solving Equation 4.3 for k_d. In other words, the current value, B_0, the annual interest, I, the par value, M, and the years to maturity, n, are known, and the yield to maturity must be found. The YTM can be found in one of three ways—by trial and error, approximation formula, or hand-held business/financial calculator. The trial-and-error approach involves finding the value of the bond at various rates until the rate causing the calculated bond value to equal its current value is

FIGURE 4.2

Relationship between time to maturity, required return, and bond value (Mars Company's 10 percent coupon interest rate, 10-year maturity, $1,000 par issue paying annual interest)

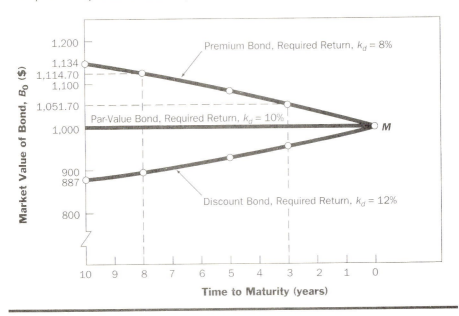

found. The approximate yield formula, given in Equation 4.4, can be used to approximate YTM:

$$Approximate\ Yield = \frac{I + \dfrac{M - B_0}{n}}{\dfrac{M + B_0}{2}} \qquad (4.4)$$

Application of the approximation method for finding YTM is demonstrated in the following example.

The Mars Company bond, which currently sells for $1,080, has a 10 percent coupon interest rate and $1,000 par value, pays interest annually, and has 10 years to maturity. Since $B_0 = \$1,080$, $I = \$100\ (.10 \times \$1,000)$, $M = \$1,000$, and $n = 10$ years, substituting into Equation 4.3a, we get:

$$\$1,080 = \$100 \times (PVIFA_{kd,10yrs}) + \$1,000 \times (PVIF_{kd,10yrs})$$

Our objective is to solve the equation for k_d—the YTM. Substituting the relevant data into the approximate yield formula given in Equation 4.4, we get:

$$Approximate\ Yield = \frac{\$100 + \dfrac{\$1,000 - \$1,080}{10}}{\dfrac{\$1,000 + \$1,080}{2}}$$

$$= \frac{\$100 + (-\$8)}{\$1,040} = \frac{\$92}{\$1,040} = 0.0885 = \underline{\underline{8.85\%}}$$

The approximate YTM is therefore 8.85 percent, which does not differ greatly from the 8.77 percent YTM computed using the regular formula.

4.3.6 Seminannual Interest and Bond Values

The procedure used to value bonds paying interest semiannually is similar to that used for compounding interest more frequently than annually—except that here we need to find present instead of future value. It involves:

1. Converting annual interest, I, to semiannual interest by dividing it by 2.
2. Converting the number of years to maturity, n, to the number of six-month periods to maturity by multiplying n by 2.
3. Converting the required stated (rather than effective) return for similar-risk bonds that also pay semiannual interest from an annual rate, k_d, to a semiannual rate by dividing it by 2.

Substituting the three changes noted above into Equation 4.3 yields:

$$B_0 = \frac{I}{2} \times \left[\sum_{t=1}^{2n} \frac{1}{\left(1+\frac{k_d}{2}\right)^t} \right] + M \times \left[\frac{1}{\left(1 + \frac{k_d}{2}\right)^{2n}} \right] \qquad (4.5)$$

$$= \frac{I}{2} \times \left(\text{PVIFA}_{\frac{k_d}{2},2n} \right) + M \times \left(\text{PVIF}_{\frac{k_d}{2},2n} \right) \qquad (4.5)$$

An example can be used to illustrate the application of this equation using either financial tables or the equation itself. Assuming that the Mars Company bond pays interest semiannually and that the required stated return, k_d, is 12 percent for similar-risk bonds that also pay semiannual interest, substituting into Equation 4.5a yields:

$$B_0 = \frac{\$100}{2} \times (\text{PVIFA}_{\frac{12\%}{2},2 \times 10\text{yrs.}}) + \$1,000 \times (\text{PVIF}_{\frac{12\%}{2},2 \times 10\text{yrs.}})$$

$$B_0 = \$50 \times (\text{PVIFA}_{6\%,20\text{periods}}) + \$1,000 \times (\text{PVIF}_{6\%,20\text{periods}})$$

$$= \$50 \times (11.470) + \$1,000 \times (.312) = \$885.50$$

Comparing the $885.30 result above with the $887.00 value found earlier by using annual compounding, we can see that the bond's value is lower when semiannual interest is used. This will always occur when the bond sells at a discount. For bonds selling at a premium, the opposite will occur (the value with semiannual interest is greater than with annual interest.)

4.4   ADVANCED BOND VALUATION TECHNIQUES

While the basic mathematics of bond valuation are quite straightforward, valuing real debt instruments in a world of fluctuating market interest rates and heterogenous investors is anything but simple. In fact, due to the almost infinite variety of debt maturities, issuer risk characteristics, bond price sensitivities to interest rate changes, and debt security terms (coupon rate, callability, indenture restrictions, etc.), bond valuation has become one of the most complex and difficult of all financial valuations. A complete description of all the techniques used in actual bond pricing is far beyond the scope of this chapter. Instead, we will examine several key concepts that directly impact the valuation of debt securities, beginning with the most basic of all interest rate equations—the Fisher Effect. We then present, discuss, and examine empirical support offered by researchers for the four main theories that have been advanced as explanations of the term structure of interest rates.

Following our discussion of term structure theories, we discuss the concept of duration and briefly examine how a bond portfolio can be immunized against changes in the level of interest rates. We then examine in turn the theoretical motivations for debt maturity structure choices by corporate issuers, the importance and valuation of bond covenants and indenture agreements (including conversion privileges), and the impact of liquidity and personal income taxation on bond valuation. Next, we discuss how mortgage-backed and floating rate debt instruments are valued. We then conclude this section with a brief overview of a variety of topics related to bond valuation—such as the economic function of ratings agencies, bond pricing models that have been presented in the literature, and the role and valuation of income and savings bonds.

4.4.1 The Fisher Effect and Expected Inflation

As mentioned above, the most basic issue in the valuation of debt claims concerns how nominal (observed) interest rates are set as a function of the real (inflation-adjusted) required return and the expected level of inflation during the life of a loan. The relationship described in Equation 4.6 below is called the **Fisher Effect** (or Fisher Equation), after Irving Fisher, the famous American economist who developed many of the basic relationships underlying interest rate theory. Fisher said that the nominal interest rate should be approximately equal to the real (inflation-adjusted) rate of interest plus a premium to compensate investors for expected inflation. The model expresses this relationship in multiplicative form (Equation 4.6), but for low inflation rates the additive form ($R_f = a + i$) is approximately correct. Formally, the Fisher Effect is:

$$(1 + R_f) = (1 + a)(1 + i) \qquad (4.6)$$

where R_f = the (default) risk-free rate of interest
  a = the real (inflation-adjusted) return required by investors
  i = the rate of inflation expected during the loan period.

Seems fairly simple, right? In theory, this relationship appears self-evident, and most investors clearly will demand a premium for saving (rather than consuming) during inflationary periods. But implicit in this model is an assumption that real interest rates should remain fairly steady for extended periods of time, and that most or all of the variation in nominal interest rates should be a result of changing inflationary expectations. Unfortunately, empirical evidence suggests that this may not always (or even usually) be the case.[4] Whereas Fama (1975), Fama and Schwert (1977), Mishkin

---

4. It is also true that more sophisticated interest rate models do not predict a simple one-for-one relationship between expected inflation and nominal interest rates. Both Benninga and Protopapadakis (1983) and Chan (1994) incorporate risk premiums for the covariance between inflation rates and real consumption opportunities. Chan's empirical evidence documents a statistically reliable premium for inflation covariability risk in short-term interest rates.

(1990), and Evans and Lewis (1995) present evidence suggesting that variations in nominal rates primarily reflect variations in inflation expectations, Pennachi (1991) finds instead that real interest rates are far more volatile than inflationary expectations, and that most fluctuations in nominal yields are therefore caused by fluctuations in real required returns.[5] Furthermore, there have been prolonged periods—particularly during the late 1970s—when nominal interest rates were almost equal to, or even below, the rate of inflation. Clearly, no model predicts negative real interest rates, so we must conclude that the empirical validity of even the most basic interest rate model, the Fisher Effect, remains in doubt—though the Evans and Lewis (1995) study increases our faith in the model's essential accuracy.

4.4.2 The Term Structure of Interest Rates

One of the most enduring regularities in bond valuation is that, at any point in time, there is a systematic relationship between the yields-to-maturity of securities in a given risk class and the terms to maturity of bonds in that risk class. Usually, yields increase with maturity so that the required return on, say, a default-risk-free Treasury bill with six months to maturity is lower than that of another T-bill with one year to maturity; and the one-year bill in turn has a lower yield than a five-year Treasury note, which itself has a lower yield than a ten-, twenty-, or thirty-year Treasury bond. The relationship between yield and maturity is called the **term structure of interest rates**, while a graphical representation of this relationship is called a **yield curve**.

Figure 4.3 presents a yield curve for three different points in time. During May 1981, the overall level of interest rates was very high, and the yield curve was downward-sloping (short-term rates were higher than long-term rates). Such an **inverted** yield curve is uncommon, and is usually observed only during recessionary periods—particularly when the central bank (such as the U.S. Federal Reserve Board) is pushing up short-term interest rates in order to dampen inflationary pressures in the economy. The yield curve during October 1993, on the other hand, documents a much lower overall level of interest rates as well as a sharply upward-sloping, or **normal**, yield curve. This is the pattern normally observed early in an economic expansion, when businesses are operating very profitably—and thus are able to finance operating expenses and capital investment spending out of current cash flow—and when inflationary pressures in the economy are weakest. Finally, in January 1995 there was an essentially **flat** yield curve—meaning that short and long-term securities offered approximately the same yield—and the level of long-term rates had increased by two full percentage points (200 basis points) from the levels observed only fifteen months before. Short-term rates had increased by an even greater amount from October 1993 to January 1995—almost four percentage points. This is the pattern commonly observed as economic expansions mature and

---

5. The Evans and Lewis study is particularly interesting, in that it employs a recently–developed time series methodology (a Markov switching model) to show that the evidence presented in Rose (1988) and Mishkin (1992)—that real rates are subject to permanent disturbances incompatible with the Fisher Effect—probably results from a small sample bias induced by a shift in the inflation-generating process during the postwar era. Evans and Lewis find that the real rate appears to be stationary after adjusting for the effects of rationally anticipated shifts in inflation.

FIGURE 4.3

Yield Curves for U.S. Treasury Securities During May 1981, October 1993, and January 1995

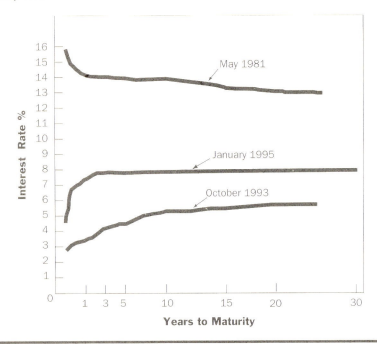

SOURCE: *MOODY'S BOND RECORD.*

inflationary pressures build: capital spending requirements force companies to borrow large sums, even as capacity constraints and other production bottlenecks cause input prices to rise and falling unemployment levels cause wage levels to first creep, and then sprint ahead.[6]

As our discussion of yield curve shapes and stages of the business cycle suggests, modern finance has developed several theories to explain the term structure of interest rates. The various theories model term structure as a function of investor expectations, macroeconomic forces, the supply and demand for debt securities of differing maturities, or the relative importance of liquidity to investors—or as a combination of one or more of these factors. Most of these theories fall into one of two categories: those which suggest that the term structure embodies investors' expectations about the course of interest rates in the future—which we will refer to as **expectations theories**—and those which model the term structure as a function of investor and issuer preferences

---

6. By January 1995 the economic expansion that began in March 1991 was almost four years old, and the U.S. economy had grown at an average annual rate of almost 3.5 percent throughout the recovery period—including growth of approximately 4 percent during 1994. For a mature economy such as the United States, growth rates much in excess of 3 percent per year have historically been very difficult to sustain without provoking serious inflationary pressures.

for securities of different, and segmented, maturity classes—which we will call **segmented markets theories**.[7] Each broad theoretical category has various "subtheories", and we will first address the unbiased expectations, liquidity premium, and the preferred habitat versions of the expectations theories before examining the market segmentation theory.

THE UNBIASED EXPECTATIONS HYPOTHESIS   According to the pure, or **unbiased expectations hypothesis** of the term structure, all points on the yield curve reflect the best prediction of market participants as to what the actual interest rate will be in the future.[8] If the yield curve has a normal shape, investors predict that interest rates will rise in coming periods. If the yield curve is inverted, investors expect rates to fall. A flat yield curve suggests that investors believe interest rates will not change in the foreseeable future. If this theory holds, then there is an entire structure of **implied forward rates** embodied in any given yield curve. This concept is best illustrated by an example. The current (period 0) observed yield to maturity for a security that matures in T periods, $_0R_T$, is assumed to be a product of one-period forward rates, $_tf_{t+1}$, as in our Equation 4.7:

$$[(1 + {_0R_T})]^T = (1 + {_0R_1})(1 + {_1f_2}) \dots (1 + {_{T-1}f_T}) \tag{4.7}$$

The forward rate $_1f_2$ is the one-period rate expected for a bond bought at the end of period one and held to maturity at the end of period two, while the last term in Equation 4.7 represents the forward rate on a bond bought at the end of period $T - 1$ and held for one period.

We can use Equation 4.7 to compute the implied forward rate for a one-year bond purchased at the end of next year, $_1f_2$, if we are given the current market rates for a one period bond, $_0R_1$, and a two-year bond, $_0R_2$. Suppose these rates are 5.00 and 6.00 percent respectively for one and two-year bonds. Equation 4.7 can be rearranged to yield an implied forward rate of:

$$(1 + {_1f_2}) = (1 + {_0R_2})^2/(1 + {_0R_1}) = (1.0600)^2/(1.0500) = 1.0701$$

---

7. Although there are several good markets and institutions textbooks which provide detailed taxonomies of term structure theories, we will use the classification scheme presented in Fabozzi, Modigliani, and Ferri (1994, chapter 12). See also chapter 14 of Bodie, Kane, and Marcus (1993), chapter 7 of Kidwell, Peterson, and Blackwell (1993), and chapter 23 of Brealey and Myers (1991). A detailed mathematical treatment of term structure theories is presented in Copeland and Weston (1988), and we will refer to their work throughout our own discussion.

8. This theory was first presented by Fisher (1896) and later amplified by Lutz (1940). More recently, Cox, Ingersoll, and Ross (CIR 1981) examine the unbiased expectations hypothesis theoretically, and find that the simplest version of this model cannot hold in a continuous time, rational expectations economy populated by risk-neutral investors, since it ignores the greater price and reinvestment risk associated with long-term securities. They find that a modified version of the expectations model, which they call the Local Expectations Hypothesis, is a better term structure model for such an economy because it only presumes unbiased expectations over finite (especially short) holding periods. The predictions of this, and a subsequent CIR (1985) model is tested, and largely supported, by Gibbons and Ramaswamy (1993). The empirical results of Pearson and Sun (1994), however, largely contradict the CIR (1985) model. Finally, Brown and Dybvig (1986) are able to estimate the CIR (1985) model using U.S. Treasury security prices, but they find the model systematically over-estimates short-term rates, and systematically overprices premium and underprices discount issues.

This formula suggests that market participants expect short-term (one-year) interest rates to rise to 7.01 percent by the end of the coming year, and will only be willing to purchase a two-year bond today if it offers a 6.00 percent yield for two periods. Similar computations can be performed to obtain any given forward rate on the yield curve.

While attractive due to its simplicity and forthrightness, there are a number of basic problems associated with the unbiased expectations hypothesis. Most significantly, this model does not account for the greater price risk, but lower reinvestment risk, associated with investing in long-term securities.[9] A long-term bond has greater **price risk** than a short-term bond because it will experience a larger percentage change in price for any given change in interest rates than will a short-term bond.[10] **Reinvestment risk** arises when an investor purchases a security with a shorter maturity than he or she actually wants, and must then reinvest the proceeds of the maturing bond in one or more other short-term securities until the desired maturity date. Suppose, for example, an investor wants to have $1,000 available upon retirement in ten years, and earn an $80 per year return in the interim. The investor can choose between buying an 8 percent, ten-year bond paying $1,000 upon maturity or investing in a series of two-year coupon bonds that mature every twenty-four months and must be **rolled over** (the proceeds must be reinvested at the going two-year interest rate) four times before the investor retires. Obviously, the ten-year bond has lower (zero) reinvestment risk than the series of two-year bonds in this example.

THE LIQUIDITY PREMIUM THEORY   An alternative to the pure or unbiased expectations hypothesis is the **liquidity premium theory** (also frequently called the liquidity preference theory), presented originally by Hicks (1946) and later refined by Langetieg (1980). This theory is also based on an expectational model of how longer-maturity interest rates are set, but it assumes that investors prefer to invest short-term and must be paid a premium—in the form of progressively higher promised yields as maturities increase—to buy and hold longer-term securities.[11] This preference for liquidity (short maturity debt

---

9. Perhaps surprisingly, the empirical support for this model is also modest. In particular, Fama (1984a) finds that in the 1975–82 period the implied forward rate has the power to forecast actual future spot rates only one month ahead. In contrast, during the 1959–1969 period forward rates are able to predict spot rates up to five months ahead. Even this feat, however, suggests implied forward rates are anything but omniscient. On the other hand, Mishkin (1989, 1990) is primarily concerned with determining what information is contained in the yield curve about expected future inflation and real returns. He finds that for maturities of six months or less, the term structure provides little information about future inflation, but provides useful information about the term structure of real returns. For longer maturities (nine to twelve months), the nominal term structure ceases to provide information about the real term structure, but begins to provide information about expected inflation. Finally, Harvey (1988) documents that the (expected) real term structure embodies more information about the growth of real consumption than either lagged consumption or the leading econometric models.

10. For example, when market interest rates change from 10 to 15 percent, a five-year bond with a $120 annual coupon payment and a $1,000 principal value will experience a 16.4 percent decline in price, from $1,075.82 to $899.44, while a ten-year bond with the same coupon payments and principal value will experience a 24.4 percent change in value, from $1122.89 to $849.44 (Copeland and Weston 1988, pages 68–69).

11. Brealey and Schaefer (1977) derive a term structure model based on uncertain future inflation that is superficially similar to the liquidity theory—in that the yield curve is upward sloping—but this is caused solely by a risk premium for inflation uncertainty and is not related to investor maturity preferences.

instruments) is rational, since investors face less price risk with short-term securities, and if held to maturity they also imply lower transactions costs (one rather than two brokerage fees) than buying and selling long-term bonds.[12]

THE PREFERRED HABITAT HYPOTHESIS   Yet another "biased" expectation model is the **preferred habitat hypothesis**, which was originally presented in Modigliani and Sutch (1966). This model also takes as given that the structure of interest rates is largely determined by expectations, but it assumes that both borrowers and lenders have maturity preferences that they will stay with unless a sufficiently higher (for investors) or lower (for issuers) rate is offered to tempt them into another maturity **habitat**. One particularly attractive feature of this model is that it can explain "kinks" in the yield curve—areas where, for example, the yield on a seven-year bond may be lower than the yields on both five- and ten-year bonds. This theory also might shed light on the tendency for yield curves to continually alter their shape, particularly over the course of a business cycle. This could be caused by changing relative supplies of and demand for securities in the various maturity habitats. Unfortunately, the "institutional" nature of this theory makes it very hard to test without detailed knowledge about the investors and issuers populating each maturity habitat, and such data is (so far) unattainable.

THE MARKET SEGMENTATION THEORY   The final term structure theory we will examine is the **market segmentation theory**, proposed by Culbertson (1957). This theory is similar to the preferred habitat theory in that both assume that investors and issuers have preferred maturities for their security issuance and investment. In contrast to the habitat model, however, the segmentation theory suggests that the different maturity zones are actually distinct, segmented markets from which investors and issuers cannot be tempted by the lure of more attractive yields. Such behavior is difficult to explain with any plausible utility of wealth model, and also ignores the voluminous evidence concerning the willingness and ability of investors (particularly bond funds) to arbitrage gross yield disparities through strategic buying of underpriced (high-yield) and short selling overpriced (low-yield) bonds. On balance, we must conclude that this theory is effectively dominated by any one of the three expectations models as a realistic theory of the term structure of interest rates, though the issue of which of the three expectations theories best describes objective reality is still unsettled.

4.4.3 Duration and Immunization

Debt securities are fiendishly difficult to value because so many different factors—coupon interest rate, market rates, issuer default risk, term to maturity, and indenture terms such as callability and convertibility—significantly impact an individual bond's

---

12. The liquidity premium theory has been examined empirically several times, and two studies in particular deserve note. First, McCulloch (1975) quantitatively estimates (and documents) liquidity premiums for U.S. government securities with maturities ranging between one month and thirty years. Second, Fama (1984b) documents that expected returns on longer-term bills systematically exceed the returns on one-month bills. He finds that expected returns on bills peak at eight or nine months, and never increase monotonically as far out as twelve months. Fama is unable to estimate longer maturity liquidity premiums because of the variability of long-term bond returns.

price. This inherent complexity has long enticed academicians and practitioners alike to attempt to develop a summary measure that combines several of these variables into a single, intuitive measure of bond price sensitivity. While no such master cypher has been, nor is likely to be developed, the concept of **duration** combines a bond's coupon and interest payments, time to maturity, and yield to maturity into a summary measure that is denominated in units of time, but can also be viewed as a measure of price sensitivity (an elasticity). Macauley (1938) coined the term "duration" and defined it as the average life of the stream of cash flows.[13] As discussed in Weil (1973, page 589), Macauley's duration is "equal to the period of time which elapses before the 'average' dollar of present value from a stream of payments is received." Using the same variable labels that we have used throughout this book, Macauley's duration can be defined as in Equation 4.8 below:[14]

$$D = \frac{\sum_{t=1}^{n} \dfrac{CF_t(t)}{(1 + k_d)^t}}{\sum_{t=1}^{n} \dfrac{CF_t}{(1 + k_d)^t}} \qquad (4.8)$$

where D = bond duration

CF_t = interest or principal payment at time t

t = time period in which cash flow is received

n = number of periods until maturity

k_d = the yield to maturity (interest rate).

The numerator of this equation is the present value of all cash flows to be paid by this bond, weighted (multiplied) by the date of that payment's receipt. The denominator is our basic formula for computing a bond's value.

One year after Macauley's work was published, Hicks (1939) independently derived an elasticity measure that is equivalent to Macauley's duration.[15] Hicks' "average period" measures the elasticity of capital value with respect to the discount rate—how much the

---

13. Cox, Ingersoll, and Ross (1979) take issue with this definition of duration, and they develop a theoretically more rigorous measure which, like Macaulay's duration, is denominated in units of time.

14. Of the several candidate presentations of Macauley's duration available, we select as our model the one presented in Kidwell, Peterson, and Blackwell (1993, page 126), though we use our symbol for the required return on debt (k_d) rather than their symbol i. These authors also provide a very good discussion of several important properties of duration that relate to bond valuation (see pages 127–129), as well as several computational examples.

15. In addition to Weil (1973), several other authors provide useful discussions of how Macauley and Hicks developed and applied their duration models—including Bierwag (1977), Bierwag, Kaufman, and Toevs (1982), and Fisher and Weil (1971). A subsequent article by Bierwag, Kaufman, and Latta (1988) provides a taxonomy of the various duration models that have been developed since Macauley, while Bierwag, Kaufman, and Toevs (1983) and Christensen and Sørensen (1994) discuss the implications of duration for bond portfolio management. Haugen and Wichern (1974) theoretically model the interest elasticity of bonds and stock, and apply their model to valuing a life insurer's equity. Finally, Williams and Pfeifer (1982) develop and test a model which uses duration and price elasticity to measure stock price risk. They present weak evidence that the higher duration of low-dividend growth stocks relative to other equities can impact returns, but they are able to explain very little of the return variability actually observed.

price of an asset with a fixed payment stream will change if market interest rates change by one unit (i.e., one percentage point). That the exact formula can be used equally well as a measure of time and of price sensitivity is a reflection of duration's usefulness both as a theoretical concept and as a practical tool for bond analysis. Unfortunately, this flexibility has also lead to confusion in the academic literature concerning duration's principal role. For example, of six leading textbooks surveyed in preparing this chapter, four define duration in terms of time and two define it in terms of price elasticity.[16] Furthermore, no two of the textbooks define (algebraically or verbally) duration in exactly the same way. Suffice it to say that duration can be defined either as (1) the length of time required to receive back, in present value of coupon and interest payments, the money invested in the purchase of a security, or (2) as the approximate percentage change in a given bond's price resulting from a one percentage point (100 basis point) change in market interest rates.

IMMUNIZATION   For bond portfolio investors, duration can be most properly used to **immunize** a bond portfolio so that its value is unaffected by a change in market interest rates. This can be done by selecting securities with a duration equal to the investment horizon of the portfolio manager.[17] One immunization strategy involves matching the maturities and as closely as possible the size of coupon interest payments for a portfolio's assets and liabilities.[18] This is particularly appropriate for financial institutions such as banks and insurance companies which must invest long term and which are particularly sensitive to interest rate changes. Intuitively, the idea behind other immunization strategies is to construct a portfolio where capital losses resulting from a rise in market interest rates will be balanced against increasingly attractive reinvestment opportunities for the intervening coupon interest payments. Alternatively, an investor wishing to perfectly immunize can do so by purchasing zero-coupon (pure discount) securities, since in this case—and only in this case—a bond's duration is equal to its maturity and such a security held until maturity will in fact have an effective, ex post yield equal to its expected, ex ante yield to maturity.

Heretofore, our discussion of bond valuation has focused primarily on investor preferences and how these influence interest rates and bond pricing. We now shift our focus to examine the decision variables that corporate *issuers* face in selecting the types of debt securities to issue. We begin with a topic that has attracted a great deal of research interest in recent years—the choice of debt maturity, and how this choice impacts the market value of the firm.

4.4.4 Debt Maturity Structure Choice

At first glance, it is unclear why and how debt maturity choice (as opposed to the choice between debt and equity issues) can impact firm valuation. However, even the

---

16. Bodie, Kane, and Marcus (1993), Brealey and Myers (1991), Kidwell, Peterson, and Blackwell (1993), and Sinkey (1992) define duration in terms of time (average present value repayment period), while Copeland and Weston (1988) and Fabozzi, Modigliani, and Ferri (1994) define duration as an elasticity.

17. Bierwag (1977) also discusses immunization techniques and describes under what conditions each strategy is likely to be successful.

18. For a discussion of this and other immunization strategies, see Bodie, Kane, and Marcus (1993, pages 492–499).

most casual analysis of observed debt issuance policies reveals systematic industry and national patterns within a wide variety of maturity classes. In the absence of market frictions, particularly informational asymmetries between managers and shareholders, Merton (1974) shows that maturity choice is irrelevant, and this result is also clearly in the spirit of the Modigliani and Miller (1963) and Stiglitz (1974) models of capital market equilibrium. All modern maturity structure models are therefore driven by market frictions, and all assume that informational asymmetry is an important factor in maturity choice. They differ primarily with respect to whether the debt maturity choice is a result of other factors—primarily the characteristics of the issuing firm itself and the richness of its investment opportunity set (IOS)—or whether managers select maturity to convey their inside information to outside investors. To use the classification scheme presented in Barclay and Smith (1995), theoretical models of maturity structure choice can be grouped into either **contracting cost models** or **signaling models**.[19] We examine each in turn below, then conclude this section with a summary of the existing empirical evidence.

CONTRACTING COST MODELS OF MATURITY STRUCTURE   Contracting cost models have in common a prediction that the debt maturity chosen by a given issuer will be related to some aspect of that firm's assets, operations, market access, or ownership structure. The first, and one of the most important articles in this research stream is by Myers (1977). While this paper is most famous for its explanation of the difficulty of financing growth options with debt—due to the fact that managers will rationally forego funding some profitable investments if most of the benefits from such investments will accrue to bondholders—Myers also shows that debt maturity choice can mitigate the under-investment problem. Specifically, by issuing debt that matures before investment opportunities expire, the stockholders can pay off the bondholder's fixed claim and capture all of the economic rents of the project by funding it themselves. Myers also provides a theoretical justification for the common practice of matching the maturities of a firm's assets with liabilities issued to finance them, since this allows debt repayments to decline in line with the future value of the assets in place.

The next paper to address debt maturity choice is Morris (1976). This author makes the case that if the covariance between a firm's net operating income and interest rates is sufficiently high—as might be the case if both interest rates and corporate profits rise during business expansions, and fall during contractions—then use of short-term debt may effectively convert interest costs into variable rather than fixed expenses, thereby lowering the firm's break-even point and its operating leverage.

Barnea, Haugen, and Senbet (1980) provide an ownership structure explanation both for the existence of call provisions in corporate bonds and for a firm's choice of debt. Specifically, they posit that these bond features allow firms to minimize, at very low cost, the agency costs of debt that result from informational asymmetries, managerial risk incentives, and foregone growth opportunities resulting from the Myers under-investment problem. Rather counter-intuitively, they find that both shortening corporate debt maturities and inserting **call provisions** (giving the firm the right to

---

19. Barclay and Smith actually present a third category of maturity choice models—tax hypotheses. We choose to discuss these in our contracting cost discussion below, since the relationships addressed by these models are also related to the investment opportunity set (IOS) of the firm.

call, or force the investor to sell back to the firm, all of the outstanding bonds in an issue) in bond issues serve identical purposes in solving agency problems.

Brick and Ravid (1985) provide a tax-based rationale for debt maturity structure. They note that, whenever the term structure of interest rates is upward-sloping, issuing long-term debt reduces the present value of expected tax liabilities, and thus maximizes the market value of the firm. This result is, however, challenged by Lewis (1990), who argues that taxes will not impact firm valuation if optimal leverage and debt maturity structure are determined simultaneously rather than sequentially.

Finally, Smith (1986) argues that a firm's average debt maturity will be longer the more heavily regulated are its activities, and Barclay and Smith (1995) predict a similar relationship between maturity and firm size. The predicted positive relationship between size and maturity is principally a function of market access. Larger firms can more easily issue long-term bonds, while smaller firms are more restricted to bank borrowing, which tends to be short-term. Regulated firms are expected to rely more on longer-term debt in order to reduce managerial discretion regarding the use of corporate assets. This restricts the ability of regulators to expropriate (and transfer to constituents) the wealth of the regulated firm's shareholders through punitive price and operational regulations. This is particularly important in the utility and transportation industries, where regulated firms must make large, long-term, and irreversible capital investments and would thus be especially vulnerable to strategic behavior by regulators unless they could contractually pre-commit to paying out the cash flows of these investments to long-term bondholders.

SIGNALING MODELS OF DEBT MATURITY CHOICE   The second main set of debt maturity models predict that the choice of maturity will be related to the degree of informational asymmetry between managers and outside investors. Though we will adopt the Barclay and Smith (1995) classification of these theories, not all of them meet the strict definition of a "signaling model" (wherein a firm employs a costly financial **signal**—an activity or cash outlay that has no intrinsic value, but is prohibitively costly for a weaker firm to employ—to convey its superior value to investors in a market characterized by great informational asymmetry). However, they do have in common a prediction that corporate managers—who have nonpublic information about the firm's future prospects—will seek to convey this information to relatively uninformed investors through maturity structure choices.

The first important paper in this stream of research, Flannery (1986), is in fact a classic signaling model where managers of the strongest firms will choose to issue more short-term debt than will managers in weaker firms. By issuing short-term debt, strong firm managers are subjecting the firm to the risk that it will be forced to refinance the debt after more information about the firm has been revealed. Managers of firms with less promising prospects will be unwilling to take this risk, and will therefore self-select into issuing long-term bonds not subject to intermediate-term renegotiation. Provided that security issuance is costly, Flannery shows that a separating equilibrium will result in which stronger firms issue short-term debt (and are rewarded with a higher market value for doing so), while weaker firms will issue long-term debt.[20]

---

20. If security issuance is costless, Flannery's model will result in a pooling equilibrium where investors cannot differentiate strong from weak firms.

Two of the most influential asymmetric information models of maturity structure choice are by Diamond (1991, 1993). In Diamond (1991a), debt maturity structure choice is modeled as a trade-off between a borrower's desire to issue short-term debt (due to private information about the firm's improving prospects) and the liquidity risk inherent in relying on short-term borrowing. **Liquidity risk** is defined as the risk that the borrower will lose non-assignable **control rents** (monetary and non-monetary benefits that accrue only to managers and which cannot be distributed to security-holders) in the event that lenders are unwilling to refinance when bad news occurs.[21] In this model, highly-rated firms will choose to issue short-term debt, and very low-rated firms have no alternative but to borrow short term, so only medium-risk firms issue long-term debt. This three-group pattern is a unique prediction of Diamond's (1991a) model.

In his later paper, Diamond (1993) models how borrowers with private information about their credit prospects choose the maturity and seniority of debt. Use of short-term debt once again increases liquidity risk for a firm's managers, and also increases the sensitivity of financing costs to new information, so only the stronger firms will employ short-term borrowings. This model predicts that short-term debt will be senior to long-term debt, and that long-term debt will allow the issuance of additional senior debt, since this strategy increases the sensitivity of finance costs to new information for a given degree of protection of managerial control.

Finally, Goswami, Noe, and Rebello (1995) model maturity structure choice as a function of the temporal distribution of informational asymmetry. For example, when asymmetry is primarily related to uncertainty regarding long-term cash flows, the firm will choose to issue long-term, coupon-paying debt that partially restricts dividend payments. On the other hand, when informational asymmetry is randomly distributed between short and long-term debt, firms rely on short-term borrowing. The authors are thus able to explain the popularity of both short- and long-term debt—as well as the existence of dividend restrictions and coupon-paying bonds (rather than pure discount securities exclusively)—without appealing to market imperfections or agency costs.

EMPIRICAL EVIDENCE ON THE CHOICE OF DEBT MATURITY STRUCTURE

We are thus left with two plausible, competing (but not necessarily mutually exclusive) explanations of debt maturity structure choice. In general, the "signaling models" predict that stronger firms will choose to issue relatively more short-term debt than will weaker firms, while the contracting cost hypotheses predict that maturity structure choice will be systematically related to a firm's IOS, regulatory status, and ownership structure.

Somewhat surprisingly, given the numerous theoretical articles discussed above, the only major empirical investigation of maturity choice is Barclay and Smith (1995). Their results offer strong support for the contracting cost model, and provide only weak support for the signaling models of Diamond (1991a, 1993).[22] Specifically, Barclay and

---

21. Diamond assumes that lenders have excessive liquidation incentives, and may choose to foreclose on firms that are economically solvent but temporarily illiquid.

22. The Diamond models are supported in that firms with potentially large information asymmetries issue more short-term debt, and the three-part tiering of maturity as a function of credit risk (high and low-risk firms issue more short-term debt, while medium-risk firms issue more long-term debt) is empirically documented.

Smith document that larger, more regulated firms—and those with fewer growth options—issue relatively more long-term debt than do smaller, growth-option-rich firms in unregulated industries. They find no support for tax explanations of debt maturity choice.

4.4.5 Bond Covenants

Apart from commercial paper, very few real debt instruments issued by corporations are simple promises to repay, in a single lump sum, a fixed amount at a given time in the future. Instead, actual debt securities exhibit a wide variety of special terms and contractual obligations which are collectively referred to as bond **covenants**. Some of these specify the basic details of the debt agreement—such as maturity date, coupon rate, payment dates, seniority status, and redemption value—while the rest are designed to either protect investors from after-issue wealth expropriation by the issuing firm, or to grant the issuing firm the power to take unilateral actions, such as the right to call an issue.[23]

Both finance theory and common sense suggest why investors will insist on bond covenants in loan agreements, since they are in effect exchanging hard cash for pieces of paper evidencing a (limited liability) corporation's promise to repay the money at a future date. Unless investors can be reasonably assured they will be repaid as promised they will not purchase debt securities, or will do so only at a prohibitively high rate of interest. Therefore, corporations seeking funds have a powerful incentive to contractually limit their own ability to expropriate bondholder wealth. Bond covenants are the legal technologies that both allow corporations to bond their benevolent intentions and permit investors to protect their repayment prospects.

Smith and Warner (1979) present what is still the classic description and analysis of bond covenants used by U.S. corporations. They examine the purpose of each type of covenant, and argue that these would only be observed in real bond issues if their benefits outweigh their demonstrable economic costs. Smith and Warner classify bond covenants into five basic categories: (1) restrictions on the firm's production/investment policy; (2) restrictions on the payment of dividends; (3) restrictions on subsequent financing policies; (4) covenants modifying the pattern of payoffs to bondholders; and (5) covenants specifying bonding activities by the firm. We will use this classification scheme in our own brief discussion of the impact of covenants on bond valuation, which follows.

RESTRICTIONS ON THE FIRM'S PRODUCTION/INVESTMENT POLICY   Investors understand that once they turn money over to a borrower they will be unable to directly monitor or control how that money is used. Bond covenants allow investors to achieve

---

23. Call provisions are examined theoretically in Barnea, Haugen, and Senbet (1980), Goswami, Noe, and Rebello (1995), and Smith and Warner (1979). Vu (1986) empirically documents that most bonds that are called are selling below their call price (the price the issuing firm must pay to force redemption) at the time, and that many bonds are called specifically in order to remove particularly restrictive bond covenants. He also finds that the stock price response to call announcements is positively related to the direction of the change in leverage.

much the same result indirectly—by limiting the discretion of borrowing-firm managers over the use of borrowed funds. Two very common such covenants are restrictions on mergers by the issuing firm and restrictions on the disposition of assets. Investors understand that managers wishing to extract capital from a corporation, and leave bondholders a bankrupt corporate shell, can accomplish this by arranging a merger or asset sale on terms that are exceedingly beneficial to the merger partner or asset purchaser.[24] Other covenants restrict the types of assets a borrower can purchase (to preclude investment in excessively risky ventures), mandate that the firm maintain the value of capital assets, and indirectly require the firm to maintain holdings of cash and other liquid assets.

RESTRICTIONS ON THE PAYMENT OF DIVIDENDS   Perhaps the easiest way for managers of a borrowing firm to expropriate creditor wealth is to issue bonds, and then pay all the proceeds raised by this issue out to shareholders as a dividend. When the bond matures (or when default triggers the first legal action by creditors), debt-holders are left with a legally enforceable claim on a worthless corporation. Furthermore, due to limited liability, bondholders cannot sue the stockholders for restitution of the money paid as a dividend. To protect themselves from this simple, but devastatingly effective fraud, bondholders almost invariably restrict the ability of the borrowing firm to pay cash dividends to shareholders.[25] As Kalay (1982) demonstrates, these dividend restricting covenants usually establish a "pool" of payable funds that managers have the unrestricted right to distribute as dividends. Effectively, dividends can be paid either out of the profits remaining after debt-service payments have been made, or out of the proceeds of new equity issues (or both), but they cannot be financed through corporate asset sales or from the proceeds of new debt issues.

RESTRICTIONS ON SUBSEQUENT FINANCING POLICIES   Yet another type of strategic behavior by borrowers that bondholders must protect themselves from is the effective dilution of their creditor status through the borrowing firm's issuance of new debt securities with the same or higher seniority status.[26] Bondholders can protect themselves from claim dilution by mandating that the borrowing firm issue only subordinated debt (bonds that receive no payments until the senior debt claim is satisfied in full), or by merely restricting the firm's ability to issue new debt of equal or higher seniority. As with all covenants, investors seeking greater protection from

---

24. This is not merely an abstract academic musing. Marais, Schipper, and Smith (1989), Asquith and Wizman (1990), and Kaplan and Stein (1990) all document that the holders of bonds lacking such event-risk protection suffered significant wealth losses during the leveraged buyout wave of the late 1980s.

25. Stock repurchase programs, which to bondholders look very much like large cash dividends, are also generally restricted.

26. If this list of predatory possibilities seems morose, one should remember that modern finance was not invented in a laboratory, but has instead evolved from actual practice over 400 years. Wisdom comes from survived pain, and each of the covenants discussed in this section was developed in response to the demonstrated cleverness and rapacity of corporate borrowers. Bond investors have learned to heed the dictum of Andrew Grove, the CEO of Intel Corporation, that "only the paranoid survive."

more restrictive bond covenants must be willing to accept a lower promised interest rate as compensation to the firm for agreeing to more severe limitations on its operational discretion. Likewise, firms seeking to insert call provisions or other favorable covenants into bond contracts must pay for this privilege by offering higher promised interest rates.[27]

COVENANTS MODIFYING THE PATTERN OF PAYOFFS TO BONDHOLDERS
Bond covenants can also be used to alter the payoff pattern of standard debt contracts in several ways that are attractive to different investor clienteles. Three of the most commonly observed such covenants are (1) sinking fund provisions, (2) call provisions, and (3) convertibility provisions. A sinking fund provision is an obligation for an issuing firm to annually retire a fixed proportion of an outstanding bond issue, either through open market purchases or by limited use of the call privilege. Sinking funds protect investors by reducing the amount of an outstanding issue over time to correspond with the decline in the economic value of the assets purchased with the issue proceeds—thereby lessening the borrower's incentive to default when the bond matures and principal repayment is expected.[28] As discussed above, call provisions allow the issuing firm to force redemption of an entire outstanding bond issue, though this usually requires the firm to pay a call premium (in addition to repaying the face value of the bond) that typically declines over time.[29] This feature is particularly valuable to corporations during periods of declining interest rates, such as the early and mid-1990s.

Convertible bonds allow investors to convert their debt securities into a fixed number of shares of stock in the issuing company. Therefore, there is an implicit exercise price at which investors "purchase" stock, and this is invariably set well above the stock price at the time the convertible bonds are issued. This gives investors a claim on exceptional firm performance without sacrificing the security of owning a fixed-income security.[30] Convertible bonds are also particularly appropriate debt securities for rapidly-growing firms—or for companies with a large number of intangible assets—to issue.[31] Explicit models for valuing convertible securities are presented in Brennan and Schwartz (1977, 1980), and the same articles describe the optimal time at which the issuing firm should call the issue. The theoretical optimal call time is reached once a bond's conversion value exceeds its call price, but empirical evidence indicates that corporations routinely

---

27. The pricing effect of bond covenants is modeled theoretically by Merton (1974) and Black and Cox (1976), among others. More generally, the optimal design of securities (the value-maximizing allocation of control and cash flow rights) is discussed theoretically in Harris and Raviv (1989) and Nachman and Noe (1994).

28. Dunn and Spatt (1984) provide a theoretical analysis of sinking fund bonds.

29. Most bonds are also call-protected for the first few years after issue, meaning that the bond cannot be called during this period.

30. As an alternative to issuing convertible securities, many corporations issue straight debt with warrants attached. These are essentially long-lived options that give investors the right to purchase a firm's common stock at a fixed price for a fixed (but typically multi-year) length of time.

31. Cornell and Shapiro (1988), Sahlman (1988), and Brennan and Schwartz (1988) all discuss the use of convertible debt in financing rapid corporate growth.

do not call convertible bonds until well after this point, and they often do not call these bonds at all.[32]

COVENANTS SPECIFYING BONDING ACTIVITIES BY THE FIRM   The final group of bond covenants are those which mandate that the borrowing firm's managers take specific steps to protect the bondholders' investment, and to generate reliable information that creditors can use for monitoring purposes. Various covenants mandate (1) that the firm must follow generally accepted accounting principles (GAAP), (2) that it must provide investors with audited financial statements, and (3) that the firm must purchase both property and key person insurance to protect against catastrophic accidental loss. Some covenants specify financial ratio measures that the firm must meet (such as minimum liquidity and maximum leverage ratios), while others spell out what constitutes default and what remedies bondholders have if default occurs. More generally, covenants that mandate what borrowing firm managers *must do* are called **positive covenants**, while those that mandate what management *must not do* are called **negative covenants**. Most real bond indenture agreements (the legal document wherein the covenants are spelled out) contain a bewildering variety of both types of covenants.[33]

4.4.6 Liquidity and Tax Effects in Bond Pricing

Our discussion of factors that influence bond valuation now shifts again—away from why corporations issue certain types of bonds (or bonds with particular features), and back to how capital market participants value certain bond features. We now focus on two such features—a bond's tax status and its liquidity—that modern research has documented are significant influences on bond valuation.

LIQUIDITY AND BOND VALUATION   While it has long seemed logical that a security's liquidity should impact its market valuation, this theoretical and empirical link was not made concretely until 1986, when Amihud and Mendelson documented that infrequently-traded (illiquid) stocks have higher risk-adjusted returns than do more frequently-traded (liquid) shares.[34] Later, Amihud and Mendelsohn (1991) document the same relationship for debt securities. Specifically, they show that U.S. Treasury notes with less than six months to maturity have higher yields than do Treasury bills with the same maturity. Since

---

32. Numerous authors present signaling and other asymmetric information models to explain why corporations delay conversion past the optimal point (see, as examples, Ingersoll [1977a,b], Mikkelson [1981], Harris and Raviv [1985], Ofer and Natarajan [1987], and Campbell, Ederington, and Vankudre [1991]). However, the empirical evidence presented in Asquith and Mullins (1991) and Campbell, Ederington, and Vankudre (1991) suggests that these delayed conversions are not as mysterious as they appear, since most issues have few bonds actually outstanding at the "optimal" conversion date and the actual incentive for a firm to force conversion is related to the difference between the after-tax coupon interest cost and the dividend yield on the firm's stock.

33. In addition to the works cited earlier, both Ho and Singer (1982) and Malitz (1986) provide empirical analyses of the use of covenants in bond indenture agreements.

34. Lippman and McCall also presented an influential analysis and definition of liquidity during 1986, though they were writing primarily for an economic, rather than finance, audience.

these two instruments have the same risk, and neither pays interest before maturity, the only explanation for the notes' higher yield is their lower liquidity. Kamara (1994) extends this study by documenting that the note-bill yield differential is systematically related to relative trading frequencies and to different tax status for the *sellers* (individual and corporate traders and investors) of notes and bills. Finally, Boudoukh and Whitelaw (1993) document surprisingly large price differtentials between almost identical Japanese government bonds. Those bonds which are part of the "benchmark issue" designated by the Japanese government typically offer yields that are 40–60 basis points lower than similar maturity, non-benchmark issues. Boudoukh and Whitelaw demonstrate the institutional restrictions on trading necessary for this to be a stable equilibrium, and conclusively document that liquidity can have significant value even in large and active capital markets.[35]

TAX EFFECTS IN BOND VALUATION   As we discuss elsewhere in this text, researchers have long been interested in the impact of taxes on security valuation and on observed corporate financial policies.[36] One aspect of this research that is particularly relevant to bond valuation involves the ratio of taxable to tax-exempt bond yields.[37] According to the Miller (1977) model of bond market equilibrium, the risk-adjusted yield on tax-exempt bonds (in the United States, principally municipal securities) should be equal to one minus the corporate tax rate times the equivalent taxable interest rate. The empirical evidence on this point is, however, contradictory. Trzcinka (1982) finds support for this hypothesis once the additional riskiness of municipal versus Treasury debt is accounted for, but Ang, Peterson, and Peterson (1985) and Buser and Hess (1986) present equally compelling evidence that the tax-exempt yield is typically higher than predicted by the Miller hypothesis.

An intriguing potential reconciliation of these two views is presented in Green (1993), who shows that rational tax arbitrage trading activities by highly-taxed individual investors will break the simple linkage between taxable and tax-exempt yield curves. In particular, Green's observation that the yield curve on tax-exempt securities *never* inverted during the 1954–1990 period is persuasive evidence that the tax-exempt market reflects factors that are idiosyncratic to a particular group of high-income investors, since taxable yield curves frequently inverted during that period.[38]

4.4.7 Valuing Mortgage-Backed and Floating Rate Securities

One of the most important capital market innovations of the past two decades has been the development of an immense and highly liquid market for **mortgage-backed**

---

35. Somewhat surprisingly, Warga (1992) documents liquidity-related yield differences of similar magnitudes in the U.S. Treasury bond market, but only for newly-issued bonds.

36. See especially the chapters on Capital Structure Theory and Dividend Policy (Chapters 7 and 8).

37. In addition to this line of research, Constantinides and Ingersoll (1984) present a model of the optimal trading strategy for an individual investor seeking to maximize his or her after-tax return from bond investments.

38. Even during the extreme months of March and April 1980, when one-year Treasuries had yields 300 basis points higher than 30-year Treasuries, long-term (30-year) municipal bond yields remained 150 (March) and 80 (April) basis points above equal-risk one-year munis (Green 1993, page 235).

securities (MBSs). These are also called **pass-through securities**, because the principal and interest payments made by mortgagors is passed through to investors (after the mortgage servicing company takes a cut, of course). McConnell and Singh (1994) report that the face amount of such securities outstanding in September 1993 exceeded $1.2 trillion. Two basic types of mortgages are securitized and sold to investors as mortgage-backed securities, **fixed rate mortgages** (FRMs) and **adjustable rate mortgages** (ARMs). Both are extremely difficult debt securities to value—FRMs because they require investors to account for both default risk and prepayment risk, and ARMs both because of default risk and because their values at any point in time can depend on the time path of interest rates leading up to the valuation date (their values are path-dependent). While almost all bond investors are subject to having their securities called whenever the general level of interest rates drops, MBS investors are especially susceptible to early redemption both because home owners can refinance mortgages at such low cost and because normal personal and professional frictions lead people to sell their homes (thus leading directly or indirectly to their mortgages being paid off) much more frequently than corporations call outstanding bond issues.

The mathematics of MBS valuation are quite intense, and in any case are far beyond our scope in this book. The interested reader is referred to Dunn and McConnell (1981), Titman and Torous (1989), Schwartz and Torous (1989), Kau, Keenan, Muller, and Epperson (1992, 1993), and McConnell and Singh (1994) for fixed-rate MBS valuation models, and to Kau, Keenan, Muller, and Epperson (1990, 1993) for adjustable-rate MBS valuation models. Finally, Ramaswamy and Sundaresan (1986) present a general model for valuing floating-rate corporate (non-mortgage-related) debt.[39]

4.4.8 Other Bond Valuation Issues

We conclude our discussion of advanced bond pricing topics with a discussion of two recent research topics. First, we discuss the role of bond rating agencies, then we examine bond pricing models which have been developed by researchers.

THE ROLE OF BOND RATING AGENCIES Most U.S. corporations that issue debt publicly choose to have that debt rated by one or more of the pre-eminent bond rating agencies. The two leading ratings services are Standard & Poor's (S&P) Corporation and Moody's Investors Service. Both provide similar default-risk ratings for individual bond issues. Although the actual inputs to these ratings processes are closely-guarded trade secrets, at least two recent studies have examined the economic functions the ratings services provide. Weinstein (1977) documents the counter-intuitive result that the announcement of a bond ratings change does not significantly impact the market value of the bond issue in question. He then points out that this is exactly what one would expect in an informationally-efficient market, since bond ratings changes *follow* changes in the economic performance of the issuing firm, and market participants are as well-

---

39. Valuation models for other specialized debt securities have also been developed and publicized. For example, Brennan and Schwartz (1977b) present a model for valuing savings, retractable, and callable bonds, while McConnell and Schlarbaum (1981a,b) analyze the reasons for the declining U.S. corporate use of **income bonds**—which are legally required to pay (tax-deductible) interest only when corporate earnings are positive, and which therefore would seem to be attractive instruments for financially-constrained firms to issue.

informed of these developments as are the ratings agencies. Wakeman (1981) reiterates this conclusion, and goes on to argue that ratings agencies provide a valuable liquidity-enhancing service by reassuring investors that the bond's true risk has been assessed and publicized. After all, a bond ratings agency places its considerable reputational capital on the line every time it certifies the riskiness of a security issue.

THE PRICING OF CORPORATE BONDS   Somewhat surprisingly, relatively few studies have attempted to document the exact pricing formula through which bond yields are determined. Following Fisher's (1959) path-breaking empirical study, Merton (1974) and Black and Cox (1976) presented theoretical bond pricing models. However, we are unaware of more recent empirical bond pricing studies, except for Edwards (1986)—who examines the pricing of bonds issued by sovereign (government), rather than corporate, borrowers. This is in sharp contrast to the literature on (bank) loan pricing, which is voluminous and which is surveyed in depth in chapter 9.[40] While the results of these studies largely confirm one's intuition (more risky and illiquid firms pay higher interest rates than less risky firms with adequate working capital), comparable results for publicly-traded bonds would be comforting.[41]

4.5   COMMON STOCK VALUATION

We now turn our focus toward several important common and preferred stock valuation issues, and there are three sections of material to be covered before concluding the chapter. First, we briefly examine basic common and preferred stock valuation techniques. Second, we describe and briefly discuss several more advanced common stock valuation issues, such as the relationship between accounting earnings and stock prices, the impact of inflation and other macroeconomic news announcements on stock valuation, and the impact of liquidity and personal taxes on stock prices. We conclude the expository part of this chapter with a summary and analysis of the burgeoning research area that has come to be called "market microstructure."

As mentioned, we begin our discussion of common stock with an overview of basic valuation techniques. Before describing these specifically, we will look again very briefly at the concept of an efficient market (discussed at length in chapter 3), which tends to dispel the belief that the prices of actively traded stocks can differ from their true values.

4.5.1 The Importance of Market Efficiency

Economically rational buyers and sellers use their assessment of an asset's risk and return to determine its value. To a buyer the asset's value represents the maximum price that he or she would pay to acquire it, while a seller views the asset's value as a minimum sale price. In competitive markets with many active participants, such as the New

---

40. In fairness, a number of studies examine the choice between public and private debt issuance and/or the choice between "inside" and "arms-length" debt financing (see, for example, Diamond 1991b).

41. Booth (1992) provides an interesting result regarding the impact on loan of interest rates having publicly-traded debt securities. He finds that firms with such public debt outstanding pay lower risk-adjusted loan interest rates than do firms without public debt. In effect, private lenders are able to free-ride on the monitoring services that public bondholders provide, and thus are able to charge the borrower lower loan rates.

York Stock Exchange, the interactions of many buyers (demanders of shares) and sellers (suppliers of shares) result in an equilibrium price or market value for each security. This price reflects the collective actions of buyers and sellers based on all available information. As new information becomes available, buyers and sellers are assumed to immediately digest such information and through their purchase and sale activities to quickly create a new market equilibrium price.

This process of market adjustment to new information can be viewed in terms of rates of return. From the discussions in chapter 3 we know that for a given level of risk, investors require a specified periodic return—the **required return**, k—which can be estimated by using beta and the CAPM. At each point in time, investors estimate the **expected return**, $\hat{k}$ (referred to in some cases as $E(R)$ in chapter 3)—the return that is expected to be earned on a given asset each period over an infinite time horizon. The expected return can be defined as the expected benefit each period divided by the current price of the asset. Whenever investors find that the expected return is not equal to the required return ($\hat{k} = k$), a market price adjustment will occur. If the expected return is less than the required return ($\hat{k} < k$), investors will sell the asset, since it is not expected to earn a return commensurate with its risk. Such action would drive the price down, which, assuming no change in expected benefits, will cause the expected return to rise to the level of the required return. If the expected return were above the required return ($\hat{k} > k$), investors would buy the asset, driving its price up and its expected return down to the point that it equals the required return. This market adjustment process can be demonstrated with an example.

The common stock of Arbitrage Industries (AI) is currently selling for $50 per share, and market participants expect it to generate benefits of $6.50 per share during each coming period. In addition the risk-free rate, R_f, is currently 7 percent; the market return, R_m, is 12 percent; and the stock's beta, β_M, is 1.20. When these values are used to calculate the firm's current expected return, $\hat{k}_0$, the result is:

$$\hat{k}_0 = \$6.50/\$50.00 = 13\%$$

When the appropriate values are substituted into the CAPM, the current required return, k_0, is:

$$\hat{k}_0 = 7\% + [1.20 \times (12\% - 7\%)] = 7\% + 6\% = 13\%$$

Since $\hat{k}_0 = \hat{k}_0$, the market is currently in equilibrium, and the stock is fairly priced at $50 per share. Assume that a just-reported earnings announcement suggests that Arbitrage Industries' cash flows are more sensitive to changes in the macroeconomic business cycle than previously thought. As a result, investors immediately adjust their risk assessment upward, raising the firm's beta from 1.20 to 1.40. The new required return, $\hat{k}_1$, becomes:

$$\hat{k}_1 = 7\% + [1.40 \times (12\% - 7\%)] = 7\% + 7\% = 14\%$$

Because the expected return of 13 percent is now below the required return of 14 percent, many investors would sell the stock—driving its price down to about $46.43—the price that would result in a 14 percent expected return, $\hat{k}_1$:

$$\hat{k}_1 = \$6.50/46.43 = 14\%$$

The new price of $46.43 brings the market back into equilibrium, since the expected return, $\hat{k}_1$, of 14 percent now equals the required return, $\hat{k}_1$, of 14 percent.

As was noted in chapter 3, active markets such as the New York Stock Exchange are efficient. They are made up of many rational investors who react quickly and objectively to new information. The Efficient Market Hypothesis, which is the basic theory describing the behavior of such a "perfect" market, states:

1. Securities are typically in equilibrium, meaning that they are fairly priced and their expected returns equal their required returns.

2. At any point in time, security prices fully reflect all public information available about the firm and its securities, and these prices react swiftly to new information.

3. Since stocks are fully and fairly priced, it follows that investors should not waste their time trying to find and capitalize on mispriced (undervalued or overvalued) securities.

With this refresher on market efficiency in mind, we are now ready to analyze the various stock pricing models that are most frequently used by financial analysts.

4.5.2 The Basic Stock Valuation Equation

Like bonds, the value of a share of common stock is equal to the present value of all future benefits it is expected to provide. Simply stated, the value of a share of common stock is equal to the present value of all future dividends it is expected to provide over an infinite time horizon.[42] Although by selling stock at a price above that originally paid, a stockholder can earn capital gains in addition to dividends, what is really sold is the right to all future dividends. Stocks that are not expected to pay dividends in the foreseeable future have a value attributable to a distant dividend that is expected to result from the sale of the company or liquidation of its assets. Therefore from a valuation viewpoint, only dividends are relevant. The basic valuation model for common stock can be specified as given in Equation 4.9:

$$P_0 = \frac{D_1}{(1+k_s)^1} + \frac{D_2}{(1+k_s)^2} + ... + \frac{D_\infty}{(1+k_s)^\infty} \qquad (4.9)$$

where P_0 = value of common stock
D_t = per-share dividend expected at the end of year t
k_s = required return on common stock

---

42. As numerous authors have demonstrated (beginning with Miller and Modigliani (1961)), stock prices can be valued using either earnings per share or dividends per share. Earnings that are retained and reinvested in the firm simply increase the size of dividends that can be paid once cash dividend payments are initiated. Over time, dividends can only be paid to shareholders out of the firm's earnings stream, and the only way to convert earnings into something valuable to shareholders is to (eventually) pay them out as dividends. To grasp this point, ask yourself what the market value of a firm with the following characteristics would be: (1) because it has a legal monopoly on the production of thundranium, the firm in question is very profitable, but it is legally prohibited from paying cash dividends and all earnings must be either reinvested internally or distributed to charity; (2) all managers are paid competitive, but fixed, salaries (no bonus or stock-related compensation); (3) all of the firm's voting stock is owned by a trust fund (though it is allowed to issue non-voting stock publicly), and the company's thundranium monopoly will end if control of the company is ever sold. No matter how profitable such a company becomes, the market value of its non-voting shares will be zero.

The equation can be simplified somewhat by redefining each year's dividend, D_t, in terms of anticipated growth. We will consider three cases here—zero growth, constant growth, and variable growth.

ZERO GROWTH   The simplest approach to dividend valuation, the zero growth model, assumes a constant, nongrowing dividend stream. In terms of the notation already introduced:

$$D_1 = D_2 = \cdots = D_\infty$$

Letting D_1 represent the amount of the annual dividend, Equation 4.9 under zero growth would reduce to:

$$P_0 = D_1 \times \left[\sum_{t=1}^{\infty} \frac{1}{(1+k_s)^t} \right] = D_1 \times (PVIFA_{k_s,\infty}) = \frac{D_1}{k_s} \tag{4.10}$$

The equation shows that with zero growth the value of a share of stock would equal the present value of a perpetuity of D_1 dollars discounted at a rate k_s. Let us look at an example.

The dividend of the Disco Company, an established wood products producer, is expected to remain constant at \$3 per share indefinitely. If the required return on its stock is 15 percent, the stock's value is \$20 (\$3/0.15).

CONSTANT GROWTH   The most widely cited dividend valuation approach, the constant growth model, assumes that dividends will grow at a constant rate, g, that is less than the required return, k_s ($g < k_s$). Letting D_0 represent the most recent dividend, Equation 4.9 can be rewritten as follows:

$$P_0 = \frac{D_0 \times (1+g)^1}{(1+k_s)^1} + \frac{D_0 \times (1+g)^2}{(1+k_s)^2} + \ldots + \frac{D_0 \times (1+g)^\infty}{(1+k_s)^\infty} \tag{4.11}$$

If we simplify Equation 4.11, it can be rewritten as follows:

$$P_0 = \frac{D_1}{k_s - g} \tag{4.12}$$

The constant growth model in Equation 4.12 is commonly called the **Gordon growth model**, after Myron Gordon, who popularized this formula during the 1960s and 1970s. An example will show how it works.

The Lazertronics Company, a small scientific instruments company, from 1991 through 1996 paid the per-share dividends shown below.

Year	Dividend per share (\$)
1996	1.40
1995	1.29
1994	1.20
1993	1.12
1992	1.05
1991	1.00

Using Appendix Table A.3 for the present-value interest factor, PVIF, the annual growth rate of dividends, which is assumed to equal the expected constant rate of dividend growth, g, is found to equal 7 percent. The company estimates that its dividend in 1995, D_1, will equal $1.50. The required return, k_s, is assumed to be 15 percent. When these values are substituted into Equation 4.12, the value of the stock is:

$$P_0 = \frac{\$1.50}{0.15-0.07} = \frac{\$1.50}{0.08} = \$18.75 \ per \ share$$

Assuming that the values of D_1, k_s, and g are accurately estimated, Lazertronics Company's stock value is $18.75.

VARIABLE GROWTH   The zero- and constant-growth common stock models presented in Equations 4.10 and 4.12, respectively, do not allow for any shift in expected growth rates. Because future growth rates might shift up or down due to changing expectations, it is useful to consider a variable growth model that allows for a change in the dividend growth rate. Letting g_1 equal the initial growth rate and g_2 equal the subsequent growth rate and assuming a single shift in growth rates (from g_1 to g_2) occurs at the end of year N, we can use the following four-step procedure to determine the value of a share of stock.

Step 1:   Find the value of the cash dividends at the end of each year, D_t, during the initial growth period—years 1 through N. This step may require adjusting the most recent dividend, D_0, using the initial growth rate, g_1, to calculate the dividend amount for each year. Therefore, for the first N years:

$$D_t = D_0 \times (1+g_1)^t = D_0 \times FVIF_{g_1,t}$$

Step 2:   Find the present value of the dividends expected during the initial growth period.   Using the notation presented earlier, this value can be given as:

$$\sum_{t=1}^{n}\left[\frac{D_0 \times (1+g_1)^t}{(1+k_s)^t}\right] = \sum_{t=1}^{n}\left[\frac{D_t}{(1+k_s)^t}\right] = \sum_{t=1}^{n}(D_t \times PVIF_{k_s,t})$$

Step 3:   Find the value of the stock at the end of the initial growth period, $P_N = D_{n+1}/(k_s-g_2)$, which is the present value of all dividends expected from year $N + 1$ to infinity—assuming a constant dividend growth rate, g_2. This value is found by applying the constant growth model (presented as Equation 4.12 in the preceding section) to the dividends expected from year $N + 1$ to infinity. The present value of P_N would represent the value today of all dividends that are expected to be received from year $N + 1$ to infinity. This value can be represented by:

$$\frac{1}{(1+k_s)^n} \times \frac{D_n+1}{k_s-g_2} = PVIF_{k_s,n} \times P_n$$

Step 4:   Add the present-value components found in steps 2 and 3 to find the value of the stock, P_0, given in Equation 4.13:

$$P_0 = \sum_{t=1}^{n}\left[\frac{D_0 \times (1+g_1)^t}{(1+k_s)^t}\right] + \left(\frac{1}{(1+k_s)^n} \times \frac{D_{n+1}}{(k_s-g_2)}\right) \qquad (4.13)$$

The application of these steps to a variable growth situation with only one growth rate change is illustrated in the following example.

The most recent (1996) annual dividend payment of Morris Industries, a rapidly growing boat manufacturer, was $1.50 per share. The firm's financial manager expects that these dividends will increase at a 10 percent annual rate, g_1, over the next three years (1997, 1998, and 1999) due to the introduction of a hot new boat. At the end of the three years (end of 1999) the firm's mature product line is expected to result in a slowing of the dividend growth rate to 5 percent per year forever (noted as g_2). The firm's required return, k_s, is 15 percent. To estimate the current (end-of-1996) value of Morris's common stock, $P_0 = P_{1996}$, the four-step procedure presented above must be applied to these data.

Step 1 The value of the cash dividends in each of the next three years is calculated in columns 1, 2, and 3 of Table 4.1. The 1997, 1998, and 1999 dividends are $1.65, $1.82, and $2.00, respectively.

Step 2 The present value of the three dividends expected during the 1995–1997 initial growth period is calculated in columns 3, 4, and 5 of Table 4.1. The sum of the present values of the three dividends is $4.14—the total of the column 5 values.

Step 3 The value of the stock at the end of the initial growth period (N = 1999) can be found by first calculating $D_N + 1 = D_{2000}$:

$$D_{2000} = D_{1999} \times (1 + .05) = \$2.00 \times (1.05) = \$2.10$$

By using $D_{2000} = \$2.10$, $k_s = 0.15$, and $g_2 = 0.05$, the value of the stock at the end of 1999 can be calculated:

$$P_{1999} = \frac{D_{2000}}{k_s - g_2} = \frac{\$2.10}{0.15 - 0.05} = \frac{\$2.10}{0.10} = \underline{\underline{\$21.00}}$$

Finally, in this step, the share value of $21 at the end of 1999 must be converted into a present (end-of-1996) value. Using the 15 percent required return, we get:

$$PVIF_{k_s,N} \times P_N = PVIF_{15\%,3} \times P_{1999} = 0.658 \times \$21.00 = \$13.82$$

Step 4 Adding the present value of the initial dividend stream (found in Step 2) to the present value of the stock at the end of the initial growth period (found in step 3) as specified in Equation 4.3, we get the current (end-of-1996) value of Morris Industries' stock:

$$P_{1996} = \$4.14 + \$13.82 = \$17.96$$

The stock is currently worth $17.96 per share.

It is important to recognize that the zero, constant, and variable growth valuation models presented above provide useful frameworks for estimating stock value. Clearly, the estimates produced cannot possibly be very precise, given that the forecasts of future growth and discount rates are themselves necessarily approximate. Looked at another way, a great deal of rounding error can be introduced into the stock price estimate as a result of rounding growth and discount rate estimates to the nearest whole percent. In applying valuation models, it is therefore advisable to carefully estimate these rates and conservatively round them, probably to the nearest tenth of a percent.

TABLE 4.1

CALCULATION OF PRESENT VALUE OF MORRIS INDUSTRIES' DIVIDENDS (1997–1999)

t	End of year	$D_0 = D_{1996}$ (1)	$PVIF_{10\%,t}$ (2)	D_t [(1) × (2)] (3)	$PVIF_{15\%,t}$ (4)	Present value of dividends [(3) × (4)] (5)
1	1997	$1.50	1.100	$1.65	.870	$1.44
2	1998	1.50	1.210	1.82	.756	1.38
3	1999	1.50	1.331	2.00	.658	1.32

$$\text{Sum of present value of dividends} = \sum_{t=1}^{3} \frac{D_0 \times (1 + g_1)^t}{(1 + k_s)^t} = \$4.14$$

4.5.3 Other Approaches to Common Stock Valuation

Many other approaches to common stock valuation exist, but only one is widely accepted. The more popular approaches include the use of book value, liquidation value, and some type of a price/earnings multiple.

BOOK VALUE   Book value per share is simply the amount per share of common stock to be received if all of the firm's assets are sold for their exact book (accounting) value and if the proceeds remaining after all liabilities (including preferred stock) are paid among the common stockholders. This method lacks sophistication and can be criticized on the basis of its reliance on historical balance sheet data. It ignores the firm's expected earnings potential and generally lacks any true relationship to the firm's value in the marketplace.[43] Let us look at an example.

The Mason Company currently (December 31, 1996) has total assets of $6 million, total liabilities including preferred stock of $4.5 million, and 100,000 shares of common stock outstanding. Its book value per share would therefore be:

$$(\$6,000,000 - \$4,500,000)/100,000 \text{ shares} = \$15 \text{ per share}$$

Since this value assumes that assets are sold for their book value, it may not represent the minimum share value. As a matter of fact, although most stocks sell above book value, it is not unusual to find stocks selling below book value.

LIQUIDATION VALUE   Liquidation value per share is the actual amount per share of common stock to be received if all of the firm's assets are sold, liabilities (including preferred stock) are paid, and any remaining money is divided among the common stockholders. This measure is more realistic than book value for firms that are not in

---

43. There is, however, one stage in a firm's life cycle when book value is appropriate—because it is all that is available. Book value is appropriate for new companies (just started), because earnings are non-existent, and the firm's **going concern value** is inestimable.

fact about to be liquidated, but it still fails to consider the earning power of the firm's assets. An example will illustrate.

The Mason Company found upon investigation that it would obtain only $5.25 million if it sold its assets today. The firm's liquidation value per share would therefore be:

$$(\$5,250,000 - \$4,500,000)/100,000 \text{ shares} = \$7.50 \text{ per share}$$

Ignoring any expenses of liquidation, this amount would be the firm's minimum value.

PRICE/EARNINGS (P/E) MULTIPLES   The price/earnings (P/E) ratio reflects the amount investors are willing to pay for each dollar of earnings. The average P/E ratio in a particular industry can be used as the guide to a firm's value if it is assumed that investors value the earnings of a given firm in the same manner as they do the "average" firm in that industry. The **price/earnings multiple approach** to value is a popular technique whereby the firm's expected earnings per share (EPS) are multiplied by the average price/earnings (P/E) ratio for the industry to estimate the firm's share value. The average P/E ratio for the industry can be obtained from a source such as **Standard & Poor's Industrial Ratios.** The use of P/E multiples is especially helpful in valuing firms that are not publicly traded, whereas the use of the market price may be preferable in the case of a publicly traded firm. In any case the price/earnings multiple approach is considered superior to the use of book or liquidation values, since it considers expected earnings. An example will demonstrate the use of price/earnings multiples.

The Mason Company is expected to earn $2.60 per share next year (1997). This expectation is based on an analysis of the firm's historical earnings trend and expected economic and industry conditions. The average price/earnings ratio for firms in the same industry is 7. Multiplying Mason's expected earnings per share (EPS) of $2.60 by this ratio gives us a value for the firm's shares of $18.20, assuming that investors will continue to measure the value of the average firm at 7 times its earnings.

It is important to recognize that professional securities analysts typically use a variety of models and techniques to value stocks. For example, an analyst might use the constant growth model, liquidation value, and price/earnings (P/E) multiples to estimate the true worth of a given stock. If the analyst feels comfortable with his or her estimates, the stock value would be viewed as being not greater than the largest estimate. Of course, should the firm's estimated liquidation value per share exceed its "going concern" value per share estimated by using one of the valuation models (zero, constant, or variable growth) or the P/E multiple approach, it would be viewed as being worth more dead than alive. In such an event the firm would lack sufficient earning power to justify its existence and should probably be liquidated. From an investor's perspective the stock in this situation would be an attractive investment only if it could be purchased at a price below its liquidation value, which in an efficient market would never occur.

4.5.4 Preferred Stock Valuation

Since preferred stock typically provides its holders with a fixed annual dividend over its assumed infinite life, Equation 4.10 can be used to find the value of preferred stock. The value of preferred stock can be estimated by substituting the stated preferred dividend and the required return on the preferred stock for D_1 and k_s, respectively, in Equation 4.10. For example, a preferred stock paying a $5 stated annual dividend and having a required return of 13 percent would have a value of $38.46 ($5/0.13). More advanced preferred stock valuation formulas are presented in Sorensen and Hawkins (1981), Emanuel (1983), and Ferreira, Spivey, and Edwards (1992). The investment performance of preferred stock is examined in Bildersee (1973), while the valuation of convertible preferred stock is studied in Lin and Rozeff (1995).

4.6   ADVANCED COMMON STOCK VALUATION TOPICS

Given the inherent complexity of common stock valuation, it is probably not surprising that researchers have examined numerous specialized valuation topics in recent years. We address several of these topics here, beginning with the broadest single area of research interest—the relationship between corporate earnings and stock prices. We then examine the theoretical and empirical relationship between stock prices and inflation, then we discuss the broader issue of the effect of macroeconomic news on stock valuation. We conclude this section with a discussion of the impacts of liquidity and personal taxation on common stock pricing.

4.6.1 Stock Prices and Corporate Earnings

As we briefly discussed earlier, common stocks can be valued as the discounted value of either dividends or earnings per share. Most empirical research on stock valuation has examined the relationship between earnings and stock prices, and in this section we survey and discuss this literature, beginning with what we will call earnings responsiveness tests—or tests of the sensitivity of stock prices to corporate earnings surprises. We then survey the literature that documents the predictive superiority of financial analysts' forecasts over simple time series extrapolations of corporate earnings. We conclude this section with a discussion of several other earnings-related studies that do not fit in either of the first two categories.

EARNINGS RESPONSIVENESS STUDIES   In a classic early paper, Ball and Brown (1968) study the information content of annual earnings reports. They conclude this number conveys economically and statistically significant information, since unexpected good news causes stock prices to increase dramatically, while negative earnings surprises cause stock prices to fall. Perhaps their most intriguing result, however, is their documentation of the fact that all but 10–15 percent of the information content of the annual earnings surprise is incorporated in stock prices *before* the number is publicly announced. Thus this study not only conclusively documents the valuation importance of corporate earnings numbers, it also indirectly documents the efficiency of the stock market—since traders rationally forecast what earnings will be, using publicly available information that predates the earnings announcement itself.

Later studies examine how quickly and efficiently stock prices react to earnings announcements. Joy, Litzenberger, and McEnally (1977) document the surprising result that the information in quarterly earnings announcements is not fully incorporated into stock price until several months after the announcement. This result is duplicated by subsequent researchers, though the ability to profit from a trading rule based on this anomaly is very questionable. On a related subject, Bernard, Thomas, and Abarbanell (1993) surveyed recent literature and concluded that the typical response to earnings announcements is too small, not too large, as those who maintain that a high-strung stock market over-reacts to earnings news would suggest. Finally, Datta and Dhillon (1993) find that earnings surprises (unexpectedly good or bad news) impact both stock and bond markets. This confirms the information content of earnings announcements for all security-holders, and suggests that gains and losses resulting from earnings surprises are shared.

FINANCIAL ANALYSTS' EARNINGS FORECASTS VS. TIME SERIES PREDICTIONS

One important subset of the earnings literature asks whether financial analysts provide more reliable forecasts of corporate earnings than do time series extrapolations or other mechanical predictions. In one sense, this is a "straw man," since brokerage firms do use highly-paid human analysts for this task, and would only do so if they provided forecasts that are superior enough to rote predictions to warrant the higher salary costs. The first authors to document the superiority of financial analysts are Brown and Rozeff (1978), and their results are echoed in the survey article by Givoly and Lakonishok (1984), and in Vander Weide and Carleton (1988).

Other researchers have used analysts' forecasts as inputs for other valuation models. An example of this is Harris and Marston (1992), who use analysts' forecasts of the S&P 500 Index value to derive average equity risk premiums over Treasury and corporate bonds during the 1982–1991 study period. They document (non-stable) market risk premiums of 6.47 and 5.13 percent per year over Treasury and corporate bonds, respectively. They also find that individual stock risk premiums are positively related to that stock's beta, as predicted by the CAPM.

OTHER EARNINGS-RELATED STUDIES   In addition to the two main streams of earnings-related research discussed above, many studies have examined other aspects of the relationship between earnings and stock prices. Beaver, Kettler, and Scholes (1970) and Bildersee (1975) document that market-determined risk measures (beta) and accounting determined risk measures (leverage, profitability ratios, etc.) are highly correlated, and both probably reflect the same underlying risk factors. Linke and Zumwalt (1984) document estimation biases in the discounted cash flow valuation formulas commonly used by analysts and utility regulators. They then present adjustment factors that can be used to correct the biases (related to the timing of dividend receipts). On a related subject, Hickman and Petry (1990) examine different models for valuing privately-held stock, and conclude that the **market comparables approach** (comparing private companies to publicly-traded firms in the same industry) favored by the courts is usually more accurate and robust than are other commonly-used valuation techniques.

More recently, Lee, Mucklow, and Ready (1993) document that NYSE specialists' bid-ask spreads widen and depths (volumes traded) fall in anticipation of earnings announcements. This clearly indicates that liquidity providers are sensitive to changes in information asymmetry risks, and use spreads and depths to manage that risk.[44] Perhaps most important of all, Fama and French (1995) find that the market, size, and book-to-market factors they document for returns (discussed in chapter 3 of this text) are mirrored in the earnings of those same firms. In other words, high book-to-market equity valuations imply poor long-term earnings prospects, consistent with rational pricing.[45] Finally,

---

44. Bid-ask spread studies are analyzed in depth in the market microstructure section of this chapter.

45. Unfortunately, due to noise in the data, Fama and French cannot prove that the book-to-market factor in earnings drive these factors in returns, though such a conclusion is clearly plausible.

Chan, Jegadeesh, and Lakonishok (1995) find that the superior stock performance of value stocks (low P/E stocks) over glamour stocks (high P/E stocks) is not merely the result of a database selection bias. This relationship persists even for actively-traded stocks, using a sample that is free of selection bias.

4.6.2 Stock Prices and Inflation

Fama and Schwert (1977) kicked off a major stream of research with their perplexing finding that common stock returns are *negatively* related to expected inflation—and probably to unexpected inflation as well. Both common sense and economic theory suggest that stocks—as claims on real assets—should serve as a hedge against inflation. But while residential real estate hedged both expected and unexpected inflation, and bonds and bills provided at least a partial hedge, stocks were clear losers. Fama (1981) suggests that the negative stock return/inflation relationship actually results from a more fundamental negative relationship between inflation and real activity (particularly capital spending). Geske and Roll (1983) point to a fiscal and monetary linkage between inflation and stock returns, where increased inflation signals lower federal government tax revenue, higher borrowing, and increased monetization of the Treasury's debt by the Federal Reserve System. This in turn leads to higher real interest rates and declining stock prices.

The true nature of the relationship between inflation and stock returns has been clarified during the past decade. First, Titman and Warga (1989) find that there is a significant positive relationship between stock returns and *future* inflation and interest rates. This finding implies that stock returns predict future price level changes, and do so in a logical way—stock price increases (decreases) predict higher (lower) inflation and interest rates. Most definitively, Boudoukh and Richardson (1993) explain the contemporaneous stock return/inflation relationship by examining the correlation between stock price changes and a measure of *long-term* inflation. Over the 1802–1990 period, they find that nominal stock returns are positively related to both ex ante and ex post inflation. Finally, Boudoukh, Richardson, and Whitelaw (1994) theoretically and empirically examine the industry-level relationship between stock returns and expected inflation, and find it is related to cyclical movements in industry output. Stock returns of non-cyclical industries tend to covary positively with expected inflation, while cyclical industry returns covary negatively.

4.6.3 Stock Returns and Macroeconomic News

One of the most challenging tasks any finance instructor faces is explaining to students the exact nature of the relationship between macroeconomic news—particularly news about the pace of economic growth—and stock returns. For example, what impact should news that the economy will grow more rapidly than previously expected have on overall stock price levels? On one hand, more rapid economic growth implies more rapid growth in corporate earnings. Since we know that a stock's price is simply the present value of all its future cash flows, higher corporate profits clearly imply higher stock prices. However, rapid economic growth also suggests increasing corporate demand for credit and higher real interest rates, which implies that the discount rate used in the stock valuation equation will also rise. Therefore, an announcement that economic growth will increase can cause stock prices to rise or fall, depending upon whether the news affects the numerator of the stock valuation equation (the stream of earnings per share) more than the denominator (the discount rate).

While we are unaware of any study that directly models and tests the relationship between earnings growth rates and discount rates in determining stock prices—which would be extremely difficult to properly specify, in any case—several authors do examine the impact of macroeconomic news announcements on stock price levels.[46] One early study is by Pearce and Roley (1985), who document that surprises related to monetary policy significantly affect stock prices, but that inflation surprises have only limited impact and news about real activity has no discernible impact at all. This last result is modified by McQueen and Roley (1993), who specifically allow for different stock price effects at different stages of the business cycle. They find that when the economy is strong the stock market responds negatively to news about higher real activity. They conclude that this negative relationship is caused by larger increases in the discount rate relative to expected cash flows, as suggested by the valuation model discussed above.

On a related note, Bartov and Bodnar (1994) examine the relationship between exchange rate changes and the stock returns of U.S. firms with significant international operations. Theoretically, internationally active firms should benefit from a depreciating dollar, both because their foreign earnings will be worth more in dollars and because the goods they produce in their U.S. factories will be cheaper on world markets—thus boosting export earnings. Bartov and Bodnar fail to document the expected correlation between contemporaneous stock returns and changes in the value of the dollar, though they do find that *lagged* changes in the dollar explain a significant fraction of current stock returns. They interpret this result as evidence that the market misprices the stocks of internationally active U.S. companies.

Two other papers on related topics deserve mention before we move on. First, Shinnar, Dressler, Feng, and Avidan (1989) present a methodology for estimating the real economic return for a sample of large U.S. industrial firms. They document a significant decline in the core profitability of these firms between the 1960s and the mid-1980s.[47] Second, French and Poterba (1991) attempt to explain the massive run-up in Japanese stock prices that occurred between 1986 and 1989, as well as the subsequent collapse in stock price levels. They can find no satisfactory explanation for either event, though the price decline is easier to rationalize than the initial increase.[48]

4.6.4 Stock prices and liquidity

As was the case with bond valuation, it was not until 1986 that the intuitively plausible relationship between stock value and liquidity was empirically verified. In that year,

---

46. Scott (1985) does suggest that changing interest rates may explain at least part of the extreme variability in stock price levels he documents, but he does not examine this empirically.

47. This has clearly been reversed during the economic expansion that began in April 1991. In fact, by 1995 the profitability of American business had reached a 45-year high.

48. French and Poterba also document that roughly half of the widely-cited difference in average P/E ratios between Japanese and American firms can be explained by accounting differences. These accounting differences cannot, however, explain the doubling of Japanese stock prices between 1986 and 1989, nor their subsequent decline.

Amihud and Mendelson documented a non-linear, negative relationship between a share's liquidity (as measured by its bid-ask spread) and its expected return. To entice investors to hold relatively illiquid shares, they must be offered a higher expected return. Amihud and Mendelson (1991) also examine the implications of their liquidity results for investors with differing time horizons.

Interestingly, 1986 was also an important year for another branch of the liquidity/stock return literature—the group of studies that examine the impact on stock prices of an exchange listing or inclusion in a major stock index. Harris and Gurel (1986) examine whether a stock's inclusion in the S&P 500 Index impacts its market value. Since these inclusions do not convey any new information about the firm's prospects, examining their valuation impact represents a clear test of Scholes' (1972) price pressure hypothesis. Since S&P inclusions are associated with an immediate 3 percent increase in value, that is almost completely reversed after two weeks, Harris and Gurel interpret their results as supporting the price pressure hypothesis. Upon inclusion, mutual fund managers (particularly managers of index funds) buy the stock in order to replicate the S&P index in their own portfolios, but this demand quickly subsides and stock prices then return to their fundamental values.

Two later studies provide general support for the Harris and Grubel findings. Kadlec and McConnell (1994) examine the valuation impact of listing on the NYSE. They find that transferring to the Big Board from one of the other markets causes stock prices to increase by 5 percent, and also leads to a significant increase in the number of shareholders and a decrease in the bid-ask spread. They conclude that both investor recognition and increased liquidity are sources of added value from an exchange listing. Beneish and Gardner (1995) find that, unlike additions to the S&P index, stocks that are included in the Dow Jones Industrial Average (DJIA) do not experience significant increases in price or trading volume. They attribute this result to the lack of index fund rebalancing (there is no major futures or options contract tied to the DJIA).[49]

In addition to the empirical studies cited above, Diamond and Verrechia (1991) examine the value of liquidity from a theoretical perspective. They examine the incentives of firms to voluntarily disclose information in order to reduce informational asymmetries and thus increase the liquidity for their securities. Not surprisingly, they find that large firms have greater incentives to disclose information, because they would gain the most from increased liquidity. On the other hand, Diamond and Verrechia also show that completely eliminating informational asymmetries would *reduce* liquidity and lower security value, since it would prompt market-makers to withdraw from trading.

4.6.5 Taxes and Stock Valuation

The final stock valuation topic we will address is the impact of personal taxes on stock pricing. Since we address this issue in depth in other chapters (particularly the risk and return, capital structure, and dividend policy chapters), as well as in our earlier discussion

---

49. Beneish and Gardner do, however, document significant negative returns when stocks are removed from the DJIA. They attribute this to increased information acquisition and trading costs for investors in these shares after they are removed from the index.

of bond valuation, our review here will be very brief and will focus on capital gains taxation. Research in this area has focused primarily on two topics—estimating the effective rate of capital gains taxation and studying how these taxes impact the trading behavior of tax-sensitive investors.

Protopapadakis (1983), Poterba (1987), Seyhun and Skinner (1994), and Bossaerts and Dammon (1994) examine the effective rate of capital gains taxes in the United States. Protopapadakis estimates the effective marginal capital gains tax rate to be between 3.4 percent and 6.6 percent during the 1960–1978 study period. He also finds that capital gains are held, on average, between 24 and 31 years before being realized. Poterba examines U.S. tax realization data to determine whether investors are able to evade capital gains taxation. He documents significant investor heterogeneity, but concludes that over 40 percent of all investors do in fact pay significant capital gains taxes. Seyhun and Skinner also examine tax realization data, and conclude that investors do face significant capital gains tax burdens—which they do not actively attempt to reduce through stock trading. Finally, Bossaerts and Dammon study whether measuring returns on an after-personal-tax basis improves the explanatory power of a consumption CAPM model. They find that a dividend tax variable improves the model's fit, but the capital gains variable's coefficient is imprecise and implausibly large.

One of the first and most important studies to examine how personal taxes can induce investor trading behavior is the work by Constantinides (1984). He described how investors should trade to minimize their personal tax liabilities, and suggested this trading behavior might be related to the January Effect (abnormally high early-year returns for small stocks) documented in stock returns. In an attempt to evaluate proposed changes in capital gains tax rates, Auerbach (1988) surveys the existing literature on tax-induced trading and the impact of capital gains taxes on stock valuation. He concludes, honestly, that we do not know nearly enough about such behavior to predict how any proposed tax change will influence either trading patterns or security valuation. As mentioned above, Seyhun and Skinner (1994) examine whether capital gains tax liabilities induce investors to actively trade, and find little evidence of this result.

On the other hand, Umlauf (1993) provides striking evidence that the imposition of a stock transactions tax by the Swedish government during the period 1980–1987 caused stock prices and trading volume to fall, without reducing price volatility. The increase in this tax's rate to 2 percent in 1986 caused much of the trading volume in Swedish shares to migrate to London. This empirical result was consistent with the predictions of Levine's (1991) model of tax policy and economic growth. Levine predicts that the imposition of taxes on financial transactions will reduce the fraction of resources devoted to firms in the economy and may also increase the incentive for firms to prematurely remove capital from productive use. The net result of a transactions tax will therefore be lower per capita economic growth rates.

4.7   MARKET MICROSTRUCTURE THEORY AND EVIDENCE

Perhaps no other area of finance has attracted as much academic and practitioner interest during the past decade as has **market microstructure**—the study of how information is incorporated into security market prices through trading activities, and how market institutional arrangements impact security pricing efficiency. This relatively new field has become the focus of intense study for (in our opinion) two principal reasons. First, the **market break of October 1987** forced policy-makers and academic researchers alike to confront the reality that markets are far more volatile (and fragile) than had previously been realized.[50] Second, during the past decade capitalism has been on the march, and many countries have recently established their first stock and bond markets. Simultaneously, deregulation and privatization have been providing a massive spur to trading volume in many other countries with established markets. This massive increase in securities trading has added urgency to the academic investigation into the workings of securities markets.

Since it is such a new field, there is not yet an established taxonomy for categorizing market microstructure research. This makes our present task particularly difficult (and potentially controversial). Rather than attempt to impose a crude classification scheme, we will instead present the six most important topics that microstructure research has attempted to address, and these will serve as the organizing focus for our subsequent literature review and discussion. In essence, microstructure research has constructed the following six types of models to address these topics:

1. **Price formation models**: These ask how relevant, non-public information is incorporated into the market price of securities, and how **market makers** (dealers who stand ready to buy and sell securities) protect themselves from losses resulting from transacting with better-informed traders.

2. **Price-volume models**: Several of these models try to explain the empirically-documented phenomenon that trading volume and price volatility are systematically higher immediately after market openings and immediately prior to market closings. Other models attempt to predict *when* (during active or inactive trading periods) and/or *how* (with one large trade or several smaller ones) an informed trader will choose to transact in order to capture as much of the value of his or her inside information as possible.

3. **Bid-Ask spread models**: In most financial markets, the compensation to market-makers for providing liquidity comes in the form of a **bid-ask spread**, which is the difference between the price they are willing to buy the security for (the bid price) and the price at which they will sell the security (the ask price). Several theoretical models have been developed to predict the size and composition of this spread—to determine the relative importance of asymmetric information, order processing, and inventory control costs—and to predict how spreads will vary between markets with different institutional settings. Empirical studies have then tested these models, with varying degrees of success.

---

50. As is widely known, on October 19, 1987 the principal U.S. stock markets lost almost 25 percent of their value in the single most hectic day of trading in history. Over 600 million NYSE shares changed hands that day, the Dow Jones Industrial Average declined by over 500 points (roughly 22 percent of its current value), and the carnage was even worse on other U.S. and international markets. The very next trading day, however, saw the markets recover about one–third of their total losses, and within a year all the major U.S. markets were hitting new all-time highs. Interestingly, by 1995 average stock market trading volumes had increased so much that new volume records were set during the bad—but hardly catastrophic—trading day of July 19. On that day, 597.5 million NASDAQ and 482.9 million NYSE shares traded hands, and the DJIA and NASDAQ indices fell by 57.41 and 46.12 points, respectively. While neither point decline set a new record, the NASDAQ volume figure was the highest ever, and this was the first day that combined NYSE and NASDAQ volume ever exceeded one billion shares.

4. **Market structure models**: It is a curious fact that the two largest U.S. stock markets have fundamentally different market-making arrangements, yet both are runaway success stories by any historical measure. On the NYSE, a single exchange-designated **specialist** is charged with maintaining an orderly market in the shares of a given company. This specialist must either match buy and sell orders submitted by market participants, or must herself become the opposite party to anyone wishing to buy or sell shares.[51] In contrast, the NASDAQ market allows multiple dealers to serve as market-makers for any given stock, and these dealers are free to enter or withdraw from the market upon short notice. Academic researchers have attempted both to explain how specialist and dealer markets can co-exist and to predict when one type of market will have a competitive advantage over the other.

5. **Non-stock market microstructure models and applications**: Several researchers have applied the tools of microstructure research—which were developed primarily to examine stock markets—to examinations of other types of financial markets. People have also studied whether heretofore unexplained financial phenomena, such as the negative return to stockholders resulting from a corporation's announcement of a new share issue, can be explained in whole or in part by microstructure effects.

6. **Optimal security market regulation models**: One of the most promising aspects of microstructure research is that it offers objective tools to analyze the effectiveness and costs of security market regulations—both those that have already been imposed and those which have been proposed or considered. As you might expect, the results to date suggest the need to oppose the regulatory imperative that policy-makers all too often seem to feel.

We examine each of these models below, beginning with the price formation models. Rather than attempt a full-scale literature review, we will instead (briefly) describe only the key theoretical models in each area, and will then summarize the theoretical extensions and empirical tests of these core models.

4.7.1 Price Formation Models

At the very heart of modern capital market theory lies a theoretical paradox. For financial markets to be informationally and allocationally efficient, they must rapidly and fully incorporate all private information into the prices they generate for financial claims. However, Grossman (1976) and Grossman and Stiglitz (1980) show that if

---

51. The historical evolution of the specialist system is described in Lindsey and Schaede (1992). It seems that in 1875 a broker named James Boyd decided to conduct trading in a single share (Western Union) from one spot on the exchange floor after a broken leg severely restricted his freedom of movement. Since other traders soon found that they could always make a market at Boyd's "post," the innovation was immediately copied by other brokers for other shares, and by 1910 over ten percent (123 of 1,100) of the NYSE members were specialists. By 1987, this percentage had increased to almost 31 percent (422 of 1366 members).

agents are price-takers and prices are fully-revealing (incorporate all relevant information), then an equilibrium with costly information acquisition does not exist.[52] No single trader has the incentive to invest in information acquisition since they will not be compensated for this investment, but without information acquisition prices cannot be informative. For financial markets to work efficiently, trading must be costly, and a mechanism must be found to compensate traders for investing in information acquisition. The theoretical models that have been advanced to motivate this type of market equilibrium are known as noisy rational expectations models (see Diamond and Verrechia 1981 and Verrechia 1982), or more simply as **price formation models**.

The earliest, and by far the most influential, fully-developed price formation model is presented in Kyle (1985). He develops a dynamic (multi-period) model of trading that allows an examination of the information content of prices, the liquidity characteristics of a speculative market, and the value of private information to an insider. Kyle's model has three types of traders: (1) a single, risk-neutral insider, (2) several competitive, risk-neutral market makers, and (3) uninformed noise traders who transact randomly. The insider makes positive profits by exploiting his or her informational monopoly power optimally in a dynamic context, where noise trading provides camouflage which conceals his or her trading from market makers. The aggregate quantities demanded by noise and insider trades is termed the **order flow**, and the insider trades in such a way that his private information is incorporated into prices gradually. The market makers rationally interpret information in the order flow, and set prices to achieve a zero profit from trading. In effect, therefore, market makers break even and insiders earn a profit at the expense of noise traders.

Kyle's model represents a real breakthrough, because it describes a trading equilibrium where informational asymmetries impact both quantities and prices. Subsequent authors who have extended this model or developed new price formation models include Easley and O'Hara (1987), Subrahmanyam (1991), Harris and Raviv (1993), Wang (1994), George, Kaul, and Nimalendran (1994), and Foster and Viswanathan (1994).[53] Collectively, these authors describe a rich variety of institutional and/or informational asymmetry settings where trading serves to incorporate all relevant information into market prices in a way that compensates insiders for the value of their information while still providing competitive returns to market makers.[54]

---

52. This theoretical paradox is discussed quite effectively in Jackson (1991).

53. Easley and O'Hara show that allowing trade size to vary introduces an adverse selection problem into trading, where informed traders wish to trade larger amounts than noise traders. Subrahmanyam extends the Kyle model to incorporate risk aversion for the market makers and informed traders, while Harris and Raviv present a model of trading in speculative markets that is based on differences of trader opinion regarding *common* (not private) information. Wang links the nature of the heterogeneity of trader informational endowments to volume and price dynamics in competitive markets, while George, Kaul, and Nimalendran show that volume can be negatively related to the degree of informational asymmetry in a specialist market where transactions costs are determined endogenously. Finally, Foster and Viswanathan describe a market equilibrium with two asymmetrically informed traders and one uninformed market maker.

54. Several other important price formation models are examined theoretically or empirically in the Market Microstructure Special Issue of the **Review of Financial Studies** (1991).

Given their theoretical nature, price formation models have not been the subjects of many empirical analyses. One important exception to this rule is the study by Jones, Kaul, and Lipson (1994), who document that trading volume is informative to traders—as predicted—but that the total number of transactions is a more important explanation of informativeness than is trade size. In fact, size has no explanatory power in explaining price variability above that accounted for by number of transactions.

4.7.2 Price-Volume Models

An important series of empirical studies—beginning with the influential paper by Wood, McInish, and Ord (1985)—document that average stock price volatility and volume are highest at the beginning and end of the trading days.[55] Several authors have attempted to explain these U-shaped volatility and volume patterns with theoretical models of informed trading.[56] Both Admati and Pfleiderer (1988) and Foster and Viswanathan (1990) develop models of time-dependent trading volume that show how information is incorporated into securities prices through the strategic activities of informed traders.[57] These studies differ in that Admati and Pfleiderer (1988) predict that informed trading will be concentrated in those periods where liquidity trading is also concentrated—at the open and close of trading, when they presume that trading costs will be low—while Foster and Viswanathan predict that informed traders will avoid these periods, since this is also the time when adverse information (and total trading) costs will be highest. Foster and Viswanathan (1993) document that adverse selection costs and return volatility are indeed highest at the opening of trading, and they interpret this finding as contradictory to Admati and Pfleiderer, but supportive of their theoretical model.[58]

Several recent empirical papers have also examined the price-volume (and volatility) relationship exhibited in intraday returns. Berry and Howe (1994) document that public information arrival (measured as news releases carried by Reuter's News Services) displays systematic intraday and seasonal patterns. They also describe a positive relationship between the amount of information released and trading volume (but not volatility). Gerety and Mulherin (1994) examine the intraday evolution of volatility

---

55. Using a new transactions-level database of trades on the NYSE, Wood, McInish, and Ord also document that average returns are highest at opening and closing, and that there is little short-term autocorrelation in stock returns once biases attributable to asynchronous trading are accounted for. The stylized facts of this article are efficiently summarized in the discussion by Tauchen (1985).

56. Spiegel and Subrahmanyam (1995) present a somewhat related model that analyzes the effect of anticipated large demand pressures on asset premia. This model also predicts that large institutions who can time their trades during a day will choose to trade at the opening—or during other times of unusually high volume.

57. Both papers also adopt Kyle's basic structural model, with informed traders, competitive market makers, and uninformed noise traders.

58. Foster and Viswanathan also document systematic differences in variance patterns over weekends and other multi-day closing periods as compared with overnight closings during the trading week. Slezak (1994) presents a theoretical model that explains these interday patterns based on delays in the resolution of uncertainty (and the attendant increased risk of holding an inventory of securities) over extended closure periods.

using 40 years of hourly observations of the Dow Jones 65 Composite Index levels. They document that transitory volatility declines steadily throughout the day, and interpret this result as supporting the idea that trading aids price formation.[59] Finally, Chang, Jain, and Locke (1995) document a U-shaped pattern of volatility in the S&P 500 futures market that occurs after the stock market itself closes. Since the futures market trades for fifteen minutes after the stock market shuts down, this pattern suggests that price discovery continues even when the underlying asset market closes.

4.7.3 Bid-Ask Spread Models

The modeling of bid-ask spreads is one area of microstructure research that has proven particularly amenable to theoretical and empirical analyses. It is also an area that is intuitively understandable, and thus represents a real "success story" for the microstructure research agenda. Conceptually, the bid-ask spread in a securities market is the economic compensation given to a market maker to ensure that he or she will continue providing liquidity services. In particular, the market-maker is expected to stand ready to buy securities whenever someone wishes to sell, as well as to sell securities whenever someone wishes to buy. The difference between the bid and ask prices the market-maker offers to a potential customer is called the **quoted spread**, while the difference between what the market-maker actually pays and receives for his or her securities inventory is called the **effective spread**. In actual practice, the effective spread is almost always less than the quoted spread. In U.S. stock markets, for example, the effective spread appears to be slightly more than half of the quoted spread.[60]

Early theoretical research into the provision of liquidity services tended to focus on the transactions costs of processing buy and sell orders (e.g., Demsetz 1968). As it became clear that these out-of-pocket and opportunity costs were only one part of the quoted spread, they became known as **order processing costs**. Likewise, early empirical research tended to compare the total spreads observed in different markets, without attempting to decompose those spreads into component parts (e.g., Branch and Freed 1977). The 1980s, however, witnessed the development of a full-scale model of the bid-ask spread. Ho and Stoll (1981, 1983) show that market-makers will use the quoted bid-ask spread to adjust their personal inventory positions—raising the bid and/or the ask price when their inventories are uncomfortably low, and lowering ask and/or bid prices

---

59. As we will discuss more fully below, they also interpret this result as compelling evidence against the wisdom of "circuit breakers" and other mandated trading halts that shut down stock markets once price levels have moved by a certain amount.

60. Stoll (1989) finds the realized spread in the NASDAQ market to be, on average, 57 percent of the quoted spread, while Petersen and Fialkowski (1994) document that effective spreads for exchange-listed stocks are even lower (roughly half the quoted spread). Petersen and Fialkowski also find that NYSE spreads are narrower (better for customers) than spreads on the regional exchange, which they interpret as evidence against the idea that U.S. equity markets are truly integrated. Finally, Campbell, LaMaster, Smith, and Van Boening (1991) document an incentive for traders in an experimental market to transact "off-floor" (privately) at prices inside the publicly-quoted bid-ask spread. This action allows them to split the gain represented by the spread without having to publicly acknowledge a willingness to make price concessions.

when inventory levels are too high. This is the **inventory control** component of the bid-ask spread, and it implies a clear pattern for the temporal evolution of bid-ask quote revisions.[61] Finally, Copeland and Galai (1983) and Glosten and Milgrom (1985) show that the possibility of information-based trading can by itself induce a positive bid-ask spread, and will increase the quoted spread in most settings. This **adverse selection** component of the bid-ask spread is designed to compensate the market-maker for the risk of doing business with a better-informed trader, and it also implies a clear pattern for bid and ask quote revisions. Since there is always the chance that any given transaction will have an informed trader as the counter-party, the market-maker will lower his or her bid price after every purchase and will raise the ask price after every sale.

Numerous empirical studies have documented the basic validity of this three-component model of the quoted bid-ask spread, though they differ on the exact importance of each component. Glosten and Harris (1988) and Hasbrouck (1988) clearly show the importance of adverse selection costs, but the most comprehensive empirical spread decomposition study presented to date is Stoll (1989). He shows that 43 percent of the quoted spread for NASDAQ stocks represents compensation for adverse selection costs, and that compensation for order processing and inventory control costs account for 47 and 10 percent of quoted spreads, respectively. Effective spreads are, on average, 57 percent of the quoted spreads.

4.7.4 Market Structure Models

For at least thirty years, a debate has been raging in American finance about the competitive advantages of specialist versus dealer markets. Only part of this debate is academic—the stakes for the two major U.S. stock exchanges are much higher, since whoever wins the debate wins assured prominence in global equity trading for decades to come.[62] In essence, the debate revolves around this question: "Which structure provides market participants with the optimal combination of the desirable liquidity features listed below?" (1) **market depth**, the ability to trade large quantities of securities with the least impact on prices; (2) **market tightness**, the ability to trade securities rapidly without great impact on prices; (3) **pricing efficiency**, the propensity of trading to incorporate relevant information into prices quickly and completely; (4) **operational efficiency**, the provision of market-making services at low cost (narrow bid-ask spreads and minimal fees); and (5) **guaranteed market-making**, the willingness of the market-maker(s) to be the trader of last resort—even in times of market panics.

Ho and Stoll (1983) are among the first researchers to examine the specialist versus multiple-dealer issue theoretically.[63] They show that spreads on comparable securities

---

61. Probably the clearest description of how the bid-ask spread should respond to order processing, inventory control, and adverse selection costs is presented in Stoll (1989).

62. Other countries also have obvious stakes in this debate, since there are a bewildering variety of trading systems worldwide that are all vying for regional or global dominance. Perhaps surprisingly, three of the largest of these markets—Tokyo, Osaka, and Frankfurt—do not employ market makers of any type for retail trading (Lindsey and Schaede 1992, page 48), yet Lehmann and Modest (1994) show that this does not prevent the Tokyo Stock Market from functioning effectively.

63. Another branch of theoretical and empirical research, exemplified by Glosten (1994), examines whether purely electronic trading systems are (or will become) competitive with exchange-based systems.

are expected to be higher in multiple-dealer markets (such as NASDAQ) than in single-dealer specialist markets (such as the NYSE and AMEX) because a multiple-dealer market stands ready to trade more shares at quoted prices. In other words, there is a trade-off between low trading cost and high trading volume. Ho and Macris (1985) and Grossman and Miller (1988) also show that multiple-dealer markets have higher aggregate inventory holdings and provide greater market depth than do specialist markets.[64] On the other hand, Leach and Madhavan (1993) predict that a specialist market will be better at price discovery, since a monopoly dealer can afford to experiment with different price levels until the correct price is obtained. The specialist will be able to recoup any early trading losses with a profitable flow of orders later in the trading period.[65] In multiple-dealer markets, however, no single dealer can afford to experiment with prices and thus every trade must break even.

Given that no clear winner to the title of most efficient market structure emerges from the theoretical literature, the issue must turn on empirical analyses—and at present the news for multiple dealer markets appears rather grim. Several studies document clear competitive advantages for specialist markets. Leach and Madhavan (1993) document the price discovery advantage they predicted theoretically for specialist markets, and Affleck-Graves, Hedge, and Miller (1994) show that order processing costs are lower on the NYSE and AMEX than on the NASDAQ (though adverse selection costs are higher). Most damning of all, however, are the studies by Christie and Schultz (1994) and Christie, Harris, and Schultz (1994). The first paper documents that odd-eighth quotes are virtually nonexistent for 70 of 100 actively-traded NASDAQ stocks. This implies that the minimum bid-ask spread is two-eighths ($0.25 per share) and clearly suggests that NASDAQ dealers implicitly collude to maintain wide spreads. Further support for this thesis is presented in Christie, Harris, and Schultz (1994). They document that effective spreads fell by nearly 50 percent for several of the largest NASDAQ stocks immediately after the results of their first study were reported in the national business media on May 26, 1994.

The empirical studies do not all favor the specialist system, however. Although Affleck-Graves, Hedge, and Miller (1994) document lower order processing costs for the NYSE, they also show that the NASDAQ market has lower adverse selection costs, and perhaps lower inventory control costs as well. Brock and Kleidon (1992), Harris (1994), and Chan, Christie, and Schultz (1995) also document clear evidence of monopoly power by exchange specialists in the intraday pattern of bid-ask spreads on the NYSE, which mirror (and are probably related to) the U-shaped patterns observed for volatility and volume. Finally, Stoll (1993) discusses the declining actual importance of specialist trading, even on the NYSE, as an ever larger fraction of total trading volume occurs off the exchange floor.[66] On balance, it seems clear that multiple-dealer markets must have important comparative advantages that

---

64. Affleck-Graves, Hedge, and Miller (1994) provide a good summary of the literature on the relative market depths of dealer and specialist markets.

65. Aitken, Garvey, and Swan (1995) document a similar benefit for long–term client/broker relationships using Australian Stock Exchange data.

66. The perceived market trends and proposed reforms discussed in Madden (1993) also clearly suggest a further lessening of the specialist's role in trading is likely in the years ahead.

academic empirical studies have not yet conclusively identified. How else can we explain the phenomenal growth of the NASDAQ, which now routinely trades more shares than the NYSE and AMEX combined?[67]

4.7.5 Non-Stock Market Microstructure Models and Applications

Although most of the core microstructure models were developed to explain trading in U.S. equity markets, several studies have used the tools of microstructure analysis to examine trading patterns in other markets. Examples include Vijh (1990) and Figlewski and Webb (1993)—who examine the role and liquidity of stock options markets—and Bollerslev and Domowitz (1993) and Bessembinder (1994), who examine bid-ask spreads in the interbank foreign exchange markets. In addition, the relationships between volume, volatility, and market depth in eight futures markets are examined in Bessembinder (1993), who finds that large open interest levels (large numbers of outstanding, "open" contracts) mitigate price volatility.

Another related stream of research re-examines previously unexplained financial phenomena to determine whether the "received results" might be explained in whole or in part by microstructure effects. Not surprisingly, many of these phenomena either disappear or become less pronounced once microstructure effects are considered. Examples of this work include Lease, Masulis, and Page (1991) [negative shareholder returns following seasoned equity issue announcements], Baker and Edelman (1992) and Cowan, Carter, Dark, and Singh (1992) [AMEX-to-NYSE and NASDAQ-to-NYSE listing decisions], Conrad and Conroy (1994) [positive excess returns to shareholders on stock split ex-days], and Han (1995) [liquidity effects of reverse stock splits]. Additionally, Huang and Stoll (1994) and Park (1995) respectively explain previously-documented intraday and interday autocorrelations in stock returns as microstructure artifacts.

4.7.6 Optimal Security Market Regulation Models

Most finance professionals, be they in business or academia, have a visceral, philosophical distaste for financial market regulation. Market microstructure research is not likely to change the visceral nature of that opposition, but it does provide a firm theoretical foundation for analyzing (and/or challenging) the effectiveness and costs of security market regulations. The most dramatic example of this application of microstructure research involves the **circuit breakers** that were adopted by the exchanges (under government pressure) after the market break of October 1987. These rules are designed to halt trading if prices change by more than a pre-specified amount during

---

67. The total daily dollar value of exchange-traded shares remains much larger, however, due to their higher average price. Furthermore, since average daily volume now exceeds 300 million shares on both the NYSE and NASDAQ, it seems clear that neither market is likely to bury the other in the foreseeable future. Proponents of each system's superiority will thus have to enjoy their financial success without the emotional satisfaction of final victory.

the trading day.[68] Lee, Ready, and Seguin (1994) and Subrahmanyam (1994) study trading halts from, respectively, empirical and theoretical viewpoints and reach a common conclusion: trading halts increase, rather than decrease, volume and volatility.[69] More generally, the proposition that the assumptions underlying rule-making at the U.S. Securities and Exchange Commission are either flawed or outdated (or both) is put forward quite persuasively in both Grundfest (1993) and Mulherin (1993).

—SUMMARY—

One of the core functions of a capital market is to generate price signals for the value of corporate debt and equity claims. In theory, stock and bond valuation is a fundamentally simple process—simply estimate the cash flows that will accrue to holders of a security, then determine the present value of those cash flows using an appropriate risk-adjusted discount rate. In the real world, valuation can be fiendishly complex, and will be dependent both upon market-wide and firm-specific factors. This chapter has discussed both types of factors, beginning with the determinants of the term structure of interest rates and concluding with an analysis of the importance of market microstructure in determining security values.

—QUESTIONS—

1. In words, describe how securities are valued in a capital market.

2. A bond with 10 years to maturity offers an 8 percent coupon interest rate, payable annually. What is the value of this bond if market interest rates are (a) 6 percent; (b) 8 percent; (c) 10 percent?

3. Define the following terms commonly used in bond valuation: (a) par value; (b) maturity date; (c) premium bonds; (d) discount bonds.

4. A 5-year bond is issued at par, when both the bond's coupon rate and market interest rates for bonds of this risk are 6 percent. Assume market interest rates then

---

68. One set of circuit breakers is tripped when the Dow Jones Industrial Average (DJIA) moves more than fifty points in a day, while the other set kicks in after a 250-point move. The first circuit breakers deny the exchange's clearing facilities to traders wishing to execute (computerized) **portfolio insurance** strategies (dynamic trading strategies involving simultaneous trading in stock index futures and options contracts, as well as the underlying stocks themselves, in order to protect the value of investment portfolios (see Brennan and Schwartz 1989). The second, more extreme circuit breaker would shut the exchange down entirely for the remainder of a trading day, once a 250-point change occurs. The first circuit breaker has been triggered many times since 1987, but the second never has been tripped-though as Power (1995) makes clear, since the rule is based on a nominal amount (250 points) rather than a percentage price change, it is sure to be tripped in the future.

69. Dutta and Madhavan (1995) reach a somewhat different conclusion about **price continuity rules** (which limit transaction price movements for individual securities) that securities markets have adopted without government pressure. Rules such as specialist-initiated trading halts need not reduce price efficiency, although they do redistribute profits among traders.

change to 9 percent. What is the percentage change in the bond's value that results from this change in interest rates?

5. Discuss how a bond's interest rate risk is related to its coupon rate and term to maturity.

6. Using the data for the 10-year bond in question 2 above, recompute the bond's value for each interest rate level assuming that interest is paid semi-annually, rather than annually.

7. What is the Fisher Effect? Has empirical testing supported or rejected the predictions of this theoretical model?

8. Define the following terms: (a) term structure of interest rates; (b) yield curve; (c) normal yield curve; (d) inverted yield curve; (e) flat yield curve.

9. [Essay question] Describe the key features of the three main expectations theories of the term structure of interest rates. What does each theory predict the "normal" shape of the yield curve will be?

10. Assume the current 1-year interest rate is 6.5 percent, and the current 2-year rate is 8.0 percent. What is the implied forward rate for a 1-year bond at the end of next year? What would the implied forward rate be if the 2-year interest rate was 5.5 percent rather than 8.0 percent?

11. What is the market segmentation hypothesis? How has it fared as a description of the term structure of interest rates?

12. [Essay question] In words, describe duration, and discuss what it implies for bond valuation. Why is it true that duration can be expressed either in years or as a price elasticity?

13. Describe how a bond portfolio can be "immunized." What does this mean, and why might a bond investor attempt to immunize a portfolio?

14. [Essay question] Describe the key features of the principal theories that have been advanced to explain debt maturity structure choice. What are the most important empirical predictions of each theoretical model? Which models have been supported by empirical testing?

15. In the context of debt maturity structure choice models, what is meant by liquidity risk?

16. [Essay question] Describe the most important types of covenants that are typically inserted into bond indenture agreements. What are these covenants designed to achieve?

17. Why are call provisions inserted into some, but not all, bond indenture agreements? Who "pays for" these provisions, and how is payment made?

18. Why are conversion features inserted into some bonds, but not into others? What empirical regularities have been documented for forced conversion of convertible bonds?

19. Discuss the difference between positive and negative covenants.

20. Describe how liquidity and personal taxes impact bond valuation.

21. What special risks do investors in mortgage-backed securities face that investors in regular corporate bonds do not have to worry about?

22. Briefly discuss the economic functions that bond ratings services are expected to perform. How effectively do they perform these missions?

23. A company with a required return on equity of 12.5 percent is expected to pay a $4.00 per share dividend indefinitely. What is this firm's stock price?

24. Assume the risk-free interest rate is currently 6.0 percent, the market (equity) risk premium is 5.0 percent, and a particular firm has a stock beta of 1.4. If this company is expected to pay a $5.00 per share dividend annually for the foreseeable future, what is its stock price?

25. Assume the ABC Company currently pays a dividend of $2.50 per share and this is expected to increase by 5 percent per year indefinitely. If this firm's required return is 12 percent, what is its stock price?

26. Instead of assuming the ABC Company's dividends will increase by 5 percent indefinitely, assume they will increase by 6 percent for four years, by 5 percent for three years, and will then setttle into a steady rate of increase of 3 percent per year thereafter. If the required return is still 12 percent, what is ABC's stock price?

27. A share of preferred stock with a stated dividend of $7.00 is selling in the market to yield 11 percent per year. What is the price of this preferred share?

28. [Essay question] Describe the empirical relationships that have been documented between corporate earnings and stock valuation.

29. How does the accuracy of financial analysts' forecasts of corporate earnings compare to that of forecasts generated by time-series extrapolations?

30. What is the relationship between inflation and stock valuation? How has this relationship been explained?

31. How does liquidity and personal income taxation affect stock valuation?

32. [Essay question] Discuss the most important topics that market microstructure research has addressed in recent years. Summarize the key findings of this research stream.

33. Discuss the key features of the Kyle price formation model. Why is this model considered to be such a breakthrough?

34. What are the three principal cost components that the quoted bid-ask spread must cover? What is the empirically-determined importance of each cost component?

35. [Essay question] You have been asked to comment on the following statement made by a fan of the New York Stock Exchange: "the NYSE's specialist system is inherently superior to multiple-dealer market-making systems." How do you respond?

36. What are circuit breakers? What are they designed to do? Have they been successful in acheiving these objectives?

—REFERENCES—

Admati, Anat R. and Paul Pfleiderer, "A Theory of Intraday Patterns: Volume and Price Variability," **Review of Financial Studies** 1 (Spring 1988), pp. 3–40.

Affleck-Graves, John, Shantaram P. Hedge, and Robert E. Miller, "Trading Mechanisms and the Components of the Bid-Ask Spread," **Journal of Finance** 49 (September 1994), pp. 1471–1488.

Aharony, Joseph and Itzhak Swary. "Quarterly Dividend And Earnings Announcements and Stockholders' Return: An Empirical Analysis." **Journal of Finance** 35 (March 1980), pp. 1–12.

Aitken, Michael J., Gerald T. Garvey, and Peter L. Swan. "How Brokers Facilitate Trade for Long-Term Clients in Competitive Securities Markets." **Journal of Business** 68 (January 1995), pp. 1–33.

Amihud, Yakov and Haim Mendelson. "Asset Pricing and the Bid-Ask Spread." **Journal of Financial Economics** 17 (December 1986), pp. 233–249.

————"Liquidity, Maturity, and the Yields on U.S. Treasury Securities." **Journal of Finance** 46 (September 1991), pp. 1411–1425.

Ang, James S., Davis W. Blackwell, and William L. Megginson. "The Effect of Taxes on the Relative Valuation of Dividends and Capital Gains: Evidence From Dual-Class British Investment Trusts." **Journal of Finance** 46 (March 1991), pp. 383–400.

Ang, James, David Peterson, and Pamela Peterson. "Marginal Tax Rates: Evidence From Nontaxable Corporate Bonds: A Note." **Journal of Finance** 40 (March 1985), pp. 327–332.

Asquith, Paul and David Mullins, Jr. "Convertible Debt: Corporate Call Policy and Voluntary Conversion." **Journal of Finance** 46 (September 1991), pp. 1273–1290.

Asquith, Paul and Thierry A. Wizman. "Event Risk, Covenants, and Bondholder Returns in Leveraged Buyouts." **Journal of Financial Economics** 27 (September 1990), pp. 195–213.

Auerbach, Alan J. "Capital Gains Taxation in the United States: Realizations, Revenue, and Rhetoric." **Brookings Papers on Economic Activity** 2 (1988), pp. 595–621.

Baker, H. Kent and Richard B. Edelman. "Amex-to-NYSE Transfers, Market Microstructure, and Shareholder Wealth." **Financial Management** 21 (Winter 1992), pp. 60–72.

Ball, Ray and Philip Brown. "An Empirical Evaluation of Accounting Income Numbers." **Journal of Accounting Research** 6 (Autumn 1968), pp. 159–178.

Barclay, Michael J. and Clifford W. Smith, Jr. "The Maturity Structure of Corporate Debt." **Journal of Finance** 50 (June 1995), pp. 609–631.

Barnea, Amir, Robert A. Haugen, and Lemma W. Senbet. "A Rationale for Debt Maturity Structure and Call Provisions in the Agency Theory Framework." **Journal of Finance** 35 (December 1980), pp. 1223–1243.

Bartov, Eli and Gordon M. Bodnar. "Firm Valuation, Earnings Expectations, and the Exchange-Rate Exposure Effect." **Journal of Finance** 44 (December 1994), pp. 1755–1785.

Beaver, William H., P. Kettler, and Myron Scholes. "The Association Between Market-Determined and Accounting-Determined Risk Measures." **Accounting Review** (October 1970), pp. 654–682.

Beneish, Messod D. and John C. Gardner. "Information Costs and Liquidity Effects From Changes in the Dow Jones Industrial Average List." **Journal of Financial and Quantitative Analysis** 30 (March 1995), pp. 125–157.

Benninga, Simon and Aris Protopapadakis. "Real and Nominal Interest Rates Under Uncertainty: The Fisher Theorem and the Term Structure." **Journal of Political Economy** 91 (October 1983), pp. 856–867.

Bernard, Victor L., Jacob K. Thomas, and Jeffery S. Abarbanell. "How Sophisticated is the Market in Interpreting Earnings News?." **Journal of Applied Corporate Finance** 6 (Summer 1993), pp. 54–63.

Berry, Thomas D. and Keith M. Howe. "Public Information Arrival." **Journal of Finance** 49 (September 1994), pp. 1331–1346.

Bessembinder, Hendrik. "Bid-Ask Spreads in the Interbank Foreign Exchange Markets." **Journal of Financial Economics** 35 (June 1994), pp. 317–348.

Bessembinder, Hendrik and Paul J. Seguin, "Price Volatility, Trading Volume, and Market Depth: Evidence From Futures Markets," **Journal of Financial and Quantitative Analysis** 28 (March 1993), pp. 21–39.

Bierwag, G. O., "Immunization, Duration, and the Term Structure of Interest Rates," **Journal of Financial and Quantitative Analysis** 12 (December 1977), pp. 725–741.

Bierwag, G.O., George G. Kaufman, and Cynthia M. Latta, "Duration Models: A Taxonomy," **Journal of Portfolio Management** 15 (Fall 1988), pp. 50–54.

Bierwag, G.O., George G. Kaufman, and Alden L. Toevs, "Single Factor Duration Models in a Discrete General Equilibrium Framework," **Journal of Finance** 37 (May 1982), pp. 325–338.

Bierwag, G.O., George G. Kaufman, and Alden Toevs, "Duration: Its Development and Use in Bond Portfolio Management," **Financial Analyst Journal** 39 (July/August 1983), pp. 113–123.

Bildersee, John S., "Some Aspects of the Performance of Non-Convertible Preferred Stock," **Journal of Finance** 28 (December 1973), pp. 1187–1201.

————"The Association Between a Market-Determined Measure of Risk and Alternative Measures of Risk," **Accounting Review** (January 1975), pp. 81–98.

Black, Fischer and John C. Cox, "Valuing Corporate Securities: Some Effects of Bond Indenture Provisions," **Journal of Finance** 31 (May 1976), pp. 351–367.

Bodie, Zvi, Alex Kane, and Alan J. Marcus, **Investments**, 2nd Edition (Richard D. Irwin, Inc.: Homewood, IL, 1993).

Bollerslev, Tim and Ian Domowitz, "Trading Patterns and Prices in the Interbank Foreign Exchange Market," **Journal of Finance** 48 (September 1993), pp. 1421–1443.

Booth, James R., "Contract Costs, Bank Loans, and the Cross-Monitoring Hypothesis," **Journal of Financial Economics** 31 (February 1992), pp. 25–42.

Bossaerts, Peter and Robert M. Dammon, "Tax-Induced Intertemporal Restrictions on Security Returns," **Journal of Finance** 49 (September 1994), pp. 1347–1371.

Boudoukh, Jacob and Matthew Richardson, "Stock Returns and Inflation: A Long-Horizon Perspective," **American Economic Review** 83 (December 1993), pp. 1346–1355.

Boudoukh, Jacob, Matthew Richardson, and Robert F. Whitelaw, "Industry Returns and the Fisher Effect," **Journal of Finance** 49 (December 1994), pp. 1595–1615.

Boudoukh, Jacob and Robert F. Whitelaw, "Liquidity as a Choice Variable: A Lesson From the Japanese Government Bond Market," **Review of Financial Studies** 6 (1993), pp. 265–292.

Branch, Ben and Walter Freed, "Bid-Asked Spreads on the AMEX and the Big Board," **Journal of Finance** 32 (March 1977), pp. 159–163.

Brealey, Richard A. and Stewart C. Myers, **Principles of Corporate Finance**, 4th Edition (McGraw Hill, Inc.: New York, 1991)

Brealey, Richard A. and Stephen Schaefer, "Term Structure With Uncertain Inflation," **Journal of Finance** 32 (May 1977), pp. 277–289.

Brennan, Michael J. and Eduardo S. Schwartz, "Convertible Bonds: Valuation and Optimal Strategies for Call and Conversion," **Journal of Finance** 32 (December 1977a), pp. 1699–1715.

————"Savings Bonds, Retractable Bonds and Callable Bonds," **Journal of Financial Economics** 5 (August 1977b), pp. 67–88.

————"Analyzing Convertible Bonds," **Journal of Financial and Quantitative Analysis** 15 (November 1980), pp. 907–929.

————"The Case for Convertibles," **Journal of Applied Corporate Finance** 1 (Summer 1988), pp. 55–64.

————— "Portfolio Insurance and Financial Market Equilibrium," **Journal of Business** 62 (October 1989), pp. 455–472.

Brick, Ivan E. and S. Abraham Ravid, "On the Relevance of Debt Maturity Structure," **Journal of Finance** 40 (December 1985), pp. 1423–1437.

Brock, William and Allan W. Kleidon, "Periodic Market Closure and Trading Volume: A Model of Intraday Bids and Asks," **Journal of Economic Dynamics and Control** 16 (1992), pp. 451–489.

Brown, Lawrence D. and Michael S. Rozeff, "The Superiority of Analysts Forecasts as Measures of Expectations: Evidence From Earnings," **Journal of Finance** 33 (March 1978), pp. 1–16.

Brown, Stephen and Philip H. Dybvig, "The Empirical Implications of the Cox, Ingersoll, Ross Theory of the Term Structure of Interest Rates," **Journal of Finance** 41 (July 1986), pp. 616–628.

Buser, Stephen A. and Patrick J. Hess, "Empirical Determinants of the Relative Yields on Taxable and Tax-Exempt Securities," **Journal of Financial Economics** 17 (December 1986), pp. 335–355.

Campbell, Cynthia, Louis H. Ederington, and Prashant Vankudre, "Tax Shields, Sample-Selection Bias, and the Information Content of Conversion-Forcing Bond Calls," **Journal of Finance** 46 (September 1991), pp. 1291–1324.

Campbell, John Y. and Robert J. Shiller, "Stock Prices, Earnings and Expected Dividends," **Journal of Finance** 43 (July 1988), pp. 661–676.

Campbell, Joseph, Shawn LaMaster, Vernon L. Smith, and Mark Van Boening, "Off-Floor Trading, Disintegration, and the Bid-Ask Spread in Experimental Markets," **Journal of Business** 64 (October 1991), pp. 495–522.

Chan, Louis K. C., "Consumption, Inflation Risk, and Real Interest Rates: An Empirical Analysis," **Journal of Business** 67 (January 1994), pp. 69–96.

Chan, Louis K. C., Narasimhan Jegadeesh, and Josef Lakonishok, "Evaluating the Performance of Value Versus Glamour Stocks: The Impact of Selection Bias," **Journal of Financial Economics** 38 (July 1995), pp. 269–296.

Chan, K.C., William G. Christie, and Paul H. Schultz, "Market Structure and the Intraday Pattern of Bid-Ask Spreads for NASDAQ Securities," **Journal of Business** 68 (January 1995), pp. 35–60.

Chang, Eric C., Prem C. Jain, and Peter R. Locke, "Standard & Poor's 500 Index Futures Volatility and Price Changes Around the New York Stock Exchange Close," **Journal of Business** 68 (January 1995), pp. 61–84.

Christensen, Peter Ove and Bjarne G. Sorensen, "Duration, Convexity, and Time Value," **Journal of Portfolio Management** 20 (Winter 1994), pp. 51–60.

Christie, William G., Jeffrey H. Harris, and Paul H. Schultz, "Why Did NASDAQ Market Makers Stop Avoiding Odd-Eighth Quotes?," **Journal of Finance** 49 (December 1994), pp. 1841–1860.

Christie, William G. and Paul H. Schultz, "Why do NASDAQ Market Makers Avoid Odd-Eighth Quotes?," **Journal of Finance** 49 (December 1994), pp. 1813–1840.

Conrad, Jennifer S. and Robert Conroy, "Market Microstructure and the Ex-Date Return," **Journal of Finance** 49 (September 1994), pp. 1507–1519.

Constantinides, George M., "Optimal Stock Trading With Personal Taxes: Implications for Prices and Abnormal January Returns," **Journal of Financial Economics** 13 (March 1984), pp. 65–89.

Constantinides, George M. and Jonathan E. Ingersoll, Jr., "Optimal Bond Trading With Personal Taxes," **Journal of Financial Economics** 13 (March 1984), pp. 299–335.

Copeland, Thomas and Dan Galai, "Information Effects on the Bid-Ask Spread," **Journal of Finance** 38 (December 1983), pp. 1457–1469.

Copeland, Thomas and J. Fred Weston, **Financial Theory and Corporate Policy,** 3rd Edition (Addison-Wesley Publishing Company: Reading, MA, 1988).

Cornell, Bradford and Marc R. Reinganum, "Forward and Futures Prices: Evidence From the Foreign Exchange Markets," **Journal of Finance** 36 (December 1981), pp. 1035–1045.

Cornell, Bradford and Alan C. Shapiro, "Financing Corporate Growth," **Journal of Applied Corporate Finance** 1 (Summer 1988), pp. 6–22.

Cowan, Arnold R., Richard B. Carter, Frederick H. Dark, Ajai K. Singh, "Explaining the NYSE Listing Choices of NASDAQ Firms," **Financial Management** 21 (Winter 1992), pp. 73–86.

Cox, John C., Jonathan E. Ingersoll, Jr., and Stephen A. Ross, "Duration and the Measurement of Basis Risk," **Journal of Business** 52 (January 1979), pp. 51–61.

———"A Re-Examination of Traditional Hypothesis About the Term Structure of Interest Rates," **Journal of Finance** 36 (September 1981), pp. 769–799.

———"A Theory of the Term Structure of Interest Rates," **Econometrica** 53 (March 1985), pp. 385–407.

Culbertson, J. M., "The Term Structure of Interest Rates," **Quarterly Journal of Economics** 67 (November 1957), pp. 485–517.

Datta, Sudip and Upinder S. Dhillon, "Bond and Stock Market Response to Unexpected Earnings Announcements," **Journal of Financial and Quantitative Analysis** 28 (December 1993), pp. 565–577.

Demsetz, Harold, "The Cost of Transacting," **Quarterly Journal of Economics** 82 (February 1968), pp. 33–53.

Diamond, Douglas W., "Debt Maturity Structure and Liquidity Risk," **Quarterly Journal of Economics** 106 (August 1991a), pp. 711–737.

———"Monitoring and Reputation: The Choice Between Bank Loans and Directly Placed Debt," **Journal of Political Economy** 99 (1991b), pp. 688–721.

———"Seniority and Maturity of Debt Contracts," **Journal of Financial Economics** 33 (June 1993), pp. 341–368.

Diamond, Douglas W. and Robert E. Verrecchia, "Disclosure, Liquidity, and the Cost of Capital," **Journal of Finance** 46 (September 1991), pp. 1325–1359.

Dunn, Kenneth B. and John J. McConnell, "Valuation of GNMA Mortgage-Backed Securities," **Journal of Finance** 36 (June 1981), pp. 599–616.

Dunn, Kenneth B. and Chester S. Spatt, "A Strategic Analysis of Sinking Fund Bonds," **Journal of Financial Economics** 13 (September 1984), pp. 399–424.

———"An Analysis of Mortgage Contracting: Prepayment Penalties and the Due-On-Sale Clause," **Journal of Finance** 40 (March 1985), pp. 293–308.

Dutta, Prajit K. and Ananth Madhavan, "Price Continuity Rules and Insider Trading," **Journal of Financial and Quantitative Analysis** 30 (June 1995), pp. 199–221.

Easley, David and Maureen O'Hara, "Price, Trade Size, and Information in Securities Markets," **Journal of Financial Economics** 19 (September 1987), pp. 69–90.

Edwards, Sebastian, "The Pricing of Bonds and Bank Loans in International Borrowing," **European Economic Review** 30 (1986), pp. 565–589.

Emanuel, David, "A Theoretical Model for Valuing Preferred Stock," **Journal of Finance** 38 (September 1983), pp. 1133–1155.

Evans, Martin D. D. and Karen K. Lewis, "Do Expected Shifts in Inflation Affect Estimates of the Long-Run Fisher Relation?," **Journal of Finance** 50 (March 1995), pp. 225–253.

Fabozzi, Frank J., Franco Modigliani, and Michael G. Ferri, **Foundations of Financial Markets and Institutions** (Prentice-Hall, Inc.: Englewood Cliffs, NJ, 1994).

Fama, Eugene F., "Short-Term Interest Rates as Predictors of Inflation," **American Economic Review** 65 (June 1975), pp. 269–282.

————"Stock Returns, Real Activity, Inflation, and Money," **American Economic Review** 71 (September 1981), pp. 545–565.

————"The Information in the Term Structure," **Journal of Financial Economics** 13 (December 1984a), pp. 509–528.

————"Term Premiums in Bond Returns," **Journal of Financial Economics** 13 (December 1984b), pp. 529–546.

Fama, Eugene F. and Kenneth R. French, "Size and Book-to-Market Factors in Earnings and Returns," **Journal of Finance** 50 (March 1995), pp. 131–155.

Fama, Eugene F. and G. William Schwert, "Asset Returns and Inflation," **Journal of Financial Economics** 5 (November 1977), pp. 115–146.

Ferreira, Eurico J., Michael F. Spivey, and Charles E. Edwards, "Pricing New-Issue and Seasoned Preferred Stocks: A Comparison of Valuation Models," **Financial Management** 21 (Summer 1992), pp. 52–62.

Figlewski, Stephen and Gwendolyn P. Webb, "Options, Short Sales, and Market Completeness," **Journal of Finance** 48 (June 1993), pp. 761–777.

Fisher, Irving, "Appreciation and Interest," **Publication of the American Economic Association** (August 1896), pp. 23–29, pp. 91–92, and pp. 427–428.

Fisher, Lawrence, "Determinants of Risk Premiums on Corporate Bonds," **Journal of Political Economy** 67 (June 1959), pp. 212–237.

Fisher, Lawrence and Roman L. Weil, "Coping with the Risk of Interest-Rate Fluctuations: Returns to Shareholders from Naive and Optimal Strategies," **Journal of Business** 44 (October 1971), pp. 408–431.

Flannery, Mark J., "Asymmetric Information and Risky Debt Maturity Choice," **Journal of Finance** 41 (March 1986), pp. 19–37.

Foster, F. Douglas and S. Viswanathan, "A Theory of the Interday Variations in Volume, Variance, and Trading Costs in Securities Markets," **Review of Financial Studies**, 3 (1990), pp. 593–624.

————"Variations in Trading Volume, Return Volatility, and Trading Costs: Evidence on Recent Price Formation Models," **Journal of Finance** 48 (March 1993), pp. 187–212.

————"Strategic Trading With Asymmetrically Informed Traders and Long-Lived Information," **Journal of Financial and Quantitative Analysis** 29 (December 1994), pp. 499–518.

French, Kenneth R. and James M. Poterba, "Were Japanese Stock Prices too High?," **Journal of Financial Economics** 29 (October 1991), pp. 337–363.

George, Thomas J., Gautam Kaul, and M. Nimalendran, "Trading Volume and Transaction Costs in Specialist Markets," **Journal of Finance** 49 (September 1994), pp. 1489–1505.

Gerety, Mason S. and J. Harold Mulherin, "Price Formation on Stock Exchanges: The Evolution of Trading Within the Day," **Review of Financial Studies** 7 (Fall 1994), pp. 609–629.

Geske, Robert and Richard Roll, "The Fiscal and Monetary Linkage Between Stock Returns and Inflation," **Journal of Finance** 38 (March 1983), pp. 1–33.

Gibbons, Michael R. and Krishna Ramaswamy, "A Test of the Cox, Ingersoll, and Ross Model of the Term Structure," **Review of Financial Studies** 6 (1993), pp. 619–658.

Gitman, Lawrence J., **Principles of Managerial Finance**, 7th Edition (HarperCollins: New York, 1994)

Givoly, Dan and Josef Lakonishok, "Earnings Expectations and Properties of Earnings Forecasts—A Review and Analysis of the Research," **Journal of Accounting Literature** (Spring 1984), pp. 85–107.

Glosten, Lawrence R., "Is the Electronic Open Limit Order Book Inevitable?," **Journal of Finance** 49 (September 1994), pp. 1127–1161.

Glosten, Lawrence R. and Lawrence E. Harris, "Estimating the Components of the Bid/Ask Spread," **Journal of Financial Economics** 21 (May 1988), pp. 123–142.

Glosten, Lawrence and Paul R. Milgrom, "Bid, Ask and Transaction Prices in a Specialist Market With Heterogenously Informed Traders," **Journal of Financial Economics** 14 (March 1985), pp. 71–100.

Goswami, Gautam, Thomas Noe, Michael Rebello, "Debt Financing Under Asymmetric Information," **Journal of Finance** 50 (June 1995), pp. 633–659.

Green, Richard C., "A Simple Model of the Taxable and Tax-Exempt Yield Curves," **Review of Financial Studies** 6 (1993). pp. 233–264.

Grossman, Sanford, "On the Efficiency of Competitive Stock Markets Where Trades Have Diverse Information," **Journal of Finance** 31 (May 1976), pp. 573–585.

Grossman, Sanford J. and Merton H. Miller, "Liquidity and Market Structure," **Journal of Finance** 43 (July 1988), pp. 617–633.

Grossman, Sanford J., and Joseph E. Stiglitz, "On the Impossibility of Informationally Efficient Markets," **American Economic Review** 70 (June 1980), pp. 393–408.

Grundfest, Joseph A., "Zen and the Art of Securities Regulation," **Journal of Applied Corporate Finance** 5 (Winter 1993), pp. 4–8.

Grundy, Bruce D. and Maureen McNichols, "Trade and Revelation of Information Through Prices and Direct Disclosure," **Review of Financial Studies** 2 (1989), pp. 495–526.

Han, Ki C., "The Effects of Reverse Splits on the Liquidity of the Stock," **Journal of Financial and Quantitative Analysis** 30 (March 1995), pp. 159–169.

Harris, Jeffrey H., "The Cost Component of Bid-Ask Spreads: An Intraday Analysis," Working paper (Ohio State University: Columbus, OH), September 1994.

Harris, Lawrence and Eitan Gurel, "Price and Volume Effects Associated With Changes in the S&P 500 List: New Evidence for the Existence of Price Pressures," **Journal of Finance** 41 (September 1986), pp. 815–829.

Harris, Milton and Artur Raviv, "A Sequential Signaling Model of Convertible Debt Call Policy," **Journal of Finance** 40 (December 1985), pp. 1263–1282.

————"The Design of Securities, **Journal of Financial Economics** 24 (October 1989), pp. 255–287.

————"Differences of Opinion Make a Horse Race," **Review of Financial Studies** 6 (1993), pp. 473–506.

Harris, Robert S., "Using Analysts' Growth Forecasts to Estimate Shareholder Required Rates of Return," **Financial Management** 17 (Spring 1988), pp. 58–67.

Harris, Robert S. and Felicia C. Marston, "Estimating Shareholder Risk Premia Using Analysts Growth Forecasts," **Financial Management** 21 (Summer 1992), pp. 63–70.

Harvey, Campbell R., "The Real Term Structure and Consumption Growth," **Journal of Financial Economics** 22 (December 1988), pp. 305–334.

Hasbrouck, Joel, "Trades, Quotes, Inventories, and Information," **Journal of Financial Economics** 22 (December 1988), pp. 229–252.

Hasbrouck, Joel and George Sofianos, "The Trades of Market Makers: An Empirical Analysis of NYSE Specialists," **Journal of Finance** 48 (December 1993), pp. 1565–1593.

Haugen, Robert A. and Dean W. Wichern, "The Elasticity of Financial Assets," **Journal of Finance** 29 (September 1974), 1229–1240.

Healy, Paul and Krishna Palepu, "Earnings Information Conveyed by Dividend Initiations and Omissions," **Journal of Financial Economics** 21 (September 1988), pp. 149–175.

Hickman, Kent and Glenn H. Petry, "A Comparison of Stock Price Predictions Using Court Accepted Formulas, Dividend Discount, and P/E Models," **Financial Management** 19 (Summer 1990), pp.76–97.

Hicks, J. R., **Value and Capital** (Oxford, England: Clarendon Press, 1939).

Hicks, James R., **Value and Capital**, Second Edition (Oxford University Press: London, 1946).

Ho, Thomas S.Y. and Richard G. Macris, "Dealer Market Structure and Performance," in Yakov Amihud, Thomas Ho, and Robert A. Schwartz, eds., **Market Making and the Changing Structure of the Securities Industries** (Lexington Books, Lexington, Mas. 1985).

Ho, Thomas S. Y. and Ronald Singer, "Bond Indenture Provisions and the Risk of Corporate Debt," **Journal of Financial Economics** 10 (December 1982), pp. 375–406.

Ho, Thomas and Hans R. Stoll, Optimal Dealer Pricing Under Transactions and Return Uncertainty," **Journal of Financial Economics** 9 (March 1981), pp. 47–73.

Ho, Thomas S. Y. and Hans R. Stoll, "The Dynamics of Dealer Markets Under Competition," **Journal of Finance** 38 (September 1983), pp. 1053–1074.

Huang, Roger D. and Hans R. Stoll, "Market Microstructure and Stock Return Predictions," **Review of Financial Studies** 7 (1994), pp. 179–213.

Ingersoll, Jonathan, "A Contingent-Claims Valuation of Convertible Securities," **Journal of Financial Economics** 7 (May 1977a), pp. 289–321.

——— —"An Examination of Corporate Call Policies on Convertible Securities," **Journal of Finance** 32 (May 1977b), pp. 463–478.

Jackson, Matthew O., "Equilibrium, Price Formation, and the Value of Private Information," **Review of Financial Studies** 4 (1991), pp. 1–16.

Jensen, Michael C. and William H. Meckling, "Theory of the Firm: Managerial Behavior, Agency Costs, and Ownership Structure," **Journal of Financial Economics** 3 (October 1976), pp. 305–360.

Jones, Charles M., Gautam Kaul, and Marc L. Lipson, "Transactions, Volume, and Volatility," **Review of Financial Studies** 7 (Winter 1994), 631–651.

Jorion, Philippe and Leonid Roisenberg, "Synthetic International Diversification," **Journal of Portfolio Management** 19 (Winter 1993), pp. 65–73.

Joy, O. Maurice, Robert H. Litzenberger, and Richard W. McEnally, "The Adjustment of Stock Prices to Announcements of Unanticipated Changes in Quarterly Earnings," **Journal of Accounting Research** (Autumn 1977), pp. 207–225.

Kadlec, Gregory B. and John J. McConnell, "The Effect of Market Segmentation and Illiquidity on Asset Prices: Evidence From Exchange Listings," **Journal of Finance** 49 (June 1994), pp. 611–636.

Kalay, Avner, "Stockholder-Bondholder Conflict and Dividend Constraints," **Journal of Financial Economics** 10 (July 1982), pp. 211–233.

Kamara, Avraham, "Liquidity, Taxes, and Short-Term Treasury Yields," **Journal of Financial and Quantitative Analysis** 29 (September 1994), pp. 403–417.

Kaplan, Steven N. and Jeremy C. Stein, "How Risky is the Debt of Highly Leveraged Transactions?," **Journal of Financial Economics** 27 (September 1990), pp. 215–246.

Kau, James B., Donald C. Keenan, Walter J. Muller III, and James F. Epperson, "The Valuation and Analysis of Adjustable Rate Mortgages," **Management Science** 36 (December 1990), pp. 1417–1431.

———"A Generalized Valuation Model for Fixed-Rate Residential Mortgages," **Journal of Money, Credit, and Banking** 24 (August 1992), pp. 279–299.

———"Option Theory and Floating-Rate Securities With a Comparison of Adjustable and Fixed-Rate Mortgages," **Journal of Business** 66 (1993), pp. 595–618.

Kaul, Gautam, "Stock Returns and Inflation: The Role of the Monetary Sector," **Journal of Financial Economics** 18 (June 1987), pp. 253–276.

Kidwell, David S., Richard L. Peterson, and David W. Blackwell, **Financial Institutions, Markets, and Money**, 5th Edition (Dryden Press: Fort Worth, TX, 1993).

Kyle, Albert S., "Continuous Auctions and Insider Trading," **Econometrica** 53 (1985), pp. 1315–1336.

Langetieg, Terence C., "A Multivariate Model of the Term Structure," **Journal of Finance** 35 (March 1980), pp. 71–97.

Leach, J. Chris and Ananth N. Madhavan, "Price Experimentation and Security Market Structure," **Review of Financial Studies** 6 (1993), pp. 375–404.

Lease, Ronald C., Ronald W. Masulis, and John R. Page, "An Investigation of Market Microstructure Impacts on Event Study Returns," **Journal of Finance** 46 (September 1991), pp. 1523–1536.

Lee, Charles M. C., Belinda Mucklow, and Mark J. Ready, "Spreads, Depth, and the Impact of Earnings Information: An Intraday Analysis," **Review of Financial Studies** 6 (1993), pp. 345–374.

Lee, Charles M.C., Mark J. Ready, and Paul Seguin, "Volume, Volatility, and New York Stock Exchange Trading Halts," **Journal of Finance** 49 (March 1994), pp. 183–214.

Lehmann, Bruce N. and David M. Modest, " Trading and Liquidity on the Tokyo Stock Exchange: A Bird's Eye View," **Journal of Finance** 49 (July 1994), pp. 951–984.

Leuthold, Raymond M., Philip Garcia, and Richard Lu, "The Return and Forecasting Ability of Large Traders in the Frozen Pork Bellies Futures Market," **Journal of Business** 67 (July 1994), pp. 459–473.

Levine, Ross, "Stock Markets, Growth, and Tax Policy," **Journal of Finance** 46 (September 1991), pp. 1445–1465.

Lewis, Craig M., "A Multiperiod Theory of Corporate Financial Policy Under Taxation," **Journal of Financial and Quantitative Analysis** 25 (March 1990), pp. 25–44.

Lin, Ji-Chai and Michael S. Rozeff, "Price Adjustment Delays and Arbitrage Costs: Evidence from the Behavior of Convertible Preferred Prices," **Journal of Financial and Quantitative Analysis** 30 (March 1995), pp. 61–80.

Lindsey, Richard R. and Ulrike Schaede, "Specialist vs, Saitori: Market-Making in New York and Tokyo," **Financial Analysts Journal** 48 (July-August 1992), pp. 48–56.

Linke, Charles M. and J. Kenton Zumwalt, "Estimation Biases in Discounted Cash Flow Analyses of Equity Capital Cost in Rate Regulation," **Financial Management** 13 (Fall 1984), pp. 15–21.

Lippman, Steven A. and John J. McCall, "An Operational Measure of Liquidity," **American Economic Review** 76 (March 1986), pp. 43–55.

Long, John B., "The Market Valuation of Cash Dividends: A Case to Consider," **Journal of Financial Economics** 6 (June-September 1978), pp. 235–264.

Lutz, F. A., "The Structure of Interest Rates," **Quarterly Journal of Economics** (November 1940), pp. 36–63.

Macauley, Frederick R., **The Movements of Interest Rates, Bond Yields and Stock Prices in the United States Since 1856** (National Bureau of Economic Research: New York, 1938).

Madden, Bartley J., "Structural Changes in Trading Stocks," **Journal of Portfolio Management** 21 (Fall 1993), pp. 19–27.

Malitz, Ileen, "On Financial Contracting: The Determinants of Bond Covenants," **Financial Management** 15 (Summer 1986), pp. 18–25.

Marais, Laurentius, Katharine Schipper, and Abbie Smith, "Wealth Effects of Going Private for Senior Securities," **Journal of Financial Economics** 23 (June 1989), pp. 155–191.

McConnell, John J. and Gary G. Schlarbaum, "Evidence on the Impact of Exchange Offers on Security Prices: The Case of Income Bonds," **Journal of Business** 54 (January 1981a), pp. 65–86.

——— "Returns, Risks, and Pricing of Income Bonds, 1956–76," **Journal of Business** 54 (January 1981), pp. 33–64.

McConnell, John J. and Manoj Singh, "Rational Prepayments and the Valuation of Collateralized Mortgage Obligations," **Journal of Finance** 49 (July 1994), pp. 891–921.

McCulloch, J. Huston, "An Estimate of the Liquidity Premium," **Journal of Political Economy** 83 (January-February 1975), pp. 95–119.

McInish, Thomas H. and Robert A. Wood, "An Analysis of Intraday Patterns in Bid Ask Spreads for NYSE Stocks," **Journal of Finance** 47 (June 1992), pp. 753–764.

McQueen, Grant and V. Vance Roley, "Stock Prices, News, and Business Conditions," **Review of Financial Studies** 6 (1993), pp. 683–707.

Merton, Robert C., "On the Pricing of Corporate Debt: The Risk Structure of Interest Rates," **Journal of Finance** 29 (May 1974), pp. 449–470.

——— "Presidential Address: A Simple Model of Capital Market Equilibrium With Incomplete Information," **Journal of Finance** 42 (July 1987), pp. 483–510.

Mikkelson, Wayne H., "Convertible Calls and Security Returns," **Journal of Financial Economics** 9 (September 1981), pp. 237–264.

Miller, Merton, "Debt and Taxes," **Journal of Finance** 32 (May 1977), pp. 261–276.

Miller, Merton and Franco Modigliani, "Dividend Policy, Growth, and the Valuation of Shares," **Journal of Business** 34 (October 1961), pp. 411–433.

Mishkin, Frederic S., "The Information in the Longer Maturity Term Structure About Future Inflation," NBER Working Paper No. 3126 (September 1989).

———"What Does the Term Structure Tell Us About Future Inflation?," **Journal of Monetary Economics** 25 (January 1990), pp. 77–96.

———"Is the Fisher Effect for Real? A Reexamination of the Relationship Between Inflation and Interest Rates," **Journal of Monetary Economics** 30 (1992), pp. 195–215.

Modigliani, Franco and Merton Miller, "Corporate Income Taxes and the Cost of Capital," **American Economic Review** 53 (June 1963), pp. 433–443.

Modigliani, Franco and Richard Sutch, "Innovations in Interest Rate Policy," **American Economic Review** (May 1966), pp. 178–197.

Morris, James R., "On Corporate Debt Maturity Policies," **Journal of Finance** 31 (March 1976), pp. 29–37.

Mulherin, J. Harold, "Market Transparency: Pros, Cons, and Property Rights," **Journal of Applied Corporate Finance** 5 (Winter 1993), pp. 94–97.

Myers, Stewart C., "The Determinants of Corporate Borrowing," **Journal of Financial Economics** 5 (November 1977), pp. 147–176.

Nachman, David C. and Thomas H. Noe, "Optimal Design of Securities Under Asymmetric Information," **Review of Financial Studies** 7 (Spring 1994), pp. 1–44.

Ofer, Aharon R. and Ashok Natarajan, "Convertible Call Policies: An Empirical Analysis of an Information-Signaling Hypothesis," **Journal of Financial Economics** 19 (September 1987), pp. 91–108.

Park, Jinwoo, "A Market Microstructure Explanation for Predictable Variations in Stock Returns Following Large Price Changes," **Journal of Financial and Quantitative Analysis** 30 (June 1995), pp. 241–256.

Pearce, Douglas K. and V. Vance Roley, "Stock Prices and Economic News," **Journal of Business** 58 (January 1985), pp. 49–68.

Pearson, Neil D. and Tong-Sheng Sun, "Exploiting the Conditional Density in Estimating the Term Structure: An Application to the Cox, Ingersoll, and Ross Model," **Journal of Finance** 49 (September 1994), pp. 1279–1304.

Pennachi, George G., "Identifying the Dynamics of Real Interest Rates and Inflation: Evidence Using Survey Data," **Review of Financial Studies** 4 (1991), pp. 53–86.

Petersen, Mitchell A. and David Fialkowski, "Posted Versus Effective Spreads: Good Prices or Bad Quotes?," **Journal of Financial Economics** 35 (June 1994), pp. 269–292.

Poterba, James, "How Burdensome are Capital Gains Taxes? Evidence From the United States," **Journal of Public Economics** 33 (July 1987), pp. 157–172.

Power, William, "SEC, Market Officials Mulling Changes in Big Board's 250-Point Trading Halt," **Wall Street Journal** (July 26, 1995), pg. C1.

Protopapadakis, Aris, "Some Indirect Evidence on Effective Capital Gains Tax Rates," **Journal of Business** 56 (April 1983), pp. 127–138.

Ramaswamy, Krishna and Suresh M. Sundaresan, "The Valuation of Floating-Rate Instruments: Theory and Evidence," **Journal of Financial Economics** 17 (December 1986), pp. 251–272.

Rose, Andrew K., "Is the Real Interest Rate Stable?," **Journal of Finance** 43 (December 1988), pp. 1095–1112.

Sahlman, William A., "Aspects of Financial Contracting in Venture Capital," **Journal of Applied Corporate Finance** 1 (Summer 1988), pp. 23–36.

Scholes, Myron S., "The Market for Securities: Substitution Versus Price Pressure and the Effects of Information on Share Prices," **Journal of Business** 45 (April 1972), pp. 179–211.

Schwartz, Eduardo S. and Walter N. Torous, "Prepayment and the Valuation of Mortgage-Backed Securities," **Journal of Finance** 44 (June 1989), pp. 375–392.

———"Prepayment, Default, and the Valuation of Mortgage Pass-Through Securities," **Journal of Business** 65 (April 1992), pp. 221–239.

Scott, Louis O., "The Present Value Model of Stock Prices: Regression Tests and Monte Carlo Results," **Review of Economics and Statistics** 67 (November 1985), pp. 599–605.

Seyhun, H. Nejat and Douglas J. Skinner, "How Do Taxes Affect Investors' Stock Market Realizations? Evidence From Tax-Return Panel Data," **Journal of Business** 67 (April 1994), pp. 231–262.

Shinnar, Reuel, Ofer Dressler, C.A. Feng, and Alan I. Avidan, "Estimation of the Economic Rate of Return for Industrial Companies," **Journal of Business** 62 (July 1989), pp. 417–445.

Sinkey, Joseph F., Jr., **Commercial Bank Financial Management**, 5th Edition (Macmillan Publishing Company: New York, 1992).

Slezak, Steve L., "A Theory of the Dynamics of Security Returns Around Market Closures," **Journal of Finance** 49 (September 1994), pp. 1163–1211.

Smith, Clifford W., Jr., "Investment Banking and the Capital Acquisition Process," **Journal of Financial Economics** 15 (January–February 1986), pp. 3–29.

Smith, Clifford W., Jr. and Jerold B. Warner, "On Financial Contracting: An Analysis of Bond Covenants," **Journal of Financial Economics** 7 (June 1979), pp. 117–161.

Sorensen, Eric H. and Clark A. Hawkins, "On the Pricing of Preferred Stock," **Journal of Financial and Quantitative Analysis** 16 (December 1981), pp. 515–528.

Spatt, Chester S., "Introduction to the Market Microstructure Symposium," **Review of Financial Studies** 4 (1991), pp. 385–388.

Spiegel, Matthew and Avinidhar Subrahmanyam, "On Intraday Risk Premia," **Journal of Finance** 50 (March 1995), pp. 319–339.

Stiglitz, Joseph E., "On the Irrelevance of Corporate Financial Policy," **American Economic Review** 64 (December 1974), pp. 851–866.

Stoll, Hans R., "Inferring the Components of the Bid-Ask Spread: Theory and Empirical Tests," **Journal of Finance** 49 (March 1989), pp. 115–134.

——"Organization of the Stock Market: Competition or Fragmentation?," **Journal of Applied Corporate Finance** 5 (Winter 1993), pp. 89–93.

Subrahmanyam, Avanidhar, "Risk Aversion, Market Liquidity, and Price Efficiency," **Review of Financial Studies** 4 (1991), pp. 417–441.

——"Circuit Breakers and Market Volatility: A Theoretical Perspective," **Journal of Finance** 49 (March 1994), pp. 237–254.

Tauchen, George, "Discussion: An Investigation of Transactions Data for NYSE Stocks," **Journal of Finance** 40 (July 1985), pp. 739–741.

Titman, Sheridan and Walter N. Torous, "Valuing Commercial Mortgages: An Empirical Investigation of the Contingent-Claims Approach to Pricing Risky Debt," **Journal of Finance** 44 (June 1989), pp. 345–373.

Titman, Sheridan and Arthur Warga, "Stock Returns as Predictors of Interest Rates and Inflation," **Journal of Financial and Quantitative Analysis** 24 (March 1989), pp. 47–58.

Trzcinka, Charles, "The Pricing of Tax-Exempt Bonds and the Miller Hypothesis," **Journal of Finance** 37 (September 1982), pp. 907–923.

Umlauf, Steven R., "Transactions Taxes and the Behavior of the Swedish Stock Market," **Journal of Financial Economics** 33 (April 1993), pp. 227–240.

Vander Weide, James H. and Willard T. Carleton, "Investor Growth Expectations: Analysis Vs. History," **Journal of Portfolio Management** 14 (Spring 1988), pp. 78–82.

Verrecchia, Robert E., "Information Acquisition in a Noisy Rational Expectations Economy," **Econometrica** 50 (1982), pp. 1415–1430.

Vijh, Anand M., "Liquidity of the CBOE Equity Options," **Journal of Finance** 45 (September 1990), pp. 1157–1179.

Vu, Joseph D., "An Empirical Investigation of Calls on Non-Convertible Bonds," **Journal of Financial Economics** 16 (June 1986), pp. 235–265.

Wakeman, L. MacDonald, "The Real Function of Bond Rating Agencies," **Chase Financial Quarterly** 1 (Fall 1981), pp. 18–26.

Wang, Jiang, "A Model of Competitive Stock Trading-Volume," **Journal of Political Economy** 102 (February 1994), pp. 127–168.

Warga, Arthur, "Bond Returns, Liquidity, and Missing Data," **Journal of Financial and Quantitative Analysis** 27 (December 1992), pp. 605–617.

Watts, Ross L., "Systematic 'Abnormal' Returns After Quarterly Earnings Announcements," **Journal of Financial Economics** 6 (June-September 1978), pp. 127–150.

Weil, Roman L. "Macaulay's Duration: An Appreciation," **Journal of Business** 46 (October 1973), pp. 589–592.

Weinstein, Mark, "The Effect of a Rating Change on Bond Prices," **Journal of Financial Economics** 5 (December 1977), pp. 329–350.

Wiggins, James B., "Beta Changes Around Stock Splits Revisited," **Journal of Financial and Quantitative Analysis** 27 (December 1992), pp. 631–640.

Williams, Alex O. and Phillip E. Pfeifer, "Estimating Security Price Risk Using Duration and Price Elasticity," **Journal of Finance** 37 (May 1982), pp. 399–412.

Wood, Robert A., Thomas H. McInish, and J. Keith Ord, "An Investigation of Transactions Data for NYSE Stocks," **Journal of Finance** 40 (July 1985), pp. 723–741.

CHAPTER

5

Option Valuation

5.1 INTRODUCTION

As the term is commonly used in finance, an **option** is the right—but not the obligation—to buy or sell a commodity at a fixed price, on or before a fixed maturity date. While the most familiar options contracts are those giving their holders the right to buy or sell stocks, bonds, or other securities, modern economies actually present investors, corporate managers, and individuals with many opportunities that have option-like characteristics. For example, corporate executives who fund research and development projects are also implicitly purchasing an option to invest in any promising new technology that emerges from the research laboratories. Likewise, students who excel in undergraduate studies create for themselves options to pursue graduate studies at the university of their choice. As these two examples make clear, the defining characteristic of an option is that it grants its holder a unilateral right—without an offsetting "delivery" obligation—to purchase something of value at a pre-determined price.[1]

This chapter will focus on financial market options, particularly options on publicly-traded common stocks. We begin in section 5.2 with definitions of the key terms and phrases commonly encountered in options market trading, and then describe the payoff patterns for investors who buy or sell options contracts. In section 5.3 we discuss how the Black-Scholes Option Pricing Model (B-S OPM) was developed, and examine how the model inputs affect option valuation. This section then concludes with a description of several boundary conditions on rational option pricing. Section 5.4 presents a discussion of empirical tests of the B-S OPM and related models based on

---

1. A fairly subtle, but important, distinction can be drawn between the two options described above and the financial market options we discuss in the rest of this chapter. Whereas these two options represent net new wealth creation, virtually all financial options are zero-sum games, where one party's gain is, by definition, another party's loss.

nonconstant return variances. Section 5.5 concludes by examining the numerous theoretical extensions and applications of the basic option pricing model that have been developed since 1973, and discussing the empirical evidence on more advanced option pricing models that has been accumulating for almost two decades.

5.2   TERMINOLOGY AND PAYOFF DIAGRAMS FOR OPTIONS TRADING

5.2.1 Terminology

Most specialties in finance have their own unique, often colorful vocabulary, and options trading is no exception. Presented below are definitions of several key terms, along with examples of their use in modern finance.

Call option. A call option is the right to *buy* an asset, at a fixed price, on or before a fixed expiration date. To illustrate the workings of this contract, assume it is Wednesday, January 11, 1995, and you have just purchased a call option giving you the right to buy Telefonos de Mexico (Telmex) stock for $40 per share on or before Saturday, February 18, 1995.[2] The market price of Telmex stock at the time of your purchase was $35.375 per share (actually quoted as $35 3/8 per share) so you, as the *holder* of this call option, hope Telmex shares will increase in value over the next five weeks so that at expiration you will be able to buy the shares for $40 and sell them in the open market at, say, $45 per share—realizing a $5 per share profit. The option buyer is also said to have established a **long position**. On the other hand, the *writer* of this call option (the person who sold you the option—or established a **short position**) is hoping that Telmex shares will not increase in price above $40 per share before February 18, since he or she will have to deliver shares at a below-market price to you if the stock price increases. Should the stock price remain unchanged or decline, the option will expire unexercised and the option writer (the short) will keep the premium.

Put option. A put option is the right to *sell* an asset, at a fixed price, on or before a fixed expiration date. To illustrate how this contract works, assume your pessimistic friend Forrest Grump purchases a February put option on Telmex shares, also with a $40 per share exercise price, at the same time you purchase a call option. Your dour friend now has the right to sell Telmex stock for $40 per share on or before February 18, and he will benefit if Telmex drops below its current $35.375 per share market price over the next five weeks. The put writer, of course, is hoping Telmex will appreciate in value—or at least remain unchanged in price. Should the stock price increase or remain unchanged, the put option will expire unexercised, and the put writer will keep the option premium.

---

2. The institutional details of options trading on the Chicago Board of Options Exchange (CBOE) are discussed in detail in chapters 19 and 20 of Bodie, Kane, and Marcus (1993). Stock options generally expire on the Saturday following the third Friday of the expiration month. Therefore, our contract, with its February expiration month, actually matures on the third Saturday of February 1995. Furthermore, the actual option contract involves delivery of 100 Telmex shares, rather than just one, but we will phrase our discussion in per share terms both because this is much easier to understand, and because option and stock prices are actually quoted this way.

Exercise price. Also referred as the **strike price**, this is the per unit (usually, per share) price that a call option holder must pay to the option writer in order to take delivery of the optioned asset. For a put option, the exercise price is the price the option holder will receive upon delivering the optioned asset to the option writer. In our examples above, $40 per share is the exercise price for both the put and call options on Telmex shares.

Expiration date. Also referred to as the *maturity date*, this is the day that the option contract expires and the option writer is no longer liable for adverse price changes. Actively traded stocks such as Telmex will usually have multiple exchange-traded options contracts outstanding, with maturity dates stretching out to one year.[3] Investors or corporate hedgers wishing to obtain longer-term stock or commodity options can often obtain them through private negotiation with commercial banks or other options dealers.

European versus **American option**. A European option can be exercised only on the expiration date, whereas an American option can be exercised at any time up to and including this date. As is probably intuitively obvious, an American option must always be at least as valuable as an otherwise-equivalent European option, and will usually be more valuable. Furthermore, the vast majority of options contracts that are actually traded—including stock options such as in our Telmex examples above—are American options, even those that are listed in European markets.[4]

Option premium. This is the option contract price that is paid by the option buyer to the option seller (writer). The option writer keeps this premium whether the option contract expires unexercised or is exercised by the buyer. The writer of the Telmex call option discussed above receives an option premium of $1.313 per share (or $131.25 for the 100-share option contract), while the writer of the Telmex put option receives a premium of $5.625 per share. As we will see later, the option premium is systematically related to the risk-free rate of interest, as well as to the option's exercise price and term to maturity, and the underlying asset's current market price and volatility.

In-the-money, out-of-the-money, and at-the-money options. These terms refer to whether or not an option contract would be valuable if the contract was currently expiring. In our put option example above, Mr. Gump's option is $4.625 **in-the-money** because the current stock price of $35.375 is that much below the exercise price of $40 per share. This difference between an option's exercise price and its current market price is called its **intrinsic value**, and the difference between an option's premium and its intrinsic value is that option's **time value**. Therefore, the Telmex put option's $5.625 per share premium can be decomposed into $4.625 of intrinsic value and $1.00 of time value, so Mr. Gump is effectively paying $1.00

---

3. Perhaps surprisingly, Telmex was the most actively-traded stock on the New York Stock Exchange in 1994—which is even more amazing given the fact that the stock was only listed on the NYSE in 1991 following Telmex's privatization and subsequent American Depository Receipt (ADR) issue.

4. A major exception to this general rule is the S&P 100 Index option contract, which began trading on the CBOE on March 11, 1983, and quickly became (and remains) the most actively traded option contract.

per share for the right to profit from a decline in Telmex share price over the next five weeks. On the other hand, the call option you purchased is out-of-the-money, meaning that it has no intrinsic value, so the entire $1.313 per share option premium represents time value. If your option expires when you finished reading this sentence, it would now be worthless (sorry). Finally, if Telmex's current stock price is exactly $40 per share, both the put and call options would be **at-the-money**, meaning that the current stock price is equal to the option's exercise price. Both options would have intrinsic values of zero in that case, so the entire option premium in each case would represent time value.

5.2.2 Payoff Diagrams for Option Writers and Buyers

Table 5.1 presents selected options quotations for Telmex shares from the January 11, 1995 **Wall Street Journal** *Listed Options Quotations* table. We also present similar quotations for Telmex shares from December 19, 1994, one day before the Mexican government devalued the peso by 15 percent (it subsequently fell an additional 20 percent before rallying slightly in early January), thereby precipitating a sharp decline in the dollar price of virtually all Mexican financial assets—including Telmex shares. We will compare the option values from these two dates later, when we discuss the importance of volatility for option valuation. Our present objective is to describe the payoff patterns for writers and holders of Telmex options for different terminal share values.

Figure 5.1 is a payoff diagram for the buyer and seller of the previously-described call option on Telmex stock with a $40 per share exercise price. The x-axis of this diagram represents the possible terminal values of Telmex stock at expiration on February 18, and the y-axis represents the profit or loss to the parties involved in this transaction. For any terminal Telmex stock price of $40 per share or less, the writer's net profit is the $1.313 per share option premium received on January 11, which is also equal to the net loss suffered by the call option holder (you). At any price above $40 per share, the call option holder earns a profit of $1 per share for each $1 increase in Telmex's stock price, and this profit comes at the expense of the option writer—who suffers a dollar-for-dollar decline in wealth as the stock price increases. Both parties break even (zero net profit or loss) at a stock price equal to the exercise price plus the option premium, $41.313 per share.

Figure 5.2 is a payoff diagram for the holder and seller of the corresponding put option on Telmex stock that we discussed earlier (also with a $40 per share exercise price). For any terminal Telmex stock price of $40 or more, the writer's net profit is the option premium received in January, $5.625 per share. This is also the put option buyer's (Forrest Gump) net loss for stock prices in this range. For any terminal stock price below $40 per share, the put option buyer (seller) earns a profit (loss) of $1 for each dollar decline in Telmex's stock price. If, during the next five weeks, the Mexican government were to renationalize Telmex without compensation to investors, the Telmex shares traded on the NYSE would have zero value and the put option holder would receive upon exercise $40 for each optioned share—yielding Mr. Gump a net profit of $34.375 per share (the $40 payoff minus the $5.625 per share option premium). If this unfortunate collapse in Telmex stock price were to occur, the put option writer would experience a net loss of equal magnitude—$34.375 per share. Both parties break even (zero net profit or loss) if the stock price at the time of expiration equals this same $34.375 per share, the exercise price minus the option premium.

TABLE 5.1

LISTED OPTIONS QUOTATIONS TABLE FOR TELEFONOS DE MEXICO (TELMEX) STOCK FOR DECEMBER 19, 1994 (PANEL A) AND JANUARY 11, 1995 (PANEL B) FROM THE *WALL STREET JOURNAL*

Closing Stock Prices	Strike Price	Expiration Month	Calls: Volume	Calls: Closing Price	Puts: Volume	Puts: Closing Price
			Panel A: December 19, 1994			
48½	45	Jan	296	4⅜	3462	¾
48½	45	Feb	25	5	529	1¼
48½	45	May	. . .	. . .	927	2 1/16
48½	45	Aug	. . .	. . .	103	2⅞
48½	50	Jan	3168	1 7/16	3363	2¾
48½	50	Feb	1053	2	953	3⅜
48½	50	May	290	3⅞	2864	4⅛
48½	50	Aug	110	5¼	1946	4⅞
48½	55	Jan	3442	⅜	1491	6½
48½	55	Feb	2257	13/16	157	6¼
48½	55	May	2180	2⅛	163	7¾
48½	55	Aug	3	3⅜	213	8⅛
48½	60	Jan	1901	⅛	2175	10⅞
48½	60	Feb	512	5/16	2004	11
48½	60	May	140	1⅛	2310	10¾
48½	65	Jan	6	1/16	2101	15⅞
48½	65	Feb	1562	⅛	2232	16
48½	65	May	232	½	16	15¾
48½	85	Jan	. . .	. . .	50	35¾
			Panel B: January 11, 1995			
35⅜	30	Feb	2114	6⅜	4941	15/16
35⅜	30	May	292	7¼	1278	1¼
35⅜	30	Aug	121	7½	588	2¼
35⅜	35	Jan	19443	1⅞	5033	1 7/16
35⅜	35	Feb	12786	3⅛	4122	2⅝
35⅜	35	May	1027	4¾	862	3⅞

(continued)

TABLE 5.1 (CONTINUED)

Closing Stock Prices	Strike Price	Expiration Month	Calls		Puts	
			Volume	Closing Price	Volume	Closing Price
$35\frac{3}{8}$	35	Aug	766	$5\frac{1}{8}$	317	$4\frac{1}{4}$
$35\frac{3}{8}$	40	Jan	5289	$\frac{5}{16}$	2099	$5\frac{1}{4}$
$35\frac{3}{8}$	40	Feb	6229	$1\frac{5}{16}$	1265	$5\frac{3}{8}$
$35\frac{3}{8}$	40	May	1423	$2\frac{9}{16}$	320	$6\frac{5}{8}$
$35\frac{3}{8}$	40	Aug	378	$3\frac{1}{4}$	114	$7\frac{1}{2}$
$35\frac{3}{8}$	45	Jan	8535	$\frac{1}{8}$	332	$10\frac{1}{4}$
$35\frac{3}{8}$	45	Feb	1239	$\frac{9}{16}$	233	$10\frac{1}{4}$
$35\frac{3}{8}$	45	May	686	$1\frac{3}{8}$	263	$10\frac{1}{2}$
$35\frac{3}{8}$	45	Aug	173	$1\frac{15}{16}$	149	11
$35\frac{3}{8}$	50	Jan	38	$\frac{1}{16}$	16	15
$35\frac{3}{8}$	50	Feb	1505	$\frac{1}{4}$	123	$14\frac{7}{8}$
$35\frac{3}{8}$	50	May	411	$\frac{3}{4}$	100	$15\frac{3}{4}$
$35\frac{3}{8}$	50	Aug	61	$1\frac{3}{16}$	43	$17\frac{3}{4}$
$35\frac{3}{8}$	55	Jan	99	$\frac{1}{16}$	6	$22\frac{1}{2}$
$35\frac{3}{8}$	55	Feb	111	$\frac{1}{8}$	30	$21\frac{1}{2}$
$35\frac{3}{8}$	55	May	139	$\frac{1}{2}$	109	$21\frac{7}{8}$
$35\frac{3}{8}$	55	Aug	146	$\frac{13}{16}$	68	22

5.2.3 Put-Call Parity

We can now demonstrate that there exists a systematic relationship between put and call prices on the same asset that must hold at all times. Consider the following strategy: (1) buy one share of Telmex stock at the current market price, S; (2) sell (write) one European call option with an exercise price, X, of $40 per share; (3) buy one European put option with the same $40 exercise price. At expiration (T periods in the future), the market price of Telmex stock, S, will either be greater than or equal to the $40 per share exercise price ($S \geq X$) or below it ($S < X$). The payoffs in each case are listed below, using both symbols and example price data ($45 or $35/share):

	$35/share	$S \geq X$	$45/share	$S < X$
Value of stock you hold	S	$45	S	$35
Value of call option written	$-(S - X)$	− $ 5	0	$ 0
Value of put option bought	0	$ 0	$(X - S)$	$ 5
Net value of position	X	$40	X	$40

FIGURE 5.1

PROFIT DIAGRAM FOR CALL OPTION ON TELMEX STOCK

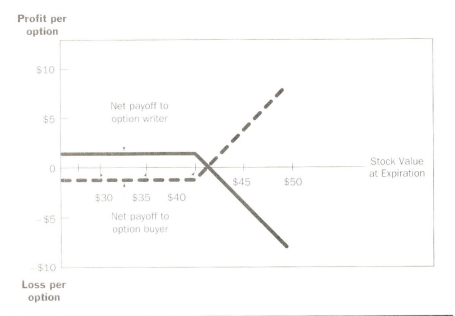

FIGURE 5.2

PROFIT DIAGRAM FOR PUT OPTION ON TELMEX STOCK

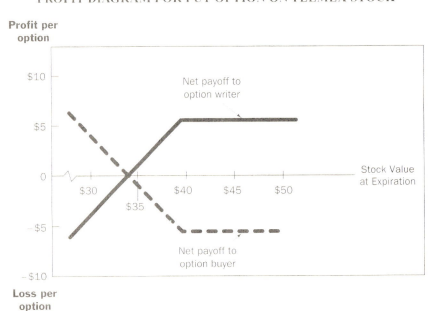

As can be seen, the payoff to this investment strategy is the same, $40, regardless of the terminal price of Telmex shares. Since this investment position will pay off $40 with certainty at time t^* (T periods ahead), we can compute its present value by discounting at the risk-free rate of interest, r_f. Using discrete discounting, the relationship between the current stock price, S_0, the current value of a put option (P_0) with exercise price X and time to maturity T, and c_0—the current market value of a European call option with the same exercise price and maturity date—can be expressed algebraically as Equation 5.1:

$$S_0 + P_0 - c_0 = X/(1 + r_f)^T \qquad (5.1)$$

This formula can be rearranged to yield Equation 5.2, which is known as the **put-call parity** formula because it expresses the proper relationship between put and call prices based on current stock price, time to maturity, and option exercise price:

$$S_0 + P_0 = c_0 + X/(1 + r_f)^T \qquad (5.2)$$

The put-call parity formula is very useful, because it allows one to compute the value of any one of the six variables in the formula—S_0, P_0, c_0, X, r_f, or T—based on observed values of the other five variables. For example, using our earlier Telmex data (with $S_0 = \$35.375$, $P_0 = \$5.625$, $X = \$40.00$, $r_f = 0.075$ [7.5 percent per year], and $T = 0.1041$ [38 days between January 11 and February 18 divided by 365 days in a year]), we can compute the call option value to be:

$$c_0 = S_0 + P_0 - X/(1 + r_f)^T = \$35.375 + \$5.625 - \$40/(1.075)^{0.1041}$$

$$= \$1.30 \text{ per share}$$

Since the market value of this call option was actually $1.313 per share, our computed value of $1.30 per share yielded a very close estimate.

5.3   THE BLACK-SCHOLES OPTION PRICING MODEL

Economists had been trying to value options for decades before Fischer Black and Myron Scholes demonstrated a closed-form valuation method in 1973.[5] All previous valuation formulas had floundered on the necessity to specify a required return for holders of options on common stocks. Options, being **derivative instruments** (their value is derived from the price of the asset on which they are written), have values that are clearly linked to the return on the underlying shares of common stock, but the precise relationship between stock and option prices was unknown prior to Black and Scholes. Two points were obvious: (1) since a call option effectively represents a levered claim on a share of stock, the option will be riskier (its price will be more variable) than the underlying stock, and (2) the expected return on the option will change continuously as the stock price changes, even if the expected (and realized) return on the stock remains constant through time.

Black and Scholes' (1973) fundamental insight was to recognize that it is possible (provided certain market efficiency and return distribution assumptions are met) to create a riskless hedge portfolio involving a long (purchased) position in the stock and a

---

5. For a detailed discussion of the pre-Black & Scholes research into option valuation, beginning with the work of the French mathematician Louis Bachelier in 1900, see Smith (1976, pages 628–633).

short (sold) position in a specific number of call options written on that stock. Once established, this risk-free hedge position can be maintained until the call option expires, using a simple dynamic trading strategy. Since a riskless investment must earn the risk-free rate of interest in equilibrium, Black and Scholes (hereafter, B-S) are able to finesse the need to compute a required return on the option itself, and are instead able to express the call option value, c, as a function of five, readily-observable (or at least computable) parameters—the current stock price, the option's exercise price and term to maturity, the risk-free interest rate, and the stock's instantaneous price volatility. Before plunging too far ahead of ourselves, however, we should pause to present the assumptions that B-S used to compute their option pricing model (OPM), and then systematically trace the logic they used to derive their call option valuation formula. We will focus on the economic logic of the B-S derivation, rather than on the (admittedly advanced) mathematics they employ, and we will use the same terminology presented in Smith (1979, pages 288–296).[6]

5.3.1 Assumptions and Development of the Black-Scholes Model

Black and Scholes made the following assumptions in order to derive their option pricing model: (1) frictionless markets—transactions costs of trading and taxes are zero; (2) there are no restrictions on short sales of stock; (3) the stock pays no dividends or other distributions; (4) the market operates continuously; (5) the stock price follows a random walk in continuous time and the distribution of possible stock prices at the end of any finite period of time is lognormal; (6) the variance rate of the return on the stock is constant; (7) the option can be exercised only at maturity (a European option); and (8) the riskless interest rate is known and is constant through time.[7] In other words, they assumed frictionless markets, stock price dynamics that follow a stationary stochastic process (prices change continuously, but within stable boundaries), and a non-stochastic (constant) interest rate and return variance.

B-S demonstrate that it is possible to create a riskless hedge, with value V_H, consisting of a long position in the stock and a short position in call options. The idea is to weight the quantity of stock held long and options sold short so that the decrease in value on one side of the position is exactly offset by an increase in value on the other. If we define Q_s as the quantity of stock in the hedge and Q_c as the quantity of call options in the hedge, the overall value, V_H, of the hedge can be expressed as in Equation 5.3 below:

$$V_H = Q_s S + Q_c c \tag{5.3}$$

where, as before, S is the price of a share of stock and c is the price of a call option to purchase one share of stock.

---

6. Students wishing a more rigorous derivation of the B-S model should see the original paper, or the derivation presented in Smith (1979). A less intensive, but more understandable, development of the model is presented in Copeland and Weston (1988, pages 296–299). Finally, an alternative derivation of the basic B-S model is presented in Merton (1973, pages 162–169).

7. While this list of assumptions seems quite extreme, the B-S model has actually proven to be quite robust to somewhat weaker restrictions, as we will discuss shortly.

If quantities of stock and options, Q_s and Q_c, are selected so that the ratio Q_s/Q_c is equal to minus the ratio of the change in option price for a given change in stock price, $- (\partial_c/\partial_s)$, then changes in the value of the hedge position (V_H) resulting from, say, an increase in the market price of stock will be exactly offset by the increased liability resulting from the rise in value of the call options written. In effect, the net equity invested in creating the hedge is rendered risk-free by the offsetting positions, and the riskless status of the hedge can be maintained through time by continuously adjusting Q_s and Q_c to maintain the equivalence of Q_s/Q_c and $- (\partial_c/\partial_s)$. Since the value of the equity invested in the hedge at option maturity can be determined with certainty, its value today can be determined by discounting the net equity investment back to the present, using the riskless rate of interest.

The logic of the risk-free hedge position allows B-S to define a differential equation for the value of the call option using only the observable variables stock price, S, exercise price of the option, X, the stock's variance rate, σ^2, the time to maturity, T—expressed as the difference between the maturity date, t^*, and the current date, t, or ($t^* - t$)—and the riskless interest rate, r.[8] Since at maturity the option must have a value of either zero or the difference between the terminal date stock price, S^*, and the exercise price ($S^* - X$), whichever is greater, we can specify the required boundary condition for the terminal value of the call option as in Equation 5.4:

$$c^* = \max [S^* - X, 0] \tag{5.4}$$

Specifying this boundary condition allows B-S to make substitutions into their (unsolvable) differential equation that transforms it into another differential equation (the heat-exchange equation in physics) with a known solution. The final model B-S derive is presented below as Equation 5.5:

$$c = SN (d_1) - e^{-rT} XN (d_2) \tag{5.5}$$

where: $d_1 = [ln(S/X) + (r + \sigma^2/2)T]/\sigma\sqrt{T}$
$d_2 = [ln(S/X) + (r - \sigma^2/2)T]/\sigma\sqrt{T}$

where c = the current call option value,
   T = time to option maturity ($t^* - t$),
   e = 2.71828, the base of the natural log function,
   ln = natural logarithm,
   $N(d)$ = the cumulative normal density function.

Variables S, X, and r are, as before, current stock price, option exercise price, and the riskless interest rate, respectively. An insight into how this valuation formula works can be obtained by interpreting the $N(d)$ terms loosely as the risk-adjusted probabilities that the option will expire in the money.[9] First, assume that the stock price is very high relative to the exercise price ($S/X >> 1.0$), suggesting a virtual certainty that the call option will expire in the money. In this case, both $N(d)$ terms will be very close to 1.0, and

---

8. Note that this is the continuously compounded riskless interest rate r, rather than the single–period, discrete-time, risk-free rate r_f we have used elsewhere.

9. Our discussion in this segment closely follows that in Bodie, Kane, and Marcus (1993, pages 681–683), which is easily the most intuitive analysis of the inner workings of the B-S model we have seen.

the call option valuation formula will collapse to $S - Xe^{-rT}$, the current stock price minus the present value of the exercise price. On the other hand, when the stock price is very low relative to the exercise price ($S/X << 1.0$), both $N(d)$ terms will be close to zero, and the call option value will also be approximately zero—as expected for deep out-of-the-money options. When values of $N(d)$ fall between 0 and 1, the value of the call option can be viewed as a trade-off between the likely payoff from owning the stock at option expiration and the discounted value of the exercise price times the probability of in-the-money option expiration.

5.3.2 Determinants of Option Values

The value of a call option can be written in more general functional form in Equation 5.6, as a function only of stock price, exercise price, time to maturity, variance, and riskless interest rate:

$$c = c(S, X, T, \sigma^2, r) \tag{5.6}$$

As it happens, the value of a put option (P) can be expressed in the same functional form, although—as we will see—the direction of the relationship between the variables and the option value is sometimes different. Expressing the call and put valuation formulas in this way allows us to clearly discuss how each of these variables impacts valuation. For example, what effect does an increase in the exercise price, X, have on the value of a call option? Clearly, for any given stock price and term to maturity, a higher exercise price decreases the value of a call option because the option is less likely to expire in-the-money (it is more likely to expire unexercised). On the other hand, the holder of a put option would prefer a higher *exercise* price to a lower one for exactly the same reason—the more likely the option is to expire in-the-money, the higher is the exercise price. We can express these same relationships mathematically by saying that the partial derivative of a call option's value with respect to (w.r.t.) the exercise price is negative ($\partial_c/\partial_X < 0$), while the partial derivative of a put option's value w.r.t. exercise price is positive ($\partial_p/\partial_X > 0$).

Table 5.2 summarizes the relationship between the five variables in Equation 5.6 and the value of call and put prices. The first column of this table lists the variable names and symbols, while columns 2 and 3 show the direction of the relationship between this variable and call option prices both verbally (positive or negative) and symbolically (as partial derivatives). Columns 4 and 5 present the same information for the relationship between the variables and put values. In our discussion below, we will also frequently refer back to Table 5.1—which lists option values for Telmex stock on two different dates—in order to amplify key points with real price data. Furthermore, our explanation of these relationships will be in intuitive terms. Those wishing a more rigorous mathematical explanation are referred to Smith (1979, pages 293–294 and 295–296).

Stock price, S. For any given exercise price and time to maturity, stock price and call values are positively related ($\partial_c/\partial_S > 0$), while stock price and put values are negatively related ($\partial_p/\partial_S < 0$). Obviously, a call option with a one-month maturity date and a $45 exercise price will be more valuable when the underlying stock price is $48.50 per share than when the stock price is $35.375 per share, while a put option with the same terms will be less valuable at $48.50. Table 5.1 makes

TABLE 5.2

DIRECTION OF RELATIONSHIP BETWEEN STOCK OPTION VALUES AND UNDERLYING PRICING FACTORS

Factor Name and Symbol	Call Options Direction of Relationship	Partial Derivative Expression	Put Options Direction of Relationship	Partial Derivative Expression
Stock Price, S	positive	$\partial_c/\partial_s > 0$	negative	$\partial_p/\partial_s < 0$
Exercise price, X	negative	$\partial_c/\partial_x < 0$	positive	$\partial_p/\partial_x > 0$
Time to expiration, T	positive	$\partial_c/\partial_T > 0$	positive or negative	$\partial_p/\partial_T \gtrless 0$
Stock return volatility, σ^2	positive	$\partial_c/\partial\sigma^2 > 0$	positive	$\partial_p/\partial\sigma^2 > 0$
Riskless rate, r	positive	$\partial_c/\partial_r > 0$	negative	$\partial_p/\partial_r < 0$

these relationships clear, since these are actual prices for Telmex stock and put options. On December 19, 1994, Telmex's stock price was $48.50 per share, the $45 January call option premium was $4.375 per share (the call was in-the-money), and the $45 January put option premium was $0.75 per share (out-of-the-money). By January 11, 1995, Telmex stock had declined in price to $35.375 per share and the $45 February (one-month maturity) call option premium was worth only $0.563 per share (the call was out-of-the-money). However, the $45 February put option was worth a whopping $10.25 per share on January 11, since the put was $9.625 per share in-the-money.

Exercise price, X . For any given stock price and time to maturity, exercise price is negatively related to call values $(\partial_c/\partial_x < 0)$ and positively related to put values $(\partial_p/\partial_x > 0)$. As discussed above, the reasoning here is quite simple—the higher the exercise price the less likely the stock price will increase in value enough over the life of the option to make a call option expire in-the-money. The exact opposite applies for put options—the higher the exercise price the greater the likelihood that the stock price will be below the exercise price at maturity (the put option will be in-the-money). Call and put values for Telmex stock on January 11, 1995 clearly demonstrate these relationships. February call options with a $35 exercise price are worth $3.125 per share when the current stock price is $35.375, while $40 February calls are worth only $1.313 per share. The opposite is true for put values—$35 February puts are worth $2.625 per share, while $40 February puts sell for $5.625 per share.

Time to expiration (maturity), T . Time to expiration actually influences options prices in two ways. First, the longer the term to option maturity the greater the likelihood that stock prices will have increased (declined) enough in price to make any given call (put) option expire in-the-money. This effect of maturity increases both put and call option values $(\partial_c/\partial_T, \partial_p/\partial_T > 0)$. The second effect of time to expiration is to lower the present value of the option exercise price. This works to further increase the value of call options, so the relationship between time to maturity and call values is unambiguously positive ($\partial_c/\partial_t > 0$). Since a put option holder hopes to *receive* a cash payment at option expiration, however, lowering the present value of the option exercise price reduces the current value of put options ($\partial_p/\partial_t < 0$). The net impact of time to maturity on put options cannot, therefore, be specified *a priori*, but will instead depend on the level of interest rates and stock volatility. Table 5.1 shows that in January 1995 put option values increase with time to maturity. For example, the $35 August 1995 puts are worth $4.25 per share, whereas the $35 February 1995 puts are worth only $2.625 per share—and the $35 May 1995 puts are worth $3.875 per share. Call option values clearly are positively related to time to option expiration: in January 1995, the $35 August call is a full $2.00 per share ($5.125 − $3.125) more valuable than the $35 February call.

Stock price volatility, σ^2. Stock price variance has an effect on put and call option valuation similar to that of maturity. The greater the volatility the greater the probability that the stock price will increase (decrease) enough to make the call (put) option expire in-the-money ($\partial_c/\partial\sigma^2, \partial_p/\partial\sigma^2 > 0$). This is where the asymmetric nature of options is most clearly contrasted with the symmetrical payoffs on most other financial assets. Most investors would prefer securities with smaller variances, since this would reduce the likelihood of suffering a large capital loss from a severe price decline during the holding period. Options, however, represent claims only on the upper (call) or lower (put) tail of the probability distribution of terminal date stock prices, so the greater the variance the better.

Riskless interest rate, r. Of all the variables that impact option values, the effect of a change in the riskless rate is the least intuitively obvious—although the effect is quite straightforward. An increase in the riskless rate reduces the present value of the exercise price the holder of an in-the-money call option will have to pay at maturity, so interest rates are positively related to call option values ($\partial_c/\partial_r > 0$). On the other hand, that same increase in the riskless rate reduces the present value of the exercise price the holder of an in-the-money put option will receive, so interest rates are negatively related to put option values ($\partial_p/\partial_r < 0$).

5.3.3 Restrictions on Rational Option Pricing

In an article that has proven almost as influential as the original Black and Scholes paper, Merton (1973) used simple dominance arguments to prove several restrictions, or boundary conditions, on rational option prices. Since most of these restrictions follow logically from the basic option pricing formulas (i.e., option values must be nonnegative; longer maturity options must be at least as valuable as shorter maturity options with the same exercise price; American options must be at least as valuable as otherwise identical European options), we will not list them here. The interested reader is referred instead to Merton's article or to the summary of these restrictions in Smith (1976, pages 620–627). Two of the restrictions are not obvious, however, and thus bear analysis here. First, Merton showed that an American call *on a non-dividend paying stock* will not be exercised before the expiration date—even if it is deeply in-the-money. However much intrinsic value an option might have today, there will always be a positive probability that it will increase even further in price and premature exercise would forfeit the remaining time value of the option. An option holder wishing to harvest a cash return on an in-the-money call would be better served by selling than by exercising the option.

On the other hand, the second of Merton's pricing restrictions we examine shows that premature exercise *will* sometimes be optimal *on a dividend-paying stock*. This will occur when the dividend payment is larger than the remaining time value of the call option after the stock goes ex-dividend. For example, assume an investor holds a call option with a $50 exercise price on a stock with a current cum-dividend price of $52, that is expected to decline to $48 per share after the firm pays its $4 per share annual dividend two days hence. Now consider how a *European* call option on this stock with, say, a nine-month maturity date and a $50 per share exercise price would be valued. Clearly, the current stock price—which reflects the imminent $4 per share dividend payment—would be irrelevant in valuing a European option. Instead, the relevant stock value would be the expected ex-dividend day share price of $48 per share, and a call option with nine months to maturity and a $50 per share exercise price would probably have a fairly low value—perhaps $0.50 per share (all of which would be time value, since intrinsic value is zero), and there would be no incentive to exercise the option prematurely.

This situation would change fundamentally, however, if the call option was an *American* rather than a European option—but was identical in all other respects. In this case, there is no rational value for the option that would entice the holder not to either sell the option or exercise it prematurely (in fact, immediately). An option value above $2 per share would be irrational—since the current, cum-dividend price is $52 per share, no rational investor would pay more than $2 for the right to buy the stock for $50 per share—so the option holder would sell it if someone was foolish enough to offer more than that price. On the other hand, it would be irrational for the option holder not to exercise the option if the option premium was less than $2 per share, since doing so would force him or her to forego receipt of a $4 per share cash dividend payment, yet still see the value of the underlying stock fall by this amount on the ex-dividend day. In fact, for any rational option valuation (between 0 and $2 per share), it would be optimal for the option holder to exercise the call, buy the stock for $50 per share, and then either receive the cash dividend or sell the stock prior to the ex-dividend day.

More generally, since most exchange-traded options are American options, and are not dividend-protected (their exercise prices are not adjusted downwards to compensate for dividend payments), call option holders will frequently find premature option exercise to be optimal. In the same paper that showed this result theoretically, Merton (1973) presented the first closed-form solution for valuing dividend-paying stocks, but he achieved this only by making the unrealistic assumption that firms paid dividends continuously (as in a discount bond) rather than in discrete lump sums. As will be discussed in the applications section below, several other authors have presented valuation models that can realistically account for dividends, though the cost of this flexibility is always additional model complexity.

5.3.4 Equity as a Call Option

As important as presenting a valuation formula for exchange-traded options was, Black and Scholes (1973) themselves realized that a potentially even more fundamental contribution of option pricing theory (OPT) lay in corporate financial analysis—specifically in valuing the equity of a levered firm. To understand how OPT can thus be used, assume that the managers of an all-equity firm decide to issue pure-discount debt that will mature at time t in the future, and then distribute the proceeds of this debt issue to the firm's shareholders—leaving the company's assets and business risk unchanged.[10] By issuing debt, the shareholders of this firm have effectively sold the assets of the company to the new bondholders, but have also purchased a call option on these assets which the shareholders can exercise at time t by paying off the maturing debt in full. The shareholders will exercise this call option if the value of the firm's assets at time t exceeds the face value of the debt. If the firm's assets are worth less than the face value of the debt at time t, the stockholders will default (as they are allowed to do in a limited liability company) and the bondholders will become the new residual claimants entitled to whatever value the assets retain. In other words, equity in a levered company is actually a call option on the assets of the firm. It is equally correct to say that stockholders in a levered, limited liability company hold a potentially valuable **option to default** on the firm's debt that they will exercise whenever the firm's economic net worth (market value of firm assets − face value of maturing debt) is negative at the option's maturity (when the debt issue matures).

Having introduced the basic Black-Scholes OPM and discussed the variables that influence option prices, we now turn to a summary of the most important empirical tests of the B-S model, and its close derivatives, that have been published during the past two decades. Even the most casual reading of the economic news headlines—with their discussions of the problems caused by inappropriate (or simply unlucky) uses of options and other "derivatives"—suggests both how important these instruments have become to a modern financial system and how complex their structures can be.

5.4 EMPIRICAL TESTS OF THE BLACK-SCHOLES OPM AND ITS EXTENSIONS

The response of both the professional and academic finance communities following the publication of the B-S OPM has been nothing short of electric, and can serve as a model of how a very robust body of knowledge can be developed both rigorously and rapidly. We begin this section with a discussion of the early tests of the B-S model itself, and then describe several important theoretical extensions of this model that have weakened the assumption of constant return variance.

5.4.1 Empirical Tests of the Black-Scholes Model

The first empirical option pricing study published in a major finance journal is actually Stoll's (1969) test of put-call parity. Although the B-S OPM had not yet even been dreamed of, Stoll was able to develop the put-call parity boundary conditions (rational

---

10. As always, the assumption that the proceeds of a debt issue be used to buy back outstanding equity is critical. If the issue proceeds are instead invested internally, the firm's investment policy and asset size have been changed, and one is no longer considering a pure capital structure change.

pricing restrictions) and empirically document that the existing over-the-counter (OTC) options markets were efficient (boundary condition violations occur infrequently). Ten years later, Klemkosky and Resnick (1979) reached a similar conclusion for the listed options markets.

Black and Scholes (1972) present the first test of their OPM, in a paper that was published almost a full year before the pricing model itself. They examine whether forming a riskless hedge by purchasing options that are "undervalued" (relative to their predicted price using the B-S OPM) by the OTC market and simultaneously selling "overvalued" options could yield positive profits. To construct this hedge, B-S first generate predicted prices using their OPM and then compare these to actual OTC option origination prices. Although this hedging strategy yields significant excess returns when options are purchased at market prices (rather than at predicted prices) and held to maturity, these profits disappear when even nominal transactions costs are assumed. Based on this, B-S conclude that the OTC options market is efficient. Galai (1977, 1978) and Bhattacharya (1983) reach similar conclusions in their tests of the efficiency of the Chicago Board Options Exchange, where listed options began trading in 1973. After transactions costs, the boundary conditions on prices in this market are not systematically violated.

Another series of empirical tests of the OPM examine whether the Black-Scholes assumption of a constant return variance can be empirically supported. MacBeth and Merville (1990) compare the B-S OPM with the Cox (1975) constant elasticity of variance model of option valuation (discussed below). They find that the Cox model, which allows return variance to be inversely related to current stock price, fits the observed option pricing data better than does the simple B-S OPM. Beckers (1980) documents that variance is in fact an inverse function of stock price for most stocks, and supports the MacBeth and Merville conclusion regarding the superiority of the constant elasticity of variance model.

In an intriguing twist of logic, Manaster and Rendleman (1982) ask whether the stock price implied by the B-S OPM is in fact a better predictor of the *equilibrium* stock price than is the stock price actually generated by trading on the NYSE and other exchanges. While this proposition may appear fantastic, there are actually several good reasons why relevant information about a stock might be incorporated into option prices before they are incorporated into stock prices. For one thing, because of the tremendous leverage involved in option trading, an investor with positive (negative) private information about a company can obtain a much higher return for each dollar of investment by purchasing call (put) options than by purchasing (shorting) the underlying stock itself. Options might also attract distinct groups of investors who wish to place a bet on the direction of a stock without being exposed to the risk of owning or shorting the stock. Finally, options trading can offer greater confidentiality for traders wishing to buy or sell shares without revealing their identities. For whatever reason, Manaster and Rendleman find that option prices incorporate relevant information up to 24 hours before that same information is incorporated into stock prices.

RECENT EMPIRICAL TESTS   Since the early 1980s, there have been relatively few published empirical tests of the B-S OPM itself, but several researchers have used the model to examine other financial issues. Ball and Torous (1984) derive a very efficient estimator of price variability using historical high, low, and closing stock prices, and then use this estimator to construct the statistically most powerful confidence interval for the B-S OPM. Barone-Adesi and Whaley (1986) use the B-S model, with Roll's (1977) dividend adjustments, to infer the *expected* ex-dividend day relative stock price decline for a large sample of stocks. They find that the expected stock price decline is not significantly different from unity (the stock price will decline by the amount of the dividend).

Skinner (1989) documents that stock return variance declines and trading volume increases significantly after the introduction of options on the underlying stock, and these results are broadly consistent with the view that options improve stock liquidity. Conrad (1989) also examines the effect of option introduction, and finds it to be associated with a permanent increase in the price of the underlying stock that occurs at the introduction itself (not at the announcement). She also documents a decline in stock volatility after option introduction. Vijh (1990) examines the liquidity of the CBOE directly, and documents excellent market depth based on the absence of price effects from large options trades. He finds that this liquidity has a cost, however, in that bid-ask spreads for options are almost as large as those on the stocks themselves, even though the average option is equal to less than half a share of stock plus borrowing.

Turning to the most recent research, Sheikh and Ronn (1994) document that option returns display systematic daily and intraday patterns, even after adjusting for patterns in the means and variances of the underlying assets. Their results are consistent with the idea that informed trading in the options market makes the order flow informative (options prices incorporate inside information), thus making options nonredundant assets. Hutchinson, Lo and Poggio (1994) propose a new, nonparametric estimation method for pricing options using learning networks. This methodology may be superior to standard pricing techniques when the underlying stock return generating process is unknown, but it suffers from the drawback that a great deal of data is required for learning networks to be developed. Finally, Brenner and Subrahmanyan (1994) provide a simplified formula for using the B-S model to construct hedges that does not require managers to understand advanced mathematics—but which is still powerful enough to accurately estimate hedge ratios and various risk factors such as volatility sensitivity.

5.4.2 Nonconstant Volatility and the Black-Scholes OPM

From the very beginning, the B-S assumption of a constant, known stock return volatility was questioned on both theoretical and empirical grounds. We now examine the ways that researchers have sought to incorporate different volatility measures into the B-S OPM. We first discuss theoretical alternatives to the constant variance assumption, and then examine empirical evidence on actual return variance.

THEORETICAL MODELS OF STOCK VOLATILITY   Perhaps surprisingly, the first major alternative variance measure presented in the theoretical literature is also the measure that has been most supported by subsequent empirical research. Cox (1975), in one of the mostly widely-cited unpublished papers in academic finance, developed a **constant elasticity of variance** (CEV) model of stock volatility, which hypothesizes that the instantaneous variance of returns is inversely related to the level of the stock price. This is described mathematically in Equation 5.7, where stock return, *dS*, is expressed as a function of time and a variance term, $\sigma S^{\alpha/2}$, where α is assumed to be less than 2.[11]

$$dS = \mu S dt + \sigma S^{\alpha/2} dz \tag{5.7}$$

The idea that variance should increase as the stock price falls makes sense both from an internal, corporate perspective—the presence of fixed operating and financial costs increases the dispersion of equity returns when equity values decline—and from a valuation perspective, since investors will be less certain of the probability distribution of possible returns on a stock that has declined in value following a period of poor financial performance. As mentioned above, the CEV model has been empirically supported by MacBeth and Merville (1980) and Beckers (1980), while the importance of leverage in determining return variance is explicitly demonstrated in Geske's (1979) compound option model.[12]

Following Cox, several other authors present theoretical models of return variance that can be incorporated into the basic B-S OPM without loss of generality. Both Merton (1976) and Cox and Ross (1976) derive mixed jump-diffusion stock return models that allow for discontinuous positive or negative stock price changes (jumps). These models incorporate an important element of reality—stock prices do indeed experience discontinuous jumps and stumbles when important information hits the market—while still preserving the basic continuous-time diffusion model for most return intervals. Rubinstein (1976) and Cox, Ross, and Rubinstein (CRR 1979) show that the B-S OPM can also hold, under special circumstances, even when trading takes place at discrete intervals, rather than in continuous time. The CRR model is especially important because it is based on the simple binomial distribution—where stock prices can take on only one of two values in the next period—and it thus allows a truly simplified approach to option pricing that can be used by ordinary managers and other mortals not blessed with a working knowledge of stochastic calculus.

Jarrow and Rudd's (1982) primary theoretical contribution to option pricing theory is to present a valuation model that weakens the assumption of a lognormal (terminal) stock price distribution and also incorporates the impact of the third and fourth moments (skewness and kurtosis) of a stock's return distribution on an option's value. They find the resulting option price is equal to the B-S model's price, plus adjustment terms that depend on the higher moments of the stochastic process generating returns.

STOCHASTIC VOLATILITY AND OTHER RECENT THEORETICAL MODELS
During the past decade, Hull and White (1987), Wiggins (1987), Scott (1987), Lamoureux and Lastrapes (1993), and Naik (1993) have all presented **stochastic volatility**

---

11. If α is equal to two, this return expression is identical to that in the basic Black-Scholes model with constant variance.

12. Geske also shows that variance will not generally be constant in option pricing formulas, because a call option on a stock is actually an option on an option—since common stock itself is a call option written on the assets of a levered firm. He also finds that stock return variance will be a function of stock prices. Galai and Masulis (1976) reach a similar conclusion—that stock betas cannot in general be stationary—in their model synthesizing the B-S OPM and the CAPM.

option pricing models (and/or empirical tests), where the stock return variance is allowed to change randomly over time—rather than simply as a function of the stock price. Hull and White present an analytical valuation formula (using Monte Carlo simulation) for European call options under the assumption that volatility risk is unpriced, whereas Wiggins presents a numerical valuation model using the finite first difference technique. Both find that stochastic volatility models will usually yield estimated option values that do not differ significantly from those generated by the B-S OPM. Scott examines the pricing of European call options on stocks with variance rates that change randomly, and documents strong evidence of intertemporal dependence in stock price volatility.[13] He finds that a random variance model yields option prices that are marginally closer to market prices than are values generated by a fixed volatility model. Lamoureux and Lastrapes present empirical evidence that volatility risk may well be priced, in contrast to the predictions of the Hull and White model. Finally, Naik develops a model where asset return volatility is subject to random and discontinuous shifts over time (resulting from takeover bids, earnings surprises, or other information shocks). This study also demonstrates trading strategies that can be used to hedge the risk of jumps in return volatilities.

The most recent theoretical and empirical advance in understanding asset volatilities involves the use of **implied binomial trees**. In his presidential address, Rubinstein (1994) develops a method for inferring risk-neutral probabilities from European options, which can be used in turn to infer unique binomial trees consistent with these probabilities. The great advantage of this methodology is its promised capability to extract far more, and far more valuable, information about the underlying stochastic process generating asset returns than has heretofore been feasible using conventional methods. Rubinstein also documents that stock return variances seem to have experienced a permanent upwards revision since 1987, which has dramatically increased the value of out-of-the-money puts. Finally, he documents that the graphical representation of implied standard deviations (ISDs, defined below) as a function of strike price departs significantly from the horizontal line implied by B-S, and instead reveals a convex pattern of measured ISDs that gives rise to the phrase **volatility smile**.

5.4.3 The Implied Standard Deviation Methodology and Its Use

One of the cleverest of all uses of the B-S OPM was pioneered by Latané and Rendleman (1976), who show that it is possible to use the OPM itself to back out an implied volatility estimate for any stock that has one or more options traded on it. To see how this is done, recall that four of the five inputs to the OPM are observable (S, X, r, and T); only variance is an unknown that must be estimated. If you then observe a market-generated option price, then you have *five* option pricing inputs (the four observable variables, plus the resulting price), and can numerically calculate the unique variance measure that will yield that price when plugged into the OPM with the other four observable variables. This is called a stock's **implied standard deviation** (ISD), or the volatility estimate implied

---

13. This means that variance changes tend to form a wave pattern, where variance increases in one period are usually followed by further increases the next period.

for that stock by observed option prices, based on the assumption that the B-S OPM is the correct option pricing model. Whenever two or more options (that differ with respect to exercise price or maturity) trade on a single underlying stock, it is possible to compute a **weighted implied standard deviation** (WISD) by averaging the ISDs computed from each traded option. Since each option will usually yield a different ISD, however, the exact weighting scheme that should be used to compute the uniquely correct WISD is unclear, and has been the subject of much debate.

Having developed the ISD methodology, Latané and Rendleman then compute WISDs for several stocks and document that these implied volatilities predict actual future variances better than do extrapolations of historical variance estimates. Chiras and Manaster (1978) also calculate the ISD of future stock returns and find them to be better predictors of subsequent, realized variances than estimates based on historical volatility measures. Somewhat surprisingly, they find that a "risk-free" trading strategy of buying underpriced options (options with ISDs that are greater than the WISD) and selling overpriced options (ISDs less than the WISD) yields significant positive excess returns. Schmalansee and Trippi (1978) use ISDs to examine the evolution of volatility over time, and document (1) that volatility is not constant, and may in fact be negatively serially correlated, and (2) that changes in expected volatility are unrelated to changes in actual current (historical) variance.

More recently, Ajinkya and Gift (1985), Day and Lewis (1988), and Resnick, Sheikh, and Song (1993) have all used ISDs to document systematic patterns in return variances. Ajinkya and Gift find that ISDs clearly reflect the contemporaneous dispersion in analyst forecasts of future earnings for a stock, and reflect this dispersion better than do historically-based forecasts. Day and Lewis document that index option (discussed below) ISDs reflect the increased stock market volatility that often accompanies quarterly expirations of stock index futures, and non-quarterly index option expirations.[14] Finally, Resnick, Sheikh, and Song (1993) find that the January effect in stock price variances documented by earlier researchers is also reflected in one-month WISDs. They use expiration-weighted WISDs rather than simple averages, and provide for the interested reader a discussion of the issues involved in selecting appropriate weighting schemes for implied volatilities.

5.5 EXTENSIONS AND APPLICATIONS OF THE BLACK-SCHOLES OPM

One of the most important trends in the option pricing literature since 1973 has been the extension of the basic B-S model to the pricing of many financial assets and investment opportunities other than non-dividend-paying common stocks. One very important application of option pricing methodology, in assessing real investment opportunities, will be discussed in the next chapter (capital budgeting and investment decisions).

---

14. When index option contracts, index futures contracts, and the stock market itself close simultaneously on four Fridays each year, the last hour of NYSE trading is called the **triple witching hour**. These periods have witnessed many dramatic price changes, up as well as down, and almost invariably show increased price volatility relative to other comparable trading periods.

We describe below how option valuation techniques can be used to value different financial assets, beginning with dividend-paying stocks, but do not present each model that has been developed. Readers interested in examining these formulas are referred to Smith (1979), where many are presented, or to the articles themselves.

5.5.1 Valuing Dividend-Paying Stocks

One disconcerting feature of the B-S OPM is its presumption that the underlying stock pays no cash dividends or other cash distribution—disconcerting because most real U.S. common stocks with listed options pay dividends regularly. Furthermore, this is not a valuation issue that can safely be ignored; Merton (1973) shows that a large enough cash dividend can result in optimal early call option exercise. Given this issue's importance, several authors have presented adjustment techniques which can account for cash dividends in the basic OPM.

Merton (1973) presents a valuation formula based on the assumption that a stock pays a continuous dividend, but this model is not often useful since dividends are almost invariably paid in discrete lump sums rather than in a continuously accruing stream.[15] Two years later, Black (1975) suggested that the approximate value of call options on dividend-paying stocks could be determined by subtracting the present value of any dividends to be received during an option's life from the current stock price, and then using this adjusted value in the B-S OPM. More exact, but also far more complex, formulas for valuing call options on dividend-paying stocks have been presented in Roll (1977), Cox, Ross, and Rubinstein (1979), Geske (1979b), Rendleman and Bartter (1979), Whaley (1981), Geske and Shastri (1985), and Boyle (1988). Tests of these models in Whaley (1982), Sterk (1982), Geske, Roll, and Shastri (1983), and Geske and Shastri (1985) tend to favor the Roll adjustment technique, but no single model works perfectly.

5.5.2 Valuing Put Options

While Black and Scholes (1973) present the basic methodology for valuing options, they do not explicitly value put options. An early derivation of the B-S OPM applied to the valuation of European put options is presented in Smith (1979), while Brennan and Schwartz (1977) present a model for valuing American puts. An analytical model for valuing American puts on dividend-paying stocks is presented in Geske and Johnson (1984).

5.5.3 Valuing Options on Debt Securities

Smith (1979) presents valuation formulas for options on debt securities, including discount bonds, collateralized loans, and lease contracts. He also values underwriting contracts and bond covenants using OPM principles. Courtadon (1982) presents a model for pricing options on bonds that are free of default risk, while Turnbull and Milne (1991) develop a discrete-time model for valuing debt options in a stochastic interest rate economy. They present closed-form solutions for ten interest rate-sensitive options, including options on bills, bonds, futures, forwards, interest rate caps, foreign exchange and stock options.

---

15. This model is useful in valuing currency options, however, as we will see later.

Dietrich-Campbell and Schwartz (1986) develop a two-factor model to describe the term structure of interest rates, and then use it to derive theoretical prices for American puts and calls on treasury bonds and bills. They then compare these model prices to actual option prices, and find their model generates more accurate prices than do other approximation techniques. Ho and Lee (1986) and Heath, Jarrow, and Morton (1992) also present single (Heath, et al) and two-factor (Ho and Lee) models of the term structure, which they then use to value interest rate-contingent claims. Flesaker (1993) tests these models, and rejects the simplest (constant variance) versions, but offers empirical support for the more complex variants. Finally, Heston (1993) develops a closed-form solution for stochastic volatility option pricing models, and applies this to the pricing of bond and foreign currency options when the underlying asset's value is correlated with its volatility.

5.5.4 Valuing Currency Options

Business is becoming truly globalized at a rate which few people can comprehend. For example, the total *daily* trading volume in the foreign exchange market now exceeds one trillion dollars, and is growing geometrically. Given this need to trade currencies, and to manage the risk that adverse currency movements can quickly destroy a company's profitability (or worse), it was perhaps inevitable that currency option contracts would be created. Exchange-traded currency options contracts began trading on the Philadelphia Stock Exchange (PHLX) in 1983, and proved to be an immediate hit— which is not surprising given the flexibility of options as a tool to: (1) hedge risk without surrendering the ability to profit from favorable price movements, (2) lock in a fixed exchange rate to cover a transaction that might occur (such as winning a construction contract bid in a foreign country), without obligating oneself if the transaction falls through, and (3) speculate on currency movements with maximum leverage and without the potentially huge delivery liability that naturally accompanies futures and forward contracts.[16]

Early academic work on the pricing of foreign currency options contracts is presented in Garman and Kohlhagen (1983) and Biger and Hull (1983), while the efficiency of the PHLX market in its early days is documented in Tucker (1985). The key to modeling currency options prices is to recast Merton's (1973) continuous dividend model—where dividend payments accrue continuously—to reflect the difference between interest rates in two countries, and the corresponding difference between spot and forward exchange rates that naturally results from interest rate differentials according to the interest rate parity condition in exchange rate theory. Briys and Crouhy (1988) use the forward rate itself in their pricing formulas, but the key to the valuation of currency-related derivatives is the interest rate differential.[17] Later empirical tests

---

16. The use of foreign currency options contracts in multinational financial setting is described in Shapiro (1992, chapter 3) and Smith, Smithson, and Wilford (1989), while the growth of options markets around the world is discussed in Abken (1991).

17. Readers conversant with the five parity conditions in international finance will probably recognize that interest rate parity will also frequently reflect inflation differentials, as per the Fisher Effect for each national interest rate market and the **International Fisher Effect** linking the two money markets. Even when the two Fisher Effects do not hold, however, interest rate parity (IRP) will whenever there is a forward market connecting two currencies, because of covered interest arbitrage opportunities that arise from IRP violations.

of the efficiency of the currency options markets and/or theoretical extensions of the basic currency option pricing models are presented in Bodurtha and Courtadon (1986), Ogden and Tucker (1988), Tucker, Peterson, and Scott (1988), Hilliard, Madura, and Tucker (1991), Turnbull and Milne (1991), and Heston (1993).

5.5.5 Valuing Index Options

On March 11, 1983 the CBOE began trading the first option contract on a stock index, in this case the S&P 100 Index. Following a by now time-honored pattern of financial market product innovation and academic pricing model response, several authors published valuation models and/or empirical studies shortly thereafter. The first theoretical study is Bailey and Stulz (1989), who develop an index option pricing model in a simple general equilibrium setting. On the empirical front, Evnine and Rudd (1985) examine the S&P 100 and Major Market Index (MMI) contracts and document frequent violations of rational boundary conditions (and of put/call parity), and find that these contracts are often mispriced relative to their theoretical values based on the underlying share prices. They conclude this inefficiency is largely due to the inability of traders to arbitrage the index (by trading in the underlying shares and buying or selling options contracts) without incurring prohibitive transactions costs. Surprisingly, two other papers—by Canina and Figlewski (1993) and Diz and Finucane (1993)—also present evidence that the index options market lacks pricing precision at the very least, and may in fact be far less than perfectly informationally efficient. This contrasts sharply with the evidence from almost all other options markets, and probably reflects the aforementioned difficulty in arbitraging an index that should reflect the values of a large number of underlying shares.

5.5.6 Valuing Other Options Contracts

Researchers have extended the B-S model to value a truly bewildering array of financial products and contracts during the past two decades, and this trend shows no sign of waning. For example, futures options have been examined theoretically and empirically by Ramaswamy and Sundaresan (1985), Whaley (1986), and Gay, Kolb, and Yung (1989), and the general consensus is that futures options markets are generally efficient, but that it is often rational to exercise the option prematurely. Additionally, Lauterbach and Schultz (1990) examine the pricing of warrants (long-maturity options to purchase newly-created stock directly from a company), and find that the B-S assumption of a constant variance is insupportable over multi-year periods. They find the CEV model yields significantly more accurate price forecasts.

Hsieh, Chen, and Ferris (1994) derive the put option values for 176 pension plan sponsors insured by the Pension Benefit Guarantee Corporation (PBGC) during the pre–1987 period, when it charged all sponsors a flat (non-risk-adjusted) premium. Not surprisingly, they document that underfunded pension plans received PBGC insurance coverage at too low a price, while overfunded plans were charged an approximately fair price. Fleming and Whaley (1994) present a model for valuing the wildcard option that is imbedded in options contracts when the settlement price is established before the option holder must declare his or her intention with respect to delivery. They document that the wildcard option can account for an economically significant fraction of total S&P 100 index value. And in perhaps the most dramatic of all weakenings of the B-S assumptions, Margrabe (1978) presents a model for pricing an option with an *uncertain exercise price*. (Who says finance cannot work miracles?) This trick is performed by expressing an option's value as the value of the right to exchange one (non-cash) asset for another, and the value of this right is a function of the correlation between the returns on the two assets in question.

As we will discuss in the next chapter, however, perhaps the most important extension of option pricing theory is in the area of capital budgeting. As the tools for valuing operating flexibility become more precise and generally useful, managers will be able to accurately assess the value of options imbedded in virtually all strategic timing, market entry/exit, and production capacity/layout decisions. They might even be able to at least conceptually understand and learn to value the untapped creativity options in their own human capital, and in that of their employees.

—SUMMARY—

The development of option pricing theory has revolutionized modern finance, both practically and theoretically. On a practical level, the total value of exchange-traded and privately-negotiated options contracts has grown exponentially since the Chicago Board Options Exchange opened for business in 1973. Firms and individuals now use options for protection against myriad pricing risks that they would have had to bear alone in years past. At a theoretical level, option pricing theory has given researchers the keys to valuing a wide variety of asymmetric payoff situations—where one party has purchased the right, but not the obligation, to buy or sell an asset at a fixed price by (or on) a certain date. Furthermore, this theory has given us a new perspective on the valuation of the equity in a levered firm, since this can be considered a call option on the assets of the firm written by the bondholders and exercisable by the stockholders through the repayment of the debt at maturity. Finally, option pricing theory has given to academics and practicing managers alike a powerful new capital budgeting tool that can be used to evaluate complex investment projects, as we will see in the next chapter.

—QUESTIONS—

1. What is the defining characteristic of an option, as compared to other derivative financial assets such as futures and forward contracts? What are some common examples of "real" options, as opposed to options on financial instruments?

2. What is the difference between a European and an American option? Which is likely to be more valuable? Why?

3. Define the following terms commonly associated with option pricing: (*a*) call option; (*b*) put option; (*c*) exercise price; (*d*) option premium; (*e*) option holder; (*f*) option writer.

4. Define the following terms commonly associated with option valuation: (*a*) in-the-money option; (*b*) at-the-money option; (*c*) out-of-the-money option; (*d*) intrinsic value; (*e*) time value.

5. Draw a payoff diagram for a call option with a $50 per share exercise price using data from Table 5.1 for December 19, 1994. Repeat this task for a $50 put option.

6. Develop put-call parity pricing relationships using Telmex put and call options with $50 per share exercise prices, assuming terminal stock prices of (*a*) $45 per share and (*b*) $55 per share.

7. Use the put-call parity pricing formulas to compute option values for the $50 January 1995 Telmex call option, using stock and put price data from Table 5.1 for December 19,1994, and assuming a risk-free rate, r_f, of 7.5 percent per year and a time to maturity, T, of 0.0904 (33 days between December 19, 1994 and January 21, 1995, divided by 365 days per year). Using these same data sources and assumptions, compute the option premium for the $50 January 1995 Telmex put option. How close are your computed values to the market generated option prices?

8. In words, describe the economic insight that allowed Black and Scholes to develop their option pricing model, whereas all previous attempts to develop a closed-form valuation model had failed.

9. List, and briefly discuss, the assumptions that Black and Scholes make in order to derive their option pricing model.

10. Your Uncle Jack—who is untutored in advanced mathematics, but is nonetheless a college graduate and a wise soul—asks you to give him a logical, one-paragraph explanation of the role that continuous portfolio rebalancing (sell options and buying stock) plays in the development of the Black-Scholes option pricing model. How do you answer?

11. List, and briefly describe, the five factors that are inputs in the Black-Scholes option pricing model. Which of these are observable, and which must be estimated? Finally, what is the direction of the relationship between each of these variables and (a) call option prices and (b) put option prices?

12. Specify, and then provide a logical explanation for, the direction of the relationship between maturity and put option valuation. Why is this relationship more ambiguous than that between call option values and term to maturity?

13. Under what circumstances will early exercise of an option be optimal for an option holder? Why?

14. Why do Black and Scholes assert that equity in a levered firm can be modeled as a call option?

15. Have empirical tests supported or refuted the Black-Scholes option pricing model?

16. Briefly describe the constant elasticity of variance model of option valuation, and discuss why this has been hailed as a more robust valuation model than the original Black-Scholes model.

17. What is an implied standard deviation (ISD)? How is it computed? Has it been supported or refuted in empirical option pricing tests?

18. List, and briefly discuss, at least four extensions of option pricing theory to the valuation of financial assets other than common stock.

—REFERENCES—

Abken, Peter A., "Globalization of Stock, Futures, and Options Markets," Federal Reserve Bank of Atlanta **Economic Review** (July/August 1991), pp. 1–22.

Ajinkya, Bipin B. and Michael J. Gift, "Dispersion of Financial Analysts' Earnings Forecasts and the (Option Model) Implied Standard Deviation of Stock Returns," **Journal of Finance** 40 (December 1985), pp. 1353–1365.

Back, Kerry, "Asymmetric Information and Options," **Review of Financial Studies** 6 (1993), pp. 435–472.

Bailey, Warren and Rene M. Stulz, "The Pricing of Stock Index Options in a General Equilibrium Model," **Journal of Financial and Quantitative Analysis** 24 (March 1989), pp. 1–12.

Ball, Clifford A. and Walter N. Torous, "The Maximum Likelihood Estimation of Security Price Volatility: Theory, Evidence, and Application to Option Pricing," **Journal of Business** 57 (January 1984), pp. 97–112.

Barone-Adesi, Giovanni and Robert E. Whaley, "The Valuation of American Call Options and the Expected Ex-Dividend Stock Price Decline," **Journal of Financial Economics** 17 (September 1986), pp. 91–111.

Beckers, Stan, "The Constant Elasticity of Variance Model and its Implications for Option Pricing," **Journal of Finance** 35 (June 1980), pp. 661–673.

Bhattacharya, Mihir, "Transactions Data Tests of Efficiency of the Chicago Board of Options Exchange," **Journal of Financial Economics** 12 (August 1983), pp. 161–185.

Biger, Nahum and John Hull, "The Valuation of Currency Options," **Financial Management** 12 (Spring 1983), pp. 24–28.

Black, Fischer, "Fact and Fantasy in the Use of Options," **Financial Analysts Journal** 31 (July-August 1975), pp. 36–41, 61–72.

————"How We Came up With the Option Formula," **Journal of Portfolio Management** 15 (Winter 1989), pp. 4–8.

Black, Fischer and Myron Scholes, "The Valuation of Option Contracts and a Test of Market Efficiency," **Journal of Finance** 27 (May 1972), pp. 399–417.

————"The Pricing of Options and Corporate Liabilities," **Journal of Political Economy** 81 (May/June 1973), pp. 637–654.

Bodie, Zvi, Alex Kane, and Alan J. Marcus, **Investments**, 2nd Edition (Richard D. Irwin, Inc.: Homewood, IL, 1993).

Bodurtha, James N., Jr. and George R. Courtadon, "Efficiency Tests of the Foreign Currency Options Market," **Journal of Finance** 41 (March 1986), pp. 151–162.

Boyle, Phelim P., "A Lattice Framework For Option Pricing With Two State Variables," **Journal of Financial and Quantitative Analysis** 23 (March 1988), pp. 1–12.

Brealey, Richard A. and Stewart C. Myers, **Principles of Corporate Finance**, 4th Edition (McGraw Hill, Inc.: New York, 1991)

Brennan, Michael J. and Eduardo S. Schwartz, " The Valuation of American Put Options," **Journal of Finance** 32 (May 1977), pp. 449–462.

Brenner, Menachem and Marti G. Subrahmanyan, "A Simple Approach to Option Valuation and Hedging in the Black-Scholes Model," **Financial Analysts Journal** 50 (March-April 1994), pp. 25–28.

Briys, Eric and Michael Crouhy, "Creating and Pricing Hybrid Foreign Currency Options," **Financial Management** 17 (Winter 1988), pp. 59–65.

Canina, Linda and Stephen Figlewski, "The Informational Content of Implied Volatility," **Review of Financial Studies** (1993), pp. 659–681.

Chiras, Donald P. and Steven Manaster, "The Information Content of Option Prices and a Test of Market Efficiency," **Journal of Financial Economics** 6 (June-September 1978), pp. 213–234.

Conrad, Jennifer, "The Price Effects of Option Introduction," **Journal of Finance** 44 (June 1989), pp. 487–498.

Copeland, Thomas and J. Fred Weston. **Financial Theory and Corporate Policy**, 3rd Edition (Addison-Wesley Publishing Company; Reading, MA, 1988).

Courtadon, Georges. "The Pricing of Options on Default-Free Bonds." **Journal of Financial and Quantitative Analysis** 17 (March 1982), pp. 75-100.

Cox, John C., "Notes on Option Pricing I: Constant Elasticity of Variance Diffusions." Working paper (Stanford University, September 1975).

Cox, John C. and Steven A. Ross. "The Valuation of Options for Alternative Stochastic Processes." **Journal of Financial Economics** 3 (January-March 1976), pp. 145-166.

Cox, John C., Stephen A. Ross, and Mark Rubinstein. "Option Pricing: A Simplified Approach." **Journal of Financial Economics** 7 (September 1979), pp. 229-263.

Day, Theodore E. and Craig M. Lewis. "The Behavior of the Volatility Implicit in the Prices of Stock Index Options." **Journal of Financial Economics** 22 (October 1988), pp. 103-122.

Dietrich-Campbell, Bruce and Eduardo Schwartz. "Valuing Debt Options: Empirical Evidence." **Journal of Financial Economics** 16 (July 1986), pp. 321-343.

Diz, Fernando, and Thomas J. Finucane. "The Rationality of Early Exercise Decisions: Evidence From the S&P 100 Index Options Market." **Review of Financial Studies** 6 (Winter 1993), pp. 765-797.

Emanuel, David C. and James D. MacBeth. "Further Results on the Constant Elasticity of Variance Call Option Pricing Model." **Journal of Financial and Quantitative Analysis** 17 (November 1982), pp. 533-554.

Evnine, Jeremy and Andrew Rudd. "Index Options: The Early Evidence." Journal of Finance 40 (July 1985), pp. 743-756.

Fleming, Jeff and Robert E. Whaley. "The Value of Wildcard Options." **Journal of Finance** 49 (March 1994), pp. 215-236.

Flesaker, Bjorn. "Testing the Heath-Jarrow-Morton Ho-Lee Model of Interest Rate Contingent Claims Pricing." **Journal of Financial and Quantitative Analysis** 28 (December 1993), pp. 483-495.

Galai, Dan. "Tests of Market Efficiency of the Chicago Board Options Exchange." **Journal of Business** 50 (April 1977), pp. 167-197.

————. "Empirical Tests of Boundary Conditions for CBOE Options." **Journal of Financial Economics** 6 (June-September 1978), pp. 187-211.

Galai, Dan and Ronald W. Masulis. "The Option Pricing Model and the Risk Factor of Stock." **Journal of Financial Economics** 3 (January-March 1976), pp. 53-81.

Garman, Mark B. and Steven W. Kohlhagen. "Foreign Currency Option Values." **Journal of International Money and Finance** 2 (1983), pp. 231-237.

Gay, Gerald D., Robert W. Kolb, and Kenneth Young. "Trader Rationality in the Exercise of Futures Options." **Journal of Financial Economics** 23 (August 1989), pp. 339-361.

Geske, Robert. "The Valuation of Compound Options." **Journal of Financial Economics** 7 (March 1979a), pp. 63-81.

————. "A Note on an Analytical Valuation Formula for Unprotected Call Options on Stocks With Known Dividends." **Journal of Financial Economics** 7 (December 1979b), pp. 375-380.

Geske, Robert and H. E. Johnson. "The American Put Option Valued Analytically." **Journal of Finance** 39 (December 1984), pp. 1511-1524.

Geske, Robert, Richard Roll, and Kuldeep Shastri. "Over-the-Counter Option Market Dividend Protection and 'Biases' in the Black-Scholes Model: A Note." **Journal of Finance** 38 (September 1983), pp. 1271-1277.

Geske, Robert and Kuldeep Shastri, "Valuation by Approximation: A Comparison of Alternative Option Valuation Techniques," **Journal of Financial and Quantitative Analysis** 20 (March 1985), pp. 45–71.

Harvey, Campbell R. and Robert E. Whaley, "Market Volatility Prediction and the Efficiency of the S&P 100 Index Option Market," **Journal of Financial Economics** 31 (February 1992), pp. 43–74.

Heath, David, Robert Jarrow, and Andrew Morton, "Bond Pricing and the Term Structure of Interest Rates: A New Methodology for Contingent Claims Valuation," **Econometrica** 60 (January 1992), pp. 77–105.

Heston, Steven L., "A Closed-Form Solution for Options With Stochastic Volatility With Applications to Bond and Currency Options," **Review of Financial Studies** 6 (1993), pp. 327–343.

Heynen, Ronald, Angelien Kemna, and Ton Vorst, "Analysis of the Term Structure of Implied Volatilities," **Journal of Financial and Quantitative Analysis** 29 (March 1994), pp. 31–56.

Hilliard, Jimmy E., Jeff Madura, and Alan L. Tucker, "Currency Option Pricing With Stochastic Domestic and Foreign Interest Rates," **Journal of Financial and Quantitative Analysis** 26 (June 1991), pp. 139–152.

Ho, Thomas S. Y. and Sang-Bin Lee, "Term Structure Movements and Pricing Interest Rate Contingent Claims," **Journal of Finance** 41 (December 1986), pp. 1011–1030.

Hsieh, Su-Jane, Andrew H. Chen, and Kenneth R. Ferris, "The Valuation of PBGC Insurance Premiums Using an Option Pricing Model," **Journal of Financial and Quantitative Analysis** 29 (March 1994), pp. 89–99.

Hull, John and Alan White, "The Pricing of Options on Assets With Stochastic Volatilities," **Journal of Finance** 42 (June 1987), pp. 281–300.

————"One-Factor Interest-Rate Models and the Valuation of Interest-Rate Derivative Securities," **Journal of Financial Analysis** 28 (June 1993), pp. 233–254.

Hutchinson, James M., Andrew W. Lo, and Tomaso Poggio, "A Nonparametric Approach to Pricing and Hedging Derivative Securities Via Learning Networks," **Journal of Finance** 49 (July 1994), pp. 851–889.

Jarrow, Robert and Andrew Rudd, "Approximate Option Valuation for Arbitrary Stochastic Processes," **Journal of Financial Economics** 10 (November 1982), pp. 347–369.

Johnson, Herb and Rene Stulz, "The Pricing of Options With Default Risk," **Journal of Finance** 42 (June 1987), pp. 281–300.

Klemkosky, Robert C. and Bruce G. Resnick, "Put-Call Parity and Market Efficiency," **Journal of Finance** 34 (December 1979), pp. 1141–1155.

Lamoureux, Christopher G. and William D. Lastrapes, "Forecasting Stock-Return Variance: Toward an Understanding of Stochastic Implied Volatilities," **Review of Financial Studies** 6 (1993), pp. 293–326.

Latané, Henry A. and Richard J. Rendleman, Jr., "Standard Deviations of Stock Price Ratios Implied in Option Prices," **Journal of Finance** 31 (May 1976), pp. 369–381.

Lauterbach, Beni and Paul Schultz, "Pricing Warrants: An Empirical Study of the Black-Scholes Model and its Alternatives," **Journal of Finance** 45 (September 1990), pp. 1181–1209.

MacBeth, James D. and Larry J. Merville, "An Empirical Examination of the Black-Scholes Call Option Pricing Model," **Journal of Finance** 34 (December 1979), pp. 1173–1186.

————"Tests of the Black-Scholes and Cox Call Option Valuation Models," **Journal of Finance** 35 (May 1980), pp. 285–303.

Manaster, Steven and Richard J. Rendleman, Jr., "Option Prices as Predictors of Equilibrium Stock Prices," **Journal of Finance** 37 (September 1982), pp. 1043–1057.

Margrabe, William, "The Value of an Option to Exchange One Asset for Another," **Journal of Finance** 33 (March 1978), pp. 177–186.

Merton, Robert C., "The Theory of Rational Option Valuation," **Bell Journal of Economics and Management Science** 4 (Spring 1973), pp. 141–183.

————"On the Pricing of Corporate Debt: The Risk Structure of Interest Rates," **Journal of Finance** 29 (May 1974), pp. 449–470.

————"Option Pricing When Underlying Stock Returns Are Discontinuous," **Journal of Financial Economics** 3 (January-March 1976), pp. 125–144.

Naik, Vasanttilak, "Option Valuation and Hedging Strategies With Jumps in the Volatilities of Asset Returns," **Journal of Finance** 48 (December 1993), pp. 1969–1984.

Ogden, Joseph P. and Alan L. Tucker, "The Relative Valuation of American Currency Spot and Futures Options: Theory and Empirical Tests," **Journal of Financial and Quantitative Analysis** 23 (December 1988), pp. 351–368.

Ramaswamy, Krishna and Suresh M. Sundaresan, "The Valuation of Options on Futures Contracts," **Journal of Finance** 40 (December 1985), pp. 1319–1340.

Rendleman, Richard J. and Brit J. Bartter, "Two-State Option Pricing," **Journal of Finance** 34 (December 1979), pp. 1093–1110.

Resnick, Bruce G., Aamir M. Sheikh, and Yo-Shin Song, "Time Varying Volatilities and Calculation of the Weighted Implied Standard Deviation," **Journal of Financial and Quantitative Analysis** 28 (September 1993), pp. 417–430.

Roll, Richard, "An Analytic Valuation for Unprotected American Call Options on Stocks With Known Dividends," **Journal of Financial Economics** 5 (November 1977), pp. 251–258.

Rubinstein, Mark, "The Valuation of Uncertain Income Streams and the Pricing of Options," **Bell Journal of Economics** (Autumn 1976), pp. 407–425.

————"Implied Binomial Trees," **Journal of Finance** 49 (July 1994), pp. 771–818.

Schmalansee, Richard and Robert R. Trippi, "Common Stock Volatility Expectations Implied by Option Premia," **Journal of Finance** 33 (March 1978), pp. 129–147.

Scott, Louis O., "Option Pricing When the Variance Changes Randomly: Theory, Estimation, and an Application," **Journal of Financial and Quantitative Analysis** 22 (December 1987), pp. 419–438.

Shapiro, Alan C., **Multinational Financial Management** (4th edition, Allyn and Bacon: Boston, 1992).

Sheikh, Aamir M. and Ehud I. Ronn, "A Characterization of the Daily and Intraday Behavior of Returns on Options," **Journal of Finance** 49 (June 1994), pp. 557–579.

Skinner, Douglas J., "Options Markets and Stock Return Volatility," **Journal of Financial Economics** 23 (June 1989), pp. 61–78.

Smith, Clifford W., Jr., "Option Pricing: A Review," **Journal of Financial Economics** 3 (January-March 1976), pp. 1–51.

————"Applications of Option Pricing Analysis," in James L. Bicksler, ed., **Handbook of Financial Economics** (North Holland Publishing Company: Amsterdam, 1979), pp. 79–121.

Smith, Clifford W., Jr., Charles W. Smithson, and D. Sykes Wilford, "Managing Financial Risk," **Journal of Applied Corporate Finance** 1 (Winter 1989), pp. 27–48.

Stein, Jeremy, "Overreactions in the Options Market," **Journal of Finance** 44 (September 1989), pp. 1011–1023.

Sterk, William, "Tests of Two Models for Valuing Call Options on Stock Dividends," **Journal of Finance** 37 (December 1982), pp. 1229–1237.

Stoll, Hans R., "The Relationship Between Put and Call Option Prices," **Journal of Finance** 24 (December 1969), pp. 801–824.

Tucker, Alan L., "Empirical Tests of the Efficiency of the Currency Option Market," **Journal of Financial Research** 8 (1985), pp. 275–285.

Tucker, Alan L., David R. Peterson, and Elton Scott, "Tests of the Black-Scholes and Constant Elasticity of Variance Currency Call Option Valuation Models," **Journal of Financial Research** 11 (1988), pp. 201–214.

Turnbull, Stuart M. and Frank Milne, "A Simple Approach to Interest-Rate Option Pricing," **Review of Financial Studies** 4 (1991), pp. 87–120.

Vijh, Anand M., "Liquidity of the CBOE Equity Options," **Journal of Finance** 45 (July 1990), pp. 1157–1179.

Whaley, Robert E., "On the Valuation of American Call Options on Stocks With Known Dividends," **Journal of Financial Economics** 9 (June 1981), pp. 207–211.

————"Valuations of American Call Options on Dividend-Paying Stocks: Empirical Tests," **Journal of Financial Economics** 10 (March 1982), pp. 29–58.

————"Valuation of American Futures Options: Theory and Empirical Tests," **Journal of Finance** 41 (March 1986), pp. 127–150.

Wiggins, James B., "Option Values Under Stochastic Volatility: Theory and Empirical Evidence," **Journal of Financial Economics** 19 (December 1987), pp. 351–372.

Xu, Xinhong and Stephen J. Taylor, "The Term Structure of Volatility Implied by Foreign Exchange Options," **Journal of Financial and Quantitative Analysis** 29 (March 1994), pp. 57–74.

Capital Budgeting and Investment Decisions

6.1 INTRODUCTION

A strong economic case can be made for the idea that modern corporations exist—and dominate economic life around the world—because they are superior instruments for generating and exploiting profitable investment opportunities. Absent this ongoing need to develop valuable "growth options", most economic activity could be conducted through open market purchases of material, capital, and labor inputs, and subsequent open market sales of product or service outputs. Such "commodity market" production would, however, almost by definition be highly competitive and only marginally profitable. The driving force of all modern economies is the exploitation of new technologies and the transfer of production to ever more capital-intensive processes, and these objectives can only be accomplished by companies with vast (and stable) pools of financial, technical, and human resources. Throughout the world, the most successful companies are those which have developed effective programs both for generating investment opportunities and for selecting the most promising projects from the set of opportunities available. This is equally true of nation-states—those countries which have provided the most attractive business investment climates have prospered relative to those which have restricted or politicized investment decision-making.[1]

---

1. Even the most casual perusal of official economic statistics (such as the International Monetary Fund's publication, **International Financial Statistics**) makes clear that the sheer amount of investment is far less important than the policy environment in which investment is made. For example, while most developing countries have gross investment rates equal to 25–30 percent of GDP, only those countries in east Asia and Latin America that have long pursued market-oriented economic policies have been able to achieve sustained, rapid growth rates. Additionally, due to its entrepreneurial culture, sophisticated financial system, and traditional reliance on private business investment, the United States has been able to retain leadership in key industries, and achieve relatively rapid growth in employment and national income—in spite of the fact that its gross investment rate (14–18 percent of GDP since the early 1980s) is the lowest of any major industrialized country.

This chapter will describe the techniques modern finance has developed for determining whether an investment opportunity should be exploited. These are collectively referred to as **capital budgeting** procedures, and we will begin our discussion with an overview of the issues involved in capital investment analysis, and with a discussion of the discounted cash flow (DCF) analytical procedures that have traditionally been the backbone of modern capital budgeting. In the final sections of the chapter we will examine several of the recent modifications to capital budgeting analysis that have been developed during the past fifteen years—especially the incorporation of agency costs, liquidity, and option pricing theory into capital investment decisions. Specifically, we will see how incorporating various options—such as flexibility options, timing options, and the value of building excess capacity—in capital budgeting processes can augment the traditional DCF procedures and improve the effectiveness of a firm's capital investment program.

6.2   THE CAPITAL BUDGETING DECISION PROCESS

The capital budgeting process involves generating long-term investment proposals; reviewing, analyzing, and selecting from them; and implementing and following up on those selected. Because long-term investments represent sizable outlays of funds that commit a firm to a given course of action, procedures are needed to analyze and select them properly. Attention must be given to measuring relevant cash flows and applying appropriate decision techniques. As time passes, fixed assets may become obsolete or may require an overhaul; at these points, too, financial decisions may be required. Capital budgeting is the process of evaluating and selecting long-term investments that are consistent with the firm's goal of owner wealth maximization. Firms typically make a variety of long-term investments, but the most common such investment for the manufacturing firm is in fixed assets, which include property (land), plant, and equipment.[2] These assets are quite often referred to as earning assets because they generally provide the basis for the firm's earning power and value.

Capital budgeting (investment) and financing decisions are treated separately, although it should become clear later that the use of the cost of capital as a discount rate links these two decisions. Typically, once a proposed investment has been determined to be acceptable, the financial manager then chooses the best financing method. Therefore we concentrate here on fixed asset acquisition without regard to the specific method of financing used. This section of the chapter discusses capital expenditure motives, the steps in the capital budgeting process, and basic capital budgeting terminology.

6.2.1 Capital Expenditure Motives

A capital expenditure is an outlay of funds by the firm that is expected to produce benefits over a period of time greater than one year. A current expenditure is an outlay resulting in benefits received within one year. Fixed-asset outlays are capital expenditures, but

---

2. Interestingly, the mix of investments has been changing rapidly in recent years, particularly in industrialized countries. In the United States, for example, Stewart (1994) reports that "Information Age" capital spending (on computers and communication equipment) first surpassed "Industrial Age" capital spending (manufacturing, mining, construction and agriculture equipment and structures) in 1991, and now exceeds it by a wide margin. Furthermore, new research reported by Stewart indicates that the returns on computer investments by U.S. manufacturing and service companies are eight times greater (48 percent per year versus less than 6 percent) than the annual returns on other tangible investments.

not all capital expenditures are classified as fixed assets. A $60,000 outlay for a new machine with a usable life of 15 years is a capital expenditure that would appear as a fixed asset on the firm's balance sheet. A $60,000 outlay for advertising that produces benefits over a long period is also a capital expenditure. However, an outlay for advertising would rarely be shown as a fixed asset.[3]

Capital expenditures are made for many reasons but, although the motives differ, the evaluation techniques are the same. The basic motives for capital expenditures are to expand, replace, or renew fixed assets or to obtain some other less tangible benefit over a long period. The capital budgeting process can be viewed as consisting of five distinct but interrelated steps, beginnning with proposal generation. This is followed by review and analysis, decision making, implementation, and follow-up. A brief description of each of these steps is given in Table 6.1.

6.2.2 Basic Terminology

Before beginning to develop the concepts, tools, and techniques related to the review and analysis and decision-making steps in the capital budgeting process, it is useful to understand some of the basic terminology of these areas. We also present a number of key assumptions that are used to simplify the discussion in the remainder of this chapter.

INDEPENDENT VS. MUTUALLY EXCLUSIVE PROJECTS   The two most common project types are (1) independent projects and (2) mutually exclusive projects.[4] Independent projects are projects whose cash flows are unrelated or independent of one another; the acceptance of one does not eliminate the others from further consideration. If a firm has unlimited funds to invest, all the independent projects that meet its minimum investment criteria can be implemented. For example, a firm with unlimited funds may be faced with three acceptable independent projects: (1) installing air conditioning in the plant, (2) acquiring a small supplier, and (3) purchasing a new computer system. Clearly, the acceptance of any one of these projects does not eliminate the others from further consideration; all three could be undertaken. Mutually exclusive projects are projects that have the same function and therefore compete with one another. The acceptance of one of a group of mutually exclusive projects eliminates all other projects in the group from further consideration. For example, a firm in need of increased production capacity could obtain it by (1) expanding its plant, (2) acquiring another com-

---

3. The economic and accounting treatment of research and development (R&D) expenditures is more ambiguous. While these usually create valuable investment opportunities that yield returns over several periods, there is no consensus regarding whether these expenditures should be capitalized as investment assets or expensed as routine operating costs. The empirical evidence regarding how markets value R&D spending will be discussed in the final section of this chapter.

4. One of the first major papers to discuss the distinction between independent and mutually exclusive projects is Lorie and Savage (1955). These authors also examined several other issues that we will discuss shortly—including the organization of capital investment decision-making processes, problems involved with using internal rate of return (IRR) rather than net present value (NPV) analysis, the existence of projects with multiple IRRs, and methods of ranking projects when firms face capital rationing.

TABLE 6.1

STEPS IN THE CAPITAL BUDGETING PROCESS

Steps (listed in order)	Description
Proposal generation	Proposals for capital expenditures are made by people at all levels within a business organization. To stimulate a flow of ideas that could result in potential cost savings, many firms offer cash rewards to employees whose proposals are ultimately adopted. Capital expenditure proposals typically travel from the originator to a reviewer at a higher level in the organization. Clearly, proposals requiring large outlays will be much more carefully scrutinized than less costly ones.
Review and analysis	Capital expenditure proposals are formally reviewed (1) to assess their appropriateness in light of the firm's overall objectives and plans and, more important, (2) to evaluate their economic validity. The proposed costs and benefits are estimated and then converted into a series of relevant cash flows to which various capital budgeting techniques are applied to measure the investment merit of the potential outlay. In addition, various aspects of the *risk* associated with the proposal are either incorporated into the economic analysis or rated and recorded along with the economic measures. Once the economic analysis is completed, a summary report, often with a recommendation, is submitted to the decision maker(s).
Decision making	The actual dollar outlay and the importance of a capital expenditure determine the organizational level at which the expenditure decision is made. Firms typically delegate capital-expenditure authority on the basis of certain dollar limits. Generally, the board of directors reserves the right to make final decisions on capital expenditures requiring outlays beyond a certain amount, while the authority for making smaller expenditures is given to other organizational levels. Inexpensive capital expenditures such as the purchase of a hammer for $15 are treated as operating outlays not requiring formal analysis.[a] Generally, firms operating under critical time constraints with respect to production often find it necessary to provide exceptions to a strict dollar-outlay scheme. In such cases the plant manager is often given the power to make decisions necessary to keep the production line moving, even though the outlays entailed are larger than he or she would normally be allowed to authorize.
Implementation	Once a proposal has been approved and funding has been made available,[b] the implementation phase begins. For minor outlays, implementation is relatively routine; the expenditure is made, and payment is rendered. For major expenditures, greater control is required to ensure that what has been proposed and approved is acquired at the budgeted costs. Often the expenditures for a single proposal may occur in phases, each outlay requiring the signed approval of company officers.

(continued)

TABLE 6.1 (CONTINUED)

Steps (listed in order)	Description
Follow-up	Involves monitoring the results during the operating phase of a project. The comparisons of actual outcomes in terms of costs and benefits with those expected and those of previous projects are vital. When actual outcomes deviate from projected outcomes, action may be required to cut costs, improve benefits, or possibly terminate the project.

THERE IS A CERTAIN DOLLAR LIMIT BEYOND WHICH OUTLAYS ARE *CAPITALIZED* (I.E., TREATED AS A FIXED ASSET) AND *DEPRECIATED* RATHER THAN *EXPENSED*. THIS DOLLAR LIMIT DEPENDS LARGELY ON WHAT THE U.S. INTERNAL REVENUE SERVICE WILL PERMIT. IN ACCOUNTING, THE ISSUE OF WHETHER TO EXPENSE OR CAPITALIZE AN OUTLAY IS RESOLVED BY USING THE *PRINCIPLE OF MATERIALITY*, WHICH SUGGESTS THAT ANY OUTLAYS DEEMED MATERIAL (I.E., LARGE) RELATIVE TO THE FIRM'S SCALE OF OPERATIONS SHOULD BE CAPITALIZED, WHEREAS OTHERS SHOULD BE EXPENSED IN THE CURRENT PERIOD.

CAPITAL EXPENDITURES ARE OFTEN APPROVED AS PART OF THE ANNUAL BUDGETING PROCESS, ALTHOUGH FUNDING WILL NOT BE MADE AVAILABLE UNTIL THE BUDGET IS IMPLEMENTED—FREQUENTLY AS LONG AS SIX MONTHS AFTER APPROVAL.

SOURCE: GITMAN, LAWRENCE J., **PRINCIPLES OF MANAGERIAL FINANCE**, SEVENTH EDITION (NEW YORK: HARPERCOLLINS, 1994)

pany, or (3) contracting with another company for production. Clearly, the acceptance of one of these alternatives eliminates the need for either of the others.

UNLIMITED FUNDS VS. CAPITAL RATIONING The availability of funds for capital expenditures affects the firm's decision environment. If a firm has unlimited funds for investment, making capital budgeting decisions is quite simple. All independent projects that will provide returns greater than some predetermined level can be accepted. Frequently, firms perceive that they are not in such a situation: they instead operate as though they face **capital rationing**. This means that they have only a fixed number of dollars available for capital expenditures and that numerous projects will compete for these limited dollars. The firm must therefore ration its funds by allocating them to projects that will maximize share value.[5] Procedures for dealing with capital rationing are presented later in this chapter. The discussions that follow assume unlimited funds.

ACCEPT-REJECT VS. RANKING APPROACHES Two basic approaches to capital budgeting decisions are available. The accept-reject approach involves evaluating capital expenditure proposals to determine whether they meet the firm's minimum acceptance criterion. This approach can be used when the firm has unlimited funds, as a preliminary step in evaluating mutually exclusive projects, or in a situation in which capital must be rationed. In these cases, only acceptable projects should be considered. The second method, the ranking approach, involves ranking projects on the basis of some predetermined measure such as net present value or internal rate of return. The project with the highest return is ranked first, and the project with the lowest return is ranked last. Only acceptable projects should be ranked. Ranking is useful in selecting

---

5. Academic researchers have traditionally been hostile to the idea that established companies routinely face capital rationing in countries with well-developed capital markets. This hostility has not, of course, prevented many of these same academics from developing exquisitely detailed procedures for dealing with capital rationing when it is encountered.

the best of a group of mutually exclusive projects and in evaluating projects with a view to capital rationing.

CONVENTIONAL VS. NONCONVENTIONAL CASH FLOW PATTERNS   Cash flow patterns associated with capital investment projects can be classified as conventional or nonconventional. A conventional cash flow pattern consists of an initial outflow followed by a series of inflows. This pattern is associated with many types of capital expenditures. For example, a firm may spend $10,000 today and as a result expect to receive cash inflows of $2,000 each year for the next eight years. A nonconventional cash flow pattern is any pattern in which an initial outflow is not followed by an uninterrupted series of inflows. For example, the purchase of a machine may require an initial cash outflow of $20,000 and may generate cash inflows of $5,000 each year for four years. In the fifth year after purchase, an outflow of $8,000 may be required to overhaul the machine, after which it generates inflows of $5,000 each year for five years.

ANNUITY VS. MIXED-STREAM CASH FLOWS   An annuity is a stream of equal annual cash flows. A series of cash flows exhibiting any pattern other than that of an annuity is a mixed stream of cash flows. The cash inflows of $2,000 per year (for eight years) in the first example are inflows from an annuity, whereas the unequal pattern of inflows in the second example represents a mixed stream. The techniques required to evaluate cash flows are much simpler to use when the pattern of flows is an annuity.

6.3   IDENTIFYING THE RELEVANT (INCREMENTAL) CASH FLOWS

To evaluate capital expenditure alternatives, the relevant cash flows, which are the incremental after-tax cash outflows and resulting subsequent inflows, must be determined. The incremental cash flows represent the additional cash flows—outflows or inflows—that are expected to result from a proposed capital expenditure. Cash flows, rather than accounting figures, are used because it is these flows that directly affect the firm's ability to pay bills and purchase assets. Furthermore, accounting figures and cash flows are not necessarily the same, due to the presence of certain noncash expenditures on the firm's income statement. The next section of this chapter is devoted to the procedures for measuring the relevant cash flows associated with proposed capital expenditures.

6.3.1 Major Cash Flow Components

The cash flows of any project having the conventional pattern can include three basic components: (1) an initial investment, (2) operating cash inflows, and (3) terminal cash flow. All projects—whether for expansion, replacement, renewal, or some other purpose—have the first two components. Some, however, lack the final component, terminal cash flow. Figure 6.1 depicts on a time line the cash flows for a project. Each of the cash flow components is labeled. The initial investment, which is the relevant cash outflow at time zero, is $50,000 for the proposed project. The operating cash inflows, which are the incremental after-tax cash inflows resulting from use of the project during its life, gradually increase from $4,000 in the first year to $10,000 in the tenth and final year of the project. The terminal cash flow, which is the after-tax nonoperating cash flow occurring in the final year of the project, usually attributable to liquidation of

FIGURE 6.1

TIMELINE FOR MAJOR CASH FLOW COMPONENTS

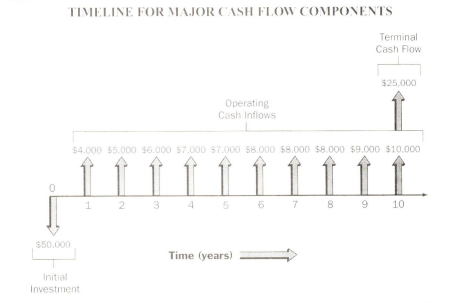

the project, is $25,000 received at the end of the project's 10-year life. Note that the terminal cash flow does not include the $10,000 operating cash inflow for year 10.

6.3.2 Expansion vs. Replacement Cash Flows

The development of relevant cash flows is most straightforward in the case of expansion decisions. In this case the initial investment, operating cash inflows, and terminal cash flow are merely the after-tax cash outflow and inflows associated with the proposed outlay. The development of relevant cash flows for replacement decisions is more complicated; the firm must find the incremental cash outflows and inflows that will result from the proposed replacement. The initial investment in this case would be found by subtracting from the initial investment needed to acquire the new asset any after-tax cash inflows expected from liquidation today of the old asset being replaced. The operating cash inflows would be found by taking the difference between the operating cash inflows from the new asset and from the replaced asset. The terminal cash flow would be found by taking the difference between the after-tax cash flows expected upon termination of the new and the old assets.

Column 1 of Table 6.2 shows the initial investment, operating cash inflows, and terminal cash flow for an example expansion decision involving the acquisition of new asset B. As a result of a $13,000 purchase price, the firm would expect operating cash inflows of $5,000 in each of the next five years and a terminal cash flow of $7,000 at the end of year 5. If new asset B is being considered as a replacement for old asset A, the relevant cash flows would be found by subtracting the expected cash

TABLE 6.2

EXPANSION AND REPLACEMENT CASH FLOWS

	Expansion	Replacement		
	New Asset B (1)	New Asset B (2)	Old Asset A (3)	Relevant Cash Flows [(2) − (3)] (4)
Initial Investment	$13,000[a]	$10,000[b]	. . .	$10,000
Year		Operating Cash Inflows		
1	$5,000	$5,000	$3,000	$2,000
2	5,000	5,000	2,500	2,500
3	5,000	5,000	2,000	3,000
4	5,000	5,000	1,500	3,500
5	5,000	5,000	1,000	4,000
Terminal cash flow	$7,000	$7,000	$2,000	$5,000

[a]PURCHASE PRICE.

[b]$13,000 PURCHASE PRICE OF NET ASSET B LESS THE $3,000 EXPECTED AFTER-TAX CASH INFLOW FROM LIQUIDATING OLD ASSET A.

flows attributed to old asset A from the expected cash flows for new asset B. The expected after-tax cash flows for new and old Asset A are shown in columns 2 and 3, respectively, of Table 6.2. Because old asset A can be liquidated for $3,000, the initial investment in new asset B is $10,000, as shown in column 2. Replacement of old asset A would eliminate both its expected operating cash inflows in years 1 through 5 of $3,000, $2,500, $2,000, $1,500, and $1,000 and its terminal cash flow of $2,000 in year 5—all shown in column 3 of Table 6.2. Therefore the relevant cash flows resulting from the replacement decision would be the difference in expected cash flows between new asset B (column 2) and old asset A (column 3), as shown in column 4 of Table 6.2.

6.3.3 International Capital Budgeting and Long-Term Investments

Although the same basic capital budgeting principles are used for domestic and international projects, several additional factors must be addressed in evaluating foreign investment opportunities.[6] International capital budgeting differs from the domestic version because: (1) cash inflows and outflows occur in a foreign currency (the dollar value of these cash flows can change radically if exchange rates fluctuate), and (2) foreign investments potentially face significant political risk, including the risk that the

---

6. A discussion of the procedures used by multinational companies in their capital budgeting programs is provided in Holland (1990), as well as in chapters 18–20 of Shapiro (1992).

company's assets may be seized. Both of these risks can be minimized through careful corporate planning.

Exchange rate risk refers to the danger that an unexpected change in the exchange rate between the dollar and the currency in which a project's cash flows are denominated can reduce the market value of that project's cash flow. While a project's initial investment can, as usual, be predicted with some certainty in either local currency or dollar value, the dollar value of future cash inflows can be dramatically altered if the local currency depreciates against the dollar. In the short term, specific cash flows can be hedged by using financial instruments such as currency futures and options. Long-term exchange rate risk can best be minimized by financing the project in whole or in part in local currency, and by sourcing production as much as possible in the currency of final sales.[7] This step ensures that the project's revenues, operating costs, and financing costs will be in the local currency, rather than having the financing costs in (for U.S. companies) dollars. Likewise, the dollar value of short-term, local currency cash flows can be protected by using special securities and strategies such as futures, forwards, and options market instruments.[8]

Political risk is much harder to protect against once a foreign project is accepted, since the foreign government can block the return of profits, seize the firm's assets (called **expropriation**), or otherwise interfere with a project's operation.[9] This inability to manage risk after the fact makes it even more important that managers account for political risks before making an investment.[10] They can do this either by adjusting a project's expected cash inflows to account for the probability of political interference or by using risk-adjusted discount rates (discussed later in this chapter) in the capital budgeting formulas. In general, it is much better to subjectively adjust individual project cash flows for political risk than to use a blanket adjustment for all projects.

More specifically, political risks in international capital budgeting can be minimized by using both financial and operating strategies. For example, by structuring the investment as a joint venture and by selecting a competent and well-connected local partner, the U.S. company can minimize the risk that its operations will be seized or harassed. Furthermore, companies can protect themselves from having their investment returns blocked by local governments by structuring the financing of such investments as debt rather than as equity. Debt-service payments are legally enforceable claims, whereas equity returns (such as dividends) are not. Even if local courts do not support the claims of the U.S. company, the company can threaten to pursue its case in U.S. courts.

---

7. For a discussion of the nature and causes of exchange rate risk, see Pringle and Connolly (1993).

8. The use of these financial instruments in hedging exchange rate risk is discussed in Smith, Smithson, and Wilford (1989).

9. Methods of pricing and hedging against expropriation risk are discussed in Mahajan (1990). The more general issue of political risk is discussed in Shapiro (1992), chapter 20.

10. American firms can obtain commercial risk insurance and political risk insurance for export sales—but not for direct investments—from the **Foreign Credit Insurance Association** (FCIA), a cooperative effort of the U.S. Export, Import Bank (Eximbank) and a group of large private insurance companies (Shapiro 1992, p. 321).

In addition to unique risks that MNCs must face, there are several other special issues that are relevant only for international capital budgeting. These include tax law differences, the importance of transfer pricing in evaluating projects, and the need to analyze international projects from a strategic as well as a financial perspective. Since only after-tax cash flows are relevant for capital budgeting, financial managers must carefully account for taxes paid to foreign governments on profits (or even on revenues) earned within their borders. They must also address the impact of these tax payments on the parent company's home-country tax liability, because full or partial credit is generally allowed for foreign tax payments.

Much of the international trade involving MNCs is, in reality, simply the shipment of goods and services from one of a parent company's wholly owned subsidiaries to another subsidiary located abroad. The parent company therefore has great discretion in setting the **transfer prices**, which are the prices that subsidiaries charge each other for the goods and services traded between them, because they are not traded in open markets with arms-length prices. The importance and widespread use of transfer pricing in international trade makes capital budgeting in MNCs very difficult unless the transfer prices used accurately reflect actual costs and incremental cash flows.

Finally, MNCs often must approach international capital projects from a strategic point of view, rather than from a strictly financial perspective. For example, an MNC may feel compelled to invest in a country to ensure continued access, even if the project itself may not have a positive net present value. This motivation was important for Japanese automakers who set up assembly plants in the United States even when the strong dollar of the early 1980s made export from Japan more economically rational. For much the same reason, U.S. investment in Europe surged during the years before the market integration of the European Community in 1992. MNCs often will invest in production facilities in the home country of major rivals to deny these competitors a profitable, uncontested home market. Finally, MNCs may feel compelled to invest in certain industries or countries to achieve a broad corporate objective such as completing a product line or diversifying raw material sources, even when the project's cash flows may not be sufficiently profitable.[11]

THE GROWING IMPORTANCE OF INTERNATIONAL INVESTMENT   In spite of the above difficulties, foreign direct investment, which involves the transfer of capital, managerial, and technical assets to a foreign country by U.S., European, Japanese, or other multinational companies, has surged in recent years. For example, the market value of foreign assets owned by U.S.-based companies now exceeds $800 billion, although because many of these investments have been in place for over 20 years, the book value of these assets is less than $400 billion.[12] Likewise, foreign direct investment in the United States now exceeds $500 billion in both market and book value, with British companies

---

11. Many of these strategic issues related to international finance and investment are discussed in detail in Lessard (1991) and Shapiro (1991).

12. Book and market value data on U.S. foreign direct investment (USFDI) is routinely (at least annually) reported in the U.S. Department of Commerce publication, **Survey of Current Business**.

holding the largest stake, followed by Japanese, Canadian, Dutch, and German companies.[13] Furthermore, foreign direct investment by U.S. companies now exceeds $50 billion per year and seems to be accelerating, particularly in East Asia and Latin America.[14]

6.4   CAPITAL BUDGETING TECHNIQUES

The relevant cash flows developed earlier in this chapter must be analyzed to assess whether a project is acceptable on its own, or whether it will be necessary to rank projects. A number of techniques are available for performing such analyses. The preferred approaches integrate time value procedures, risk and return considerations, and valuation concepts to select capital expenditures that are consistent with the firm's goal of maximizing owners' wealth. This and the following section focus on the use of these techniques to evaluate capital expenditure proposals for decision-making purposes.

We shall use the same basic problem to illustrate the application of all the techniques described in this chapter. The problem concerns the Delta Company, a medium-sized metal fabricator that is currently contemplating two projects—project A, requiring an initial investment of $42,000, and project B, requiring an initial investment of $45,000. The projected incremental (relevant) operating cash inflows for the two projects are presented in Table 6.3. The projects exhibit conventional cash flow patterns. In addition, we assume that all projects' cash flows have the same level of risk, that projects being compared have equal usable lives, and that the firm has unlimited funds (it is not in a capital rationing situation). Since very few decisions are actually made under such conditions, these simplifying assumptions are relaxed in later sections of the chapter. Here we begin with a look at the three most popular capital budgeting techniques—payback period, net present value, and internal rate of return.

6.4.1 Payback Period

Payback periods are a commonly used criterion for evaluating proposed investments. The payback period is the exact amount of time required for the firm to recover its initial investment in a project, as calculated from its projected cash inflows. In the

---

13. Coughlin (1992) discusses the dominant patterns observed in foreign direct investment into the United States (FDIUS), and makes clear that the overall impact of FDIUS on the American economy is overwhelmingly positive. Furthermore, the attractiveness of the United States as a base for export-oriented manufacturing investment by international MNCs has increased dramatically in recent years as low inflation, an expanding economy, and a stable or depreciating dollar (stable versus most European currencies; depreciating against the Japanese yen) has made the U.S. the low-cost producer among major industrialized economies.

14. Mandel (1994) reports that American companies invested $58 billion in foreign operations in 1993, and for the first nine months of 1994 direct investment by U.S. firms was on track to reach an annual total of $65 billion. Flanders (1994) reports that total world FDI for 1993 topped $170 billion, with approximately 40 percent of that being targeted for developing countries (over $20 billion was invested in China alone in 1993). Even more impressive than FDI capital flows are the total values of international portfolio capital flows. Flanders reports that these essentially passive investment flows increased from less than $200 billion per year in the late 1980s to almost $600 billion in 1993—with approximately $100 billion being invested in developing countries. During the 1990s, American investors have claimed the lion's share of these international investments, due largely to the desire of U.S. pension fund managers to increase their international stock ownership from less than 2 percent to 5 percent or more of their aggregate equity holdings.

TABLE 6.3		
CAPITAL EXPENDITURE DATA FOR DELTA COMPANY		
	Project A	**Project B**
Initial Investment	$42,000	$45,000
Year	**Operating Cash Inflows**	
1	$14,000	$28,000
2	14,000	12,000
3	14,000	10,000
4	14,000	10,000
5	14,000	10,000
Average	**$14,000**	**$14,000**

case of an annuity the payback period can be found by dividing the initial investment by the annual cash inflow; for a mixed stream the yearly cash inflows must be accumulated until the initial investment is recovered. Although popular, the payback period is generally viewed as an unsophisticated capital budgeting technique, since it does not explicitly consider the time value of money by discounting cash flows to find present value.[15]

The decision criterion when payback is used to make accept-reject decisions is as follows: If the payback period is less than the maximum acceptable payback period, accept the project; if the payback period is greater than the maximum acceptable payback period, reject the project. As an example, the data for Delta Company's projects A and B presented in Table 6.3 can be used to demonstrate the calculation of the payback period. For project A, which is an annuity, the payback period is 3.0 years ($42,000 initial investment / $14,000 annual cash inflow). Since project B generates a mixed stream of cash inflows, the calculation of the payback period is not quite as clear-cut. In year 1 the firm will recover $28,000 of its $45,000 initial investment. At the end of year 2, $40,000 ($28,000 from year 1 + $12,000 from year 2) will have been recovered. At the end of year 3, $50,000 ($40,000 from years 1 and 2 + $10,000 from year 3) will have been recovered. Since the amount received by the end of year 3 is greater than the initial investment of $45,000, the payback period is somewhere between two and three

15. In spite of its lack of sophistication, Gitman and Maxwell (1987) report that the use of payback period ranks second only to internal rate of return as a capital budgeting tool in their survey of U.S companies' investment decision-making processes. Payback period was used more frequently than net present value or any other technique (besides IRR). Additionally, Hodder (1986) reports that most large Japanese manufacturing firms do not use IRR or NPV, but instead rely on less sophisticated accounting profitability measures that either ignore the time value of money, or account for it indirectly with an interest charge. In spite of this, few people would claim that Japanese manufacturers are backwards—financially or technologically.

years. Only $5,000 ($45,000 − $40,000) must be recovered during year 3. Actually, $10,000 is recovered, but only 50 percent of this cash inflow ($5,000 / $10,000) is needed to complete the payback of the initial $45,000. The payback period for project B is therefore 2.5 years (2 years + 50 percent of year 3).

If Delta's maximum acceptable payback period is 2.75 years, project A would be rejected, and project B would be accepted. If the maximum payback were 2.25 years, both projects would be rejected. If the projects were being ranked, project B would be preferred over project A, since it has a shorter payback period (2.5 years versus 3.0 years).

PROS AND CONS OF PAYBACK PERIODS   The payback period's popularity, particularly among small firms, results from its ease of calculation and simple intuitive appeal.[16] It is appealing in light of the fact that it considers cash flows rather than accounting profits; it also gives some implicit consideration to the timing of cash flows and therefore to the time value of money. Because it can be viewed as a measure of risk exposure, many firms use the payback period as a decision criterion or as a supplement to sophisticated decision techniques. The longer the firm must wait to recover its invested funds, the greater the possibility of a calamity. Therefore the shorter the payback period, the lower the firm's exposure to such risk.

The major weakness of payback is that the appropriate payback period cannot be specified in light of the shareholder wealth maximization goal (modern finance's Prime Directive) because it is not based upon discounting cash flows to determine whether they add to the firm's value. Instead, the appropriate payback period is merely a subjectively determined maximum acceptable period of time over which a project's cash flows must break even (i.e., just equal the initial investment). A second weakness is that this approach fails to take fully into account the time factor in the value of money; by measuring how quickly the firm recovers its initial investment, it only implicitly considers the timing of cash flows. A third weakness is the failure to recognize cash flows that occur after the payback period.

6.4.2 Net Present Value (NPV)

Because net present value (NPV) gives explicit consideration to the time value of money, it is considered a more sophisticated capital budgeting technique than payback period. This and other techniques (such as internal rate of return) in one way or another discount the firm's cash flows at a specified rate. This rate—often called the discount rate, opportunity cost, or cost of capital—refers to the minimum return that must be earned on a project to leave the firm's market value unchanged. The net present value

---

16. This author had a personal experience with management's fixation on payback period early in his professional career, when he heard a senior vice president of a major international petroleum company announce that the company would only be willing to accept projects with a three-year payback period. This occurred at a time (the late 1970s) when real interest rates were often negative, and when oil prices—and thus the profitability of petroleum-related investments—were rising rapidly. Adding to the surreal nature of this announcement was the fact that it was made on the premises of the world's largest and most modern styrene monomer manufacturing facility (where the author was a rookie production chemist) and the statement was made by an accomplished and intelligent engineer.

(NPV), as noted in Equation 6.1, is found by subtracting the initial investment (II) from the present value of the net cash inflows (CF_t) discounted at a rate equal to the firm's cost of capital (k).

$$\text{NPV} = \textit{Present value of cash inflows} - \textit{initial investment} \qquad (6.1)$$

Using NPV, both inflows and outflows are measured in terms of present dollars. Since we are dealing with conventional investments, the initial investment is automatically stated in terms of today's dollars. If it were not, the present value of a project would be found by subtracting the present value of outflows from the present value of inflows.

The decision criterion when NPV is used to make accept-reject decisions is as follows: If NPV is greater than $0, accept the project; if NPV is less than $0, reject the project. If NPV is greater than zero, the firm will earn a return greater than its cost of capital. Such action should enhance the market value of the firm and therefore the wealth of its owners. The net present value (NPV) approach can be illustrated by using the Delta Company data presented in Table 6.4. If the firm has a 10 percent cost of capital, the net present values for projects A (an annuity) and B (a mixed stream) are calculated to be $11,074 and $10,914 respectively. Both projects are acceptable, since the net present value of each is greater than zero. If the projects were being ranked, however, project A would be considered superior to B, since it has a higher net present value ($11,074 versus $10,914) than that of B.

6.4.3 Internal Rate of Return (IRR)

The internal rate of return (IRR), although considerably more difficult to calculate by hand than NPV, is probably the most commonly used capital budgeting technique that explicitly accounts for the time value of money.[17] The internal rate of return (IRR) is defined as the discount rate that equates the present value of net cash inflows with the initial investment associated with a project. The IRR, in other words, is the discount rate that equates the NPV of an investment opportunity with zero (since the present value of cash inflows equals the initial investment). Mathematically, the IRR is found by solving Equation 6.2 for the value of k that causes NPV to equal zero.

$$0 = \sum_{t=1}^{n} \frac{CF_t}{(1 + IRR)^t} - II$$

$$\sum_{t=1}^{n} \frac{CF_t}{(1 + IRR)^t} = II \qquad (6.2)$$

The decision criterion, when the IRR is used in making accept-reject decisions, is as follows: If the IRR is greater than the cost of capital, accept the project; if the IRR is

17. This is the finding that Gitman and Maxwell (1987) and other studies document. It should be stressed, however, that in most cases the most difficult aspect of capital budgeting is not deciding on a technique to use, or even deciding on the appropriate discount rate. Rather, the forecasting of future cash inflows and outflows with adequate precision is both the most difficult and most important step in capital budgeting decision-making, as Butler and Schacter (1989), Pohlman, Santiago, and Markel (1988) and Pruitt and Gitman (1987) make clear.

TABLE 6.4

THE CALCULATION OF NPVS FOR DELTA COMPANY'S CAPITAL EXPENDITURE ALTERNATIVES

Project A

Annual cash inflow	$14,000
× Present-value annuity interest factor, PVIFA[a]	3.791
Present value of cash inflows	$53,074
− Initial investment	42,000
Net present value (NPV)	$11,074

Project B

Year	Cash Inflows (1)	Present-Value Interest Factor, PVIF[b] (2)	Present Value [(1) × (2)] (3)
1	$28,000	.909	$25,452
2	12,000	.826	9,912
3	10,000	.751	7,510
4	10,000	.683	6,830
5	10,000	.621	6,210
		Present value of cash inflows	$55,914
		− Initial investment	45,000
		Net present value (NPV)	$10,914

[a]FROM TABLE A-4, FOR 5 YEARS AND 10 PERCENT.
[b]FROM TABLE A-3, FOR GIVEN YEAR AND 10 PERCENT.

less than the cost of capital, reject the project. This criterion guarantees that the firm earns at least its required return. Such an outcome should enhance the market value of the firm and therefore the wealth of its owners.

The IRR can be found either by using trial-and-error techniques or with the aid of a financial calculator or a computer. We will assume throughout that readers have access to a calculator, but will also discuss the use of present and future value tables.[18] Finding the internal rate of return of a mixed stream of cash inflows can be illustrated by using Delta Company's project B cash flows given in Table 6.3. For this project, the exact IRR would be 21.65 percent. Project B is acceptable, since its IRR of approximately 22 percent is greater than the Delta Company's 10 percent cost of capital. This

---

18. A thorough discussion of calculating IRRs using trial-and-error techniques is presented in Gitman (1992, pp. 347–352).

is the same conclusion as was reached by using the NPV criterion. It is interesting to note that the IRR suggests that project B is preferable to project A, which has an IRR of approximately 20 percent. This conflicts with the rankings of the projects obtained by using NPV. Such conflicts are not unusual; there is no guarantee that these two techniques (NPV and IRR) will rank projects in the same order. However, both methods should reach the same conclusion about the acceptability or nonacceptability of the vast majority of real world projects.

6.5   COMPARING NPV AND IRR TECHNIQUES

For conventional projects, net present value (NPV) and internal rate of return (IRR) will always generate the same accept-reject decision, but differences in their underlying assumptions can cause them to rank projects differently. To understand the differences and preferences surrounding these techniques, we need to look at net present value profiles and the issue of conflicting rankings to answer the question of which approach is better.

6.5.1 Net Present Value Profiles

Projects can be compared by constructing net present value profiles that graphically depict the net present values for various discount rates. These profiles are useful in evaluating and comparing projects, especially when conflicting rankings exist, as the following example will demonstrate. To prepare net present value profiles for Delta Company's two projects, A and B, the first step is to develop a number of discount-rate-net-present-value coordinates. Three coordinates can easily be obtained for each project; they are at discount rates of 0 percent, 10 percent (the cost of capital, k), and the IRR. The net present value at a 0 percent discount rate is found by merely adding all the cash inflows and subtracting the initial investment. Using the data in Table 6.3, for project A we get:

$$(\$14{,}000 + \$14{,}000 + \$14{,}000 + \$14{,}000 + \$14{,}000) - \$42{,}000 = \$28{,}000$$

and for project B we get:

$$(\$28{,}000 + \$12{,}000 + \$10{,}000 + \$10{,}000 + \$10{,}000) - \$45{,}000 = \$25{,}000$$

The net present values for projects A and B at the 10 percent cost of capital were found to be \$11,074 and \$10,914, respectively (in Table 6.4). Since the IRR is the discount rate for which net present value equals zero, the IRRs of 20 percent for project A and 22 percent for project B result in \$0 NPVs.

Plotting the data generated above on a set of discount rate-NPV axes results in the net present value profiles for projects A and B plotted in Figure 6.2. An analysis of this figure indicates that for any discount rate less than approximately 10.7 percent, the NPV for project A is greater than the NPV for project B. Beyond this point, the NPV for project B is greater than that for project A. Since the net present value profiles for projects A and B cross at a positive NPV, the IRRs for the projects cause conflicting rankings whenever they are compared to NPVs calculated at discount rates below 10.7 percent.

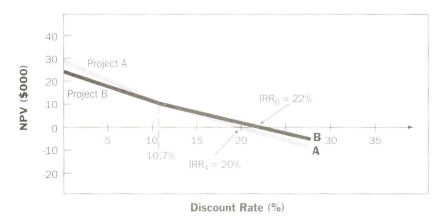

FIGURE 6.2

NET PRESENT VALUE PROFILES FOR DELTA COMPANY'S PROJECTS A AND B

6.5.2 Conflicting Rankings

The possibility of conflicting rankings of projects by NPV and IRR should be clear from the Delta Company example. Ranking is an important consideration when projects are mutually exclusive or when capital rationing is necessary.[19] Conflicting rankings using NPV and IRR result from differences in the magnitude and timing of cash flows. Although these two factors can be used to explain conflicting rankings, the underlying cause results from the implicit assumption concerning the reinvestment of intermediate cash inflows—cash inflows received before the termination of a project. NPV assumes that intermediate cash inflows are reinvested at the cost of capital, whereas IRR assumes that intermediate cash inflows can be invested at a rate equal to the project's IRR. These differing assumptions can be demonstrated with an example.

A project requiring a $170,000 initial investment is expected to provide operating cash inflows of $52,000, $78,000, and $100,000 at the end of each of the next three years. The NPV of the project (at the firm's 10 percent cost of capital) is $16,867, and its IRR is 15 percent. Clearly, the project is acceptable (NPV = $16,867 > $0 and IRR = 15 percent > 10 percent cost of capital). Table 6.5 demonstrates calculation of the project's future value at the end of its three-year life, assuming both a 10 percent (its cost of capital) and a 15 percent (its IRR) rate of return. A future value of $248,720 results from reinvestment at the 10 percent cost of capital (total in column 5), and a future value of $258,496 results from reinvestment at the 15 percent IRR (total in column 7).

If the future value in each case in Table 6.5 is viewed as the return received three years from today from the $170,000 initial investment, the cash flows are those given in

---

19. Lorie and Savage (1955) recognized this point four decades ago.

TABLE 6.5

REINVESTMENT RATE COMPARISONS FOR A PROJECT

			Reinvestment Rate			
			10%		**15%**	
Year (1)	Cash Inflows (2)	Number of Years Earning Interest (t) [3 − (1)] (3)	$FVIF_{10\%,t}$ (4)	Future Value [(2) × (4)] (5)	$FVIF_{15\%,t}$ (6)	Future Value [(2) × (6)] (7)
1	$ 52,000	2	1.210	$ 62,920	1.323	$ 68,796
2	78,000	1	1.100	85,800	1.150	89,700
3	100,000	0	1.000	100,000	1.000	100,000
		Future value at end of year 3		$248,720		$258,496

NPV @ 10% = $16,867

IRR = 15%

TABLE 6.6

PROJECT CASH FLOWS AFTER REINVESTMENT

	Reinvestment Rate	
	10%	**15%**
Initial Investment	$170,000	
Year	Operating Cash Inflows	
1	$0	$0
2	0	0
3	248,720	258,496
NPV @ 10%	$ 16,867	$ 24,213
IRR	13.5%	15.0%

Table 6.6. The NPVs and IRRs in each case are shown below the cash flows in Table 6.6. It can be seen that when the 10 percent reinvestment rate is used, the NPV remains at $16,867, while a different NPV ($24,213) results from reinvestment at the 15 percent IRR. From this it should be clear that NPV assumes reinvestment at the cost of capital (10 percent in this example). Note that with reinvestment at 10 percent, the IRR would be 13.5 percent rather than the 15 percent value that results with the 15 percent reinvestment rate. It should be clear that the IRR assumes an ability to reinvest intermediate cash inflows at the IRR; if reinvestment does not occur at this rate, the IRR will differ from 15 percent. Reinvestment at a rate below the IRR would (as demonstrated in Table 6.6)

result in an IRR below that calculated, and reinvestment at a rate above the IRR would result in an IRR above that calculated.[20]

In general, projects with similar-sized investments and lower early-year cash inflows (lower cash inflows in the early years) tend to be preferred at lower discount rates. Projects having higher early-year cash inflows (higher cash inflows in the early years) tend to be preferred at higher discount rates. These behaviors can be explained by the fact that at high discount rates, later-year cash inflows tend to be severely penalized in present-value terms.[21] Of course, annuities (projects with level cash inflows) cannot be characterized in this fashion; they can best be evaluated in comparison to other cash inflow streams. In an earlier example, the Delta Company's projects A and B were found to have conflicting rankings at the firm's 10 percent cost of capital. This finding is depicted in Figure 6.2. If we review each project's cash inflow pattern as presented in Table 6.3, we see that although the projects require similar initial investments, they have dissimilar cash inflow patterns—project A has level cash inflows, and project B has higher early-year cash inflows. Our logic indicates that project B would be preferred over project A at higher discount rates. Figure 6.2 shows that this is in fact the case. At a discount rate in excess of 10.7 percent, project B's NPV is above that of project A. Clearly, the magnitude and timing of the projects' cash inflows do affect their rankings.

Although this classification of cash inflow patterns is useful in explaining conflicting rankings, differences in the magnitude and timing of cash inflows do not guarantee conflicts in ranking. In general, the greater the difference between the magnitude and timing of cash inflows, the greater the likelihood of conflicting rankings. Conflicts based on NPV and IRR can be reconciled computationally; to do so, one creates and analyzes an incremental project reflecting the difference in cash flows between the two mutually exclusive projects.

6.5.3 Multiple IRRs

As if conflicting rankings was not enough of a problem, several authors—beginning with Lorie and Savage (1955) and Hirshleifer (1958)—have documented that certain cash flow streams may have two or more internal rates of return. To demonstrate this, Hirshleifer presented the investment option of $-1, 5, -6$ in periods 0, 1, and 2. This

---

20. This issue of the reinvestment assumption in IRR calculations is actually far more pervasive and important than might be apparent, because the IRR calculation methodology represents finance's principal technique for pricing bonds and other fixed payment streams. While usually not stressed, the yield-to-maturity (YTM) method for valuing corporate bonds implicitly assumes that intermediate cash flows can be reinvested at the calculated yield. Therefore, *realized* yields from bond investments will usually be greater or less than *calculated* yields. The only way an investor can be certain of earning exactly the promised yield, regardless of the level of or changes in market interest rates, is by purchasing a zero-coupon (pure discount) bond, and holding it to maturity.

21. This factor might partially explain why Japanese firms seemed much more willing than U.S. firms to commit to long-term investment projects during the 1980s—the Japanese firms had a lower cost of capital and this lower discount rate imposed lower penalties on cash flows far in the future. Frankel (1991) discusses this hypothesis, and finds modest support for it, but concludes that other financial, demographic, and corporate governance factors explained more of the investment rate difference between Japanese and U.S. firms.

project has IRRs of 100 percent *and* 200 percent. Additionally, Hirshleifer demonstrated that certain projects (such as −1, 3, −2.5) may have no real internal rates. More generally, IRR can fail to yield a unique solution in many circumstances involving multiple cash flow sign changes. In contrast, the NPV rule works whenever IRR does, and also works perfectly well in most instances where IRR fails.

6.5.4 Which Approach is Better?

The better approach for evaluating capital expenditures is difficult to determine because the theoretical and practical strengths of the approaches differ. It is therefore wise to view both NPV and IRR techniques in light of each of the following dimensions. On a purely theoretical basis, NPV is the better approach to capital budgeting. Its theoretical superiority is attributed to a number of factors. Most important is the fact that the use of NPV implicitly assumes that any intermediate cash inflows generated by an investment are reinvested at the firm's cost of capital. The use of IRR assumes reinvestment at the often high rate specified by the IRR. Since the cost of capital tends to be a reasonable estimate of the rate at which the firm could actually reinvest intermediate cash inflows, the use of NPV with its more conservative and realistic reinvestment rate is in theory preferable. In addition, certain mathematical properties may cause a project with nonconventional cash flows to have zero or more than one IRR; this problem does not occur with the NPV approach.

Evidence suggests that in spite of the theoretical superiority of NPV, financial managers prefer to use IRR. The preference for IRR is attributable to the general disposition of business people toward rates of return rather than actual dollar returns. Because interest rates, profitability, and so on are most often expressed as annual rates of return, the use of IRR makes sense to financial decision makers. They tend to find NPV more difficult to use because it does not really measure benefits relative to the amount invested. Because a variety of methods and techniques are available for avoiding the pitfalls of the IRR, its widespread use should not be viewed as reflecting a lack of sophistication on the part of financial decision makers.

6.6   RISK-ADJUSTMENT TECHNIQUES

There are several "behavioral" approaches for dealing with risk that allow the financial manager to get a feel for project risk by allowing the cash inflows to have different risk levels than that of the firm itself.[22] These include NPV simulation and sensitivity and scenario analyses.[23] Unfortunately, they do not really provide a straightforward basis

---

22. Various authors have proposed methods of risk adjusting project cash flows that have risk levels different from that of the firm itself. Hill and Stone (1980) propose an "accounting beta" approach that uses income statement measures of correlation and risk, while Fuller and Kerr (1981) propose a "pure-play" or analogous firm method that treats each project as a stand-alone firm. Both of these techniques are discussed in Ehrhardt and Bhagwat (1991), who propose their own risk-adjustment method that models the firm as a portfolio of projects. The firm's beta is thus simply a weighted average of its project betas, with or without the new project included.

23. These are described in depth in chapter 9, pages 357–362, of Gitman (1994).

for evaluating risky projects. We will now illustrate the two major risk-adjustment techniques using the net present value (NPV) decision method. The NPV decision rule of accepting only those projects with NPVs > $0 will continue to hold. The basic equation for NPV was presented in Equation 6.1. Close examination of that equation should make it clear that since the initial investment (II), which occurs at time zero, is known with certainty, a project's risk is embodied in the present value of cash inflows:

$$\sum_{t=1}^{n} \frac{CF_t}{(1 + k)^t}$$ (6.3)

Two opportunities to adjust the present value of cash inflows for risk exist: (1) the cash inflows, CF_t, can be adjusted, or (2) the discount rate, k, can be adjusted. Here we describe and compare two techniques—the cash inflow adjustment process, using certainty equivalents, and the discount rate adjustment process, using risk-adjusted discount rates. In addition, we consider the portfolio effects of project analysis as well as the practical aspects of certainty equivalents and risk-adjusted discount rates.

6.6.1 Certainty Equivalents (CEs)

One of the most direct and theoretically preferred approaches for risk adjustment is the use of **certainty equivalents** (CEs), which represent the percent of estimated cash inflow that investors would be satisfied to receive for certain (without risk), rather than the cash inflows that are possible for each year. Equation 6.4 presents the basic expression for NPV when certainty equivalents are used for risk adjustment:

$$NPV = \sum_{t=1}^{n} \frac{\alpha_t \times CF_t}{(1 + R_f)^t} - II$$ (6.4)

where α_t = certainty equivalent factor in year t $(0 < \alpha < 1)$
CF_t = relevant cash inflow in year t
R_f = risk-free rate of return

The equation shows that the project is adjusted for risk by first converting the expected cash inflows to certain amounts, $\alpha_t \times CF_t$, and then discounting the cash inflows at the risk-free rate, R_f, which is the rate of return that one would earn on a virtually riskless investment such as a U.S. Treasury bill. This procedure is used to discount the certain cash inflows and is not to be confused with a risk-adjusted discount rate. (If a risk-adjusted rate were used, the risk would in effect be counted twice.) Although the process described here of converting risky cash inflows to certain cash inflows is somewhat subjective, the technique is theoretically sound—as an example will demonstrate.[24]

Delta Company wishes to consider risk in the analysis of two projects, A and B. The basic data for these projects were initially presented in Table 6.3, and the analysis of the

---

24. Bogue and Roll (1974) discuss the use of certainty equivalents in capital budgeting, and describe how their basic valuation model must be modified if there are not perfect secondary markets for corporate assets (if perfect secondary markets exist, most multi-period valuation formulas can be collapsed to a one-period model with a cash inflow during period 1 and a sale of the asset at its capitalized value at the end of the period). Sick (1986) presents a more recent, and less theoretical, discussion of the use of certainty equivalents in assessing capital investment projects.

projects using net present value and assuming that the projects had equivalent risks was presented in Table 6.4. By ignoring risk differences and using net present value, it was shown earlier that at the firm's 10 percent cost of capital, project A was preferred over project B, since its NPV of $11,074 was greater than B's NPV of $10,914. Assume, however, that on further analysis the firm found that project A was actually more risky than project B. To consider the differing risks, the firm estimated the certainty equivalent factors for each project's cash inflows for each year. Columns 2 and 7 of Table 6.7 show the estimated values for projects A and B, respectively. Multiplying the risky cash inflows (given in columns 1 and 6) by the corresponding certainty equivalent factors (CEs) (columns 2 and 7, respectively) gives the certain cash inflows for projects A and B shown in columns 3 and 8, respectively.

Upon investigation, Delta's management estimated the prevailing risk-free rate of return, R_f, to be 6 percent. Using the 6 percent risk-free rate to discount the certain cash inflows for each of the projects results in the net present values of $4,541 for project A and $10,141 for project B, as calculated in Table 6.7. Note that as a result of the risk adjustment, project B is now preferred. The usefulness of the certainty equivalent approach for risk adjustment should be quite clear; the only difficulty lies in the need to make subjective estimates of the certainty equivalent factors.

6.6.2 Risk-Adjusted Discount Rates (RADRs)

A more practical approach for risk adjustment involves the use of risk-adjusted discount rates (RADRs). Instead of adjusting the cash inflows for risk, as was done in the certainty equivalent approach, this approach adjusts the discount rate. Equation 6.5 presents the basic expression for NPV when risk-adjusted discount rates are used:

$$NPV = \sum_{t=1}^{n} \frac{CF_t}{(1 + RADR)^t} - II \tag{6.5}$$

The **risk-adjusted discount rate** (RADR) is the rate of return that must be earned on a given project to compensate the firm's owners adequately, thereby resulting in the maintenance or improvement of share price. The higher the risk of a project, the higher the RADR and therefore the lower the net present value for a given stream of cash inflows. Because the logic underlying the use of RADRs is closely linked to the Capital Asset Pricing Model developed in chapter 3, we will review some of its basic constructs here before demonstrating the development and use of RADRs. It is, of course, important to recognize that because real corporate assets, unlike securities, are not traded in an efficient market, the CAPM cannot always be directly applied in making real asset decisions.[25]

RADR AND CAPM   In chapter 3 the Capital Asset Pricing Model (CAPM) was used to link the relevant risk and return for all assets traded in efficient markets. In the development of the CAPM, the total risk of an asset was defined as:

$$Total\ risk = nondiversifiable\ risk + diversifiable\ risk \tag{6.6}$$

---

25. In addition to the authors cited in footnote 22, several other researchers have examined risk-adjustment (and valuation) techniques for non-traded projects and real assets. These include Timme and Eisemann (1989) and Weaver, Clemmens, Gunn, and Dannenburg (1989).

TABLE 6.7

ANALYSIS OF DELTA COMPANY'S PROJECTS A AND B USING CERTAINTY EQUIVALENTS

Project A

Year (t)	Cash Inflows (1)	Certainty Equivalent Factors[a] (2)	Certain Cash Inflows [(1) × (2)] (3)	$PVIF_{6\%,t}$ (4)	Present Value [(3) × (4)] (5)
1	$14.000	.90	$12.600	.943	$11.882
2	14.000	.90	12.600	.890	11.214
3	14.000	.80	11.200	.840	9.408
4	14.000	.70	9.800	.792	7.762
5	14.000	.60	8.400	.747	6.275
				Present value of cash inflows	$46.541
				− Initial investment	42.000
				Net present value (NPV)	$4.541

Project B

Year (t)	Cash Inflows (6)	Certainty Equivalent Factors[a] (7)	Certain Cash Inflows [(6) × (7)] (8)	$PVIF_{6\%,t}$ (9)	Present Value [(8) × (9)] (10)
1	$28.000	1.00	$28.000	.943	$26.404
2	12.000	.90	10.800	.890	9.612
3	10.000	.90	9.000	.840	7.560
4	10.000	.80	8.000	.792	6.336
5	10.000	.70	7.000	.747	5.229
				Present value of cash inflows	$55.141
				− Initial investment	45.000
				Net present value (NPV)	$10.141

NOTE: THE BASIC CASH FLOWS FOR THESE PROJECTS WERE PRESENTED IN TABLE 6.3, AND THE ANALYSIS OF THE PROJECTS USING NPV AND ASSUMING EQUAL RISK WAS PRESENTED IN TABLE 6.4.

[a]THESE VALUES WERE ESTIMATED BY MANAGEMENT; THEY REFLECT THE RISK THAT MANAGERS PERCEIVE IN THE CASH INFLOWS.

For assets traded in an efficient market, the diversifiable risk, which results from uncontrollable or random events, can be eliminated through diversification. The relevant risk is therefore the nondiversifiable risk— the risk for which owners of these assets are rewarded. Nondiversifiable risk for securities is commonly measured by using beta, which is an index of the degree of movement of an asset's return in response to a change in the market return.

By using beta, β_j, to measure the relevant risk of any asset j, the CAPM is:

$$k_j = R_f + [\beta_j \times (k_m - R_f)] \tag{6.7}$$

where k_j = required return on asset j
  R_f = risk-free rate of return
  β_j = beta coefficient for asset j
  k_m = return on the market portfolio of assets.

In chapter 3 we demonstrated that the required return on any asset, j, could be determined by substituting values of R_f, β_j, and k_m into the CAPM—Equation 6.7. Any security that is expected to earn in excess of its required return would be acceptable, and those that are expected to earn an inferior return would be rejected.

If we assume for a moment that real corporate assets such as computers, machine tools, and special-purpose machinery are traded in efficient markets, the CAPM could be redefined as noted in Equation 6.8:

$$k_{project\,j} = R_f + [\beta_{project\,j} \times (k_m - R_f)] \tag{6.8}$$

The Security Market Line (SML), which is a graphic depiction of the CAPM, is shown for Equation 6.8 in Figure 6.3. As noted, any project having an IRR falling above the security market line (SML) would be acceptable, since its IRR would exceed the required return, $k_{project}$; any project with an IRR below $k_{project}$ would be rejected.[26] In terms of NPV, any project falling above the SML would have a positive NPV, and any project falling below the SML would have a negative NPV. Two projects, L and R, are shown in Figure 6.3. Project L has a beta, β_L, and generates an internal rate of return, IRR_L. The required return for a project with risk β_L is k_L.[27] Since project L generates a return greater than that required ($IRR_L > k_L$), project L would be acceptable. Project L would have a positive NPV when its cash inflows are discounted at its required return, k_L. Project R, on the other hand, generates an IRR below that required for its risk, β_R ($IRR_R < k_R$). This project would have a negative

26. Rubinstein (1973) was the first author to fully incorporate the CAPM with other areas of corporate finance, including capital budgeting. Fama (1977) later presented what is still the standard discussion of the use (and misuse) of risk-adjusted discount rates in capital budgeting decisions. More recently, Butler and Schacter (1989) also discuss RADRs.

27. Several authors have addressed the issue of which of its betas a firm should use in capital investment decision-making—its *actual* stock beta (computed as the correlation between the stock's return and the overall market's return) or its *unlevered* stock beta, which abstracts from the firm's current level of financial leverage and essentially measures the beta of the firm's assets. Most authors—beginning with Modigliani and Miller (1958) and Hirshleifer (1964)—recommend using unlevered betas, and Hamada (1972) demonstrates how unlevered betas can be computed from measured betas. The recommended use of unlevered betas is based on the traditional assumption that investment and financial decisions should be separated—managers should first decide which projects have sufficiently high risk-adjusted returns, and then should finance those projects using an appropriate mix of internal and external funding. As Myers (1974), DeAngelo and Masulis (1980), Mackie-Mason (1990) and many others make clear, however, this separation between finance and investment may break down if, for example, the tax code imparts a major incentive to use debt rather than equity financing. This issue will be discussed later in this chapter.

FIGURE 6.3

CAPM AND SML IN CAPITAL BUDGETING DECISION MAKING

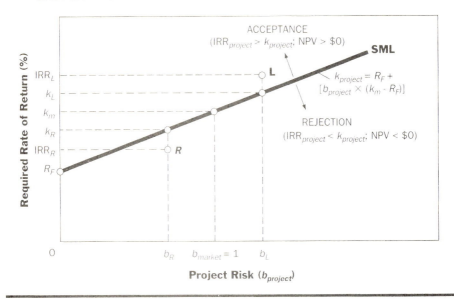

NPV when its cash inflows are discounted at its required return, k_R. Project R should be rejected.

PORTFOLIO EFFECTS   As was noted in chapter 3, since investors are not rewarded for taking diversifiable risk, they should hold a diversified portfolio of securities. Since a business firm can be viewed as a portfolio of assets, is it similarly important that the firm maintain a diversified portfolio of assets? By holding a diversified portfolio the firm could reduce the variability of its cash flows. By combining two projects with negatively correlated cash inflows, the combined cash inflow variability—and therefore the risk—could be reduced. But are firms rewarded for diversifying risk in this fashion? If they are, the value of the firm could be enhanced through diversification into other lines of business. Surprisingly, the value of the stock of firms whose shares are traded publicly in an efficient marketplace is generally not affected by diversification. In other words, diversification is not normally rewarded and therefore is generally not necessary.[28]

The lack of reward for diversification results from the fact that investors themselves can diversify by holding securities in a variety of firms; they do not need to have the firm do it for them. Investors can diversify more readily due to the ease of making transactions and at a lower cost because of the greater availability of information and trading mechanisms. Of course, if as a result of acquiring a new line of business the firm's cash flows tend to respond more to changing economic conditions (i.e., greater

---

28. This point is made quite elegantly in Galai and Masulis (1976).

nondiversifiable risk), greater returns would be expected. If, for the additional risk, the firm earned a return in excess of that required (IRR $> k$), the value of the firm could be enhanced. Also, other benefits such as increased cash, greater borrowing capacity, guaranteed availability of raw materials, and so forth, could result from, and therefore justify, diversification in spite of any immediate cash flow impact.

CE VS. RADR IN PRACTICE   Certainty equivalents (CEs) are generally the theoretically preferred approach for project risk adjustment because they separately adjust for risk and time; they first eliminate risk from the cash flows and then discount the certain cash flows at a risk-free rate. Risk-adjusted discount rates (RADRs), on the other hand, have a major theoretical problem: They combine the risk and time adjustments in a single discount-rate adjustment. Because of the basic mathematics of compounding and discounting, the RADR approach therefore implicitly assumes that risk is an increasing function of time. Partly because of this implicit assumption, CEs are considered to be theoretically superior to RADRs.

However, because of the complexity of developing CEs, RADRs are most often used in practice. Their popularity stems from two major facts: (1) They are consistent with the general disposition of financial decision makers toward rates of return, and (2) they are easily estimated and applied. The first reason is clearly a matter of personal preference, but the second is based on the computational convenience and well-developed procedures involved in the use of RADRs.

6.7   CAPITAL BUDGETING REFINEMENTS

Refinements must often be made in the analysis of capital budgeting projects to accommodate special circumstances. These adjustments permit the relaxation of certain simplifying assumptions presented earlier. Two areas in which special forms of analysis are frequently needed are (1) comparison of mutually exclusive projects having unequal lives and (2) capital rationing caused by a binding budget constraint.

6.7.1   Comparing Projects with Unequal Lives

The financial manager must often select the best of a group of unequal-lived projects. If the projects are independent, the length of the project lives is not critical. But when unequal-lived projects are mutually exclusive, the impact of differing lives must be considered because the projects do not provide service over comparable time periods. This is especially important when continuing service is needed from the project under consideration. The discussions that follow assume that the unequal-lived mutually exclusive projects being compared are ongoing. If such were not the case, the project with the highest net present value (NPV) would be selected.

A simple example will demonstrate the basic problem of noncomparability caused by the need to select the best of a group of mutually exclusive projects with differing usable lives. The CTV Company, a regional cable television company, is in the process of evaluating two projects, X and Y. The relevant cash flows for each project are given in Table 6.8. The applicable cost of capital for use in evaluating these equally risky

TABLE 6.8

COMPARING PROJECTS X AND Y FOR THE CTV COMPANY USING THE ANNUALIZED NET PRESENT VALUE APPROACH

	Project X	Project Y
Initial Investment	$70,000	$85,000
Year	Cash Inflows	
1	$28,000	$35,000
2	33,000	30,000
3	38,000	25,000
4	—	20,000
5	—	15,000
6	—	10,000

projects is 10 percent. The net present value (NPV) of each project at the 10 percent cost of capital is found to be:

$$NPV_X = [\$28,000 \times (.909)] + [\$33,000 \times (.826)] + [\$38,000 \times (.751)] - \$70,000$$

$$= (\$25,452 + \$27,258 + \$28,538) - \$70,000$$

$$= \$81,248 - \$70,000 = \$11,248$$

$$NPV_Y = [\$35,000 \times (.909)] + [\$30,000 \times (.826)] + [\$25,000 \times (.751)]$$

$$+ [\$20,000 \times (.683)] + [\$15,000 \times (.621)]$$

$$+ [\$10,000 \times (.564)] - \$85,000$$

$$= (\$31,815 + \$24,780 + \$18,775 + \$13,660 + \$9,315 + \$5,640) - \$85,000$$

$$= \$103,985 - \$85,000 = \$18,985$$

The NPV for project X is $11,248; that for project Y is $18,985. Ignoring the differences in project lives, we can see that both projects are acceptable (NPVs greater than zero) and that project Y is preferred over project X. In other words, if the projects are independent and, due to limited funds, only one can be accepted, project Y, with the larger NPV, will be preferred. On the other hand, if the projects are mutually exclusive, their differing lives must be considered; project X provides three years of service, and project Y provides six years of service.

The analysis in this example is incomplete if the projects are mutually exclusive (which will be our assumption throughout the remaining discussions). To compare these unequal-lived, mutually exclusive projects correctly, the differing lives must be considered in the analysis; an incorrect decision could result from use of NPV to select the better project. Although a number of approaches are available for dealing with unequal lives, here we present only the most efficient technique—the annualized net present value (ANPV) approach.

6.7.2 Annualized Net Present Value (ANPV) Approach

The **annualized net present value** (ANPV) **approach** converts the net present value of unequal-lived projects into an equivalent (in NPV terms) annual amount that can be used to select the best project. This net-present-value-based approach can be applied to unequal-lived, mutually exclusive projects by using the following steps.

STEP 1 Calculate the net present value of each project j, NPV_j, over its life, n_j, using the appropriate cost of capital, k.

STEP 2 Divide the net present value of each project having a positive NPV by the present-value interest factor for an annuity at the given cost of capital and the project's life to get the annualized net present value for each project j, $ANPV_j$:

$$ANPV_j = \frac{NPV_j}{PVIFA_{k,nj}} \tag{6.9}$$

STEP 3 Rank order and select the best projects. The project having the highest ANPV would be the best, followed by the project with the next highest ANPV, and so on.

Application of these steps can be illustrated by using data from the preceding example. Using the CTV Company data presented earlier for projects X and Y, the three-step ANPV approach can be applied as follows:

STEP 1 The net present values of projects X and Y discounted at 10 percent—calculated in the preceding example for a single purchase of each asset—are:

$$NPV_X = \$11,248$$

$$NPV_Y = \$18,985$$

As was noted earlier, on the basis of these NPVs, which ignore the differing lives, project Y is preferred over project X.

STEP 2 By applying Equation 6.10 to the NPVs, the annualized net present value for each project can be calculated:

$$ANPV_x = \frac{\$11,248}{PVIFA_{10\%,3}} = \frac{\$11,248}{2.487} = \$4,523$$

$$ANPV_y = \frac{\$18,985}{PVIFA_{10\%,6}} = \frac{\$18,985}{4.355} = \$4,359$$

STEP 3 Reviewing the ANPVs calculated in Step 2, we can see that project X would be preferred over project Y. Given that projects X and Y are mutually exclusive, project X would be the recommended project because it provides the higher annualized net present value.

6.7.3 Capital Rationing

Firms commonly operate under real or imagined capital rationing—they have more acceptable independent projects than they can fund. In theory, capital rationing should not exist.[29] Firms should accept all projects that have positive NPVs (or IRRs > the cost of capital). However, in practice many firms operate as if they face capital rationing. Generally, firms attempt to isolate and select the best acceptable projects subject to a capital expenditure budget set by management. Research has found that management internally imposes capital expenditure constraints to avoid what it deems to be "excessive" levels of new financing, particularly debt. In spite of the fact that failing to fund all acceptable independent projects is theoretically inconsistent with the goal of owner wealth maximization, here we discuss capital rationing procedures because they are widely used in practice.

The objective of capital rationing is to select the group of projects that provides the highest overall net present value and does not require more dollars than are budgeted. As a prerequisite to capital rationing, the best of any mutually exclusive projects must be chosen and placed in the group of independent projects. Two basic approaches to project selection under capital rationing are discussed here.

6.7.4 Internal Rate of Return Approach

The internal rate of return approach involves graphically plotting IRRs in descending order against the total dollar investment. This graph is called the investment opportunities schedule. By drawing the cost of capital line and then imposing a budget constraint, the financial manager can determine the group of acceptable projects. The problem with this technique is that it does not guarantee the maximum dollar return to the firm. It merely provides a satisfactory solution to capital rationing problems. An example illustrates this technique.

The Sigma Company, a fast-growing plastics company, is confronted with six projects competing for its fixed budget of $250,000. The initial investment and IRR for each project are as follows:

Project	Initial Investment	IRR
A	$ 80,000	12%
B	70,000	20
C	100,000	16
D	40,000	8
E	60,000	15
F	110,000	11

The firm has a cost of capital of 10 percent. Figure 6.4 presents the investment opportunities schedule (IOS) resulting from ranking the six projects in descending order

---

29. Capital rationing research is surveyed and assessed in Weingartner (1977). In spite of the theoretical implausibility of capital rationing, recent research has documented a very strong relationship between investment and various measures of liquidity (or cash flow) at the individual firm level, with the correlation being most pronounced for smaller firms. We will discuss this important issue at length in the next section of this chapter.

FIGURE 6.4

INVESTMENT OPPORTUNITIES SCHEDULE (IOS) FOR SIGMA COMPANY PROJECTS

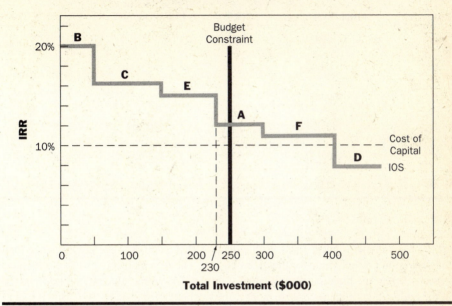

Total Investment ($000)

based on IRRs. According to the schedule, only projects B, C, and E should be accepted. Together they will absorb $230,000 of the $250,000 budget. Project D is not worthy of consideration, since its IRR is less than the firm's 10 percent cost of capital. The drawback of this approach, however, is that there is no guarantee that the acceptance of projects B, C, and E will maximize total dollar returns and therefore owners' wealth.

6.7.5 Net Present Value Approach

The net present value approach is based on the use of present values to determine the group of projects that will maximize owners' wealth. It is implemented by ranking projects on the basis of IRRs and then evaluating the present value of the benefits from each potential project to determine the combination of projects with the highest overall present value. This is the same as maximizing net present value, since, whether the entire budget is used or not, it is viewed as the total initial investment. The portion of the firm's budget that is not used does not increase the firm's value. At best, the unused money can be invested in marketable securities or returned to the owners in the form of cash dividends. In either case the wealth of the owners is not likely to be enhanced.

The group of projects described in the preceding example is ranked in Table 6.9 on the basis of IRRs. The present value of the cash inflows associated with the projects is also included in the table. Projects B, C, and E, which together require $230,000, yield a present value of $336,000. However, if projects B, C, and A were implemented, the total budget of $250,000 would be used, and the present value of the cash inflows would be $357,000. This is greater than the return expected from selecting the projects

	TABLE 6.9		
RANKING FOR SIGMA COMPANY PROJECTS			
Project	Initial Investment	IRR	Present Value of Inflows at 10%
B	$ 70,000	20%	$112,000
C	100,000	16	145,000
E	60,000	15	79,000
A	80,000	12	100,000
F	110,000	11	126,500	Cutoff point
D	40,000	8	36,000	(IRR < 10%)

on the basis of the highest IRRs. Implementing B, C, and A is preferable, since they maximize the present value for the given budget. The firm's objective is to use its budget to generate the highest present value of inflows. Assuming that any unused portion of the budget does not gain or lose money, the total NPV for projects B, C, and E would be $106,000 ($336,000 − $230,000), whereas for projects B, C, and A the total NPV would be $107,000 ($357,000 − $250,000). Selection of projects B, C, and A will therefore maximize NPV.

6.8   ADVANCED CAPITAL BUDGETING ISSUES: INTERACTIONS BETWEEN FINANCE AND INVESTMENT

So far in this chapter, all of the capital budgeting techniques we have examined are based on the classic assumption in modern finance—tracing back to Modigliani and Miller (1958)—that a firm's investment and financing decisions are, and rightly should be, separable. In the M&M world, which was constructed theoretically prior to the development of the CAPM, corporate managers are instructed to assess individual investment projects using the discount rate (required return on investment) of an unlevered firm in the same business risk class as the project itself.[30] After the development of the CAPM, the discount rate to be used for an individual project was related to the correlation of the project's cash flows with the return on the full market for risky assets. In either case, all projects with risk-adjusted expected returns greater than their required rates of return were to be accepted by a firm's managers, who then financed the set of acceptable investment opportunities by accessing perfectly competitive (hence friction-

---

30. Since M&M did not explicitly examine investment policies for projects with business risks that differ from the firm's own risk, this interpretation is taking some liberties with their original model—though our interpretation is clearly implied.

less) capital markets. Since capital structure is irrelevant in the M&M world of perfect capital markets, there was no link between financing and investment decisions.

Even after finance theory relaxed M&M's perfect markets assumption, the separation between finance and investment remained intact, with the single modification that a firm's managers should use the weighted average cost of capital derived from its "preferred" capital structure as the discount rate to be used for assessing projects with the same level of risk as the firm itself. Even if capital structure "matters" for tax or other reasons, it remained fairly easy to show that there should be no direct link between any single investment project and a single financing decision, but rather that an investment program should be decided on first and then financed afterwards.[31]

Beginning with Myers (1974, 1977), however, finance theory began to dramatically change the way it approached capital investments—to the point that one of finance's leading academic researchers, Stephen Ross, recently stated that traditional discounted cash flow analysis was probably appropriate only for the very simplest investment projects. To adequately assess most real investment projects, Ross asserted that the analyst must account for various project interactions and imbedded options—not the least important of which is the option of delaying the project's implementation (the option to delay).[32]

We will use the remainder of this chapter to discuss several of the more advanced capital budgeting issues that have been developed recently, beginning in this section with the interactions between financial and investment policies resulting from (1) characteristics of the firm's investment opportunity set—particularly the collateralizability of investment project assets; (2) agency costs of the manager-shareholder relationship; (3) the profitability and liquidity position of the investing firm; and (4) taxation policy. We then briefly examine how investment policy has been used as an information revelation tool in various signalling models of corporate capital structure, dividend, and equity valuation models, after which we discuss empirical findings regarding how the stock market values corporate investment programs. We conclude this section with a brief discussion of one of the newest investment analysis techniques—economic value added, or EVA. The next section of this chapter discusses several of the options that are inherently a part of most investment decisions, including options to open or shut down a mining or production process, timing options (including the option to delay a project), flexibility options regarding inputs

---

31. To demonstrate this, assume a company can issue up to $1 million in debt at an after-tax cost of 7 percent, but then must raise additional funds by issuing equity—at a cost of 13 percent. Furthermore, assume this company currently has (and is content with) a 50 percent debt, 50 percent equity capital structure, so its weighted average cost of capital (WACC) is 10 percent. Then assume that two investment projects present themselves to the firm's managers in the following order: project A costs $1 million and promises an after-tax return of 9 percent, while project B also costs $1 million but yields 12 percent. If this company's managers are as well-trained as you, they will know to use the 10 percent WACC as a discount rate for both projects, and will thus correctly accept project B and reject project A. If, however, the managers assess the first project that arrives using the firm's cost of debt (which is available for use), they will accept project A—since the project's 9 percent yield exceeds the debt's 7 percent cost—but will then be forced to reject project B, since its 12 percent yield is less than the 13 percent required return on new equity. Clearly, not separating individual financings from individual projects can yield perverse investment outcomes.

32. Ross made these comments in his Keynote Address to the Financial Management Association in St. Louis, October 1994.

or outputs, and the valuation of growth options—particularly the options created by research and development expenditures.

6.8.1 The Investment Opportunity Set (IOS) and Financing Policies

Prior to 1977, one of the unanswered questions in finance was why firms do not finance their operations almost exclusively with debt, given the seemingly massive tax incentives favoring levered financing. Myers (1977) was able to show that many real investment projects require ongoing financial investment for their full exploitation, and he demonstrated that managers of highly-levered firms would often rationally choose not to continue funding these growth options if most of the benefits from these investments would accrue to bondholders—but would have to be financed with stockholders' funds. In other words, growth options that require ongoing discretionary funding should be financed with equity capital, while tangible assets—that can be easily monitored and/or disposed of in liquid secondary markets following firm liquidation—can be financed almost completely with debt. The principal empirical prediction of Myers' model is that high-tech and other growth option-rich firms (computer software, pharmaceuticals, aerospace companies) should have lower leverage ratios than real estate, transportation, or other tangible asset-rich companies. This empirical relationship is convincingly documented in Smith and Watts (1992), Baker (1993), Gaver and Gaver (1993), and Skinner (1993).

Another branch of financial research has established relationships between the business risk inherent in a firm's production technology and its optimal leverage levels. Dotan and Ravid (1985) model this relationship theoretically, Ravid (1988) summarizes early literature on production/finance interactions, and Kale, Noe, and Ramirez (1991) find a U-shaped, non-linear relationship between operating and financial leverage. On the other hand, Green (1984) and Berkovitch and Kim (1990) show that a firm's decision to use debt financing can significantly (often negatively) impact a firm's investment incentives, meaning that a levered firm may have an incentive to pass up positive NPV investment opportunities. Finally, Baldwin and Ruback (1986) survey the literature examining the generally negative empirical relationship between inflation and investment.

6.8.2 Agency Problems and Corporate Investment Policy

In a world without agency problems, managers (1) would invest in all positive NPV investment opportunities and would forego all negative NPV projects; (2) they would concentrate only on the systematic risk of a project's cash flow (which investors cannot diversify away) rather than assessing projects based on their *total* risk (the unsystematic portion of which investors can costlessly diversify away); and (3) managers would pay out as dividends the free cash flow remaining after all positive NPV projects had been funded. In other words, managers would pursue a market value-maximizing capital investment policy, even when this policy was not in the personal best interests of the managers themselves.

In the real world, of course, there are significant agency problems between managers and shareholders, and managers have incentives to pursue low risk/low profit investment projects rather than more valuable high risk/high profit projects—because this lowers the overall variability of the firm's cash flow, and thus reduces the risk to the manager's tenure in office. For the same reason, managers will also prefer to assess a project based on its total risk than on systematic risk alone. Investors may be able to diversify a project's nonsystematic risk by investing in several different companies, but a manager has much of his or her human capital at risk in one firm that could be destroyed by a single sour investment. In a related vein, managers rationally prefer to invest in projects that are difficult for outside monitors to objectively assess, since this makes it harder for monitors (i.e., shareholders) to accurately measure managerial ability. Finally, the vast majority of managers prefer to retain free cash flow (cash flow remaining after all positive NPV projects have been funded) in the firm rather than pay it out to shareholders as dividends, since this both increases the amount of resources under management's discretionary control and reduces the risk that the firm will encounter liquidity problems. Unfortunately, such retention by definition implies that funds are invested in negative NPV projects.[33]

As the above list of perils illustrates, there is vast scope for managerial mischief regarding a firm's investment policy, and the discretionary nature of capital investment programs makes these agency problems even more severe. These problems, and potential solutions, are discussed at length in Jensen (1986, 1993) and Fama and Jensen (1985).[34] Perhaps the single most important method of aligning managerial and shareholder interests regarding investment policy is with an appropriately-structured management compensation package that includes stock options (to lessen management's fear of total risk and to focus on value maximization) and deferred compensation (to avoid the temptation of foregoing profitable investments to pump up current earnings).[35] There are no perfect answers, however, and potential agency problems must always be considered in real world investment planning and analysis.

6.8.3 Liquidity and Investment

One of the most intriguing empirical regularities that financial researchers have documented during the past decade is the significant link between the liquidity and investment levels of many firms.[36] In a world with frictionless capital markets, a firm's level of liquidity (defined variously as cash on hand, free cash flow, or unused borrowing capacity) should be unrelated to its ability to finance—internally or externally—its positive NPV

---

33. Empirical support for this idea—that retained free cash flow is often invested foolishly—is provided in Cooper and Richards (1988) and Jensen (1993).

34. For an intriguing analysis of the special investment policy problems that bedevil labor-managed firms, see Jensen and Meckling (1979).

35. Larcker (1983), Baker, Jensen, and Murphy (1988), Smith and Watts (1992), Gaver and Gaver (1993), and Skinner (1993) all document the inter-relatedness of compensation and investment policies.

36. An earlier stream of literature had examined whether a similar link exists between firm dividend and investment policies. Fama (1974) finds no such relationship, and concludes that paying dividends do not cause firms to become financially constrained. Peterson and Benesh (1983), on the other hand, find a statistically significant relationship.

investment opportunities. Evidence presented in Fazzari, Hubbard, and Petersen (1988), Whited (1992), Fazzari and Petersen (1993), Petersen and Rajan (1994), and Vogt (1994) regarding American firms—and in Hoshi, Kashyap, and Scharfstein (1990) regarding Japanese companies—clearly document that investment is directly related to liquidity, at least for smaller firms with imperfect access to capital markets.[37] Such a relationship not only has clear policy implications for individual firms—(for example, it provides an obvious rationale for the observed tendency for firms to hold otherwise perplexingly high levels of cash and marketable securities), it has equally clear macroeconomic and regulatory policy implications for governments. Policy-makers concerned with maximizing the economy's level of fixed investment should assure that adequate liquidity is provided to the nation's banking system, and that competition among institutions and markets will assure that deserving firms are able to obtain adequate, timely financing.

6.8.4 Taxes and Investment

Few areas of economics have attracted as much scholarly attention over the years as has the theoretical and empirical relationship between the level of business investment and the level (and incidence) of corporate taxation. Finance, however, has only recently begun seriously researching this issue using firm-level data and financial models of corporate behavior. Myers (1974) is the first major paper that documents how the U.S. tax code's massive subsidy for the use of debt impacts the capital structure and investment policies of individual firms. DeAngelo and Masulis (1980) document theoretically that non-debt tax shields such as depreciation and amortization can substitute for debt in a firm's capital structure decision, though Dammon and Senbet (1985) show that the net effect of taxes and depreciation on corporate investment and financial leverage is far from unambiguous due to various substitution and income effects. Dotan and Ravid (1985) also theoretically examine the impact of corporate income taxes on a firm's optimal level of operating and financial leverage, and reach similarly ambiguous results. Somewhat surprisingly, Mackie-Mason (1990) is the first finance researcher to unequivocably document that debt-related and non-debt-related tax shields are, at the margin, substitutes for one another in a firm's investment and capital structure decision-making process.

By far the most comprehensive (and damning) analysis of the impact of current U.S. tax policy on corporate investment is provided in Poterba (1987). He shows that the Tax Reform Act of 1986's repeal of the income tax credit, combined with less rapid depreciation rates and lowered tax rates of distributed profits (dividends) could be expected to lower equilibrium levels of corporate investment in the ecomomy. Although cause and effect is notoriously difficult to isolate in macroeconomic data, Poterba's prediction seemed to be borne out by events during the late 1980s and early 1990s—since gross investment, as reported in the International Monetary Fund's **In-**

---

37. Barro (1990) documents a seemingly related phenomena—that changes in stock prices are significantly positively related to investment levels of U.S. and Canadian firms. The fact that this relationship remains even after cash flow variables are included in the model suggests that stock price increases are important in their own right, and are not merely a proxy for increased ability to raise equity capital.

ternational Financial Statistics, did fall by about two percentage points relative to GDP during that period (from an average 19.7 percent during 1981–1986 to 17.5 percent during 1987–1991).[38]

6.8.5 Signaling Models of Corporate Investment

Given its importance to long-term firm performance, and the fact that it is a highly visible cash flow variable that is completely under management's discretion, it was probably inevitable that several researchers would develop signaling models where capital investment is one of the key signals (or the only signal) management can use to convey information about the firm's profitability to investors in a market characterized by asymmetric information. John and Nachman (1985), Miller and Rock (1985), and Ambarish, John, and Williams (1987) develop models where the level of investment spending chosen by management serves as a credible sign of the level of a firm's cash flow, since it is a signal weaker firms cannot mimic without exhausting their cash reserves. As such, investment increases convey positive news to investors, and investment decreases signal bad news.

6.8.6 Market Valuation of Capital Investment Spending

One of the most important criticisms that has frequently been levied against the American finance system is its perceived unwillingness to support managers wishing to make long-term investments in research and development and/or capital equipment. A well-articulated (though unsophisticated) statement of this "finance is strangling American business" hypothesis is presented in Porter (1992). So what does the empirical evidence say about financial market valuations of capital investment spending? It certainly does not support Porter's thesis—quite the reverse! In the most comprehensive such test, McConnell and Muscarella (1985) document a significantly positive stock price reaction to corporate announcements of plans to increase capital investment spending (including R&D), and a negative reaction to investment spending cuts.[39] Furthermore, Jarrell, Lehn, and Marr (1985) find that high R&D spending does not increase the likelihood that a firm will become a takeover target—one of the principal charges levied against finance as practiced during the 1980s. Chan, Martin, and Kensinger (1990) further document that most R&D spending is valued positively by stock market investors, though Hall (1993) shows the market's very high historical valuation of R&D spending

---

38. Since 1991, however, American capital spending has been increasing dramatically, though it is unclear whether this is due to a rapidly expanding economy, a more favorable export climate, the increased profitability and reduced cost of information processing capital goods, declining interest rates resulting from a uniquely favorable inflationary outlook, or some combination of all of these factors. The beauty of tax research is that there are never any final answers—just new data with which to address old questions.

39. The single important exception to this pattern regards oil and gas exploration expenditures. Stock market investors react negatively to announcements of plans to increase such spending, which is consistent with Jensen's (1986) thesis that oil companies were particularly prone to squander free cash flow (reinvesting high current earnings in declining businesses) during the 1980s.

declined precipitously during the 1980s.[40] Finally, Pilotte (1992) shows that firms which issue common stock in order to fund growth options face a less negative stock market response than do mature companies announcing seasoned stock issues.

6.8.7 Economic Value Added (EVA)

One of the newest methods proposed for analyzing the effectiveness of a firm's capital spending program is to measure the **economic value added** (EVA) by its investments. As popularized by Joel Stern and Bennett Stewart, and discussed in Walbert (1994), EVA is a measure of economic profits which subtracts a company's cost of capital (equity and debt) from its net operating profits after tax. A positive EVA implies a firm is earning a return on its investments that exceeds the (explicit and implicit) cost of the funds used to fund those investments, while a negative EVA suggests a firm is squandering investment capital. The stock market's assessment of how well management is applying EVA principles is measured by **market value added** (MVA), which is calculated as the difference between a company's total market value and the total capital contributed by investors. The future seems very bright for EVA and MVA, both because these techniques provide effective analytical tools to focus on the critical financial decisions that managers need to make correctly (investment decisions) and because the rankings provided by MVA correspond closely with the rankings more comprehensive surveys (and informed opinion) yield.[41]

6.9   CONTINGENT CLAIMS ANALYSIS IN CAPITAL BUDGETING

At the risk of sounding overly dramatic, it seems clear that the incorporation of contingent claims analysis into capital budgeting decision-making promises to revolutionize the way corporations organize and assess their investment programs. No technique previously available offers so much flexibility in addressing (and eventually valuing) the numerous options that inevitably arise when one searches for projects in which to productively invest a firm's capital.[42] In this final section, we will briefly address three key

---

40. Hall is unable to conclusively document the reason for this decline in relative valuation—to the point where R&D and advertising expenditures were valued roughly equally during the 1980s—but takeover pressures could not be completely ruled out. There is, of course, a vast literature on the macroeconomic importance of R&D spending in the economics literature that is not directly relevant to our current discussion (see especially Griliches (1986)). Finally, **Business Week** provides a very useful annual survey of R&D spending by U.S. firms (see Mandel 1994).

41. Walbert documents that Wal-Mart, Coca-Cola, Philip Morris, General Electric, and Merck were the five firms with the greatest market value added in 1992, while Digital Equipment, General Motors, and IBM occupied the three lowest positions among the 1,000 firms examined.

42. We refer parenthetically to "eventually valuing" these options with good reason. At present, most articles on this subject either use stylized numerical examples or adopt a purely conceptual approach to describing how option pricing can be used in capital budgeting. Actually valuing the various options requires parameterizing all of the option payoffs and costs, as well as all of the probability distributions describing outcome possibilities. The assumptions that would be required to obtain tractable closed-form solutions (bounded variation, lognormal distributions, continuous trading of hedge portfolios, etc.) are likely to deter formal application of quantitative models in most instances. Nonetheless, even incorporating option pricing techniques into capital budgeting at a purely conceptual level adds perspective to the analysis, since it makes clear what other investment possibilities or interactions might exist.

issues in the emerging investment options literature, beginning with the general topic of real option analysis, and then including timing options and flexibility options. At this stage of development, a formula-based approach to investment options is not appropriate, though in a few years these are likely to figure prominently even in introductory corporate finance textbooks.

6.9.1 Real Option Analysis

The classic applications of contingent claims analysis to capital budgeting are presented in Brennan and Schwartz (1985).[43] Marsh and Merton provide a general overview, but Brennan and Schwartz actually examine how option pricing techniques can generate optimal opening, closing, and operating rules for a mining operation based solely on the price of the mine's output—once the variable costs of operating, and the fixed costs of opening, closing, and mothballing the mine are specified. Subsequently, Siegel and Smith (1987) and Hampson, Parsons, and Blitzer (1991) extend the Brennan and Schwartz model to the analysis of petroleum exploration and development projects. More generally, these techniques seem particularly applicable to most types of natural resource investment projects, though numerous researchers have employed variations of these models in evaluating non-resource-related manufacturing, marketing, and product-development projects. Examples of this work include Chung and Charoenwong (1991), Baldwin and Clark (1992), Kulatilaka and Marcus (1992), Kasanen (1993), Quigg (1993), Trigeorgis (1993), Kemma (1993), and Lee, Martin, and Senchak (1993).

6.9.2 Timing Options

Classic NPV analysis assumes (implicitly or explicitly) that a given investment opportunity must be accepted immediately or lost forever. In other words, NPV analysis ignores the possibility of delaying acceptance of a project one or more periods in order to resolve some uncertainty or to see if interest rates will change. It also ignores the ability of management to accelerate or slow a project's development in response to new information arrival. Finally, traditional analysis ignores a firm's option to temporarily shut down a project's operation if output price temporarily falls below economic levels, or to temporarily maximize output if prices increase. All of these options have recently been modeled. Majd and Pindyck (1987) examine the option to accelerate or delay the construction of a multiperiod project, while Laughton and Jacoby (1993) examine timing options that depend on a mean-reverting underlying variable. By far the most important paper in this research stream, however, is Ingersoll and Ross (1992), who demonstrate the pervasive importance of the option to delay a project—in other words, to compare a project with itself delayed.

---

43. The intellectually-retentive reader will recall that the first author to discuss the value of growth options in an investment context was Myers (1977), but we do not discuss that work again here because Myers' objective was to show how the presence of growth options impacted the optimal financing decision—not to examine the characteristics of the option itself.

6.9.3 Flexibility Options

The final types of options that have recently come to prominence in capital budgeting analyses are collectively referred to as **flexibility options**—or the ability to incorporate flexibility into production processes. Three of these options have attracted particular attention. First, the value of the ability to use multiple inputs is described by Kulatilaka (1993), who specifically examines the value (net of additional purchase price) of installing an industrial boiler capable of using either oil or gas as a fuel rather than a single-fuel boiler (*input flexibility*). Second, Trigeorgis and Mason (1987), Triantis and Hodder (1990), Baldwin and Clark (1992), and Kulatilaka (1993) demonstrate the value of a flexible production technology that is able to produce a variety of outputs using the same basic processing plant and equipment in different configurations (*operating and/or output flexibility*). Finally, McLaughlin and Taggart (1992) and Kogut and Kulatilaka (1994) document the value that can be created by maintaining excess production capacity that can be utilized quickly to meet peak demand shocks (*capacity flexibility*). While costly to purchase and retain, excess capacity can be immensely valuable in capital-intensive industries subject to wide swings in output demand and long lead times in building new capacity from scratch. Kogut and Kulatilaka's paper is particularly important, because it studies the profit opportunities a multinational firm can exploit if it has excess capacity that allows it to move production around the world in response to exchange rate changes.

All of the options we have discussed above have a common implication for capital budgeting—they work to increase the value of almost all investment opportunities. This point is extremely important, given the criticisms that have been levied against the static NPV analytical techniques. By incorporating—even if only conceptually—option pricing into capital budgeting processes, managers are able to account for the value of all these production and timing opportunities and to examine how the various options interact with each other. The result of this augmented analysis should be better capital budgeting by individual firms, and more efficient allocation of capital at the macroeconomic level.

—SUMMARY—

Developing a method of generating, and then selecting, the best possible capital investment projects is critical to the long-run success of corporations around the world. It is equally vital for nation states to develop a legal, political, and regulatory climate that is hospitable to entrepreneurial risk-taking and business investment. Only by nurturing the most promising new technologies and by expanding existing capacity can businesses and countries continue to enjoy rising levels of prosperity. This chapter both examines the capital budgeting techniques that modern corporations currently employ and surveys the newest option-pricing based methods of evaluating investment projects. These new techniques, which explicitly value such things as manufacturing flexibility, excess capacity, and timing options (the option to delay investment) promise to revolutionize capital budgeting in future years—but are in their infancy today. For the near future, managers around the world will have to use the tried-and-true techniques of net present value analysis and internal rate of return criteria for choosing which capital projects to fund. Despite their limitations, the proper use of these proven techniques will yield value-enhancing capital investment decisions.

—QUESTIONS—

1. What does a firm's "capital budgeting program" entail? What should the objective(s) of this program be?

2. List the five steps in a firm's capital budgeting process. At which step does an investment decision become irreversible?

3. Define the following terms relating to capital budgeting: (*a*) capital rationing; (*b*) mutually exclusive projects; (*c*) nonconventional cash flow pattern; (*d*) mixed stream cash flow pattern.

4. What are the three major cash flow components in most capital budgeting problems? Which of these can be estimated with the greatest accuracy?

5. [Essay question] Compare and contrast exchange rate risk and political risk in an international capital budgeting context. What tools are most appropriate for dealing with each type of risk?

6. [Problem] In order to expand production, a firm buys a machine tool that costs $20,000 to purchase and install. This machine will increase profits by $5,000 per year for five years, after which the firm expects to sell the used machine tool for $7,000. Calculate the following for this machine tool: (*a*) payback period; (*b*) net present value; (*c*) internal rate of return on the assumption that the firm has a cost of capital of 10 percent.

7. What are the strengths and weaknesses of payback period as a capital budgeting technique?

8. **NPV for varying required returns** Athenia Printing Company is evaluating a new offset printing machine. The asset requires an initial investment of $24,000 and will generate after-tax cash inflows of $5,000 per year for eight years. For each of the required rates of return listed below, (1) calculate the net present value (NPV) and (2) indicate whether to accept or reject the machine.

a. The cost of capital is 10 percent.

b. The cost of capital is 12 percent.

c. The cost of capital is 14 percent.

9. **Internal rate of return** For each of the following projects, calculate the internal rate of return (IRR), and indicate for each project the maximum cost of capital that the firm could have and find the IRR acceptable.

	Project A	Project B	Project C	Project D
Initial Investment (II)	$90,000	$490,000	$20,000	$240,000
Year (*t*)		Cash Inflows (CF$_t$)		
1	$20,000	$150,000	$ 7,500	$120,000
2	25,000	150,000	7,500	100,000
3	30,000	150,000	7,500	80,000
4	35,000	150,000	7,500	60,000
5	40,000	—	7,500	—

10. Compare and contrast net present value (NPV) and internal rate of return (IRR) as capital budgeting techniques. Which is theoretically superior (and why)? Which is more commonly used (and why)?

11. **NPV, IRR, and NPV profiles** Gamma Company is considering two mutually exclusive projects. The firm, which has a 12 percent cost of capital, has estimated its cash flows as shown in the table below:

	Project A	Project B
Initial Investment (II)	$130,000	$85,000
Year (t)	Cash Inflows (CF$_t$)	
1	$ 25,000	$40,000
2	35,000	35,000
3	45,000	30,000
4	50,000	10,000
5	55,000	5,000

a. Calculate the NPV of each project, and assess its acceptability.

b. Calculate the IRR for each project, and assess its acceptability.

c. Draw the NPV profile for each project on the same set of axes.

d. Evaluate and discuss the rankings of the two projects based on your findings in a, b, and c.

12. What can cause a capital budgeting project to have multiple internal rates of return (IRR)? Why does this not happen with NPV analysis?

13. **Certainty equivalents** Acme Manufacturing is considering investing in either of two mutually exclusive projects, C and D. The firm has a 14 percent cost of capital, and the risk-free rate is currently 9 percent. The initial investment, expected cash inflows, and certainty equivalents associated with each project are presented in the table below:

	Project C		Project D	
Initial Investment (II)	$40,000		$56,000	
Year (t)	Cash Inflows (CF$_t$)	Certainty Equivalent Factors (α_t)	Cash Inflows (CF$_t$)	Certainty Equivalent Factors (α_t)
1	$20,000	.90	$20,000	.95
2	16,000	.80	25,000	.90
3	12,000	.60	15,000	.85
4	10,000	.50	20,000	.80
5	10,000	.40	10,000	.80

a. Find the net present value (unadjusted for risk) for each project. Which is preferred according to this measure?

b. Find the certainty equivalent net present value for each project. Which is preferred according to this risk-adjustment technique?

c. Compare and discuss your findings in a and b. Which, if either, of the projects would you recommend that the firm accept?

14. **Risk-adjusted discount rates** Euphoric Industries is considering investment in one of three mutually exclusive projects, E, F, and G. The firm's cost of capital is 15 percent, and the risk-free rate, R_f, is 10 percent. The firm has gathered the following basic cash flow and risk index data for each project:

	Project (j)		
	E	F	G
Initial Investment (II)	$15,000	$11,000	$19,000
Year (*t*)		Cash Inflows (CF₁)	
1	$ 6,000	$ 6,000	$ 4,000
2	6,000	4,000	6,000
3	6,000	5,000	8,000
4	6,000	2,000	12,000
Risk Index (RI_j)	1.80	1.00	0.60

a. Find the net present value (NPV) of each project using the firm's cost of capital. Which project is preferred in this situation?

b. The firm uses the following equation to determine the risk-adjusted discount rate, RADR_j, for each project j:

$$RADR_j = R_f + [RI_j \times (k - R_f)]$$

where: R_f = risk-free rate of return
  RI_j = risk index for project j
  k = cost of capital

Substitute each project's risk index into this equation to determine its RADR.

c. Use the RADR for each project to determine its risk-adjusted NPV. Which project is preferable in this situation?

d. Compare and discuss your findings in a and c. Which project would you recommend that the firm accept?

15. Compare and contrast certainty equivalents (CE) and risk-adjusted discount rates (RADR) as capital budgeting risk adjustment techniques. Which is more theoretically correct (and why)? Which is easier to use?

16. **Unequal lives—ANPV approach** Evans Industries wishes to select the best of three possible machines, each expected to fulfill the firm's ongoing need for additional aluminum-extrusion capacity. The three machines—A, B, and C—are equally risky. The firm plans to use a 12 percent cost of capital to evaluate each of them. The initial investment and annual cash inflows over the life of each machine are given in the following table:

	Machine A	Machine B	Machine C
Initial Investment (II)	$92,000	$65,000	$100,500
Year (*t*)		Cash Inflows (CF$_t$)	
1	$12,000	$10,000	$ 30,000
2	12,000	20,000	30,000
3	12,000	30,000	30,000
4	12,000	40,000	30,000
5	12,000	——	30,000
6	12,000	——	

a. Calculate the NPV for each machine over its life. Rank the machines in descending order based on NPV.

b. Use the annualized net present value (ANPV) approach to evaluate and rank the machines in descending order based on the ANPV.

c. Compare and contrast your findings in a and b. Which machine would you recommend that the firm acquire? Why?

17. **Capital rationing—IRR and NPV approaches** Utopia Corporation is attempting to select the best of a group of independent projects competing for the firm's fixed capital budget of $4.5 million. The firm recognizes that any unused portion of this budget will earn less than its 15 percent cost of capital, thereby resulting in a present value of inflows that is less than the initial investment. The firm has summarized the key data to be used in selecting the best group of projects in the following table:

Project	Initial Investment	IRR	Present Value of Inflows at 15 %
A	$5,000,000	17%	$5,400,000
B	800,000	18	1,100,000
C	2,000,000	19	2,300,000
D	1,500,000	16	1,600,000
E	800,000	22	900,000
F	2,500,000	23	3,000,000
G	1,200,000	20	1,300,000

a. Use the internal rate of return (IRR) approach to select the best group of projects.

b. Use the net present value (NPV) approach to select the best group of projects.

c. Compare, contrast, and discuss your findings in a and b.

d. Which projects should the firm implement? Why?

18. What is the theoretical justification for separating a firm's investment and financing decisions? What real-world factors can cause this separation to break down in practice?

19. [Essay question] Describe how a firm's investment opportunity set can influence a firm's optimal investment, financing (capital structure), and dividend policies.

20. Briefly describe how agency problems between managers and shareholders can impact observed corporate capital investment policies.

21. Describe the relationship between firm-level liquidity and capital investment spending that has been documented by empirical testing. What economic policy implications can be developed from these results?

22. [Essay question] A reporter asks you to comment on the proposition that the influence of capital markets in American corporate governance is imparting a "short-term bias" to the investment spending of U.S. companies. How do you respond?

23. [Essay question] Describe three types of flexibility options, and discuss how each impacts a firm's optimal investment policies.

—REFERENCES—

Ambarish, Ramasatry, Kose John, and Joseph Williams, "Efficient Signalling With Dividends and Investments," **Journal of Finance** 42 (June 1987), pp. 321–343.

Baker, George P., "Growth, Corporate Policies, and the Investment Opportunity Set," **Journal of Accounting and Economics** 16 (January/April/July 1993), pp. 161–165.

Baker, George P., Michael C. Jensen, and Kevin J. Murphy, "Compensation and Incentives: Practice vs. Theory," **Journal of Finance** 43 (July 1988), pp. 593–616.

Baldwin, Carliss Y. and Richard S. Ruback, "Inflation, Uncertainty and Investment," **Journal of Finance** 41 (July 1986), pp. 657–667.

Baldwin, Carliss Y. and Kim B. Clark, "Capabilities and Capital Investment: New Perspectives on Capital Budgeting," **Journal of Applied Corporate Finance** 15 (Summer 1992), pp. 67–82.

Barro, Robert J., "The Stock Market and Investment," **Review of Financial Studies** 3 (1990), pp. 115–131.

Berkovitch, Elazar and E. Han Kim, "Financial Contracting and Leverage Induced Over-and Under-Investment Incentives," **Journal of Finance** 45 (July 1990), pp. 765–794.

Bogue, Marcus C. and Richard Roll, "Capital Budgeting of Risky Projects With 'Imperfect' Markets for Physical Capital," **Journal of Finance** 29 (May 1974), pp. 601–613.

Brennan, Michael J. and Eduardo S. Schwartz, "Evaluating Natural Resource Investments," **Journal of Business** 58 (April 1985), pp. 135–157.

Butler, J. S. and Barry Schacter, "The Investment Decision: Estimation Risk and Risk Adjusted Discount Rates," **Financial Management** 18 (Winter 1989), pp. 13–22.

Chan, Su Han, John D. Martin, and John W. Kensinger, "Corporate Research and Development Expenditures and Share Value," **Journal of Financial Economics** 26 (August 1990), pp. 255–276.

Chung, Kee H. and Charlie Charoenwong, "Investment Options, Assets in Place, and Risk of Stocks," **Financial Management** 20 (Autumn 1991), pp. 21–33.

Cooper, Kerry and R. Malcolm Richards, "Investing the Alaskan Project Cash Flows: The Sohio Experience," **Financial Management** 17 (Spring 1988), pp. 58–70.

Coughlin, Cletis C., "Foreign-Owned Companies in the United States: Malign or Benign?," Federal Reserve Bank of St. Louis **Review** (May/June 1992), pp. 17–31.

Coy, Peter, Neil Gross, Silvia Sansom, and Kevin Kelly, "R&D Scoreboard," **Business Week** (June 27, 1994), pp. 78–103.

Dammon, Robert M. and Lemma W. Senbet, "The Effect of Taxes and Depreciation on Corporate Investment and Financial Leverage," **Journal of Finance** 43 (June 1985), pp. 357–371.

DeAngelo, Harry and Ronald W. Masulis, "Optimal Capital Structure Under Corporate and Personal Taxation," **Journal of Financial Economics** 8 (March 1980), pp. 3–30.

Dotan, Amihud and S. Abraham Ravid, "On the Interaction of Real and Financial Decisions of the Firm Under Uncertainty," **Journal of Finance** 40 (June 1985), pp. 501–517.

Ehrhardt, Michael C. and Yatin N. Bhagwat, "A Full-Information Approach for Estimating Divisional Betas," **Financial Management** 20 (Summer 1991), pp. 60–69.

Fama, Eugene F., "The Empirical Relationship Between the Dividend and Investment Decisions of Firms," **American Economic Review** 64 (June 1974), pp. 304–318.

————"Risk-Adjusted Discount Rates and Capital Budgeting Under Uncertainty," **Journal of Financial Economics** 5 (August 1977), pp. 3–24.

Fama, Eugene F. and Michael C. Jensen, "Organizational Forms and Investment Decisions," **Journal of Financial Economics** 14 (March 1985), pp. 101–118.

Farrell, Christopher, "21st Century Capitalism—The Triple Revolution," **Business Week** (Special 1994 Bonus Issue), pp.16–25.

Fazzari, Steven M. and B. Petersen, "Investment Smoothing with Working Capital: New Evidence on the Impact of Financial Constraints," **RAND Journal of Economics** (Autumn 1993), pp. 328–342.

Fazzari, Steven M., R. Glenn Hubbard, and B. Petersen, "Financing Constraints and Corporate Investment," **Brookings Papers on Economic Activity** 1 (1988), pp. 141–206.

Flanders, Stefanie, "Strategies Build Upon Knowledge Base," World Economy and Finance Special Report, **Financial Times** (September 30, 1994), pp. XII.

Frankel, Jeffrey A., "The Japanese Cost of Finance: A Survey," **Financial Management** 20 (Spring 1991), pp. 95–127.

Fuller, Russell J. and Halbert S. Kerr, "Estimating the Divisional Cost of Capital: An Analysis of the Pure-Play Technique," **Journal of Finance** 36 (December 1981), pp. 997–1008.

Galai, Dan and Ronald W. Masulis, "The Option Pricing Model and the Risk Factor of Stock," **Journal of Financial Economics** 3 (January/March 1976), pp. 53–81.

Gaver, Jennifer J. and Kenneth M. Gaver, "Additional Evidence on the Association Between the Investment Opportunity Set and Corporate Financing, Dividend, and Compensation Policies," **Journal of Accounting and Economics** 16 (January/April/July 1993), pp. 125–160.

Gitman, Lawrence J., **Basic Managerial Finance** (3rd edition, Harper Collins: New York, 1992)

————**Principles of Managerial Finance**, Seventh edition (New York: Harper Collins, 1994).

Gitman, Lawrence J. and Charles E. Maxwell, "A Longitudinal Comparison of Capital Budgeting Techniques Used by Major U.S. Firms: 1986 versus 1976," **Journal of Applied Business Research** (Fall 1987), pp. 41–50.

Green, Richard C., "Investment Incentives, Debt, and Warrants," **Journal of Financial Economics** 13 (March 1984), pp. 115–136.

Griliches, Zvi, "Productivity, R&D, and Basic Research at the Firm Level in the 1970s," **American Economic Review** 76 (March 1986), pp. 141–154.

Hall, Bronwyn H., "The Stock Markets' Valuation of R&D Investment During the 1980s," **American Economic Review** 83 (May 1993), pp. 259–264.

Hamada, Robert S., "The Effect of the Firm's Capital Structure on the Systematic Risk of Common Stocks," **Journal of Finance** 27 (May 1972), pp. 435–452.

Hampson, Philip, John Parsons, and Charles Blitzer, "A Case Study in the Design of an Optimal Production Sharing Rule for a Petroleum Exploration Venture," **Journal of Financial Economics** 30 (November 1991), pp. 45–67.

Hill, Ned C. and Bernell K. Stone, "Accounting Betas, Systematic Operating Risk, and Financial Leverage: A Risk-Composition Approach to the Determinants of Systematic Risk," **Journal of Financial and Quantitative Analysis** 15 (September 1980), pp. 595–637.

Hirshleifer, Jack, "On the Theory of Optimal Investment Decisions," **Journal of Political Economy** 66 (August 1958), pp. 329–352.

————"Efficient Allocation of Capital in an Uncertain World," **American Economic Review** 54 (May 1964), pp. 77–85.

Hodder, James E., "Evaluation of Manufacturing Investments: A Comparison of U.S. and Japanese Practices," **Financial Management** 15 (Spring 1986), pp. 17–24.

Holland, John, "Capital Budgeting for International Business: A Framework for Analysis," **Managerial Finance** 16 (1990), pp. 1–6.

Hoshi, Takeo, Anil Kashyap, and David Scharfstein, "The Role of Banks in Reducing Financial Distress in Japan," **Journal of Financial Economics** 27 (September 1990), pp. 67–88.

Ingersoll, Jonathan E., Jr. and Stephen A. Ross, "Waiting to Invest: Investment and Uncertainty," **Journal of Business** 65 (March 1992), pp. 1–29.

Jarrell, Gregg A., Ken Lehn, and M. Wayne Marr, "Institutional Ownership, Tender Offers, and Long-Term Investments," Office of the Chief Economist: U.S. Securities and Exchange Commission (April 1985).

Javetski, Bill and William Glasgall, "21st Century Capitalism—Borderless Finance: Fuel for Growth," **Business Week** (Special 1994 Bonus Issue), pp.40–50.

Jensen, Michael C., "Agency Cost of Free Cash Flow, Corporate Finance, and Takeovers," **American Economic Review** 76 (May 1986), pp. 323–329.

————"The Modern Industrial Revolution, Exit, and the Failure of Internal Control Systems," **Journal of Finance** 48 (July 1993), pp. 831–880.

Jensen, Michael C. and William H. Meckling, "Rights and Production Functions: An Application to Labor-Managed Firms and Codetermination," **Journal of Business** 52 (October 1979), pp. 469–506.

John, Kose and David C. Nachman, "Risky Debt, Investment Incentives, and Reputation in a Sequential Equilibrium," **Journal of Finance** 40 (July 1985), pp. 863–878.

Kahn, Joseph, "A Tale of Three Cities: Beijing Warily Pushes Shanghai to Resume Role in Global Finance," **Wall Street Journal** (November 25, 1994), p. A1.

Kale, Jaynat R., Thomas H. Noe, and Gabriel G. Ramirez, "The Effect of Business Risk on Corporate Capital Structure: Theory and Evidence," **Journal of Finance** 46 (December 1991), pp. 1693–1715.

Kasanen, Eero, "Creating Value by Spawning Investment Opportunities," **Financial Management** 22 (Autumn 1993), pp. 251–258.

Kemma, Angelien G. Z., "Case Studies on Real Options," **Financial Management** 22 (Autumn 1993), pp. 259–270.

Kogut, Bruce and Nalin Kulatilaka, "Operating Flexibility, Global Manufacturing, and the Option Value of a Multinational Network," **Managemenmt Science** 40 (January 1994), pp. 123–139.

Kulatilaka, Nalin, "The Value of Flexibility: The Case of a Dual-Fuel Industrial Steam Boiler," **Financial Management** 22 (Autumn 1993), pp. 271–280.

Kulatilaka, Nalin and Alan J. Marcus, "Project Valuation Under Uncertainty: When Does DCF Fail?," **Journal of Applied Corporate Finance** 5 (Fall 1992), pp. 92–100.

Larcker, David, "The Association Between Performance Plan Adoption and Corporate Capital Investment," **Journal of Accounting and Economics** 5 (April 1983), pp. 3–30.

Laughton, David G. and Henry D. Jacoby, "Reversion, Timing Options, and Long-Term Decision-Making," **Financial Management** 22 (Autumn 1993), pp. 225–240.

Lee, Wayne Y., John D. Martin, and Andrew J. Senchak, "The Case for Using Options to Evaluate Salvage Values in Financial Leases," **Financial Management** 22 (Autumn 1993), pp. 33–41.

Lessard, Donald R., "Global Competition and Corporate Finance in the 1990s," **Journal of Applied Corporate Finance** 3 (Winter 1991), pp. 59–72.

Lorie, James H. and Leonard J. Savage, "Three Problems in Rationing Capital," **Journal of Business** 28 (October 1955), pp. 229–239.

Mackie-Mason, Jeffrey K., "Do Taxes Affect Corporate Financing Decisions?," **Journal of Finance** 45 (December 1990), pp. 1471–1493.

Mahajan, Arvind, "Pricing Expropriation Risk," **Financial Management** 19 (Winter 1990), pp. 77–86.

Majd, Saman and Robert S. Pindyck, "Time to Build, Option Value, and Investment Decisions," **Journal of Financial Economics** 18 (March 1987), pp. 7–28.

Mandel, Michael J., "Business Rolls the Dice," **Business Week** (October 17, 1994), pp. 88–90.

Mason, Scott P. and Robert C. Merton, "The Role of Contingent Claims Analysis in Corporate Finance," in Edwin Altman and Marti Subrahmanyan, eds., **Recent Advances in Corporate Finance** (Richard D. Irwin, Inc.: Homewood, IL, 1985), pp. 7–54.

McConnell, John J. and Chris J. Muscarella, "Corporate Capital Expenditure Decisions and the Market Value of the Firm," **Journal of Financial Economics** 14 (September 1985), pp. 399–422.

McLaughlin, Robyn and Robert A. Taggart, Jr., "The Opportunity Cost of Excess Capacity," **Financial Management** 21 (Summer 1992), pp. 12–23.

Miller, Merton H. and Kevin Rock, "Dividend Policy Under Asymmetric Information," **Journal of Finance** 40 (September 1985), pp. 1031–1051.

Modigliani, Franco and Merton Miller, "The Cost of Capital, Corporation Finance, and the Theory of Investment," **American Economic Review** 48 (June 1958), pp. 261–297.

Myers, Stewart, "Interactions of Corporate Financing and Investment Decisions—Implications for Capital Budgeting," **Journal of Finance** 29 (March 1974), pp. 1–25.

———— "The Determinants of Corporate Borrowing," **Journal of Financial Economics** 5 (November 1977), pp. 147–176.

Pakes, Ariel, "On Patents, R and D, and the Stock Market Rate of Return," **Journal of Political Economy** 93 (1985), pp. 390–409.

Petersen, Mitchell A. and Raghuram G. Rajan, "The Benefits of Lending Relationships: Evidence From Small Business Data," **Journal of Finance** 49 (March 1994), pp. 3–37.

Peterson, Pamela and Gary Benesh, "A Reexamination of the Empirical Relationship Between Investment and Financing Decisions," **Journal of Financial and Quantitative Analysis** 18 (December 1983), pp. 439–453.

Pilotte, Eugene, "Growth Opportunities and the Stock Price Response to New Financing," **Journal of Business** 65 (July 1992), pp. 371–394.

Pindyck, Robert S., "Irreversibility, Uncertainty, and Investment," **Journal of Economic Literature** 29 (September 1991), pp. 1110–1152.

Pohlman, Randolph A., Emmanuel S. Santiago, and F. Lynn Markel, "Cash Flow Estimation Practices of Large Firms," **Financial Management** 17 (Summer 1988), pp. 71–79.

Porter, Michael E., "Capital Disadvantage: America's Failing Capital Investment System," **Harvard Business Review** (September/October 1992), pp. 65–82.

Poterba, James, "Tax Policy and Corporate Savings," **Brookings Papers on Economic Activity** 2 (December 1987), pp. 455–515.

Pringle, John J. and Robert A. Connolly, "The Nature and Causes of Foreign Currency Exposure," **Journal of Applied Corporate Finance** 6 (Fall 1993), pp. 61–72.

Pruitt, Stephen W. and Lawrence J. Gitman, "Capital Budgeting Forecast Biases: Evidence From the Fortune 500," **Financial Management** 16 (Spring 1987), pp. 46–51.

Ravid, S. Abraham, "On Interactions of Production and Financial Decisions," **Financial Management** 17 (Fall 1988), pp. 87–99.

Quigg, Laura, "Empirical Testing of Real Option-Pricing Models," **Journal of Finance** 48 (June 1993), pp. 621–640.

Rubinstein, Mark E., "A Mean-Variance Synthesis of Corporate Financial Theory," **Journal of Finance** 28 (March 1973), pp. 167–181.

Shapiro, Alan C., "The Economic Import of Europe 1992," **Journal of Applied Corporate Finance** 3 (Winter 1991), pp. 25–36.

————**Multinational Financial Management**, Fourth edition (Boston: Allyn and Bacon, 1992).

Sick, Gordon A., "A Certainty-Equivalent Approach to Capital Budgeting," **Financial Management** 15 (Winter 1986), pp. 23–32.

Siegel, Daniel R. and James L. Smith, "Valuing Offshore Oil Properties With Option Pricing Models," **Midland Corporate Finance Journal** 5 (Spring 1987), pp. 22–30.

Skinner, Douglas J., "The Investment Opportunity Set and Accounting Procedure Choice," **Journal of Accounting and Economics** 16 (January/April/July 1993), pp. 407–445.

Smith, Clifford W., Jr., Charles W. Smithson, and D. Sykes Wilford, "Managing Financial Risk," **Journal of Applied Corporate Finance** 1 (Winter 1989), pp. 27–48.

Smith, Clifford W., Jr. and Ross L. Watts, "The Investment Opportunity Set and Corporate Financing, Dividend, and Compensation Policies," **Journal of Financial Economics** 32 (October 1992), pp. 263–292.

Stewart, Thomas A., "The Information Age in Charts," **Fortune** (April 4, 1994), pp. 75–79.

Timme, Stephen G. and Peter C. Eisemann, "On the Use of Consensus Forecasts of Growth in the Constant Growth Model: The Case of Electric Utilities," **Financial Management** 18 (Winter 1989), pp. 23–35.

Triantis, Alexander J. and James E. Hodder, "Valuing Flexibility as a Complex Option," **Journal of Finance** 45 (June 1990), pp. 549–565.

Trigeorgis, Lenos, "The Nature of Option Interactions and the Valuation of Investments With Multiple Real Options," **Journal of Financial and Quantitative Analysis** 28 (March 1993), pp. 1–20.

Trigeorgis, Lenos and Scott P. Mason, "Valuing Managerial Flexibility," **Midland Corporate Finance Journal** 5 (Spring 1987), pp. 14–21.

Vogt, Stephen C., "The Cash Flow/Investment Relationship: Evidence From U.S. Manufacturing Firms," **Financial Management** 23 (Summer 1994), pp. 3–20.

Walbert, Laura, "The Stern Stewart Performance 1000: Using EVA™ to Build Market Value," **Journal of Applied Corporate Finance** 6 (Winter 1994), pp. 109–116.

Weaver, Samuel C., Peter J. Clemmens III, Jack A. Gunn, and Bruce D. Dannenburg, "Divisional Hurdle Rates and the Cost of Capital," **Financial Management** 18 (Spring 1989), pp. 18–25.

Weingartner, H. Martin, "Capital Rationing: Authors in Search of a Plot," **Journal of Finance** 32 (December 1977), pp. 1403–1431.

Whited, Toni M., "Debt, Liquidity Constraints, and Corporate Investment: Evidence From Panel Data," **Journal of Finance** 47 (September 1992), pp. 1425–1460.

CHAPTER

7

Capital Structure Theory

7.1 INTRODUCTION

The phrase **capital structure** refers to the relative mix of debt and equity securities in the long-term financial structure of a company. As contrasted with terms such as debt ratio, leverage ratio, and other more general measures of a company's total indebtedness, capital structure usually is applied strictly to the "permanent" or long-run **capital** that undergirds a company's operations. While a capital structure measure can be computed for any company sophisticated enough to generate a balance sheet, the focus of both academic research and practical financial analysis has been on those large corporations with publicly-traded debt and equity securities that dominate economic life throughout the developed world. And everywhere the same two fundamental questions are asked: (1) Does capital structure matter—can the total market value of a firm's securities be increased or decreased by changing the mix of debt and equity financing? And, (2) if capital structure does matter, what factors determine the optimal mix of debt and equity that will maximize the firm's market value and thus minimize its cost of capital?

Providing clear answers to these two positive economic questions is transcendingly important. If capital structure does matter, and if we could determine precisely which factors were critical, the benefits to society would be immense. Corporate managers could always ensure that their companies were being financed at the lowest possible cost, investors could confidently entrust their savings to financial markets that guaranteed maximum return for minimum risk, and public policy-makers could design a regulatory and taxation regime that maximized aggregate output at the minimum possible risk to the nation's economic stability. Financial decision-making could be made with mathematical precision, and a nation's stock of investment capital could be allocated to its highest and best use.

Unfortunately, academic finance cannot yet provide unambiguous answers to the two key capital structure questions, despite the fact that this topic has been the focus of intense research for almost four decades. This is not to suggest that we can offer no practical advice to either the practicing manager or the policy-maker: much has been learned since Franco Modigliani and Merton Miller (1958) published their seminal capital structure theory, and each year brings an increase in our understanding of the forces that influence the corporate financing behavior of American firms. Of even greater importance is the fact that capital structure research has become increasingly internationalized in recent years, because this provides researchers the opportunity to make cross-sectional comparisons between countries and between various industries around the world.[1] Nonetheless, we are unlikely to ever be able to describe observed capital structures with scientific certainty, and every time a consensus seemed ready to emerge among capital structure researchers in the past, financial changes and innovations in the real business world conspired to render agreement impossible. While frustrating, this also makes the study of capital structure a fascinating and challenging pursuit.

This chapter investigates the theoretical models that have been advanced to explain capital structure patterns, and also examines the empirical evidence concerning each of these theoretical models. We focus our attention on the "mainstream" model of corporate leverage, the Agency Cost/Tax Shield Trade-Off Model, but we also examine two other theoretical contenders—the Pecking Order Hypothesis and the Signaling Models of capital structure.

7.2   OBSERVED CAPITAL STRUCTURE PATTERNS

Before examining capital structure theory, let's first summarize exactly what capital structure patterns are actually observed around the world. This will in turn make clear what a viable theory of capital structure should be able to explain. This will also provide us with an objective standard for judging the usefulness of the various theories that have been put forward over the years to explain actual corporate behavior. A robust theory should be able to explain the following empirical regularities.

1. **Observed capital structures show distinct national patterns.** Among industrialized nations, American, British, German, Australian and Canadian companies have lower average *book value* debt ratios than do their counterparts in Japan, France, Italy and other European countries. On the other hand, British and German firms have by far the lowest market value leverage ratios. Among developing (or newly-industrialized) countries, debt ratios in Singapore, Malaysia, Chile and Mexico are typically lower than in Brazil, India or Pakistan.[2] The exact reasons for these differences are unclear,

---

1. An excellent empirical analysis of international capital structure patterns is provided in Rajan and Zingales (1994). A model of international capital structure equilibrium is presented in Hodder and Senbet (1990).

2. See Rutterford (1988), Sekely and Collins (1988), Frankel (1991), and Rajan and Zingales (1994) for book value data, which is fairly noncontroversial. Much controversy remains, however, concerning whether market value (rather than book value) capital structure ratios are significantly different between countries, particularly between the U.S. and Japan. See, as examples, Michel and Shaked (1985), Kester (1986), and Kester and Luehrman (1992). As Frankel points out, once you adjust for different accounting rules and express Japanese leverage ratios in market value terms, debt ratios in Japan were actually lower than those of U.S. corporations in the late 1980s, and virtually identical to U.S. ratios after the crash of the Tokyo Stock Exchange in the early 1990s. Probably the best overall empirical study of international capital structure differences is Rajan and Zingales (1994), who conjecture that the extremely low leverage ratios of British and German firms results from the immense power banks and other creditors have over borrowers who encounter financial distress.

but historical, institutional, and even cultural factors all probably play a part, as does a nation's reliance on capital markets versus banks for corporate financing.[3] Table 7.1 presents various measures of debt ratios for the G-7 (group of seven large industrial) countries in 1991.

2. **Capital structures have pronounced industry patterns, and these are the same around the world.** In all developed countries, certain industries are characterized by high debt-to-equity ratios (utilities, transportation companies, and mature, capital-intensive manufacturing firms), while other industries employ little or no long-term debt financing (service firms, mining companies, and most rapidly growing or technology-based manufacturing companies). These patterns are very strong, suggesting that characteristics of an industry's optimal asset mix, plus the variability of its operating environment, significantly influence the actual capital structures chosen by firms in that industry anywhere in the world.[4]

3. **Within industries, leverage is inversely related to profitability.** Regardless of the industry in question, the most profitable companies borrow the least.[5] While this may not seem surprising, finance theory suggests that firms with access to well-functioning capital markets should be able (at least over time) to set their debt ratios at any level they desire—or at any level that is "best" for the industry. In addition, tax-based capital structure theories suggest profitable firms should borrow *more*, since they have greater need to shelter income from corporate taxes.[6] This empirical relationship between profitability and leverage suggests that observed capital structures are at least partly **residual** in nature—meaning they are artifacts of a company's historic profitability (and dividend policy) rather than the result of a deliberate capital structure policy choice. This distinction is crucial because it goes to the heart of whether a firm's capital structure is the cause or the result of its other financial policy choices.

4. **Taxes clearly influence capital structures, but are not alone decisive.** This may seem counter-intuitive, since corporate and personal income tax changes (particularly extreme changes) can so dramatically change both the inherent profitability of a company's operations and the relative attractiveness of issuing debt versus equity securities. And, indeed, research has shown that increases in corporate

---

3. See Roe (1990), Prowse (1990), Kester (1992), and Bhide (1993). Frankel (1991) also provides a detailed comparison of the ownership structures of U.S. and Japanese companies. For a more complete listing of academic papers that examine corporate governance systems in Japan, Germany, and the United States, see chapter 2.

4. The classic article documenting these relationships is Bradley, Jarrell, and Kim (1984). More recent articles documenting similar relationships include Long and Malitz (1985), Titman and Wessels (1988), Smith and Watts (1992), Gaver and Gaver (1993), and Rajan and Zingales (1994). An historical listing of average U.S. capital structures, by industry, is provided in Table 14 of Bernanke and Campbell (1988). Finally, a very thorough survey of the non-tax-related capital structure literature is provided in Harris and Raviv (1991).

5. See Myers (1993), especially page 6 and footnote 5, for a summary of the literature on the relationship between leverage and profitability. Myers particularly stresses Kester's (1986) finding that leverage is inversely related to profitability in both the U.S. and Japan.

6. This is a straightforward implication of all tax-based models, but several recent papers have presented more sophisticated analyses of the interaction between earnings volatility and the value of debt-related tax shields. As examples, see Bradley, Jarrell and Kim (1984), as well as Smith and Stulz (1985), MacKie-Mason (1990), and Kale, Noe, and Ramirez (1991).

TABLE 7.1

LEVERAGE MEASURES FOR PUBLICLY-TRADED FIRMS IN THE G-7 COUNTRIES, 1991

Extent of leverage in different countries.

Leverage measures are calculated for all non-financial companies reporting consolidated balance sheets in 1991. In this 'book' column, equity is measured at book value. In the 'market' column, equity is measured at market value. For instance, this alters the value of assets as follows: the (quasi) market value of assets is obtained by subtracting the book value of common equity from book assets and adding back the market value of common equity. Non-equity liabilities to total assets is the sum of all liabilities divided by the value of assets. Debt to total assets is the value of short-term plus long-term debt divided by total assets. Debt to net assets is the book value of debt divided by net assets where net assets is assets minus accounts payables and other current liabilities. Debt to capital is the book value of debt divided by the sum of the book value of debt and equity. EBIT is earnings before interest and taxes. EBITDA is earnings before interest, taxes, and depreciation. Aggregate ratios are obtained by summing the numerator across all reporting firms in the country and dividing by the denominator summed across the same firms.

Country	Number of Firms	Non-Equity Liabilities to Total Assets Medians (Means) Aggregate		Debt to Total Assets Medians (Means) Aggregate		Debt to Net Assets Medians (Means) Aggregate		Debt to Capital Medians (Means) Aggregate		Interest Coverage Ratio Medians Aggregate	
		Book	Market	Book	Market	Book	Market	Book	Market	EBIT/ Interest	EBITDA/ Interest
U.S.A.	2580	0.58 (0.66) 0.69	0.44 (0.44) 0.49	0.27 (0.31) 0.37	0.20 (0.24) 0.26	0.34 (0.38) 0.44	0.24 (0.27) 0.29	0.37 (0.37) 0.53	0.28 (0.32) 0.34	2.41 2.19	4.05 3.66
Japan	514	0.69 (0.67) 0.75	0.45 (0.45) 0.55	0.35 (0.35) 0.42	0.22 (0.24) 0.31	0.48 (0.35) 0.58	0.27 (0.29) 0.39	0.53 (0.52) 0.63	0.29 (0.31) 0.41	2.46 2.20	4.66 3.71

(continued)

TABLE 7.1 (CONTINUED)

Country	Number of Firms	Non-Equity Liabilities to Total Assets Medians (Means) Aggregate		Debt to Total Assets Medians (Means) Aggregate		Debt to Net Assets Medians (Means) Aggregate		Debt to Capital Medians (Means) Aggregate		Interest Coverage Ratio Medians Aggregate	
		Book	Market	Book	Market	Book	Market	Book	Market	EBIT/ Interest	EBITDA/ Interest
Germany	191	0.73 (0.72) 0.76	0.60 (0.56) 0.65	0.16 (0.20) 0.16	0.12 (0.16) 0.13	0.21 (0.25) 0.19	0.15 (0.19) 0.16	0.38 (0.39) 0.39	0.23 (0.28) 0.28	3.20 3.29	6.81 6.74
France	225	0.71 (0.69) 0.78	0.64 (0.61) 0.68	0.25 (0.26) 0.29	0.21 (0.23) 0.25	0.39 (0.39) 0.43	0.32 (0.33) 0.34	0.48 (0.46) 0.57	0.41 (0.41) 0.45	2.64 2.15	4.35 3.47
Italy	118	0.70 (0.67) 0.73	0.70 (0.67) 0.73	0.27 (0.28) 0.30	0.29 (0.28) 0.30	0.38 (0.38) 0.43	0.38 (0.39) 0.43	0.47 (0.46) 0.53	0.46 (0.47) 0.52	1.81 1.55	3.24 2.62
U.K.	608	0.54 (0.57) 0.56	0.40 (0.42) 0.42	0.18 (0.21) 0.24	0.14 (0.16) 0.18	0.26 (0.31) 0.32	0.18 (0.21) 0.22	0.28 (0.29) 0.34	0.19 (0.23) 0.24	4.79 3.98	6.44 5.29
Canada	318	0.56 (0.61) 0.64	0.49 (0.47) 0.55	0.32 (0.36) 0.38	0.28 (0.27) 0.33	0.37 (0.39) 0.44	0.32 (0.31) 0.37	0.39 (0.39) 0.50	0.35 (0.36) 0.43	1.55 1.19	3.05 2.55

SOURCE: RAJAN AND ZINGALES (1994, TABLE IIIC).

income tax rates are associated with increased debt usage by corporations—at least in those countries where interest is a tax-deductible expense—and that decreases in the personal tax rates on equity income (dividends and capital gains) relative to those on interest income are associated with decreased corporate debt usage.[7] On the other hand, American corporations apparently used no less debt prior to the introduction of the income tax in 1913 than they did when corporate and personal tax rates peaked (at over 60% and 90%, respectively) during World War II, so taxes clearly neither caused nor prevented levered capital structures. In fact, apart from the extreme (market value) leverage ratios found during the Great Depression, Panels A (book values) and B (market values) of Figures 7.1A and 7.1B reveal that capital structures of American companies have been remarkably constant over the period 1929–1980—especially compared to the dramatic changes in tax rates (and regulatory structures) that have occurred this century.[8] Table 7.2 presents book and market value long-term debt-to-asset ratios for U.S. companies over the period 1969–1988.

5. **Leverage ratios appear to be inversely related to the perceived costs of financial distress.** Both across industries and across countries, the larger the perceived costs of bankruptcy and financial distress, the less debt will be used. In countries such as Japan, where banks play dominant roles in corporate finance and bankruptcy laws strongly favor creditors over debtors, healthy companies routinely operate with leverage ratios that would be considered far too high for comparable American firms.[9] Furthermore, some industries seem able to tolerate far higher leverage ratios than others because they can pass through periods of financial stress (or even bankruptcy) with relatively little dead weight loss in economic value. For example, companies rich in collateralizeable assets such as commercial real estate and transportation equipment typically are far less sensitive to financial distress than are companies whose principal assets are the human capital of its employees, the brand image of its products, or other intangible assets.[10]

6. **Existing shareholders invariably consider leverage-increasing events to be "good news" and leverage-decreasing events to be "bad news".** Almost every major published empirical study shows that stock prices rise when a company announces leverage-increasing events, such as debt-for-equity exchange offers, debt-financed share repurchase programs, and debt-financed cash tender offers to acquire control of another company.[11] On the other hand, leverage decreasing

---

7. See Feldstein, Green, and Sheshinski (1979), Fung and Theobald (1984), Hamada and Scholes (1985), and Ang and Megginson (1990).

8. For historical information on U.S. capital structure measures, see Taggart (1985) and Bernanke and Campbell (1988).

9. See Hoshi, Kashyap, and Scharfstein (1990), Prowse (1990, 1992), Frankel (1991), Kester (1992), and Berglof and Perotti (1994).

10. See Titman (1984), Bradley, Jarrell, and Kim (1984), Titman and Wessels (1988), and Maksimovic and Titman (1991).

11. The first major paper documenting this phenomenon is Masulis (1980). Subsequent articles showing similar results include Dann (1981), Mikkelson and Partch (1986), and Travlos (1987). While Eckbo (1986) shows that "plain vanilla" bond offerings yield insignificant abnormal returns to shareholders, James (1987) documents that announcements of bank loans are associated with positive abnormal shareholder returns for corporate borrowers.

FIGURE 7.1A

(PANEL A): BOOK VALUE LONG-TERM DEBT-TO-TOTAL CAPITALIZATION AND PREFERRED STOCK-TO-TOTAL CAPITALIZATION RATIOS FOR U.S. CORPORATIONS, 1926–1980

This figure plots the book value long-term debt (LD) and preferred stock (P) to total capitalization (TC) measures for U.S. corporations over the period 1926–1980. The graphs present data for manufacturing and for all U.S. companies with available data.

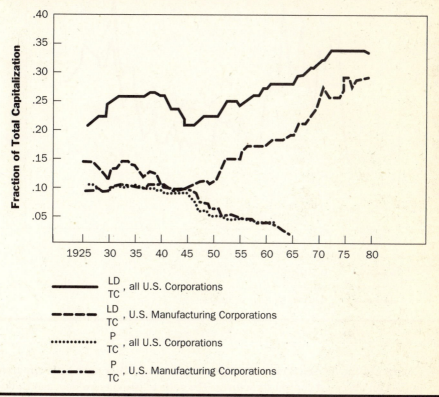

SOURCE: TAGGART (1985, FIGURE 1.1).

events such as equity-for-debt exchange offers, new stock offerings, and acquisition offers involving payment with a firm's own shares are almost always associated with share price declines.[12] This perplexes serious capital structure researchers, because it clearly indicates that such actions are counter to shareholders' best interests, but continue nonetheless. The actual cause of the stock price decline is also unclear. Obviously, adverse information is released, but precisely what information?

---

12. See Dann and Mikkelson (1984), Finnerty (1985), Asquith and Mullins (1986), Masulis and Korwar (1986), Mikkelson and Partch (1986), Barclay and Litzenberger (1988), Linn and Pinegar (1988), Lucas and McDonald (1990), and Loughran and Ritter (1995). Interestingly, Shah (1994) documents that leverage-increasing and leverage-decreasing intrafirm exchange offers convey fundamentally different types of information.

FIGURE 7.1B

(PANEL B): MARKET VALUE DEBT-TO-TOTAL CAPITALIZATION RATIO FOR U.S. CORPORATIONS, 1926–1980.

This figure plots the market value of total debt-to-total capitalization measures for U.S. corporations over the period 1926–1980. Total capitalization is defined as the sum of total debt (D), preferred stock (P), and common equity (E).

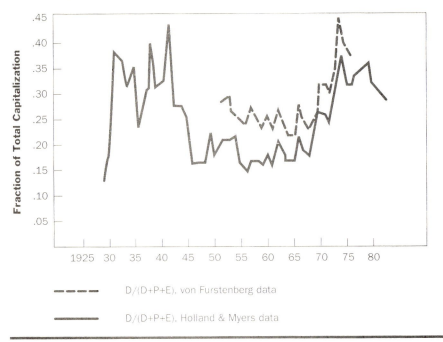

D/(D+P+E), von Furstenberg data

D/(D+P+E), Holland & Myers data

SOURCE: TAGGART (1985, FIGURE 1.1).

7. **Changes in the transactions costs of issuing new securities have little apparent impact on observed capital structures.** The costs of issuing new debt and equity securities have declined dramatically in recent decades throughout the world, particularly in the United States, but this has had little effect either on individual firm leverage ratios or on the types of securities issued.[13] Transactions costs may influence the size or frequency of security issues, but not capital structure choice.

8. **Ownership structure clearly seems to influence capital structures, though the true relationship is ambiguous.** Generally speaking, the more concentrated a firm's

---

13. While little direct evidence has been published documenting declines in issuance costs over time, there can be little doubt that both the direct (out-of-pocket expenses) and indirect (underpricing, information disclosure) costs of issuing corporate securities have declined sharply, particularly for debt securities. The one article we know of that directly examines the impact of transactions costs on capital structure decisions—Fischer, Heinkel, and Zechner (1989)—shows that these costs set leverage ratio "ranges" within which the firm will allow its debt ratios to fluctuate, but transactions costs do not imply that any one range is optimal for a given firm. Furthermore, Amihud and Mendelsohn (1986) present empirical evidence that security valuation is directly related to market liquidity, suggesting that corporations could maximize their market valuations by issuing only a few highly liquid debt and equity security classes in carefully selected proportions.

TABLE 7.2

BOOK VALUE AND MARKET VALUE DEBT-TO-ASSET RATIOS FOR PUBLICLY-TRADED U.S. FIRMS, 1969–1988

This table provides average annual debt-to-asset ratios, measured using both book and market values for debt and total assets. These are value-weighted averages of firms that are listed in the COMPUSTAT files. Sources: Bernanke and Campbell (1988, Table 4) for 1969–1986 data, and Bernanke, Campbell, and Whited (1988, Table 3) for 1987–1988 data.

| Year | Book Value | Market Value | | Number of Firms in Sample |
		Method A[1]	Method B[2]	
1969	0.300	0.260	0.254	643
1970	0.290	0.257	0.247	695
1971	0.281	0.247	0.234	747
1972	0.268	0.235	0.219	800
1973	0.257	0.270	0.267	859
1974	0.283	0.368	0.388	902
1975	0.287	0.325	0.334	932
1976	0.272	0.303	0.308	966
1977	0.273	0.345	0.354	1,013
1978	0.266	0.350	0.365	1,051
1979	0.264	0.336	0.351	1,085
1980	0.251	0.286	0.308	1,122
1981	0.263	0.317	0.344	1,169
1982	0.257	0.308	0.330	1,197
1983	0.241	0.286	0.303	1,259
1984	0.248	0.304	0.309	1,321
1985	0.256	0.298	0.288	1,386
1986	0.273	0.311	0.298	1,386
1987	na	0.305	0.276	1,179
1988	na	0.297	0.271	1,179

[1] VALUE OF LONG-TERM DEBT IS CALCULATED ON THE ASSUMPTION OF A 20-YEAR MATURITY, UNLESS SAMPLE DATA INDICATES OTHERWISE.

[2] MARKET VALUE OF DEBT MEASURED BY CAPITALIZING REPORTED INTEREST PAYMENTS.

ownership structure (the tighter the pattern of share ownership) the more debt it seems to desire and to be able to tolerate. Therefore, family-controlled firms tend to be more levered than similar publicly-traded firms with more atomized share ownership; and individual managers who place a high value on the personal benefits of controlling a corporation will tend to prefer new debt to new equity issues for financing, because this minimizes dilution of their ownership stake.[14] Furthermore, in countries where banks and other financial institutions are allowed to own both debt and equity stakes in client firms, observed debt ratios tend to be higher than in the U.S.—where there is generally a sharp distinction between equity and debt investors. The principal American examples of mixed investment structures—leveraged buyouts (LBOs), where debt ratios are very high and ownership is tightly concentrated—are the exceptions that prove this general rule.[15]

9. **Corporations that are forced away from a preferred capital structure tend to return to that structure over time.** This forced departure from a preferred debt ratio has occurred frequently in recent years, particularly for American corporations that have taken on large amounts of new debt to finance (or defend against) take overs of other companies or to fund major new ventures. The first priority of these companies after the acquisition is complete usually becomes paying down the debt incurred to a more comfortable level.[16] More generally, there is evidence that corporations like to operate within **target leverage zones**, and will issue new equity when debt ratios get too high and will issue debt if they fall too low. However, the single best predictor of new equity issues is the recent trend in stock prices. Companies tend to issue equity following unusually large increases in their stock prices, and essentially refuse to issue new equity after share prices have fallen.[17]

7.2.1 Theoretical Explanations for Observed Capital Structures

Not surprisingly, devising a single theory to explain all of the phenomena described above is extremely difficult. Nonetheless, three major theoretical models of capital structure choice have been developed, and we will introduce each one in turn below, and then discuss them in more depth in subsequent sections.

---

14. The relationship between ownership structure and financial structure has been examined theoretically in Stulz (1988), and empirically in Kim and Sorensen (1986) and Friend and Lang (1988). Stulz shows that managers who value control very highly will rely primarily on debt financing in order to minimize dilution of their own equity stakes in the firm, thus making the firm (and themselves) less vulnerable to hostile take over. Kim and Sorensen clearly document a direct relationship between insider ownership and corporate debt ratios. The empirical evidence does not unambiguously support this finding, however. Friend and Lang, for example, document that family-owned firms are much more likely to be all-equity-financed than are other companies, and Smith and Watts (1992) and Rajan and Zingales (1994) find a direct relationship between size and leverage ratios—though their explanation for this relationship relies on reduced bankruptcy costs, not ownership considerations.

15. See Kaplan (1989), Baker and Wruck (1989), Lehn, Netter, and Poulsen (1990), and Opler and Titman (1993) for recent evidence on the causes and consequences of leveraged buy-outs.

16. The most dramatic example of this phenomenon has occurred in leveraged buyouts, since the debt levels at the start of life as private companies are often extremely high. See, in particular, Muscarella and Vetsuypens (1990). Furthermore, Fischer, Heinkel, and Zechner (1989) document that corporate security issuance patterns indicate firms have preferred leverage ratio ranges that they return to over time with new debt and equity issues.

17. This pattern is documented both by Marsh (1982), for British firms, and by Asquith and Mullins (1986) and Korajczyk, Lucas, and McDonald (1991) for U.S. companies. On a prospective basis, Hansen and Crutchley (1990) show that firms tend to issue new stock immediately before they experience significant earnings declines, suggesting these issues are at least partly made to cover a cash flow shortfall resulting from lower-than-expected earnings.

THE AGENCY COST/TAX SHIELD TRADE-OFF MODEL   The first model, which we will call the **Agency Cost/Tax Shield Trade-Off model** (or simply "the trade-off model"), assumes that observed capital structures are the result of individual firms trading off the tax benefits of increased debt usage against the increasingly severe agency costs that result as debt ratios approach critical levels. This model has evolved from modifications to the original Modigliani and Miller (M&M) capital structure irrelevance hypothesis, and is the "mainstream" choice of most academics and financial practitioners. It also has the attractive feature of being based solidly on a capital market equilibrium and value maximizing arguments.

THE PECKING ORDER HYPOTHESIS   A very strong challenger has emerged during the past decade as the shortcomings of the simple trade-off model have become apparent. The **Pecking Order Hypothesis** has been developed almost single-handedly by Stewart Myers (1984), who first coined the term in his American Finance Association presidential address. It is based on two key assumptions: (1) managers are better informed about the investment opportunities faced by their firms than are outside investors (an asymmetric information assumption); and (2) managers act in the best interests of *existing* shareholders. Given these assumptions, Myers demonstrated that a firm will sometimes forego positive-NPV projects, if accepting these projects means the firm will have to issue new equity at a price that does not reflect the true value of the company's investment opportunities. This in turn provides a rationale for firms to value **financial slack**, such as large cash and marketable security holdings, and even unused debt capacity. This model has won converts because it can explain: (1) why debt ratios and profitability are inversely related; (2) why markets react negatively to all new equity issues and why managers seem to make such issues only when they either have no choice (following an unexpected earnings decline) or they feel the firm's shares are over-valued; and (3) why managers of even highly-regarded firms choose to hold more cash—and issue less debt—than either the trade-off theory or common sense suggest they should. Whereas the trade-off theory explains observed corporate debt *levels* fairly well, the pecking order theory offers a far superior explanation for observed capital structure *changes*—especially those involving security issues.

THE SIGNALING MODEL OF FINANCIAL STRUCTURE   The third and final capital structure theory we will examine is the **Signaling Model of Financial Structure**. This hypothesis is also based on the assumption of asymmetric information between managers and investors (as in the pecking order model), but in this case managers use costly signals to differentiate their firms from weaker competitors. One such signal, that is both costly and credible, is to adopt a highly levered capital structure. Only the strongest firms can afford to risk financial distress with such a structure, and investors are thus willing to assign a separate, higher valuation to highly levered companies rather than assigning them the low average valuation given to other firms. Although this model is intuitively appealing, it does not explain observed capital structures very well—at least not in its simplest form—so we will present it faithfully, but briefly.

A separate, though somewhat related, body of literature describes observed capital structure patterns in game theory terms. In essence, this body of literature models real industries as **oligopolies** (less than perfectly competitive industries, where individual firms have some market power), and examines how firms can use capital structure decisions to cooperate and communicate with each other so as to maximize aggregate industry profits. In this setting, leverage ratios can communicate either a willingness to cooperate with or a commitment to punish other firms if they choose to take a particular action. Although we will not review this literature in depth in this chapter, the interested reader is referred to Brander and Lewis (1986), Maksimovic (1988), and Maksimovic and Zechner (1991), among others.

Our first task will be to present and explain the original Modigliani & Miller capital structure irrelevance model in some depth. We do this both to nail down the brilliant intuition that underlies this proposition and because the M&M model serves as a starting point for all three of the subsequent, competing capital structure theories.

7.3   THE MODIGLIANI AND MILLER CAPITAL STRUCTURE IRRELEVANCE PROPOSITIONS

In their original 1958 article, Modigliani and Miller (henceforth M&M) set out to provide "an operational definition of the cost of capital and a workable theory of investment" that would explicitly recognize uncertainty, and would be solidly based on the principle of market value maximization.

7.3.1 Assumptions of the M&M (1958) Capital Structure Model

M&M begin by making the following assumptions either explicitly or implicitly:

1. All physical assets are owned by corporations;
2. Capital markets are frictionless. There are no corporate or personal income taxes, securities can be purchased or sold costlessly and instantaneously, and there are no bankruptcy costs;
3. Corporations can issue only two types of securities, risky equity and risk-free debt;
4. Both individuals and corporations can borrow or lend at the risk-free interest rate;
5. Investors have homogeneous expectations about the future stream of corporate profits;
6. There is no growth, so all cash flow streams are perpetuities;
7. All corporations can be classified into one of several "equivalent return classes" such that the returns on shares of all firms in that class are proportional to, and perfectly correlated with, all other firms in that class.[18]

Like most students, your first reaction to this list is probably to consider it almost laughably unrealistic. We will shortly present an example demonstrating that reality may be less at variance with these assumptions than it seems, but first let's examine how M&M originally achieve their irrelevance result. The key to their model is assumption 7, which states that shares of firms within a given risk class have both the

---

18. A logical question to ask is why M&M did not use the capital asset pricing model (CAPM), or some other asset pricing model, to adjust for risk. The answer, of course, is that the CAPM did not exist in 1958, and their article predated the development of arbitrage pricing theory by almost two decades. For a development of the M&M capital structure irrelevance propositions in a mean-variance (CAPM) framework, see Rubinstein (1973).

same expected return and the same probability distribution of expected returns, and can therefore be considered perfect substitutes for each other. Companies within a risk class thus differ from each other only in scale—they have the same expected profit per dollar of invested capital, and investors can expect their per share returns to be identical. M&M suggested that these classes might be comparable to industrial classifications, and this is a useful and intuitive analogy.

7.3.2 M&M's Proposition I

To arrive at Proposition I, let us assume that a company j, belonging to class c, is expected to earn operating profits (Net Operating Income, NOI) averaging NOI_j each period for the foreseeable future. We will denote the market value of this firm's debt as D_j, its equity as S_j, and the total value of its outstanding securities as V_j, where $V_j = S_j + D_j$. This can also be labeled the market value of the firm. M&M's Proposition I, then, asserts that:

$$V_j = (S_j + D_j) = \frac{NOI_j}{\rho_k}, \text{ for any firm } j \text{ in class } k. \tag{7.1}$$

Meaning, *"the market value of any firm is independent of its capital structure and is given by capitalizing its expected return at the rate ρ appropriate to its class."*

Making an assertion is one thing, proving it is quite another. M&M proved their proposition using an **arbitrage** argument. In economics, arbitrage is the (riskless, instantaneous) process of buying a good in one market at a low price, and then reselling it in another market where the identical good is selling at a higher price. Arbitrage promises infinite profits, and therefore is a powerful force ensuring that the **law of one price** (the same goods must sell within transactions costs of each other in two different markets) holds in well-functioning markets. M&M demonstrate that an arbitrage opportunity exists if the market value of the combined debt and equity of a levered firm differs from that of an otherwise identical all-equity firm. This is easiest to show with an example.

COMPUTING RETURNS TO LEVERED AND UNLEVERED SHAREHOLDERS   Consider two firms, U and L, that belong to the same risk class and have the same level of expected operating profit, $100,000 per year. Furthermore, assume that the required return ρ for firms of this risk class is 10%, implying that both firms should have market valuations of $100,000/0.10 = $1,000,000. Firm U has no debt outstanding. Instead, it has 20,000 shares outstanding, each of which should be worth $50 since this price would offer investors an expected return of 10%. Levered firm L, on the other hand, has both debt and equity outstanding. Assume it recently issued $500,000 worth of debt at a promised interest rate of 6% per year, and used the proceeds of this issue to repurchase half of its outstanding equity—10,000 shares at $50 each.[19] It therefore has 10,000 shares remaining outstanding that should also be worth $50 each, for a total of $500,000.

---

19. To keep this analysis clearly focused on pure capital structure changes, it is vital to assume that any money raised through the issuance of debt be used strictly to retire outstanding equity, and vice versa. This keeps the total value of the firm's assets constant, and allows one to examine financial changes in isolation.

But what return can firm L's shareholders expect to receive on their levered shares? As we will see, M&M's Proposition II could tell us directly, but instead let's reason through to the answer. To compute an expected return, we must first account for the fact that the firm is obligated to pay $0.06 \times \$500,000 = \$30,000$ in interest from its expected NOI of $100,000 before any money can be claimed by shareholders. The remaining $\$100,000 - \$30,000 = \$70,000$ in net income (NI) can either be distributed to shareholders or reinvested in the firm on their behalf. The expected return to firm L's shareholders is therefore NI divided by the market value of its shares, $\$70,000/\$500,000 = 0.14$, or 14%. We will refer to this as k_l, the required return on levered equity for firms in this risk class. Let us now summarize in Table 7.3 what the financial values *should* be for our two firms in a world where M&M's assumptions hold.

Now that we know what the market values of the securities of firms U and L should be, let's see how an "arbitrageur" (one who engages in arbitrage) could profit from any other valuation. Let's assume, as most authors did prior to 1958, that investors are willing to pay a premium price for the shares of levered firms. This is exactly the same as saying that investors would accept "too low" an expected return k_l, so let's say firm L's shares are selling to yield a 12.5% expected return. This implies a market valuation for firm L's equity (computed using the formula NI/k_l) of $\$70,000/0.125 = \$560,000$, or $56 per share. Added to the market value of the firm's debt ($500,000), this implies a total market valuation for firm L of $\$560,000 + \$500,000 = \$1,060,000$, while firm U's market value remains $1,000,000. These "disequilibrium" relative valuations are summarized in Table 7.4.

7.3.3 Proving Proposition I Using "Homemade Leverage"

How can an individual investor arbitrage these valuations? To understand how, keep in mind that the two firms in question are industrially equivalent, and must therefore have the same business and operating risk. Remember also that investors can borrow on their own account at the risk-free rate of interest. This allows them to make or unmake any corporate leverage ratio they want within their own portfolios. Therefore, an individual investor who currently owns some of firm L's stock (say, for simplicity, 1% of the total outstanding) expects to earn a 12.5% return on that investment, or $0.125 \times \$5,600 = \$700$. He or she could earn an arbitrage profit from the following transactions:

1. Sell all the firm L shares currently owned (1% of 10,000 = 100 shares), receiving $56 per share, for a total of $5,600.

2. Borrow an amount equivalent to 1% of firm L's debt (1% of $500,000 = $5,000), promising to pay 6% interest, or $300 ($0.06 \times \$500,000$).

3. Use $10,000 of the proceeds from steps 1 and 2 to purchase 1% (200 shares) of firm U's stock at $50 per share ($0.01 \times 20,000$ shares $\times \$50/share = \$10,000$). Ignore for now the $600 remaining from steps 1 and 2 ($5,600 + $5,000 − $10,000).

What, in financial terms has our investor/arbitrageur accomplished with this series of transactions? He or she initially held 1% of the stock of a company with a 50% debt: 50% equity capital structure, or a levered equity position. Steps 1–3 transformed this into an equally risky levered equity stake (also 1%) in the all-equity firm U, but now the leverage is all on personal account. Using **homemade leverage** (borrowing on per-

TABLE 7.3

EQUILIBRIUM EXPECTED VALUES FOR FIRMS U AND L

	Firm U	Firm L
Net Operating Income (NOI)	$100,000	$100,000
Interest Paid $(r \times D)$	0	$30,000
Net Income $(NOI - rD)$	$100,000	$70,000
Required Return on Assets for Firms in Risk Class (ρ)	10%	10%
Total Firm Value (NOI/ρ)	$1,000,000	$1,000,000
Required Return on Equity (k)	10%	14%
Market Value of Equity (S)	$1,000,000	$500,000
Interest Rate on Debt (r)	–	6%
Market Value of Debt (D)	0	$500,000

TABLE 7.4

DISEQUILIBRIUM VALUES FOR FIRMS U AND L ALLOWING ARBITRAGE

	Firm U	Firm L
Net Operating Income (NOI)	$100,000	$100,000
Interest Paid $(r \times D)$	0	$30,000
Net Income $(NOI - rD)$	$100,000	$70,000
Required Return on Assets for Firms in Risk Class (ρ)	10%	9.43%
Total Firm Value (NOI/ρ)	$1,000,000	$1,060,000
Required Return on Equity (k)	10%	**12.5%**
Market Value of Equity (S)	$1,000,000	**$560,000**
Interest Rate on Debt (r)	–	6%
Market Value of Debt (D)	0	$500,000

sonal account), the investor has constructed a portfolio consisting of $10,000 worth of firm U's stock—which should earn 10%, or $1,000—and $5,000 in debt, on which he or she must pay $300 interest. The net return to this new portfolio is therefore $1,000 − $300 = $700, exactly the same return expected on the original 1% stake in firm L's levered shares.

But our intrepid arbitrageur is still not through. He or she still has $600 remaining after investing only $10,000 of the $10,600 raised in steps 1 and 2. Let's assume this is invested back into firm L stock to earn 12.5%, or 0.125 × $600 = $75. This brings the total return from the arbitrage transactions to $700 + $75 = $775, which exceeds the return on the original 1% stake in firm L's stock, for no additional risk. Such an arbitrage opportunity is a money machine that will force prices back into equilibrium. This can only occur when the expected return on firm L's stock rises to 14%, yielding a total equity value of $500,000 and a total firm L market value of $1,000,000.

Obviously, if the expected return on firm L's shares was originally set *too high*—say, at 16%—arbitrage would proceed in the opposite direction. An investor/arbitrageur would sell firm U shares and then purchase 1% of both the equity and the debt of firm L, to create an equally low-risk portfolio that has a higher expected return than firm U shares alone. In other words, the investor would "unmake" firm L's leverage by lending on personal account. The key point in all of these examples is that the profit-maximizing activities of individual investors/arbitrageurs will force M&M's Proposition I to hold and will yield capital structure irrelevance whenever their no-tax, perfect capital markets assumptions are met.

7.3.4 Proposition II

So far, we have dwelt almost exclusively on M&M's Proposition I, and have barely mentioned their second famous proposition, which specifies what the expected return on levered equity must be for market equilibrium to hold. This is no oversight. We place greater relative emphasis on Proposition I because it is by far the more basic. In fact, if you accept Proposition I you have also accepted Proposition II, because it follows tautologically (by definition). We will demonstrate this, but first let's define Proposition II. It asserts that the expected return, k_j, on a levered firm's equity is a linear function of that firm's debt-to-equity ratio:

$$k_j = \rho_t + \frac{(\rho_t - r)\, D_j}{S_j} \tag{7.2}$$

In M&M's words, "*the expected yield of a share of stock is equal to the appropriate capitalization rate ρ_t for a pure equity stream in the class, plus a premium related to financial risk equal to the debt-to-equity ratio times the spread between ρ_t and r.*"

We should not find this definition of the required return surprising, because it yields exactly the same return we computed in our examples above to bring the market prices of firms U and L into equilibrium. If capital structure is irrelevant (if Proposition I holds), Proposition II tells us what the required return on levered equity must be for total firm market value to be unchanged—and for the overall cost of capital to remain constant—as debt is substituted for equity in a firm's capital structure.

In describing the capital structure irrelevance propositions, we have found a graph like that presented in Figure 7.2 to be helpful. This figure represents the expected net operating income of a firm over time as a mean value and a probability distribution of possible outcomes. Since we are representing a stream of risky cash flows stretching far into the future, the area under this bell-shaped curve is the financial value an investor sees when he or she evaluates an investment in this company. The firm's assets will generate this stream of profits, and an investor will assign a present value to this income stream by discounting each cash flow back to the present using a discount rate appropriate to a company with this degree of *business* risk.

So what, we hear you ask with a yawn. The importance of this valuation procedure is its assertion that economic value derives solely from the stream of operating profits a

FIGURE 7.2

GRAPHICAL DESCRIPTION OF THE VALUATION OF NET OPERATING CASH FLOWS IN THE MODIGLIANI AND MILLER (1958) MODEL

The bell-shaped distribution of expected net operating cash flows that will accrue to a firm in risk class k clearly reveals that it is this distribution of expected returns—characterized by a mean expected net operating income, E(NOI), and standard deviation, σ—that investors value, not how that distribution is carved into "equity" and "debt" cash flow streams. For example, the value of this firm would be the same whether the firm promised bondholders a cumulative cash flow claim of D or D*. In either case, the value of the firm is equal to E(NOI)/ρ, the capitalization rate of an all-equity firm with this level of business risk.

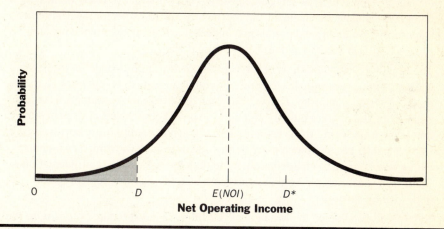

Net Operating Income

firm's assets will generate. This fundamental valuation cannot be either increased or decreased by repackaging ownership claims on the cash flow stream into "debt" and "equity" income streams. Value is derived from a company's investments and operations, not from financial marketing decisions.

7.3.5 Capital Structure Irrelevance in Real Financial Markets

Okay, you're convinced capital structure is irrelevant in a world with "perfect" markets, but what about the real world—where taxes must be paid and financial exchange is both noisy (filled with uncertainty) and costly? We will now try to demonstrate that, for certain types of companies and certain taxation regimes, the M&M assumptions may not be radically different from objective reality. To visualize this, assume that you are now an American private investor in the year 2006, and you are trying to assign valuations to two similar-sized hotel companies, one of which has no debt and one of which has a 90% debt: 10% equity capital structure. Both are large, well-managed companies that are routinely followed and reported on by dozens of security analysts, and both companies expect revenues to grow by no more than the rate of inflation (which itself is approaching zero percent). Now make three additional assumptions about legislation that was enacted early in the 21st century:

1. In the Third Millennium Tax Reform Act (TRA) of 2001, Congress replaced the current tax system—with its numerous different taxes—with a new system that raised the same revenue from only two taxes: a 20% value-added-tax (effectively a sales tax) on all business sales and a proportional income tax on all earned individual income. In order to make the U.S. more "capital friendly" in the fiercely competitive new century, the corporate profits tax was eliminated, as was the individual income tax on investment income (dividends, capital gains, and interest).[20]

2. The Bankruptcy Reform Act (BRA) of 2003 revised the U.S. bankruptcy code to more closely parallel those in other developed countries. The code in force during the late 1990s had been widely denounced as both wasteful and tilted too heavily in favor of incumbent management teams. The new law provided for much speedier bankruptcy resolutions and promised to reduce deadweight costs in the process, such as legal and accounting fees paid to third parties.

3. The Banking Deregulation Act (BDA) of 2005 allowed full-scale investment banking, and also eliminated several other impediments to competition in the financial services industry. Barriers between different money markets were also either removed or were quickly competed away. The net result of this act was that interest rates paid to savers and rates charged to creditworthy borrowers (like yourself) became much more nearly equal. In fact, for valued customers, banks were willing to charge barely more than the risk-free rate of interest on funds borrowed, and paid only slightly less than the risk-free rate on funds deposited by savers.

Under these conditions, the Modigliani & Miller capital structure propositions will hold even in the "real world". And lest you think our three legislative assumptions above are unrealistic, we should point out that all three have either been seriously proposed in the U.S. Congress or are currently the law of the land in other developed countries, or both.[21] More importantly, the assumptions we made above make clear what is required for capital structure to be irrelevant. Or, to turn this statement around, our assumptions point to factors that can make capital structure *relevant*.

---

20. While most business people are aware that corporate and personal tax *rates* in the United States are relatively low by international standards (see Rajan and Zingales 1994, Table IV), few realize that the American tax *system* is quite punitive in its treatment of corporate source income. The most egregious example of this is the system's walloping of dividends, which are taxed once when earned (at the corporate level, where federal, state, and local corporate income taxes take up to 47 percent) and then again when distributed to investors (where personal taxes on investment income take up to another 50 percent, depending upon the state of residence). Furthermore, individuals must pay capital gains taxes, at rates up to 36 percent, on all realized capital gains—and these gains are calculated on a nominal, not an inflation-adjusted, basis. Finally, all interest earned by individuals is taxed at their full marginal tax rates, while certain forms of interest paid on personal borrowings (mortgage interest payments, in particular) are tax deductible. In total, it is hard to imagine a tax system which does more to encourage borrowing and consumption, and discourage savings and investment, than that of the United States, and American corporations are at a significant disadvantage in their competition with companies based in more business-friendly countries.

21. We should also say that, in our opinion, all three proposals have great merit and should be adopted. Furthermore, we support most of the "flat tax" and/or national sales tax proposals currently (mid–1995) percolating through Congress.

7.3.6 What Can Make Capital Structure Relevant in the M&M Model?

In order to determine what can make capital structure matter in a M&M world, we need to examine what assumptions we needed in order to make leverage *irrelevant* in our example. Specifically: (1) we assumed that the companies in question were hotels with zero real growth rates because this allowed us to assume away the need for the firms to make large research and development expenditures or other intangible asset investments. Hotels are standardized, easily-valued, real assets that lose relatively little value in bankruptcy, and hotel management firms are unlikely to have access to many positive NPV investment opportunities. Therefore, *investment policy* differences were relatively unimportant in our example. (2) We assumed the companies were large and widely followed by security analysts because this (plus the fact that the hotel business is fairly easy to understand) allowed us to assume away the importance of *asymmetric information* between managers and shareholders. (3) We assumed the provisions of the TRA of 2001 because this made *taxes* irrelevant to corporate financing or personal investment decisions. Taxes exist, but they do not differentially affect corporate profits or investor income. (4) We assumed the provisions of the BRA of 2003 because this neutralized the importance of both the **tangible costs** (out-of-pocket cash payments) and **intangible costs of corporate bankruptcy** (lost sales due to lost customer confidence, the loss of key employees, diversion of management's attention, etc.). If a firm's value will be reduced by going through the bankruptcy *process*—as opposed to the decline in value that led to distress in the first place— then bankruptcy costs can reduce the amount of leverage most firms would wish to have. (5) We assumed the provisions of the BDA of 2005 to remove any benefit from corporations being able to borrow at lower interest rates than individuals. **Differential borrowing rates** (different borrowing and lending rates, or different borrowing rates for corporations and individuals) might also preclude investors from homemade leverage arbitrage.

Having examined the M&M capital structure propositions in a world of perfect capital markets, and having shown how they can still hold in an imperfect world, we will now examine the three main theories that have been put forth to explain observed capital structures. This is a good jumping-off point, because all three models take M&M as their base—they just disagree about which elements of reality are most important.

7.4 THE AGENCY COST/TAX SHIELD TRADE-OFF MODEL OF CORPORATE LEVERAGE

As we mentioned in the introduction to this chapter, finance researchers have been perplexed by capital structure questions for almost four decades. The M&M propositions suggest leverage should be irrelevant, but the real business world offers convincing evidence that corporate financial structures are neither random nor treated as minor, irrelevant details by corporate executives. In ongoing attempts to explain observed leverage ratios with an internally consistent theoretical model, finance academics and practitioners have incorporated more and more elements of reality into the basic M&M propositions. We will examine the impact that incorporating each of the topics below has on the original irrelevance model, and will then conclude this section with a summary of the current state of the Agency Cost/Tax Shield Trade-Off Model:

1. Corporate income taxes;

2. Personal taxes on investment income (dividends, capital gains, and interest);

3. Deadweight costs of bankruptcy and financial distress;

4. Agency problems (and costs) between managers, stockholders, and bondholders;

5. Contracting costs associated with writing and enforcing financial agreements;

6. Asset characteristics, earnings volatility, and a firm's investment opportunity set;

7. Ownership structure and corporate control.

7.4.1 Capital Structure with Corporate Income Taxes

The easiest way to demonstrate the impact of corporate income taxes is to refer back to the two firms, U and L, we used to develop capital structure irrelevance in perfect markets. We will use the same logic that Modigliani and Miller (1963) used in their "corrected" capital structure model, which explicitly incorporated a tax on corporate profits. Absent taxes, each of the firms in Table 7.3 has assets with a market value of $1,000,000. Firm U financed these assets completely with equity, while firm L used 50% equity and 50% debt, yielding a debt-to-total capital (debt plus equity) ratio of 50%. Each firm generates $100,000 in net operating income (NOI) each year, all of which goes to firm U's shareholders. Firm L, however, must pay $30,000 in interest on its debt ($500,000 with a 6% interest rate), leaving $70,000 for firm L's shareholders. Into this idealized world, let's incorporate a tax on corporate profits at a rate of 35%, τ_c = 0.35. This yields income statements for firms U and L as given in Table 7.5.

We can now compute the value of firm U, V_U, using the basic M&M valuation formula we used before, modified to discount profit after taxes (NI) rather than net operating income. We can also assume that investors still require an expected return (after tax) of 10 percent for firms in this risk class, so $\rho = 0.10$ as before. This yields:

$$V_U = \frac{[NOI(1 - \tau_c)]}{\rho} = \frac{NI}{\rho} = \frac{\$65,000}{0.10} = \$650,000 \qquad (7.3)$$

Therefore, the introduction of a 35 percent corporate profits tax causes an immediate $350,000 reduction in the market value of our all-equity company, Firm U. This represents a pure wealth transfer from firm U's shareholders to the government.

But what about firm L? How can we modify our valuation formula to reflect the ongoing value of the tax shield resulting from interest deductions? If the debt is assumed to be permanent (it will always be renewed at maturity), the interest deduction represents a perpetual tax shield equal to the tax rate times the amount of interest paid, $\tau_c \times rD = 0.35 \times (\$30,000) = \$10,500$ each year. To find the present value of this perpetuity, we capitalize this stream of benefits at r, the rate of interest charged on the firm's risk-free debt. If the debt were risky, we would still use the rate charged on the bonds, since the tax benefits are no riskier than the debt itself. With these assumptions, we can compute the present value of the interest tax shields to be:

$$PV \ Interest \ Tax \ Shields = \frac{(\tau_c \times rD)}{r} = \tau_c \times D$$

$$= 0.35(\$500,000) = \$175,000 \qquad (7.4)$$

In other words, the present value of interest tax shields on (perpetual) debt is equal to the tax rate times the face value of the debt outstanding. Therefore, the value of our

TABLE 7.5

INCOME STATEMENTS FOR FIRMS U AND L WITH CORPORATE INCOME TAXES

	Firm U	Firm L
Net Operating Income (NOI)	$100,000	$100,000
Interest Paid ($r \times D$)	0	$30,000
Taxable Income (NOI − rD)	$100,000	$70,000
Tax at 35% ($\tau_c = 0.35$)	($35,000)	($24,500)
Net Income (NI)	$65,000	$45,500
Total Income to Private Investors (Interest + Net Income)	$65,000	$75,500
Value of Tax Shield Each Period ($\tau_c \times r$D = 0.35 × Interest)	0	$10,500

levered firm L, V_L, is equal to the value of our unlevered firm plus the present value of the interest tax shields:

$$V_L = V_U + PV \text{ Tax Shield} = V_U + \tau_{cD}$$

$$= \$650,000 + \$175,000 = \$825,000 \tag{7.5}$$

What a deal! In essence, the government has given firm L's shareholders a $175,000 subsidy to employ debt financing rather than equity. But this cannot be an equilibrium. If a 50 percent debt-to-capital ratio increases total firm value by $175,000 over that of an otherwise equivalent unlevered firm, and each additional $1 of debt increases value by 35 cents, then the optimal leverage ratio for any firm is embarrassingly obvious—100 percent debt! This is the result M&M arrived at in 1963, though they never quite said as much, and it was this result more than any other which lessened initial acceptance of their propositions.

7.4.2 Capital Structure with Corporate *and* Personal Income Taxes

For fourteen years after the second M&M paper was published, finance authors and researchers were in a quandary. Their best theoretical models said capital structure was either irrelevant or should be set at 100 percent debt, but objective reality clearly suggested neither alternative was correct.[22] Then Miller (1977) offered an explanation for the fact that U.S. corporate leverage ratios had averaged between 30 and 40 percent of total capital for several decades (except during the Depression), in spite of the fact that

---

22. Several excellent theoretical extensions or modifications of the M&M theories were published during this period. As examples, see Farrar and Selwyn (1967), Hamada (1969), Stiglitz (1969), Kraus and Litzenberger (1973), and Stiglitz (1974). Three other papers tied capital structure theory to new developments in asset pricing and option pricing theory. See Hamada (1972), Rubinstein (1973), and Galai and Masulis (1976).

corporate tax rates had varied between zero (prior to 1913) and over 50 percent (during the 1950s) during the same period. He pointed out that personal tax rates on investment income had almost invariably been changed simultaneously with, and in the same direction as, changes in corporate tax rates.[23] Miller showed that a more sophisticated model that incorporated personal taxes could explain observed capital structure, without having to assume the presence of very large costs of financial distress. Empirical research had documented that the direct costs of corporate bankruptcy (discussed more fully in subsequent sections), at 1–5% of pre-bankruptcy firm value, were simply too small to offset the seemingly massive tax subsidy offered to corporations to use debt financing. Something else was clearly relevant, and Miller provided the following formula for computing the gains from using leverage, G_L, both for individual companies and for the corporate sector as a whole:

$$G_L \left[1 - \frac{(1 - \tau_c)(1 - \tau_{ps})}{(1 - \tau_{pd})} \right] D_L \tag{7.6}$$

where τ_c = Tax rate on corporate profits, as before
  τ_{ps} = Personal tax rate on income from stock (capital gains and dividends)
  τ_{pd} = Personal tax rate on income from debt (interest income)
  D_L = Market value of a firm's outstanding debt.

This is, in fact, a very general formulation. In a no-tax world ($\tau_c = \tau_{PS} = \tau_{PD} = 0$), the original M&M irrelevance proposition holds, while in a world with only corporate income taxes ($\tau_c = 0.35$, $\tau_{PS} = \tau_{PD} = 0$) the 100 percent optimal debt result again obtains. If, however, personal tax rates on interest income are sufficiently high, and personal tax rates on equity income are sufficiently low, the gains to corporate leverage can be dramatically reduced, or even offset entirely. To see this, assume for a moment (as Miller did) that $\tau_{ps} = 0$, which is not as wild as it might sound since investors only pay capital gains taxes upon realization (and taxes can be skipped entirely with careful estate planning), and can choose non-dividend-paying stocks to avoid personal taxes on equity income. With this assumption, we can plug into the gain-from-leverage formula the top corporate and personal income tax rates set forth in the Tax Reform Act of 1993, $\tau_c = 0.35$ and $\tau_{PD} = 0.40$ (actually, 39.6 percent, but 40 percent is easier to work with):

$$G_L = \left[1 - \frac{(1 - 0.35)(1 - 0)}{(1 - 0.4)} \right] D_L = (-0.083)D_L \tag{7.7}$$

As can be seen, with this set of tax rates, the "gain" from leverage is actually negative! Even with a personal tax on equity income of 7.7 percent, the gain from leverage is zero and capital structure is again irrelevant.

BOND MARKET EQUILIBRIUM IN THE MILLER (1977) MODEL   As important as Miller's gain-to-leverage model is, however, the most important contribution of his

---

23. For a listing of U.S. corporate and personal tax rates during the twentieth century, see Table 1.6 of Taggart (1985), while Beatty (1995) provides empirical evidence that the stock market values financial policies (i.e., employee stock ownership plans) that minimize corporate tax payments.

paper is to make clear what the interaction of corporate and personal taxes implied the equilibrium level of interest rates would be in a market economy. Consider what happens immediately after corporate income taxes are introduced into a previously untaxed economy. Whereas before, firms were indifferent between debt and equity, now income destined for shareholders is worth only $(1 - \tau_C)(NOI)$, while interest paid to bondholders escapes corporate taxation entirely. This means that firms have a massive incentive to issue debt, and will continue to do so until their additional supply drives up interest rates to the point where the tax advantages of the interest deduction are completely off-set by higher rates. This occurs when pre-tax, nominal interest rates are **grossed up** (increased to provide a given after-tax yield) from r to $r/(1 - \tau_C)$. At that point individual firms are again indifferent between issuing debt and equity, but the equilibrium level of debt in the economy—as well as average corporate leverage ratios—is far higher than in the no-tax case.

The more perceptive of you have probably noticed that we have not said anything yet about personal taxes due on interest income received by investors. Wouldn't taxable investors also demand that the rate paid to them be grossed up as compensation for taxes due? The answer is, yes—but. The reason why interest rates are not bid up immediately is that Miller makes two additional (and quite realistic) assumptions about capital market participants in his model. First, he assumes the existence of a sizable group of investors who do not have to pay tax on interest income. Real world examples of such investors include university endowment funds, certain trust funds, and corporate and public sector pension funds (American pension funds currently have assets of over $4 trillion). Second, he assumes that ordinary investors (subject to personal income tax) can choose to invest in risk- and personal-tax-free **municipal bonds** (bonds issued by American state and local governments). These bonds pay an interest rate of r_0, which is equal to the after-personal-tax return on riskless corporate bonds, or $(1 - \tau_{PD}) r$.

Given these assumptions, we can graphically represent the relationship between D, the total amount of corporate debt outstanding in an economy (shown on the horizontal axis of Figure 7.3) and the level of interest rates—shown on Figure 7.3's vertical axis. The horizontal line labeled $r_S(D)$ is the supply curve for corporate debt. As we argued above, corporations have an incentive to issue debt as long as equilibrium interest rates are less than or equal to this interest rate. The upward-sloping curve $r_D(D)$ is the demand curve for debt, and requires some explanation. Immediately after the imposition of corporate and personal income taxes, the economy would be at point r_0. Here corporations have a huge incentive to issue debt, tax-exempt investors are willing to buy debt (lend money) at this rate, and taxable investors shun taxable corporate debt in favor of tax-free municipal bonds.

This is not an equilibrium, however, because corporations still have the incentive to issue more debt—or, more precisely, to keep investment policy fixed, to issue debt and use the proceeds to repurchase equity. As this occurs, we move farther and farther out (to the right) on the flat portion of curve $r_D(D)$, until all tax-exempt demand for bonds has been met. What then? Corporations can no longer issue debt at rate r_0, but debt is still cheaper than issuing equity (r is still below $r_0/(1 - \tau_C)$). Companies must therefore entice taxable investors to purchase debt, beginning with those investors in the lowest tax brackets, by offering interest rates high enough to compensate them for the taxes they will have to pay. Once that demand is exhausted, corporations will raise rates further to entice investors in the next tax bracket, and so on until the marginal interest rate paid has been grossed up to equal $r_0 / (1 - \tau_c)$. At this point, represented as B^*, corporations are again indifferent between issuing debt and equity, and capital market equilibrium has been re-established. To put this another way, the first corporations to issue bonds after passage of the Income Tax Amendment to the U.S. Constitution in 1913 were able to issue debt at unusually low rates (at rates between r_0 and $r_0/(1 - \tau_c)$). But from that time forward equilibrium interest rates fully reflected investor tax rates, and capital structure has been irrelevant—from a tax standpoint—ever since.

EMPIRICAL EVIDENCE ON THE MILLER MODEL   While few people suggest that the Miller model is a perfect reflection of objective reality, the model is both intuitively appealing and supported by some (but not all) empirical research. For example, over long periods of time U.S. tax-exempt municipal bonds have generally offered nominal yields that are between 65 and 80 percent of the yield on corporate bonds of comparable risk and maturity, suggesting that the personal tax rate (τ_{PB}) of the marginal bond investor has fluctuated between 20 and 35 percent.[24] Further support for the need to consider both personal and corporate income taxes in economic models comes from research using data from countries such as Great Britain which have tax systems that seek to partially offset the tax incentive for corporate debt by giving investors a tax credit (for corporate taxes paid) on dividends received.[25] Tax changes which penalize equity income are apparently associated with declines in aggregate debt ratios, while the reverse is true for changes that increase tax rates on equity income. Only the arrogant among us, however, would claim anything like a precise understanding of exactly how taxes influence corporate decision-making. In a complex, $7 trillion economy like that of the United States, incremental effects of even something as important as a change in corporate tax rates is very hard to measure precisely.

FURTHER TAX EFFECT MODELS   Following Miller, several authors developed tax-based extensions of the basic capital structure models. The most important of these, DeAngelo and Masulis (1980), incorporates non-debt tax shields as substitutes for debt in corporate financial structures. The principal hypothesis in this model is that companies with large amounts of depreciation, investment tax credits, R&D expenditures, and other non-debt tax shields (NDTS) should employ less debt financing than otherwise equivalent companies with fewer such shields. Plausible as this hypothesis is, however, early research by Bradley, Jarrell, and Kim (1984) and Titman and Wessels (1988) found just the reverse. Leverage seemed to be directly, not inversely, related to the availability of NDTS. This was interpreted as evidence that assets which generated such tax shields could also be used as collateral for additional debt, so firms rich in tangible assets were able to use higher levels of (secured) debt. This **secured debt hypothesis** was first put forward by Scott (1977), and was later supported theoretically by Stulz and Johnson (1985) and empirically by Rajan and Zingales (1994). More recent research by MacKie-Mason (1990) has been able to measure the separate effects of NDTS and collateralizeable assets, and provides support for both the secured debt and the non-debt tax shields hypotheses.

24. See Trzcinka (1982), Ang, Peterson, and Peterson (1985), and Buser and Hess (1986).

25. See Peles and Sarnat (1978), Poterba and Summers (1985), and Ang and Megginson (1990).

FIGURE 7.3

BOND MARKET EQUILIBRIUM IN THE MILLER (1977) MODEL

This figure describes the demand curve for fully-taxable corporate bonds, yielding a nominal rate $r_d(B)$, as a function of the tax-exempt rate r_0, the supply of corporate bonds described by the ray $r_s(B)$, the corporate tax rate τ_c, and the personal tax rate on interest income τ^d_{PB}. Equilibrium occurs at B^* level of corporate debt outstanding, which itself occurs after the demand by tax-exempt investors for corporate bonds yielding r_0 is exhausted, and corporations must entice investors who face positive taxes on interest income. When the marginal investor's personal tax rate τ^d_{PB} equals the corporate tax rate, supply equals demand in the bond market, and capital structure is once again irrelevant for individual firms.

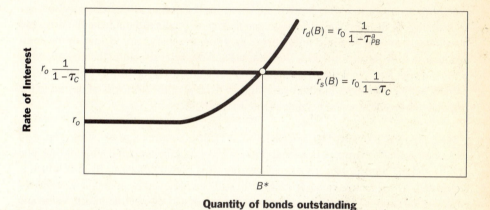

$$r_d(B) = r_0 \frac{1}{1 - T^a_{PB}}$$

$$r_0 \frac{1}{1 - \tau_c}$$

$$r_s(B) = r_0 \frac{1}{1 - \tau_c}$$

$$r_0$$

Rate of Interest

B^*

Quantity of bonds outstanding

SOURCE: "DEBT AND TAXES" BY MERTON H. MILLER, THE JOURNAL OF FINANCE, MAY 1977, VOL. XXXII, NO. 2, PAGE 269.

7.4.3 Costs of Bankruptcy and Financial Distress

Finance theorists have long realized that sufficiently large costs of bankruptcy and financial distress could dramatically reduce the incentive for firms to use debt financing, even in a world of otherwise perfect capital markets.[26] Furthermore, in the real world of finance, it seems painfully clear that overly-indebted companies can be severely penalized if they cease being able to service their debts, and managers of failed companies usually face bleak subsequent career prospects.[27] Practical experience also suggests that a bankrupt company's security-holders, even supposedly protected senior bondholders, frequently lose their entire investment in a firm. This problem seems particularly severe in the United States, where bankruptcy court protection often allows a company to continue operating (unprofitably) long after economic logic suggests it should be liquidated. Surely, then, the perceived costs of

---

26. The first major paper to prove this is Stiglitz (1969), who shows that all the other original M&M assumptions can be relaxed and the irrelevance results still obtain, but bankruptcy costs are critical.

27. See Altman (1984), Gilson, John, and Lang (1990), Opler and Titman (1994), and Hotchkiss (1995) for evidence that bankruptcy is costly for firms. Gilson (1989) and Gilson and Vetsuypens (1993) document that bankruptcy can be similarly painful for managers.

bankruptcy and financial distress can cause firms in one type of industry to employ less debt than similar-sized firms in other industries, right?

Perhaps. Before proceeding much farther in our discussion of how bankruptcy costs impact actual firm capital structures, we need to clearly differentiate between the decline in firm value that led to financial distress in the first place and the costs associated with the event of bankruptcy itself. To do this, we must briefly explain the legal process of bankruptcy. In the United States, a firm becomes bankrupt when it comes under the supervision of the federal government's bankruptcy courts, and ceases to operate as a separate, independently-contracting legal entity. A failing company can either file for bankruptcy protection itself (a voluntary filing) or, under certain conditions, the firm can be forced into bankruptcy court by its creditors (an involuntary filing). In either case, if the court accepts the petition, the court itself assumes ultimate supervisory responsibility for the company. The court can then choose either to liquidate the firm, and distribute the money received to the firm's creditors to satisfy their claims, or the court can choose to reorganize the firm's operations and financial structure, thereby allowing it to reemerge from bankruptcy as a new company. In theory, the firm's original shareholders will be wiped out in either case, and ownership of the firm will be passed to the original bondholders—who become the new stockholders.

WHAT MAKES BANKRUPTCY COSTS MATTER?   So what's your point, you ask? The point is that bankruptcy is a legal process involving the reorganization of financial claims and the transfer of corporate ownership. It is not a cremation. Even if a firm is liquidated, its remaining valuable assets will still be employed by someone else. Bankruptcy is the result of economic failure, not the cause, and the decline in firm value and loss of jobs commonly associated with the event of bankruptcy is actually what pushes the firm into bankruptcy court in the first place. In fact, think about what a bankruptcy filing actually means for a firm's shareholders. It means they are exercising their option to default on the company's debt, which is a key benefit of the limited liability feature of the corporate form of organization. Absent this feature, shareholders would have to pay off the firm's creditors out of their own pockets, instead of simply handing creditors the assets of the company in bankruptcy court. Consider also that most shareholders have well-diversified portfolios, so the possibility of loss on a single investment must surely be tolerable if the potential benefits of leverage and risk-taking are sufficiently attractive.

Therefore, unless the *process* of bankruptcy imposes costs on a company that would not be borne by a similarly-distressed, non-bankrupt firm, the mere possibility of falling into bankruptcy cannot significantly influence capital structure decision-making.[28] Similarly, financial leverage itself cannot be considered dangerous—and therefore something to be avoided—unless debt financing somehow makes encountering financial distress more painful for a levered company than it would be for an all-equity company. Since losing $10 million per quarter would be painful for either type of firm, the special significance of debt financing is far from obvious.

As the discussion above hopefully makes clear, costs associated with bankruptcy and financial distress will discourage the use of financial leverage only if: (1) encoun-

---

28. The classic exposition of this point is provided in Haugen and Senbet (1978).

tering financial distress would reduce market demand for a firm's products or increase its costs of production; (2) financial distress would give the firm's managers, operating as agents of the firm's shareholders, perverse operating or financial incentives to take actions likely to reduce overall firm value; or (3) entering bankruptcy would impose deadweight costs on a firm that would not be borne by an identical, non-bankrupt firm. This provides us with a useful way to discuss how financial distress might influence capital structures in the real world and, as you might imagine, empirical research indicates that these costs do significantly impact observed leverage ratios.[29]

Intuitively, it seems clear that certain types of firms should be able to weather financial distress better than others. If, for example, you wish to purchase a commodity item (unprocessed corn, pulpwood, basic machinery) or use a service only once (to print a set of business cards, to ship a load of goods to a single destination), you would care little whether the company you purchased that good or service from remained in existence after your transaction. If, on the other hand, you are contemplating the purchase of a large new computer system, or are choosing which airplane manufacturer's equipment to purchase, the long-term viability of the supplier becomes very important. As a general rule, therefore, producers of goods requiring warranties will have an incentive to use less debt than will firms producing non-durable goods or services, since it is more important for durable goods producers to assure customers that they will be able to provide ongoing service, warranty and repair work, and product improvements.

ASSET CHARACTERISTICS AND BANKRUPTCY COSTS   A firm's asset characteristics also influence its willingness to court financial distress by using relatively large amounts of debt financing. Companies which have assets that are mostly tangible in nature, and that have well-established secondary markets, should be less fearful of financial distress than companies whose assets are mostly intangible in nature. Therefore, trucking companies, airlines, construction firms, pipeline companies, and railroads can all employ relatively more debt than can companies with few if any tangible assets, such as pharmaceutical manufacturers, food distributors (what is the collateral value of week-old tomatoes?), or pure service companies. Financial distress can be particularly damaging to firms that produce research-and-development intensive goods and services, for two reasons. First, most of the expenses incurred in producing the good or service are **sunk costs** (which have already been spent, and thus should not affect prospective decisions), which can only be recovered with a long period of profitable sales. Second, "cutting edge" goods and services typically require ongoing research and development spending to ensure market acceptance, and a bankrupt (or impoverished) firm will be unable to finance such spending. One should also keep in mind that some intangible assets—such as patents, trademarks, and reputation—are both extremely valuable and very unlikely to survive financial distress or bankruptcy intact.

Financial distress can also dramatically increase the costs of production for many companies. Suppliers may be unwilling to extend credit to a company perceived as too

---

29. Direct evidence that firms have an incentive to avoid the deadweight costs of formal bankruptcy is provided in Gilson, John, and Lang (1990) and John, Lang, and Netter (1992). Financial contracting problems encountered by firms in or approaching bankruptcy are examined in Gilson, John, and Lang (1990), Brown, James, and Mooradian (1993), Franks and Torous (1994), Mooradian (1994), Denis and Denis (1995), and Hotchkiss (1995).

risky, or may do so only under very restrictive conditions. The firm may be unable to attract business partners for joint ventures or risk-sharing developmental projects. Perhaps most important of all, a highly-indebted firm may be unable to attract talented new employees, and may even see its own best people (who, by definition, are the most mobile) leave for more promising careers elsewhere. Any firm that is dependent upon the creativity, loyalty, and stability of its work force is thus particularly vulnerable to leverage-induced financial distress, and can be expected to employ less debt than other firms.

THE ASSET SUBSTITUTION PROBLEM   One of the most insidious problems associated with financial distress is that it provides otherwise-trustworthy managers with perverse, but rational, incentives to play a variety of financial and operating "games", mostly at bondholders' expense. Two such games are particularly important and potentially damaging. Both typically begin when a company first encounters financial difficulties and its managers realize the firm will probably be unable to pay off its debt to bondholders when the bonds mature. Assume that the firm still has some cash on hand that can either be simply held in reserve or be invested in one of two projects. Project *Boring* is a low-risk, positive-NPV investment opportunity that will increase firm value, but which does not itself offer a return high enough to fully pay off the maturing bonds. Project *Vegas*, on the other hand, is basically a gamble. It is an extremely risky, negative-NPV investment opportunity, but if the gamble is successful the project's return will be more than sufficient to fully pay off the firm's bonds when they mature.

Consider the manager's incentives in this case. Clearly, bondholders want the manager to either select project *Boring* or retain the firm's cash in reserve. But this is manifestly not in the interests of the firm's shareholders. Since they are effectively "playing with the bondholders' money", shareholders want the manager to accept project *Vegas*. If successful, the project will yield enough for shareholders to pay off the creditors and retain ownership of the firm. On the other hand, if project *Vegas* is unsuccessful, the shareholders will simply hand the (valueless) firm over to bondholders after defaulting on the maturing bonds. Shareholders have everything to gain and nothing to lose from this strategy, and their agent (the manager) controls the firm's investment policy until default actually occurs, so there is no way for the bondholders to prevent shareholders from executing the strategy that benefits them at bondholder expense.[30]

THE UNDERINVESTMENT PROBLEM   The second game set up by financial distress arises in similar circumstances—when a firm's managers realize default is likely, but still control investment policy until default actually occurs. Assume the firm gains access to a very profitable (but perishable) investment opportunity that promises to have a return sufficiently high to fully repay the firm's bonds when they mature, but financing the project would require the shareholders themselves to contribute all the cash needed. Accepting this project would maximize overall firm value, and would clearly benefit

---

30. For descriptions of the often exquisitely detailed terms that are inserted into bond covenants by bondholders to protect themselves from strategic behavior by shareholders (and managers, their agents), see Smith and Warner (1979), Asquith and Wizman (1990), Crabbe (1991), and Bae, Klein, and Padmaraj (1994). In a related vein, Leland (1994) uses bond covenants to derive a closed-form analytical model of long-term debt values and optimal capital structure.

the bondholders, but the shareholders would rationally choose not to accept the project, since they would have to finance the investment but most of the benefit would accrue to the bondholders.[31]

An all-equity firm would not be vulnerable to either of the two games associated with financial distress discussed above. Managers would always choose the firm-value-maximizing project in the first example, and would always contribute cash for positive-NPV projects in the second example. Because these costs of financial distress are related to conflicts of interest between two groups of security-holders, they are also referred to as *agency costs* of the relationship between bondholders and stockholders.

DIRECT AND INDIRECT COSTS OF BANKRUPTCY   Finally, if the process of bankruptcy is itself sufficiently costly, firms can have a reason to limit financial leverage in order to minimize the possibility of being forced into the bankruptcy courts. To make clear how this might be possible, we need to differentiate between the **direct** and **indirect costs of bankruptcy**. Direct costs are out-of-pocket cash expenses directly related to bankruptcy filing and administration. Document printing and filing expenses, as well as professional fees paid to lawyers, accountants, investment bankers, and court personnel are all examples of direct bankruptcy costs. While these can run to several million dollars per month for complex cases, empirical research indicates that they are much too small—relative to the pre-bankruptcy market value of large firms—to provide an effective deterrent to the use of debt financing.[32] Indirect bankruptcy costs, as the name implies, are expenses or economic losses that result from bankruptcy but are not cash expenses spent on the process itself. These include the diversion of management's time while bankruptcy is underway, lost sales during and after bankruptcy, constrained capital investment and R&D spending, and the loss of key employees after a firm becomes bankrupt.

EMPIRICAL EVIDENCE ON BANKRUPTCY COSTS   While indirect bankruptcy costs are inherently difficult to measure, empirical research clearly suggests they are quite significant.[33] Recent studies have documented that: (1) firms entering bankruptcy have lower sales in the years after filing than they were expected to have based upon an extrapolation of pre-bankruptcy sales growth rates; (2) managers of bankrupt firms lose their jobs much more frequently than do managers of non-bankrupt firms, the pay of those managers who retain their jobs is dramatically reduced in comparison with managers in other firms, and their chances of being rehired by other large companies are virtually nil; (3) American courts frequently deviate from the absolute priority rules that are supposed to govern wealth distributions among security-holders. This adds uncertainty to the predicted outcomes of bankruptcy, increasing the risk to all claimants and increasing the incentives for some parties—particularly shareholders

---

31. This incentive problem associated with leverage is first described in Myers (1977).

32. See Warner (1977) for evidence that the direct costs of bankruptcy are usually of essentially trivial magnitude for large firms.

33. Altman (1984) provides the best *empirical* evidence to date that the indirect costs of financial distress are large enough to discourage excessive use of financial leverage. Indirect evidence that high leverage weakens a firm's industrial competitiveness is provided by Lang and Stulz (1992), Opler and Titman (1994), and Phillips (1995).

and employees—to engage in "strategic behavior"; (4) bankruptcy costs are much higher in the U.S. than in other advanced countries, and court decisions generally favor managers over creditors in determining when a company should be liquidated; and (5) bankruptcy reduces a firm's debt levels far less than might be expected, and far less than is usually needed, leaving many firms vulnerable to re-entering bankruptcy a second or even third time.[34]

Other studies provide indirect evidence that increasing risk of bankruptcy is associated with lower observed leverage levels. Specifically, researchers have documented that: (6) firms with highly variable earnings use less debt than do those with more stable profits; (7) observed leverage ratios across industries are systematically related to that industry's investment opportunity set in the way we expect—capital-intensive industries with few growth options tend to be highly levered, while technology-based industries with many growth options employ relatively little debt; and (8) leverage ratios appear to be directly related to the ease with which a firm's assets can pass through bankruptcy without losing value. Clearly, bankruptcy costs significantly influence capital structure decisions in complex, but largely predictable ways. This allows us to expand our basic valuation formula to express the value of a levered firm, V_L, in terms of the value of an unlevered firm, V_t, the present value of the benefits from debt and non-debt tax shields, and the present value of expected bankruptcy costs:

$$V_l = V_t + PV\ Tax\ Shields - PV\ Bankruptcy\ Costs \qquad (7.8)$$

One can clearly begin to understand why the theory we are developing is referred to as the "trade-off" model of corporate capital structure, since it assumes that firm managers trade off the tax-related benefits of increasing leverage against the bankruptcy and agency costs that grow progressively worse as leverage rises.

7.4.4 Agency Costs and Capital Structure

An agency cost theory of financial structure is put forward by Jensen and Meckling (1976). Few papers in the history of finance (or even economics) have had a comparable impact on how we view issues of corporate control, capital structure, or financial contracting. Jensen and Meckling observe that when an entrepreneur owns 100 percent of the stock of a company there is no separation between corporate ownership and control. In plain English, this means that the entrepreneur bears all of the costs, and reaps all of the benefits, of his or her actions. Once a fraction, α, of the firm's stock is sold to outside investors, however, the entrepreneur bears only $1 - \alpha$ of the consequences of his or her actions. This gives the entrepreneur a clear incentive to, in Jensen and Meckling's tactful phrasing, "consume perquisites" (goof off, purchase a corporate jet, frequently tour the firm's plant in Hawaii, become a regular "business commentator" on television). By selling off a stake in the company the entrepreneur lowers the cost of engaging in such activity by α times the dollar cost, so he or she bears only $(1 - \alpha)$ times the cost. Nice deal for the entrepreneur, right?

---

34. The predilection of American bankruptcy courts to violate absolute priority rules is documented in Eberhart, Moore, and Roenfeldt (1990), Franks and Torous (1989), Weiss (1990), Hotchkiss (1995), and Betker (1995).

Not in an efficient market! Informed investors expect the entrepreneur's performance to change after they purchase their α stake in the firm, and they will thus only pay a price per share that fully reflects the expected induced decline in firm value that will result from the entrepreneur's consumption of "perks". In other words, the entrepreneur is charged in advance for the perks he or she is expected to consume after the equity sale, so the entrepreneur once again bears the full costs of his or her actions. Furthermore, society suffers because these **agency costs of (outside) equity** reduce the market value of corporate assets by $(1 - \alpha)$ times the expected value of entrepreneurial perquisite consumption. We are therefore at an impasse. Selling stock to outside investors creates agency costs of equity, which are borne solely by the entrepreneur, but which also harm society by reducing the value of corporate assets and discouraging additional entrepreneurship. Selling external equity is vital for entrepreneurs, however, both because of individual portfolio diversification demands and because of the need to finance corporate growth once it outstrips personal wealth constraints.

USING DEBT TO OVERCOME THE AGENCY COSTS OF OUTSIDE EQUITY
Jensen and Meckling point out that using debt financing can help overcome the agency costs of external equity in two ways. First, using debt by definition means that less external equity will have to be sold to raise a given dollar amount of external financing. If agency costs of outside equity rise more than proportionally as α increases, then economizing on the amount of outside equity sold will reduce the deadweight agency costs of the manager/stockholder relationship. The second, and more important, effect of employing outside debt rather than equity financing is that this reduces the scope for excessive managerial perquisite consumption. The burden of having to make regular, contractually-enforceable, debt service payments serves as a very effective tool for disciplining entrepreneurs. With debt outstanding, the cost of excessive perk consumption might well include the entrepreneur losing control of his or her company following default and bondholder seizure of the company's assets. In Jensen and Meckling's words, external debt serves as a **bonding mechanism** for managers to convey their good intentions to outside shareholders. Because taking on debt validates that managers are willing to risk losing control of their firm if they fail to perform effectively, shareholders are willing to pay a higher price for the firm's shares.

Lest you think this is all esoteric theory, consider for a minute just how important the agency costs of equity are for the typical large, publicly-traded American corporation. Insiders (managers and directors) of most *Fortune 500* companies own less than 5 percent of their company's shares (in a majority of cases, less than 2 percent), yet they reap all of the financial and non-financial benefits of controlling a large, prestigious organization.[35] The typical CEO of such a company makes over $2,000,000 per year in salary, bonuses, and stock options, and some directors receive fees and services worth as much as $100,000 per year for attending fewer than a dozen meetings.[36]

---

35. The literature in this area is vast. For a sampling of the best papers on the impact of insider shareholdings on corporate financial policies, see Demsetz and Lehn (1985), Jensen (1986), Mikkelson and Partch (1989), and Barclay and Holderness (1989). Finally, Maloney, McCormick, and Mitchell (1993) document that leverage improves managerial decision-making in key situations (i.e., acquisitions).

36. See, for example, Jensen and Murphy (1990) and Kaplan (1994).

CAPITAL MARKET MONITORING OF CORPORATE MANAGERS   Now, consider what you as a shareholder can do to discipline management if you become dissatisfied with the performance of one of the companies you have invested in. Virtually nothing! Even if you represent an institutional investor with a $10,000,000 stake in a large company, your shares represent a tiny fraction of the total outstanding, and management can ignore you with virtual impunity. You can vote against management at the annual shareholders meeting, but—given that the rules of corporate governance stack the deck in management's favor—the question again becomes, so what? You can sell your shares on the open market, but if management's actions have driven down their market price, who suffers when you sell at a loss? You can try to sue management for malfeasance, but this is extremely hard to prove and the **Business Judgement Rule** (which gives directors broad legal discretion to use their business judgement) protects boards of directors from shareholder second-guessing in all but egregious cases of abuse. Besides, who can hire the best team of lawyers—you or a *Fortune 500* company? Furthermore, even if you were to "win" either in court or by directly challenging management, you would have borne all of the financial costs of improving corporate performance personally (and been "dragged through the mud" by management in the process), but the vast bulk of the benefits of your actions would go to the other, passive shareholders.

You are probably thinking that an active takeover market might rescue you as a shareholder from the grip of an entrenched, self-enriching management team. Think again! The takeover wars of the 1980's are over, and it is tempting to conclude that management won. Court decisions, state antitakeover laws, the development of poison pills and other defensive innovations, federal regulations, and the general tightening of credit in the 1990s have all combined to make it extremely difficult to mount a successful, hostile takeover of a company controlled by managers intent on remaining in place.[37] Furthermore, the fact that bidding firms were able to offer target firm shareholders such huge premiums during the 1980s only suggests just how important agency problems between managers and shareholders had become. Without even the threat of hostile takeover, how serious have these agency problems become today?

The point of the tirade above is not to berate inept management teams (therapeutic as that might be), but to make clear that agency costs between managers and stockholders are real, pervasive, and very difficult to effectively reduce. One way to control these costs is for the firm to issue debt. This actually accomplishes two things. First, it forces managers to directly confront and be monitored by the public capital market (see Easterbrook 1984). If investors have a negative view of management's competence, they will charge a high interest rate on the money they lend to the firm, or they will insist on restrictive bond covenants to constrain management's freedom of action, or both. Second, outstanding debt effectively limits management's ability to reduce firm value through incompetence or perquisite consumption. If management is unable to operate the firm well enough to at least cover debt service payments (interest and principal repayments), the firm will be forced into bankruptcy, the bondholders will take control of the firm, and the offending managers will be invited to seek employment elsewhere. By choosing to issue debt, managers voluntarily accept this risk of being replaced, and this reduces the agency costs of the manager/stockholder relationship (see Jensen 1986).

---

37. An overview and description of the corporate control market in the United States is provided in chapter 2.

AGENCY COSTS OF OUTSIDE DEBT   Why then don't firms use "maximum debt" financing? Good question. The answer is because there are also agency costs of debt, some of which we alluded to in our earlier discussion of bankruptcy costs. As the fraction of debt in a firm's capital structure increases, bondholders begin taking on an increasing fraction of the firm's business and operating risk, but shareholders and managers still control the firm's investment and operating decisions. This gives managers a variety of incentives to expropriate bondholder wealth for the benefit of themselves and the shareholders they represent. The easiest way to do this would be to float a bond issue, then pay out the money raised to shareholders as a dividend. After default, the bondholders would be left with an empty corporate shell, and limited liability would prevent the bondholders from trying to collect directly from shareholders.[38]

Another way the shareholders can separate gullible bondholders from their wealth is to borrow money on the promise that it will be used to finance a "safe" investment (remember project *Boring*), and then actually invest in a risky project (such as project *Vegas*). If lenders are convinced their money will be employed prudently, they will accept a lower interest rate on the funds they lend. Therefore, if managers and stockholders can find enough naive bondholders, they can borrow at a "safe" interest rate and then make high risk/high return investments. If these investments are successful, shareholders can fully repay bondholders and pocket any excess project returns. If the project is unsuccessful, shareholders simply default and bondholders take over an empty corporate shell. This game of promising to accept a safe project, then accepting a risky project after securing low-cost financing is called **bait-and-switch**, and it can be devastating for bondholders.

As you might imagine, very few naive bondholders are still around (wisdom comes from survived pain), and the remaining bond investors take steps to effectively prevent managers from playing these games with their money. The most effective preventive steps bond investors can take involve writing very detailed **covenants** into bond contracts, which sharply constrain the ability of the borrowing firm's managers to engage in expropriative behavior.[39] Unfortunately, these covenants make bond agreements immensely costly to negotiate and enforce, and in constraining management's ability to make value-decreasing investment decisions these covenants often also prevent managers from making value-increasing investments (see Smith and Warner 1979). For example, if a bond covenant limits a firm's ability to issue additional debt of equal seniority (a frequently observed bond covenant), managers may be forced to pass up value-increasing investments such as synergistic mergers or major capital expenditures for new plant and equipment if these investments would have to be financed in part with newly-issued bonds. Other covenants almost invariably restrict (but do not prevent) dividend payments, even for very profitable firms (see Kalay 1982). This means a firm may be forced to over-invest (in negative-NPV projects) if current profits are high and positive-NPV investment opportunities

---

38. See Kalay (1982) for a description of how bondholders protect themselves from expropriative dividend policies. Bathala, Moon, and Rao (1994) discuss the interaction between insider ownership, institutional shareholdings, and debt policy in an agency cost framework.

39. These may be classified as either **positive** or **negative covenants**, depending upon whether they mandate what the borrowing *must do* (provide audited financial statements, maintain the firm's assets, purchase business and liability insurance) or *must not do* (merge or sell off assets, issue new senior debt, allow key financial ratios to reach danger levels). These are described in more depth in chapter 9.

are exhausted. These **agency costs of debt** can be quite real, and become progressively more important as a firm's leverage ratio increases.

BALANCING THE AGENCY COSTS OF OUTSIDE EQUITY AND DEBT   You can probably see where we are headed. Jensen and Meckling's model predicts that managers of an individual firm, starting from an all-equity position, will substitute bonds for stock in the firm's capital structure in order to reduce the agency costs of equity. As this process continues, however, the agency costs of debt begin to rise at an increasing rate. The firm's optimal (value-maximizing) debt-to-equity ratio is reached at the point where the agency cost of an additional dollar of debt exactly equals the agency cost of the dollar of equity retired.

We are now ready to tie together all of the threads of the modern Agency Cost/Tax Shield Trade-off Model of corporate capital structure. This model expresses the value of a levered firm in terms of the value of an unlevered firm, adjusted for the present values of tax shields, bankruptcy costs, and the agency costs of debt and equity as follows:

$$V_L = V_U + \frac{PV\ Tax}{Shields} - \frac{PV\ Bankruptcy}{Costs}$$

$$+ \frac{PV\ Agency\ Costs}{of\ Outside\ Equity} - \frac{PV\ Agency\ Costs}{of\ Outside\ Debt} \tag{7.9}$$

This model provides an understandable and intuitively attractive explanation for how capital structures are actually set by real corporations. While no one pretends the individual components of this model are easy to estimate empirically, much of the available research on capital structure both in the United States and internationally is consistent with the model's predictions (see, especially, Rajan and Zingales 1994).

7.5   THE PECKING ORDER HYPOTHESIS OF CORPORATE CAPITAL STRUCTURE

While the trade-off model of corporate leverage has to be considered the "mainstream" choice as the dominant capital structure theory today, there are several embarrassing regularities in observed corporate behavior that it cannot explain. Three real-world patterns are particularly hard to reconcile with even the most sophisticated trade-off model: (1) within virtually every industry, the most profitable firms have the lowest debt ratios—which is exactly the opposite of what a tax-effect trade-off model predicts; (2) leverage-increasing events, such as stock repurchases and debt-for-equity exchange offers, are almost invariably associated with large positive abnormal returns for a company's stockholders, while leverage-decreasing events lead to stock price declines. According to the trade-off model, these events should both net out to zero abnormal returns, since some firms will be below their "optimal" debt level when they increase leverage while others will be above the optimum; (3) firms issue debt securities frequently, but seasoned equity issues are very rare.[40] In fact, few American companies

---

40. For example, Pratt (1995) reports that while American issuers sold securities worth $708.6 billion in U.S. capital markets during 1994 (versus $1,056 *trillion* in 1993), only $27.5 billion ($44.6 billion) of this was seasoned common equity sold by publicly-traded companies.

issue new stock as frequently as once per decade, and non-U.S. firms are even shier about new equity issues. Furthermore, announcements of new issues of seasoned equity are invariably greeted with a decline in the firm's stock price—sometimes the stock price decline represents one-third or more of the amount of new capital that the issue is intended to raise.[41]

7.5.1 Assumptions Underlying the Pecking Order Hypothesis

How do we as financial economists account for these perplexing facts about observed capital structures? One answer to this question was put forward by Stewart Myers (1984), when he proposed the **Pecking Order Hypothesis of Corporate Leverage**. This model is based on four observations and/or assumptions about corporate financial behavior: (1) Dividend policy is "sticky". Managers try at all costs to maintain a constant dollar-per-share dividend payment, and will neither increase nor decrease dividends in response to temporary fluctuations in current profits;[42] (2) firms prefer internal financing (retained earnings and depreciation) to external financings of any sort, debt or equity; (3) if a firm must obtain external financing, it will choose the safest security first; (4) as a firm is required to obtain more external financing, it will work down the pecking order of securities, beginning with very safe debt, then progressing through risky debt, convertible securities, preferred stock, and finally common stock as a last resort. This model focuses on the motivations of the corporate manager, rather than on capital market valuation principles.

In its crudest form, this pecking order theory had been in circulation for many years prior to Myers' presidential address, but had largely been ignored by modern economists because it seemed to be based on irrational, value-decreasing corporate behavior that financial natural selection should have excised long before. And, indeed, the simple pecking order model presumes severe market imperfections (very high transactions costs, uninformed investors, and managers who are completely insensitive to the firm's stock market valuation) that are hard to accept as accurate portraits of modern capital markets. Myers provides a viable theoretical justification for the pecking order theory, based on asymmetric information, in Myers and Majluf (1984). Myers and Majluf make two key (and plausible) assumptions about corporate managers. First, they assumed a firm's managers know more about the company's current earnings and investment opportunities than do outside investors. Second, they assumed managers act in the best interests of the firm's *existing* shareholders.

Why are these two assumptions crucial? The asymmetric information assumption implies that managers who develop or discover a marvelous new positive-NPV investment opportunity are unable to convey that information to outside shareholders because the managers' statements will not be believed. After all, every management team has an incentive to announce wondrous new projects in order to bid up the firm's stock price, so they can sell shares at an unjustifiably high price. And, since investors are unable to verify these claims until long after the fact, they will assign a low average value to the

---

41. See especially Asquith and Mullins (1986).

42. This is one of the most constant phenomena in all of finance. In fact, corporate managers are as intent on maintaining stable nominal dividend payments today as they were when Lintner (1956) first documented this behavior in the 1950s.

stocks of all firms and will buy new equity issues only at a large discount from their equilibrium values without informational asymmetries. Corporate managers understand these problems, and in certain cases will refuse to accept positive-NPV investment opportunities if this would entail issuing new equity, since this would give away too much of the project's value to the new shareholders at the expense of the old.

What a mess! Investors cannot trust managers, so they place a low value on common stocks, and managers are forced to forego valuable investment opportunities because they cannot credibly convey their private information to existing (old) shareholders. Furthermore, information problems in financial markets are problems caused by human nature, and thus are not soluble through reductions in transactions costs or other capital market innovations. So what is the solution to this pervasive problem of modern corporate finance? According to Myers and Majluf, the solution is for corporations to retain sufficient *financial slack* to be able to fund positive-NPV projects internally.

Financial slack is defined to include a firm's cash and marketable securities holdings, as well as unused (risk-free) debt capacity. Firms with sufficient financial slack will never have to issue risky debt or equity securities in order to fund their investment projects, and they are thus able to finesse asymmetric information problems between managers and investors. In addition, the Fisherian optimal investment rule is once again in force, since managers can accept all positive-NPV projects without harming existing shareholders. Perhaps most important, this model provides an explanation for the observed pattern of profitable firms retaining their earnings as equity and building up their cash reserves—they are building both financial slack and financial flexibility.[43]

The Myers and Majluf model also explains stock market reactions to leverage-increasing and leverage-decreasing events. Since firms with valuable investment opportunities find a way to finance their projects internally, or use the least risky securities possible if they have to obtain financing externally, the only firms that will issue equity are those with managers who consider the firm's shares to be over-valued. Investors understand these incentives, and also realize that managers are better informed about a firm's prospects than they are, and therefore investors always greet the announcement of a new equity issue as "bad news" (as a sign that management considers the firm's shares to be over-valued).

7.5.2 Implications of the Pecking Order Hypothesis

Taking the Pecking Order model a step further explains several other observed patterns of behavior. Since we know that new equity issues are punished by the stock market, it follows that managers will issue stock—or undertake other leverage-decreasing activities—only if they are either forced to do so by an earnings shortfall or are voluntarily acting against the interests of their existing shareholders in order to enrich themselves. In either case, this explains why leverage-decreasing events are associated with stock price declines. Conversely, the announcement of a leverage-increasing event suggests that a corporation's managers are confident enough of the firm's future earnings power that they

---

43. The impact of financial slack on takeover decisions is described in Bruner (1988), Lang, Stulz, and Walkling (1991), and Smith and Kim (1994).

can increase corporate debt levels without impairing the firm's ability to fund its investments internally. Therefore, leverage-increasing events are greeted warmly by stock market traders.

The pervasiveness of the informational asymmetry between corporate managers and shareholders also provides a rationale for the development of financial intermediaries. Not all companies with positive-NPV investment opportunities will be lucky enough to have financial slack on hand to finance these projects. Young, entrepreneurial growth companies are especially likely to have more valuable investment projects than they can finance through retained earnings, and these companies are also the most prone to experience serious informational asymmetry problems. Banks and other financial intermediaries are able to effectively overcome these information problems by becoming corporate "insiders" through repeated contact with the firm's managers, and by having proprietary access to the firm's financial statements and operating plans. As mutual trust between management and the intermediary develops, the intermediary is able to assess, and meet, the company's financial needs with one or more credit instruments (or even through direct equity investment, in countries where this is allowed). The intermediary is also in a position to monitor managerial performance, and to directly intervene in the firm's operations at the first sign of serious trouble. A financial intermediary is therefore able to directly finance, and monitor the performance of, corporate borrowers without having to overcome the problems of capital market informational asymmetries. This helps explain the pattern of bank-related corporate financing observed in most advanced countries besides the United States, and also explains why American corporations that maintain close relationships with banks and other intermediaries seem to enjoy higher market valuations than do other firms that rely strictly on capital markets for their external financing.

7.5.3 Limitations of the Pecking Order Hypothesis

Unfortunately, the Pecking Order Theory cannot explain all the capital structure regularities observed in practice. For example, it suffers in comparison with the trade-off theory in its inability to explain how taxes, bankruptcy costs, security issuance costs, and an individual firm's investment opportunity set influence that company's actual debt ratio.[44] Furthermore, the theory ignores significant agency problems that can easily arise when a firm's managers accumulate so much financial slack that they become immune to market discipline. This can occur if a firm has no need to raise new external funds, and thus cannot be directly penalized via a low security price, and has amassed so much financial slack (augmented with non-financial take over defenses) that its managers are immune to forced removal following a hostile acquisition.[45] Nonetheless, the Pecking Order Hypothesis of capital structure seems to explain certain aspects of observed corporate behavior better than any other models do, and this is particularly true of corporate financing choices (what types of securities firms choose to issue) and market responses to security issues.

---

44. On the other hand, Shyam-Sunder and Myers (1993) empirically compare the Pecking Order and Trade-off models of corporate leverage, and find the Trade-off model wanting. In fact, their tests show that the power of some usual tests of the Trade-off model to be virtually nil.

45. Several examples of this are provided in Jensen (1989, 1993).

7.6   SIGNALING AND OTHER ASYMMETRIC INFORMATION MODELS OF CORPORATE LEVERAGE

Beginning in the late 1970s, Ross (1979) and other authors developed a signaling model of corporate capital structure based on asymmetric information problems between well-informed managers and poorly-informed outside shareholders.[46] These models are based on the idea that corporate executives with favorable inside information about their firms have a clear incentive to somehow convey this positive information to outside investors, in order to cause an increase in the firm's stock price. Given the asymmetric information problems, however, managers cannot simply announce that they have good news because every other manager has the same incentives, and shareholders will be properly skeptical about any self-serving statement that can only be validated with the passage of time (talk really is cheap).

7.6.1   How Signaling with Capital Structure Can Convey Information

One solution to this problem is for managers of high-value firms to *signal* this information to investors by taking some action—or adopting some financial policy—that is prohibitively costly for less valuable firms to duplicate ("mimic"). As used in the finance and economics literature, a **signal** is an action that imposes deadweight costs on the signaler in order to convey value to relatively poorly informed outsiders (usually investors). The signal is credible if it is prohibitively costly for a weaker firm to attempt to mimic. Ross (1977) shows that it is possible to design an incentive-based compensation contract for managers of high-value firms that will induce them to adopt a heavily-leveraged capital structure for their companies. Less valuable companies are unwilling to assume so much debt because they are much more likely to fall into bankruptcy, with all its deadweight costs. Given these assumptions, a **separating equilibrium** occurs where high-value firms use a great deal of debt financing and less valuable companies rely more on equity financing.[47] Investors are able to differentiate between high- and low-value firms by observing their capital structures, and are willing to assign higher valuations to highly levered firms. Finally, since weaker firms are unwilling to mimic the stronger ones (by taking on extra debt), the equilibrium is stable.

7.6.2   Empirical Evidence on Capital Structure Signaling Models

While this model, and the other signaling models that follow, are intuitively attractive, observed capital structure patterns suggest they are poor predictors of actual behavior. As we have seen, leverage ratios are inversely related to profitability in almost every industry—not directly related as the signaling models predict. Furthermore, the signaling model predicts that industries rich in growth options and other intangible assets

---

46. In addition to Ross, later papers include John (1987), Blazenko (1987), Noe (1988), and Narayanan (1988).

47. The alternative to a separating equilibrium is a **pooling equilibrium**, which occurs when signalling cannot differentiate between good and bad firms. Instead, all firms are pooled, and treated as a single group.

should employ more debt than mature, tangible-asset-rich industries because growth companies have more severe information asymmetry problems, and thus greater need to signal. As we know, exactly the opposite pattern is observed—asset-rich companies use far more debt than do growth companies.

On the other hand, the signaling models do explain market responses to the different types of security issues quite well. Debt issues signal good news (managers are confident about the future), and are greeted with a positive stock price response, while equity issues signal bad news (earnings will decline in the future), and are met with significant stock price declines. Signaling models will surely be refined further in the future, and could well benefit from an emerging literature that ties capital structure to specific characteristics of the product and factor markets that a given firm operates in.[48] For now, however, we must look primarily to the Agency Cost/Tax Shield Trade-Off and the Pecking Order theories for consistent explanations of how capital structures are set in the all-too-real world of modern corporate finance. In theory, as in the financial markets, may the best model win!

—SUMMARY—

Modern corporate finance theory was born with the publication of Modigliani and Miller's capital structure theoretical model in 1958. They showed that, in a capital market free of taxes, transactions costs, and other frictions, the choice of a firm's capital structure could not affect its market valuation—because investors could make or unmake any level of leverage they desired by borrowing or lending on personal account. Much of the history of capital structure theory during the past forty years has involved examining how robust the model is to more realistic assumptions regarding market frictions and the information sets available to managers and shareholders. The development of agency theory in the 1980s, coupled with detailed research into the extent and effects of bankruptcy costs during the 1980s, lead to a yet more detailed view of the utility of the basic M&M capital structure theory. Finally, cross-cultural examination of observed capital structure patterns in non-U.S. industrialized countries has lead to our current mainstream view that corporations act as if there is a unique, optimal capital structure for individual firms that results from a trade-off between the tax benefits of increasing leverage and increasing agency and bankruptcy costs that higher debt entails.

This is not to suggest that the mainstream trade-off model reigns unchallenged. Numerous researchers—particularly Stewart Myers—have pointed out real "blind spots" that the trade-off theory cannot explain. This is particularly true of the observed stock market reaction to leverage-increasing and leverage-decreasing (i.e., seasoned equity issues) transactions, which consistently yield stock price increases and decreases, respectively. As an alternative to the trade-off model, Myers has put forth his Pecking Order hypothesis of Corporate Leverage. It predicts that firms will prefer internal financing to issuing securities, and if forced to resort to external financing will use debt

---

48. See, as examples, Wedig, Sloan, Hassan, and Morrisey (1988), Kim and Maksimovic (1990), and Maksimovic and Titman (1991). Harris and Raviv (1991) provide a thorough review of these and other information-based leverage models.

before equity. This model explains many observed patterns in corporate finance, including the tendency of firms not to issue stock and their choice to hold surprisingly large cash reserves and other forms of "financial slack." While promising, the Pecking Order model has its own drawbacks, and is not yet a potent challenger to the trade-off model.

Finally, various signaling models of capital structure have also been proposed which suggest that managers use leverage to signal firm prospects to poorly informed outside investors—who believe these signals because they are prohibitively costly for weak firms to mimic. Unfortunately, these models (or at least the early versions) generally predict that the firms with the best earnings and growth prospects will employ the most leverage—which is the opposite of observed behavior. To date, the trade-off theory of corporate capital structure is the reigning champion, but we should all stay tuned!

—QUESTIONS—

1. How would the development of a truly comprehensive and accurate theory of capital structure help policy-makers and corporate executives around the world?

2. List and briefly describe at least five of the "stylized facts" about international capital structure patterns.

3. What would it mean to say that capital structure is a "residual?" If true, what would this imply about observed capital structure patterns?

4. Discuss the evidence concerning the stock market reaction to leverage-changing events (security issues, methods of takeover financing, etc.). What does this evidence suggest about capital structure theory?

5. Briefly discuss the empirical evidence regarding the relationship between ownership structure and capital structure.

6. [Essay question] List and briefly discuss the assumptions underlying the Modigliani and Miller (1958) capital structure model. Your discussion should describe *why* each assumption is made.

7. You have been asked by a friend who lacks your mastery of finance theory to describe what Modigliani & Miller's Proposition I really means, and what it implies about the existence of one true "optimal" capital structure for a given firm.

8. Develop an example of "home-made leverage" showing (1) initial capital structure disequilibrium, (2) the specific arbitrage process involved in correcting this disequilibrium, and (3) the new capital structure equilibrium that will result from this process.

9. [Numerical problem] Assume you are trying to value a firm with the following characteristics: NOI = $500,000, k_1 = 0.15, r = 0.08, and D = $2,000,000. Calculate V_u, S_l, V_l, and p for this levered firm. Then describe the exact arbitrage process that will bring the value of this firm back to equality with the value of an otherwise equivalent unlevered firm.

10. In words, describe how the process of "homemade leverage" is expected to work.

11. Why is it true that M&M's Proposition II follows logically from Proposition I, and that if you "accept" Proposition I you must automatically accept Proposition II?

12. Discuss the difference between the direct and indirect costs of corporate bankruptcy. Then discuss the empirical evidence regarding the relative importance of these two costs of corporate financial distress.

13. [Numerical problem] Calculate the value of the tax shield generated by the corporate borrowing of a firm with the following characteristics: NOI = $500,000, D = $1,000,000, $r = 0.08$, and $\tau_c = 0.30$. Then calculate V_L for this firm and V_U for an otherwise equivalent unlevered firm if $\rho = 0.10$.

14. Using both words and equations, describe the Miller (1977) model of bond market equilibrium. Then discuss what this model implies about optimal capital structures for individual firms.

15. [Numerical problem] Compute the gain to leverage, G_L, when $\tau_C = 0.35$, $\tau_{ps} = 0.05$, $\tau_{pd} = 0.30$ and $D_L = $1,000,000$. What would τ_{pd} have to be to make $G_L = 0$, assuming the other variables remain constant?

16. What does it mean to state that an interest rate must be "grossed up" to reflect personal income taxes (use examples as needed)?

17. What is the "secured debt hypothesis?" What empirical regularities does this hypothesis help to explain?

18. Respond to the following statement: "Unless there are deadweight (out-of-pocket) costs to the bankruptcy *process*, then the threat of entering bankruptcy cannot itself affect capital structure decisions."

19. What is required for bankruptcy and/or financial distress to be costly enough to discourage firms from increasing their leverage past some "safe" level?

20. What is the "asset substitution problem" in corporate debt policy, and how does it influence bondholder behavior?

21. How do asset characteristics affect corporate capital structure?

22. [Essay question] List and briefly discuss at least five of the most important empirical regularities that have been documented regarding the costs of bankruptcy and financial distress for American firms and managers.

23. Why do Jensen and Meckling (1976) assert that managers will bear all of the agency costs resulting from the separation of ownership and control resulting from the sale of equity to outside investors?

24. In the Jensen and Meckling model, how can debt be used to overcome the agency costs of outside equity?

25. Describe the agency costs of outside debt identified by Jensen and Meckling (1976). How can these costs be minimized?

26. [Essay question] Describe, verbally and algebraically, the Agency Cost/Tax Shield Trade-Off Theory of Capital Structure.

27. What empirical capital structure regularities are left unanswered by the "Trade-Off Theory" of corporate leverage? How does the Pecking Order Hypothesis explain these regularities?

28. What four assumptions underlie the Pecking Order Hypothesis of Capital Structure?

29. What is "financial slack," and what role does it play in the Pecking Order Hypothesis of corporate leverage?

30. What are the principal empirical predictions of the Pecking Order Hypothesis?

31. In finance theory, what is a "signal," and what characteristics must it have to be useful in capital structure decision-making?

32. Discuss the empirical evidence regarding signaling models of corporate leverage.

—REFERENCES—

Altman, Edward, "A Further Empirical Investigation of the Bankruptcy Cost Question," **Journal of Finance** 39 (September 1984), pp. 1067–1089.

Amihud, Yakov and Haim Mendelsohn, "Asset Pricing and the Bid-Ask Spread," **Journal of Financial Economics** 17 (December 1986), pp. 223–249.

Ang, James and William L. Megginson, "A Test of the Before-Tax Versus After-Tax Equilibrium Models of Corporate Debt," **Research in Finance** 8 (JAI Press, 1990).

Ang, James, David Peterson, and Pamela Peterson, "Marginal Tax Rates: Evidence From Nontaxable Corporate Bonds: A Note," **Journal of Finance** 40 (March 1985), pp. 327–332.

Asquith, Paul and David W. Mullins, "Equity Issues and Stock Price Dilution," **Journal of Financial Economics** 15 (January/February 1986), pp. 61–89.

Asquith, Paul and Thierry A. Wizman, "Event Risk, Covenants, and Bondholder Returns in Leveraged Buyouts," **Journal of Financial Economics** 27 (September 1990), pp. 195–214.

Bae, Sung C., Daniel P. Klein, and Raj Padmaraj, "Event Risk Bond Covenants, Agency Costs of Debt and Equity, and Stockholder Wealth," **Financial Management** 23 (Winter 1994), pp. 28–41.

Baker, George P. and Karen H. Wruck, "Organizational Changes and Value Creation in Leveraged Buyouts: The Case of The O. M. Scott Company," **Journal of Financial Economics** 25 (December 1989), pp. 163–190.

Barclay, Michael J. and Clifford Holderness, "Private Benefits From Control of Public Corporations," **Journal of Financial Economics** 25 (December 1989), pp. 371–396.

Barclay, Michael J. and Robert H. Litzenberger, "Announcement Effects of New Equity Issues and the Use of Intraday Price Data," **Journal of Financial Economics** 21 (May 1988), pp. 71–100.

Bathala, Chenchuramaiah, Kenneth P. Moon, and Ramesh P. Rao, "Managerial Ownership, Debt Policy, and the Impact of Institutional Holdings: An Agency Perspective," **Financial Management** 23 (Autumn 1994), pp. 38–50.

Beatty, Anne, "The Cash Flow and Informational Effects of Employee Stock Ownership Plans," **Journal of Financial Economics** 38 (June 1995), pp. 211–240.

Berglof, Eric and Enrico Perotti, "The Governance Structure of the Japanese Financial Keiretsu," **Journal of Financial Economics** 36 (October 1994), pp. 259–284.

Bernanke, Ben S. and John Y. Campbell, "Is There a Corporate Debt Crisis?," **Brookings Papers on Economic Activity** 1: 1988, pp. 83–125.

Bernanke, Ben S. and John Y. Campbell, and Toni M. Whited, "U.S. Corporate Leverage: Developments in 1987 and 1988," **Brookings Papers on Economic Activity** 1 (1988), pp. 255–278.

Betker, Brian L., "Management's Incentives, Equity's Bargaining Power, and Deviations From Absolute Priority in Chapter 11 Bankruptcies," **Journal of Business** 68 (April 1995), pp. 161–183.

Bhide, Amar, "The Hidden Costs of Stock Market Liquidity," **Journal of Financial Economics** 34 (August 1993), pp. 31–51.

Blazenko, George W., "Managerial Preference, Asymmetric Information, and Financial Structure," **Journal of Finance** 42 (September 1987), pp. 839–862.

Bradley, Michael, Gregg Jarrell, and E. Han Kim, "On the Existence of an Optimal Capital Structure: Theory and Evidence," **Journal of Finance** 39 (May 1984), pp. 857–878.

Brander, J. A. and T. R. Lewis, "Oligopoly and Financial Structure," **American Economic Review** 76 (1986), pp. 956–971.

Brown, David T., Christopher M. James, and Robert M. Mooradian, "The Informational Content of Distressed Restructurings Involving Public and Private Debt Claims," **Journal of Financial Economics** 33 (1993), pp. 93–118.

Bruner, Robert F., "The Use of Excess Cash and Debt Capacity as a Motive for Merger," **Journal of Financial and Quantitative Analysis** 23 (June 1988), pp. 199–219.

Buser, Stephen A. and Patrick J. Hess, "Empirical Determinants of the Relative Yields on Taxable and Tax-Exempt Securities," **Journal of Financial Economics** 17 (December 1986), pp. 335–355.

Crabbe, Leland, "Event Risk: An Analysis of Losses to Bondholders and 'Super Poison Put' Bond Covenants," **Journal of Finance** 46 (June 1991), pp. 689–706.

Dann, Larry, "Common Stock Repurchases: An Analysis of Returns to Bondholders and Stockholders," **Journal of Financial Economics** 9 (June 1981), pp. 113–138.

Dann, Larry and Wayne Mikkelson, "Convertible Debt Issuance, Capital Structure Change and Financing Related Information: Some New Evidence," **Journal of Financial Economics** 13 (June 1984), pp. 157–186.

DeAngelo, Harry and Ronald W. Masulis, "Optimal Capital Structure Under Corporate and Personal Taxation," **Journal of Financial Economics** 8 (March 1980), pp. 3–30.

Demsetz, Harold and Kenneth Lehn, "The Structure of Corporate Ownership: Causes and Consequences," **Journal of Political Economy** 93 (December 1985), pp. 1155–1177.

Denis, David J. and Diane K. Denis, "Causes of Financial Distress Following Leveraged Recapitalizations," **Journal of Financial Economics** 37 (February 1995), pp. 129–157.

Easterbrook, Frank H., "Two Agency-Cost Explanations of Dividends," **American Economic Review** 74 (September 1984), pp. 650–659.

Eberhart, Allen, William Moore, and Rodney Roenfeldt, "Security Pricing and Deviations From the Absolute Priority Rule in Bankruptcy Proceedings," **Journal of Finance** 45 (December 1990), pp. 1457–1469.

Eckbo, Espen B., "Valuation Effects of Corporate Debt Offerings," **Journal of Financial Economics** 15 (January/February 1986), pp. 119–152.

Farrar, Donald E. and Lee L. Selwyn, "Taxes, Corporate Financial Policy, and Return to Investors," **National Tax Journal** 20 (December 1967), pp. 444–454.

Feldstein, Martin, Jerry Green, and Eytan Sheshinski, "Corporate Financial Policy and Taxation in a Growing Economy," **Quarterly Journal of Economics** 93 (August 1979), pp. 411–432.

Finnerty, John D., "Stock-for-Debt Swaps and Shareholder Returns," **Financial Management** 14 (Winter 1985), pp. 5–17.

Fischer, Edwin O., Robert Heinkel, and Josef Zechner, "Dynamic Capital Structure Choice: Theory and Tests," **Journal of Finance** 44 (March 1989), pp. 19–40.

Frankel, Jeffrey A., "The Japanese Cost of Finance: A Survey," **Financial Management** 20 (Spring 1991), pp. 95–127.

Franks, Julian R. and Walter N. Torous, "An Empirical Investigation of U.S. Firms in Reorganization," **Journal of Finance** 44 (July 1989), pp. 747–770.

————"A Comparison of Financial Recontracting in Distressed Exchanges and Chapter 11 Reorganizations," **Journal of Financial Economics** 35 (June 1994), pp. 349–370.

Friend, Irwin and Larry H. P. Lang, "An Empirical Test of the Impact of Managerial Self-Interest on Corporate Capital Structure," **Journal of Finance** 43 (June 1988), pp. 271–281.

Fung, William K. H. and Michael F. Theobald, "Dividends and Debt Under Alternative Tax Systems," **Journal of Financial and Quantitative Analysis** 19 (March 1984), pp. 59–72.

Galai, Dan and Ronald W. Masulis, "The Option Pricing Model and the Risk Factor of Stock," **Journal of Financial Economics** 3 (January/March 1976), pp. 53–81.

Gaver, Jennifer J. and Kenneth M. Gaver, "Additional Evidence on the Association Between the Opportunity Set and Corporate Financing, Dividend, and Compensation Policies," **Journal of Accounting and Economics** 16 (January/April/July 1993), pp. 125–160.

Gertner, Robert and David Scharfstein, "A Theory of Workouts and the Effects of Reorganization Law," **Journal of Finance** 46 (September 1991), pp. 1189–1222.

Gilson, Stuart C., "Management Turnover and Financial Distress," **Journal of Financial Economics** 25 (December 1989), pp. 241–262.

————"Debt Renegotiation, Leverage Costs, and Optimal Capital Structure: An Analysis of Leverage Choices by Financially Distressed Firms," Working paper (Harvard Universtiy, October 1994).

Gilson, Stuart C., Kose John, and Larry H. P. Lang, "Troubled Debt Restructurings: An Empirical Study of Private Reorganization of Firms in Default," **Journal of Financial Economics** 27 (September 1990), pp. 315–353.

Gilson, Stuart C. and Michael R. Vetsuypens, "CEO Compensation in Financially Distressed Firms: An Empirical Analysis," **Journal of Finance** 48 (June 1993), pp. 425–458.

Goh, Jeremy C. and Louis H. Ederington, "Is a Bond Rating Downgrade Bad News, Good News, or No News for Stockholders?," **Journal of Finance** 48 (December 1993), pp. 2001–2008.

Hamada, Robert S., "Portfolio Analysis, Market Equilibrium, and Corporation Finance," **Journal of Finance** 24 (March 1969), pp. 13–31.

————"The Effect of the Firm's Capital Structure on the Systematic Risk of Common Stock," **Journal of Finance** 27 (May 1972), pp. 435–452.

Hamada, Robert S. and Myron S. Scholes, "Taxes and Corporate Financial Management," in Edward I. Altman and Marti Subrahmanyam, eds., **Recent Advances in Corporate Finance** (Homewood, Illinois: Richard D. Irwin, 1985).

Hansen, Robert S. and Claire Crutchley, "Corporate Earnings and Financings: An Empirical Analysis," **Journal of Business** 63 (July 1990), pp. 347–371.

Harris, Milton and Artur Raviv, "The Theory of Capital Structure," **Journal of Finance** 46 (March 1991), pp. 297–355.

Haugen, Robert A. and Lemma W. Senbet, "The Insignificance of Bankruptcy Costs in the Theory of Optimal Capital Structure," **Journal of Finance** 33 (May 1978), pp. 383–393.

Hodder, James E. and Lemma W. Senbet, "International Capital Structure Equilibrium," **Journal of Finance** 45 (December 1990), pp. 1495–1516.

Hoshi, Takeo, Anil Kashyap, and David Scharfstein, "The Role of Banks in Reducing the Costs of Financial Distress in Japan," **Journal of Financial Economics** 27 (September 1990), pp. 67–88.

Hotchkiss, Edith Shwalb, "Postbankruptcy Performance and Management Turnover," **Journal of Finance** 50 (March 1995), pp. 3–21.

"How Sweet it Was," **Investment Dealers' Digest** (January 11, 1993), pp. 14–30.

James, Christopher, "Some Evidence on the Uniqueness of Bank Loans," **Journal of Financial Economics** 19 (December 1987), pp. 217–235.

Jensen, Michael C., "Agency Costs of Free Cash Flow, Corporate Finance and Takeovers," **American Economic Review** 76 (May 1986), pp. 323–329.

————"Eclipse of the Public Corporation," **Harvard Business Review** 67 (September/October 1989), pp. 61–74.

————"Presidential Address: The Modern Industrial Revolution, Exit, and the Failure of Internal Control Systems," **Journal of Finance** 48 (July 1993), pp. 831–880.

Jensen, Michael C. and William H. Meckling, "Theory of the Firm: Managerial Behavior, Agency Costs, and Ownership Structure," **Journal of Financial Economics** 3 (October 1976), pp. 305–360.

Jensen, Michael C. and Kevin J. Murphy, "Performance Pay and Top-Management Incentives," **Journal of Political Economy** 98 (April 1990), pp. 225–264.

John, Kose, "Risk-Shifting Incentives and Signalling Through Corporate Capital Structure," **Journal of Finance** 42 (July 1987), pp. 623–641.

John, Kose, Larry H. P. Lang, and Jeffrey M. Netter, "Voluntary Restructuring of Large Firms in Response to Performance Decline," **Journal of Finance** 47 (July 1992), pp. 891–917.

Kalay, Avner, "Stockholder-Bondholder Conflict and Dividend Constraints," **Journal of Financial Economics** 10 (July 1982), pp. 211–233.

Kale, Jayant R., Thomas H. Noe, and Gabriel G. Ramirez, "The Effect of Business Risk on Corporate Capital Structure: Theory and Evidence," **Journal of Finance** 46 (December 1991), pp. 1693–1715.

Kaplan, Steven, "The Effect of Management Buyouts on Operating Performance and Value," **Journal of Financial Economics** 24 (October 1989), pp. 217–254.

Kaplan, Steven N., "Top Executive Rewards and Firm Performance: A Comparison of Japan and the United States," **Journal of Political Economy** 102 (June 1994), pp. 510–546.

Kester, W. Carl, "Capital and Ownership Structure: A Comparison of United States and Japanese Manufacturing Corporations," **Financial Management** 15 (Spring 1986), pp. 17–24.

————"Governance, Contracting, and Investment Horizons: A Look at Japan and Germany," **Journal of Applied Corporate Finance** 5 (Summer 1992), pp. 83–98.

Kester, W. Carl and Timothy A. Luehrman, "What Makes You Think U.S. Capital is So Expensive?," **Journal of Applied Corporate Finance** 5 (Summer 1992), pp. 29–41.

Kim, Moshe and Vojislav Maksimovic, "Debt and Input Misallocation," **Journal of Finance** 45 (July 1990), pp. 795–816.

Kim, Wi Saeng and Eric H. Sorensen, "Evidence on the Impact of The Agency Costs of Debt on Corporate Debt Policy," **Journal of Financial and Quantitative Analysis** 21 (June 1986), pp. 131–144.

Korajczyk, Robert A., Deborah J. Lucas, and Robert L. McDonald, "The Effect of Information Releases on the Pricing and Timing of Equity Issues," **Review of Financial Studies** 4 (1991), pp. 685–708.

Kraus, Alan and Robert H. Litzenberger, "A State-Preference Model of Optimal Financial Leverage," **Journal of Finance** 28 (September 1973), pp. 911–922.

Lang, Larry H. P. and René M. Stulz, "Contagion and Competitive Intra-Industry Effects of Bankruptcy Announcements," **Journal of Financial Economics** 32 (August 1992), pp. 45–60.

Lang, Larry H. P., René M. Stulz, and Ralph A. Walkling, "A Test of the Free Cash Flow Hypothesis: The Case of Bidder Returns," **Journal of Financial Economics** 29 (October 1991), pp. 315–335.

Lehn, Kenneth, Jeffrey Netter, and Annette Poulsen, "Consolidating Corporate Control: Dual-Class Recapitalizations Versus Leveraged Buyouts," **Journal of Financial Economics** 27 (September 1990), pp. 557–580.

Leland, Hayne E., "Corporate Debt Value, Bond Covenants, and Optimal Capital Structure," **Journal of Finance** 49 (September 1994), pp. 1213–1252.

Linn, Scott C. and J. Michael Pinegar, "The Effect of Issuing Preferred Stock on Common Stockholder Wealth," **Journal of Financial Economics** 22 (October 1988), pp. 155–184.

Lintner, John, "Distribution of Incomes of Corporations Among Dividends, Retained Earnings, and Taxes," **American Economic Review** 46 (May 1956), pp. 97–113.

Long, Michael and Ileen Malitz, "The Investment-Financing Nexus: Some Empirical Evidence," **Midland Corporate Finance Journal** 3 (Spring 1985), pp. 53–59.

Loughran, Tim and Jay R. Ritter, "The New Issues Puzzle," **Journal of Finance** 50 (March 1995), pp. 23–51.

Lucas, Deborah J. and Robert L. McDonald, "Equity Issues and Stock Price Dynamics," **Journal of Finance** 45 (September 1990), pp. 1020–1043.

MacKie-Mason, Jeffrey K., "Do Taxes Affect Corporate Financing Decisions?," **Journal of Finance** 45 (December 1990), pp. 1471–1493.

Maksimovic, Vojislav, "Capital Structure in Repeated Oligopolies," **RAND Journal of Economics** 19 (Autumn 1988), pp. 389–407.

Maksimovic, Vojislav and Sheridan Titman, "Financial Policy and Reputation for Product Quality," **Review of Financial Studies** 4 (1991), pp. 175–200.

Maksimovic, Vojislav and Josef Zechner, "Debt, Agency Costs, and Industry Equilibrium," **Journal of Finance** 46 (December 1991), pp. 1619–1644.

Maloney, Michael T., Robert E. McCormick, and Mark L. Mitchell, "Managerial Decision Making and Capital Structure," **Journal of Business** 66 (April 1993), pp. 189–217.

Marsh, Paul, "The Choice Between Equity and Debt: An Empirical Study," **Journal of Finance** 37 (March 1982), pp. 121–144.

Masulis, Ronald W., "The Effect of Capital Structure Change on Security Prices: A Study of Exchange Offers," **Journal of Financial Economics** 8 (June 1980), pp. 139–177.

Masulis, Ronald W. and Ashok N. Korwar, "Seasoned Equity Offerings: An Empirical Investigation," **Journal of Financial Economics** 15 (January/February 1986), pp. 91–118.

Michel, Allen and Israel Shaked, "Japanese Leverage: Myth or Reality?," **Financial Analysts Journal** 41 (Winter 1985), pp. 61–67.

Mikkelson, Wayne and M. Megan Partch, "Valuation Effects of Security Offerings and the Issuance Process," **Journal of Financial Economics** 15 (January/February 1986), pp. 31–60.

————"Managers' Voting Rights and Corporate Control," **Journal of Financial Economics** 25 (December 1989), pp. 263–290.

Miller, Merton, "Debt and Taxes," **Journal of Finance** 32 (May 1977), pp. 261–276.

Modigliani, Franco and Merton Miller, "The Cost of Capital, Corporation Finance, and the Theory of Investment," **American Economic Review** 48 (June 1958), pp. 261–297.

————"Corporate Income Taxes and the Cost of Capital," **American Economic Review** 53 (June 1963), pp. 433–443.

Muscarella, Christopher J. and Michael R. Vetsuypens, "Efficiency and Organizational Structure: A Study of Reverse LBOs," **Journal of Finance** 45 (December 1990), pp. 1389–1413.

Myers, Stewart C., "The Determinants of Corporate Borrowing," **Journal of Financial Economics** 5 (November 1977), pp. 147–176.

———"The Capital Structure Puzzle," **Journal of Finance** 39 (July 1984), pp. 575–592.

———"Still Searching for an Optimal Capital Structure," **Journal of Applied Corporate Finance** 6 (Spring 1993), pp. 4–14.

Myers, Stewart C. and Nicholas S. Majluf, "Corporate Financing and Investment Decisions When Firms Have Information Investors Do Not Have," **Journal of Financial Economics** 13 (June 1984), pp. 187–221.

Narayanan, M. P., "Debt Versus Equity Under Asymmetric Information," **Journal of Financial and Quantitative Analysis** 23 (March 1988), pp. 39–52.

Noe, Thomas H., "Capital Structure and Signalling Game Equilibria," **Review of Financial Studies** 1 (1988), pp. 331–355.

Opler, Tim and Sheridan Titman, "The Determinants of Leveraged Buyout Activity: Free Cash Flow vs. Financial Distress Costs," **Journal of Finance** 48 (December 1993), pp. 1985–1999.

———"Financial Distress and Corporate Performance," **Journal of Finance** 49 (July 1994), pp. 1015–1040.

Peles, Yoram C. and Marshall Sarnat, "Corporate Taxes and Capital Structure: Some Evidence Drawn From the British Experience," **Review of Economics and Statistics** (1978), pp. 118–120.

Petersen, Mitchell A., "Cash Flow Variability and Firm's Choice: A Role for Operating Leverage," **Journal of Financial Economics** 36 (December 1994), pp. 361–383.

Phillips, Gordon M., "Increased Debt and Industry Product Markets: An Empirical Analysis," **Journal of Financial Economics** 37 (February 1995), pp. 189–238.

Poterba, James M. and Lawrence H. Summers, "The Economic Effects of Dividend Taxation," in Edwin Elton and Marti Subrahmanyan, eds., **Recent Advances in Corporate Finance** (Homewood, IL: Richard D. Irwin, 1985).

Pratt, Tom, "Wall Street's Deep Freeze," **Investment Dealers' Digest** (January 9, 1995), pp. 12–33.

Prowse, Stephen D., "Institutional Investment Patterns and Corporate Financial Behavior in the United States and Japan," **Journal of Financial Economics** 27 (September 1990), pp. 43–66.

———"The Structure of Corporate Ownership in Japan," **Journal of Finance** 47 (July 1992), pp. 1121–1140.

Rajan, Raghuram G. and Luigi Zingales, "What Do We Know About Capital Structure? Some Evidence From International Data," NBER Working Paper (October 1994).

Roe, Mark J., "Political and Legal Restraints on Ownership and Control of Public Companies," **Journal of Financial Economics** 27 (September 1990), pp. 7–41.

Ross, Stephen A., "The Determination of Financial Structure: The Incentive-Signaling Approach," **Bell Journal of Economics** 8 (Spring 1977), pp. 23–40.

Rubinstein, Mark E., "A Mean-Variance Synthesis of Corporate Financial Theory," **Journal of Finance** 28 (March 1973), pp. 167–181.

Rutterford, Janette, "An International Perspective on the Capital Structure Puzzle," in Joel M. Stern and Donald H. Chew, Jr., eds., **New Developments in International Finance** (New York: Basil Blackwell, 1988).

Scott, James, "Bankruptcy, Secured Debt, and Optimal Capital Structure," **Journal of Finance** 32 (March 1977), pp. 1–20.

Sekely, William S. and J. Markham Collins, "Cultural Influences on International Capital Structure," **Journal of International Business Studies** (Spring 1988), pp. 87–100.

Shah, Kshitij, "The Nature of Information Conveyed by Pure Capital Structure Changes," **Journal of Financial Economics** 36 (August 1994), pp. 89–126.

Shyam-Sunder, Lakshmi and Stewart C. Myers, "Testing Static Trade-Off Against Pecking Order Models of Capital Structure," Working paper, Massachusetts Institute of Technology (March 1993).

Smith, Jr., Clifford W. and René M. Stulz, "The Determinants of Firms' Hedging Policies," **Journal of Financial and Quantitative Analysis** 20 (December 1985), pp. 391–405.

Smith, Jr., Clifford W. and Jerold B. Warner, "On Financial Contracting: An Analysis of Bond Covenants," **Journal of Financial Economics** 7 (June 1979), pp. 117–161.

Smith, Jr., Clifford W. and Ross L. Watts, "The Investment Opportunity Set and Corporate Financing, Dividend, and Compensation Policies," **Journal of Financial Economics** 32 (December 1992), pp. 263–292.

Smith, Richard L. and Joo-Hyun Kim, **Journal of Business** 67 (April 1994), pp. 281–310.

Stiglitz, Joseph E., "A Reexamination of the Modigliani-Miller Theorem," **American Economic Review** 54 (December 1969), pp. 784–793.

     "On the Irrelevance of Corporate Financial Policy," **American Economic Review** 64 (December 1974), pp. 851–866.

Stulz, René M., "Managerial Control of Voting Rights: Financing Policies and the Market for Corporate Control," **Journal of Financial Economics** 20 (January/March 1988), pp. 25–54.

Stulz, René M. and Herb Johnson, "An Analysis of Secured Debt," **Journal of Financial Economics** 14 (December 1985), pp. 501–521.

Taggart, Jr., Robert A., "Secular Patterns in the Financing of U.S. Corporations," in Bejamin M. Friedman, ed., **Corporate Capital Structures in the United States** (Chicago: University of Chicago Press, 1985).

Titman, Sheridan, "The Effect of Capital Structure on a Firm's Liquidation Decision," **Journal of Financial Economics** 13 (March 1984), pp. 137–151.

Titman, Sheridan and Roberto Wessels, "The Determinants of Capital Structure Choice," **Journal of Finance** 43 (March 1988), pp. 1–19.

Travlos, Nickolas G., "Corporate Takeover Bids, Methods of Payment, and Bidding Firms' Stock Returns," **Journal of Finance** 42 (September 1987), pp. 943–963.

Trzcinka, Charles, "The Pricing of Tax-Exempt Bonds and the Miller Hypothesis," **Journal of Finance** 37 (September 1982), pp. 907–923.

Warner, Jerold B., "Bankruptcy Costs: Some Evidence," **Journal of Finance** 32 (May 1977), pp. 337–347.

Wedig, Gerard, Frank A. Sloan, Mahmud Hassan, and Michael A. Morrisey, "Capital Structure, Ownership, and Capital Payment Policy: The Case of Hospitals," **Journal of Finance** 43 (March 1988), pp. 21–40.

Weiss, Lawrence, "Bankruptcy Resolution: Direct Costs and Violation of Priority of Claims," **Journal of Financial Economics** 27 (October 1990), pp. 285–314.

CHAPTER
8

Dividend Policy

8.1 INTRODUCTION

The phrase **dividend policy** has historically referred to a corporation's choice of whether to pay its shareholders a cash dividend and, if so, how much to pay and with what frequency (annually, semiannually, or quarterly). In recent years, dividend policy has come to include many more variables, such as whether to distribute cash to investors via share repurchases or specially-designated dividends rather than regular dividends, whether to rely on stock rather than cash distributions, and how to balance the cash flow preferences of highly-taxed individuals with those of the untaxed institutional investors who are becoming increasingly dominant in capital markets around the world. In spite of today's complexity, however, most corporations still have to struggle with the same issues that John Lintner (1956) found to be important for corporate managers in the 1950s—should my firm's dividend payment be maintained at its current level or be changed? If the payment is increased, will corporate profits remain high enough to sustain it? How will the stock market interpret any changes the firm announces regarding its dividend? Do investors prefer a stable nominal dividend payment per share or is it acceptable to allow payments to fluctuate along with a firm's earnings? Finally, should my firm's dividend policy favor older investors, who are often retired and prefer a high dividend payout; or younger investors who face higher marginal tax rates and have a longer investment horizon, and thus prefer that profits be reinvested in the firm rather than being paid out as dividends? As you might expect, there are few easy answers to these real and pressing questions.

Along with capital structure, dividend policy was one of the first areas of corporate finance to be analyzed with a rigorous theoretical model, and it has since become one of the most thoroughly-researched issues in modern finance. In spite of this, much remains unexplained about the role cash dividends play in conveying information to investors about corporate prospects, how markets value high- versus low-dividend-paying stocks, how corporate and personal income taxes affect the demand for and supply of cash dividends, how dividends interact with other corporate financial variables (such as leverage and investment levels) by way of the firm's cash flow identity, and why dividend payout ratios are so vastly different for different industries and between different countries. Our objective in this chapter is to present two competing modern theories of dividend policy, discuss how well each is supported by existing empirical evidence, and then attempt to address the issues raised above about the role of dividend policy in real world decision-making and financial valuation. We will be seeking answers to two fundamental questions: (1) Does dividend policy matter—can the total market value of a firm's securities be increased or decreased by changes in its dividend payments? And, (2) if dividend policy does matter, what factors determine the optimal payout level that will maximize firm value and thus minimize its cost of capital? We will begin our analysis by first examining patterns in dividend policy that are actually observed around the world.

8.2   OBSERVED DIVIDEND POLICY PATTERNS

Summarizing observed dividend payment patterns will make clear exactly what a viable theory of dividend policy must be able to explain, and will also provide a framework for discussing the relevance of recent empirical research. As the following details make clear, dividend policy shows remarkable similarities throughout the non-communist world, but equally fascinating differences also exist. The perceptive student will also notice that the patterns observed for dividend policy are generally similar to those documented in chapter 7 for capital structure.

1. **Observed dividend policies show distinct national patterns.** As Figure 8.1 makes clear, British firms generally have the highest payouts in the industrialized world, and North American companies tend to have higher payouts than western European or Japanese companies.[1] Companies headquartered in developing countries typically have very low dividend payouts, if they pay dividends at all.[2] Many factors influence these patterns, though one of the strongest seems to be that countries such as Britain, Canada, and the U.S. that rely on capital markets for financing their corporations tend to observe higher dividend payments than do countries such as Germany, Japan, and South Korea that rely more on intermediated financing. Not surprisingly, countries with a strong socialist tradition (such as France), or those with a long history of state involvement in the economy (such as Italy), tend to discourage dividend payments to private investors.[3]

---

1. Differences in the financial management of Anglo-American and other developed country firms are discussed in Berglof and Perotti (1994), Frankel (1991), Kaplan and Minton (1994), Kester (1992), Petersen and Rajan (1994), and Prowse (1992), among others.

2. An in-depth discussion of the difference in payouts between American and Japanese firms is provided in Frankel (1991), while Koretz (1993) provides a more summarized comparison.

3. A recent study documents that state-owned enterprises that are privatized significantly increase dividend payouts after divestment, some making dividend payments for the first time. See Megginson, Nash, and Randenborgh (1994).

FIGURE 8.1

INTERNATIONAL DIVIDEND PAY-OUT COMPARISONS

This figure describes the average dividend pay-out ratio, as a percent of after-tax corporate profits for companies headquartered in Great Britain, the United States, Japan, and (West) Germany over the period 1975–1994.

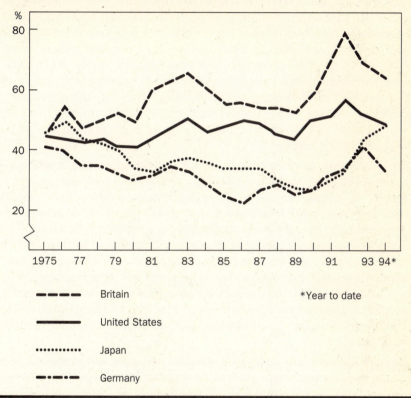

- – – – – Britain   *Year to date

—————— United States

•••••••••••• Japan

– • – • – Germany

SOURCE: "COMPANY DIVIDENDS," *THE ECONOMIST* (JUNE 4, 1994), PG. 109.

2. **Dividend policies have pronounced industry patterns, and these are the same worldwide.** In general, profitable firms in mature industries tend to pay out much larger fractions of their earnings than do firms in younger, rapidly-growing industries, and utility companies have very high dividend payouts in almost every country. The most important influences on dividend payout appear to be industry growth rate, capital investment needs, profitability, earnings variability, and asset characteristics (the mix between tangible and intangible assets).[4] In the United States, an industry's

---

4. Two recent empirical studies document these relationships. See Smith and Watts (1992) and Gaver and Gaver (1993). The survey results detailed in Baker, Farrelly, and Edelman (1985) offer further support for these inter-industry dividend patterns. The interrelationship between a firm's dividend payment and capital investment spending is examined in Fama (1974) and in Peterson and Benesh (1983). Fama shows that investment spending and dividend payments are independent, but Peterson and Benesh suggest that such a link might exist.

average dividend payout ratio is positively related to the richness of its investment opportunity set (whether the industry has many valuable investment opportunities) and to the degree to which the industry is regulated.[5] Table 8.1 lists average dividend payout ratios for several American industries during the mid-1990s.

3. **Within industries, dividend payout tends to be directly related to size and asset intensity, but is inversely related to growth rate.** Large firms pay out, on average, larger fractions of their earnings than do small firms. Asset-rich companies (those where tangible assets represent a large fraction of total firm value) tend to have higher dividend payouts than do companies where intangible assets, such as growth options, represent a large fraction of total firm market value. Furthermore, regulated companies (particularly utilities) pay out more of their earnings than do non-regulated companies.[6] The relationship between dividend payout and growth rate is equally clear—rapidly growing firms horde cash and select zero or very low dividend payouts. As these companies mature, dividend payouts increase.

4. **Almost all firms maintain constant nominal dividend payments per share for long periods of time.** Put another way, companies everywhere tend to "smooth" dividend payments, and these payments show far less variability than do the corporate profits upon which they ultimately are based.[7] Managers will not increase per share dividends until they are convinced that "permanent" earnings have increased enough to support a higher dividend level, and they will then gradually increase dividend payments until a new per share equilibrium payment is reached. Likewise, corporate managers will try to maintain nominal per share dividend payments, even in the face of temporary net losses, until it becomes clear that earnings will not revive. Managers will then reduce (but almost never eliminate) dividend payments, and will make the full adjustment in one large cut.[8]

5. **The stock market reacts positively to dividend initiations and increases, and has a strong negative reaction to dividend decreases or eliminations.** When a company announces either its first regular cash dividend payment (an initiation) or an increase

5. These relationships are inferred primarily from the firm-level results presented in a recent study by Barclay, Smith, and Watts (1995).

6. These relationships are documented in Smith and Watts (1992), Gaver and Gaver (1993), and Barclay, Smith, and Watts (1995).

7. This is one of the first important empirical regularities to be documented in the dividend literature, in that it was suggested by the work of Lintner (1956), and then documented by Fama and Babiak (1968). Aharony and Swary (1980) later exploit this predictability to model unexpected dividend changes as any change in nominal dividends per share—thereby making their sample construction simpler and cleaner. Fudenberg and Tirole (1995) provide a theoretical rationale for why managers would choose to smooth (not merely inflate) reported income and dividend payments, while the empirical importance of dividend smoothing is addressed in Kao and Wu (1994).

8. The extreme reluctance of managers to reduce or eliminate dividends is documented in DeAngelo and DeAngelo (1990, pp. 1415–1431) and DeAngelo, DeAngelo, and Skinner (1992). Michaely, Thaler, and Womack (1995) document that the (negative) stock price reaction to a dividend omission is much larger than the (positive) reaction to its mirror image, a dividend initiation, but Christie (1994) presents the intriguing (and unexplained) result that the stock market reaction to a dividend omission is less negative than that for a large dividend reduction.

TABLE 8.1

AVERAGE DIVIDEND PAYOUT RATIOS, YIELDS, AND PRICE/EARNINGS (P/E) RATIOS FOR SELECTED U.S. INDUSTRIES, 1994–95

Industry	Payout Ratio	Dividend Yield	P/E Ratio
Electric utilities	86%	6.7%	12.9
Basic chemicals	83	4.0	23.5
Petroleum	80	4.0	20.7
Distilling	71	5.0	14.3
Natural gas	61	4.9	13.7
Telecommunications	57	3.9	22.3
Pharmaceuticals	47	2.9	19.0
Electrical equipment	44	2.6	17.0
Food processing	42	2.2	24.3
Banking	38	3.6	10.6
Paper & forest products	37	2.6	17.0
Household products	37	2.2	18.1
Retail stores	32	2.0	17.1
Auto & truck manufacturing	16	3.1	5.9
Software & services	8	0.3	30.4
Semiconductors	7	0.4	17.9
Broadcasting	7	0.3	24.7
Computer software	7	0.3	32.5
Medical services	6	0.3	28.0
Health care services	5	0.3	23.5
Air transport	4	0.3	24.2

SOURCES: BOONE, RONALD, JR., "MONEY & INVESTMENTS: THE DIVIDEND REVIEW," FORBES (JUNE 5, 1995), PG. 174. KLEIN, MICHAEL E., "DIVIDEND REVIEW," FORBES (NOVEMBER 21, 1994), PG. 228. STEEDLEY, GILBERT, "DIVIDEND REVIEW," FORBES (JUNE 20, 1994), PG. 258.

in its existing per share dividend, that company's stock price typically increases by one to three percent.[9] However, firms that cut or eliminate their dividends are severely punished by the stock market, sometimes witnessing stock price declines of up to fifty percent.

9. Dividend initiations have been studied in Asquith and Mullins (1983), Richardson, Sefcik, and Thompson (1986), Healy and Palepu (1988), Venkatesh (1989), Michaely, Thaler, and Womack (1995), and Lipson, Maquieira and Megginson (1995), while Ghosh and Woolridge (1988), Healy and Palepu (1988), Christie (1994) and Michaely, Thaler, and Womack (1995) examine dividend omissions. The classic empirical study of the market response to dividend changes is Aharony and Swary (1980), with later such studies including Handjinicolaou and Kalay (1984), and Ofer and Siegel (1987).

6. **Dividend changes clearly convey information about management's expectations regarding the firm's current and future earnings.** Investors understand that managers smooth dividends, and their reactions to dividend changes reflect rational assessments of managerial signals. Put another way, dividend changes convey information to investors who are less well-informed about company affairs than are managers, and dividends thus help to overcome informational asymmetries in modern capital markets.[10] Dividend increases imply that management expects higher earnings in the future, while decreases imply declining earnings prospects. All modern dividend theories assign an information revelation role to dividend changes, but they differ on the exact mechanism of information transmission and about the complementary or supplementary information-conveying role of other firm announcements—such as earnings and investment policy announcements.[11]

7. **Taxes clearly influence dividend payouts, but the net effect is ambiguous and taxes neither cause nor prevent companies from initiating dividend payments.** It might seem obvious that levying income taxes on investors who receive dividend payments would reduce the demand for dividends, and thus prompt corporations to retain a larger share of their profits. In the extreme, very high tax rates should cause corporations to stop paying dividends entirely.[12] Plausible though these arguments may be, they are not supported by empirical evidence—and in fact some studies show that dividend payments actually increase following tax increases. Furthermore, American corporations paid dividends long before the adoption of the personal income tax on dividends in 1936, and they continued paying dividends even when marginal tax rates

---

10. The information-revelation function of dividend payments is examined theoretically and/or empirically in numerous studies, including Watts (1973), Brickley (1983), Kalay and Loewenstein (1985, 1986), Asquith and Mullins (1986), Healy and Palepu (1988), Kumar (1988), Lang and Litzenberger (1989), Bajaj and Vijh (1990, 1995), Kao and Wu (1994), and Lee (1995).

11. The two major theoretical models of dividend payment (and, implicitly, information production) are described in detail later in this chapter. Precisely what information is revealed by dividend changes is somewhat unclear, but Handjimicolaou and Kalay (1984) indicate that dividend increases cause both stock and bond prices to increase, suggesting that dividend payments do not represent attempts to expropriate bondholder wealth but are instead firm value-maximizing steps by corporate managers. This result is rather convincingly attacked, however, by Dhillon and Johnson (1994), who show that large dividend increases do transfer wealth from bondholders to stockholders.

12. Tax-related dividend studies have actually tried to answer two distinct, but related, economic questions. First, how do personal taxes on cash dividend payments affect the market valuation of high-dividend-paying stocks versus that of stocks paying smaller dividends (or none at all)? These studies have usually examined whether high-dividend stocks earned a higher pre-tax, risk-adjusted return in a CAPM context than did low-dividend stocks or whether stock prices fell by less than the dividend payment on their ex-dividend day, as would be expected if dividends were taxed at a higher rate than capital gains income. The second type of tax study seeks to answer a more basic question—do high rates of tax on dividend income reduce market valuations of corporate equity, thereby reducing the equilibrium level of corporate capital investment that would otherwise be achieved? Ex-dividend day studies and after-tax CAPM studies will be surveyed in later sections. Examples of studies that examine the valuation and investment-reduction impact of dividend taxation include Feldstein (1970), Feldstein and Fane (1973), Auerbach (1983), Poterba and Summers (1983, 1985), Poterba (1987), Ang, Blackwell, and Megginson (1991), and Christie and Nanda (1994).

increased to over 90 percent.[13] Table 8.2 presents decade-average payout ratios for U.S. firms over the period 1929–1986, while Table 8.3 presents aggregate profit and dividend payout levels for American companies since 1983.

8. **In spite of intensive research, it is unclear exactly how dividend payments affect the required return on a firm's common stock.** Both common sense and a variety of after-tax asset pricing models suggest that high-dividend-yield stocks will have a higher nominal (pre-personal-tax) required rate of return than will similar low-yield stocks, since investors have to pay income taxes on dividends received, but can effectively defer tax payments on capital gains. While some empirical research has supported this prediction, other research has contradicted it, and the net effect of dividend taxes on the valuation of corporate equity appears to be far more complex than once supposed.[14]

9. **Changes in transactions costs or in the technical efficiency of capital markets seem to have very little impact on dividend payouts.** In the aggregate, American corporations pay out roughly the same fraction (approximately half) of their total earnings as dividends today as they did in the 1920s or 1950s, in spite of the fact that the U.S. financial system is far more efficient, and offers far greater investment and payment flexibility today than in years past (see Tables 8.3 and 8.4). If dividend payments were originally designed to provide investors with a regular cash return on an otherwise illiquid stock investment, then dividend payments should have declined over time as stock trading became less costly and as higher-yielding competitive investments (i.e., money market mutual funds) became available. Clearly, technical market imperfections do not cause dividends, and do not even seem to significantly influence them.[15]

10. **Ownership structure matters.** One of the most enduring dividend regularities, both inside the United States and around the world, is that private or closely-held companies rarely pay any dividends at all, while publicly-traded companies

---

13. Poterba (1987) provides a detailed listing of dividend tax rates on aggregate dividend payout ratios in the United States for the period 1929–1986 (see table 4). The most striking aspect of this data is the fact that dividend payouts have been so stable for so many decades, in spite of dramatic changes in marginal tax rates, investment incentives, and economic growth rates. Eades, Hess, and Kim (1994) also document that four major U.S. tax law changes over the period 1977 to 1987 had very little impact on dividend valuation—as measured using ex-dividend day returns. Finally, Barclay (1987) documents that dividends were paid, and were apparently valued much the same as today, in the pre-tax years of the early 1900s.

14. The research in this area has been voluminous. The first after-tax capital asset pricing model was presented in Brennan (1970). This model was further developed explicitly with dividends in mind by Litzenberger and Ramaswamy (1979), who document empirically that high-dividend-yield stocks have a higher required rate of return than do stocks paying lower dividends, as predicted by the after-tax CAPM. This result is echoed in Blume (1980), and Ang and Peterson (1985). Several other authors cast doubt on the empirical validity of the after-tax CAPM, however, and these researchers ask the simple and awkward question, why do managers of firms pay dividends if they could lower the required rate of return on its equity simply by eliminating dividend payments? See Black and Scholes (1974) and Miller and Scholes (1982).

15. Eades, Hess, and Kim (1984, 1994) document that the cost of trading stocks dropped precipitously for most investors when fixed commissions on the NYSE were eliminated May 1, 1975, but no significant change was observed in the payout ratios of American corporations, or in the valuation of cash dividend payments.

TABLE 8.2

AVERAGE DIVIDEND PAYOUT RATIOS FOR U.S. COMPANIES, 1929–1986

This table presents average dividend payout ratios for U.S. companies for the years 1929 and 1986; for the decades 1930–39 through 1970–79; and for the period 1980–86. The table also presents the share of corporate equity owned by individuals (rather than institutions) for each period, as well as the relative after-tax income from dividends versus retained earnings, computed using the maximum marginal tax rates in effect for each period.

Year(s)	Dividend Payout Ratio[a]		Share of Corporate Equity Owned by Individuals	Relative After-Tax Income from Dividends vs. Retained Earnings
	Accounting Earnings	Adjusted Earnings		
1929	0.67	0.70	0.915	0.901[b]
1930–39	0.70	1.49	0.909	0.842
1940–49	0.39	0.52	0.902	0.643
1950–59	0.39	0.46	0.885	0.633
1960–69	0.42	0.40	0.853	0.677
1970–79	0.34	0.45	0.753	0.711
1980–86	0.59	0.61	0.647	0.752
1986	0.77	0.50	0.634	0.783

NOTES: THE PAYOUT SHARE OF ACCOUNTING EARNINGS IS DEFINED AS DIVIDEND PAYMENTS BY DOMESTIC BUSINESS DIVIDED BY AFTER-TAX PROFITS PLUS NOMINAL INTEREST PAYMENTS. THE PAYOUT SHARE OF ADJUSTED EARNINGS ADJUSTS THE AFTER-TAX PROFITS PLUS NOMINAL INTEREST SERIES IN THE DENOMINATOR FOR THE INVENTORY VALUATION ADJUSTMENT AND CAPITAL CONSUMPTION ADJUSTMENT IN THE NATIONAL INCOME ACCOUNTS.
[b]THIS RATIO MEANS THAT AN INDIVIDUAL INVESTOR IN THE TOP MARGINAL INCOME TAX BRACKET WOULD RECEIVE 90.1 CENTS OF DISPOSABLE (AFTER PERSONAL-TAX) INCOME FROM NET CORPORATE PROFITS DISTRIBUTED AS DIVIDENDS VERSUS $1.00 OF AFTER-PERSONAL-TAX INCOME IF THOSE SAME CORPORATE PROFITS WERE RETAINED AND REINVESTED BY THE CORPORATION.

SOURCE: TABLE 4 IN POTERBA, JAMES M., "TAX POLICY AND CORPORATE SAVINGS," BROOKINGS PAPERS ON ECONOMIC ACTIVITY 2 (DECEMBER 1987), PP. 455–515.

everywhere pay out substantial fractions of their earnings as dividends each year.[16] Even after other factors (growth rate, asset characteristics, firm size) are controlled for, ownership structure is still a very strong influence on observed dividend policy.[17] In almost every country and every industry, firms with tightly-knit control

16. This relationship is documented in Walker and Petty (1978) and in Dwyer and Lynn (1989), while Lipson, Maquieira, and Megginson (1995) examine the reasons why managers of newly-public companies decide to take the essentially irreversible step of initiating regular cash dividend payments.

17. The relationship between dividend payout and ownership structure is documented most clearly for American companies in Rozeff (1982), while Megginson, Nash, and van Randenborgh (1994) document that newly-privatized, non-U.S. (mostly European) firms significantly increase dividend payouts once they switch from state-owned to privately-owned enterprises.

TABLE 8.3

PROFITS, TAXES, DIVIDENDS, AND DIVIDEND PAYOUT RATIOS OF U.S. CORPORATIONS, 1983–93

This table details the aggregate profits, taxes, and dividends paid by U.S. corporations for the period 1983–93. From these data, annual average dividend payout ratios are computed. All values, except payout ratios, are in billions of current dollars.

Item	1983	1984	1985	1986	1987	1988	1989	1990	1991	1992	1993
Profits before taxes	210.7	240.5	225.0	217.8	287.9	347.5	342.9	365.7	362.3	395.4	449.4
Less: Income tax liab.	77.2	94.0	96.5	106.5	127.1	137.0	141.3	138.7	129.8	146.3	174.0
Equals: Profits after tax	133.5	146.4	128.5	111.3	160.8	210.5	201.6	227.1	232.5	249.1	275.4
Less: Net dividends[a]	81.2	82.7	92.4	109.8	106.2	115.3	134.6	153.5	137.4	150.5	169.0
Equals: Undistrib. Profits	52.3	63.8	36.1	1.6	54.6	95.2	67.1	73.6	95.2	98.6	106.4
Dividend Payout Ratio	60.8%	56.5%	83.0%	98.7%	66.0%	54.8%	66.8%	67.6%	59.1%	60.4%	61.4%

NOTE: [a]DISBURSEMENTS TO U.S. RESIDENTS, MEASURED AFTER ELIMINATIONS OF INTERCORPORATE DIVIDENDS.

SOURCE: STATISTICAL ABSTRACT OF THE UNITED STATES, 1994 (U.S. DEPARTMENT OF COMMERCE, WASHINGTON, D.C.), PG. 560.

coalitions tend to have very low dividend payouts, while companies with more diffuse ownership structures tend to need higher payouts.

8.2.1 Theoretical Explanations for Observed Patterns

It is very hard to conceive of a single theoretical model that can explain all of the empirical regularities described above. Nonetheless, two internally-consistent theoretical models have been developed, and each will be discussed in turn. Greater attention will be given to the first of these, the **Agency Cost/Contracting Model of Dividends** (or simply the "agency cost model"), since it represents the mainstream of current economic thought. This model assumes that dividend payments arise as an attempt to overcome the agency problems that result when there is a separation of corporate ownership and control. In privately held companies with tight ownership coalitions these agency costs are not important, so dividends are not needed. As ownership becomes more atomistic, however, few investors have the incentive or the ability to monitor and control corporate managers, and agency problems become more important. These problems are especially severe in large, slowly-growing firms that generate large quantities of free cash flow. The natural tendency of corporate managers is to spend this cash flow (calling it "investment", of course) rather than pay it out to shareholders.[18] Investors understand these incentives, however, and will thus pay a low price for manager-controlled firms that horde cash, but they are willing to pay higher prices for stock in companies with more responsive managers. Therefore, announcements of dividend initiations or increases are associated with stock price increases, and managers who pay out cash rather than horde it are rewarded through stock options or other stock-related compensation. Other aspects of this model help explain cross-sectional variations in dividend payments based upon industry growth rates or asset characteristics.

The competing **Dividend Signaling Model** assumes that dividends are needed to convey positive information from well-informed managers to poorly-informed shareholders in capital markets characterized by asymmetric information. Cash dividend payments are costly both to the paying firms (since this reduces the amount of money the firm can use for investment) and to shareholders receiving the dividends, since they will have to pay taxes on the dividends received. This means that only the "best" (most profitable) firms can afford to pay dividends, in the sense that they can bear the cost of these payments in terms of reduced investment. Since weaker firms have no incentive to try to mimic the dividend payments of the best firms, a separating equilibrium will result where the most profitable firms (and those with the most valuable investment opportunities) will pay out the most dividends.

Before examining either of these modern theories, however, we must begin by examining the role of dividend policy in a world of perfect capital markets. As you prob-

---

18. The importance of these managerial incentives to over-invest in marginal projects rather than paying excess cash flow out as dividends is hard to over-estimate. Christie and Nanda (1994) document the amazing fact that the unexpected imposition of a tax by the federal government on retained corporate profits in 1936 caused stock prices to *rise* significantly —particularly for low-payout firms. In spite of its direct costs, investors welcomed the tax because it would presumably force recalcitrant managers to pay out cash that they had been effectively hoarding. The fact that firms judged to be subject to the highest agency costs raised dividend payouts less than better-managed firms gives another indication of the power of the incentives weak managers have to retain more than a value-maximizing amount of free cash flow.

ably have already guessed, this model was first put forth by Merton Miller and Franco Modigliani (1961) and, as with capital structure, they came up with an irrelevant result. In a world of perfect information and frictionless capital markets, dividend policy cannot affect the market value of the firm, which is determined solely by the inherent profitability of the firm's assets and the competence of its management team. Even though markets are not frictionless, examining this model will be useful because doing so will allow us to say more conclusively under what conditions dividend policy *will* matter, how it will matter, and to at least suggest how managers should set dividend policy to maximize firm market value.

8.3   DIVIDEND POLICY IN FRICTIONLESS CAPITAL MARKETS

Miller and Modigliani (hereafter M&M) began their analysis of dividend policy by assuming a world with perfect markets, rational behavior, and perfect certainty. For precision, they spelled out their assumptions by defining the phrases *perfect markets* (assumptions 1–4 below), *rational behavior* (assumptions 5–6), and *perfect certainty* (assumptions 7–8). Their model assumed a world where:

1. No buyer or seller (or issuer) of securities is large enough to influence market prices;

2. all traders have equal and costless access to the same information set;

3. there are no transactions costs, such as brokerage costs or transfer fees involved in trading securities;

4. there are no tax differentials between dividends and capital gains or between distributed and undistributed profits;

5. investors prefer more wealth to less, and;

6. investors are indifferent whether wealth increases come about through dividends or through capital gains;

7. every investor has complete assurance as to the future investment program and future profits of every corporation, and;

8. because of this certainty, all corporations issue a single class of security, called common stock.

After you have finished rolling your eyes in disbelief, keep in mind that the purpose of this model is to establish the effect of dividend policy in an idealized world, and then examine how the results change as elements of reality are introduced. Based on their assumptions, M&M spell out their **fundamental principle of valuation**, which states that, "the price of each share must be such that the rate of return (dividends plus capital gains per dollar invested) on every share will be the same throughout the market over any given interval of time." As assumption 7 implies, they assumed away risk differences between shares by assuming perfect certainty about future profits, but it is simple enough to modify this principle to state that the risk-adjusted return, $\rho(t)$, for all shares will be equal. Either way, this required return can be computed as follows:

$$\rho(t) = \left[\frac{d_j(t) + p_j(t+1) - p_j(t)}{p_j(t)} \right] \tag{8.1}$$

where $d_j(t)$ = dividend per share paid by firm j during period t, and
   $p_j(t)$ = the price of a share in firm j at the start of period t.

Equation 8.1 can then be rearranged to formulate the fundamental valuation principle by expressing the price of a firm j share as the sum of its dividend in the current period, $d_j(t)$, plus the share price at the beginning of the next period, $p_j(t + 1)$, discounted back to the present at one plus the required rate of return, $\rho(t)$:

$$p_j(t) = \left[\frac{d_j(t) + p_j(t + 1)}{1 + \rho(t)} \right] \tag{8.2}$$

This expression of a firm's stock price as a function of current period dividend payments and the (expected) stock price at the end of the period is both simple and intuitive, but some of you may have sensed that it is a rather circular valuation formula. Why? To answer that, ask yourself what determines the firm's stock price at the beginning of period $(t + 1)$. Once again, the fundamental principle of valuation says that period's stock price will be the dividend payment during period $(t + 1)$ plus the expected stock price at the beginning of period $(t + 2)$, which itself will be a function of period $(t + 2)$ dividends and the expected end of period stock price. The formula can be cranked ahead as many periods as desired, and the result will always be the same. Ultimately, the value of a firm's stock will be equal to the present value of the stream of dividends that firm will pay on each share for the foreseeable future. This is true even for a company that is not currently paying any dividends at all but instead is reinvesting all profits in the firm. The stream of dividends is still the only source of value to stock market participants, only in this case the stream will not begin until far in the future, at which time it will be very large indeed.

But if cash dividends are the only source of value to market participants, how did M&M arrive at a dividend irrelevant result? As was the case for capital structure, the answer to this question is that the economic value of a firm will always be derived solely from the operating profits the firm is currently generating, and will continue to generate in the future as its investment policy unfolds. As long as the firm accepts all positive-NPV investment projects, and has costless access to capital markets, it can pay any level of dividends it desires each period—but if dividends are paid, the firm must issue new shares to raise the cash required to finance its ongoing investment projects. In M&M's world, a company can choose to retain all its profits and finance its investments with internally-generated cash flow, or that same company can pay out all of its earnings as dividends and raise the cash needed for investment by selling new shares. Since there are no taxes or transactions costs, either strategy produces the same total market value for the firm's shares, although there will be fewer shares outstanding for the retention strategy and each share will be more valuable.

8.3.1 Dividends and aggregate firm value

Before illustrating this point with an example, we must make one more modification to equations 8.1 and 8.2 in order to express the total value of the firm at the beginning of period t, $V(t)$, as a function of the number of shares outstanding at the start of the period, $n(t)$, the price per firm share at the end of period t (which we will call the beginning of period $t + 1$), $p(t + 1)$, and the total dollar amount of dividends paid during period t,

$D(t)$. This last variable is also equal to the dividend per share times the number of shares outstanding, or $D(t) = n(t)d(t)$. Algebraically, total firm value is computed as follows:

$$V(t) = \left[\frac{D(t) + n(t)p(t + 1)}{1 + \rho(t)} \right] \tag{8.3}$$

This formulation allows us to demonstrate how a firm can choose any desired level of dividend payments without affecting firm value, provided investment policy is held constant.

8.3.2 An Example of Dividend Irrelevance in the M&M Model

To make this key point clearly, we will use an example. Consider two firms that are currently the same size, are in the same industry, and have access to the same investment opportunities. Both companies currently have assets worth $20 million and these assets generate operating profits of $2 million each period (providing a steady-state return on investment of 10 percent). Furthermore, assume that the return required by investors, $\rho(t)$, is 10 percent per period for both companies, and that each company is presented with the opportunity to make a $2 million, positive-NPV investment during period t. Assume also that at the start of period t, each firm has 1 million shares outstanding, implying that shares in both firms are initially worth $20 each. The managers of firm P (for payout) want to pay all of the firm's earnings out as dividends, but they also intend to finance the company's $2 million investment opportunity by issuing as many new shares as necessary. The managers of firm R (for retention) would rather not pay dividends, preferring instead to retain the firm's operating profits for use in funding the planned $2 million investment program. Can each management team pursue its preferred strategy and still have the market values of the two firms be identical at the end of the period?

Yes. To see how, we will first examine firm R's strategy, then firm P's, and then we will provide a summary table describing exactly what each strategy involved. Since firm R's managers decide to retain the $2 million ($2.00 per share) profit the firm earns in period t in order to internally finance the $2 million investment project that period, total dividends paid (and dividends per share) are zero and the market value of the firm at the end of period t (beginning of period $t + 1$) is equal to the $20 million beginning value plus the $2 million investment plus the net present value of the investment opportunity. For simplicity, we will assume for now that the project's NPV is positive but small enough to be ignored. Therefore the beginning of period $t + 1$ value of firm R is equal to $22 million ($20 million + $2 million), which is equal to $22 per share since the firm did not have to issue any new shares during period t. Plugging these values into equation 8.1 verifies that firm R shareholders indeed earn the 10 percent return on investment they require in period t:

$$\rho(t) = \left[\frac{d_r(t) + p_r(t + 1) - p_r(t)}{p_r(t)} \right] = \left[\frac{0 + \$22 - \$20}{\$20} \right] = 10\%$$

Furthermore, we can use our computed figures to work backwards to verify that the beginning of period t firm value is indeed the $20 million ($mm$) we assumed in our example:

$$V_r(t) = \left[\frac{D_r(t) + n_r(t)p_r(t + 1)}{1 + \rho(t)} \right] = \left[\frac{0 + (1\ mm)\ (\$22)}{1.10} \right] = \$20\ mm$$

So far, so good, but what about firm P? This firm's managers decide to pay out as a $2 per share dividend the total period t firm profit of $2 million, so they must raise the $2 million needed to finance the investment project by selling new shares. But how many shares must they sell? To answer that, we must reason through what the beginning of period $t + 1$ price of firm P's shares will be. We know that firm P's existing assets at the end of period t will still be worth $20 million, and so the price of the existing firm P shares at that time will still be $20 each. Therefore, the firm must raise $2 million ($2 mm) by selling 100,000 shares at $20 each, and the total number of shares outstanding at the beginning of period $t + 1$ will be 1,100,000. This yields a total firm market value at that time of $20 per share $\times$ 1.1 million shares $=$ $22 million. Once again, we can verify that firm P shareholders earned the required 10 percent return during period t, and that all of our computed values are consistent with the initial firm valuation we assumed:

$$\rho(t) = \left[\frac{d_p(t) + p_p(t + 1) - p_p(t)}{p_p(t)} \right] = \left[\frac{\$2 + \$20 - \$20}{\$20} \right] = 10\%$$

and

$$V_p(t) = \left[\frac{D_p(t) + n_p(t)p_p(t + 1)}{1 + \rho(t)} \right] = \left[\frac{\$2\ mm + (1\ mm)(\$20)}{1.10} \right] = \$20\ mm$$

By now, you are probably thinking this has all been done with mirrors, but the essential points of this comparative example are really quite simple. Investors are indifferent between (1) allowing the firm to retain corporate profits to fund positive-NPV investment opportunities and (2) receiving cash dividends and allowing the firm to fund its investment project with a new share issue. In the former case, initial investors earn their 10 percent required return exclusively as a capital gain on the shares they hold, and their proportional stake in the firm will be unchanged—someone who owned 10,000 shares, or 1 percent, of the company initially would still own 1 percent at the end. In the second case, initial shareholders would receive their 10 percent period t return exclusively as a dividend, and an initial 10,000 share, 1 percent stake in the firm would be diluted to a 10,000/1,100,000 = 0.91 percent stake after the firm issued new shares. Given frictionless markets and perfect certainty, there is no reason to expect investors to prefer either the full-payout or the full-retention strategy or, for that matter, any combination of partial payout and partial retention. As long as *investment policy is fixed*, dividend policy is truly irrelevant since it cannot affect firm value.

8.3.3 The importance of holding investment policy fixed

The problem most people run into in understanding dividend policy irrelevance is that they fail to keep investment policy truly fixed. A common error is, using our example, to compare firm R with firm P without requiring that firm P finance an investment equivalent to firm R's through the issue of new shares. If additional investment in firm P is not required, one is in fact valuing a bond that yields a steady $2 million return on $20 million of assets for a return of 10 percent per period. This will give the same return as for firm R in our example, but firm R is actually a company that is growing in size by 10 percent per period and will cease to be comparable with firm P in a single period. Another common error is to assume that firms which retain their earnings are able to earn a higher return on their investments than can firms which pay their earnings out. Not surprisingly, this error will demonstrate that high-retention firms are more valuable than high-payout companies, but this is caused by a difference in investment policy, not dividend policy. In the M&M world, we always return to the same fundamental conclusion—value is created by investing in productive assets, not by financial manipulations such as changing capital structures or altering dividend payouts.

8.4 EFFECTS OF MARKET IMPERFECTIONS

Few of us have ever transacted in frictionless capital markets, so our next task is to examine how robust the M&M dividend policy irrelevance propositions are under more realistic market conditions. We will examine how weakening each of the major perfect market assumptions we made earlier impacts a firm's optimal dividend policy. Our final goal will be to determine whether a given firm has an "optimal" (value-maximizing) dividend policy and, if so, how that policy should be set. As we proceed, most of you will notice a puzzling fact: almost all of the "real world" issues we incorporate—such as taxes, transactions costs for issuing new securities, and uncertainty about a firm's investment opportunities—argue *against* the payment of cash dividends, and yet American corporations have been paying out roughly half of their annual earnings for many decades. We will show that observed dividend policies can best be explained with agency costs, asymmetric information, and ownership structure arguments.

8.4.1 Personal Income Taxes

Incorporating only personal taxes on dividend income into the M&M model yields an unambiguous result—firms should retain all earnings and shareholders should reap their investment returns in the form of capital gains resulting from stock appreciation. To see this, consider the company we discussed above that generates $2 million in operating profits each period which it can either reinvest or pay out as dividends (and then fund investment with a new stock issue). In a no-tax world, investors are indifferent between full corporate retention and full payout, because in the first case $2 million is reinvested at the required 10 percent return in the firm and the shareholders experience a $2 increase in the value of their shares, while in the second case shareholders receive $2 million (net) in cash dividends and then experience a proportional decline in their fractional ownership of the company. If a personal income tax on dividend income of say, 40 percent is now imposed, the irrelevance between the retention and payout strategy disappears. The payoff to the retention strategy is unchanged, but now the shareholders of the payout firm receive only $2,000,000 (1 − tax rate) = $2,000,000 (0.6) = $1,200,000 each period rather than $2 million. Furthermore, unless firm P (the payout company) promises to change to a full retention policy, new investors will value the shares being offered to finance investment as securities that yield a fully taxable return, and they will offer only $20 (0.6) = $12 per share rather than $20 for each new share purchased. Dividend payments become dominated cash flows, and all taxable investors prefer capital gains income to dividend income.[19]

But what if a large capital gains tax is also imposed—won't that re-establish dividend policy irrelevance? (Before reading on, see if you can reason through to an answer). Apparently, imposing a 40 percent capital gains tax will again make investors indifferent between taxable dividends and taxable capital gains, but this will only happen if the tax on stock appreciation is levied every period, regardless of whether the shares are sold or not. In fact, capital gains taxes are almost invariably taxed only upon *realization* (when the shares are sold), and a tax payment delayed is a tax payment rendered less valuable. Furthermore, in the United States stock-related capital gains taxes can often be escaped entirely if shares are passed on to an investor's heirs at his or her death. Therefore, there generally remains a very large tax preference for capital gains over cash dividends, even if the nominal tax rates for both types of income are the same.

STOCK REPURCHASES   American capital markets provide yet another quirky example of why dividends should be tax-dominated cash flows. The U.S. tax code treats a cash dividend received as ordinary income (which is taxed at the full marginal personal tax rate), but the law considers cash received through a share repurchase program as capital gains income (which historically has been taxed at a preferential rate).[20] In a share repurchase program, the firm itself generally makes an open market offer to repurchase shares from investors at an above-market price. Investors who sell their shares receive a premium price, and pay capital gains taxes rather than ordinary income taxes. Non-participating shareholders experience a large (unrealized) capital gain, since there remain fewer shares outstanding after the repurchase is completed and their fractional ownership has increased. In other words, share repurchase programs seemingly represent an alternative (and tax-advantaged) method of distributing cash to those investors who need a liquid return on their investment, while simultaneously minimizing the tax liabilities of non-participating shareholders.[21]

So why don't more U.S. companies substitute share repurchase programs for cash dividend payments? There are three answers to this question. First, many companies do have large, ongoing repurchase programs and the total value of shares repurchased often exceeds $10 billion per year. Second, the Internal Revenue Service has the power to rule that a given company's share repurchase program is merely an attempt to avoid taxes, and it can then impose the higher personal income tax rates on all income received by in-

---

19. Even if one assumes that investors desire a cash return on their investment portfolios, this alone does not "rescue" cash dividend payments from being irrational, since investors can also receive cash payments through corporate share repurchase programs. In the United States, investors who sell shares that have been held for at least a year are subject only to tax on the realized profit on the trade, and then only at the long-term capital gains tax rate—which has almost always been lower than the personal tax rate on cash dividend income. See footnote 21 for a full citation listing.

20. In many of the most important European and Asian countries, company-sponsored share repurchases are illegal.

21. Numerous studies document significant positive abnormal returns to shareholders at the announcement of (even during) repurchase programs. See, as examples, Dann (1981), Vermaelen (1981), Lakonishok and Vermaelen (1990), Bagwell (1992), and Denis (1990). Repurchases are examined theoretically in Ofer and Thakor (1987) and Brennan and Thakor (1990).

vestors under the program. In other words, companies that adopt routine share repurchase programs in lieu of dividend payments can theoretically be imposing large supplemental tax liabilities on their shareholders. The actual importance of this rule in deterring repurchases is questionable, however, because the IRS almost never invokes it in actual cases. The third reason for not substituting repurchases for dividend payments is that a repurchase program can discourage specialists from making a market in the firm's stock, because they would often be forced to trade with a seller (a company insider/manager) who had superior information about the firm's prospects. To protect himself or herself, the specialist would have to charge a higher price to make a market in such a firm's shares, and this would hurt individual investors wishing to trade shares at the lowest possible price.[22] In spite of these three problems, however, it still remains something of a puzzle why more firms do not eliminate (or at least reduce) dividend payments in favor of the share repurchase strategy, since the latter seems to have such obvious tax advantages.[23]

8.4.2 Tests for Tax Effects

Having introduced the issue of personal taxes and dividend payments, many of you are probably wondering whether empirical studies have documented systematic tax effects in studies of dividend valuation. The answer to this question is—perhaps. Researchers have employed two principal methodologies to study tax effects. The first method is to employ a variant of the capital asset pricing model (CAPM) to see if investors demand a higher pre-tax return on high-versus low-dividend-paying stocks, as would be expected if investors paid a higher effective tax rate on cash dividend income than on capital gains income. Numerous studies have examined precisely this issue, and most have documented a positive relation between dividend yield and stock returns, but there is no consensus regarding whether this is in fact a tax effect or some other phenomenon.[24] Furthermore, proponents of a tax effect model have great difficulty explaining why rational corporate managers would ever pay cash dividends if doing so resulted in a higher pre-tax required return. It would seem that these managers could increase stock prices, and thus lower the firm's cost of capital simply by cutting dividend payouts. The survival of dividend payments in modern economies suggests that the tax-effect models of dividend valuation must be missing something important.

EX-DIVIDEND DAY STUDIES   The second methodology used to study the differential effects of capital gains versus dividend income taxation on common stock valuation is to examine the average change in a firm's stock price on its ex-dividend day. Prior to this day, an investor who buys the stock is entitled to receive the next dividend payment.

---

22. This point is made by Barclay and Smith (1988).

23. Another issue that has puzzled researchers is why firms pay stock dividends (distributing additional shares to existing stockholders), and why the stock market seems to react positively to these share distributions—since they should be financial non-events. Similarly, it is unclear why companies split the value of their stocks, since this merely doubles (or more) the number of shares outstanding, and should simply cause the value of each share to decline by half. Instead stock prices decline by a less than proportional amount. Stock dividends and splits are examined in Grinblatt, Masulis, and Titman (1984), Lakonishok and Lev (1987), Brennan and Copeland (1988), and McNichols and Dravid (1990).

24. See the studies cited in footnote 11 above.

After the stock goes ex-dividend, the dividend is paid to the former owner. Therefore, a taxable investor who owns a stock about to go ex-dividend faces a choice between selling the stock at the higher cum-dividend (with dividend) price, thus taking his or her return in the form of a capital gain, or waiting until the stock goes ex-dividend, selling the stock at a lower price, and receiving a return in the form of cash dividends. If stock prices fall by the full amount of the dividend payment, most taxable investors would prefer to sell shares before they go ex-dividend, thereby earning a higher after-tax return on a capital gain than on a cash dividend. The empirical observation that stock prices fall on ex-dividend days by significantly less than the amount of the dividend (on average, by about 60–70 cents on the dollar) has often been interpreted as evidence of a tax effect in dividend valuation.[25]

While ex-dividend day studies show plausible average results, there is reason to be suspicious of these studies as definitive evidence of differential tax effects, most tellingly because transactions costs must be very high for a pure tax effect to be observed. This is because of the incentive a tax-free trader (or a corporate investor, who faces lower taxes on dividends than on capital gains) has to buy stocks just before they go ex-dividend if the price is expected to decline by less than the amount of the dividend payment. Such an investor could make huge, virtually risk-free profits by, for example, purchasing a stock that has promised a $1.00 per share dividend payment before the ex-day, receiving the dividend payment, and then selling it on the ex-dividend day for only $0.65 per share less. As long as this investor's trading costs are less than $0.35 per share, such "dividend arbitrage" is very profitable, and it is more profitable the higher is the nominal per share dividend payment. For example, a $50 per share stock that pays only a $0.25 per share quarterly dividend (a 2 percent per year dividend yield) will be unlikely to attract arbitrageurs, while a similar $50 per share stock that pays $1.00 per share (an 8 percent annual yield) will probably attract many such traders— particularly since the per share trading costs will be similar for both stocks.[26]

Another conceptual flaw in these ex-dividend studies is their inability to explain why relative ex-day price drops have not increased (become closer to matching the nominal dividend payment) over time as tax-free investors have risen to prominence in modern stock markets. Since institutional investors currently account for as much as ninety percent of average trading volume on the New York Stock Exchange, and these investors face very low trading costs, it is not clear why a differential tax-effect that is only relevant for certain individual investors should continue to be observed.

To summarize this section, phenomena that can plausibly be considered tax effects have been documented in some, but not all, empirical dividend valuation studies, but

25. Modern ex-dividend studies trace their roots to Elton and Gruber (1970). Subsequent studies that examine the Elton and Gruber model of the ex-day price drop as a reflection of relative personal tax rates on dividends and capital gains income include Hess (1982), Kalay (1982a), Eades, Hess, and Kim (1984, 1994), Booth and Johnston (1984), Poterba and Summers (1984), Lakonishok and Vermaelen (1983, 1986), Poterba (1986), Barclay (1987), Karpoff and Walkling (1988, 1990), Michaely (1991), Robin (1991), and Stickel (1991).

26. Papers supporting this trading cost explanation of why ex-day price drops do not directly reflect tax differentials include Lakonishok and Vermaelen (1983, 1986), Poterba and Summers (1984), Eades, Hess, and Kim (1984, 1994), and Karpoff and Walkling (1988, 1990). The ex-dividend day behavior of options prices is examined in a paper with that title by Kalay and Subrahmanyan (1984), while an option pricing explanation of the ex-day price drop of common stocks is provided in Heath and Jarrow (1988).

the interpretation of these results remains controversial. Furthermore, even if these phenomena are tax-related, they are almost surely contaminated by differences in transactions costs and other influences, and cannot be used to directly infer marginal tax rates for any individual firm's shareholders.

8.4.3 Transactions Costs

We have seen that personal taxes cannot explain observed dividend payments, but what about transactions costs? Positive security trading costs affect expected dividend payouts in two, potentially offsetting ways. First, if routinely selling small share lots is costly—in terms of deadweight brokerage costs—then an investor wishing to achieve a cash return on his or her investment would find dividend payments an attractive way to achieve liquidity. Regular cash dividend payments would represent a costless way to receive a cash return on the investor's stock portfolio, and this cash could be used either for consumption or to rebalance the investor's portfolio. A serious flaw in this argument, however, is that it suggests dividend payments should be highest in relatively undeveloped markets characterized by the highest transactions costs, but in reality dividend payments are the highest in the United States, Britain, and Canada—three countries with highly liquid, low-cost stock markets (see Bhide 1993). Furthermore, a transactions cost argument cannot easily explain why aggregate dividend payouts in the U.S. have remained relatively constant over time, even as American stock markets have become vastly more efficient and the costs of trading have declined precipitously.

The second effect of transactions costs on dividend payments is unambiguously negative. This relates to a corporation's need to replace cash paid out as dividends with cash raised by new share sales. Remember that the M&M dividend irrelevance result depends critically on a company being able to fund its investment either by retaining corporate profits or paying out profits as dividends and replacing this cash with funds received from new share sales. As long as share issues are costless, investors will be indifferent between receiving returns in the form of capital gains (on non-dividend-paying shares) or as cash dividends on shares. If issuing securities entails large, deadweight costs, however, all parties should prefer a full retention strategy, and no corporation should ever both pay dividends and raise funds for investment by issuing new securities (especially stock, since this has the highest issuance cost).[27] Since most large American corporations do just that, it is obvious that transactions costs alone do not explain observed dividend policy.

8.4.4 The residual theory of dividend payments

The discussion above suggests another possible explanation of observed dividend payments. Might they simply be a residual—the cash left over after corporations have funded all their positive-NPV investments? This would be a rational, value-maximizing strategy, and would help explain why firms in rapidly-growing industries retain almost all of their profits while firms in mature, slow-growing industries tend to have very

---

27. Interestingly, an important dividend theory paper suggests that corporations pay dividends precisely because this will force them into the capital market for financing (rather than being able to rely solely on internal financing), where investors have the incentive and ability to monitor and discipline corporate management. See Easterbrook (1984).

high dividend payouts. It would also explain the "life-cycle" pattern of dividend payments for individual firms. Young companies that are growing rapidly rarely pay any dividends, but those same companies typically change to a high payout strategy once they mature and their growth rate slows.

An alternative explanation is that dividend policy is a **residual** of a more fundamentally important capital structure policy. For example, if a particular firm decides (for whatever reason) that it wishes to maintain a fifty percent debt-to-total-capital ratio over time, then each period it will finance half of its new investment needs with borrowed funds and half with retained earnings (or new share issues, if earnings are too low). Any remaining corporate profits will be paid out to shareholders as dividends. To nail this point down conceptually, keep in mind that some aspect of a firm's financial policy *must* be a residual. Since profits fluctuate each period, and value-maximizing firms will fund all positive-NPV investment opportunities, management must consciously set a firm's capital structure, dividend, and security issuance policies each period in such a way that the firm's cash inflows equal its cash outflows (to satisfy the cash flow identity).[28] With given profit and investment levels, management can set any two of these three variables at any desired level, but the third must then become a residual.

As an example of the decisions a firm must make each period, consider a company with annual profits of \$4,000,000 and positive investment opportunities equal to \$5,000,000. It can choose any desired level of two of the three variables discussed above. If, say, the firm desired a debt-to-total-capital ratio of fifty percent and a dividend payout equal to half (50%) of corporate profits (or, equivalently, a constant dividend payment of \$2,000,000 per year), then it would pay shareholders \$2,000,000 of its profits as dividends, it would retain \$2,000,000 of those profits to finance its investment, and it would issue \$2,500,000 in debt and \$500,000 in new equity. In this case, security issuance policy is the residual. If, on the other hand, the firm wanted the same capital structure policy (50% debt, 50% equity), and also wanted to refrain from any new stock issues, this could be achieved by allowing dividends to become a residual. In this case, the firm would issue new debt worth \$2,500,000, and would match that with \$2,500,000 of retained profits, thereby funding its investments with the desired ratio of debt and equity. Obviously, the remaining \$1,500,000 in profits would be paid out as cash dividends to shareholders. See if you can apply this logic to determine the firm's strategy if it wishes to achieve a fifty percent dividend payout without issuing any new stock (thereby making capital structure the residual variable).

The residual theory of dividends probably has merit, but it suffers from one massive empirical problem. Dividend payments simply are not as variable as they would be if firms were viewing them as residuals from the cash flow identity. In fact, dividend payments are the most stable of any cash flow into or out of a firm, and all available evidence suggest that corporate managers both smooth dividends (keep the nominal dividend payment per share constant) and are very cautious about changing established dividend payout levels.

---

28. The constraints placed on a firm's dividend payout policy by the cash flow identity play a prominent role in Kalay's (1982b) study of the relationship between bond covenants and dividend payments in a large, random sample of companies. Kalay documents that bond indenture agreements establish a "pool" of funds—mostly retained earnings, but also including equity financings—that can be paid out to shareholders as cash dividends, and he argues that these covenants are designed to minimize the natural conflict of interest between creditors and shareholders.

Furthermore, companies routinely issue new equity even as they maintain constant dividend payments—actions that should be irrational in a world with positive security issuance costs. Clearly, the residual theory is not the sole explanation of observed dividend payments, and is probably not even an important explanation. On the other hand, a modern "cousin" of the residual theory—the free cash flow theory of dividend payout, developed by Michael Jensen and others—has proven much more robust. This theory is discussed in depth later in this section.

8.4.5 Dividends as Transmitters of Information

Sooner or later, every intellectually curious person who studies the question of why firms pay dividends is drawn to the idea that dividends exist so that managers, who have a better understanding of the firm's true financial condition than shareholders do, can convey this information to shareholders in a way that will be both believable and hard for weaker firms to duplicate. Phrased in economic terms, in a world that is characterized by informational asymmetries between managers and investors, cash dividend payments serve as a credible transmitter of information from corporate insiders (officers and directors) to the company's shareholders. Viewed this way, every aspect of a firm's dividend policy conveys significant new information. When a company begins paying dividends (a dividend initiation), this act conveys management's confidence that the firm is now profitable enough to both fund its investment projects and pay out cash. Furthermore, since investors and managers both understand that once a particular dividend payment strategy is initiated it is rarely cut back later, a dividend initiation also implies that management is confident that earnings will be high enough in the future to support the newly adopted payment level.

The same logic applies to dividend increases. Since everyone understands that dividend cuts are to be avoided at almost all costs, the fact that management is willing to increase dividend payments clearly implies it is confident profits will remain high enough to support the new payment level. Dividend increases therefore suggest a *permanent* increase in the firm's normal level of profitability. Unfortunately, this logic applies even more forcefully to dividend decreases. Because all concerned understand that dividend cuts are perceived as being very bad news, managers will only reduce dividend payments when they have no choice—when the financial health of the firm is declining, and no turnaround is in sight—and the stock market's reaction to dividend cuts is nothing short of foul.[29]

There is much empirical support for the informational role of dividend payments, beginning with John Lintner's (1956) classic article documenting that corporate managers approach dividend decisions with great care and with the idea that the level of dividend payments selected will become a fixed expense of the company for the foreseeable future. Lintner shows that managers are far more concerned with *changing* an established per share dividend payment than they are with finding the theoretically "correct" level of dividend payout (what fraction of profits should be paid out each period). A later study by Fama and Babiak (1968) documents that managers do in fact have target payout ratios in mind and that dividend payments per share track the course

---

29. For documentation of these points, see the articles cited in footnotes 7–11 above.

of corporate profits quite closely over time. However, Fama and Babiak also show that managers employ a **partial adjustment** strategy in adjusting dividend payments to changes in corporate profits, wherein an increase in profit levels will not be fully reflected in a higher equilibrium dividend per share until several quarters have elapsed. This strategy allows management to become confident that profits have in fact permanently increased before fully committing to higher dividend payments. Naturally, over time, knowledge of this corporate behavior pattern is incorporated into investor perceptions of dividend policy changes.

The third path-breaking empirical article on dividend policy, by Aharony and Swary (1980), documents how stock market investors react to dividend increases, decreases, and continuations. They show that dividend increases result, on average, in a statistically significant 0.35 percent positive stock price change (abnormal return), while dividend continuations (no change in dividends per share) are financial non-events causing essentially no measurable change in stock prices. Dividend cuts (or eliminations), on the other hand, are viewed as true disasters—yielding statistically significant average stock price declines of between 1.13 and 1.46 percent on the announcement day, and cumulative stock price declines of between 4.62 and 5.39 percent over the two-week period preceding and including the day the dividend cut is announced. These basic results are verified by later studies, some of which instead examine dividend initiations (technically, a dividend increase) and document significantly positive stock price changes in the range of 1.5 to 3.5 percent.[30] We can therefore conclude that markets react to announcements of dividend changes in systematic, predictable ways that are consistent with the hypothesis that dividends convey relevant information in markets characterized by informational asymmetries.

8.4.6 Ownership Structure and Dividend Policy

While dividends clearly serve an information revelation function, this cannot be the only explanation either for the existence of dividends or for their cross-sectional variability, since several empirical regularities are not consistent with this theory. First, this rationale cannot explain why dividend payments are so much higher in the United States, Canada, and Great Britain than they are in other developed economies, since Anglo-American firms are no more profitable than other companies. While better investment opportunities in certain Asian economies may explain some of this difference, differential investment spending certainly cannot explain why continental European or Japanese companies pay less of their earnings out as dividends than do North American and British firms. An even more telling argument against a pure information revelation story is the fact that, within the U.S. economy, private and newly-public firms rarely pay any dividends, while virtually all large, established companies pay out sizable fractions of their earnings as cash dividends.[31] Differences in investment opportunities again explain some of this difference, but such a sharp dichotomy between small and large, or private and public, firms suggests that the structure of a firm's ownership critically impacts its need to pay regular cash dividends.

---

30. See the articles cited in footnote 9 above.

31. See the articles cited in footnotes 16 and 17 above.

CONTROL COALITION COHESIVENESS   An ownership structure explanation for dividend policy is in fact very attractive, particularly if one allows a role for other influences—especially information revelation. This is because ownership structure can influence the need for a firm to pay dividends in two ways. First, in a tightly-knit ownership coalition, there is relatively little informational asymmetry between corporate insiders and outsiders, so there is little need to use dividends to convey information. This is true both in family-owned businesses, where shareholders and managers tend to be the same people, and in larger companies where banks and industrial groups exercise great authority in corporate governance. In both cases, a relatively few people make decisions and communications between them can be very rapid and very credible. Based on this logic, differences in the dispersion of stock ownership can help explain differences in dividend payout between American, British, and Canadian companies on the one hand—which rely very heavily on capital markets for financing and have dispersed ownership structures—and continental European, Japanese, Korean, and other Asian firms on the other hand, since these firms typically rely much more on bank financing and have much tighter ownership structures. Similar logic helps explain the difference between public and private American companies. If a firm has an ownership structure characterized by a small number of principal shareholders, who know each other well and who can communicate privately with each other, there is very little informational asymmetry between shareholders and managers and thus little need for managers to use dividend payments to convey information.

The second, and probably more basic, reason ownership structure might impact the need to pay dividends is that in firms with tightly-knit ownership coalitions there is little separation between corporate ownership and control, while in large public companies with diffuse ownership structures the separation is almost complete. As we have seen many times in this book already, whenever there is a separation between ownership and control, potentially serious agency problems almost always arise because corporate managers bear less than the full cost of any poor performance, and they reap less than the full benefit resulting from exceptionally good performance. These agency problems become more serious as the firm's ownership structure becomes more diffuse, both because managers own increasingly smaller fractions of their own firms' shares and because fewer and fewer shareholders have the proper incentives to monitor corporate managers as the average size of an ownership stake falls. Therefore, deadweight agency costs grow as the firm's ownership structure splinters, and this becomes even more serious in firms that are generating large amounts of free cash flow (cash flow in excess of that needed to fund all positive-NPV investment opportunities.)

DIVIDENDS AS BONDING MECHANISMS   The existence of these deadweight costs gives managers an incentive to find a method of **bonding** (credibly committing) themselves to a value-maximizing strategy. One very effective bonding technique is to commit to the payment of a fixed cash dividend each period, since this is much more credible than any statements managers might try to make.[32] This promise is also self-enforcing, since any move to "cheat" by reducing dividend payments is likely to be

---

32. The basic logic of this agency cost minimization role of dividend payments is developed, in a capital structure context, by Jensen (1986).

met by an immediate stock price decline, followed by unpleasant meetings with unhappy shareholders. Once again this logic helps explain observed cross-sectional differences in dividend payout, especially the difference between public and private firms. Since in private firms there is little separation between ownership and control, few agency problems arise that must be overcome with dividend payments, whereas the agency problems that arise in large publicly-traded companies are severe enough to warrant very sizable dividend payouts.

Even if agency costs were not a problem in corporate finance, modern capital markets offer yet one more reason why a firm's ownership structure might impact its dividend decisions. The reason is that roughly half of the outstanding equity of large American companies is owned by institutional investors—primarily pension funds, insurance companies, and mutual funds, who often have different investment cash flow preferences than do ordinary individual investors.[33] While this is less important for mutual funds, which essentially act as a manager of individuals' funds, the distinction is very important for other institutional investors, for four reasons. First, they are effectively untaxed on their investment returns, and thus have little reason to prefer capital gains to dividend income, or vice versa. Second, their investment horizon is, almost by definition, very long-term in nature, suggesting that their preferences will generally be for companies with opportunities to profitably reinvest earnings, rather than for companies with large dividend payouts. Third, the toughest investment problem for many of these investors is not illiquidity, but rather finding a profitable home for all of the cash pouring in as premium income or pension contributions. Therefore, it is hard to see why these investors would prefer high-dividend-paying stocks to low-paying shares, since high dividend payments merely compound their problem. Finally, institutional investors, who often trade equity in 10,000 share blocs, face transactions costs of trading that are almost zero, and thus should place little value on the transactions-cost-minimizing role that dividends might play for other investors.

The practical importance of the issues raised above is somewhat questionable, both because the influences partially offset each other and because the determinants of the investment patterns of institutional investors, as well as their impact on the financial policies chosen by corporations, remain two of the great unanswered questions of modern finance. It is also true that the scale and impact of institutional investment differs greatly around the world, so sweeping statements about how their global rise to prominence should have influenced dividend payouts must naturally be carefully hedged. Nonetheless, it is somewhat puzzling that dividend payouts in most countries have remained relatively constant over time even as investment has become increasingly institutionalized, since dividend payments should be less important to these investors than to individual stockholders. As they have become more preeminent, their demand for lower-dividend-paying firms should have caused these companies to appreciate in value relative to high-payout companies, which over time should have caused a reduction in the average dividend payout of all firms. This has not happened. Perhaps, as Miller and Modigliani first

33. Black (1992) presents summary evidence showing that institutional equity ownership as a percent of total U.S market capitalization has increased from 38.0 percent in 1981 to 53.3 percent in 1990, and that one-third of the 1,000 largest companies had more than 69 percent institutional ownership in 1990. Furthermore, he documents that levels of institutional ownership (and clout) are much higher in Germany, Japan, and Britain than in the United States.

suggested in their seminal dividend policy article, the need for all investors to have well-diversified portfolios will prevent dividend "clienteles" from forming, or at least will keep one type of dividend-paying firm from establishing dominance.[34]

8.5   THE AGENCY COST/CONTRACTING MODEL

The Agency Cost/Contracting Model of Dividends (or agency cost model) is currently the leading mainstream economic model for explaining observed dividend payouts. In many ways, it is simply a restatement of the net effects of the influences discussed above that modify the basic M&M dividend irrelevance model to account for real world market imperfections. Therefore, it lacks the elegance, simplicity, and innate internal consistency of the competing signaling model, or of other equilibrium models in economics, but it offers a rational and robust explanation both for why dividends exist and why they have the cross-sectional patterns actually observed.

In a nutshell, the agency cost model explains cash dividend payments as value-maximizing attempts by managers of certain companies to minimize the deadweight costs of the agency conflict between managers and shareholders that arises naturally in large public companies where there is a separation of ownership and control. The severity of these agency problems—which show up primarily as a tendency to retain cash flow by over-investing in zero- or negative-NPV projects—is in turn a function of (1) the industry the firm operates in, the company's size, the capital intensity of the firm's production process, the free cash flow generated, and the availability of positive-NPV investment opportunities to the firm; and (2) the number of shareholders, their relative "tightness" or "diffuseness", and the presence or absence of an active, large share bloc-holder willing and able to directly monitor corporate management.[35]

Other factors that influence dividend payments include high transactions costs involved in buying, selling, or issuing securities; the tax treatment of capital gains versus dividend income; the relative importance of institutional investors in a firm's ownership structure, and the rôle national law and tradition allows them to play in corporate governance; the amount of information corporations are mandated to disclose; and the relative importance of capital markets versus financial intermediaries in financing corporate activities. Corporate managers who pursue a dividend payment policy that is in the shareholders' best interests will be rewarded by increasing share prices and greater professional tenure, while managers who ignore investor preferences regarding dividends will see their firm's share price decline and will soon find themselves out of a job. Dividend payments clearly have survival value, but the optimum level for individual firms can only be determined by market trial and error. The predictions of the agency cost model

---

34. Several other dividend "puzzles" remain unanswered. While we have clearly progressed in our understanding since Fischer Black (1976) wrote his famous paper, "The Dividend Puzzle," we still cannot conclusively answer the questions posed in the first two lines of his article: Why do corporations pay dividends? Why do investors pay attention to dividends? The only published paper that sought to directly answer the first question—Feldstein and Green (1983)—was roundly criticized by subsequent researchers for its view that dividends exist primarily to offer investors diversification opportunities unavailable elsewhere. The second question was addressed indirectly by Shefrin and Statman (1984), and by Long (1978). Long finds a preference for cash dividends, but a somewhat contrary finding is reported in Ang, Blackwell, and Megginson (1991).

35. Perhaps the best statement, and empirical test, of this model is in Barclay, Smith, and Watts (1995).

about the relationship between corporate-level variables and expected dividend payout are summarized below:

Increases in This Firm-Level Variable	Impact Dividend Payout as Follows
Asset growth rate	Reduce
Positive-NPV investment opportunities	Reduce
Capital intensity of the production process	Increase
Free cash flow generated	Increase
Number of individual shareholders	Increase
Relative "tightness" of ownership coalition	Reduce
Size of largest bloc-holder	Reduce

In addition to firm-level variables, macroeconomic and national financial variables also influence equilibrium dividend payments. The predictions of the agency cost/contracting model concerning these variables are detailed below:

Increases in This Macroeconomic Variable	Impact Dividend Payout as Follows
Transactions costs of security trading	Increase
Personal tax rates on dividend income	Reduce
Personal tax rates on capital gains income	Increase
Importance of institutional investors	Reduce
Power of institutional investors in corporate governance	Reduce
Relative importance of capital markets versus intermediated financing	Increase
Amount of corporate information disclosure	Reduce

As our discussion in the text and footnotes of previous sections makes clear, we interpret the vast bulk of the available empirical evidence on dividend payments and valuation as being supportive of the agency cost model. We now turn to an examination of the signaling model of dividend policy, which has arisen as a serious competitor to the agency cost model during the last two decades.

8.6   THE SIGNALING MODEL

As in the case of capital structure theory, finance theorists have recently developed full-scale economic models of dividend payments as value-maximizing responses to pervasive informational asymmetries between corporate managers and shareholders.[36] This model is

---

36. The first major dividend signaling paper was Bhattacharya (1979). Important subsequent signaling models were developed in Miller and Rock (1985), John and Williams (1985), Ambarish, John, and Williams (1987), Williams (1988), and John and Lang (1991).

based on the idea that managers of firms with exceptionally good financial prospects cannot costlessly and credibly convey that information to uninformed shareholders, because any costless action they might take—such as publicly announcing the firm's prospects—could also be costlessly mimicked by weaker firms. Since investors understand the incentives of weaker firms to mimic stronger ones (to profit from stock price increases that, if believed, would greet good news), they will not believe any public announcement and all firms will be "pooled" in investors' eyes into one average quality class.

In order to overcome this market failure, a strong firm has an incentive to employ a **signal** that would be costly, but affordable, for it to employ but which would be prohibitively expensive for a weaker firm to mimic. Dividends fit this definition of a signal very well, and several finance authors have built dividend signaling models on the classic papers by Akerlof, Spence, and Riley.[37] Cash distributions are costly to the dividend-paying firm, both because the company must generate enough cash to support a permanently high dividend payout and because paying this cash out prevents it from being used to finance positive-NPV investment opportunities. Less profitable firms either do not generate enough cash to mimic this dividend payout, or they would find the cost in foregone investment prohibitively expensive, or both. The net result is a **separating equilibrium**, in which stronger firms employ a signal, and are rewarded by a higher stock price, while weaker firms choose not to signal and are valued accordingly.[38] This equilibrium is both stable—no party can profit by inappropriate signaling behavior—and efficient, in that the values of all companies correctly reflect their true prospects and investors are able to differentiate strong from weak firms.

As you have probably gathered, employing a signal is akin to **burning money**—it is wasteful for everyone, but firms with good financial prospects can look forward to recouping this cost in the future (through subsequent share issues at the new, higher share prices), while weaker firms cannot. The importance of using cash flow from operations as a signal is stressed by Bhattacharya (1979), while Miller and Rock (1985) emphasize the importance of foregone investment spending in their model. Other authors, particularly John and Williams (1985) and Ambarish, John, and Williams (1987), stress the importance of the dissipative costs of personal taxes on dividend income in making dividend payments a viable signal. While the details of each model vary, the basic idea is the same in each case. Dividends serve as costly (indeed, wasteful) signals of firm value in markets characterized by asymmetric information between managers and shareholders, but they survive because they are the least expensive way to credibly convey quality differences between firms to uninformed investors.

8.6.1 Empirical Assessments

So how well do these signaling models explain observed dividend behavior? They have some successes. For example, the cash flow signaling models are consistent with the observation that dividend payout tends to be directly related to firm profitability, and

---

37. The real "grandfather" of all signaling models in economics is Akerlof (1970). Pivotal subsequent signaling models in economics include Spence (1973) and Riley (1979). The first significant application of signaling theory in the finance literature (in a capital structure setting) is by Leland and Pyle (1977).

38. If signaling cannot yield a separating equilibrium, all firms will be considered to be part of a single, average-quality group of firms. This result is called a **pooling equilibrium.**

that companies which generate significant amounts of free cash flow benefit the most from higher dividend payments. Furthermore, signaling models are completely consistent with the core observation that the market response to dividend initiations and increases is significantly positive, while dividend cuts are almost invariably greeted by large stock price declines.

On the other hand, signaling models also have several empirical weaknesses. For one thing, they are not unique in predicting positive responses to dividend increases and negative responses to decreases—this is also what the Agency Cost/Contracting Model predicts. Furthermore, signaling models offer few predictions concerning the cross-sectional variability of dividend payments across industries, countries, or ownership structures, and they beg the question of why less costly (but equally effective) methods of conveying information to shareholders have not evolved. Also left unanswered is why dividend payments have remained relatively constant in spite of vast improvements in information processing technology, and in the informational efficiency of capital markets the world over. Finally, even the most casual observation suggests that firms in those industries with the best growth prospects, and the greatest number of positive-NPV investment opportunities (computers, pharmaceuticals, entertainment, telecommunications, etc.), pay out lower fractions of their earnings as dividends—while signaling models predict just the opposite result. On balance, the weight of empirical evidence currently favors the Agency Cost/Contracting Model over the various signaling models, and we will treat the former as the finance "standard" throughout this textbook.

—SUMMARY—

Even though corporate dividend policies have been subjected to intense theoretical and empirical investigation for over thirty years, they remain fundamentally unexplained. In all the world's market economies, publicly-held companies pay regular cash dividends to stockholders—even as they search diligently for external financing to help fund ongoing investment opportunities. Furthermore, while national average dividend payouts vary wildly, dividend payment policies show the same basic patterns throughout the world—larger, slowly growing, regulated companies with excess cash flow and diffuse ownership structures pay out larger fractions of their earnings as cash dividends than do smaller, rapidly growing, unregulated private or closely-held firms with many valuable investment opportunities and little excess internally-generated cash flow. Dividend changes also convey information to shareholders about management's assessment of the course of current and future earnings, so they have an important information revelation function. They seem to also have an important role to play in resolving agency problems between corporate shareholders (principals) and managers (agents), though the severity of these agency problems varies a great deal between countries. Clearly, dividend policy is systematically related to firm size, ownership structure, the richness of a firm's investment opportunity set, the degree of informational asymmetry between shareholders and managers, and the severity of industrial regulation, but researchers have not yet documented the exact relationship between any of these variables and corporate dividend policy.

In addition to examining the determinants of payout policy, modern research has explored how dividends are valued by capital markets. Much of this research has focused on the importance of firm and individual-level income taxation on dividend valuation. The principal tools used by researchers are (1) ex-dividend day studies, which attempt to explain the less than dollar-for-dollar share price drop that occurs on ex-days in terms of differential taxation, and (2) after-tax CAPM models, which examine whether high-dividend stocks offer a higher pre-tax return than low-dividend stocks as compensation to investors for higher personal taxes due on dividend versus capital gains income. In spite of voluminous research, the effect of taxes on dividend payouts and valuation remains as ambiguous as most other areas of dividend policy theory. Clearly, this important and interesting area of corporate finance theory will attract academic researchers—and perplex practicing corporate managers—for many years to come.

—QUESTIONS—

1. What two fundamental questions are dividend policy researchers trying to answer?

2. Do dividend payout ratios show national patterns? If so, discuss these patterns and suggest possible explanations for the observed patterns.

3. [Essay question] Describe and discuss industrial patterns observed in dividend payouts worldwide. What are the most important influences on industry and firm-level dividend payouts?

4. Describe what dividend smoothing means, and discuss the empirical significance of this phenomenon.

5. How does the stock market respond to dividend changes? Is the response different for dividend initiations and omissions as compared with dividend increases and decreases?

6. [Essay question] A reporter asks you whether dividends (and dividend changes) convey information, and, if so, what information. How do you respond?

7. What evidence do we have that dividends are not primarily designed to overcome transactions costs involved in selling shares to finance current consumption?

8. How does a firm's ownership structure affect its incentives to pay dividends?

9. List the major assumptions that Miller and Modigliani (1961) make in order to derive their dividend irrelevance proposition. What purpose do you think each major assumption serves (why is it included)?

10. [Essay question] Using words and formulas as necessary, develop the M&M fundamental principle of valuation.

11. [Numerical problem] Assume that two firms, A and B, are equivalent in every way—except that they wish to pursue different dividend payout policies. Both firms have a 12.5 percent required return (ρ); both have steady-state, after-tax (corporate) earnings of $5,000,000; both currently have 2,000,000 shares outstanding; and both have access to a positive-NPV investment opportunity that will cost $5,000,000 to fund. Firm A wishes to finance all investments internally, while firm B wishes to follow a policy of paying all earnings out as dividends and financing investment externally. (1) Show what each firm will do, and determine each company's value—both before and after funding the investment opportunity (assume its NPV = 0 for convenience). Then, (2) using these values, demonstrate how the M&M dividend irrelevance proposition "works". [Extra credit: repeat the first part of this exercise,

assuming that each firm has an investment opportunity costing (a) $3,000,000 and (b) $8,000,000].

12. [Essay question] How do personal income taxes affect the market valuation of high versus low-dividend stocks? What methodologies have been employed to examine this issue? What have they found?

13. What is a share repurchase program? How does the stock market usually react to such a program? How do you explain this reaction?

14. What is an ex-dividend day study, and what economic phenomena are examined with these studies? What have these studies documented?

15. What is the residual theory of dividend payments? What is the major empirical problem with this theory?

16. What is a partial adjustment dividend payment strategy? Does the empirical evidence suggest that corporate managers actually pursue such a strategy?

17. [Essay question] How can dividend payments help overcome agency problems between managers and shareholders? What evidence do we have that dividends actually serve this purpose?

18. Other things equal, what type of dividend policy (high versus low-payout) should pension fund managers prefer? What policy should a high-income individual investor prefer? Why?

19. [Essay question] A friend of yours—who is intelligent, but not well-versed in business theory—asks you to describe (in clear English) the key predictions of the Agency Cost/Contracting Model of Dividends. How do you respond?

20. What are the principal predictions of the Signaling Model of Dividend Payments? Have these predictions been borne out by empirical testing?

21. What is a separating equilibrium? How are dividend payments supposed to generate this equilibrium in the dividend signaling model?

—REFERENCES—

Aharony, Joseph and Itzhak Swary, "Quarterly Dividend and Earnings Announcements and Stockholders' Returns: An Empirical Analysis," **Journal of Finance** 35 (March 1980), pp. 1–12.

Akerlof, George, "The Market for 'Lemons', Qualitative Uncertainty and the Market Mechanism," **Quarterly Journal of Economics** 87 (August 1970), pp. 488–500.

Ambarish, Ramasastry, Kose John, and Joseph Williams, "Efficient Signaling with Dividends and Investments," **Journal of Finance** 42 (June 1987), pp. 321–343.

Ang, James S. and David Peterson, "Return, Risk, and Yield: Evidence From Ex Ante Data," **Journal of Finance** 40 (June 1985), pp. 537–548.

Ang, James S., David W. Blackwell, and William L. Megginson, "The Effects of Taxes on the Relative Valuation of Dividends and Capital Gains: Evidence From Dual-Class British Investment Trusts," **Journal of Finance** 46 (March 1991), pp. 383–399.

Asquith, Paul and David W. Mullins, Jr., "The Impact of Initiating Dividend Payments on Shareholders' Wealth," **Journal of Business** 56 (January 1983), pp. 77–96.

————"Signaling With Dividends, Stock Repurchases, and Equity Issues," **Financial Management** 15 (Autumn 1986), pp. 27–44.

Auerbach, Alan J., "Stockholders Tax Rates and Firm Attributes," **Journal of Public Economics** 21 (July 1983), pp. 107–128.

Bagwell, Laurie Simon, "Dutch Auction Repurchases: An Analysis of Shareholder Heterogeneity," **Journal of Finance** 47 (March 1992), pp. 71–106.

Bajaj, Mukesk and Anand M. Vijh, "Dividend Clienteles and the Information Content of Dividend Changes," **Journal of Financial Economics** 26 (August 1990), pp. 193–219.

————"Trading Behavior and the Unbiasedness of the Market Reaction to Dividend Announcements," **Journal of Finance** 50 (March 1995), pp. 255–279.

Baker, H. Kent, Gail E. Farrelly, and Richard B. Edelman, "A Survey of Management Views on Dividend Policy," **Financial Management** 14 (Autumn 1985), pp. 78–84.

Barclay, Michael J., "Dividends, Taxes, and Common Stock Prices Before the Income Tax," **Journal of Financial Economics** 19 (September 1987), pp. 31–44.

Barclay, Michael J. and Clifford W. Smith, Jr., "Corporate Payout Policy: Cash Dividends Versus Open Market Repurchases," **Journal of Financial Economics** 22 (October 1988), pp. 61–82.

Barclay, Michael J., Clifford W. Smith, and Ross L. Watts, "The Determinants of Corporate Leverage and Dividend Policies," **Journal of Applied Corporate Finance** 17 (Winter 1995), pp. 4–19.

Berglöf, Erik and Enrico Perotti, "The Governance Structure of the Japanese Keiretsu," **Journal of Financial Economics** 36 (October 1994), pp. 259–284.

Bhattacharya, Sudipto, "Imperfect Information, Dividend Policy, and the 'Bird in the Hand' Fallacy," **Bell Journal of Economics** 10 (Spring 1979), pp. 259–270.

Bhide, Amar, "The Hidden Costs of Stock Market Liquidity," **Journal of Financial Economics** 34 (August 1993), pp. 31–51.

Black, Bernard, "Agents Watching Agents," **UCLA Law Review** 39 (1992), pp. 811–893.

Black, Fischer, "The Dividend Puzzle," **Journal of Portfolio Management** 2 (Winter 1976), pp. 72–77.

Black, Fischer and Myron S. Scholes, "The Effects of Dividend Yield and Dividend Policy on Common Stock Prices and Returns," **Journal of Financial Economics** 1 (May 1974), pp. 1–22.

Blume, Marshall E., "Stock Returns and Dividend Yields: Some More Evidence," **Review of Economics and Statistics** 62 (November 1980), pp. 567–577.

Booth, Laurence D. and David J. Johnston, "The Ex-Dividend Behavior of Canadian Stock Prices: Tax Changes and Clientele Effects," **Journal of Finance** 39 (June 1984), pp. 457–476.

Brennan, Michael J., "Taxes, Market Valuation and Corporate Financial Policy," **National Tax Journal** 23 (December 1970), pp. 417–427.

Brennan, Michael J. and Thomas E. Copeland, "Stock Splits, Stock Prices, and Transaction Costs," **Journal of Financial Economics** 22 (October 1988), pp. 83–102.

Brennan, Michael J. and Anjan V. Thakor, "Shareholder Preferences and Dividend Policy," **Journal of Finance** 45 (September 1990), pp. 993–1019.

Brickley, James A., "Shareholder Wealth, Information Signaling and the Specially Designated Dividend: An Empirical Study," **Journal of Financial Economics** 12 (August 1983), pp. 187–209.

Christie, William G., "Are Dividend Omissions Truly the Cruelest Cut of All?," **Journal of Financial and Quantitative Analysis** 29 (September 1994), pp. 459–480.

Christie, William G. and Vikram Nanda, "Free Cash Flow, Shareholder Value, and the Undistributed Profits Tax of 1936 and 1937," **Journal of Finance** 49 (December 1994), pp. 1727–1754.

Dann, Larry, "Common Stock Repurchases: An Analysis of Returns to Bondholders and Stockholders," **Journal of Financial Economics** 9 (June 1981), pp. 113–138.

DeAngelo, Harry and Linda DeAngelo, "Dividend Policy and Financial Distress: An Empirical Investigation of Troubled NYSE Firms," **Journal of Finance** 45 (December 1990), pp.1415–1431.

DeAngelo, Harry, Linda DeAngelo, and Douglas J. Skinner, "Dividends and Losses," **Journal of Finance** 47 (December 1992), pp. 1837–1863.

Denis, David J., "Defensive Changes in Corporate Payout Policy: Share Repurchases and Special Dividends," **Journal of Finance** 45 (December 1990), pp. 1433–1456.

Dhillon, Upinder S. and Herb Johnson, "The Effect of Dividend Changes on Stock and Bond Prices," **Journal of Finance** 49 (March 1994), pp. 281–289.

Dwyer, Hubert J. and Richard Lynn, "Small Capitalization Companies: What Does Financial Analysis Tell Us About Them?," **Financial Review** 24 (1989), pp. 397–414.

Eades, Kenneth M., Patrick Hess, and E. Han Kim, "On Interpreting Security Returns During the Ex-Dividend Day Period," **Journal of Financial Economics** 13 (March 1984), pp. 3–34.

———, "Time Series Variation in Dividend Pricing," **Journal of Finance** 49 (December 1994), pp. 1617–1638.

Easterbrook, Frank H., "Two Agency-Cost Explanations of Dividends," **American Economic Review** 74 (September 1984), pp. 650–659.

"Company Dividends," **The Economist** (June 4, 1994), pg. 109.

Elton, Edwin J. and Martin J. Gruber, "Marginal Stockholder Tax Rates and the Clientel Effect," **Review of Economics and Statistics** 52 (February 1970), pp. 68–74.

Fama, Eugene F., "The Empirical Relationships Between the Dividend and Investment Decisions of Firms," **American Economic Review** 64 (June 1974), pp. 304–318.

Fama, Eugene F. and Harvey Babiak, "Dividend Policy: An Empirical Analysis," **Journal of the American Statistical Association** 63 (December 1968), pp. 1132–1161.

Feldstein, Martin, "Corporate Taxation and Dividend Behavior," **Review of Economic Studies** 37 (January 1970), pp. 57–72.

Feldstein, Martin and George Fane, "Taxes, Corporate Dividend Policy, and Personal Savings: The British Postwar Experience," **Review of Economics and Statistics** 55 (November 1973), pp. 399–411.

Feldstein, Martin and Jerry Green, "Why Do Companies Pay Dividends?," **American Economic Review** 73 (March 1983), pp. 17–30.

Frankel, Jeffrey A., "The Japanese Cost of Finance: A Survey," **Financial Management** 20 (Spring 1991), pp. 95–127.

Fudenberg, Drew and Jean Tirole, "A Theory of Income and Dividend Smoothing Based on Incumbency Rents," **Journal of Political Economy** 103 (February 1995), pp. 75–93.

Gaver, Jennifer J. and Kenneth M. Gaver, "Additional Evidence on the Association Between the Investment Opportunity Set and Corporate Financing, Dividend, and Compensation Policies," **Journal of Accounting and Economics** 16 (January April July 1993), pp. 125–160.

Ghosh, Chinmoy and J. Randall Woolridge, "An Analysis of Shareholder Reaction to Dividend Cuts and Omissions," **Journal of Financial Research** 11 (Winter 1988), pp. 281–294.

Grinblatt, Mark S., Robert W. Masulis, and Sheridan Titman, "The Valuation of Stock Splits and Stock Dividends," **Journal of Financial Economics** 13 (December 1984), pp. 461–490.

Handjinicolaou, George and Avner Kalay, "Wealth Redistributions or Changes in Firm Value: An Analysis of Returns to Bondholders and Stockholders Around Dividend Announcements," **Journal of Financial Economics** 13 (March 1984), pp. 35–63.

Healy, Paul M. and Krishna Palepu, "Earnings Information Conveyed by Dividend Initiations and Omissions," **Journal of Financial Economics** 21 (September 1988), pp. 149–175.

Heath, David C. and Robert A. Jarrow, "Ex-Dividend Stock Price Behavior and Arbitrage Opportunities," **Journal of Business** 61 (January 1988), pp. 95–108.

Hess, Patrick J., "The Ex-Dividend Behavior of Stock Returns: Further Evidence on Tax Effects," **Journal of Finance** 37 (May 1982), pp. 445–456.

Jensen, Michael C., "Agency Costs of Free Cash Flow, Corporate Finance and Takeovers," **American Economic Review** 76 (May 1986), pp. 323–329.

John, Kose and Larry H. P. Lang, "Insider Trading Around Dividend Announcements: Theory and Evidence," **Journal of Finance** 46 (September 1991), pp. 1361–1389.

John, Kose and Joseph Williams, "Dividends, Dilution and Taxes: A Signaling Equilibrium," Journal of Finance 40 (September 1985), pp. 1053–1070.

Kalay, Avner, "The Ex-Dividend Day Behavior of Stock Prices: A Reexamination of the Clientele Effect," **Journal of Finance** 37 (September 1982a), pp. 1059–1070.

————"Stockholder-Bondholder Conflict and Dividend Constraints," **Journal of Financial Economics** 10 (July 1982b), pp. 211–233.

Kalay, Avner and Uri Lowenstein, "Predictable Events and Excess Returns: The Case of Dividend Announcements," **Journal of Financial Economics** 14 (September 1985), pp. 423–449.

————"The Informational Content of the Timing of Dividend Announcements," **Journal of Financial Economics** 16 (July 1986), pp. 373–388.

Kalay, Avner and Marti G. Subrahmanyan, "The Ex-Dividend Day Behavior of Options Prices," **Journal of Business** 57 (January 1984), pp. 113–128.

Kaplan, Steven N. and Bernadette A. Minton, "Appointments of Outsiders to Japanese Boards: Determinants and Implications for Managers," **Journal of Financial Economics** 36 (October 1994), pp. 225–258.

Karpoff, Jonathan M. and Ralph A. Walkling, "Short-Term Trading Around Ex-Dividend Days: Additional Evidence," **Journal of Financial Economics** 21 (September 1988), pp. 291–298.

————"Dividend Capture in NASDAQ Stocks," **Journal of Financial Economics** 28 (November/December 1990), pp. 39–66.

Kao, Chihwa and Chunchi Wu, "Tests of Dividend Signaling Using the Marsh-Merton Model: A Generalized Friction Approach," **Journal of Business** 67 (January 1994), pp. 45–68.

Kester, W. Carl, "Governance, Contracting, and Investment Horizons: A look at Japan and Germany," **Journal of Applied Corporate Finance** 5 (Summer 1992), 83–98.

Koretz, Gene, "Economic Trends," **Business Week** (August 16, 1993), pg. 18.

Kumar, Praveen, "Shareholder-Manager Conflict and the Information Content of Dividends," **Review of Financial Studies** 1 (1988), pp. 111–136.

Lakonishok, Josef and Baruch Lev, "Stock Splits and Stock Dividends: Why, Who, and When," **Journal of Finance** 42 (September 1987), pp. 913–932.

Lakonishok, Josef and Theo Vermaelen, "Tax Reform and Ex-Dividend Day Behavior," **Journal of Finance** 38 (September 1983), pp. 1157–1175.

————— "Tax-Induced Trading Around Ex-Dividend Days," **Journal of Financial Economics** 16 (July 1986), pp. 287–319.

————— "Anamolous Price Behavior Around Repurchase Tender Offers," **Journal of Finance** 45 (June 1990), pp. 455–478.

Lang, Larry H. P. and Robert H. Litzenberger, "Dividend Announcements: Cash Flow Signaling Vs. Free Cash Flow Hypothesis?," **Journal of Financial Economics** 24 (September 1989), pp. 181–192.

Lee, Bong-Soo, "The Response of Stock Prices to Permanent and Temporary Shocks to Dividends," **Journal of Financial and Quantitative Analysis** 30 (March 1995), pp. 1–22.

Leland, Hayne E. and David H. Pyle, "Informational Asymmetries, Financial Structure, and Financial Intermediation," **Journal of Finance** 32 (May 1977), pp. 371–387.

Lintner, John, "Distribution of Incomes of Corporations Among Dividends, Retained Earnings, and Taxes," **American Economic Review** 46 (May 1956), pp. 97–113.

Lipson, Marc L., Maquieira, Carlos P., and William L. Megginson, "Why Do Public Companies Begin Paying Dividends?," working paper, the University of Georgia and the University of Chile (July, 1995).

Litzenberger, Robert H. and Krishna Ramaswamy, "The Effect of Personal Taxes and Dividends on Capital Asset Prices: Theory and Empirical Evidence," **Journal of Financial Economics** 7 (June 1979), pp. 163–195.

Long, Jr., John B., "The Market Valuation of Cash Dividends: A Case to Consider," **Journal of Financial Economics** 6 (June-September 1978), pp. 235–264.

McNichols, Maureen and Ajay Dravid, "Stock Dividends, Stock Splits, and Signaling," **Journal of Finance** 45 (July 1990), pp. 857–880.

Megginson, William L., Robert C. Nash, and Matthias van Randenborgh, "The Financial and Operating Performance of Newly-Privatized Firms: An International Empirical Analysis," **Journal of Finance** 49 (June 1994), pp. 403–452.

Michaely, Roni, "Ex-Dividend Day Stock Price Behavior: The Case of the Tax Reform Act," **Journal of Finance** 46 (July 1991), pp. 845–860.

Michaely, Roni, Richard H. Thaler, and Kent L. Womack, "Price Reactions to Dividend Initiations and Omissions: Overreaction or Drift," **Journal of Finance** 50 (June 1995), pp. 573–608.

Miller, Merton H. and Franco Modigliani, "Dividend Policy, Growth and the Valuation of Shares," **Journal of Business** 34 (October 1961), pp. 411–433.

Miller, Merton H. and Kevin Rock, "Dividend Policy Under Asymmetric Information," **Journal of Finance** 40 (September 1985), pp. 1021–1051.

Miller, Merton H. and Myron S. Scholes, "Dividends and Taxes: Some Empirical Evidence," **Journal of Political Economy** 90 (December 1982), pp. 1118–1141.

Ofer, Aharon R. and Daniel R. Siegel, "Corporate Financial Policy, Information, and Market Expectations: An Empirical Explanation of Dividends," **Journal of Finance** 42 (September 1987), pp. 889–911.

Ofer, Aharon R. and Anjan V. Thakor, "A Theory of Stock Price Responses to Alternative Corporate Cash Disbursement Methods: Stock Repurchases and Dividends," **Journal of Finance** 42 (June 1987), pp. 365–394.

Petersen, Mitchell A. and Raghuram G. Rajan, "The Benefits of Lending Relationships: Evidence From Small Business Data," **Journal of Finance** 49 (March 1994), pp. 3–37.

Peterson, Pamela P. and Gary A. Benesh, "A Reexamination of the Empirical Relationship Between Investment and Financing Decisions," **Journal of Financial and Quantitative Analysis** 18 (December 1983), pp. 439–454.

Poterba, James M., "The Market Valuation of Cash Dividends: The Citizens Utilities Case Reconsidered," **Journal of Financial Economics** 15 (March 1986), pp. 395–405.

———"Tax Policy and Corporate Savings," **Brookings Papers on Economic Activity** 2 (December 1987), pp. 455–515.

Poterba, James M. and Lawrence H. Summers, "Dividend Taxes, Corporate Investment, and 'Q'," **Journal of Public Economics** 22 (September 1983), pp. 135–167.

———"New Evidence That Taxes Effect the Valuation of Dividends," **Journal of Finance** 39 (December 1984), pp. 1397–1415.

———"The Economic Effects of Dividend Taxation," in E.I. Altman and M.G. Subrahmanyan, eds., **Recent Advances in Corporate Finance** (Homewood, IL: Richard D. Irwin, 1985), pp. 227–284.

Prowse, Michael, "Is America in Decline?," **Harvard Business Review** (July/August 1992), pp. 34–45.

Richardson, Gordon, Stephen Sefcik, and Rex Thompson, "A Test of Dividend Irrelevance Using Volume Reactions to a Change in Dividend Policy," **Journal of Financial Economics** 17 (December 1986), pp. 313–333.

Riley, John, "Informational Equilibrium," **Econometrica** 47 (March 1979), pp. 331–359.

Robin, Ashok J., "The Impact of the 1986 Tax Reform On Ex-Dividend Day Returns," **Financial Management** 20 (Spring 1991), pp. 60–70.

Rozeff, Michael, "Growth, Beta and Agency Costs as Determinants of Dividend Payout Ratios," **Journal of Financial Research** 5 (Fall 1982), pp. 249–259.

Shefrin, Hersh M. and Meir Statman, "Explaining Investor Preference for Cash Dividends," **Journal of Financial Economics** 13 (June 1984), pp. 253–282.

Smith, Jr., Clifford W. and Ross L. Watts, "The Investment Opportunity Set and Corporate Financing, Dividend, and Compensation Policies," **Journal of Financial Economics** 32 (October 1992), pp. 263–292.

Spence, Michael, "Job Market Signaling," **Quarterly Journal of Economics** 87 (August 1973), pp. 355–374.

Stickel, Scott E., "The Ex-Dividend Behavior of Nonconvertible Preferred Stock Returns and Trading Volume," **Journal of Financial and Quantitative Analysis** 26 (March 1991), pp. 45–62.

Venkatesh, P. C., "The Impact of Dividend Initiation on the Information Content of Earnings Announcements and Returns Volatility," **Journal of Business** 62 (April 1989), pp. 175–197.

Vermaelen, Theo, "Common Stock Repurchases and Market Signaling," **Journal of Financial Economics** 9 (June 1981), pp. 139–183.

Walker, Ernest W. and J. William Petty II, "Financial Differences Between Large and Small Firms," **Financial Management** 7 (Winter 1978), pp. 61–68.

Watts, Ross L., "The Information Content of Dividends," **Journal of Business** 46 (April 1973), pp. 191–211.

Williams, Joseph, "Efficient Signaling with Dividends, Investment, and Stock Repurchases," **Journal of Finance** 43 (July 1988), pp. 737–747.

CHAPTER
9

Under-standing and Accessing Financial Markets

9.1 INTRODUCTION

Financial markets play vital roles in the economic lives of developed and developing countries alike. At the most basic level, financial markets serve to channel funds from individual and corporate savers with surplus funds to invest to corporate, government and individual borrowers seeking money to finance investment opportunities that exceed internally-generated cash flow. The more efficiently financial markets provide this service the more productive the economy will be and the higher will be the net returns to borrowers and savers alike. Financial markets also allow individuals to transfer consumption through time. As a practical matter, this usually means that people can borrow money to finance college, buy homes, and start families when they are young adults, then save increasingly large fractions of their income during their most productive middle years, and finally live comfortably off the returns from their savings during retirement. Countries with competitive and efficient consumer financial markets are able to offer their citizens higher average standards of living than can countries that lack such markets.

Although consumer-oriented financial markets are very important, our focus in this chapter will be on financial markets that are designed to service corporate borrowers and savers. While the number, variety, and capacity of these markets have grown steadily since they first arose during medieval times, the past twenty-five years have witnessed an almost incredible surge of financial market innovation and volume—both in the United States and in the international markets. Never before have corporate financial executives faced such a rich choice of financing options, and never before have the challenges and opportunities been greater for apprentice (or practicing) finance professionals like yourselves.

Before describing our objectives for this chapter, we should make clear that we do not intend to develop a full-scale "theory of financial markets", or even to provide a comprehensive descriptive survey of financial market instruments and practices. Either objective would be far beyond the scope of a single chapter. Instead, this chapter attempts to accomplish four objectives. First, it provides an overview of the scale and scope of modern financial markets, and describes key empirical regularities that have been documented in these markets around the world. Second, it provides a "taxonomy" or classification of modern financial markets as a way of organizing a discussion of the services each market provides and the financial instruments each market employs. This section also defines key terms that are frequently encountered by financial market pilgrims.

Third, we discuss the roles that **financial intermediaries** (institutions that raise funds by selling claims against themselves, then lend the funds so raised to government, corporate and individual borrowers) currently play in corporate financial systems in the United States, in other advanced countries, and in many of the rapidly growing economies of Asia and Latin America. We begin by incorporating a brief discussion of the principal theoretical models that have been advanced to explain the existence of financial intermediaries (especially commercial banks), and we also discuss how regulation, history, and new product developments have affected their relative importance in the corporate finance systems of the United States versus those of other countries. Our discussion of intermediaries includes an analysis of the various risk management and hedging products offered by these institutions, and a description of how each of the four "building blocks" (forwards, futures, options, and swaps) of risk management works. We conclude by examining whether commercial banks, in particular, are a declining force in international corporate finance or whether they have enduring competitive advantages that ensure their continued pre-eminence as financiers of the world's commerce.

Finally, we examine the expanding global role of securities markets, and discuss why these markets have been developing so rapidly during the past two decades. We provide summary data documenting the current size and growth rates of American and international securities markets, and discuss why certain investment banking practices have demonstrated survival value throughout the world. This section also discusses the immense body of academic research that has examined the stock price effects of various types of securities issues, the impact of information releases on securities prices, and how managers select the types of securities to issue (or repurchase) in order to overcome (or exploit) agency problems resulting from informational asymmetries between corporate managers and investors. As you read this chapter, see if you can formulate your own explanation of why security market financing might be preferred to intermediary market financing for certain financial transactions, and why intermediated financing might logically be preferred in others.

9.2 OBSERVED PATTERNS IN FINANCIAL MARKETS

Before diving into the theory and terminology of financial markets, it is useful to stand back and describe several patterns that these markets present. Doing so not only allows us to comprehend the immense scale and diversity of modern financial markets, it also provides us with a benchmark set of empirical facts that a theory must be able to explain to be accepted as viable.

1. **Financial markets are colossal in scale and scope, and the relative importance of financial services in the world economy has increased dramatically during the past two decades.** The world's 100 largest banks alone had assets of $15.0

trillion in 1993, and the total market value of world stock and corporate bond markets was $9.5 trillion and $6.0 trillion, respectively.[1] Furthermore, at the end of 1994 the total notional value of derivative products outstanding exceeded $23 trillion—split roughly equally between exchange-traded instruments and those traded over-the-counter (created by a financial institution specifically for a corporate client).[2] Finally, the total value of Euro-syndicated credit facilities in place at the end of 1991 was roughly $3.6 trillion. To put these numbers in perspective, total world gross domestic product probably amounted to $25–30 trillion in 1994, and the total value of financial services as a fraction of world and national GDP has been growing steadily for several decades—rapidly since 1973[3].

2. **Bonds and commercial paper have become the most important sources of external finance for American corporations. Outside of the United States, commercial banks are the preeminent sources of external finance for corporations, though their degree of dominance varies considerably.** In 1960, the total debt of American corporations was split roughly evenly between bonds and bank loans. By the 1990s, bank loans represented less than 30 percent of the total debt of U.S. firms, while bonds' share had remained stable and non-bank corporate loans and commercial paper had grabbed market shares of approximately 15 and 5 percent, respectively.[4] Since no other country has a national bond market comparable to America's, non-U.S. corporations continue to place far greater reliance on banks for external financing than U.S. firms do.

3. **The direct financing role of commercial banks is shrinking in most advanced economies (particularly in the United States), but their role as providers of corporate risk management and other sophisticated financial products is increasing.** Though no other country has witnessed as dramatic a degree of disintermediation as has the United States, there has been a global trend towards direct security market financing of corporate capital needs. Commercial banks have, however, demonstrated real competitive strengths as providers of financial

1. The bank total asset figure is from the 1994 **Euromoney** 500 bank survey (Piggott 1994), the stock market capitalization total is from a monthly Goldman Sachs investment report (Zurack and Foote 1994), and the world bond market valuation is derived from year-end 1991 data presented in a fixed income almanac compiled by Douglas (1993). McKinsey and Company (cited in the **Economist** November 5, 1994) provide similar results. They estimate the total value of world financial assets to be $35 trillion in 1992, and predict this will grow to $83 trillion ($53 trillion in 1992 dollars) by 2000.

2. The derivative product totals are from the Bank for International Settlements, as reported in the **Economist** (March 4, 1995). A General Accounting Office report presented to the U.S. Congress in May 1994, as reported in Shirreff (1994), provides a more detailed breakdown and description of this market.

3. Syndicated credit totals are reported in the 1993 Update to the **Handbook of Modern Finance** (Sundaram 1993). World GDP figures for 1994 are extrapolated from a 1991 figure of approximately $20 trillion reported in **Hoover's Handbook of World Business** 1993, based on recent national growth rates published in various issues of the **Economist**. Finally, the dramatic increase in financial intermediation as a fraction of American GDP is described in Boyd and Gertler (1994).

4. See page 11 of the International Banking Survey published in the **Economist** (April 30, 1994). Similar financing patterns for American non-financial corporations are also presented in Boyd and Gertler (1994, Table 6). The **Economist** article also describes financing patterns in other advanced economies (particularly in western Europe).

products needed by corporations to cope with the input price, foreign exchange, and interest rate risks modern corporations face throughout the world[5].

4. **Banks in other developed countries tend to be much larger than U.S. banks, and play more central roles in their national corporate finance system.** The United States is unique among developed countries in that—for a variety of historical and political reasons—it has never allowed truly national banks to be formed. As a consequence, the largest American banks are far smaller than the largest European and Japanese banks, with only one American bank (Citicorp) making the list of the 25 largest banks in the world (ranked by asset size) in 1994.[6] Furthermore, since U.S. banks are also prohibited from owning corporate equity and have become relatively high-cost (compared to commercial paper) sources of short-term funds, they play a much smaller role in financing large American corporations than do their non-U.S. counterparts. American banks remain very important to the entrepreneurial and small business sectors of the U.S. economy, however, and are globally-competitive providers of many types of non-credit financial services.

5. **Worldwide corporate securities issue volume more than tripled (to $1.502 trillion) from 1988 to 1993, and U.S. issuers accounted for over two-thirds ($1.048 trillion) of the 1993 total.**[7] This little-noted phenomenon is even more remarkable since the total number of issues increased by less than 80 percent—implying that the average size of new security issues has dramatically increased.[8] Since municipal bond and mortgage-backed securities accounted for $707 billion of the 1993 U.S. total, this means that American corporations floated new stock and bond issues worth $341 billion in 1993, while all non-U.S. companies combined issued only an additional $454 billion. In addition, American companies issued over

---

5. The changing role of banks in national and international finance is described in the articles cited above, as well as in several articles in the 25th anniversary issue of **Euromoney** (June 1994). A quick measure of the relative importance of banks in the U.S. economy is provided by Wheelock (1993), who reports that at year-end 1992, American commercial banks had financial assets of $2.775 trillion, while nonbank institutions had financial assets totaling $10.012 trillion—including $3.322 trillion held by private and public pension funds. More recently, the Federal Deposit Insurance Corporation (FDIC) reported that American banks had total assets of $3.9 trillion and Tier-1 capital (primarily equity) of $300 billion in September 1994, up 43 percent and 16 percent, respectively, since 1990 (see **Economist** February 25, 1995).

6. No fewer than eleven of the world's 25 largest banks are Japanese, including the seven largest. Ranking by shareholders' equity (book value) yields similar conclusions (see Piggott 1994). The announced merger between Bank of Tokyo and Mitsubishi Bank in March 1995 will make this size disparity even more compelling. The merger will create the world's largest bank which, with $701.3 billion in assets, will be over three times the size of Citicorp (see Baker 1995).

7. In 1988, corporations raised $483.1 billion with 5,551 issues worldwide; the 1993 total dollar volume was raised through 9,969 issues. Each January, the **Investment Dealers' Digest** publishes a summary of the total number and value of securities issued the previous year, in both U.S. and international capital markets. These surveys are the sources for most of the figures cited in this and subsequent footnotes.

8. While total issue volumes shrank by roughly a third during the very difficult year of 1994 (to $1.09 trillion and $708.6 billion, respectively, for worldwide and U.S. domestic offerings), the overall trend towards vastly greater security issue volumes remains intact (see Pratt 1995a). Furthermore, issue volumes in specific market segments seem to be picking up again during 1995, in response to falling interest rates and continued strong economic growth in most regions of the world.

$500 billion worth of commercial paper (short-term money market instruments) in 1993, which greatly exceeded the non-U.S. total[9].

6. **U.S. corporations have been issuing record volumes of all types of securities this decade, with leverage reductions and debt refinancings being principal objectives.** American firms issued $85.7 billion of new common stock in 1993 (a record), of which almost half ($41.5 billion) represented a record volume of initial public offerings. In addition, U.S. firms issued $54.3 billion in "junk bonds" (speculative grade debt), $22.4 billion in nonconvertible preferred stock, and $15.2 billion in convertible debt and preferred stock. Mirroring patterns observed in other years, American industrial and utility companies issued far larger volumes of investment grade debt—$175.8 billion and $75.2 billion, respectively.[10] Since interest rates in the United States declined continuously (and dramatically) during the early 1990s (until February 1994), and since American companies entered the decade with unusually high leverage ratios, most of these security issues probably represent refinancings to achieve lower debt service payments or alterations in corporate capital structures, rather than net new financings.

7. **Though still dwarfed by the volume of American corporate issuers, non-U.S. companies have also been issuing record volumes of securities during the 1990s—primarily on international capital markets.** In 1993, non-U.S. corporations issued $356.2 billion worth of Eurobonds, foreign bonds (sold outside of the United States) worth $33.8 billion, and Euro common stock worth $17.9 billion.[11] In addition, foreign companies have successfully tapped U.S. capital markets—raising $60.6 billion and $9.8 billion through "Yankee" bonds and common stock, respectively, in 1993.[12] All told, almost 1,400 non-U.S. companies see their common stock trade in American markets in the form of American Depository Receipts (ADRs)[13].

---

9. Sharpe (1994) reports that the total value of Euro-commercial paper outstanding at the end of March 1994 was $81 billion, while the comparable U.S. total was $570 billion. See page IV of the International Capital Markets Survey (May 26, 1994). Furthermore, commercial paper issuance by U.S. companies jumped again in 1994, reaching $605.8 billion outstanding by year-end (see Pratt 1995b). This figure includes a record $8 billion program arranged in November for American Home Products in about two hours.

10. All of the figures quoted here are from the January 10, 1994 **Investment Dealers' Digest** securities issuance survey (Pratt 1994). As was true for the overall volume figures, issue volumes for all of these individual categories dropped significantly in 1994 (see Pratt 1995a). A full tabulation of security issue statistics for the period 1990–1994 is presented in Table 9.3.

11. As was true for American issues, the total volume of non-U.S. security issues fell during 1994 (from a total of $481.4 billion to $404.4 billion), but the percentage decline was much smaller and certain categories actually experienced increasing volumes—including foreign bonds, Yankee common and Euro common stock, and Euro asset-backed securities (see Pratt 1995a).

12. See Pratt (1994, pages 39–42).

13. **Euromoney** reports there were 1,162 active ADR programs at the end of 1993, and approximately 200 new programs were expected to be set up in 1994 (see Marray 1994). Furthermore, ADRs represented 7.5 percent of the $2.25 trillion worth of common shares traded on the New York Stock Exchange in 1993, and Telefonos de Mexico—an ADR—was the most actively-traded NYSE stock in 1994. The **Financial Times** (January 9, 1995) reports that 285 companies from 43 countries raised more than $20 billion in ADRs during 1994, and Harverson (1994) documents that Bank of New York has solidified its position as the leading ADR bank, handling over 800 programs for companies from 44 countries.

8. **In addition to securities issues, corporate and governmental borrowers arranged a record total of $604.8 billion in syndicated bank loans in 1993.** These loans differ from traditional single-bank credits both in size—syndicated loans are usually for at least $100 million, and often exceed $1 billion—and in the fact that a large group (syndicate) of international banks typically arranges what amounts to a line of credit that the borrower is allowed to draw against as needed over a period of several years. While American banks lead-managed (arranged) over two-thirds of the issues in 1993, they provided very little of the actual funding. The 1993 total also included the largest single syndicated loan in history—the $20.6 billion credit arranged for General Motors by Chemical Bank[14].

9. **There are distinct, systematic patterns in the response of a firm's stock price to announcements of new security issues and bank financings.** Announcements of new common stock and convertible debt issues are associated with unambiguously negative abnormal stock returns, while preferred stock issue announcements yield generally negative returns and debt issues yield insignificant, slightly negative returns. In stark contrast, announcements of bank financing agreements—particularly renewals of existing agreements—are associated with significant, positive abnormal stock returns[15].

10. **Privatization stock issues with a total value in excess of $400 billion have been sold since 1977, and these have dramatically promoted the growth of stock markets around the world.** Privatization issues are those where a government sells off some or all of the shares it owns in a state-owned firm directly to private investors through a public share offering. Most sales are pure "secondary issues", in that the government sells existing shares and no new cash flows to the firm itself. Many of the roughly 200 such issues have been colossal in size and importance to the local market—in fact, the $40 billion Nippon Telegraph and Telephone issue in November 1987 was the largest security issue ever floated by a corporate entity.[16] Largely due to the impetus of these programs, the total trading volume and market capitalization of stock exchanges outside of the United States has increased more than tenfold since 1970[17].

11. **Over half of the trading volume of the world's organized financial markets involves financial instruments that did not exist prior to 1973**. As astonishing as it seems, exchange-trading options and financial futures contracts are less than 25 years old, and most of the floating rate, high yield, and medium term debt securities that trade in American and international markets have been developed during the past two decades. Additionally, almost all of the sophisticated financial products—such as interest rate swaps, commodity-linked bonds, and long-dated options

---

14. The same **Investment Dealers' Digest** issue that presented these totals also provides a breakdown of the leading syndicators of these loans (Hintze 1994).

15. A full listing of the academic articles which present these results is provided in section 9.5 of this chapter.

16. These issues are described in depth in Jones, Megginson, Nash, and Netter (1995).

17. According to the Morgan Stanley Capital International Index (Quarter I 1994), the market value of stock markets outside of the United States and Canada increased from an index level normalized to equal 100 in January 1970 to a value of approximately 1,010 at the end of March 1994. By comparison, U.S. stock markets increased from 100 to slightly over 400 during the same period.

contracts—that are tailor-made for individual customers by financial intermediaries have been developed since the late 1970s. No other period in world history has witnessed such an explosion of financial innovation.[18]

The facts presented above suggest that financial markets are very large and are vital to the functioning of a modern economy, but their role and importance differs greatly across countries. We now attempt to classify financial markets by function, by type of financial instrument involved, by original maturity of the instrument, and by whether the market involves sales of new or existing securities. We also define several key terms that are frequently used in financial markets around the world.

9.3   FINANCIAL MARKET CLASSIFICATIONS AND TERMINOLOGY

As you surely have noticed, financial markets come in an immense variety of sizes and flavors—far beyond our ability to completely categorize or describe here. Instead, we will focus on only the major distinctions among markets and will tell our story from a corporate finance perspective. In other words, we will ask, "how do companies around the world obtain external financing, and what determines the particular market(s) that individual firms will choose to tap?"

9.3.1 Intermediated vs. Security Markets

The most basic and important classification scheme for financial markets is to distinguish between **intermediated financial markets** and **security markets**. In intermediated financial markets, a financial intermediary—usually a commercial bank—will raise capital by issuing liabilities against itself, usually in the form of demand or savings deposits. The intermediary will then pool the funds raised and use these to make loans to corporate borrowers. Borrowers, in turn, will repay the intermediary, meaning that they have no direct contact with the individual savers who actually funded the loans. Both borrowers and savers thus deal directly with the intermediary, which is therefore able to specialize in credit analysis and collection, even as it offers specialized financial instruments tailored to the needs of both borrowers and savers.

Intermediated markets have natural competitive advantages over security markets for many routine financial transactions, and tend to be preeminent in corporate financing everywhere except the United States, where—as we will see—political considerations have hamstrung banks with regulations other countries have chosen to forego. One important characteristic of intermediated financial markets is transaction and information processing efficiency. Individual investors do not have to invest in acquiring credit information on numerous potential borrowers, nor do these borrowers have to assume the search costs involved with identifying and reassuring large numbers of individual investors. Instead, both parties are able to delegate these functions to intermedi-

---

18. In addition to the derivatives markets discussed in item 1 and the new products described above, virtually the entire collateralized asset market (including mortgage-backed securities) has been developed since the collapse of the Bretton Woods fixed exchange rate system in 1973. For a description of the securitization process that is transforming American corporate financing patterns, see Liebowitz (1992b).

aries capable of providing these and other services at very low transactions cost. Furthermore, if there are a sufficient number of intermediaries in competition, investors will receive high returns for their savings and borrowers will acquire capital at minimum cost.

Intermediaries also find it rational to invest in acquiring the human and technological skills needed to provide higher-value-added financial services such as risk management, currency trading, trust and custodial services, cash management, and data processing—in addition to basic commercial and consumer lending. Commercial banks, in particular, have the specialized personnel and organizational missions that facilitate innovation. Intermediaries also enjoy a natural competitive advantage over security markets in the acquisition and exploitation of information. If information on a potential borrower is costly to acquire—due either to the borrower's concern with keeping confidential information from reaching competitors or the inherent difficulty in verifying borrower veracity without direct and extended observation—a financial intermediary (FI) can effectively overcome both problems by becoming an "insider" in the borrower's operations. The FI is then in a position to make more informed (and therefore more profitable in the long term) investment decisions.

In markets outside the United States, commercial banks typically play much larger roles in corporate finance—both as lenders and as active shareholders and monitors of corporate management—than is allowed in America. In most countries, a relative handful of very large banks service the entire population of a nation's firms, and the size and competence of these institutions—coupled with bank-friendly regulation—give them tremendous influence over corporate financial and even operating policies.[19] This power is further strengthened by the ability of most non-U.S. banks to underwrite corporate security issues and make direct equity investments in commercial firms, in addition to making ordinary commercial loans. Banks that offer all of these services are often referred to as **merchant banks** (or, in several European countries, **universal banks**). A listing of the twenty largest banks in the world in 1994 is provided in Table 9.1.

We will return to intermediated market financing again later in the next section of this chapter, when we discuss banking regulation and financing patterns in U.S. and non-U.S. markets. We will then examine the various types of loans and other financial services these intermediaries offer, and discuss their relative merits vis-à-vis security markets. For now, the concept we want to nail down is that with intermediated financing there is no direct link between the ultimate saver (individual investors) and the ultimate borrower (commercial firms). Instead, each deals only with an intermediary that issues liabilities against itself to savers and then lends (or invests) directly to corporate borrowers.

Our focus now turns to security market financing, where corporations raise funds by selling securities directly to investors. The critical distinction with intermediated market financing is that in security markets there is a direct financial link between the ultimate borrower (the issuing corporation) and the ultimate saver (the individual investor). Money flows directly from the investor to the issuer when a security is initially

---

19. For a description of how banking regulation influences the competitiveness of internationally-active financial institutions, see Hirtle (1991). A description of how banking is evolving around the world is provided in Pavel and McElravey (1990), while an overview of banking regulation in Britain, Japan, Germany, and the United States is provided in chapter 3 of Fabozzi, Modigliani, and Ferri (1994).

TABLE 9.1

INTERNATIONAL BANKS, RANKED BY ASSET AND CAPITAL SIZE, 1994

This table documents the asset size, Tier 1 capital, return on assets, and Bank for International Settlements (BIS) capital ratio for the world's 25 largest banks—ranked by asset size.[1] Asset size and capital amounts are in billion US dollars, using the exchange rate in effect during July 1994. The source of this data is the July 1994 issue of **The Banker**.

Size Rank	Bank Name	Country	Asset Size	Tier 1 Capital	Return On Assets (%)	BIS Capital (%)
1	Bank of Tokyo/Mitsubishi Bank[2]	Japan	$701.3bn	$28.2bn	0.25%	9.91%
2	Fuji Bank	Japan	507.2	19.4	0.12	9.66
3	Dai-Ichi Kangyo Bank	Japan	506.6	19.4	0.13	9.40
4	Sumitomo Bank	Japan	497.8	22.1	0.18	9.89
5	Sakura Bank	Japan	496.0	18.5	0.12	9.50
6	Sanwa Bank	Japan	493.6	19.6	0.19	9.94
7	Norinchukin Bank	Japan	429.3	3.4	0.14	na
8	Industrial Bank of Japan	Japan	386.9	13.6	0.11	9.10
9	Crédit Lyonnais	France	338.8	10.4	−0.26	8.30
10	Indust. & Commel. Bank of China	China	337.8	16.8	0.42	10.38
11	Deutsche Bank	Germany	322.4	11.7	0.83	11.30
12	Tokai Bank	Japan	311.5	10.9	0.15	9.49

(continued)

TABLE 9.1 (CONTINUED)

Size Rank	Bank Name	Country	Asset Size	Tier 1 Capital	Return On Assets (%)	BIS Capital (%)
13	HSBC Holdings	UK	305.2	14.6	1.25	13.20
14	Long-Term Credit Bank of Japan	Japan	302.2	10.9	0.20	9.46
15	Crédit Agricole	France	282.9	14.7	0.54	9.80
16	Asahi Bank	Japan	262.0	10.3	0.17	9.60
17	Société Génerale	France	260.2	7.9	0.38	na
18	ABN-AMRO Bank	Netherlands	253.0	10.2	0.64	11.20
19	Banque Nationale de Paris	France	250.4	9.7	0.11	9.50
20	Barclays Bank	UK	245.9	9.1	0.40	9.80
21	CS Holding (Crédit Suisse)	Switzerland	234.2	9.3	0.84	na
22	Bank of China	China	234.0	10.3	0.72	na
23	Compagnie Financiére de Paribas	France	229.9	9.3	0.32	9.00
24	National Westminster Bank	UK	226.4	8.7	0.65	10.80
25	Dresdner Bank	Germany	220.6	7.1	0.48	11.20

[1]IF BANKS WERE RANKED BY CAPITAL, RATHER THAN ASSETS, FOUR AMERICAN BANKS WOULD BE IN THE TOP 25, BUT THE RESULTS WOULD OTHERWISE BE SIMILAR. INTERESTINGLY, THE FOUR U.S. BANKS—CITICORP, BANKAMERICA CORP., CHEMICAL BANKING CORP., AND J. P. MORGAN—ALL HAVE RETURN ON ASSETS OF AT LEAST 1.33% AND CAPITAL RATIOS OF AT LEAST 11.45%.

[2]THIS BANK WAS FORMED THROUGH A MERGER ANNOUNCED IN MARCH 1995. ASSET AND CAPITAL AMOUNTS ARE THE SUMMED VALUES OF THE TWO BANKS, WHILE THE RETURN ON ASSETS AND CAPITAL RATIOS ARE WEIGHTED AVERAGES OF THE MERGING FIRMS.

purchased, and then the financial returns on that investment are paid directly by the corporation to the investor. Even when—as is usually the case—an **investment bank** assists the issuing corporation in selling its securities by **underwriting** (guaranteeing the amount of money that will be raised) and selling the issue, the investment bank is essentially a passive broker bringing together buyers and sellers of the securities. Once the sale is completed, the investment bank is no longer directly involved in the investment relationship—though many investment bankers continue making a market in the securities they have underwritten, and also provide ongoing financial advice to issuing firms after the specific underwriting is completed. Rather than digressing at this point into a detailed taxonomy of securities markets, we will allow our ongoing classification of financial markets below to perform this task as we now turn to the distinction between money and capital markets.

9.3.2 Money vs. Capital Markets

Given that a firm has decided to raise funds externally, it must decide whether it needs short or long-term funding. If the company needs money to help finance inventory build-ups or for other working capital needs, it will probably obtain funding by turning to the **money markets**. Technically, these are defined as markets for securities with original maturities of one year or less and, by definition, involve only debt securities (equity securities have no maturity date). For small and mid-size companies, the principal source of short-term debt financing is usually borrowing from a commercial bank or a non-bank FI. These credits are either secured loans, where the corporation pledges accounts receivable or inventory as collateral for the debt, or unsecured lines of credit that the corporation can borrow against—and then repay—as its funding needs evolve.

Large companies, however, are able to tap the money markets directly, principally by issuing **commercial paper**. This is a short-term debt instrument that is sold by companies directly to individual and corporate investors, usually without using the services of an investment bank. American companies issue more than one-half trillion dollars worth of commercial paper each year, and the non-U.S. **Euro commercial paper** market now handles almost $100 billion each year.[20] In addition to bank loans and commercial paper, corporate borrowers are able to access the money markets using a variety of other financial instruments, such as **repurchase agreements** (selling and simultaneously agreeing to repurchase a marketable security later at a higher price) and **factoring** (selling to an intermediary) the firm's accounts receivables. The composition of short-term credit market debt used by American corporations for several years since 1950 is presented in Table 9.2.

Capital markets are defined as financial markets involved in the sale or trading of equity securities or debt securities with an original maturity of more than one year.

---

20. A description of the historical evolution of commercial paper as a funding source both in the United States and in Europe is provided in Heller (1988), while Crabbe and Post (1994) document that U.S. companies operate in an allocationally efficient commercial paper market by showing that a ratings downgrade leads to an economically and statistically significant decline in the volume of new paper issued by the bank holding companies in their sample. No such decline is documented in the volume of large certificate of deposit issuance by these companies, suggesting that deposit insurance may have removed market discipline from the CD market.

Table 9.2					
COMPOSITION OF SHORT-TERM CREDIT MARKET DEBT OF U.S. NONFINANCIAL CORPORATIONS, 1950–1992					
	1950	**1960**	**1970**	**1980**	**1990**	**1992**

	1950	1960	1970	1980	1990	1992
	percent					
Bank loans	91	87	83	71	59	59
Nonbank finance loans	6	9	9	14	17	18
Commercial paper	1	2	6	9	12	12
Foreign loans	—	—	—	1	9	9
Bankers' acceptances	2	2	2	5	3	2
Total	**100**	**100**	**100**	**100**	**100**	**100**
Billion dollars	20	43	125	324	951	882

SOURCE: BOARD OF GOVERNORS OF THE FEDERAL RESERVE SYSTEM, **BALANCE SHEETS FOR THE U.S. ECONOMY, 1945–92** (MARCH 10, 1993), AS REPORTED IN KAUFMAN AND MOTE (1994).

Since equity securities do not "mature" in the normal sense of the word, they can only trade on capital markets. For debt securities, the distinction between capital and money market instruments is sometimes less clear-cut. Intermediate-term debt securities with original maturities of between one and seven years are often called **notes**, while longer-term securities are generally called **bonds**. Further distinctions between types of debt securities can be made depending upon the seniority status of the security, whether the security being issued is backed by specific collateral or merely by a firm's promise to repay, whether it can be resold by an investor or must be held until maturity, whether and at what price the security can be "called" by the issuer, and whether the bond or note is convertible into common stock at the investor's or the issuer's discretion. Each of these items will be briefly discussed below, where we examine the differences between debt and equity markets.

9.3.3 Debt vs. Equity Markets

The economic function of equity capital is to bear most of a firm's financial risk and thus to provide a "cushion" of safety for the firm's creditors.[21] There are two types of equity capital—common stock and preferred stock—though only common stockholders are true **residual claimants** who bear all of the firm's business and financial risk

---

21. Many authors have made this or similar points. See, especially, Jensen and Meckling (1976), Fama and Jensen (1983), and Fama (1990).

and are entitled to all firm value remaining after senior claims are satisfied in full. While preferred stockholders are typically promised a fixed cash payment every period and a fixed redemption value for their shares upon firm liquidation, their claim is considered to be an equity security for two principal reasons. First, their right to preferred dividend payments is not a legally-enforceable claim in the way that a bond coupon payment is, but must instead be approved by a firm's board of directors each period. Generally, preferred stockholders' only legal rights are to be paid before common stockholders receive cash dividends and to be paid the face value of their claims before any money is distributed to common stockholders upon liquidation. Second, preferred stock is a **perpetual security**, meaning that it has no fixed maturity date. Preferred stock is, however, often structured to be convertible into common stock at the holder's or the issuer's discretion.[22]

Every company has equity capital, even though it may be called something else. For example, American companies that executed leveraged buyouts (LBOs) during the 1980s ended up with very high debt-to-equity ratios, but the junior debt in these capital structures (derisively called **junk bonds** by LBO critics) actually served the risk-bearing and cushioning role of equity capital.[23] Many non-U.S. companies also have heavily-indebted capitalization, but this occurs most frequently when some other factor—such as a protected product market position, a government guarantee, or a strong bank monitor—reduces the firm's business risk to the point that equity risk capital is less financially vital.[24] In the more general case, almost every company has a sizeable financial base of common stock that supports the firm's borrowing and absorbs most of the risk of business fluctuations.

This common stock usually comes from one or more of three principal sources. First, when a company is initially organized, the founders invest cash and other valuable assets (including their labor, or **sweat equity**) in the company and receive a substantial block of common stock in return. Subsequent rounds of private stock sales may also expand the firm's equity base. The second, and usually most important source of equity capital is retained earnings. This represents net operating profits that the firm's owners have deliberately chosen to reinvest in the company rather than paying out to themselves as cash dividends. Many finance authors have likened retained earnings to a fully-subscribed issue of new common stock that is paid for with the cash dividends that the owners forego through retention.

The final source of equity capital is a public sale of equity securities to unaffiliated investors. The first such sale is called an **initial public offering**, or IPO, and it is almost always a transforming event for any company that lives through the experience. While different countries have different financial disclosure and exchange listing requirements, the basic results of an IPO are universal. First, a company generally raises a relatively gargantuan amount of money that can be used to repay existing debt, finance fixed asset and working capital expansion, or serve as a base for future borrowing. The

22. Linn and Pinegar (1988) report that, generally, industrial firms issue convertible preferred, utilities issue non-convertible preferred, and financial companies issue adjustable-rate preferred stock.

23. High-yield bonds are examined in several articles, including Altman (1987, 1992), Asquith, Mullins, and Wolff (1989), Blume, Keim, and Patel (1991), Cornell and Green (1991), and Fridson (1994).

24. The importance of this ability to operate at a higher optimal leverage ratio is discussed at length in Lessard (1991).

typical American IPO, for example, will raise $10–30 million in equity financing for a company with annual sales and assets of less than $50 million.[25] Second, the firm becomes a **public company**, meaning that it is listed for trading on a public stock market and thus has a direct means to sell new equity issues to investors whenever it wishes—though these issues must generally be "registered" with the securities regulatory authorities and, in some countries (including Japan), the firm wishing to issue stock must obtain special permission to sell shares and thus "disrupt" capital markets. An important side benefit of a public listing is that it provides the firm's owners with a chance to acheive personal liquidity for the shares they own.

The third, and usually least pleasant, result of an IPO is that a newly-public company finds that it has very demanding new shareholders to answer to, and must also publicly disclose heretofore highly confidential financial information. This disclosure requirement is most extreme in the United States, since the **Securities and Exchange Commission** (SEC) mandates that any firm (including non-U.S. companies) wishing to sell securities on American capital markets must not only disclose all pertinent *financial* data (profits, financing patterns, taxes, etc.), it must also provide detailed descriptions of its ownership structure (officer and director shareholdings, principal outside shareholdings, and biographical sketches of all directors), compensation plans (salary and bonus payments to top officers, executive stock option plans, and employee stock purchase and pension plans), and interest in affiliated companies.[26] In spite of these requirements, increasing numbers of foreign companies have begun to tap American stock and bond markets in recent years, though most do indeed cringe at the degree of information disclosure required.[27]

As mentioned above, one of the principal benefits of being a public company is that the firm (usually) has the right to sell new equity securities either to its existing shareholders—through what is called a **rights issue**—or to any investor wishing to buy new shares.[28] These share sales are referred to as **seasoned issues**, and can be important sources of equity capital, particularly for rapidly growing firms. Seasoned equity issues are surprisingly rare for both U.S. and non-U.S. companies, however, and the typical large American company will not sell new equity even as frequently as once per

---

25. While relatively small IPOs are the most common, inclusion of several very large issues raises the average proceeds much higher. However, it also seems clear that IPOs are becoming larger over time. In 1993, for example, 707 operating companies raised $41.5 billion, for an average issue size of $58.7 million.

26. A summary of the information required by the two principal types of public security registration statements (Forms S-1 and S-18) is provided in Peat Marwick Main & Company (1987).

27. After a long tug-of-war, the Securities and Exchange Commission won an important victory in October 1993, when Daimler-Benz finally agreed to comply with the SEC's information disclosure and accounting requirements in order to obtain a listing on the New York Stock Exchange (see Raghavan and Sesit 1993). After this, several other German companies expressed an interest in following, though none did immediately. Furthermore, the wisdom of mandating such dramatically greater disclosure than other countries require is challenged on practical and theoretical grounds by Baumol and Malkiel (1993) and Edwards (1993).

28. In spite of the fact that rights issues appear to have significantly lower issuance costs than underwritten offerings, rights issues have been declining monotonically for decades. This phenomenon is examined by Smith (1977), Hansen and Pinkerton (1982), and Hansen (1989), and the most likely explanation is that firms announcing rights issues suffer larger price drops than do firms announcing underwritten offers—thereby negating the benefits of lower underwriting fees (Hansen 1989).

decade.[29] In fact, the total value of all seasoned equity issues by U.S. companies rarely exceeds $30 billion per year (as compared to over $250 billion in corporate bond issues in recent years), and the total volume has actually been barely larger than the total volume of IPOs (also called **unseasoned equity issues**) so far this decade. Part of the reason for the reluctance of managers to suggest new seasoned issues is the fact that their announcement generally triggers a sizeable stock price decline. In the United States, the average dollar value of this price decline is equal to almost one-third of the dollar value of the issue itself. Clearly, the announcement of seasoned equity issues conveys negative information to investors, though precisely what information is transmitted is not always clear. The most likely message being conveyed is either that management—which is presumably better informed about a company's true prospects than are outside investors—believes the firm's current stock price is too high (thus giving management the opportunity to sell over-valued shares), or that the firm's earnings will be lower-than-expected in the future and management is issuing stock to make up for the lower-than-expected internal cash flow, or both. The stock price responses to both debt and equity issues are discussed in depth in section 9.5.

DEBT MARKETS   Debt markets are usually categorized by type of issuer, loan maturity, loan purpose and collateral backing, and special features. We will briefly look at each category, beginning with type of issuer. Specialized debt markets have developed to cater to corporate, government and individual (consumer) borrowers. In the United States, these markets are almost perfectly segmented from each other, and even within each broad category there are myriad variations. The federal government and its agencies, for example, tap different financial markets than do state and local governments. Outside of the United States, the distinction between corporate and government debt markets is often less precise—particularly for borrowing by the national government, which is often referred to as **sovereign borrowing**.[30] For example, many governments borrow in the Eurobond and Eurocurrency syndicated loan markets (discussed below), even though they are primarily designed to service corporate borrowers.[31] American

---

29. For example, Mikkelson and Partch (1986) report only 80 common stock offerings for their sample of 360 companies over the eleven-year period 1972–1982. On the other hand, there were 205 public debt offerings (33 convertible and 172 nonconvertible) and 296 private debt placements by these same companies during the study period.

30. The most famous (infamous?) examples of sovereign borrowing in international markets, of course, involve developing countries borrowing from western commercial banks in the Eurocurrency syndicated loan markets during the 1970s and early 1980s. The buildup, and subsequent meltdown, of these credits has been documented in Lessard and Williamson (1985), Sachs (1986), Sachs and Huizinga (1987), and Dillon and Oliveros (1987). An excellent analysis of the theoretical problems involved with sovereign lending is provided in Eaton, Gersovitz, and Stiglitz (1986), while Bulow and Rogoff (1989), Chowdhry (1991), Grossman and Van Huyck (1988), and Shapiro (1985, 1988) also present theoretical analyses of sovereign lending. Finally, empirical tests of sovereign loan pricing models are presented in Edwards (1984, 1986) and Boehmer and Megginson (1990).

31. Western European countries with good credit ratings but small financial markets, such as Denmark and Sweden, rely quite heavily on Eurobond financing. Many other European countries tap this market as one part of their deficit-financing programs. While creditworthy sovereign borrowers tend to prefer Eurobond issues to Eurocurrency loans, the latter's ability to raise large volumes of cash on short notice caused the Saudi Arabian and Kuwaiti governments to negotiate jumbo (billion dollar plus) loans to meet their acute reconstruction and working capital needs shortly after the Persian Gulf War ended in 1991.

consumers also enjoy generally better access to debt markets designed specifically for their needs than is true for citizens of other countries, though many over-indebted American families have found this access to be a two-edged sword.

Although consumer and government debt markets are important to a nation's economy, more important by far are the debt markets that service the needs of corporate borrowers, because limited liability companies are the principal vehicles used for producing the goods and services demanded by societies all the world over. In most countries, commercial banks still provide the bulk of the loan capital that even large companies need. In the United States, and in the international financial markets that service multinational companies, specialized debt markets play much larger roles in corporate finance. As mentioned above, American companies can issue short-term debt securities in the commercial paper market and long-term debt securities in any of several corporate bond markets. Large American and non-U.S. companies that operate in many different countries are usually called **multinational companies**, or MNCs, and these firms have a veritable smorgasbord of debt markets and instruments to choose from. The most important of these are the Eurobond, foreign bond, and Eurocurrency syndicated loan markets. A **Eurobond** is a long-term debt security that is issued simultaneously in several countries—usually not including the home country of the corporate (or sovereign) issuer—but is denominated in a single currency.[32] The classic example of a Eurobond issue is a dollar-denominated bond issued by an American corporation to investors in several Western European countries.

Foreign bonds are debt securities issued by a foreign company in a single national market and denominated in the host country's currency. A dollar-denominated bond issued in the United States by a German company would be an example of a foreign bond, as would a yen-denominated bond issued by an American company in Japan. Many of these issues have colorful names. For example, the two bonds described above would be called **Yankee bonds** and **Samurai bonds**, respectively. Similar issues in Britain would be called **Bulldog bonds**, while issues in Switzerland and the Netherlands would be referred to as **Heidi** and **Rembrandt bonds**.

The single largest and most important international debt market is the Eurocurrency syndicated loan market. The **Eurocurrency market** is a bank deposit and loan market where international banks accept deposits and make loans in currencies other than that of their home country.[33] For example, a British bank that accepts a dollar-denominated deposit in London is creating a Eurodollar deposit, and if it then relends the deposit to another bank or corporate borrower it is making a Eurodollar loan. The principal credit instrument used in this market is the syndicated loan, which is actually a large (credits of $1 billion or more are common and credits of $5 billion or more are not unheard of), intermediate-term line of credit arranged by a syndicate of international

---

32. Academic papers that examine Eurobond pricing and issuance patterns include Finnerty, Schneeweis, and Hedge (1980), Kidwell, Marr, and Thompson (1985), and Kim and Stulz (1988).

33. According to estimates provided by Morgan Stanley, the gross value of Eurocurrency deposits at the end of 1991 was $6.100 trillion, and the net value (canceling out interbank loans) of these deposits was $1.408 trillion. In contrast, the corresponding gross and net values for the Eurocurrency markets in 1970 were $110 billion and $35 billion, respectively, yielding compound annual growth rates of 20.0 and 18.3 percent over the 22 year period from 1970 to 1991.

banks for a single sovereign or corporate borrower.[34] These loans are highly valued by borrowers because of their low cost and great flexibility.

MATURITY   Debt instruments are usually classified according to original maturity into short-, intermediate-, and long-term securities.[35] As mentioned above, the principal short-term corporate debt markets are those for commercial paper and working capital loans from commercial banks. Intermediate-term debt markets can also be categorized into securitized and bank loan markets, with **term loans**—borrowings tied to the purchase of a specific asset, with a fixed term and equal periodic principal and interest payments—being the most important examples of intermediate-term bank loans.[36] Intermediate-term note and bond markets have also become increasingly attractive financing options for corporations in recent decades, as investors have come to see medium-term securities as attractive compromises between the lower interest rates offered on short-term securities and the much greater price volatility and risk of loss from inflation inherent in long-term bond investments. In particular, the development of the **medium-term note** (MTN) market—where corporations can issue securities directly to investors, without using an investment banking underwriter—has dramatically expanded the financing opportunities of firms wishing to raise intermediate-term capital.[37]

All this is not to suggest that the classic long-term corporate bond is becoming obsolete—far from it. In fact, as inflationary expectations in the American economy steadily declined in the late 1980s and early 1990s, several large companies, including Walt Disney, began to experiment with the issuance of very long-term (100 years) bonds. Given the enthusiastic reception these bonds received, more such nearly perpetual bonds will probably be forthcoming.[38] Far more common are corporate bonds with maturities of between ten and thirty years. Most such bonds issued by American corporations have fixed coupon interest rates (paid semi-annually) and a final repayment of principal at the bond's maturity, though **zero-coupon** bonds that pay no explicit interest but rather are purchased at a discount and mature at par several years later experienced a burst of popularity after they were introduced in the early 1980s.[39]

34. The historical evolution of the syndicated loan market is described in Mendelson (1980), Sarver (1988), and Winkler (1991), while Pavey and Humphreys (1988) and Grabbe (1991) describe the mechanics of syndicated lending. Finally, Megginson, Poulsen, and Sinkey (1995) examine stock market responses to bank announcements that they are participating in syndicated loans to sovereign or corporate borrowers.

35. One of the first authors to provide a theoretical analysis of the choice of debt maturity structure was Myers (1977). Since that time, numerous other researchers have provided either theoretical or empirical analyses of maturity choice. Three recent examples are Brick and Ravid (1991), Diamond (1993), and Houston and Venkataram (1994).

36. The pricing of bank loans has been examined theoretically by Smith (1980), and empirically by Scott and Smith (1986), Booth (1992), and Petersen and Rajan (1994). The types of business loans offered by U.S. commercial banks are described in Sinkey (1992), chapter 18.

37. The historical development and current status of the medium-term loan market is described in Crabbe (1992).

38. On July 20, 1993, Disney was able to easily sell $150 million worth of these bonds at a coupon rate only 95 basis points (0.95 percentage points) higher than 30-year Treasury bond yields (Vogel 1993). Two days later, Coca-Cola Company followed Disney's lead with another 100-year, $150 million bond issue.

Outside of the United States, investors seem to prefer shorter-maturity bonds with floating, rather than fixed, interest payments.[40] This is particularly true in countries with a history of high and/or volatile inflation rates.

U.S. corporate bonds are usually also **callable**—meaning that the corporation has the right (subject to the terms in the bond issuance contract) to repurchase the bonds from investors at a fixed price after a fixed length of time from original issuance.[41] This right is most valuable to corporations, and most painful to investors, when market interest rates decline sharply, since this provides the corporation with an opportunity to call high-interest-rate debt inexpensively and replace it with a bond issue carrying a lower coupon rate. Investors lose out on the capital gain that would accrue to them following an interest rate decline if their bonds were not callable. Naturally, corporations must purchase this right—which is effectively a call option—from investors at the time of issue by offering bond buyers a higher coupon interest rate than would be required on similar-risk bonds without this call feature.

Although American corporations (and non-U.S. companies that can issue bonds in American markets) have the opportunity to issue longer-maturity bonds than their international competitors, the actual average maturity of the typical American bond issue is far less than its stated maturity would imply due to the pervasiveness of mandated **sinking funds** on long-term U.S. debt security issues.[42] These programs require corporate issuers to repurchase a given fraction of each outstanding bond issue each year, either through open market purchases or by selective calls on individual investors. Therefore, the typical bond issue with, say, $100 million principal amount and a fifteen-year maturity will probably have only a few million dollars worth of bonds still outstanding when the last bonds are redeemed a decade and a half after issuance. Depending upon the terms of the sinking fund, the actual average maturity of this issue (the weighted average years outstanding) will probably be less than ten years, rather than the fifteen years advertised. By forcing the corporation to redeem part of each issue early, sinking funds reduce the risk of default on an individual issue, for two reasons. First, sinking funds increase the likelihood that any financial difficulties an issuing firm encounters will be trumpeted to investors early rather than late (by the firm missing a sinking fund payment), thus triggering the demand for effective corrective action, up to and including the removal of the issuing firm's incumbent management team. Second, since at maturity only a fraction of a given bond issue will remain outstanding, the issuing firm's managers will have less incentive to default on the issue and attempt to expropriate bondholder wealth by filing for bankruptcy protection.

---

39. The exciting birth and recent demise of the zero-coupon bond is discussed in Finnerty (1992) and Sundaram (1993).

40. Analyses of the pricing of floating rate debt are provided in Ramaswamy and Sundaresan (1986) and Kaufold and Smirlock (1991).

41. For recent examples of the academic literature on the callability of corporate bonds, see Mitchell (1991), Kish and Livingston (1993) and Mauer (1993). The Mitchell and Mauer articles also provide references of earlier articles examining the reasons why call options are included in bond contracts. The best-known empirical study examining calls of corporate bonds is by Vu (1986).

42. Sinking funds are examined theoretically by Dunn and Spatt (1984), and empirically by Dyl and Joehnk (1979), Smith (1979), Ho and Singer (1984), Ogden (1987), and Mitchell (1991).

SECURITY, SENIORITY, AND RATING STATUS OF CORPORATE BONDS   Most bank loans to corporations, regardless of maturity, are **secured** by specific collateral.[43] This collateral might be an individual asset (a machine tool) or it might be an asset category, such as the firm's inventory or accounts receivable. While this is often referred to as **asset-backed lending**, banks in reality are primarily cash flow lenders. They hope and expect to be repaid out of cash flow, but require collateral both as an alternative source of repayment and as "ransom" to decrease the incentive of borrowing firms to default (since a defaulting borrower would lose the use of valuable corporate assets). Most pledged assets are secured by a **lien**, which is a legal contract specifying under what conditions the lender can take title to the asset if the loan is not repaid and prohibiting the borrowing firm from selling or disposing of the asset without the lender's consent. Not all assets make acceptable collateral, of course. For an asset to be useful as collateral, it should (1) be nonperishable, (2) be relatively homogeneous in quality, (3) have a high value relative to its bulk, and (4) have a well-established secondary market where seized assets can be turned into cash without a severe price penalty.

In contrast to ordinary bank loans, corporate bond issues and syndicated bank loans usually are not secured by explicit collateral, but are instead backed by the full faith and credit of the issuing corporation—meaning they are backed only by the assets and earning power of the issuing firm.[44] Unsecured corporate bonds are often called **debentures** to distinguish them from **mortgage bonds**, which are secured by real assets (land and structures attached to it), and **collateral trust bonds**, which are debt securities issued against specific pledged assets such as aircraft, barges, rolling stock, and other transportation equipment. Also in contrast to bank loans, corporate bonds are often explicitly structured to have a junior, or subordinated, status relative to senior debt securities. This means that such **subordinated debentures** will not receive any periodic interest or principal payments until all the claims of the senior securities are satisfied in full. Obviously, these securities have coupon interest rates commensurate with the risk their purchasers are expected to bear.

Most large U.S. corporate bond issues are also **rated**—given a relative default risk score—by credit analysis and rating services such as Moody's, Standard and Poor's, and Fitch Investors' Services.[45] The highest grade (lowest risk) bonds are given a rating of Aaa by Moody's and AAA by Standard and Poor's. Increasingly risky bonds are given ratings of Aa, A, Baa, Ba, B, Caa, Ca, and C by Moody's, with bonds rated in the Aaa through Baa range being referred to as **investment grade**. Standard and Poor's (S&P) gives similar ratings, with the exceptions that the ratings are all capital letters (AA, A, BBB, BB, B, CCC, CC, C) and S&P also has a rating of D, meaning the bond is in de-

---

43. The use of collateral as backing for a loan has been analyzed theoretically by Scott (1977), Stulz and Johnson (1985), and Igawa and Kanatas (1990), and empirically by Berger and Udell (1990) and Booth (1992). Both of these empirical studies support earlier findings that collateral is associated with *higher,* rather than lower, interest rates (spreads over a base rate) on secured loans. This implies that collateral allows riskier borrowers to receive credit that would not be granted to them through unsecured lending.

44. For a discussion of the relative bargaining power of Eurobond issuers versus borrowers in the Eurocurrency syndicated loan market, and how this impacts the severity of debt restrictions and collateral requirements, see Lee (1994).

45. Bond ratings have been examined in numerous academic studies, including Pinches and Mingo (1973), Weinstein (1977), Kaplan and Urwitz (1979), Wakeman (1981), Ogden (1987), and Gentry, Whitford, and Newbold (1988).

fault. Since few other countries have large, actively-traded corporate bond markets, ratings are not as important outside the United States. As non-U.S. bond markets grow in issue and trading volume, however, it is virtually certain that investors elsewhere will find bond ratings as efficient and indispensable as U.S. investors have.

COVENANTS, CONVERSION OPTIONS, AND OTHER SPECIAL FEATURES   The final method of classifying debt securities is by the covenants, conversion options, and other special features that corporate issuers often insert into bond contracts in order to appeal to (or address the risk concerns of) certain investor clienteles. The variety of these special features that have actually been observed in recent years is astonishing, but we will examine only a few key issues. First, almost all bank loan and bond issue contracts contain often detailed covenants that limit the corporate borrower's operating and financial discretion while they have outstanding borrowings under the debt contract.[46] **Positive covenants** mandate what a borrower *must do*, while **negative covenants** mandate what the borrower *must not do*. As examples, mandates that the borrowing firm must provide creditors with audited financial statements, purchase insurance against fire damage to the firm's property, and maintain minimum working capital ratios are all positive covenants, while mandates that the borrowing firm's management team must not dispose of the firm's assets without permission, acquire another company without prior approval, or issue new debt with equal or higher seniority status are all commonly employed negative covenants.

More generally, positive and negative covenants can be grouped into one of four categories: (1) default triggers, which specify what constitutes a loan default and spell out what remedial actions the creditors can then take; (2) cash flow controls, which limit the borrower's ability to reinvest or distribute (as dividends or share repurchases) its operating cash flows; (3) operating controls, which mandate that management act responsibly to safeguard the firm's physical and intangible assets; and (4) strategy controls, which limit the firm's ability to pursue mergers, acquisitions, divestitures, or other strategies that would substantially change the nature of the firm's operations. In all cases, the covenant's purpose is to protect the creditor by limiting the borrower's ability to expropriate the creditor's wealth, and the borrower is willing to accept these provisions because debt financing would be either more expensive or unattainable in their absence.

A special form of debt covenant is a **conversion option**. Such an option gives an investor the right to convert each bond held into a fixed number of common shares of the issuing corporation.[47] Dividing the face value of the bond by the number of shares to be received upon conversion determines the implied exercise price of the conversion option,

---

46. Debt covenants have been extensively examined in the finance literature, beginning with what remains a classic analysis by Smith and Warner (1979). Subsequent papers include Kalay (1982), Malitz (1986), Berlin and Loeys (1988), Press and Weintrop (1990), and El-Gazzar and Pastena (1990).

47. Pricing models for convertible securities are presented in Brennan and Schwartz (1980) and Ingersoll (1977a), and a theoretical analysis of their use in corporate finance is provided in Stein (1992). Several authors—including Ingersoll (1977b), Brennan and Schwartz (1977), and Dunn and Eades (1984)— document that corporations tend to delay calling convertible bonds longer than they should, based on theoretical models, but Asquith and Mullins (1991) show this behavior is mostly the result of very small quantities of bonds remaining outstanding at the time calls would be optimal. Several authors have also performed event study analyses of the stock price responses to convertible security issues (Mikkelson 1981, Dann and Mikkelson 1984) and calls (Ofer and Natarajan 1987, Mais, Moore, and Rogers 1989, and Cowan, Nayar, and Singh 1990).

and the value of the option itself depends upon the volatility of the firm's share price, the number of years to the bond's maturity, and how far the current stock price is below the implied exercise price. Current research suggests that **convertible bonds** are most commonly issued by relatively rapidly growing firms that face significant operating uncertainty, and that must raise external capital in order to finance valuable growth options.[48] As we know, such an operating environment naturally generates agency problems between managers and investors—who have great difficulty monitoring managers in the face of such informational asymmetries—and convertible securities help control these agency problems by giving investors a claim on the firm's upside potential. A similar objective can be achieved by issuing bonds with **warrants**, that give an investor the right to purchase shares of stock at a fixed price for a fixed period of time. These warrants are often **detachable**, meaning that they can be sold separately from the underlying bond itself. Both warrants and conversion options are valuable to investors, and corporations usually can lower the coupon rate they must pay on debt by including these features in their bond offerings. The cost, of course, is potential dilution of existing shareholder claims when and if the bonds are converted or the warrants are exercised.

In recent years, corporations have developed a plethora of new debt instruments that are designed to attract unique bond investor clienteles, whose members presumably would be willing to pay a higher price for a given special feature. Examples of this trend include **floating rate bonds** (and notes) that protect investors from interest rate risk, **multi-currency bonds** that pay interest in one currency and repay principal in another (or pay both interest and principal in a basket of different currencies), and **puttable bonds** that allows an investor to force the issuing firm to repurchase the bond at face value if the issuing firm's credit rating should slip after the bonds are issued.[49] An additional force driving debt security innovations is the desire of corporations to issue claims that alter the firm's operating risk profile. A classic example of this is a **commodity-linked bond** whose payoff at maturity is linked to the contemporaneous market value of the commodity in question. Such a feature would allow, say, an oil company to issue bonds that paid off at maturity either the face value of the bond or the market value of fifty barrels of petroleum. At least some investors would value the opportunity to purchase such a bond as an opportunity to speculate on the future value of petroleum, while the oil company would find the feature attractive because it would only have to pay off in barrels of petroleum when it could best afford to do so—after the commodity's price had risen dramatically. Many other bonds with payoffs linked to interest rates, exchange rates, commodity prices, or other risk factors have also been developed in recent years.[50]

---

48. For example, Brennan and Schwartz (1988) present an excellent intuitive discussion of the appropriate corporate uses of convertible securities.

49. Another example of financial innovation was provided in March 1995, when the Hong Kong and Shanghai Banking Corporation (HSBC) issued Eurobonds with payments linked to the British retail price index (RPI). These were designed to appeal to U.K. pension fund managers seeking a long-term investment that is protected from inflation risk (see Sharpe 1995).

50. Many of the newly-developed financial products discussed here are described and analyzed in the Winter 1992 Financial Innovation issue of the **Journal of Applied Corporate Finance**. In particular, Finnerty provides an overview of the types of securities that have been issued, and Miller and Merton each analyze the economic value of financial innovation. Separately, Sundaram (1993) describes new securities developed for international capital markets, while Tufano (1989) analyzes innovation from the perspective of the investment bank that develops a new product and Shirreff (1994) discusses how financial products are likely to evolve in the coming decades.

9.3.4 Primary vs. Secondary Markets

Yet another way to classify financial markets is to draw a distinction between primary and secondary markets, and between primary and secondary security sales. A **primary market** is a market where newly-issued securities are sold for cash to their initial purchaser, while existing securities are traded between investors on a **secondary market**. Likewise, a **primary security issue** (or primary sale) is a capital-raising event for an issuer in that the issuing firm sells a financial claim against itself to an original investor in exchange for cash. If that investor later decides to sell the security to another investor, such a transaction is called a **secondary security sale** (as are all subsequent trades), and it has no direct cash flow effect on the issuing corporation whatsoever.[51] Most routine secondary security sales (i.e., when an individual investor decides to sell 100 shares of common stock) involve the use of a broker to bring together buyer and seller, but some large secondary sales are structured as **secondary issues** that are actually underwritten by investment bankers. In recent years, the most economically important secondary security issues have been the share-issue privatizations that governments around the world have executed. The vast majority of these have involved the government selling existing shares rather than being capital-raising events for the newly-privatized companies themselves.

Of course, very few real security markets are exclusively either primary or secondary markets, although there is a greater degree of differentiation than you might expect. Since common and preferred stocks are perpetual securities, and since seasoned equity issues are rare for any single company, the overwhelming majority of transactions on the world's stock markets involve secondary trades of existing shares. On the other hand, only a relatively tiny fraction of all the debt securities that are outstanding at any point in time actively trade on truly liquid secondary markets, and most short-term debt instruments (including commercial paper) are purchased with the intention of being held until maturity. Since liquidity is a property that investors often value highly, corporate treasurers trying to design the optimal capital-raising strategy for their firm face a real choice between issuing a limited number of highly liquid securities or issuing multiple classes of (relatively illiquid) securities with special features designed to attract diverse investor clienteles.[52]

9.3.5 Markets for Hedging and Risk Management Products

While trading in virtually all types of financial instruments has increased over the past two decades, no markets have experienced growth rates as explosive as those for the financial instruments used for hedging and risk management. Since the collapse of the

---

51. While a secondary sale may have no direct cash flow effect on a firm, the announcement of such a sale can cause stock prices to decline if the sale is being made by a presumably well-informed insider (officer, director, or blocholder), or if there is a less than perfectly elastic demand curve for shares. Secondary distributions are examined by Scholes (1972), Dann, Mayers, and Raab (1977), Holthausen, Leftwich, and Mayers (1987), Easley and O'Hara (1987), Kumar, Sarin, and Shastri (1992), and Hudson, Jensen, and Pugh (1993).

52. The first major finance article to both provide a theoretical explanation of why liquidity should be valuable to investors, and to document its empirical relevance, is Amihud and Mendelson (1986). Further indirect evidence that liquidity increases value is provided in Sanger and McConnell (1986), while liquidity is modeled theoretically by Grossman and Miller (1988).

Bretton Woods fixed exchange rate regime in 1973, corporations have been exposed to extreme fluctuations in interest rates, exchange rates, and in the prices of virtually all important raw materials.[53] This increased risk has led to a mushrooming demand for financial instruments and strategies that corporations can use to **hedge**, or offset, their underlying operating and financial exposures.[54] The four principal risk management "building blocks" are forwards, futures, options, and swaps.[55] We will discuss each of these instruments below, but before proceeding it is worth noting that organized markets did not exist for any of these financial products (except currency forward contracts) prior to 1973.

A **forward contract** involves two parties agreeing today on a price at which the purchaser will buy a given amount of a commodity or financial instrument from the seller at a fixed date sometime in the future. For example, a multinational company's treasurer who expects to receive a ten million Swiss Franc (SF) payment in sixty days might choose to sell that payment forward at, say, $0.70 per Swiss Franc. By doing this, the treasurer has hedged the company's foreign exchange risk associated with this payment by locking in the dollar price the company will receive for its foreign currency cash flow. In sixty days, the company will deliver SF10,000,000 and receive in exchange $7,000,000 ($0.70/SF x SF10,000,000), regardless of what the spot (immediate delivery) $/SF exchange rate happens to be at that time. Most forward contracts are individually negotiated between corporations and financial intermediaries, but there are active markets for standard denomination and maturity forward contracts on several currencies and raw materials which institutions (including the bank market-makers themselves) can use to hedge their own exposures.

In contrast to forwards, a **futures contract** is an *exchange-traded* contract that promises the delivery of a *standardized volume* of a commodity or financial instrument on a *standardized date* (i.e., the third Wednesday) of the month in which the contract expires. The economic rationale for designing futures contracts in this way is that it provides a standardized, high trading volume (hence low transactions cost) financial instrument that can be used by both individuals and businesses to hedge underlying commercial risks, as well as by speculators wishing to place a highly-leveraged bet on the direction of commodity prices. While both futures and forwards impose delivery obligations on their holders, the default risk of a futures contract is much lower, for two reasons.[56] First, every major futures exchange operates a clearinghouse that acts as the counter-party to all buyers and all sellers. While individual traders interact with each other face-to-face in a futures "pit"

---

53. The dramatic increase in the volatility of financial assets (including currencies) is illustrated graphically in Smithson and Chew (1992).

54. Several papers discuss how a firm might first assess, then use, financial contracts to help minimize exposure, including Kaufold and Smirlock (1986), Rawls and Smithson (1990), Pringle (1991), Smithson and Chew (1992), Dolde (1993), Pringle and Connolly (1993), and Acheson (1994). A practitioner-oriented discussion of the increased perceived risk in using derivatives to hedge financial risks is provided in a **Business Week** (October 31, 1994) special report on managing risk.

55. The four building blocks are described in Smith, Smithson, and Wilford (1989). These authors also describe how managers can "mix and match" these instruments to achieve specific risk management objectives.

56. An intuitive discussion of the pricing of financial futures is provided in French (1989), while Cox, Ingersoll, and Ross (1981) and Meulbroek (1992) provide comparisons of forward and futures prices.

(trading area), the actual contract drawn up to formalize this trade will break this direct link between buyer and seller, and will instead insert the clearinghouse as the opposite party. This means that traders need not worry about the credit-worthiness of the party they trade with (as forward market traders must), but only about the credit-worthiness of the exchange itself. Daily cash settlement of all contracts, called **marking-to-market**, is the second factor limiting default risk on futures exchanges. By its very nature, a futures contract is a zero-sum game in that whenever the market price of a commodity changes, the underlying value of a long (purchase) or short (sale) position also changes—and one party's gain is the other party's loss. By requiring each contract's loser to pay the winner the net amount of this change each day, futures exchanges eliminate the possibility that large unrealized losses will build up over time.

In addition to the distinctions listed above, futures differ from forward contracts in two other important respects. First, futures contracts are designed to have a value (usually around $100,000) that will appeal to a "retail" market of individuals and smaller companies, whereas most actively-traded forward contracts have minimum denominations of $1,000,000 or more. This small contract size is rarely a problem for futures traders, however, since those wishing to hedge large exposures can simply purchase multiple contracts. Second, while most forward contracts are settled by actual delivery, this rarely occurs with futures contracts. Instead, futures market hedgers will execute an offsetting trade to close out their position in the futures market whenever they have closed out their underlying commercial risk through delivery in the normal course of their business.

For example, the multinational company with the SF10,000,000 exposure discussed earlier could have chosen to hedge that exposure in the futures market rather than with a forward contract by purchasing eighty Swiss Franc futures contracts (each mandating delivery of SF125,000) that expire *after* the date on which it will receive the SF payment (since futures contracts have fixed delivery dates, they will only rarely exactly match a trader's desired payment date). When the SF payment is received, the company will exchange it for dollars at whatever the spot $/SF exchange rate happens to be at the time, and will simultaneously sell eighty SF futures contracts with the same delivery date as the contracts purchased earlier—thereby offsetting or canceling out its futures position. If the dollar value of the Swiss Franc has declined from $0.70/SF to say $0.50/SF during the sixty days in question then the company will lose $0.20/SF, or a total of $2,000,000, on its cash market sale of the SF payment. But this loss will be exactly offset by the $2,000,000 profit the company will acheive on its futures position. If the Swiss Franc appreciates rather than depreciates against the dollar, then the company will gain on its cash market transaction and lose on its futures contracts. Either way, hedgers can use a financial contract to hedge an underlying commercial risk without actually having to take physical delivery on the futures contract.

In a **swap contract** two parties agree to exchange payment obligations on two underlying financial liabilities that are equal in principal amount but differ in payment patterns. The most common such transaction is an interest rate swap, under which one party who has floating rate debt outstanding will exchange payment obligations with the other party, who has a fixed rate debt issue outstanding.[57] The first party would have

---

57. Swaps are examined in several academic papers, including Bicksler and Chen (1986), Litzenberger (1992), McNulty (1990), and Titman (1992).

liked to issue fixed rate debt, but chose instead to issue floating rate debt either because the fixed rate market was closed to this issuer or it was more costly. By entering a swap agreement, the floating rate issuer can effectively obtain a fixed rate payment obligation, while the counter-party (who has better access to fixed rate debt markets) achieves a preferred floating rate pattern of payments. Rather than exchange gross amounts, the two parties will instead exchange only the net difference between the two payment obligations, so the party that has swapped a fixed rate payment obligation for a floating rate one will lose (have to increase payment amounts) if market interest rates rise and will benefit if market rates fall. The second most common type of swap contract is a currency swap, in which two parties exchange payment obligations denominated in different currencies. For example, an American company wishing to invest in Switzerland would prefer to borrow in Swiss Francs rather than in dollars. If, however, the company could borrow on more attractive terms in dollars (as is often the case) than in francs, a logical strategy for this company would be to borrow the money needed for investment in dollars, and then swap payment obligations with a Swiss company seeking dollars for investment in the United States.

Option contracts are the final risk management building block, and these are truly pervasive in modern financial systems. There are exchange-traded options contracts on individual common stocks, on stock indexes, on numerous currencies and interest rates, on a bewildering number of industrial and agricultural commodities, and even on futures contracts. Even more options are custom designed by financial institutions to meet the needs of their customers (these are often called over-the-counter, or OTC options). A **call** option gives its holder the right to buy a fixed amount of a commodity at a fixed price, on (with a European option) or by (with an American option) a fixed date in the future, while a **put** option entails a similar right to sell that commodity.[58] The valuation and payoff pattern of an option is discussed in depth in chapter 5. For our purposes here, the key feature of an option as a hedging tool is that it provides protection against adverse price risk (one has the right to exercise the option if price changes make it optimal to do so) without having to forfeit the right to profit if the price on the underlying commodity moves in your favor (in which case, you allow the option to expire unexercised).

Modern corporations, and the financial institutions that cater to them, have become extremely adept at combining these risk management building blocks in complex patterns in order either to achieve specific risk profiles that benefit corporate issuers or to offer investors unique payoff structures that help complete the capital markets, or both. Given that the returns to successful financial innovation can be very high, a great many new financial products are developed every year. Most of these fail, or at least do not meet expectations, but enough succeed that we can identify certain trends which are likely to continue for the foreseeable future. First, longer-maturity risk management

---

58. The treasurer of the company in our earlier example wishing to hedge the dollar value of an expected Swiss Franc cash flow could also do this by purchasing a SF put option, giving the company the right to sell francs at a fixed price (say, $0.70/SF). If, at expiration, the spot price of Swiss Francs was less than $0.70/SF, the company would exercise its right to sell SF for $0.70/SF. If, however, the spot SF price was more than $0.70/SF (say $0.80/SF), the company would allow the option to expire unexercised and would instead sell SF on the open market. The gross profit from this transaction would be $0.80 − $0.70 = $0.10/SF, or $0.10/SF × SF10,000,000 $1,000,000, and the net profit per SF would be $0.10/SF minus the per SF option premium.

products will continue to be developed. While standard futures, forwards, and options are all short-term contracts, recent years have seen the introduction of much longer-dated contracts as well as the development of intermediate- and long-term securities that effectively perform hedging roles. Second, ever more complex securities will be developed to hedge multiple interest rate, currency, and input/output pricing risks—particularly in the international arena. Third, new techniques for hedging pricing and underwriting risks in the issuance of new securities will continue to be developed as the securitization trend accelerates around the world. Finally, it seems inevitable that new methods of hedging the strategic and currency risks of investing in small, politically-unstable, or financially under developed countries will be developed in the coming decade as Western capital is committed to the transformation of the formerly socialist or mixed economies of China, India, Russia, and eastern Europe.

WHY SHOULD PUBLIC COMPANIES HEDGE?   While it is clear that the corporate demand for hedging and risk management products has grown dramatically in recent years, it is less clear why a public company would choose to hedge at all. Risk aversion can explain why individuals and private firms hedge, but this cannot explain why a company that is presumably being run in the interest of a large number of well-diversified shareholders would expend valuable resources to hedge unsystematic risk. Clifford Smith and René Stulz describe three reasons why public companies can benefit from hedging.[59] First, if a firm's effective tax rate is a convex function of pre-tax profit (the effective marginal tax rate increases as income increases), hedging can reduce the present value of expected tax liabilities by smoothing the profit stream and reducing the likelihood that the firm will pay high taxes in one period while having to forego (or delay) the benefits of tax shields in another period. Second, hedging can increase firm value by reducing the likelihood that the firm will encounter bankruptcy or financial distress. For example, a credible promise to hedge operating and financial risks can sometimes entice creditors to lend the firm money on more favorable terms than they would be willing to lend to an unconstrained borrower. Finally, hedging helps to alleviate the incentive and monitoring problems caused by managerial risk aversion. By reducing the risk that bankruptcy will damage or destroy managers' firm-specific human capital, firms can attract better managers, pay them lower wages than would otherwise be necessary, and/or entice them to make greater investment in acquiring firm-specific expertise than would otherwise be individually rational.

9.4   THE ROLE OF FINANCIAL INTERMEDIARIES IN MODERN ECONOMIES

A financial intermediary is a commercial bank or other financial institution which breaks the direct funding link between savers and borrowers by transforming the financial claims borrowers prefer to issue into claims that savers prefer to hold. This process is called

---

59. This theory is presented in Smith and Stulz (1985) and tested empirically in Nance, Smith, and Smithson (1993). Other theoretical papers examining rationales for corporations to engage in costly risk management activities include Campbell and Kracaw (1990) and Froot, Scharfstein, and Stein (1993). In a related vein, Mayers and Smith (1982, 1990) also examine why corporations purchase insurance.

qualitative asset transformation, and it distinguishes an intermediary from a financial **broker**, who merely brings together a buyer and seller and does not change the nature of the financial claim being traded.[60] While intermediaries sometimes provide brokerage as well as asset transformation services, our focus as corporate finance theorists will be on the latter. In an economic sense, financial intermediaries (hereafter, FIs) raise funds by selling claims against themselves and then invest these funds in the debt and equity securities issued by individuals, governments, and non-financial corporations. FIs play important roles in all modern economies, but their relative importance and market power varies immensely from country to country. Our primary objectives in this section are to describe the financial services intermediaries provide to corporations, to explain why the role of FIs is so much different in the corporate finance system of the United States than it is in other advanced and developing countries, and to assess the relative competitive advantages of FIs vis-à-vis security markets in the provision of the products and services that will increasingly be needed by globally competitive companies.

Modern FIs provide five principal types of qualitative asset transformation services.[61] First, FIs provide **liquidity** and **payment intermediation** that is valuable both to individuals and to corporations. Depository institutions, for example, issue highly-liquid, nearly risk-free claims against themselves that claimholders can use (in lieu of cash) as payment for goods and services. These institutions then purchase relatively illiquid claims issued by corporations and other borrowers. Second, FIs provide **maturity intermediation** in that they issue relatively short-term liabilities (certificates of deposit, money market mutual fund shares, transactions deposits, etc.) and purchase financial and real assets with much longer lives. Commercial banks, in particular, can be crudely viewed as making a living by exploiting the yield curve—borrowing short term at low rates and lending longer term where the credit-risk-adjusted returns are usually higher. Third, FIs provide **denomination intermediation** since they offer investors a choice of small-denomination savings vehicles (what is the minimum positive balance your checking account has ever reached?), but are also able to finance the working capital and investment needs of even the largest corporations. This obviously eliminates the cost and risk of assembling a large group of small investors each time a corporation needs to finance a capital spending program. Fourth, FIs provide low-cost **diversification intermediation** to individual savers, who might otherwise be unable to purchase a broadly-diversified investment portfolio with the small sums they have to invest at any one time. Instead of incurring the search and transactions costs of investing in multiple assets, investors can simply purchase a claim against an intermediary that itself has a broadly-diversified portfolio.[62]

The fifth and final service that FIs provide is also the most important. This is **information intermediation**, and most modern theories of financial intermediation

---

60. For a full discussion of qualitative asset transformation, and a survey of intermediation theory, see Bhattacharya and Thakor (1993).

61. A good overview of the intermediation services provided by financial institutions is presented in Fabozzi, Modigliani, and Ferri (1994). A very revealing list of the different products and services offered by American FIs in 1990, compared with 1950, is presented in Shirreff (1994).

62. These four types of intermediation have been extensively researched in the financial literature. The first major article presenting a transactions cost explanation for FIs was Benston and Smith (1976). Subsequent papers include Morgan and Smith (1987), and Gorton and Pennacchi (1990).

consider it to be the central reason that FIs have developed and prospered.[63] In financial markets characterized by informational asymmetries between corporate managers and individual investors, it is very difficult for investors either to assess the true credit worthiness of borrowers prior to lending them money (or making an equity investment) or to monitor subsequent corporate use of the funds so raised. Faced with this inability to differentiate between high- and low-risk borrowers, investors will either choose not to lend (or invest) at all or will do so only at very high promised rates of return. Financial intermediaries are able to acquire the specialized expertise and personnel needed to overcome these informational asymmetries, determine which borrowers have the most promising investment opportunities, directly supply the funds needed to exploit these opportunities, and monitor the compliance of corporate managers with the terms of the investment/lending agreement.

Economists have long realized that it is very difficult to sell information on the open market since potential buyers are unwilling to purchase the information until its value is revealed by disclosure—but revealing the information's value through generalized disclosure makes it a public good that anyone can exploit without payment. One way of overcoming this public good aspect of information is to combine in an intermediary the economic functions of (1) credit information acquisition and analysis, (2) direct provision of funding, and (3) monitoring of borrower performance. Over time, the borrowing firm can develop a positive reputation with the intermediary (through prompt repayment of loans, by adopting prudent working capital management policies, or as a savvy user of sophisticated financial products), which in turn will give the FI the confidence to increase the amount it is willing to lend the firm and to invest time and resources into developing an ongoing business relationship. A commercial bank or other FI can thus become a **corporate insider**, trusted with confidential information about the borrowing firm's operations and opportunities and well positioned to first assess, then meet, the firm's evolving financial needs. Petersen and Rajan (1994) clearly show the value of banking relationships, particularly to small firms.

In many countries—but not in the United States—intermediaries also play an extremely important **corporate governance** role, distinct from their activities in granting credit and monitoring loan repayment.[64] Commercial banks, in particular, frequently help set operating as well as financial policies of firms they have invested in by serving on corporate boards and monitoring the performance of individual managers. In countries such as Germany, where banks can both own large equity stakes directly and vote the shares held in trust for individual customers, financial institutions wield tremendous economic power. And in countries with a long tradition of state ownership of corporate

---

63. The literature examining informational rationales for the existence of FIs is vast, but the classic finance paper on this topic is Leland and Pyle (1977). Since that time, several other pivotal articles examining the importance of informational asymmetries on the demand for intermediation have been published, including Diamond (1984, 1989), Fama (1980), Campbell and Kracaw (1980), and Allen (1990).

64. For overviews of the Japanese corporate finance (and control) system, see Hodder and Tschoegl (1985) or Frankel (1991). For a comparative analysis of corporate governance in Germany and Japan—plus a tabulation of share ownership patterns in these two countries, the U.S. and U.K.—see Kester (1992). This paper shows that U.S. banks own (mostly in trust for their customers) 0.3 percent of all traded equity, while the corresponding figures for German and Japanese banks are 8.9 and 25.2 percent, respectively. A more complete discussion of the importance of ownership structure is presented in chapter 2 of this text.

assets, state-owned banks are usually the chosen instrument for exercising financial control. For political and historical reasons, however, the United States has chosen to prohibit commercial banks from exercising a corporate governance role, even as it has discouraged other intermediaries—insurance companies, pension funds, mutual funds, etc.—from actively monitoring and disciplining corporate management.[65] We now briefly examine the regulatory environment that American FIs must operate in as a prelude to examining the role intermediaries play in the corporate financial system of the United States.

9.4.1 Regulation and the Role of Intermediaries in U.S. Corporate Finance

Americans have a long history of distrust for concentrated economic power, and this has dramatically influenced how the nation's financial institutions have been regulated. In response to public opinion, policy-makers have consistently discouraged the growth of large intermediaries (especially commercial banks), in part by imposing on them severe geographical restrictions.[66] In **unit-banking states**, for example, commercial banks are allowed to have only one office (branching is prohibited), and even today relatively few American states allow unrestricted statewide branching. In 1927, geographical restrictions were codified into national law when Congress passed the **McFadden Act**, which prohibited interstate banking. This legislation effectively guaranteed that a truly national bank—one with integrated operations spanning all or a large fraction of the states—would not be created as long as the law was in force. Over the years, several banks have been able to cobble together multi-state systems either by exploiting regulatory loopholes or by expanding into adjacent states as allowed by several regional "compacts", but even these systems must be structured as separate corporations within a holding company framework and none can be considered a seamless nationwide network. After numerous failed attempts to repeal the McFadden Act over the years, a bill allowing full interstate branch banking was finally approved by Congress in July 1994.[67]

The second pivotal law affecting American FIs is the **Glass-Steagall Act**, which was passed in 1933 in response to perceived banking abuses during the Great Depression. This legislation mandated the separation of investment and commercial banking, thereby prohibiting commercial banks from underwriting corporate security issues, providing security brokerage services to their customers, or even owning voting equity securities on their own account. Banking's corporate financing role was thus effectively restricted to making commercial loans and to providing closely related services such as leasing. As

---

65. For a description of these rules, and a discussion of their impact, see Grundfest (1990), Roe (1990), Black (1990, 1992), Jensen (1993), and Bhide (1993).

66. The historical evolution of banking regulation is ably summarized in Wheelock (1993), who also surveys the current state of American banking. Similar surveys that seek to answer the question, "is banking a declining industry?", include Kaufman and Mote (1994) and Boyd and Gertler (1994).

67. A wave of bank mergers may well be one of the first major effects of this bill's passage, as institutions try to quickly create nationwide branch networks (see Knecht 1994). Some commentators even predicted that within three to five years a handful (eight to ten) of large banks would control 50–80 percent of the national banking market.

with the McFadden Act, there have been repeated attempts to repeal Glass-Steagall, and in 1995 both parties introduced bills in Congress to repeal all or most of the Act's provisions. At this writing, however, the law remains in force—though several banks have been able to skirt its severest restrictions.

It is hard to over-estimate the impact that these two laws have had on the development of the modern American financial system. Some of these effects have been positive. For example, it is doubtful that U.S. securities markets would be as efficient, or that American investment banks would be as large and globally-competitive, if the Glass-Steagall Act had not restricted financial competition from established commercial banks.[68] The McFadden Act's geographic restrictions have also allowed far more local banks (which are perceived as being more willing to finance small businesses than are larger banks) to survive as independent institutions than would otherwise have been the case. Most disinterested observers would conclude, however, that the regulations imposed on American banks by these two acts have not served the financial needs of the nation's non-financial corporations well.

The geographic restrictions of the McFadden Act and the product line restrictions of the Glass-Steagall Act (plus corporate governance restrictions placed on non-bank FIs) have negatively affected American corporate finance in three principal ways. First, by disallowing the evolution of banks large enough to effectively service the giant American corporations that emerged after World War II, these laws promoted far greater reliance on security market financing by U.S. companies than would likely have occurred otherwise. While security markets clearly have a place in modern financial systems, common sense and the experience of other advanced nations suggest that intermediated financing has real competitive advantages in most routine business settings.[69] The fact that no other country has security markets as large or commercial banks as relatively small as the United States suggests that the politically-inspired neutering of American financial institutions has imposed real efficiency costs on the nation's businesses. While commercial banks are still critical to small and medium-sized firms (discussed below), and they are central to the nation's payments system, their direct financing role for the largest U.S. corporations is essentially limited to arranging syndicated loans, hedging risks, and providing advanced cash management services.

The separation of commercial and investment banking and the prohibition of interstate banking has also arguably increased the brittleness of the American financial system

---

68. The extent of American dominance of worldwide investment banking is made clear by an October 1993 **Euromoney** poll of corporate financial officers published in an **Economist** (April 30, 1994) international banking survey. This poll rated investment banks on underwriting, trading, and advisory capabilities. Four of the top five, and ten of the top twenty, investment banks in the poll were American firms (Goldman Sachs, Merrill Lynch, and J.P. Morgan were the top three). Market share data published in the **Investment Dealers' Digest** (T. Kershaw 1994) shows an even greater American dominance, since U.S. firms occupy the top three positions (CS First Boston/Crédit Suisse, partly American-owned, was fourth), and eleven of the top thirteen ranks. These eleven companies lead-managed 5,351 (53.7 percent) of the 9,969 issues sold worldwide in 1993, and these issues accounted for 64.1 percent of the $1.5 trillion raised in that year. Perhaps most persuasively, an **Economist** (April 15, 1995) special Wall Street survey argues that American investment banks are the world's most competitive financial institutions, and seem poised to dominate the new world of corporate finance—both domestically and globally.

69. The relative merits of securitized versus bank financing in monitoring and controlling corporate managers are examined in Seward (1990) and Diamond (1994).

because it produced comparatively weak commercial banks.[70] The fact that large U.S. banks (often called **money-center banks**) could not diversify geographically or into new product lines lead them during the late 1970s to become increasingly dependent on large-denomination, "purchased" money (negotiable certificates of deposit, Eurodollar deposits) for their financing, and also promoted an excessive reliance on international lending as a growth strategy. When the developing country debt crisis broke during the early 1980s, the effect on U.S. money center banks was calamitous.[71] Not only did several of their largest borrowers default or declare debt service moratoriums, but the weakness of their funding base was graphically revealed when numerous large depositors either withdrew their funds or demanded higher risk premiums. Even when the banks recovered somewhat during the middle 1980s, their limited business opportunities lead them once again to excessive reliance on two high-risk industries with voracious appetites for credit—real estate and oil and gas—both of which suffered major financial traumas towards the end of the decade. Since few other American industries are saddled with the regulatory millstones banks must carry, it is perhaps no surprise that today many large U.S. non-financial corporations have better credit ratings—and are thus able to borrow on more favorable terms—than do the large commercial banks that theoretically exist to serve them. The declining interest rates and rising profits enjoyed by banks during the early 1990s have ameliorated this situation somewhat, but the long-term prognosis for many American banks remains grim. The declining market shares of commercial banks in the American financial services industry is graphically demonstrated in Table 9.3, which presents the asset shares of various U.S. financial institutions for selected years since 1860.

The third, and by far most serious, problem caused by sixty years of U.S. financial regulation is that it has lead to a very weak corporate governance system.[72] Since banks are prohibited from owning common stock, and since insurance companies and other non-bank FIs are discouraged by regulation from playing an active corporate oversight role, managers of large U.S. non-financial corporations do not have to answer to financial intermediaries in the way their non-U.S. counterparts do.

---

70. Unlike most other advanced nations, the United States has experienced a series of banking crises this century. During the 1920s, bank failures (mostly in rural areas) dropped the number of commercial banks from their all-time peak of 30,456 in 1921 to 24,970 in December 1929 (Wheelock 1993). The Great Depression caused an additional 43 percent of these banks to fail by the end of 1933, resulting in a decline of over 50 percent in the number of U.S. banks (to 14,207) between 1921 and 1933. In contrast, Canada—which experienced similar economic hardship but which had nationwide branch banking—experienced only one bank failure during the Depression. Bank failures were relatively uncommon from the mid 1930s to the early 1980s in the United States, but the past decade has seen an upsurge in bank failures. As before, these were concentrated in a few states that were either heavily reliant on agriculture or which severely restricted bank branching (Texas alone had over one-third of the nation's bank failures during the 1980s). By year-end 1992, the number of banks in the United States had declined to 11,461.

71. For an analysis of the effect of the LDC debt crisis on U.S. money center banks, see Sachs and Huizinga (1987).

72. In addition to the papers cited earlier, see Jensen (1986, 1989) for analyses of the financial and operating problems a weak corporate governance system can create. Of course, even if banks and other creditors cannot exercise control rights as stockholders, they can indirectly influence corporate policies through the design of the covenants they insert into loan contracts, and through the vigor with which they enforce those rights. An earlier footnote provides citations on debt covenants, while Diamond (1994) examines how taxes and bankruptcy costs impact the control roles of bank versus public debt.

TABLE 9.3
SHARES OF ASSETS OF FINANCIAL INSTITUTIONS IN THE UNITED STATES, 1860–1993

	1860	1880	1900	1912	1929	1939	1948	1960	1970	1980	1993
						percent					
Commercial banks	**71.4**	**60.6**	**62.9**	**64.5**	**53.7**	**51.2**	**55.9**	**38.2**	**37.9**	**34.8**	**25.4**
U.S.-chartered banks and bank holding companies	71.4	60.6	62.9	64.5	53.7	51.2	55.3	37.6	37.2	32.4	21.7
U.S. offices of foreign banks	—	—	—	—	0.0	0.0	0.6	0.6	0.7	2.4	3.7
Thrift institutions	**17.8**	**22.8**	**18.2**	**14.8**	**14.0**	**13.6**	**12.3**	**19.7**	**20.4**	**21.4**	**9.4**
Savings and loan associations	0.0	2.2	3.1	3.0	6.0	4.2	4.7	11.8	13.0	15.5	7.4[a]
Savings banks	17.8	20.6	15.1	11.8	8.0	9.2	7.4	6.9	6.0	4.2	
Credit unions	—	—	—	—	0.0	0.2	0.2	1.1	1.4	1.7	2.0

(continued)

TABLE 9.3 (CONTINUED)

SHARES OF ASSETS OF FINANCIAL INSTITUTIONS IN THE UNITED STATES, 1860–1993

	1860	1880	1900	1912	1929	1939	1948	1960	1970	1980	1993
						percent					
Insurance companies	**10.7**	**13.9**	**13.8**	**16.6**	**18.6**	**27.2**	**24.3**	**23.8**	**18.9**	**16.1**	**17.4**
Life insurance	1.8	9.4	10.7	13.6	14.8	23.5	20.6	19.4	15.1	11.5	12.8
Property/casualty	8.9	4.5	3.1	3.0	3.8	3.7	3.7	4.4	3.8	4.5	4.6
Investment companies	—	—	—	—	**2.4**c	**1.9**c	**1.3**c	**2.9**	**3.5**	**3.6**	**14.9**
Mutual funds	—	—	—	—	—	—	—	2.9	3.5	3.4	14.2
Stock and bond	—	—	—	—	—	—	—	2.9	3.5	1.5	10.2
Money market	—	—	—	—	—	—	—	—	—	1.9	4.0
Closed-end funds	—	—	—	—	—	—	—	b	b	0.2	0.7
Pension funds	—	—	**0.0**	**0.0**	**0.7**	**2.1**	**3.1**	**9.7**	**13.0**	**17.4**	**24.4**
Private	—	—	—	—	0.4	0.8	1.6	6.4	8.4	12.5	16.7
State and local government	—	—	0.0	0.0	0.3	1.3	1.5	3.3	4.5	4.9	7.6
Finance companies	—	**0.0**	**0.0**	**0.0**	**2.0**	**2.2**	**2.0**	**4.6**	**4.8**	**5.1**	**4.7**

(continued)

TABLE 9.3 (CONTINUED)

SHARES OF ASSETS OF FINANCIAL INSTITUTIONS IN THE UNITED STATES, 1860–1993

	1860	1880	1900	1912	1929	1939	1948	1960	1970	1980	1993
						percent					
Securities brokers and dealers	0.0	0.0	3.8	3.0	8.1	1.5	1.0	1.1	1.2	1.1	3.3
Mortgage companies	0.0	2.7	1.3	1.2	0.6	0.3	0.1	b	b	0.4	0.2
Real estate investment trusts	—	—	—	—	—	—	—	0.0	0.3	0.1	0.1
Total (percent)	100.0	100.0	100.0	100.0	100.0	100.0	100.0	100.0	100.0	100.0	100.0
Total (trillion dollars)	.001	.005	.016	.034	.123	.129	.281	.596	1.328	4.025	13.952

[a] THE END OF THE FIRST QUARTER OF 1993 WAS THE LAST DATE FOR WHICH DATA FOR SAVINGS AND LOAN ASSOCIATIONS AND SAVINGS BANKS WERE REPORTED SEPARATELY. THE FIGURES FOR THAT DATE WERE: SAVINGS AND LOANS, 6.0 PERCENT; SAVINGS BANKS, 1.9 PERCENT.

[b] DATA NOT AVAILABLE.

[c] BREAKDOWN BETWEEN OPEN- AND CLOSED-END FUNDS NOT AVAILABLE.

SOURCES: DATA FOR 1860–1948 FROM RAYMOND W. GOLDSMITH, *FINANCIAL STRUCTURE AND DEVELOPMENT*, STUDIES IN COMPARATIVE ECONOMICS, NEW HAVEN, CT: YALE UNIVERSITY PRESS, 1969, TABLE D–33, PP. 548–9. DATA FOR 1960–1993 FROM BOARD OF GOVERNORS OF THE FERDERAL RESERVE SYSTEM, "FLOW OF FUNDS ACCOUNTS," VARIOUS YEARS. THE DATA FOR THIS TABLE COMES FROM KAUFMAN AND MOTE (1994).

Instead, American managers only have to answer to the company's shareholders, no one of whom has the proper incentive to monitor or discipline management, because he or she would bear all the monitoring costs but would receive only a small share of the benefits of more effective governance. In the absence of effective monitoring by either shareholders or financial institutions, American finance has been forced to rely on hostile takeovers and proxy contests for disciplining or removing inefficient management teams. Not only are these crude and expensive techniques of corporate control, but the hostile takeovers of the late 1980s generated such serious political hostility that they too have now been rendered much more difficult to mount by regulation and by the passage of anti-takeover laws by several key states.[73] While the increased activism of a few dozen large institutional investors—particularly state pension funds—during this decade offers some hope for improved corporate monitoring, the lack of a strong counterweight to entrenched managerial power is the central problem of American corporate finance.[74]

COMPETITIVE ADVANTAGES OF U.S. FINANCIAL INTERMEDIARIES   The rather dismal discussion above should not lead one to conclude that American FIs are helpless souls lost in a financial world they can neither compete in nor understand. In fact, U.S. bank and non-bank intermediaries not only successfully service large swathes of American business, they have also proven to be world leaders in developing and purveying high-value-added financial products to international business customers. Commercial banks, for example, remain the most important sources of external financing for the entrepreneurial and small business sectors of the U.S. economy. Since these sectors represent over half of America's GDP, and employ over 60 percent of the nation's work force, their financial care and feeding is critical to U.S. economic performance.[75]

Banks have also led the charge into securitization by pooling—and then selling claims against—car loans, accounts receivable loans, and other traditional bank credit instruments.[76] These products have not only proven to be real hits with investors, they

---

73. Many of our colleagues will surely take issue with the proposition that capital market monitoring is inadequate, but the same articles that can be enlisted to support the optimality of an unrestricted corporate control market also prove that massive incentive and monitoring problems exist in American corporate finance (if these problems aren't pervasive, how can acquirers consistently pay 30–50 percent takeover premiums in cash acquisitions?). Clearly, hostile takeovers and proxy contests are very blunt control instruments to be used only as a last resort.

74. While we by no means agree with all the conclusions and recommendations made in Porter (1992), the papers surveyed in his article do provide a coherent analysis of the weaknesses in America's capital investment spending, and his recommendations on a strengthened role for institutions in corporate governance are sound [a similar point is made in Black (1992)]. Several other authors have taken issue with Porter (or at least with the "finance is killing American business" school of thought), including Wooldridge (1988), Miller (1994), and Bernstein (1992).

75. The importance of banks to small and medium-sized U.S. businesses is discussed in Elliehausen and Wolken (1990) and Petersen and Rajan (1994), while the importance of corporate liquidity to optimal corporate investment policies is documented by Whited (1992). Other very informative papers that examine the special difficulties of entrepreneurial finance include Pettit and Singer (1985), Timmons and Sander (1989), Posner (1992), Bhide (1993), and Petty, Bygrave, and Shulman (1994), while the special challenges involved in financing corporate growth are addressed in Cornell and Shapiro (1988).

76. A theoretical analysis of why banks might choose to sell loans (as well as limits on their ability to do so), is provided in Pennachi (1988), while a breakdown of asset-backed security issue volumes by type of loan (credit cards, autos, home equity, and other loans) for 1992 is provided in Douglas (1993).

have also allowed banks to continue originating, servicing, and profiting from commercial and consumer lending without having to keep these assets on their own balance sheets. Even the immense U.S. commercial paper market, the very existence of which seems to symbolize banking's obsolescence, is actually a major bank profit center—since virtually all commercial paper issues are backed by bank lines of credit. In fact, several recent studies have found that American banking, far from being a declining industry, has actually been increasing its importance in the U.S. economy, when its output is measured as a percent of GNP or its employment is measured as a percent of the U.S. total.[77] While banking's share of the total assets held by financial institutions has indeed been declining monotonically for decades, this is more than offset by the fact that the relative importance of financial intermediation in the American economy has been dramatically increasing throughout the post-war era—and may even be accelerating today.

U.S. commercial banks have also been successful in the international financial arena. While they are no longer even near the top ranks in sheer size, they are still preeminent in foreign exchange trading, the arranging (but not the funding) of syndicated loans for corporate and sovereign borrowers, and international cash management.[78] Furthermore, six large American banks dominate the world market for currency and interest rate swaps, and these same institutions have pioneeered the development of many of the high-tech, high-profit securities and derivative financial products that have been introduced in recent years.[79] Ironically, U.S. commercial banks have even enjoyed considerable success (but not dominance) in security issue underwriting in the Eurobond markets—the very activity denied to them in their home market.

Non-bank financial institutions also play important roles in American corporate finance, both as creditors and as equity investors.[80] Insurance companies not only provide much of the long-term financing for large real estate development and factory

---

77. See especially Wheelock (1993), Kaufman and Mote (1994), and Boyd and Gertler (1994). In addition, Hunter and Timme (1991) document significant ongoing improvements in the operating efficiency of large U.S. banks, while Berger, Hunter, and Timme (1993) provide a more general survey of the vast literature on the efficiency of financial institutions.

78. In the May 1994 **Euromoney** rankings of foreign exchange banks, American institutions held five of the top six (including the top two), and eight of the top twenty places on the list of customers' favorite banks (van Duyn 1994). Listings by foreign exchange trading volume or market share show similar rankings. Furthermore, in the January 17, 1994 **Investment Dealers' Digest** ranking of global loan syndicators, American banks held the top six, and ten of the top twenty-five, positions. Plender (1994), writing in the **Financial Times,** asserts that, "few on Wall Street or in London doubt that the U.S. banks have mapped out the future of wholesale finance," while a **Wall Street Journal** staff reporter (1991) attempting to pick the twelve banks that would make up the "Global Elite" in the year 2000 selected Citicorp, J.P. Morgan, and Bankers Trust as American members of the group.

79. Factors influencing the use of derivatives by commercial banks are examined in Sinkey and Carter (1994), and this paper also describes the market dominance of the six large U.S. banks. This dominance is under challenge today, not from bank competitors, but from regulators in the United States and Europe who are responding to a series of derivative-related financial losses suffered by several large companies in early 1994 (see Cohen 1994 and Lipin 1993).

80. Wheelock (1993) reports that, at the end of 1992, U.S. financial institutions held financial assets totaling $12,089 billion, distributed as follows: commercial banks ($2,775 billion), thrift institutions ($1,345 billion), life insurance companies ($1,623 billion), other insurance companies ($624 billion), private pension plans ($2,349 billion), public pension funds ($972 billion), finance companies ($807 billion), mutual funds ($1,050 billion), and money market mutual funds ($544 billion).

construction, they also directly own roughly 5 percent of all publicly-traded corporate equity. Specialized finance companies such as General Electric Credit Corporation and General Motors Acceptance Corporation have carved out very successful niches as secured lenders for large-scale equipment purchases. Money market mutual funds indirectly finance businesses by purchasing large fractions of the negotiable certificates of deposit issued by commercial banks. There are now twice as many equity mutual funds as there are stocks listed on the New York Stock Exchange, and these funds own another 10 percent of all traded equity. However, public and private pension funds have emerged in recent years as by far the most important single class of equity investor in the United States (they own one-quarter of all publicly-traded common stock and control assets worth $4.3 trillion), and it is precisely these institutions that have assumed the role of activist monitors of corporate managers.

VENTURE CAPITALISTS   Perhaps the most interesting American non-bank financial intermediaries are the institutional venture capital funds.[81] These funds are widely considered to be national treasures due to the remarkable success they have enjoyed over the years in identifying, financing, and nurturing to maturity many of the best-known high technology start-up companies—including Digital Equipment, Intel, Federal Express, Apple Computers, Microsoft, Compaq Computers, Genentech, Amgen, and Sun Microsystems. The ability of these funds to use specialized contracting technology and convertible preferred stock to help overcome the pervasive incentive and asymmetric information problems that bedevil rapidly-growing private companies has attracted so much academic, political, and practitioner interest that most people are surprised to learn that venture capital funds have never raised more than $4 billion in any single year (and only did that once, in 1987), and usually raise and invest only about $2 billion annually.[82] In the $7 trillion U.S. economy, such sums amount to little more than round-off error.[83]

9.4.2 The Role of Intermediaries Outside the United States

Although actual practices vary considerably from country to country, FIs tend to play much greater roles in the corporate finance systems of other developed countries than they do in the United States. In particular, no other major Western country has chosen to impose serious geographic restrictions on the ability of commercial banks to branch nationwide, and all but Japan allow commercial banks either to underwrite security issues

---

81. There have been several academic articles on venture capital published recently, including Chan (1983), Sahlman (1988, 1990), Barry, Muscarella, Peavy, and Vetsuypens (1990), Megginson and Weiss (1991) and Lerner (1994).

82. The specialized financial contracting technology venture capitalists use is described in depth in Sahlman (1988, 1990), Gompers and Lerner (1994), while Mull (1990) presents evidence on the frequency of convertible preferred stock usage by venture capitalists. Chapter 2 of this text also discusses venture capital in more depth.

83. While venture capitalists attract the most attention from academics and from the news media, "angel capitalists" (non-institutional private investors, usually successful local business people) actually provide an order of magnitude more in direct equity funding to private companies. For example, Freear and Wetzel (1991) report that individual investors provide over $30 billion in funding to over 100,000 ventures each year.

of non-financial corporations or invest directly in corporate equity securities, or both.[84] Even in Japan's case, banks are allowed to own small equity stakes (currently no more than 5 percent) directly, and the rule prohibiting banks from security underwriting (Article 65) was not adopted after a rational consideration of its economic merits, but was instead inserted into Japan's post-war constitution by the American occupation authorities. In other words, most non-U.S. Western countries allow commercial banks to act as true **merchant banks** capable of providing the full range of financial services, including (1) payment and cash management services; (2) short-, intermediate-, and long-term commercial lending; (3) trade and project finance; (4) securities underwriting; and (5) direct private placement of equity capital. Where America has promoted the development of security market-based corporate finance system, most other advanced countries have chosen to emphasize intermediated systems.

Several factors have influenced the differing evolution of financial intermediation in the United States and in other Western capitalist democracies. Cultural, historical, and geographic influences have all played a role. Culturally, concentrated private wealth seems to be perceived as less a threat by Canadian, European, and Japanese citizens than by their U.S. counterparts, perhaps because these societies have also historically allowed government to play a greater role as a counterweight to private economic power than Americans have. Probably the most important historical influence on the financial development of modern Europe and Japan, as compared to the United States, is the vastly differing impact World War II had on these societies. Whereas the United States emerged from World War II both triumphant and rich, Europe and Asia emerged physically shattered and financially bankrupt (even the other "victors"). In order to rebuild rapidly, the governments of all these countries felt compelled to rely on a handful of strong private or state-owned financial institutions to directly allocate domestic and foreign savings (including Marshall Plan funding) to those sectors of their economies considered to be most strategically vital. This imperative, plus the fact that the war had destroyed the value of most privately-held financial assets, meant that security markets played very little role in financing the post-war Japanese and European economic miracles (see Hentzler 1992). Finally, the sheer geographic size of the United States, and the vast amounts of capital required for its agricultural and industrial development during the nineteenth and early twentieth centuries, would have promoted a reliance on securitized rather than intermediated finance even absent discriminatory banking regulations, since capital markets are relatively better vehicles for raising very large increments of high-risk financing.

Several effects flow from the historical preference of non-U.S. industrialized countries for intermediated systems of corporate finance, and from their generally more relaxed bank regulatory regimes.[85] First, Canadian, European, and Japanese commercial banks are much larger on average than American banks, and there tend to be far fewer of them. Since banks in these countries faced few geographic or product line restrictions, only the largest

---

84. A brief overview of banking regulations in Britain, Japan, and Germany is provided at the end of chapter 3 in Fabozzi, Modigliani, and Ferri (1994).

85. This is not to imply that banks in any real country are free from politically-motivated intervention by government regulators. No government of any advanced country has been able to resist the temptation to mandate certain lending policies for banks in order to channel low-cost funds to politically-favored groups, though some governments (France, Italy, the United States) are clearly worse than others.

and most efficient have survived over the years. Therefore, most countries have a banking system composed of a relative handful of large universal banks, most of which have nationwide branch networks. Second, non-financial corporations in other countries have traditionally been much more dependent on commercial banks for both short and long-term financing than have American corporations. This difference should not be overstated, however, since the direct financing role of banks in all countries has been declining for the past two decades, and top-flight non-U.S. corporations have long been able to tap international security markets directly (for example, by issuing Eurobonds). Third, banks in other western countries play much larger corporate governance roles than do American banks. This role is particularly important in Germany, where bank representatives frequently sit on the supervisory boards of client firms. Corporate governance is also important in Japan—where banks often effectively control large industrial groupings (*Keiretsu*), even though their direct shareholdings in any one group company cannot exceed 5 percent.

Finally, non-U.S. banks typically have far greater power vis-à-vis corporate borrowers than American banks do, and they play more central roles in the resolution of client firm bankruptcy or financial distress.[86] While this may seem to be bad news for borrowers, research on Japanese banking relationships suggests just the opposite. Given their strong investor and creditor positions, Japanese banks are far more willing to continue lending money to financially distressed borrowers than are American banks, and the ability of Japanese banks to intervene directly in a troubled firm's operations means they are often able to intervene in time to avert disaster—or at least minimize financial loss.[87]

The intermediary-based corporate finance system described above has many important strengths (particularly in the areas of corporate governance and financial distress resolution), and it has served Canada, Japan, and western Europe well throughout the post-war era, but a pure intermediated system of corporate finance is probably becoming an anachronism for advanced economies. Due to the tremendous advances in telecommunications and information-processing technology that have been made in recent years, the trend in western corporate finance clearly seems to be towards the American security-market-based model.[88] As will be discussed more fully in part 9.5

---

86. A comparison of bankruptcy law and procedure in Germany versus the United States is provided in Rösseler (1993), and the effect of differential bankruptcy procedures on observed national capital structure patterns is examined in Rajan and Zingales (1994).

87. The role of banks in the Japanese financial system is discussed in Frankel (1991) and Berglof and Perotti (1994), while their specific role in the resolution of financial distress is detailed in Hoshi, Kashyap, and Scharfstein (1990). Interestingly, these same authors later (1993) document a dramatic shift away from bank towards public debt financing by Japanese firms during the 1980s, and the authors find the shift to public markets to be most pronounced for the largest, most successful *Keiretsu* members. Weaker *Keiretsu* firms continued borrowing from their lead banks. This phenomenon of larger firms "graduating" from bank financing, and the attendant decline in the average creditworthiness of bank clients, has been observed in virtually every major Western country—though it first appeared, and has progressed furthest, in the United States.

88. An intriguing illustration of the strategic dimensions of the choice between bank and capital market financing is provided by Szopo (1994), who reports that policy-makers in the newly-independent countries of central and eastern Europe must decide whether to build their corporate finance system on a "Anglo-Saxon" (capital market) or "continental European" (commercial bank) model. He predicts these countries will opt for the capital market model both because of the vast amounts of financing that will be needed during the coming decade and because large-scale privatizations in Poland, Hungary, and the Czech Republic have already made possible (and necessary) an active market for trading corporate ownership claims.

below, securitization naturally seems to occur whenever individual property rights are well-established and financial information on potential borrowers can be disseminated credibly and at low cost. Furthermore, the reputations of many once-vaunted European and Japanese banks have been severely tarnished by a series of recent scandals in Germany (Metallgeschaft, Schneider), by massive losses at Crédit Lyonnais and other European state-owned banks, and by the disastrous real estate loan loss experiences of almost all Japanese banks.

FINANCIAL INTERMEDIATION IN DEVELOPING COUNTRIES   The intermediary model will, however, probably continue to be quite viable for developing countries for many years to come. Most developing countries have corporate finance systems that differ from those of advanced countries in several important ways. First, while several of the most advanced developing countries such as Singapore, Hong Kong, and Chile have efficient banking systems more or less open to foreign investment, most developing countries have highly concentrated, technologically backward banking systems that are totally or partially protected from foreign competition. Nowhere is this more of a problem than in China, where a communist government must try to control an extraordinarily rapidly growing capitalist economy with a command-economy banking system. Second, many developing country banking systems are state-owned monopolies (or near monopolies), that are often more concerned with political objectives than with providing adequate funding to local businesses. Even where banks have been privatized, governments have often retained significant influence over their credit-granting and staffing decisions. Third, almost all of the banking systems of former Soviet bloc countries are in a painful period of transition, where they are unable to adequately provide business funding due to inexperience with modern banking practices and the legacy of large numbers of bad loans to state-owned firms.[89] In spite of this, the banks in these countries are usually expected to play central roles in the voucher privatization programs most formerly-communist nations have adopted. Finally, bond, option, and commercial paper markets are either nonexistent or rudimentary in almost all developing countries.[90]

On the other hand, there have been several positive financial developments in many developing countries during the past fifteen years. For example, many governments are indeed trying to modernize their nations' banking systems, both through internal reforms and by opening them up to foreign investment.[91] The critical role that efficient banking systems have played in helping several developing countries achieve rapid and sustained economic growth serves as a powerful spur for reform in other countries. In addition, most large developing countries now have stock markets, and many of these have experienced phenomenal growth in market capitalization (fueled in part by foreign, particularly

---

89. In an article entitled, "First Sort Out the Banks," Rudnick (1994) describes some of the difficulties the Russian government has encountered in trying to establish a modern banking system.

90. Several Moslem countries have attempted an even more radical break with Western banking practice than these points suggest, in that they have adopted (wholly or in part) **Islamic banking** laws based on the Koran's prohibition against lending money for interest. While alien to Western eyes, the actual experience of countries that have adopted this code has not been completely negative (see Iqbal and Mirakhor 1987, Haladjian 1994, Khalaf 1994, and Thompson 1994).

91. Grosse and Venkataramany (1993) provide a tabular summary (Figure F4–4) of the current restrictions on foreign investment in the banking systems of 38 developed and developing countries.

American, portfolio investment) in recent years due to price appreciation and large privatization issues.[92] While few of these are yet capable of providing sufficient equity capital to local businesses, they have helped institutionalize privatization programs and other market-oriented economic policies, and have helped promote risk-taking business cultures in many societies traditionally hostile to capitalism. Furthermore, many Latin American and Asian countries have been able to achieve truly phenomenal (and sustained) economic growth rates—fueled in Asia's case partly by the dynamism and vast financial resources of the region's 53 million "overseas Chinese" (ethnic Chinese living outside of mainland China).[93]

9.4.3 International Banking

Our discussion so far has focused on the domestic financial markets of various countries. We now examine the financial products and services offered by a group of several hundred very large North American, European, and Asian banks that specialize in whole or in part in international finance.[94] The size and power of these international banks grew steadily from the immediate post-World War II era until the collapse of the Bretton Woods exchange rate system in 1973, but their growth since then has been incredibly rapid. While most of these banks are also important in at least their own domestic markets, many derive a majority of their income from international activities such as (1) foreign exchange trading, (2) accepting Eurocurrency deposits and making Eurocurrency syndicated loans, (3) arranging project financing for sovereign and corporate borrowers, (4) providing global cash management and trade financing services, (5) underwriting of and market-making in new security issues, and (6) providing specialized risk management products—especially currency swaps. Eurocurrency transactions and currency swaps were discussed earlier, but we describe the other products below.

The **foreign exchange market** is by far the largest financial market the world has ever seen, with *daily* turnover estimated to be approximately $1 trillion![95] Although

---

92. Cross-border portfolio investment flows have surged in recent years, hitting a record net $159.2 billion in 1993 (see Sesit 1994). American investors accounted for 42 percent of that total, or $66.4 billion. While these funds flowed to capital markets in the developed and developing countries alike, the impact of the flows was naturally greatest in the relatively less liquid emerging stock markets of the Pacific Rim, Latin America, Eastern Europe, the Middle East and Africa—which collectively attracted 33 percent of the investment total.

93. The rapid pace of China's economic development, and the role of overseas Chinese in promoting and funding the transformation, is discussed in Barnathan (1994) and Tanzer (1994). A summary of the economic strengths, weaknesses, and development plans of ten major East Asian countries is provided in Rountree (1994).

94. A survey of the academic literature on international banking is provided in Aliber (1984), while Pavel and McElravey (1990) and Lessard (1991) describe the products and processes involved in the globalization of finance and Hirtle (1991) examines the factors that lead to international competitiveness for financial institutions.

95. While this daily turnover figure seems incredible, it has been separately reported both by the **Economist** (1992)—which cited a Bank for International Settlements (BIS) study—and by **Euromoney** (Fallon 1994). For comparison purposes, note that daily foreign exchange trading volume in 1969 was a mere $20 billion, so volume has increased *fifty-fold* in a quarter century.

trading is centered in the major financial centers of London, New York and Tokyo, this is actually a global telecommunications market involving traders in many different areas. Trades are classified as either forward (future delivery) or spot market (immediate delivery) transactions. Historically, almost all trading has involved the U.S. dollar as the **numeraire currency**, meaning that a company wishing, for example, to exchange Swiss Francs for German Marks would first trade Francs for dollars, and then dollars for Marks. Such a practice has inherent efficiencies (since only one market is needed for each currency, that market will have great depth), and is still employed exclusively for infreqently-traded currencies. In recent years, however, an increasing fraction of foreign exchange (FOREX) trading has involved direct exchange of major currencies for each other. Perhaps because of the historical importance of the U.S. dollar, American banks have long dominated foreign exchange trading and are consistently rated as the most capable forex traders by corporate treasurers.

Project finance is a specialized method of allocating financial risk among creditors, borrowers, investors and operating companies involved in risky, capital-intensive infrastructure and resource-based projects throughout the world.[96] The distinguishing feature of project finance is the creation of a vehicle company, legally separate from the project's sponsors, that arranges limited or non-recourse construction financing, and then operates the project and pays off its debt after completion.[97] This technique was first used on a large international scale in the financing of the North Sea oil field developments of the 1970s—which involved both great risk and vast amounts of capital—and is most commonly used today either for major road, bridge, tunnel, and other infrastructure projects or for construction of processing facilities for minerals (including petroleum) that have well-developed world markets. A specialized form of project finance is called **build, operate, transfer (BOT)**, because a vehicle company will be formed to finance and construct, say, a major toll road, and will then be responsible for operating the road, collecting the tolls, and using these to repay the original financing. BOT has enjoyed many successes, particularly in Asia, where it was used to build the North-South Highway in Malaysia as well as the main road connecting Hong Kong and south China. On the other hand, there have been several spectacular financial disasters associated with project finance in general (EuroDisneyland), and BOT in particular (the Channel Tunnel). International banks have been key players in both the successes and the failures, with European and Japanese banks holding by far the largest market shares.

International cash management and trade financing is, as you might expect, rooted in domestic banking practices—with the additional twist that more than one currency and legal system is involved in every transaction. The key competitive tools for banks in global cash management are strong information processing capabilities and large multi-national (preferably multi-continent) branch banking networks. Not surprisingly, American banks do quite well in this market. Success in trade financing is far more dependent on a bank's knowledge of the legal, financial, and even social practices of

---

96. An excellent overview of project finance is provided in Smith and Walter (1990), while Chemmanur and John (1993) present a more theoretical analysis. Other academic and practitioner articles on project finance include Kensinger and Martin (1988), Bennett (1993), Peagam (1994), Edwards (1995), Kleimeier and Megginson (1995), Marray (1995), Röel (1995), and van Duyn (1995).

97. The costs and benefits of various vehicle company formats are discussed at length in Kleimeier (1993).

many different countries than it is on high-tech financial capabilities. There are several specialized financial instruments and documents that are commonly used in trade finance (letters of credit, bills of lading, bankers' acceptances), and expertise in this field takes many years to develop. Perhaps because international trade has historically been much more important to European companies than to Japanese and American firms, European banks tend to dominate trade finance worldwide.

Banks have become increasingly important in the international issuing and trading of securities during the past fifteen years. As mentioned earlier, American banks often participate in Eurobond underwriting syndicates (as do European, Japanese, and Canadian commercial banks), and banks are the principal issuers or underwriters (or both) of several types of short- and intermediate-term debt securities. Commercial banks have also led the charge into the securitization of many classical credit-granting transactions.[98] A good example of this has been the (partial) transformation of syndicated lending into securitized borrowing. Where before banks would purchase shares of large loan packages and hold these as assets on their own books, today many large syndicated credits are structured as **note issuance facilities** wherein the issuing corporation draws funding by selling securities (notes) to banks in the underwriting syndicate.[99] The banks can then either re-sell these notes to their own customers or retain them as assets on their own books. Banks also act as market-makers (brokers and dealers) for various financial instruments—including some of their own mistakes. One of the most rapidly-growing markets today involves the secondary market trading of developing country syndicated loans, which international banks made in the 1970s and which could not be repaid during the 1980s. Investors now trade these loans at a fraction of face value, and banks participate in this market both as broker/dealers and as sellers of their own uncollectible syndicated loans.[100]

International banking has been one of the great growth industries of the late twentieth century, and the future looks very bright. Ten years ago, the open world economy consisted of roughly one billion people in Western Europe, North America, Japan, and certain countries in southeast Asia, the Middle East, and Latin America. Today over five billion people are part of this open world economy, which now also includes most of Asia, Latin America, Eastern Europe, and several parts of Africa. Finally, the financial intermediation opportunities offered by economic transitions in China, India, and Russia (among many other places) are truly vast. Lest you think, however, that all of the "action" in finance during the course of your professional career will be in banking, let us now begin exam-

---

98. One factor encouraging banks to shift further away from classical bank lending (holding loans as assets on bank balance sheets) has been the adoption of the risk-based bank capital standards recommended by the Basle Committee on Banking Regulations and Supervisory Practices in July 1988. These standards are described in Sinkey (1992, chapters 21 and 22), and the stock price effect of their adoption is assessed in Cooper, Kolari, and Wagster (1991). In a related vein, Dimson and Marsh (1993) provide a very good critique of the differing regulatory approaches that several Western countries are taking towards applying capital standards to securities firms. They clearly show that the SEC's "comprehensive" approach is far less efficient than the Basle Committee's "building block" approach, which itself is less effective than the Bank of England's "portfolio" approach.

99. Note issuance facilities are discussed in several of the papers cited in an earlier footnote, and in chapter 15 of Grabbe (1991).

100. The development of, and the prices generated by trading in, this market are examined in Boehmer and Megginson (1990).

ining security market financing—which offers challenges and opportunities at least as great as banking for people with drive, intellect, discipline, and integrity.

9.5   THE EXPANDING ROLE OF SECURITIES MARKETS IN THE GLOBAL ECONOMY

No trend in modern finance is as clear or as transforming as the worldwide shift towards corporate reliance on securities markets (rather than intermediaries) for external financing. We begin by documenting, and analyzing the forces driving, this global trend towards securitization, and then look specifically at security issue techniques in U.S. capital markets. Next, we describe security issue patterns in other advanced countries as well as in developing countries. We then describe the stock market reactions to different corporate security issues that have been documented by academic researchers and conclude with a discussion of the theoretical explanations for the systematic stock market responses researchers have documented surrounding security issues.

9.5.1 Overview of Securities Issues Worldwide

Table 9.4A, 9.4B presents summary information from the **Investment Dealers' Digest** on securities issues worldwide, and for the United States alone, for the years 1990–1994. The total value of all issues around the world in 1993 was a record $1.502 trillion, up from $1.161 trillion in 1992 (itself a record at the time), and less than $500 billion as recently as 1988.[101] This total dipped to $1.092 trillion in 1994, as interest rates increased dramatically throughout the year, but such a total is still the third highest in history. The almost incredible surge in security market financing over the 1988–1993 period was not matched by a remotely comparable increase in world trade, investment, or economic activity, but instead graphically illustrates the power of the trend toward securitization of corporate finance. Besides rapid recent growth, another major trend that can be observed from these data is that it has, to date, been concentrated in U.S. capital markets, since American issuers accounted for $1.049 trillion (69.8 percent) of the 1993 total and $708.6 billion (64.9 percent) of the 1994 total.

Looking more closely at the issuance statistics for the United States alone, we can identify several other trends that are working to transform American finance. First, actual capital-raising issues by corporations accounted for slightly more than half ($545 billion) of the 1993 total, while issues of collateralized securities (primarily mortgage-backed securities) accounted for most ($478.9 billion) of the remaining amount. While not directly related to corporate financing, the rapid growth of collateralized security issues during the past two decades can be taken as evidence reinforcing our claim made earlier about the impact of securitization on American financial intermediaries. Rather than holding car loans and home mortgages on their books as assets, banks and savings institutions today originate these loans, then repackage and sell the loans and mortgages to security market investors.

Second, within the category of capital-raising security issues, most of the recent growth has been concentrated in various forms of debt, rather than equity, issues.

---

101. If one adds in the $604.8 billion in syndicated loans raised by American and international borrowers, the total value of underwritten external financings by (mostly) non-sovereign issuers exceeded $2.1 trillion in 1993 (data from Pratt 1994 and Hintze 1994).

TABLE 9.4A

SECURITIES ISSUES ON U.S. CAPITAL MARKETS, 1990–1994

This table details the total value, in billions of U.S. dollars, and number (in parentheses) of securities issues on American capital markets for each year in the period 1990–1994. The data are taken from early-January issues of the **Investment Dealers' Digest**—specifically, articles by Liebowitz (1992a) and Pratt (1994, 1995a).

Type of Security Issue	1994	1993	1992	1991	1990
All domestic issues	$708.6 (6,221)	$1,055.6 (7,220)	$856.1 (5,235)	$586.0 (11,968)	$312.1 (6,064)
All domestic capital-raising issues	440.9 (5,058)	542.1 (5,562)	396.9 (3,846)	327.4 (3,101)	171.0 (1,586)
Investment-grade debt	342.5 (3,786)	386.2 (3,637)	281.1 (2,444)	200.8 (1,939)	109.1 (1,016)
High-yield debt	31.8 (195)	54.5 (345)	38.2 (236)	9.9 (44)	0.5 (7)
Nonconvertible preferred stock	9.6 (75)	22.5 (301)	20.9 (231)	10.7 (109)	4.2 (73)
Collateralized securities	252.5 (1,040)	474.5 (1,285)	427.7 (1,123)	294.1 (8,958)	174.5 (4,542)
Mortgage-backed securities	177.4 (732)	415.2 (1,087)	376.7 (983)	246.2 (8,779)	133.9 (4,406)
Asset-backed securities	75.2 (308)	59.4 (198)	50.9 (140)	46.6 (155)	40.1 (114)
Common stock[1]	56.0 (1,009)	85.6 (1,374)	56.6 (996)	45.6 (812)	13.6 (362)
Initial public offerings[1]	28.5 (608)	41.4 (707)	24.1 (517)	16.4 (360)	4.6 (174)
Convertible debt and preferred stock	10.6 (74)	15.2 (162)	15.5 (113)	16.8 (90)	5.0 (43)
Revenue bond issues	103.6 (5,242)	198.0 (6,795)	151.5 (6,286)	107.2 (4,191)	84.8 (4,127)
General obligation bonds	57.8 (5,233)	91.4 (7,204)	80.6 (6,306)	57.2 (4,597)	40.2 (4,212)

[1]EXCLUDING CLOSED-END FUNDS

American corporations issued $389.2 billion in investment-grade debt, $54.3 billion in junk bonds, and $15.2 billion in convertible securities (including preferred stock) in 1993, representing 71.4, 10.0, and 2.8 percent of the capital raising total, respectively. On the other hand, U.S. companies issued only $85.7 billion in new common stock and $22.4 billion in nonconvertible preferred stock in 1993, respectively 15.7 and 4.1 percent of the capital raising total. Since bank loans and retained earnings together account for roughly two-thirds of the capital American corporations need for investment each

TABLE 9.4B

WORLDWIDE SECURITIES ISSUES, 1990–1994

This table details the total value, in billions of U.S. dollars, and number (in parentheses) of securities issues worldwide (including the United States) for each year in the period 1990–1994. The data are taken from early-January issues of the **Investment Dealers' Digest**—specifically, articles by Liebowitz (1992a) and Pratt (1994, 1995a).

Type of Security Issue	1994	1993	1992	1991	1990
Worldwide offerings (debt & equity)	$1,092.3 (8,972)	$1,502.5 (9,969)	$1,161.5 (7,158)	$857.8 (13,716)	$503.7 (7,574)
U.S. issuers worldwide	687.9 (6,204)	1,048.6 (7,378)	853.5 (5,403)	588.7 (12,076)	313.2 (6,141)
International debt	405.6 (2,689)	479.1 (2,701)	335.9 (1,861)	261.0 (1,549)	184.3 (1,376)
Eurobonds	324.1 (2,035)	388.3 (2,162)	268.7 (1,421)	250.7 (1,391)	172.1 (1,213)
Fixed-rate, $-denominated Eurobonds	64.9 (337)	77.6 (403)	57.1 (253)	68.8 (344)	48.1 (253)
Foreign bonds	36.6 (415)	34.7 (302)	23.0 (234)	10.3 (158)	12.2 (163)
Yankee bonds	46.4 (268)	58.9 (270)	44.3 (206)	2.1 (174)	13.4 (81)
Yankee common	10.2 (97)	9.7 (91)	5.5 (50)	22.1 (174)	13.4 (81)
Euro common stock	22.1 (292)	18.8 (309)	12.3 (261)	10.6 (197)	7.2 (132)
Euro mortgage-backed securities	4.5 (31)	3.9 (41)	1.8 (15)	5.2 (29)	4.4 (13)
Euro asset-backed securities	5.7 (46)	4.3 (25)	2.0 (16)	2.6 (9)	5.8 (18)

year, the net contribution of public equity issues to the financing of business operations is even smaller than these numbers suggest—probably less than 7 percent per year. Clearly, corporations that must raise capital through security market issues greatly prefer to issue debt rather than common or preferred stock.[102]

---

102. Myers (1984) also documents this tendency to issue debt before equity, and labels it the "pecking order" model of external financing. Myers and Majluf (1984) provide a theoretical explanation for the immense reluctance to issue common stock, while Marsh (1982) and others document that managers choose to issue equity following a sharp increase in their firm's stock price—suggesting that managers consider the stock to be over-valued. For this and other information-revelation reasons, the stock price response to new equity issue announcements is significantly and consistently negative, as discussed below.

Third, the relative insignificance of new equity issues as a financing source for U.S. corporations is further accentuated by the fact that initial public offerings (excluding closed-end investment funds) accounted for almost half, $41.5 billion, of the $85.7 billion in common stock issued by companies in 1993. While IPO issue volumes fluctuate wildly from year to year (1993 was easily a record), the key point here is that seasoned common stock issues typically represent only 2–4 percent of the total capital raised (internally and externally) by American corporations each year, and preferred stock issues account for an even smaller, and shrinking, fraction.[103] Bond issues are by far the largest source of external funding for U.S. firms, with bank loans and commercial paper following behind.

INITIAL PUBLIC OFFERINGS Before turning to international security issues, let's briefly examine several empirical regularities that have been documented in the American IPO market in recent years. First, the number and dollar value of unseasoned equity issues shows phenomenal year-to-year variability. During "hot issue markets" (1983, 1986–87, 1991–93) the total dollar value of IPOs can exceed $20 billion per year, while in cold markets (1981–82, 1984–85, 1988–90, and most of the 1970s) issue volume can fall to almost trivial levels.[104] Within this cyclical pattern, there also seems to be a secular trend towards greater total issue volume and average IPO size that began in the early 1980s, and shows no sign of slowing. Second, a vast number of academic papers have documented a perplexing phenomenon that has come to be called **underpricing**. IPO shares are sold to investors at an offering price that is, on average, about 15 percent below the closing price of the shares after the first day of trading.[105] This implies that underwriters deliberately (and consistently) sell shares to investors for only six-sevenths of their value. More recent research has lessened the depths of this puzzle by showing that much of the underpricing can be explained by underwriter price stabilization in the immediate aftermarket.[106] In any

---

103. In fact, net equity issues by U.S. corporations were actually negative for the last half of the 1980s, due to the massive corporate purchases of individually-held shares through cash acquisitions and stock repurchases.

104. An excellent overview of the empirical issues we will discuss here is provided in Ibbotson, Sindelar, and Ritter (1994), which updates an earlier (1988) summary. They document that 10,626 companies went public in the United States during the period 1960–1992, and raised over $140 billion (unadjusted for inflation) in that 33-year period. Ritter (1987) documents that going public is a very costly undertaking, while Ibbotson and Jaffe (1975) and Ritter (1984) provide early evidence on hot issue markets.

105. This phenomenon was first documented by Ibbotson (1975), and has since been the subject of an astounding number of empirical and theoretical papers. The empirical studies are summarized in Ibbotson, Sindelar, and Ritter (1988, 1994), while the first theoretical models were presented in Baron (1982), Rock (1986) and Beatty and Ritter (1986). Interestingly, one of the few applications of signaling theory in the area of capital raising has been in attempting to explain IPO underpricing. These models generally predict that issuing firms will underprice deliberately to signal their intrinsic value to investors. Later, once their true value is revealed these firms can recoup the underpricing through subsequent, highly-valued equity issues. Signaling models were presented by Downes and Heinkel (1982), and later by Allen and Faulhaber (1989), Grinblatt and Hwang (1989), and Welch (1989), but the theoretical plausibility of underpricing signaling models was challenged by Gale and Stiglitz (1989). These models have not fared well in empirical testing, either, as Ritter (1984), Garfinkel (1993), and even one of the signaling studies—by Jegadeesh, Weinstein, and Welch (1993)—all find evidence contradictory to the predictions of the signaling models.

106. Aftermarket support by underwriters is described, and its empirical relevance is fairly conclusively documented, in Ruud (1993), Hanley, Kumar, and Seguin (1993), and Schultz and Zaman (1994).

case, only about 60 percent of all IPOs are underpriced and the median initial return to investors is much lower than the average, implying that there is tremendous excess demand (and subsequent rationing of shares) for severely underpriced issues, whereas investors are able to purchase all they want of overpriced issues. This is called the **winner's curse**—if you receive all the shares you want, it is because better-informed investors are not buying.

A third perplexing phenomenon in the IPO market, which has not yet been satisfactorily explained, is the significant negative long-run performance of new issues. Compared to other small stocks (or even compared to NYSE companies), IPOs yield negative abnormal stock returns over a three-year period following their initial offering.[107] This result seems to suggest that investors systematically pay too much for IPOs, and never learn that they will lose money on their investment over time. Documenting such a result in American markets is especially troubling since IPOs in non-U.S. markets have exploded in value and volume during the past fifteen years.[108] Most of these have been share-issue privatizations, but many others have been classic new share issues by entrepreneurial companies. Clearly, more research needs to be focused on documenting and explaining long-run new issue investment performance.

NON-U.S. SECURITY ISSUES   Returning to Table 9.4, we can also identify a number of issue patterns in international security markets. First, the Eurobond market is easily the largest security market outside of the United States, with the foreign bond market ranking second. Corporations (and some governments) issued $388.3 billion in Eurobonds in 1993, up almost 45 percent from the $268.7 total in 1992. Furthermore, U.S. issuers accounted for only $32.1 billion (8.3 percent) of the 1993 total—which is a radical change from the early and mid-1980s, when American firms accounted for roughly half of total Eurobond issue volume, and issued almost as much debt internationally as in the domestic bond market. This is almost surely a reflection of the fact that shelf registration (discussed later in the chapter) has lowered bond issue costs for U.S. borrowers in their home market. The patterns for 1994 are similar, though the volume figures are lower. While Table 9.4 does not present a nationality breakdown of the non-U.S. Eurobond issuers, other sources make one fact clear: Japanese corporations are no longer major Eurobond issuers, as they were during the late 1980s when they were able to issue very low-cost convertible debt to investors wishing to indirectly buy into the surging Japanese stock market. Today, many Japanese companies must face the difficult challenge of refunding maturing Eurobond issues at significantly higher interest rates.[109]

A second pattern observable in international finance is that **Euro common stock** issues raised $17.9 billion in 1993, up from $12.3 billion in 1992. These are equity issues

---

107. This result is first presented in Ritter (1991), and reiterated for both IPOs and seasoned offerings in Loughran and Ritter (1995). Brav and Gompers (1995), however, cast doubt on whether a value-weighted (rather than equally-weighted) sample of IPOs underperforms the market at all.

108. Examples of international IPO studies include Koh and Walter (1989), Saunders and Lim (1990), McGuinness (1992), Aggarwal, Leal, and Hernandez (1993), Levis (1993), Keloharju (1993), and Kim, Krinsky, and Lee (1993). A survey of international studies is presented in Loughran, Ritter, and Rydqvist (1994).

109. Sundaram (1993) provides details on Japanese firm Eurobond issuance and redemption patterns (Figures F3–3 and F3–4).

that are sold in more than one country (excluding the United States) by non-U.S. corporations. While this total has grown steadily over the years, it is both small by American standards and less than twice as large as the volume of **Yankee common stock** ($9.8 billion) issued by foreign firms in the U.S. market in 1993. The rather surprising importance of American capital markets to non-U.S. issuers is further illustrated by the fact that Yankee bond issues (bonds sold publicly to U.S. investors by foreign companies) raised almost twice as much ($60.6 billion versus $33.8 billion) as all other foreign bond issues combined. Finally, the rather small totals for Euro mortgage-backed securities ($2.9 billion) and other asset-backed securities ($4.4 billion) add to the impression that securitization is far less developed outside the United States than it is in American markets.

This observation leads to two obvious questions: (1) why has securitization progressed so far in the United States, and (2) why has its progress been much slower elsewhere? While we are unaware of any academic studies that have examined either question directly, market commentators have suggested that securitization is being propelled in U.S. markets primarily by the rapid spread of information processing technology and the partial deregulation of American financial markets in the early 1980s. Today, anyone with access to a modern computer is able to obtain detailed financial information on a vast number of public companies, and potential creditors and investors who are tied into any of several online information services are able to obtain financial information on thousands of private companies as well. Because investors are able to obtain credible financial information on corporate borrowers themselves, they are less dependent on banks and other intermediaries for credit analysis or investment advice. Financial deregulation in the United States during the early–1980s also promoted securitization both by permitting securities firms to develop innovative new financial products and by promoting cost-reducing competition among all types of financial companies for the dollars of investors. While many other Western countries have computer-literate populations, and several have partially deregulated their financial systems, both of these trends are far more advanced in the United States than in other developed or developing countries—though probably not for long.

U.S. SECURITY ISSUES   The methods corporations use to issue securities are both interesting in their own right and important for the theoretical insights they give us about survival values of seemingly costly contracting forms in modern corporate finance. Security issue techniques can be categorized in various ways, but the most basic classification deals with whether an issuing firm employs an investment banker to help it sell securities to investors, or attempts such a sale without assistance. In the United States, most commercial paper is sold directly by the issuing corporation itself, and issuers of medium-term notes either sell these securities directly or employ agents rather than investment bankers.[110] In almost all other types of security issues, the issuing corporation will obtain the services of an investment banker to help with the planning and execu-

---

110. Standard issue procedures for medium-term notes (MTN) are described in Crabbe (1992), while the extraordinary growth in worldwide MTN issue volume from less than $20 billion in 1985 to $540.0 billion in 1994 is documented in Schwimmer (1995).

tion of security sales. Investment bankers help the firm determine what type of security should be issued, and the banker's knowledge of market conditions gives it a unique ability to advise clients on the likely optimal size and pricing of the issue, as well as to help actually sell the issue to final investors.[111]

Having decided to issue a particular type and size of security, the issuing firm must then choose whether to **register** the securities (obtain Securities and Exchange Commission authorization) for sale on the nation's public securities markets or to try to sell securities through a private placement.[112] A **public offering** is invariably costly, since a great deal of information must be disclosed in specific legal documents filed with the SEC, which must explicitly allow the offering to proceed (to "go effective").[113] A security registration also involves many legal, printing, and other out-of-pocket costs, not to mention the competitive damage to a firm that may result from virtually total disclosure of financial and operating information. The reason most firms choose public to private offerings is that more money can generally be raised, and at lower required rate of return, through a public offering.

The cost advantage of large public issues may be shrinking, however, largely because of new placement techniques and the increasing appetite of investors (especially institutional investors) for unregistered securities. For example, U.S. private placements totaled $174.0 billion in 1993, up 59 percent from 1992's level of $109.5 billion. As in other cases, the 1994 total of $133.9 billion represented a significant drop from 1993—though it was the second largest total ever. Table 9.5 provides a breakdown of these data for the years 1990–1994, revealing that medium-term notes ($34.8 billion), "plain vanilla" debt ($49.3 billion), "plain vanilla" equity ($20.3 billion), and securitized issues ($37.2 billion) accounted for 20.0, 28.3, 11.7, and 21.4 percent of the total 1993 private placement volume, respectively. Yankee private placements (issues by foreign firms) represented $50.9 billion, or 29.3 percent, of the 1993 total. The most important recent development in the private placement market has been the popularity of **Rule 144A** issues, which accounted for 52.5 percent ($91.3 billion) of the 1993 issue volume.[114] These unregistered issues require limited information disclosure, and are designed to be traded strictly among sophisticated institutional investors. They were first authorized by the SEC in April 1990, and have proven very popular with foreign and U.S. issuers alike—who issued $24.5 billion and $66.8 billion, respectively, in 1993. Similar patterns for the securities discussed above are observed in 1994.

If a company decides to make a public rather than private issue, it must then decide whether to have the issue underwritten or sold on a best-efforts basis. As the terms

---

111. Theoretical models of the demand for investment banking services are provided in Mandelker and Raviv (1977), Baron and Holmstrom (1980), Baron (1982), and Benveniste and Spindt (1989).

112. Academic studies that have examined the choice between public issues and private placements (or bank loans) include Blackwell and Kidwell (1988), Giammarino and Lewis (1989), Easterwood and Kadapakkam (1991), Hertzel and Smith (1993), and Chemmanur and Fulghieri (1994). Dyer (1994), T. Kershaw (1994), and Keegan (1995) provide practitioner-oriented discussions of private placements.

113. The historical impact of SEC disclosure and registration requirements is described in Simon (1989), while Zeune (1992) presents a good description both of the types of private placements that can be made and of the information required for various types of public security issues.

114. T. Kershaw (1994) provides a breakdown of private placement issue volumes for 1992 and 1993, including an analysis of Rule 144A issues both by U.S. and international issuers.

TABLE 9.5

PRIVATE PLACEMENTS IN THE UNITED STATES, 1990–1994

This table details the total value, in billions of U.S. dollars, and number (in parentheses) of private placements in the United States for each year in the period 1990–1994. The data are taken from late-February or early-March issues of the **Investment Dealers' Digest** specifically, articles by Bavaria (1992), T. Kershaw (1994), and Keegan (1995).

Type of Security	1994	1993	1992	1991	1990
Overall private placements	$133.9 (2,730)	$173.3 (3,402)	$109.5 (2,414)	110.4 (2,315)	128.6 (2,253)
Plain vanilla debt	37.0 (709)	49.5 (951)	37.1 (728)	38.6 (673)	50.9 (809)
Plain vanilla equity	20.1 (384)	19.3 (347)	13.8 (283)	12.0 (257)	15.7 (217)
Securitized private placements	24.9 (664)	37.5 (866)	22.2 (444)	29.4 (525)	21.6 (338)
Yankee private placements	44.4 (901)	50.9 (955)	30.9 (719)	21.8 (447)	21.3 (322)
Acquisition-related placements	11.8 (117)	6.4 (88)	5.3 (91)	6.2 (112)	13.1 (276)
Rule 144A issues	65.5 (1,046)	90.6 (1,434)	41.7 (727)	20.9 (364)	3.7 (38)
Rule 144A by U.S. issuers	44.7 (692)	66.9 (1,038)	30.3 (508)	na	na

imply, in an **underwritten issue** the lead investment banker will guarantee (underwrite) that the issuer will receive a fixed amount of money whether the securities are all sold or not, while in a **best-efforts issue** the investment banker makes no such guarantee and instead promises only to makes its best sales effort.[115] Not surprisingly, most issuing corporations prefer underwritten to best-efforts contracts, so the actual decision on issue type falls to the investment banker— who usually only forces the smallest and riskiest issues to be handled on a best-efforts basis. After agreeing to an underwriting contract, the lead investment banker usually organizes an underwriting syndicate composed of several other bankers, and the syndicate purchases the entire issue from the corporate client prior to public sale. The syndicate members then sell their portions of the issue to their own individual and institutional investors, and also support the offer price for several days after the issue is sold.

The underwriting syndicate members are compensated in two ways. First, they are reimbursed for their out-of-pocket expenses by the issuing firm either as these expenses

---

115. Public best-efforts issues are usually observed only in IPOs and non-underwritten rights issues. IPOs are examined theoretically in Bower (1989) and empirically in Chalk and Peavy (1987), while Smith (1977), Hansen and Pinkerton (1982), and Hansen (1988) examine rights issues. Private equity issues by public companies are also not underwritten (Wruck, 1989).

are incurred (during the planning period) or out of the proceeds of the offering. Second, the syndicate's profit comes from the **underwriter spread**, which is the difference between the security price promised to the issuing company and the **offer price** at which the securities are sold to the public.[116] Expressed as a percentage of the offer price, the spread is inversely related to offer size, and is much larger for equity than for debt issues.

Another decision that must be made by a corporation wishing to make an underwritten security is whether to solicit investment banking services through **competitive bidding**, where the issuer publicly announces a desire to sell securities and solicits offers from several investment banking firms, or through direct negotiation with a single investment banker. Although academic research indicates that competitive bidding yields at least superficially lower total issuance costs, virtually all corporations that have a real choice (utilities frequently are legally required to use competitive bidding) choose **negotiated bidding** procedures.[117] This seemingly irrational choice can be explained by the fact that investment bankers must invest in performing **due diligence** examinations of potential security issuers, meaning that they are legally required to diligently search out and disclose all relevant information about an issuer before securities are sold to the public—or the underwriter can be held legally responsible for investor losses that occur after the issue is sold. Since investors understand that the most prestigious investment bankers have the most to lose from inadequate due diligence, the mere fact that these firms are willing to underwite an issue provides valuable **certification** that the issuing company is in fact disclosing all material information. With so much to lose, top-tier investment bankers are unlikely to be enticed by competitive bid issues that entail the same risk—but far less profit—as negotiated bids, so issuing firms are willing to pay the higher direct issuance costs of a negotiated bid to obtain the services of a prestigious underwiter.[118]

The final decision that most large U.S. firms wishing to float a security issue must make is whether or not to use **shelf registration** (SEC Rule 415) for the issue. This procedure allows a qualifying company to register a large bloc of securities for sale over a two-year period. Once the SEC approves the issue, it is placed "on the shelf" and the company can sell securities out of inventory (off the shelf) to investors as needed anytime over the next two years.[119] This has proven to be immensely popular with issuing corporations, which previously had to incur the costs (including costs of

---

116. Smith (1986) provides an excellent survey of academic research on capital-raising procedures (including underwriting techniques and costs) and stock price effects of security issue announcements.

117. The choice between competitive and underwritten offerings is examined in Bhagat (1986), Bhagat and Frost (1986), and Hansen and Khanna (1994).

118. The certification role of investment bankers, and other third parties such as auditors and creditors, in conveying the true value of security issues in markets characterized by asymmetric information is examined in Booth and Smith (1986), Titman and Trueman (1986), Hughes (1986), Blackwell, Marr, and Spivey (1990), Slovin and Young (1990), and Megginson and Weiss (1991).

119. Several academic studies have examined shelf registration, usually to determine whether this technique yields higher or lower underwriting costs. Kidwell, Marr, and Thompson (1984), Bhagat, Marr, and Thompson (1985), Moore, Peterson, and Peterson (1986), and Foster (1989) find that shelf registration lowers underwriting costs, while Allen, Lamy, and Thompson (1990) and Blackwell, Marr, and Spivey (1990) document insignificantly different and higher costs to shelf registrations, respectively.

delay) of filing separate SEC registrations for each new security issue. Interestingly, academic research has documented both that underwriting expenses are lower for shelf registrations than for traditional security issues and that very few equity issues are shelf-registered, whereas most qualifying bond issues do use shelf registration. This last result is explained by the greater need for underwriter certification of individual equity issues than of debt issues, due to greater uncertainty about the financial position and prospects of a company seeking to issue common stock.[120]

INTERNATIONAL MARKETS In general, security issuance practices do not differ greatly from those for similar security classes in American markets—which is not surprising, since many international procedures were adapted from U.S. practices. There are, however, a few important differences. First, Eurobonds and non-U.S. foreign bonds are bearer securities, whereas all debt issues sold on American markets must be in registered form. Furthermore, since most Eurobond investors are individuals (rather than institutions), and the issues are often sold in many different national markets, underwriting syndicates tend to be very large and the syndicate members tend to be chosen largely due to their distribution capabilities in their home markets. Second, international security issues typically are governed by British rather than American securities laws, since London is the center of Eurobond and Euro equity issuance. Third, equity issues by foreign corporations in U.S. markets are usually structured as **American depository receipts** (ADRs), which are dollar-denominated claims issued against shares of the foreign firm that are held on deposit by a bank in the issuing firm's home country.[121]

ADRs have proven to be very popular with U.S. investors, at least partly because they allow investors to diversify internationally while still holding a claim that is covered by American securities laws and that pays dividends in dollars (dividends on the underlying shares are converted from local currency into dollars and then paid to U.S investors). Since an ADR can always be converted into ownership of the underlying shares, arbitrage ensures rational dollar valuation of this claim against foreign-currency-denominated stock. Given the success of ADRs, many large international equity issues use this form even for share **tranches** (portions of the issue) that are destined for sale outside of the United States. Very large international issues that use this form are often called **Global depository receipts** (GDRs) to emphasize their multi-national characteristics.

Finally, the single most important security issuance phenomenon in international finance during the past fifteen years has been the emergence of very large **privatization share issues**, many of which have significant stakes reserved for international investors.[122]

---

120. Denis (1991) presents this rather striking dichotomy between equity and debt issuers' use of shelf registration.

121. A very informative practitioner-oriented description of ADRs, their importance in U.S. markets, and their likely future role is provided in Marray (1994), while Jayaraman, Shastri, and Tandon (1993) present evidence that listings of ADRs are associated with positive abnormal returns on the underlying shares in their home markets. Hargis (1994) and Parisi (1995) also examine ADRs in academic works.

122. The economic benefits of privatization have been examined, and generally documented to be substantial, in Yarrow (1986), Kikeri, Nellis, and Shirley (1992), and Megginson, Nash, and van Randenborgh (1994). Voucher privatization schemes are described in Boycko, Shleifer, and Vishny (1993), while share issue privatizations are described in Perotti and Guney (1993) and Jones, Megginson, Nash, and Netter (1995).

Over 200 such issues have been floated by some 45 governments since 1979, and these issues have raised over $250 billion for the governments selling shares (most of these have been pure secondary issues). Privatizations have been the largest share issues ever in almost all of these 45 countries, and many of the issues have been truly colossal in size. For examples, the November 1987 and October 1988 Nippon Telegraph and Telephone issues raised $40.3 billion and $22.4 billion, respectively, making these the two largest security issues ever floated in any capital market. At least thirty other privatizing share issues have raised $1 billion or more (either in local currency or dollars), and the international tranches in these issues have increased on average during recent years. This worldwide trend towards privatizing state-owned enterprises shows no sign of slackening, and may well be accelerating.

9.5.2 Stock Price Response to Security Issue Announcements

We now conclude this chapter by examining how investors react to the announcements of new security issues, and then seeing how the evidence fits existing theoretical models. Event study methodology is the standard tool academic finance researchers employ to determine whether, on average, corporate managers are acting in the best interests of their firm's shareholders when they take certain actions or announce policy changes. A truly impressive number of event studies using U.S. data have examined the average stock price response to announcements of many different types of security issues, exchanges, and repurchases, and the results of these studies have lead to an unusual degree of consensus among finance theorists concerning managerial motivations for, and capital market valuation of, various capital market transactions. The overall conclusions about American securities markets that can be drawn from this body of research are quite easy to state.

1. **Announcements of new equity issues and other leverage-decreasing events are associated with negative abnormal stock returns.** Seasoned common stock issue announcements yield, on average, very large stock price declines (approximately 3 percent in most studies), and the losses suffered by existing shareholders are equal to roughly one-third of the new issue proceeds.[123] Preferred stock issue announcements by industrial firms (but not utilities or financial institutions) also yield negative stock returns, as do convertible debt issue announcements and equity-for-debt exchange offer announcements.[124]

2. **Announcements of new debt issues yield insignificant abnormal returns, but other leverage-increasing events are associated with positive abnormal**

---

123. Numerous academic papers have examined the stock price responses to common equity issue announcements, and a variety of interactions have been considered (the impact of issue size, utility versus industrial company, the use of proceeds, the presence of bank creditor or other monitor, etc.). In all cases, the stock price reaction is consistently and significantly negative, and the type of issue (debt versus equity) is the only important factor. See, as examples, Mikkelson and Partch (1986), Asquith and Mullins (1986a, b), Hess and Bhagat (1986), Slovin, Sushka, and Hudson (1990), Mann and Sicherman (1991), Cooney and Kalay (1993), and Denis (1994).

124. The stock price responses to preferred stock and convertible debt issue announcements are examined by Linn and Pinegar (1988) and Dann and Mikkelson (1984), respectively, while negative abnormal returns associated with leverage-decreasing security exchange offers are documented by Masulis (1980) and Cornett and Travlos (1989).

returns to stockholders. Straight debt issue announcements are essentially financial non-events that do not affect the stock prices of issuing firms.[125] The same is true for announcements of nonconvertible preferred stock issues by utility companies.[126] Almost all other leverage-increasing events are greeted as good news by shareholders—stock prices increase on average when firms announce (non-targeted) share repurchase programs, bank financing agreement renewals, and debt-for-equity exchange offers.[127]

3. **All security issue announcements reveal new information to market participants, and the information conveyed is usually interpreted negatively.** As predicted by Myers and Majluf (1984) and Miller and Rock (1985), security issue announcements are interpreted as a sign from management that the firm's earnings will be lower than expected in the future, and that the firm needs the issue proceeds to make its cash flow identity balance.[128] Equity issue announcements convey the worst news, but unanticipated debt issues can also be interpreted negatively.[129]

4. **Announcements of transactions that concentrate firm ownership or improve the ability of shareholders to monitor corporate managers are associated**

---

125. Both Eckbo (1986) and Shyam-Sunder (1991) document insignificantly negative stock price responses to straight debt issue announcements, and both studies find no relationship between the riskiness of the bond issue and abnormal announcement period stock returns.

126. See Linn and Pinegar (1988).

127. Positive abnormal returns to shareholders of companies announcing nondiscriminatory (open market or tender offer) share repurchase programs are documented by Dann (1981), Vermaelen (1981), and Lakonishok and Vermaelen (1990), while Asquith and Mullins (1986b) compare the stock price results for repurchases with those from dividend initiation and seasoned equity issue announcements. Mikkelson and Partch (1986) and James (1987) find significantly positive abnormal returns associated with the announcement of bank loan approvals, while Lummer and McConnell (1989) document that the positive returns are due specifically to loan *renewal* announcements. Debt-for-equity exchange offers are examined, and positive abnormal returns are documented, by Masulis (1980) and Cornett and Travlos (1989).

128. Academic studies have documented both that security issue announcements convey information to market participants and that the degree of information asymmetry between managers and shareholders in turn influences management's decision whether to issue securities at all. Jain (1992) finds that analysts revise earnings forecasts downwards when firms announce equity issues, and Hansen and Crutchley (1990) show that earnings are lower than expected after all types of security issues—indicating that external financings are motivated by earnings declines. Korajczyk, Lucas, and McDonald (1991) find that companies prefer to issue stock only when the market is most informed about a company's prospects, while Dierkens (1991) verifies that stock price declines associated with seasoned equity issue announcements are larger for companies with the greatest informational asymmetries between shareholders and managers. Further, Cornett and Tehranian (1994) find that stock price declines are greater for commercial banks announcing voluntary common stock issues than for banks announcing involuntary common stock injections. Finally, Kalay and Shimrat (1987) document significant negative abnormal returns to *bondholders* following announcements of common stock issues, in spite of the fact that additional equity should make the bondholders' claim against the firm less risky.

129. Chaplinsky and Hansen (1993) show that truly unanticipated debt issue announcements yield significantly negative abnormal returns to a firm's stockholders because of what these issues reveal about the firm's cash flow needs. Many other debt issues are partially anticipated by investors because their announcements coincide with other information releases (earnings, capital investment, or bond refunding announcements, etc.), and this may explain why other studies find debt issue announcements to be insignificant events.

with positive abnormal returns. Only two types of equity issue announcements, private placements and partial divestitures of subsidiary firm shares by parent companies (called **equity carve-outs**, or ECOs), yield average stock price increases.[130] Furthermore, ownership-concentrating transactions, such as negotiated sales of control share blocs or open market share purchases by large blocholders or corporate investors, yield positive average abnormal returns, as do share repurchases designed to reduce the number of small shareholdings. On the other hand, concentration-reducing transactions such as secondary market stock sales by large blocholders yield stock price declines, as do targeted share repurchases (also known as greenmail) that reduce the probability the firm will be acquired through a hostile takeover.[131]

5. **Announcements of non-public financing transactions are associated with positive abnormal stock returns.** Privately-placed debt and equity financings and announcements of bank loan renewals yield positive returns, probably because investors perceive that these creditors or investors have superior, inside information about the capital-raising firm's true prospects.[132] The fact that these people (or institutions) are willing to financially back the firm provides credible certification of its value.

All of these results fit neatly in an agency cost/contracting model of corporate finance.[133] In financial markets characterized by asymmetric information between corporate managers and outside investors, security issuance and repurchase transactions are interpreted by investors as strong signs of management's intentions and beliefs about the firm's current health and future prospects. Managers, as agents of the firm's shareholders, are charged with running the firm in the shareholders' best interests, and the overall pattern of security transactions suggests that most managers try to accomplish this objective. The most value-decreasing security issues—new common stock sales—are also the rarest, whereas leverage-increasing transactions such as straight debt sales and bank loan renewals that benefit (or at least do not harm) shareholders are the most common. We also observe that managers frequently announce programs to repurchase their firm's common stock as a sign that they believe it to be under-valued, and this action yields strong positive stock returns. Furthermore, when unforeseen operating problems force

---

130. Wruck (1989) and Hertzel and Smith (1993) document significant positive returns to private placements of new equity, in spite of the fact that these shares are typically sold at a discount, while Schipper and Smith (1986) find a similar result for equity carve-outs. The most likely explanation of these results is that they increase the ability of the buyers of privately-placed shares (usually other corporations or large institutional investors) and buyers of ECOs to monitor and discipline corporate managers.

131. Negative abnormal stock returns associated with targeted share repurchases (greenmail) are documented by Bradley and Wakeman (1983), Dann and DeAngelo (1983), Klein and Rosenfeld (1988), and Denis (1990). Dann and DeAngelo (1988) find that ownership changes that are perceived to be takeover defenses yield negative returns to shareholders, while Holthausen, Leftwich, and Mayers (1987) demonstrate that the identities of the parties involved in large-bloc share transactions systematically influence how the market reacts to these transactions.

132. See the articles by Wruck (1989), Hertzel and Smith (1993), Mikkelson and Partch (1986), James (1987), and Lummer and McConnell (1989) cited above.

133. The agency cost/contracting model is described in depth in Smith and Watts (1992) and in chapter 2 of this text.

the firm to raise funds externally, managers pursue a clear pecking order in their choice of issuing senior securities first, and only issuing equity securities as a last resort.

On the other hand, managers have many incentives to pursue their own best interests, rather than their firms' shareholders, and security market transactions provide many opportunities to do this. By engineering new equity issues and other leverage-decreasing transactions, managers can lessen the risk that bankruptcy or financial distress will damage their firm-specific human capital, and by reducing ownership concentration or shareholder monitoring capabilities managers are also able to reduce the threat to their tenure in office. Shareholders understand these incentives, and respond rationally to these managerial actions by bidding down the firm's stock price. Third parties to security market transactions, such as prestigious investment bankers and buyers of privately-placed shares, are also able to help overcome agency problems between managers and investors. Given the ever-increasing size and efficiency of securities markets, it is likely that new methods of solving these asymmetric information problems will continue to be developed.

—SUMMARY—

Immensely large, efficient, and complex financial markets are now a key characteristic of all developed economies, and are becoming increasingly visible in developing countries as well. Around the world, financial intermediation and security market transacting have captured steadily larger shares of national output as nations have embraced democratic capitalism, and as economic development has promoted the development of efficient methods of channeling savings towards productive investment. This trend towards ever larger and more complex financial markets shows no evidence of slowing—and in fact is probably gaining strength as experience with sophisticated hedging and risk management tools spreads, and as new securities are developed and adapted to specific economic needs. No period in history has witnessed as much financial innovation as has the last quarter century, and the pace of change seems likely to accelerate and become more multi-cultural in the coming decades.

This chapter has examined and classified financial markets in several ways. Perhaps most important has been its evaluation of the merits of intermediated versus security market-based systems of financing corporate activities, and how the once sharp line between these two types of finance has been steadily blurring. A discussion of the stock market response to the announcements of various financing activities (arranging bank loans versus issuing new debt or equity securities) is provided, and the chapter concludes with an analysis of why the stock market reaction to new equity issues should be so much more negative than to all other financings. Hopefully, this chapter has conveyed a sense of wonder at the diversity, power, and efficiency of modern financial markets. These are truly exciting times to be a finance professional.

—QUESTIONS—

1. You have been asked to succinctly describe the importance of financial markets in modern economies, and to discuss their recent growth rates. How do you respond?

2. Briefly discuss how the role of commercial banks in advanced economies (particularly the United States) has changed in recent years.

3. Briefly discuss the most important U.S. securities issuance patterns (types and volumes of securities issued) observed since the late 1980s.

4. [Essay question] Describe the most important similarities and differences between intermediated financial markets and security markets. As sources of financing for a nation's corporations, what are the strengths and weaknesses of each financial model (intermediated versus capital-market-based financing systems)?

5. List and briefly describe the most important money market instruments used in modern financial markets.

6. Define the following terms: (a) residual claimant; (b) perpetual security; (c) junk bond; (d) underwriter; (e) investment bank; (f) universal bank; (g) sweat equity.

7. Why do you think that an initial public offering (IPO) is usually considered a fundamentally transforming event for most companies? What are the most important costs and benefits of an IPO?

8. Define the following terms: (a) sovereign borrowing; (b) Eurobonds; (c) foreign bonds; (d) Yankee bonds; (e) Eurocurrency market; (f) syndicated loans.

9. What is callable debt? Why do you think most U.S. corporations issue callable bonds? What is the principal cost of this type of debt for the issuing firm?

10. What economic roles do bond rating agencies play? Why do you think that corporations are willing to pay to have their debt rated?

11. Discuss the difference between positive and negative covenants in debt contracts. Why are these provisions inserted into the contracts? Finally, give two examples of each type of covenant.

12. Define the following: (a) primary market; (b) secondary market; (c) primary issue (sale); (d) secondary issue; (e) secondary market sale.

13. Describe the most important risk management instruments. Under what circumstances would each be most appropriate?

14. Why should public companies hedge?

15. List and briefly describe the five principal types of qualitative asset transformation services that financial intermediaries provide.

16. Briefly discuss the corporate governance role that financial intermediaries—particularly commercial banks—play in countries other than the United States. Why don't American intermediaries play a similar role?

17. How have the provisions of the McFadden and Glass-Steagall Acts influenced the development of the American financial system? Overall, do you think these acts have weakened or strengthened American finance? Why?

18. List and briefly discuss the comparative advantages enjoyed by U.S. investment and commercial banks, and other financial intermediaries.

19. How do the powers granted to financial intermediaries in other G–7 countries differ from those granted to American intermediaries?

20. Why are developing countries likely to retain intermediary-based corporate financing systems for the foreseeable future, even as G–7 countries move towards greater reliance on capital market financing?

21. List and briefly describe the international banking activities that generate most of the profits for large, globally-active banks.

22. What is project finance? Why has it become such an important means of funding large infrastructure and natural resource projects around the world? Under what circumstances would the build-operate-transfer (BOT) method of financing be particularly appropriate?

23. List and briefly describe the most important empirical regularities identified for initial public offerings in the United States.

24. List and briefly describe the most important empirical regularities identified regarding non-U.S. securities issues.

25. List and briefly discuss the most important securities issuance techniques (i.e., firm commitment underwriting) commonly observed in U.S. capital markets. When would one type be more appropriate than another?

26. What is shelf registration? Why has it proven so popular with issuing corporations? For what types of security issues are corporations most and least likely to use shelf registration?

27. What are ADRs and GDRs, and why have they grown so much in importance in recent years?

28. [Essay question] How do stock market participants react to the announcement that a corporation intends to issue new securities? How do these reactions differ based on: (a) type of security being offered; (b) impact of offer on the issuing firm's ownership structure; (c) whether the security is issued publicly or privately?

—REFERENCES—

Acheson, Marcus W. IV, "The Growing Middle Market Demand for Sophisticated Financial Products," **Journal of Applied Corporate Finance** 7 (Spring 1994), pp. 4–15.

Admati, Anat R. and Paul Pfleiderer, "Robust Financial Contracting and the Role of Venture Capitalists," **Journal of Finance** 49 (June 1994), pp. 371–402.

Afshar, K. A., R. F. Taffler, and P. S. Sundarsanam, "The Effect of Corporate Diversification on Shareholder Wealth: The UK Experience," **Journal of Banking and Finance** 16 (1992), pp. 115–135.

Aggarwal, Reena, Ricardo Leal, and Leonardo Hernandez, "The Aftermarket Performance of IPOs in Latin America," **Financial Management** 22 (Spring 1993), pp. 42–53.

Alderson, Michael J., Keith C. Brown, and Scott Lummer, "Dutch Auction Rate Preferred Stock," **Financial Management** 16 (Summer 1987), pp. 68–73.

Aliber, Robert Z., "International Banking: A Survey," **Journal of Money, Credit, and Banking** 16 (November 1984), pp. 661–678.

Allen, David S., Robert E. Lamy, and G. Robert Thompson, "The Shelf Registration of Debt and Shelf Selection Bias," **Journal of Finance** 45 (March 1990), pp. 275–287.

Allen, Franklin, "The Market for Information and the Origin of Financial Intermediation," **Journal of Financial Intermediation** 1 (March 1990), pp. 3–30.

Allen, Franklin and Gerald R. Faulhaber, "Signaling by Underpricing in the IPO Market," **Journal of Financial Economics** 23 (August 1989), pp. 303–324.

Allen, Franklin and Douglas Gale, "Optimal Security Design," **Review of Financial Studies** 1 (Fall 1989), pp. 229–263.

Altman, Edward E., "Revisiting the High-Yield Bond Market," **Financial Management** 21 (Summer 1992), pp. 78–92.

Altman, Edward I., "The Anatomy of the High-Yield Bond Market," **Financial Analysts Journal** 43 (July-August 1987), pp. 12–25.

Amihud, Yakov and Haim Mendelsohn, "Asset Pricing and the Bid-Ask Spread," **Journal of Financial Economics** 17 (December 1986), pp. 223–249.

Arnold, Jasper H. III, "How to Negotiate a Term Loan," **Harvard Business Review** (March/April 1982), pp. 131–137.

Arnold, Jerry L., "Exempt Offerings: Going Public Privately," **Harvard Business Review** (January/February 1985), pp. 16–30.

Asquith, Paul and David W. Mullins, Jr., "Equity Issues and Offering Dilution," **Journal of Financial Economics** 15 (January/February 1986a), pp. 61–89.

————"Signalling With Dividends, Stock Repurchases, and Equity Issues," **Financial Management** 15 (Autumn 1986b), pp. 27–44.

————"Convertible Debt: Corporate Call Policy and Voluntary Conversion," **Journal of Finance** 46 (September 1991), pp. 1273–1290.

Asquith, Paul, David W. Mullins, Jr., and Eric D. Wolff, "Original Issue High Yield Bonds: Aging Analyses of Defaults, Exchanges, and Calls," **Journal of Finance** 44 (September 1989), pp. 923–952.

Asquith, Paul and Thierry A. Wizman, "Event Risk, Covenants, and Bondholder Returns in Leveraged Buyouts," **Journal of Financial Economics** 27 (September 1990), pp. 195–213.

Bagnani, Elizabeth Strock, Nikolaos T. Milonas, Anthony Saunders, and Nickolaos G. Travlos, "Managers, Owners, and the Pricing of Risky Debt: An Empirical Analysis," **Journal of Finance** 49 (June 94), pp. 453–477.

Baker, Gerard, "Size Isn't Everything," **Financial Times** (March 29, 1995), p. 13.

Barclay, Michael J. and Clifford G. Holderness, "Private Benefits From Control of Public Corporations," **Journal of Financial Economics** 29 (December 1989), pp. 371–395.

Barnathan, Joyce, "China: Is Prosperity Creating a Freer Society?," **Business Week** (June 6, 1994), pp. 94–99.

Baron, David P., "A Model of the Demand for Investment Banking Advising and Distribution Services for New Issues," **Journal of Finance** 37 (September 1982), pp. 955–976.

Baron, David P. and Bengt Holmstrom, "The Investment Banking Contract for New Issues Under Asymmetric Information: Delegation and the Incentive Problem," **Journal of Finance** 35 (December 1980), pp. 1115–1138.

Barry, Christopher B., Chris J. Muscarella, John W. Peavy III, and Michael R. Vetsuypens, "The Role of Venture Capital in the Creation of Public Companies: Evidence From the Going Public Process," **Journal of Financial Economics** 27 (October 1990), pp. 447–471.

Barry, Christopher B., Chris J. Muscarella, and Michael R. Vetsuypens, "Underwriter Warrants, Underwriter Compensation, and the Costs of Going Public," **Journal of Financial Economics** 29 (March 1991), pp. 113–135.

Baumol, William J. and Burton Malkiel, "Redundant Regulation of Foreign Security Trading and U.S. Competitiveness," **Journal of Applied Corporate Finance** 5 (Winter 1993), pp. 19–27.

Bavaria, Steven, "Slipping Away," **Investment Dealers' Digest** (March 9, 1992), pp. 18–25.

Beatty, Randolph P. and Jay R. Ritter, "Investment Banking, Reputation, and the Underpricing of Initial Public Offerings," **Journal of Financial Economics** 15 (January/February 1986), pp. 213–232.

Bennett, Rosemary, "Project Finance: Morton's Folly," **Euromoney** (June 1993), pp. 59–63.

Benston, George J. and Clifford W. Smith, Jr., "A Transactions Cost Approach to the Theory of Financial Intermediation," **Journal of Finance** 31 (May 1976), pp. 215–231.

Benveniste, Lawrence M. and Paul A. Spindt, "How Investment Bankers Determine the Offer Price and Allocation of New Issues," **Journal of Financial Economics** 24 (October 1989), pp. 343–361.

Berger, Allen N., William C. Hunter, and Stephen G. Timme, "The Efficiency of Financial Institutions: A Review and Preview of Research Past, Present, and Future," **Journal of Banking and Finance** 17 (April 1993), pp. 221–249.

Berger, Allen N. and Gregory F. Udell, "Collateral, Loan Quality, and Bank Risk," **Journal of Monetary Economics** 25 (January 1990), 21–42.

Berglöf, Eric and Enrico Perotti, "The Governance Structure of Japanese Financial Keiretsu," **Journal of Financial Economics** 36 (October 1994), pp. 259–284.

Berlin, Mitchell and Jan Loeys, "Bond Covenants and Delegated Monitoring," **Journal of Finance** 43 (June 1988), pp. 397–412.

Bernstein, Peter L., "Are Financial Markets the Problem or the Solution? A Reply to Michael Porter," **Journal of Applied Corporate Finance** 5 (Summer 1992), pp. 17–22.

Bhagat, Sanjai, "The Effect of Management's Choice Between Negotiated and Competitive Equity Offerings on Shareholder Wealth," **Journal of Financial and Quantitative Analysis** 21 (June 1986), pp. 181–196.

Bhagat, Sanjai and Peter Frost, "Issuing Costs to Existing Shareholders in Competitive and Negotiated Underwritten Public Utility Equity Offerings," **Journal of Financial Economics** 15 (January/February 1986), pp. 233–259.

Bhagat, Sanjai, M. Wayne Marr, and G. Rodney Thompson, "The Rule 415 Experiment: Equity Markets," **Journal of Finance** 40 (December 1985), pp. 1385–1401.

Bhattacharya, Sudipto and Anjan V. Thakor, "Contemporary Banking Theory," **Journal of Financial Intermediation** 3 (October 1993), pp. 2–50.

Bhide, Amar, "Bootstrap Finance: The Art of Start-Ups," **Harvard Business Review** (November/December 1992), pp. 109–117.

————"The Hidden Costs of Stock Market Liquidity," **Journal of Financial Economics** 34 (August 1993), pp. 31–51.

Bicksler, James and Andrew H. Chen, "An Economic Analysis of Interest Rate Swaps," **Journal of Finance** 41 (July 1986), pp. 645–656.

Black, Bernard, "Shareholder Passivity Reexamined," **Michigan Law Review** 89 (December 1990), pp. 521–608.

Black, Bernard S., "Institutional Investors and Corporate Governance: The Case for Institutional Voice," **Journal of Applied Corporate Finance** 5 (Fall 1992), pp. 19–32.

Blackwell, David W. and David S. Kidwell, "An Investigation of Cost Differences Between Public Sales and Private Placements of Debt," **Journal of Financial Economics** 22 (December 1988), pp. 253–278.

Blackwell, David W., M. Wayne Marr, and Michael F. Spivey, "Shelf Registration and the Reduced Due Diligence Argument: Implications of the Underwriter Certification and the Implicit Insurance Hypothesis," **Journal of Financial and Quantitative Analysis** 25 (June 1990), pp. 245–259.

Blume, Marshall E., Donald B. Keim, and Sandeep A. Patel, "Returns and Volatility of Low-Grade Bonds, 1977–1989," **Journal of Finance** 46 (March 1991), pp. 49–74.

Boehmer, Ekkehart and William L. Megginson, "Determinants of Secondary Market Prices for Developing Country Syndicated Loans," **Journal of Finance** 45 (December 1990), pp. 1517–1540.

Booth, James R., "Contract Costs, Bank Loans, and the Cross-Monitoring Hypothesis," **Journal of Financial Economics** 31 (February 1992), pp. 25–41.

Booth, James R. and Richard L. Smith, Jr., "Capital Raising, Underwriting and the Certification Hypothesis," **Journal of Financial Economics** 15 (January/February 1986), pp. 261–281.

Bower, Nancy L., "Firm Value and the Choice of Offering Method in IPOs," **Journal of Finance** 44 (July 1989), pp. 647–662.

Boycko, Maxim, Andrei Shleifer, and Robert W. Vishny, "A Theory of Privatization," Working paper (The Russian State Committee on the Management of Property, Harvard University, and the University of Chicago, 1993).

Boyd, John H. and Mark Gertler, "Are Banks Dead? Or, Are the Reports Greatly Exaggerated?," in the **Proceedings of the 30th Annual Conference on Bank Structure and Competition,** Federal Reserve Bank of Chicago (May 1994), pp. 85–117.

Bradley, Michael and L. MacDonald Wakeman, "The Wealth Effects of Targeted Share Repurchases," **Journal of Financial Economics** 11 (April 1983), pp. 301–328.

Brav, Alon, "Myth or Reality? The Long-Run Underperformance of Initial Public Offerings: Evidence From Venture and Nonventure Capital-Backed Companies," Working paper (University of Chicago, March 1995).

Brav, Alon and Paul A. Gompers, "Myth or Reality? The Long-Run Underperformance of Initial Public Offerings: Evidence From Venture and Nonventure Capital-backed Companies" (Working paper; University of Chicago, 1995).

Brennan, Michael J. and Eduardo S. Schwartz, "Analyzing Convertible Bonds," **Journal of Financial and Quantitative Analysis** 15 (November 1980), pp. 907–929.

Brennan, Michael J. and Eduardo S. Schwartz, "The Case for Convertibles," **Journal of Applied Corporate Finance** 1 (Summer 1988), pp. 55–64.

Brick, Ivan E. and S. Abraham Ravid, "Interest Rate Uncertainty and the Optimal Debt Maturity Structure," **Journal of Financial and Quantitative Analysis** 26 (March 1991), pp. 63–82.

Bulow, Jeremy and Kenneth Rogoff, "A Constant Recontracting Model of Sovereign Debt," **Journal of Political Economy** 97 (1989), pp. 155–178.

Business Week (October 31, 1994), "Managing Risk (Special Report)," pp. 86–104.

Campbell, Tim S. and William A. Kracaw, "Information Production, Market Signalling, and the Theory of Financial Intermediation," **Journal of Finance** 35 (September 1980), pp. 863–882.

————"Corporate Risk Management and the Incentive Effects of Debt," **Journal of Finance** 45 (December 1990), pp. 1673–1686.

Chalk, Andrew J. and John W. Peavy III, "Initial Public Offerings, Daily Returns, Offering Types and the Price Effect," **Financial Analysts Journal** 43 (1987), pp. 65–69.

Chan, Yuk-Shee, "On the Positive Role of Financial Intermediation in Allocation of Venture Capital in a Market With Imperfect Information," **Journal of Finance** 38 (December 1983), pp. 1548–1568.

Chaplinsky, Susan and Robert S. Hansen, "Partial Anticipation, the Flow of Information and the Economic Impact of Corporate Debt Sales," **Review of Financial Studies** 6 (1993), pp. 709–732.

Chemmanur, Thomas J. and Paolo Fulghieri, "Reputation, Renegotiation, and the Choice Between Bank Loans and Publicly Traded Debt," **Review of Financial Studies** 7 (Fall 1994), pp. 475–506.

Chemmanur, Thomas J. and Kose John, "Optimal Incorporation, Structure of Debt Contracts, and Limited-Recourse Project Finance," unpublished working paper (New York University; New York, March 1993).

Chowdhry, Bhagwan, "What is Different About International Lending?," **Review of Financial Studies** 4 (1991), pp. 121–148.

Cohen, Norma, "Bank Rules to Reflect New Derivatives Risks," **Financial Times** (July 15, 1994), p. 15.

Cooney, John W., Jr. and Avner Kalay, "Positive Information From Equity Issue Announcements," **Journal of Financial Economics** 33 (April 1993), pp. 149–172.

Cooper, Kerry, James Kolari, and John Wagster, "A Note on the Stock Market Effects of the Adoption of Risk-Based Capital Requirements on International Banks in Different Countries," **Journal of Banking and Finance** 15 (April 1991), pp. 367–381.

Cornell, Bradford and Kevin Green, "The Investment Performance of Low-Grade Bond Funds," **Journal of Finance** 46 (March 1991), pp. 29–48.

Cornell, Bradford and Alan C. Shapiro, "Financing Corporate Growth," **Journal of Applied Corporate Finance** 1 (Summer 1988), pp. 6–22.

Cornett, Marcia Millon and Hassan Tehranian, "An Examination of Voluntary Versus Involuntary Security Issuances by Commercial Banks," **Journal of Financial Economics** 35 (February 1994), pp. 99–122.

Cornett, Marcia Millon and Nickolaos G. Travlos, "Information Effects Associated With Debt-for-Equity and Equity-for-Debt Exchange Offers," **Journal of Finance** 44 (June 1989), pp. 451–468.

Corrigan, Tracy, "Privatization the Driving Force," **Financial Times** International Capital Markets Survey (May 26, 1994), p. IV.

Cowan, Arnold R., Nandkumar Nayar, and Ajai K. Singh, "Stock Returns Before and After Calls of Convertible Bonds," **Journal of Financial and Quantitative Analysis** 25 (December 1990), pp. 549–554.

Cox, John C., Jonathan E. Ingersoll, Jr., and Stephen A. Ross, "The Relation Between Forward Prices and Futures Prices," **Journal of Financial Economics** 9 (December 1981), pp. 321–346.

Crabbe, Leland, "Corporate Medium-Term Notes," **Journal of Applied Corporate Finance** 4 (Winter 1992), pp. 90–102.

Crabbe, Leland and Mitchell A. Post, "The Effect of a Rating Downgrade on Outstanding Commercial Paper," **Journal of Finance** 39 (March 1994), pp. 39–56.

Dann, Larry, "Common Stock Repurchases: An Analysis of Returns to Bondholders and Shareholders," **Journal of Financial Economics** 9 (January 1981), pp. 113–138.

Dann, Larry and Harry DeAngelo, "Standstill Agreements, Privately Negotiated Stock Repurchases and the Market for Corporate Control," **Journal of Financial Economics** 11 (April 1983), pp. 295–300.

Dann, Larry Y. and Harry DeAngelo, "Corporate Financial Policy and Corporate Control: A Study of Defensive Adjustments in Asset and Ownership Structure," **Journal of Financial Economics** 20 (January/March 1988), pp. 87–128.

Dann, Larry Y., David Mayers, and Robert J. Raab, Jr., "Trading Rules, Large Blocks, and the Speed of Price Adjustment," **Journal of Financial Economics** 4 (January 1977), pp. 3–22.

Dann, Larry Y. and Wayne H. Mikkelson, "Convertible Debt Issuance, Capital Structure Change and Financing-Related Information: Some New Evidence," **Journal of Financial Economics** 13 (June 1984), pp. 157–186.

Datta, Sudip and Upinder S. Dhillon, "Bond and Stock Market Response to Unexpected Earnings Announcement," **Journal of Financial and Quantitative Analysis** 28 (December 1993), pp. 565–577.

Denis, David J., "Defensive Changes in Corporate Payout Policy: Share Repurchases and Special Dividends," **Journal of Finance** 45 (December 1990), pp. 1433–1456.

————"Shelf Registration and the Market for Seasoned Equity Offerings," **Journal of Business** 64 (April 1991), pp. 189–212.

————"Investment Opportunities and the Market for Seasoned Equity Offerings," **Journal of Financial and Quantitative Analysis** 29 (June 1994), pp. 159–177.

Diamond, Douglas, "Financial Intermediation and Delegated Monitoring," **Review of Economic Studies** 51 (1984), pp. 393–414.

Diamond, Douglas W., "Reputation Acquisition in Debt Markets," **Journal of Political Economy** 97 (August 1989), pp. 828–862.

————"Seniority and Maturity of Debt Contracts," **Journal of Financial Economics** 33 (June 1993), pp. 341–368.

————"Corporate Capital Structure: The Control Roles of Bank and Public Debt With Taxes and Costly Bankruptcy," Federal Reserve Bank of Richmond **Economic Quarterly** 80 (Spring 1994), pp. 11–37.

Dierkens, Nathalie, "Information Asymmetry and Equity Issues," **Journal of Financial and Quantitative Analysis** 26 (June 1991), pp. 181–199.

Dillon, Burke and Gumersindo Oliveros, **Recent Experiences With Multilateral Official Debt Rescheduling** (International Monetary Fund; Washington, DC, 1987).

Dimson, Elroy and Paul Marsh, "The Debate on International Capital Requirements: Evidence on Equity Position Risk for UK Securities Firms," unpublished working paper (London Business School; London, June 1993).

Dolde, Walter, "The Trajectory of Corporate Financial Risk Management," **Journal of Applied Corporate Finance** 6 (Fall 1993), pp. 33–41.

Douglas, Livingston G., **The Fixed Income Almanac 1993** (Probus Publishing Company; Chicago, 1993).

Downes, David H. and Robert Heinkel, "Signaling and the Valuation of Unseasoned New Issues," **Journal of Finance** 37 (March 1982), pp. 1–10.

Dunn, Kenneth B. and Kenneth M. Eades, "Voluntary Conversion of Convertible Securities and the Optimal Call Strategy," **Journal of Financial Economics** 23 (August 1989), pp. 273–302.

Dunn, Kenneth B. and Chester S. Spatt, "A Strategic Analysis of Sinking Fund Bonds," **Journal of Financial Economics** 13 (September 1984), pp. 399–424.

Dyer, Geoff, "After Global Bonds, Global Private Placements?," **Euromoney** (April 1994), pp. 75–78.

Dyl, Edward A. and Michael D. Joehnk, "Sinking Funds and the Cost of Corporate Debt," **Journal of Finance** 34 (September 1979), pp. 887–893.

Easley, David and Maureen O'Hara, "Price, Trade Size, and Information in Securities Markets," **Journal of Financial Economics** 19 (September 1987), pp. 69–90.

Easterwood, John C. and Palami-Rajan Kadapakkam, "The Role of Private and Public Debt in Corporate Capital Structures," **Financial Management** 20 (Autumn 1991), pp. 49–57.

Eaton, Jonathan, Mark Gersovitz, and Joseph Stiglitz, "The Pure Theory of Country Risk," **European Economic Review** 30 (June 1986), pp. 481–513.

Eckbo, B. Espen, "Valuation Effects of Corporate Debt Offerings," **Journal of Financial Economics** 15 (January/February 1986), pp. 119–151.

Economist (September 26, 1992), "Realignment Merchants," p. 94.

Economist (April 30, 1994), "International Banking Survey."

Economist (July 9, 1994), "Japan Survey."

Economist (November 5, 1994), "The Intermediary's Lot," pp. 16–18.

Economist (February 25, 1995), "Loan Arrangers Ride Again," p. 81.

Economist (March 4, 1995), "The Collapse of Barings," pp. 19–21.

Economist (April 15, 1995), "Wall Street Survey."

Edwards, Ben, "Too Much Money, Too Few Deals," **Euromoney** (March 1995), pp. 109–115.

Edwards, Franklin R., "Listing of Foreign Securities On U.S. Exchanges," **Journal of Applied Corporate Finance** 5 (Winter 1993), pp. 28–36.

Edwards, Sebastian, "LDC Foreign Borrowing and Default Risk: An Empirical Investigation: 1976–80," **American Economic Review** 74 (September 1984), pp. 726–734.

————"The Pricing of Bonds and Bank Loans in International Markets: An Empirical Analysis of Developing Countries' Foreign Borrowing," **European Economic Review** 30 (June 1986), pp. 565–589.

El-Gazzar, Samir and Victor Pastena, "Negotiated Accounting Rules in Private Financial Contracts," **Journal of Accounting and Economics** 12 (March 1990), pp. 381–396.

Ellichausen, Gregory E. and John D. Wolken, "Banking Markets and the Use of Financial Services by Small and Medium-Sized Businesses," unpublished working paper (Federal Reserve System; Washington, September 1990).

Euromoney Supplement (May 1988), "Syndicated Loans: A Competitive Business."

Euromoney (June 1994), "Markets: All Change," pp. 89–101.

Evans, Richard and Paula Dwyer, "NASDAQ With a European Accent?," **Business Week** (June 27, 1994), p. 73.

Fabozzi, Frank J., Franco Modigliani, and Michael G. Ferri, **Foundations of Financial Markets and Institutions** (Prentice Hall, Inc.: Englewood Cliffs, NJ, 1994).

Fallon, Padraic, "The Age of Economic Reason," **Euromoney** (June 1994), pp. 28–35.

Fama, Eugene F., "Banking in the Theory of Finance," **Journal of Monetary Economics** 6 (1980), pp. 39–57.

————"Contract Costs and Financing Decisions," **Journal of Business** 63 (January 1990), pp. S71–S91.

Fama, Eugene F. and Michael C. Jensen, "Agency Problems and Residual Claims," **Journal of Law and Economics** 26 (June 1983), pp.327–349.

Financial Times (January 9, 1995), "ADR Issues," p. 17.

Finnerty, John D., "An Overview of Corporate Securities Innovation," **Journal of Applied Corporate Finance** 4 (Winter 1992), pp. 23–39.

Finnerty, Joseph E., Thomas Schneeweis, and Shantaram P. Hedge, "Interest Rates in the Eurobond Market," **Journal of Financial and Quantitative Analysis** 15 (September 1980), pp. 743–755.

Foster, F. Douglas, "Syndicate Size, Spreads, and Market Power During the Introduction of Shelf Registration," **Journal of Finance** 44 (March 1989), pp. 195–204.

Frankel, Jeffrey A., "The Japanese Cost of Finance: A Survey," **Financial Management** 20 (Spring 1991), pp. 95–127.

Freear, John and William E. Wetzel, Jr., "The Informal Venture Capital Market in the Year 2000", unpublished working paper (University of New Hampshire, April 1991).

French, Kenneth R., "Pricing Financial Futures Contracts: An Introduction," **Journal of Applied Corporate Finance** 1 (Winter 1989), pp. 59–66.

Fridson, Martin S., "The State of the High Yield Bond Market: Overshooting or Return to Normalcy?," **Journal of Applied Corporate Finance** 7 (Spring 1994), pp. 85–97.

Froot, Kenneth A., David S. Scharfstein, and Jeremy C. Stein, "Risk Management: Coordinating Corporate Investment and Financing Policies," **Journal of Finance** 48 (December 1993), pp. 1629–1658.

Gale, Ian and Joseph E. Stiglitz, "The Informational Content of Initial Public Offerings," **Journal of Finance** 44 (June 1989), pp. 469–477.

Garfinkel, Jon A., "IPO Underpricing, Insider Selling and Subsequent Equity Offerings: Is Underpricing a Signal of Quality?," **Financial Management** 22 (Spring 1993), pp. 74–83.

Gentry, James A., David T. Whitford, and Paul Newbold, "Predicting Industrial Bond Ratings With A Probit Model and Fund Flow Components," **Financial Review** 23 (August 1988), pp. 269–286.

Ghosh, Chimnoy, Raj Varma, and J. Randall Woolridge, "An Analysis of Exhangeable Debt Offers," **Journal of Financial Economics** 28 (November/December 1990), pp. 251–263.

Giammarino, Ronald M. and Tracy Lewis, "A Theory of Negotiated Equity Financing," **Review of Financial Studies** 1 (1989), pp. 265–288.

Gompers, Paul and Josh Lerner, "An Analysis of Compensation in the U.S. Venture Capital Partnership," Working paper (University of Chicago, 1994).

Gorton, Gary and George Pennacchi, "Financial Intermediation and Liquidity Creation," **Journal of Finance** 45 (March 1990), pp. 48–71.

Grabbe, J. Orlin, "Syndicated Eurocredits," Chapter 15 of **International Financial Markets,** 2nd edition (Elsevier Science Publishing Co.; New York, 1991), pp. 287–298.

Grinblatt, Mark and Chuan Yang Hwang, "Signalling and the Pricing of New Issues," **Journal of Finance** 44 (June 1989), pp. 393–420.

Grosse, Robert and Sivakumar Venkataramany, "International Banking," in Dennis E. Logue, ed., **Handbook of Modern Finance,** Third Edition (Warren Gorham Lamont: Boston, 1993).

Grossman, Herschel and John B. van Huyck, "Sovereign Debt as a Contingent Claim: Excusable Default, Repudiation and Reputation," **American Economic Review** 78 (1988), pp. 1088–1097.

Grossman, Sanford J. and Merton H. Miller, "Liquidity and Market Structure," **Journal of Finance** 43 (July 1988), pp. 617–633.

Grundfest, Joseph A., "Subordination of American Capital," **Journal of Financial Economics** 27 (September 1990), pp. 89–114.

Haladjan, Mardig, "Middle East Mixes Oil and Water," **Euromoney** (June 1994), pp. 134–135.

Hanley, Kathleen Weiss, A. Arun Kumar, and Paul J. Seguin, "Price Stabilization in the Market for New Issues," **Journal of Financial Economics** 34 (October 1993), pp. 177–197.

Hansen, Robert S., "The Demise of the Rights Issue," **Review of Financial Studies** 1 (1988), pp. 289–309.

Hansen, Robert S. and Claire Crutchley, "Corporate Earnings and Financings: An Empirical Analysis," **Journal of Business** 63 (July 1990), pp. 347–371.

Hansen, Robert S. and Naveen Khanna, "Why Negotiation With a Single Syndicate May Be Preferred to Making Syndicates Compete: The Problem of Trapped Bidders," **Journal of Business** 67 (July 1994), pp. 423–457.

Hansen, Robert S. and John M. Pinkerton, "Direct Equity Financing: A Resolution of a Paradox," **Journal of Finance** 37 (June 1982), pp. 651–665.

Hargis, Kent, "The Internationalization of Emerging Equity Markets: Domestic Market Development or Retardation," Working paper (University of Illinois at Urbana–Champaign), October 1994.

Harris, Milton and Artur Raviv, "The Design of Securities," **Journal of Financial Economics** 24 (October 1989), pp. 255–287.

Harverson, Patrick, "Bank of NY Cements Role in ADR Sales," **Financial Times** (December 29, 1994), p. 12.

Heinkel, Robert and Josef Zechner, "The Role of Debt and Preferred Stock as a Solution to Adverse Investment Incentives," **Journal of Financial and Quantitative Analysis** 25 (March 1990), pp. 1–24.

Heller, Lucy, "The History and Development of the Eurocommercial Paper Market," Chapter One in **Eurocommercial Paper** (Euromoney Publications: London, 1988).

Hentzler, Herbert A., "The New Era of Eurocapitalism," **Harvard Business Review** (January/February 1992), pp. 57–68.

Hertzel, Michael and Richard L. Smith, "Market Discounts and Shareholder Gains for Placing Equity Privately," **Journal of Finance** 48 (June 1993), pp. 459–485.

Hess, Alan C. and Sanjai Bhagat, "Size Effects of Seasoned Stock Issues: Empirical Evidence," **Journal of Business** 59 (1986), pp. 567–584.

Hintze, John, "Loan Syndication Swelled by 74% in 1993," **Investment Dealers' Digest** (January 17, 1994), p. 21.

Hirschey, Mark and Janis K. Zaima, "Insider Trading, Ownership Structure, and the Market Assessment of Corporate Sell-Offs," **Journal of Finance** 44 (September 1989), pp. 971–980.

Hirtle, Beverly, "Factors Affecting the Competitiveness of Internationally Active Financial Intermediaries," Federal Reserve Bank of New York **Quarterly Review** (Spring 1991), pp. 38–51.

Hite, Gailen L., James E. Owers, and Ronald C. Rogers, "The Market for Interfirm Asset Sales: Partial Sell-Offs and Total Liquidations," **Journal of Financial Economics** 18 (1987), pp. 229–252.

Ho, Thomas and Donald E. Singer, "The Value of Corporate Debt With a Sinking-Fund Provision," **Journal of Business** 57 (September 1984), pp. 315–336.

Hodder, James E. and Adrian E. Tschoegl, "Some Aspects of Japanese Corporate Finance," **Journal of Financial and Quantitative Analysis** 20 (June 1985), pp. 173–191.

Holderness, Clifford G. and Dennis P. Sheehan, "The Role of Majority Shareholders in Publicly Held Corporations: An Exploratory Analysis," **Journal of Financial Economics** 20 (January–March 1988), pp. 317–346.

Holthausen, Robert W., Richard W. Leftwich, and David Mayers, "The Effects of Large Block Transactions on Security Prices: A Cross-Sectional Analysis," **Journal of Financial Economics** 19 (December 1987), pp. 237–268.

Hoover's Handbook of World Business (The Reference Press: Austin, TX, 1993).

Hoshi, Takeo, Anil Kashyap, and David Scharfstein, "The Role of Banks in Reducing the Costs of Financial Distress in Japan," **Journal of Financial Economics** 27 (September 1990), pp. 67–88.

————"The Choice Between Public and Private Debt: An Analysis of Post-Deregulation Corporate Financing in Japan," unpublished working paper (National Bureau of Economic Research: Cambridge, MA, 1993).

Houston, Joel F. and S. Venkataram, "Optimal Maturity Structure With Multiple Debt Claims," **Journal of Financial and Quantitative Analysis** 29 (June 1994), pp. 179–197.

Hudson, Carl D., Marlin R. H. Jensen, and William N. Pugh, "Informational Versus Price-Pressure Effects: Evidence From Secondary Offerings, " **Journal of Financial Research** 16 (1993), pp. 193–207.

Hughes, Patricia J., "Signalling By Direct Disclosure Under Asymmetric Information," **Journal of Accounting and Economics** 8 (June 1986), pp. 119–142.

Hunter, William C. and Stephen G. Timme, "Technological Change in Large U.S. Commercial Banks," **Journal of Business** 64 (July 1991), pp. 339–362.

Ibbotson, Roger G., "Price Performance of Common Stock New Issues," **Journal of Financial Economics** 2 (September 1975), pp. 235–272.

Ibbotson, Roger G. and Jeffrey F. Jaffe, "Hot Issue Markets," **Journal of Finance** 30 (Spring 1975), pp. 1027–1042.

Ibbotson, Roger G., Jody L. Sindelar, and Jay R. Ritter, "Initial Public Offerings," **Journal of Applied Corporate Finance** 1 (Summer 1988), pp. 37–45.

————"The Market's Problems With the Pricing of Initial Public Offerings," **Journal of Applied Corporate Finance** 7 (Spring 1994), pp. 66–74.

Igawa, Kazuhiro and George Kanatas, "Asymmetric Information, Collateral, and Moral Hazard," **Journal of Financial and Quantitative Analysis** 25 (December 1990), pp. 469–490.

Ingersoll, Jonathan E., Jr., "A Contingent-Claims Valuation of Convertible Securities," **Journal of Financial Economics** 4 (May 1977a), pp. 289–322.

————"An Examination of Corporate Call Policies on Convertible Securities," **Journal of Finance** 32 (May 1977b), pp. 463–478.

Iqbal, Zubair and Abbas Mirakhor, **Islamic Banking,** Occasional Paper # 49 (International Monetary Fund: Washington, DC, 1987).

Jacque, Laurent and Gabriel Hawawini, "Myths and Realities of the Global Capital Market: Lessons for Financial Managers," **Journal of Applied Corporate Finance** 6 (Fall 1993), pp. 81–90.

Jain, Prem C., "Equity Issues and Changes in Expectations of Earnings by Financial Analysts," **Review of Financial Studies** 5 (1992), pp. 669–683.

James, Christopher, "Some Evidence on the Uniqueness of Bank Loans," **Journal of Financial Economics** 19 (December 1987), pp. 217–235.

James, Christopher and Peggy Wier, "Borrowing Relationships, Intermediation, and the Cost of Issuing Public Securities," **Journal of Financial Economics** 28 (November/December 1990), pp. 149–171.

Jayaraman, Narayanan, Kuldeep Shastri, and Kishore Tandon, "The Impact of International Cross Listings on Risk and Returns: The Evidence of American Depository Receipts," **Journal of Banking and Finance** 17 (February 1993), pp. 91–103.

Jegadeesh, Narasimhan, Mark Weinstein, and Ivo Welch, "An Empirical Investigation of IPO Returns and Subsequent Equity Offerings," **Journal of Financial Economics** 34 (October 1993), pp. 153–175.

Jensen, Michael C., "Agency Costs of Free Cash Flow, Corporate Finance, and Takeovers," **American Economic Review** 76 (May 1986), pp. 659–665.

"Eclipse of the Public Corporation," **Harvard Business Review** 67 (September-October 1989), pp. 61–74.

"Presidential Address: The Modern Industrial Revolution, Exit, and the Failure of Internal Control Systems," **Journal of Finance** 48 (July 1993), pp. 831–880.

Jensen, Michael C. and William Meckling, "Theory of the Firm: Managerial Behavior, Agency Costs and Ownership Structure," **Journal of Financial Economics** 3 (October 1976), pp. 305–360.

Jones, Steven L., William L. Megginson, Robert C. Nash, and Jeffry M. Netter, "Financial Means to Political and Economic Ends in Share Issue Privatizations," Working paper (University of Georgia, Athens), June 1995.

Kalay, Avner, "Stockholder-Bondholder Conflicts and Dividend Constraints," **Journal of Financial Economics** 10 (July 1982), pp. 211–233.

Kalay, Avner and Adam Shimrat, "Firm Value and Seasoned Equity Issues: Price Pressure, Wealth Redistributions, or Negative Information," **Journal of Financial Economics** 19 (September 1987), pp. 109–126.

Kaplan, Robert S. and Gabriel Urwitz, "Statistical Models of Bond Ratings: A Methodologicial Inquiry," **Journal of Business** 52 (April 1979), pp. 231–262.

Kaufman, George G. and Larry R. Mote, "Is Banking a Declining Industry? A Historical Perspective," Federal Reserve Bank of Chicago **Economic Perspectives** (May/June 1994), pp. 2–21.

Kaufold, Howard and Michael Smirlock, "Managing Corporate Exchange and Interest Rate Exposure," **Financial Management** 15 (Autumn 1986), pp. 64–72.

"The Impact of Credit Risk on the Pricing and Duration of Floating-Rate Notes," **Journal of Banking and Finance** 15 (1991), pp. 43–52.

Keegan, Jeffrey, "Beset by Change and Erosion, Private Placements Endure," **Investment Dealers' Digest** (February 27, 1995), pp. 14–24.

Keloharju, Matti, "The Winner's Curse, Legal Liability, and the Long-Run Price Performance of Initial Public Offerings in Finland," **Journal of Financial Economics** 34 (October 1993), pp. 251–277.

Kensinger, John W. and John D. Martin, "Project Finance: Raising Money the Old-Fashioned Way," **Journal of Applied Corporate Finance** 1 (Fall 1988), pp. 69–81.

Kershaw, Gene, "German Banks Are Not Such Alert Watchdogs After All," **Business Week** (June 27, 1994), p. 18.

Kershaw, Tom, "Scouring the Globe for the Traditional Private Market," **Investment Dealers' Digest** (March 7, 1994), pp. 16–24.

Kester, W. Carl, "Governance, Contracting, and Investment Horizons: A Look at Japan and Germany," **Journal of Applied Corporate Finance** 5 (Summer 1992), pp. 83–98.

Khalaf, Roula, "An Inherent Contradiction," **Financial Times** (December 15, 1994), p. 36.

Kidwell, David S., M. Wayne Marr, and G. Rodney Thompson, "SEC Rule 415: The Ultimate Competitive Bid," **Journal of Financial and Quantitative Analysis** 19 (June 1984), pp. 183–195.

———"Eurodollar Bonds: Alternative Financing for U.S. Companies," **Financial Management** 14 (Winter 1985), pp. 18–27.

Kikeri, Sunita, John Nellis, and Mary Shirley, **Privatization: The Lesson of Experience** (The World Bank: Washington, DC, 1992).

Kim, Jeong-Bon, Itzhak Krinsky, and Jason Lee, "Motives for Going Public and Underpricing: New Findings From Korea," **Journal of Business, Finance, and Accounting** 20 (January 1993), pp. 195–211.

Kim, Yong Choel and René M. Stulz, "The Eurobond Market and Corporate Financial Policy: A Test of the Clientele Hypothesis," **Journal of Financial Economics** 22 (December 1988), pp. 189–205.

Kish, Richard J. and Miles Livingston, "Estimating the Value of Call Options on Corporate Bonds," **Journal of Applied Corporate Finance** 6 (Fall 1993), pp. 95–99.

Kleimeier, Stefanie, **Essays in Project Finance,** Unpublished dissertation (University of Georgia: Athens, GA), 1993.

Kleimeier, Stefanie and William L. Megginson, "An Economic Analysis of Project Finance," Working paper (Maastricht School of Management, The Netherlands), May 1995.

Klein, April and James Rosenfeld, "Targeted Share Repurchases and Top Management Changes," **Journal of Financial Economics** 20 (January/March 1988), pp. 493–506.

Knecht, G. Bruce, "Nationwide Banking is Around the Corner, But Obstacles Remain," **Wall Street Journal** (July 26, 1994), p. A1.

Koh, Francis and Terry Walter, "A Direct Test of Rock's Model of the Pricing of Unseasoned Issues," **Journal of Financial Economics** 23 (August 1989), pp. 251–272.

Korajczyk, Robert A., Deborah J. Lucas, and Robert L. McDonald, "The Effect of Information Releases on the Pricing and Timing of Equity Issues," **Review of Financial Studies** 4 (1991), pp. 685–708.

Koretz, Gene, "German Banks Are Not Such Alert Watchdogs After All," **Business Week** (June 27, 1994), p. 18.

Kumar, Raman, Atulya Sarin, and Kuldeep Shastri, "The Behavior of Optimal Price Around Large Block Transactions in the Underlying Security," **Journal of Finance** 47 (July 1992), pp. 879–889.

Lakonishok, Josef and Theo Vermaelen, "Anomalous Price Behavior Around Repurchase Tender Offers," **Journal of Finance** 45 (June 1990), pp. 455–477.

Lang, Larry, Annette B. Poulsen, and René M. Stulz, "Assets Sales, Firm Performance, and the Agency Costs of Managerial Discretion," **Journal of Financial Economics** 37 (1995), pp. 3–37.

Lee, Peter, "The Brakes Fail Again," **Euromoney** (August 1994), pp. 24–27.

Leland, Hayne and David Pyle, "Information Asymmetries, Financial Structure, and Financial Intermediation," **Journal of Finance** 32 (May 1977), pp. 371–387.

Lerner, Joshua, "Venture Capitalists and the Decision to Go Public," **Journal of Financial Economics** 35 (June 1994), pp. 293–316.

Lessard, Donald R., "Global Competition and Corporate Finance in the 1990s," **Journal of Applied Corporate Finance** 3 (Winter 1991), pp. 59–72.

Lessard, Donald R. and John Williamson, **Financial Intermediation Beyond the Debt Crisis** (Institute for International Economics; Washington, DC, 1985).

Levis, Mario, "The Long-Run Performance of Initial Public Offerings: The UK Experience 1980–1988," **Financial Management** 22 (Spring 1993), pp. 28–41.

Liebowitz, Michael, "Reversing Four-Year Trend and Swooning Economy, Wall Street Explodes in 1991," **Investment Dealers' Digest** (January 6, 1992a), pp. 16–41.

————"Can Corporate America Securitize . . . Itself?," **Investment Dealers' Digest** (January 27, 1992b), pp. 14–21.

Linn, Scott C. and J. Michael Pinegar, "The Effect of Issuing Preferred Stock on Common and Preferred Stockholder Wealth," **Journal of Financial Economics** 22 (October 1988), pp. 155–184.

Lipin, Steven, "Banks Try to Avoid Rules on Derivatives," **Wall Street Journal** (July 21, 1993), p. C1.

Litzenberger, Robert H., Presidential Address: Swaps: Plain and Fanciful," **Journal of Finance** 47 (July 1992), pp. 831–850.

Loderer, Claudio, Dennis P. Sheehan, and Gregory B. Kadlec, "The Pricing of Equity Offerings," **Journal of Financial Economics** 29 (March 1991), pp. 35–57.

Long, Michael S., Ileen B. Malitz, and Stephen E. Sefcik, "An Empirical Examination of Dividend Policy Following Debt Issues," **Journal of Financial and Quantitative Analysis** 29 (March 1994), pp. 131–144.

Loughran, Tim and Jay R. Ritter, "The New Issues Puzzle," **Journal of Finance** 50 (March 1995), pp. 23–51.

Loughran, Tim, Jay R. Ritter, and Kristian Rydqvist, "Initial Public Offerings: International Insights," **Pacific-Basin Finance Journal** 2 (1994), pp. 165–199.

Lummer, Scott C. and John J. McConnell, "Further Evidence on the Bank Lending Process and the Capital Market Responses to Bank Loan Agreements," **Journal of Financial Economics** 25 (November 1989), pp. 99–122.

Mais, Eric L., William T. Moore, and Ronald C. Rogers, "A Re-Examination of Shareholder Wealth Effects of Calls of Convertible Preferred Stock," **Journal of Finance** 44 (December 1989), pp. 1401–1410.

Malitz, Ileen, "On Financial Contracting: The Determinants of Bond Covenants," **Financial Management** 15 (Summer 1986), pp. 18–25.

Mandelker, Gershon and Artur Raviv, "Investment Banking: An Economic Analysis of Optimal Underwriting Contracts," **Journal of Finance** 32 (June 1977), pp. 683–694.

Mann, Steven V. and Neil W. Sicherman, "The Agency Costs of Free Cash Flow: Acquisition Activity and Equity Issues," **Journal of Business** 64 (April 1991), pp. 213–228.

Marais, Laurentius, Katharine Schipper, and Abbie Smith, "Wealth Effects of Going Private for Senior Securities," **Journal of Financial Economics** 23 (June 1989), pp. 155–191.

Marray, Michael, "Depositary Receipts: The US Welcomes the Alien Invasion," **Euromoney** (April 1994), pp. 61–63.

———"Life After Mexico," **Euromoney** (March 1995), pp. 121–127.

Marsh, Paul, "The Choice Between Equity and Debt: An Empirical Study," **Journal of Finance** 37 (March 1982), pp. 121–144.

Masulis, Ronald W., "The Effects of Capital Structure Change on Security Prices: A Study of Exchange Offers," **Journal of Financial Economics** 8 (June 1980), pp. 139–177.

Mauer, David C., "Optimal Bond Call Policies Under Transactions Costs," **Journal of Financial Research** 16 (Spring 1993), pp. 23–37.

Mayers, David and Clifford W. Smith, Jr., "On the Corporate Demand for Insurance," **Journal of Business** 55 (April 1982), pp. 281–296.

Mayers, David C. and Clifford W. Smith, Jr., "On the Corporate Demand for Insurance: Evidence From the Reinsurance Market," **Journal of Business** 63 (January 1990), pp. 19–40.

McGuinness, Paul, "An Examination of the Underpricing of Initial Public Offerings in Hong Kong," **Journal of Business Finance and Accounting** 19 (January 1992), pp. 165–186.

McLaughlin, Robyn M., "Investment Banking Contracts in Tender Offers," **Journal of Financial Economics** 28 (November/December 1990), pp. 209–232.

McNulty, James E., "The Pricing of Interest Rate Swaps," **Journal of Financial Services Research** 4 (March 1990), pp. 53–63.

Megginson, William L., Robert C. Nash, and Matthias van Randenborgh, "The Financial and Operating Performance of Newly-Privatized Firms: An International Empirical Analysis," **Journal of Finance** 49 (June 1994), pp. 403–452.

Megginson, William L., Annette B. Poulsen, and Joseph F. Sinkey, Jr., "Syndicated Loan Announcements and the Market Value of the Banking Firm," **Journal of Money, Credit, and Banking** 27 (May 1995), pp. 457–475.

Megginson, William L. and Kathleen A. Weiss, "Venture Capitalist Certification in Initial Public Offerings," **Journal of Finance** 46 (July 1991), pp. 879–903.

Mendelson, M. S., **Money on the Move—The Modern International Capital Market** (McGraw Hill; New York, 1980).

Merton, Robert C., "Financial Innovation and Economic Performance," **Journal of Applied Corporate Finance** 4 (Winter 1992), pp. 12–22.

Meulbroek, Lisa, "A Comparison of Forward and Futures Prices of an Interest Rate Sensitive Financial Asset," **Journal of Finance** 47 (March 1992), pp. 381–396.

Mian, Shehzad and Clifford W. Smith, Jr., "Accounts Receivable Management Policy: Theory and Evidence," **Journal of Finance** 47 (March 1992), pp. 169–200.

Mikkelson, Wayne, "Convertible Calls and Security Returns," **Journal of Financial Economics** 9 (September 1981), pp. 237–264.

Mikkelson, Wayne H. and M. Megan Partch, "Valuation Effects of Security Offerings and the Issuance Process," **Journal of Financial Economics** 15 (January/February 1986), pp. 31–60.

Miller, Merton, "Is American Corporate Governance Fatally Flawed?," **Journal of Applied Corporate Finance** 6 (Winter 1994), pp. 32–39.

Miller, Merton H., "Financial Innovation: Achievements and Prospects," **Journal of Applied Corporate Finance** 4 (Winter 1992), pp. 4–11.

Miller, Merton H. and Kevin Rock, "Dividend Policy Under Asymmetric Information," **Journal of Finance** 40 (September 1985), pp. 1031–1051.

Mitchell, Karlyn, "The Call, Sinking Fund, and Term-to-Maturity Features of Corporate Bonds: An Empirical Investigation," **Journal of Financial and Quantitative Analysis** 26 (June 1991), pp. 201–222.

Moore, Norman H., David R. Peterson, and Pamela P. Peterson, "Shelf Registration and Shareholder Wealth: A Comparison of Shelf and Traditional Equity Offerings," **Journal of Finance** 41 (June 1986), pp. 451–464.

Morgan, George Emir and Stephen D. Smith, "Maturity Intermediation and Intertemporal Lending Policies of Financial Intermediaries," **Journal of Finance** 42 (September 1987), pp. 1023–1034.

Mull, Frederick H., **Towards a Positive Theory of Venture Capital** (Unpublished dissertation; University of Georgia, 1990).

Muscarella, Chris J. and Michael R. Vetsuypens, "A Simple Test of Baron's Model of IPO Underpricing," **Journal of Financial Economics** 24 (September 1989), pp. 125–135.

———"Efficiency and Organizational Structure: A Study of Reverse LBOs," **Journal of Finance** 45 (December 1990), pp. 1389–1413.

Myers, Stewart C., "Determinants of Corporate Borrowing," **Journal of Financial Economics** 5 (November 1977), pp. 147–176.

————"Presidential Address: The Capital Structure Puzzle," **Journal of Finance** 39 (July 1984), pp. 575–592.

Myers, Stewart C. and Nicholas S. Majluf, "Corporate Financing and Investment Decisions When Firms Have Information Investors Do Not Have," **Journal of Financial Economics** 13 (June 1984), pp. 187–221.

Nance, Deana R., Clifford W. Smith, Jr., Charles W. Smithson, "On the Determinants of Corporate Hedging," **Journal of Finance** 48 (March 1993), pp. 267–284.

Ofer, Aharon R. and Ashok Natarajan, "Convertible Call Policies: An Empirical Analysis of an Information-Signaling Hypothesis," **Journal of Financial Economics** 19 (September 1987), pp. 91–108.

Ogden, Joseph P., "Determinants of the Ratings and Yields on Corporate Bonds: Tests of the Contingent Claims Model," **Journal of Financial Research** 10 (Winter 1987), pp. 329–339.

Parisi, Franco, "Time-Varying Transmission of Pricing and Volatility in ADRs," Unpublished dissertation (University of Georgia, August 1995).

Pavel, Christine and John N. McElravey, "Globalization in the Financial Services Industry," Federal Reserve Bank of Chicago **Economic Perspectives** (May/June 1990), pp. 3–18.

Pavey, Nigel and Gary Humphries, "Syndicated Loans: A Competitive Business," **Euromoney** (Special Supplement, May 1988).

Peagam, Norman, "Project Finance: The Hunt for a New Source of Capital," **Euromoney** (June 1994), pp. 221–224.

Peat Marwick Main & Company, **Going Public: What the High Technology CEO Needs to Know** (KPMG Peat Marwick: Chicago, 1987).

Pennacchi, George G., "Loan Sales and the Cost of Bank Capital," **Journal of Finance** 43 (June 1988), pp. 375–396.

Perrotti, Enrico C. and Serhat E. Guney, "The Structure of Privatization Plans," **Financial Management** 22 (Spring 1993), pp. 84–98.

Petersen, Mitchell A. and Raghuram G. Rajan, "The Benefits of Lending Relationships: Evidence From Small Business Data," **Journal of Finance** 39 (March 1994), pp. 3–37.

Pettit, R. Richardson and Ronald F. Singer, "Small Business Finance: A Research Agenda," **Financial Management** 14 (Autumn 1985), pp. 47–60.

Petty, J. William, William D. Bygrave, and Joel Shulman, "Harvesting the Entrepreneurial Venture: A Time for Creating Value," **Journal of Applied Corporate Finance** 7 (Spring 1994), pp. 48–58.

Piggott, Charles, "Euromoney Five Hundred: What a Difference a Decade Makes," **Euromoney** (June 1994), pp. 137–169.

Pinches, George E. and Kent A. Mingo, "A Multivariate Analysis of Industrial Bond Ratings," **Journal of Finance** 28 (March 1973), pp. 1–18.

Plender, John, "High Wire Act in a Bear Garden," **Financial Times** (May 19, 1994), p. 13.

Porter, Michael E., "Capital Disadvantage: America's Failing Capital Investment System," **Harvard Business Review** (September/October 1992), pp. 65–82.

Posner, Bruce G., "How to Finance Anything," **Inc.** (April 1992), pp. 51–62.

Pratt, Tom, "A Knockout Year for Wall Street," **Investment Dealers' Digest** (January 10, 1994), pp. 18–38.

————"Wall Street's Deep Freeze," **Investment Dealers' Digest** (January 9, 1995a), pp. 12–33.

————"Liquidity and Creativity Keep CP Market Thriving," **Investment Dealers' Digest** (January 30, 1995b), p. 13.

Press, Eric G. and Joseph B. Weintrop, "Accounting-Based Constraints in Public and Private Debt Agreements: Their Association With Leverage and Impact on Accounting Choice," **Journal of Accounting and Economics** 12 (January 1990), pp. 65–95.

Pringle, John J., "Managing Foreign Exchange Exposure," **Journal of Applied Corporate Finance** 3 (Winter 1991), pp. 73–82.

Pringle, John J. and Robert A. Connolly, "The Nature and Causes of Foreign Currency Exposure," **Journal of Applied Corporate Finance** 6 (Fall 1993), pp. 61–72.

Prowse, Stephen D., "Institutional Investment Patterns and Corporate Financial Behavior in the United States and Japan," **Journal of Financial Economics** 27 (September 1990), pp. 43–66.

Rajan, Raghuram and Luigi Zingales, "What Do We Know About Capital Structure? Some Evidence From International Data," NBER Working paper (October 1994).

Raghavan, Anita and Michael R. Sesit, "Financing Boom: Foreign Firms Raise More and More Money in the U.S. Markets," **Wall Street Journal** (October 5, 1993), p. A1.

Ramaswamy, Krishna and Suresh M. Sundaresan, "The Valuation of Floating-Rate Instruments: Theory and Evidence," **Journal of Financial Economics** 17 (December 1986), pp. 251–272.

Rawls, S. Waite III and Charles W. Smithson, "Strategic Risk Management," **Journal of Applied Corporate Finance** 2 (Winter 1990), pp. 6–18.

Ritter, Jay R., "The 'Hot Issue' Market of 1980," **Journal of Business** 57 (October 1984), pp. 215–240.

————"The Costs of Going Public," **Journal of Financial Economics** 19 (December 1987), pp. 269–281.

————"The Long-Run Performance of Initial Public Offerings," **Journal of Finance** 46 (March 1991), pp. 3–28.

Robertson, Jamie, "The Coming Shake-Out in ECP," **Euromoney** (December 1987), pp. 161–172.

Rock, Kevin, "Why New Issues are Underpriced," **Journal of Financial Economics** 15 (January/February 1986), pp. 187–212.

Roe, Mark J., "Political and Legal Restraints on Ownership and Control of Public Companies," **Journal of Financial Economics** 27 (September 1990), pp. 7–41.

Röel, Sophie, "Where, When—and How Much," **Euromoney** (March 1995), pp. 116–120.

Rösseler, Benedikt, **Bankruptcy Law in Germany and the United States: A Comparison of Different Legal Approaches to Resolve Financial Distress,** (Unpublished thesis: University of Georgia, 1993).

Rountree, Robert, "Southeast Asia Gets More Neighbourly," **Euromoney** (June 1994), pp. 124–126.

Rudnick, David, "First Sort Out the Banks," **Euromoney** (March 1994), pp. 157–163.

Ruud, Judith S., "Underwriter Price Support and the IPO Underwriter Puzzle," **Journal of Financial Economics** 34 (October 1993), pp. 135–151.

Sachs, Jeffrey D., "Managing the LDC Debt Crisis," **Brookings Papers on Economic Activity** 2 (1986), pp. 397–440.

Sachs, Jeffrey D. and Harry Huizinga, "U.S. Commercial Banks and the Developing-Country Debt Crisis," **Brookings Papers on Economic Activity** 2 (1987), 555–601.

Sahlman, William A., "Aspects of Financial Contracting in Venture Capital," **Journal of Applied Corporate Finance** 1 (Summer 1988), pp. 23–36.

————"The Structure and Governance of Venture-Capital Organizations," **Journal of Financial Economics** 27 (October 1990), pp. 473–522.

Sanger, Gary C. and John J. McConnell, "Stock Exchange Listings, Firm Value, and Security Market Efficiency: The Impact of NASDAQ," **Journal of Financial and Quantitative Analysis** 21 (March 1986), pp. 1–25.

Sarver, Eugen, **The Eurocurrency Handbook** (Institute of Finance: New York, 1988).

Saunders, Anthony and Joseph Lim, "Underpricing and the New Issues Process in Singapore," **Journal of Banking and Finance** 14 (1990), pp. 291–310.

Schipper, Katharine and Abbie Smith, "A Comparison of Equity Carve-Outs and Seasoned Equity Offerings: Share Price Effects and Corporate Restructuring," **Journal of Financial Economics** 15 (January/February 1986), pp. 153–186.

Scholes, Myron S., "The Market for Securities: Substitution Versus Price Pressure and the Effects of Information on Share Prices," **Journal of Business** 45 (April 1972), pp. 179–211.

Schultz, Paul H. and Mir A. Zaman, "Aftermarket Support and the Underpricing of Initial Public Offerings," **Journal of Financial Economics** 35 (April 1994), pp. 199–219.

Schwimmer, Anne, "Shelter From the Storm," **Investment Dealers' Digest** (January 23, 1995), pp. 10–14.

Scott, James, "Bankruptcy, Secured Debt, and Optimal Capital Structure," **Journal of Finance** 32 (March 1977), pp. 1–20.

Scott, Jonathan A. and Terrence C. Smith, "The Effect of the Bankruptcy Reform Act of 1976 On Small Business Loan Pricing," **Journal of Financial Economics** 16 (May 1986), pp. 119–140.

Sesit, Michael R., "Americans Pour Money Into Foreign Markets," **Wall Street Journal** (April 14, 1994), p. C1.

Seward, James K., "Corporate Financial Policy and the Theory of Financial Intermediation," **Journal of Finance** 45 (June 1990), pp. 351–377.

Shapiro, Alan C., "Currency Risk and Country Risk in International Banking," **Journal of Finance** 40 (July 1985), pp. 881–893.

——"International Banking and Country Risk Analysis," in Joel Stern and Donald Chew, eds., **New Developments in International Finance** (Basil Blackwell, Inc.: New York, 1988).

——"The Economic Import of Europe 1992," **Journal of Applied Corporate Finance** 3 (Winter 1991), pp. 25–36.

Sharpe, Antonia, "Commercial Paper: Cash Haven Lures Investors," **Financial Times** (International Capital Markets Survey; May 24, 1994), pp. IV–V.

——"RPI-Linked Bonds From HBSC," **Financial Times** (May 17, 1995), p. 22.

Shirreff, David, "The Metamorphosis of Finance," **Euromoney** (June 1994), pp. 36–46.

Shyam-Sunder, Lakshmi, "The Stock Price Effect of Risky Versus Safe Debt," **Journal of Financial and Quantitative Analysis** 26 (December 1991), pp. 549–558.

Simon, Carol J., "The Effect of the 1933 Securities Act on Investor Information and the Performance of New Issues," **American Economic Review** 79 (June 1989), pp. 295–318.

Sinkey, Joseph F., Jr., **Commercial Bank Financial Management in the Financial Services Industry,** Fourth Edition (MacMillan Publishing Company: New York, 1992).

Sinkey, Joseph and David A. Carter, "On the Use and Determinants of Bank Derivatives," unpublished working paper (University of Georgia: Athens, 1994).

Slovin, Myron B., Marie E. Sushka, and Carl D. Hudson, "External Monitoring and its Effect on Seasoned Common Stock Issues," **Journal of Accounting and Economics** 12 (1990), pp. 391–417.

Slovin, Myron B., Marie E. Sushka, and John A. Polonchek, "Informational Externalities of Seasoned Equity Issues: Differences Between Banks and Industrial Firms," **Journal of Financial Economics** 32 (August 1992), pp. 87–101.

Slovin, Myron B. and John Young, "Bank Lending and Initial Public Offerings," **Journal of Banking and Finance** 14 (October 1990), pp. 729–740.

Smith, Clifford W., Jr., "Alternative Methods for Raising Capital: Rights Versus Underwritten Offerings," **Journal of Financial Economics** 5 (December 1977), pp. 273–307.

————"On the Theory of Financial Contracting—The Personal Loan Market," **Journal of Monetary Economics** 6 (1980), pp. 333–357.

————"Investment Banking and the Capital Acquisition Process," **Journal of Financial Economics** 15 (January/February 1986), pp. 3–29.

Smith, Clifford W., Jr., Charles W. Smithson, and D. Sykes Wilford, "Managing Financial Risk," **Journal of Applied Corporate Finance** 1 (Winter 1989), pp. 27–48.

Smith, Clifford W., Jr., and René M. Stulz, " The Determinants of Firms' Hedging Policies," **Journal of Financial and Quantitative Analysis** 20 (December 1985), pp. 391–405.

Smith, Clifford W., Jr. and Jerold Warner, "On Financial Contracting: An Analysis of Bond Covenants," **Journal of Financial Economics** 7 (June 1979), pp. 117–161.

Smith, Clifford W., Jr. and Ross L. Watts, "The Investment Opportunity Set and Corporate Financing, Dividend, and Compensation Policies," **Journal of Financial Economics** 32 (October 1992), pp. 263–292.

Smith, Roy C. and Ingo Walter, "Project Finance," Chapter 9 in **Global Financial Services** (Harper Business Publications: New York, 1990), pp. 191–281.

Smithson, Charles W. and Donald H. Chew, "The Uses of Hybrid Debt in Managing Corporate Risk," **Journal of Applied Corporate Finance** 4 (Winter 1992), pp. 79–89.

Stein, Jeremy C., "Convertible Debt as Backdoor Equity Financing," **Journal of Financial Economics** 32 (August 1992), pp. 3–21.

Stulz, René M. and Herb Johnson, "An Analysis of Secured Debt," **Journal of Financial Economics** 14 (December 1985), pp. 501–521.

Sundaram, Anant, "International Financial Markets," in Dennis E. Logue, ed., **Handbook of Modern Finance**, Third Edition (Warren Gorham Lamont: Boston, 1993).

Szopo, Peter, "Central and Eastern Europe is Climbing Back," **Euromoney** (June 1994), pp. 130–134.

Tang, Alex P. and Ronald F. Singer, "Valuation Effects of Issuing Nonsubordinated Versus Subordinated Debt," **Journal of Financial Research** 16 (Spring 1993), pp. 11–21.

Tanzer, Andrew, "The Bamboo Network," **Forbes** (July 18, 1994), pp. 138–145.

Testa, Richard J., "The Legal Process of Venture Capital Investment," in Yong Lim and Ted Weinsberg, eds., **Pratt's Guide to Venture Capital Sources** (Venture Economics: Boston, 1994), pp. 65–79.

Thompson, Jason, "Serving God and Mammon," **Euromoney** (November 1994), pp. 46–49.

Timmons, Jeffry A. and Dale A. Sander, "Everything You (Don't) Want to Know About Raising Capital," **Harvard Business Review** (November/December 1989), pp. 70–73.

Titman, Sheridan, "Interest Rate Swaps and Corporate Financing Choices," **Journal of Finance** 47 (September 1992), pp. 1503–1516.

Titman, Sheridan and Brett Trueman, "Information Quality and the Valuation of New Issues," **Journal of Accounting and Economics** 8 (June 1986), pp. 159–172.

Tufano, Peter, "Financial Innovation and First Mover Advantages," **Journal of Financial Economics** 25 (December 1989), pp. 213–240.

van Duyn, Aline, "Foreign Exchange: Working for Their Money," **Euromoney** (May 1994), pp. 49–58.

van Duyn, Aline, "Investors Play Hard to Get," **Euromoney** (February 1995), pp. 72–75.

Vermaelen, Theo, "Common Stock Repurchases and Market Signalling: An Empirical Study," **Journal of Financial Economics** 9 (June 1981), pp. 139–183.

Viscione, Jerry A., "How Long Should You Borrow Short Term?" **Harvard Business Review** (March/April 1986), pp. 20–24.

Viswanath, P. V., "Strategic Considerations, the Pecking Order Hypothesis, and Market Reactions to Equity Financing," **Journal of Financial and Quantitative Analysis** 28 (June 1993), pp. 213–234.

Vogel, Thomas T., "Disney Amazes Investors With Sale of 100-Year Bonds," **Wall Street Journal** (July 21, 1993), p. C1.

Vu, Joseph D., "An Examination of Corporate Call Behavior of Nonconvertible Bonds," **Journal of Financial Economics** 16 (June 1986), pp. 235–265.

Wakeman, Lee Macdonald, "The Real Function of Bond Rating Agencies," **Chase Financial Quarterly** (Fall 1981), pp. 19–25.

Waller, David, "Resisting the Bait of Equity Ownership," **Financial Times** (July 14, 1994), p. 19.

Wall Street Journal, "Experts Pick Banks They Expect to be Global Elite by 2000" (March 25, 1991), p. A4.

Weinstein, Mark I., "The Effect of a Rating Change Announcement on Bond Price," **Journal of Financial Economics** 5 (December 1977), pp. 329–350.

Welch, Ivo, "Seasoned Offerings, Imitation Costs, and the Underpricing of Initial Public Offerings," **Journal of Finance** 44 (June 1989), pp. 421–449.

Wheelock, David C., "Is the Banking Industry in Decline? Recent Trends and Future Prospects From a Historical Perspective," Federal Reserve Bank of St. Louis **Economic Review** (September/October 1993), pp. 3–22.

Whited, Toni M., "Debt, Liquidity Constraints, and Corporate Investment: Evidence From Panel Data," **Journal of Finance** 47 (September 1992), pp. 1425–1460.

Winkler, Andreas, **The Pricing of Syndicated Bank Loans in the Euromarket** (Unpublished thesis; University of Georgia, 1991).

Woolridge, J. Randall, "Competitive Decline and Corporate Restructuring: Is a Myopic Stock Market to Blame?" **Journal of Applied Corporate Finance** 1 (Spring 1988), pp. 26–36.

Wruck, Karen H., "Equity Ownership Concentration and Firm Value: Evidence From Private Equity Financings," **Journal of Financial Economics** 23 (June 1989), pp. 3–28.

Yarrow, George, "Privatization in Theory and Practice," **Economic Policy** 2 (1986), pp. 324–364.

Zeune, Gary D., "Accessing the Capital Markets," Chapter 31 in Richard Bort, ed., **Corporate Cash Management Handbook** (Warren Gorham Lamont: Boston, 1992).

Zurack, Mark A. and Kevin F. Foote, **The Goldman Sachs Extended Global Bond Market Indices** (Goldman Sachs & Company: London, July 1994).

APPENDIX

*Financial
Tables*

Table A.1 Future-Value Interest Factors for One Dollar Compounded at k Percent for n Periods: $FVIF_{k,n} = (1 + k)^n$

Interest Rate

Period	1%	2%	3%	4%	5%	6%	7%	8%	9%	10%
1	1.010	1.020	1.030	1.040	1.050	1.060	1.070	1.080	1.090	1.100
2	1.020	1.040	1.061	1.082	1.102	1.124	1.145	1.166	1.188	1.210
3	1.030	1.061	1.093	1.125	1.158	1.191	1.225	1.260	1.295	1.331
4	1.041	1.082	1.126	1.170	1.216	1.262	1.311	1.360	1.412	1.464
5	1.051	1.104	1.159	1.217	1.276	1.338	1.403	1.469	1.539	1.611
6	1.062	1.126	1.194	1.265	1.340	1.419	1.501	1.587	1.677	1.772
7	1.072	1.149	1.230	1.316	1.407	1.504	1.606	1.714	1.828	1.949
8	1.083	1.172	1.267	1.369	1.477	1.594	1.718	1.851	1.993	2.144
9	1.094	1.195	1.305	1.423	1.551	1.689	1.838	1.999	2.172	2.358
10	1.105	1.219	1.344	1.480	1.629	1.791	1.967	2.159	2.367	2.594
11	1.116	1.243	1.384	1.539	1.710	1.898	2.105	2.332	2.580	2.853
12	1.127	1.268	1.426	1.601	1.796	2.012	2.252	2.518	2.813	3.138
13	1.138	1.294	1.469	1.665	1.886	2.133	2.410	2.720	3.066	3.452
14	1.149	1.319	1.513	1.732	1.980	2.261	2.579	2.937	3.342	3.797
15	1.161	1.346	1.558	1.801	2.079	2.397	2.759	3.172	3.642	4.177
16	1.173	1.373	1.605	1.873	2.183	2.540	2.952	3.426	3.970	4.595
17	1.184	1.400	1.653	1.948	2.292	2.693	3.159	3.700	4.328	5.054
18	1.196	1.428	1.702	2.026	2.407	2.854	3.380	3.996	4.717	5.560
19	1.208	1.457	1.753	2.107	2.527	3.026	3.616	4.316	5.142	6.116
20	1.220	1.486	1.806	2.191	2.653	3.207	3.870	4.661	5.604	6.727
21	1.232	1.516	1.860	2.279	2.786	3.399	4.140	5.034	6.109	7.400
22	1.245	1.546	1.916	2.370	2.925	3.603	4.430	5.436	6.658	8.140
23	1.257	1.577	1.974	2.465	3.071	3.820	4.740	5.871	7.258	8.954
24	1.270	1.608	2.033	2.563	3.225	4.049	5.072	6.341	7.911	9.850
25	1.282	1.641	2.094	2.666	3.386	4.292	5.427	6.848	8.623	10.834
30	1.348	1.811	2.427	3.243	4.322	5.743	7.612	10.062	13.267	17.449
35	1.417	2.000	2.814	3.946	5.516	7.686	10.676	14.785	20.413	28.102
40	1.489	2.208	3.262	4.801	7.040	10.285	14.974	21.724	31.408	45.258
45	1.565	2.438	3.781	5.841	8.985	13.764	21.002	31.920	48.325	72.888
50	1.645	2.691	4.384	7.106	11.467	18.419	29.456	46.900	74.354	117.386

Table A.1 Future-Value Interest Factors for One Dollar Compounded at k Percent for n Periods: $FVIF_{k,n} = (1 + k)^n$ (continued)

Period						Interest Rate					
	11%	12%	13%	14%	15%	16%	17%	18%	19%	20%
1	1.110	1.120	1.130	1.140	1.150	1.160	1.170	1.180	1.190	1.200
2	1.232	1.254	1.277	1.300	1.322	1.346	1.369	1.392	1.416	1.440
3	1.368	1.405	1.443	1.482	1.521	1.561	1.602	1.643	1.685	1.728
4	1.518	1.574	1.630	1.689	1.749	1.811	1.874	1.939	2.005	2.074
5	1.685	1.762	1.842	1.925	2.011	2.100	2.192	2.288	2.386	2.488
6	1.870	1.974	2.082	2.195	2.313	2.436	2.565	2.700	2.840	2.986
7	2.076	2.211	2.353	2.502	2.660	2.826	3.001	3.185	3.379	3.583
8	2.305	2.476	2.658	2.853	3.059	3.278	3.511	3.759	4.021	4.300
9	2.558	2.773	3.004	3.252	3.518	3.803	4.108	4.435	4.785	5.160
10	2.839	3.106	3.395	3.707	4.046	4.411	4.807	5.234	5.695	6.192
11	3.152	3.479	3.836	4.226	4.652	5.117	5.624	6.176	6.777	7.430
12	3.498	3.896	4.334	4.818	5.350	5.936	6.580	7.288	8.064	8.916
13	3.883	4.363	4.898	5.492	6.153	6.886	7.699	8.599	9.596	10.699
14	4.310	4.887	5.535	6.261	7.076	7.987	9.007	10.147	11.420	12.839
15	4.785	5.474	6.254	7.138	8.137	9.265	10.539	11.974	13.589	15.407
16	5.311	6.130	7.067	8.137	9.358	10.748	12.330	14.129	16.171	18.488
17	5.895	6.866	7.986	9.276	10.761	12.468	14.426	16.672	19.244	22.186
18	6.543	7.690	9.024	10.575	12.375	14.462	16.879	19.673	22.900	26.623
19	7.263	8.613	10.197	12.055	14.232	16.776	19.748	23.214	27.251	31.948
20	8.062	9.646	11.523	13.743	16.366	19.461	23.105	27.393	32.429	38.337
21	8.949	10.804	13.021	15.667	18.821	22.574	27.033	32.323	38.591	46.005
22	9.933	12.100	14.713	17.861	21.644	26.186	31.629	38.141	45.923	55.205
23	11.026	13.552	16.626	20.361	24.891	30.376	37.005	45.007	54.648	66.247
24	12.239	15.178	18.788	23.212	28.625	35.236	43.296	53.108	65.031	79.496
25	13.585	17.000	21.230	26.461	32.918	40.874	50.656	62.667	77.387	95.395
30	22.892	29.960	39.115	50.949	66.210	85.849	111.061	143.367	184.672	237.373
35	38.574	52.799	72.066	98.097	133.172	180.311	243.495	327.988	440.691	590.657
40	64.999	93.049	132.776	188.876	267.856	378.715	533.846	750.353	1051.642	1469.740
45	109.527	163.985	244.629	363.662	538.752	795.429	1170.425	1716.619	2509.583	3657.176
50	184.559	288.996	450.711	700.197	1083.619	1670.669	2566.080	3927.189	5988.730	9100.191

Table A.1 Future-Value Interest Factors for One Dollar Compounded at k Percent for n Periods: $FVIF_{k,n} = (1 + k)^n$ *(continued)*

Interest Rate

Period	21%	22%	23%	24%	25%	30%	35%	40%	45%	50%
1	1.210	1.220	1.230	1.240	1.250	1.300	1.350	1.400	1.450	1.500
2	1.464	1.488	1.513	1.538	1.562	1.690	1.822	1.960	2.102	2.250
3	1.772	1.816	1.861	1.907	1.953	2.197	2.460	2.744	3.049	3.375
4	2.144	2.215	2.289	2.364	2.441	2.856	3.321	3.842	4.421	5.063
5	2.594	2.703	2.815	2.932	3.052	3.713	4.484	5.378	6.410	7.594
6	3.138	3.297	3.463	3.635	3.815	4.827	6.053	7.530	9.294	11.391
7	3.797	4.023	4.259	4.508	4.768	6.275	8.172	10.541	13.476	17.086
8	4.595	4.908	5.239	5.589	5.960	8.157	11.032	14.758	19.541	25.629
9	5.560	5.987	6.444	6.931	7.451	10.604	14.894	20.661	28.334	38.443
10	6.727	7.305	7.926	8.594	9.313	13.786	20.106	28.925	41.085	57.665
11	8.140	8.912	9.749	10.657	11.642	17.921	27.144	40.495	59.573	86.498
12	9.850	10.872	11.991	13.215	14.552	23.298	36.644	56.694	86.380	129.746
13	11.918	13.264	14.749	16.386	18.190	30.287	49.469	79.371	125.251	194.620
14	14.421	16.182	18.141	20.319	22.737	39.373	66.784	111.119	181.614	291.929
15	17.449	19.742	22.314	25.195	28.422	51.185	90.158	155.567	263.341	437.894
16	21.113	24.085	27.446	31.242	35.527	66.541	121.713	217.793	381.844	656.841
17	25.547	29.384	33.758	38.740	44.409	86.503	164.312	304.911	553.674	985.261
18	30.912	35.848	41.523	48.038	55.511	112.454	221.822	426.875	802.826	1477.892
19	37.404	43.735	51.073	59.567	69.389	146.190	299.459	597.625	1164.098	2216.838
20	45.258	53.357	62.820	73.863	86.736	190.047	404.270	836.674	1687.942	3325.257
21	54.762	65.095	77.268	91.591	108.420	247.061	545.764	1171.343	2247.515	4987.883
22	66.262	79.416	95.040	113.572	135.525	321.178	736.781	1639.878	3548.896	7481.824
23	80.178	96.887	116.899	140.829	169.407	417.531	994.653	2295.829	5145.898	11222.738
24	97.015	118.203	143.786	174.628	211.758	542.791	1342.781	3214.158	7461.547	16834.109
25	117.388	144.207	176.857	216.539	264.698	705.627	1812.754	4499.816	10819.242	25251.164
30	304.471	389.748	497.904	634.810	807.793	2619.936	8128.426	24201.043	69348.375	*
35	789.716	1053.370	1401.749	1861.020	2465.189	9727.598	36448.051	*	*	*
40	2048.309	2846.941	3946.340	5455.797	7523.156	36117.754	*	*	*	*
45	5312.758	7694.418	11110.121	15994.316	22958.844	*	*	*	*	*
50	13779.844	20795.680	31278.301	46889.207	70064.812	*	*	*	*	*

*FVIF > 99,999.

Table A.2 Future-Value Interest Factors for a One-Dollar Annuity Compounded at k Percent for n Periods: $FVIFA_{k,n} = \sum_{t=1}^{n} (1 + k)^{t-1}$

Period					Interest Rate					
	1%	2%	3%	4%	5%	6%	7%	8%	9%	10%
1	1.000	1.000	1.000	1.000	1.000	1.000	1.000	1.000	1.000	1.000
2	2.010	2.020	2.030	2.040	2.050	2.060	2.070	2.080	2.090	2.100
3	3.030	3.060	3.091	3.122	3.152	3.184	3.215	3.246	3.278	3.310
4	4.060	4.122	4.184	4.246	4.310	4.375	4.440	4.506	4.573	4.641
5	5.101	5.204	5.309	5.416	5.526	5.637	5.751	5.867	5.985	6.105
6	6.152	6.308	6.468	6.633	6.802	6.975	7.153	7.336	7.523	7.716
7	7.214	7.434	7.662	7.898	8.142	8.394	8.654	8.923	9.200	9.487
8	8.286	8.583	8.892	9.214	9.549	9.897	10.260	10.637	11.028	11.436
9	9.368	9.755	10.159	10.583	11.027	11.491	11.978	12.488	13.021	13.579
10	10.462	10.950	11.464	12.006	12.578	13.181	13.816	14.487	15.193	15.937
11	11.567	12.169	12.808	13.486	14.207	14.972	15.784	16.645	17.560	18.531
12	12.682	13.412	14.192	15.026	15.917	16.870	17.888	18.977	20.141	21.384
13	13.809	14.680	15.618	16.627	17.713	18.882	20.141	21.495	22.953	24.523
14	14.947	15.974	17.086	18.292	19.598	21.015	22.550	24.215	26.019	27.975
15	16.097	17.293	18.599	20.023	21.578	23.276	25.129	27.152	29.361	31.772
16	17.258	18.639	20.157	21.824	23.657	25.672	27.888	30.324	33.003	35.949
17	18.430	20.012	21.761	23.697	25.840	28.213	30.840	33.750	36.973	40.544
18	19.614	21.412	23.414	25.645	28.132	30.905	33.999	37.450	41.301	45.599
19	20.811	22.840	25.117	27.671	30.539	33.760	37.379	41.446	46.018	51.158
20	22.019	24.297	26.870	29.778	33.066	36.785	40.995	45.762	51.159	57.274
21	23.239	25.783	28.676	31.969	35.719	39.992	44.865	50.422	56.764	64.002
22	24.471	27.299	30.536	34.248	38.505	43.392	49.005	55.456	62.872	71.402
23	25.716	28.845	32.452	36.618	41.430	46.995	53.435	60.893	69.531	79.542
24	26.973	30.421	34.426	39.082	44.501	50.815	58.176	66.764	76.789	88.496
25	28.243	32.030	36.459	41.645	47.726	54.864	63.248	73.105	84.699	98.346
30	34.784	40.567	47.575	56.084	66.438	79.057	94.459	113.282	136.305	164.491
35	41.659	49.994	60.461	73.651	90.318	111.432	138.234	172.314	215.705	271.018
40	48.885	60.401	75.400	95.024	120.797	154.758	199.630	259.052	337.872	442.580
45	56.479	71.891	92.718	121.027	159.695	212.737	285.741	386.497	525.840	718.881
50	64.461	84.577	112.794	152.664	209.341	290.325	406.516	573.756	815.051	1163.865

Table A.2 Future-Value Interest Factors for a One-Dollar Annuity Compounded at k Percent for n Periods: $FVIFA_{k,n} = \sum_{t=1}^{n}(1+k)^{t-1}$ (continued)

Interest Rate

Period	11%	12%	13%	14%	15%	16%	17%	18%	19%	20%
1	1.000	1.000	1.000	1.000	1.000	1.000	1.000	1.000	1.000	1.000
2	2.110	2.120	2.130	2.140	2.150	2.160	2.170	2.180	2.190	2.200
3	3.342	3.374	3.407	3.440	3.472	3.506	3.539	3.572	3.606	3.640
4	4.710	4.779	4.850	4.921	4.993	5.066	5.141	5.215	5.291	5.368
5	6.228	6.353	6.480	6.610	6.742	6.877	7.014	7.154	7.297	7.442
6	7.913	8.115	8.323	8.535	8.754	8.977	9.207	9.442	9.683	9.930
7	9.783	10.089	10.405	10.730	11.067	11.414	11.772	12.141	12.523	12.916
8	11.859	12.300	12.757	13.233	13.727	14.240	14.773	15.327	15.902	16.499
9	14.164	14.776	15.416	16.085	16.786	17.518	18.285	19.086	19.923	20.799
10	16.722	17.549	18.420	19.337	20.304	21.321	22.393	23.521	24.709	25.959
11	19.561	20.655	21.814	23.044	24.349	25.733	27.200	28.755	30.403	32.150
12	22.713	24.133	25.650	27.271	29.001	30.850	32.824	34.931	37.180	39.580
13	26.211	28.029	29.984	32.088	34.352	36.786	39.404	42.218	45.244	48.496
14	30.095	32.392	34.882	37.581	40.504	43.672	47.102	50.818	54.841	59.196
15	34.405	37.280	40.417	43.842	47.580	51.659	56.109	60.965	66.260	72.035
16	39.190	42.753	46.671	50.980	55.717	60.925	66.648	72.938	79.850	87.442
17	44.500	48.883	53.738	59.117	65.075	71.673	78.978	87.067	96.021	105.930
18	50.396	55.749	61.724	68.393	75.836	84.140	93.404	103.739	115.265	128.116
19	56.939	63.439	70.748	78.968	88.211	98.603	110.283	123.412	138.165	154.739
20	64.202	72.052	80.946	91.024	102.443	115.379	130.031	146.626	165.417	186.687
21	72.264	81.698	92.468	104.767	118.809	134.840	153.136	174.019	197.846	225.024
22	81.213	92.502	105.489	120.434	137.630	157.414	180.169	206.342	236.436	271.028
23	91.147	104.602	120.203	138.295	159.274	183.600	211.798	244.483	282.359	326.234
24	102.173	118.154	136.829	158.656	184.166	213.976	248.803	289.490	337.007	392.480
25	114.412	133.333	155.616	181.867	212.790	249.212	292.099	342.598	402.038	471.976
30	199.018	241.330	293.192	356.778	434.738	530.306	647.423	790.932	966.698	1181.865
35	341.583	431.658	546.663	693.552	881.152	1120.699	1426.448	1816.607	2314.173	2948.294
40	581.812	767.080	1013.667	1341.979	1779.048	2360.724	3134.412	4163.094	5529.711	7343.715
45	986.613	1358.208	1874.086	2590.464	3585.031	4965.191	6879.008	9531.258	13203.105	18280.914
50	1668.723	2399.975	3459.344	4994.301	7217.488	10435.449	15088.805	21812.273	31514.492	45496.094

Table A.2 Future-Value Interest Factors for a One-Dollar Annuity Compounded at k Percent for n Periods: $FVIFA_{k,n} = \sum_{t=1}^{n} (1 + k)^{t-1}$ *(continued)*

Period	21%	22%	23%	24%	25%	30%	35%	40%	45%	50%
1	1.000	1.000	1.000	1.000	1.000	1.000	1.000	1.000	1.000	1.000
2	2.210	2.220	2.230	2.240	2.250	2.300	2.350	2.400	2.450	2.500
3	3.674	3.708	3.743	3.778	3.813	3.990	4.172	4.360	4.552	4.750
4	5.446	5.524	5.604	5.684	5.766	6.187	6.633	7.104	7.601	8.125
5	7.589	7.740	7.893	8.048	8.207	9.043	9.954	10.946	12.022	13.188
6	10.183	10.442	10.708	10.980	11.259	12.756	14.438	16.324	18.431	20.781
7	13.321	13.740	14.171	14.615	15.073	17.583	20.492	23.853	27.725	32.172
8	17.119	17.762	18.430	19.123	19.842	23.858	28.664	34.395	41.202	49.258
9	21.714	22.670	23.669	24.712	25.802	32.015	39.696	49.152	60.743	74.887
10	27.274	28.657	30.113	31.643	33.253	42.619	54.590	69.813	89.077	113.330
11	34.001	35.962	38.039	40.238	42.566	56.405	74.696	98.739	130.161	170.995
12	42.141	44.873	47.787	50.895	54.208	74.326	101.840	139.234	189.734	257.493
13	51.991	55.745	59.778	64.109	68.760	97.624	138.484	195.928	276.114	387.239
14	63.909	69.009	74.528	80.496	86.949	127.912	187.953	275.299	401.365	581.858
15	78.330	85.191	92.669	100.815	109.687	167.285	254.737	386.418	582.980	873.788
16	95.779	104.933	114.983	126.010	138.109	218.470	344.895	541.985	846.321	1311.681
17	116.892	129.019	142.428	157.252	173.636	285.011	466.608	759.778	1228.165	1968.522
18	142.439	158.403	176.187	195.993	218.045	371.514	630.920	1064.689	1781.838	2953.783
19	173.351	194.251	217.710	244.031	273.556	483.968	852.741	1491.563	2584.665	4431.672
20	210.755	237.986	268.783	303.598	342.945	630.157	1152.200	2089.188	3748.763	6648.508
21	256.013	291.343	331.603	377.461	429.681	820.204	1556.470	2925.862	5436.703	9973.762
22	310.775	356.438	408.871	469.052	538.101	1067.265	2102.234	4097.203	7884.215	14961.645
23	377.038	435.854	503.911	582.624	673.626	1388.443	2839.014	5737.078	11433.109	22443.469
24	457.215	532.741	620.810	723.453	843.032	1805.975	3833.667	8032.906	16579.008	33666.207
25	554.230	650.944	764.596	898.082	1054.791	2348.765	5176.445	11247.062	24040.555	50500.316
30	1445.111	1767.044	2160.459	2640.881	3227.172	8729.805	23221.258	60500.207	*	*
35	3755.814	4783.520	6090.227	7750.094	9856.746	32422.090	*	*	*	*
40	9749.141	12936.141	17153.691	22728.367	30088.621	*	*	*	*	*
45	25294.223	34970.230	48300.660	66638.937	91831.312	*	*	*	*	*
50	65617.202	94525.279	*	*	*	*	*	*	*	*

Interest Rate

* $FVIFA > 99,999$.

Table A.3 Present Value Interest Factors for One Dollar Discounted at k Percent for n Periods: $PVIF_{k,n} = \dfrac{1}{(1+k)^n}$

Period	Discount (Interest) Rate									
	1%	2%	3%	4%	5%	6%	7%	8%	9%	10%
1	.990	.980	.971	.962	.952	.943	.935	.926	.917	.909
2	.980	.961	.943	.925	.907	.890	.873	.857	.842	.826
3	.971	.942	.915	.889	.864	.840	.816	.794	.772	.751
4	.961	.924	.888	.855	.823	.792	.763	.735	.708	.683
5	.951	.906	.863	.822	.784	.747	.713	.681	.650	.621
6	.942	.888	.837	.790	.746	.705	.666	.630	.596	.564
7	.933	.871	.813	.760	.711	.665	.623	.583	.547	.513
8	.923	.853	.789	.731	.677	.627	.582	.540	.502	.467
9	.914	.837	.766	.703	.645	.592	.544	.500	.460	.424
10	.905	.820	.744	.676	.614	.558	.508	.463	.422	.386
11	.896	.804	.722	.650	.585	.527	.475	.429	.388	.350
12	.887	.789	.701	.625	.557	.497	.444	.397	.356	.319
13	.879	.773	.681	.601	.530	.469	.415	.368	.326	.290
14	.870	.758	.661	.577	.505	.442	.388	.340	.299	.263
15	.861	.743	.642	.555	.481	.417	.362	.315	.275	.239
16	.853	.728	.623	.534	.458	.394	.339	.292	.252	.218
17	.844	.714	.605	.513	.436	.371	.317	.270	.231	.198
18	.836	.700	.587	.494	.416	.350	.296	.250	.212	.180
19	.828	.686	.570	.475	.396	.331	.277	.232	.194	.164
20	.820	.673	.554	.456	.377	.312	.258	.215	.178	.149
21	.811	.660	.538	.439	.359	.294	.242	.199	.164	.135
22	.803	.647	.522	.422	.342	.278	.226	.184	.150	.123
23	.795	.634	.507	.406	.326	.262	.211	.170	.138	.112
24	.788	.622	.492	.390	.310	.247	.197	.158	.126	.102
25	.780	.610	.478	.375	.295	.233	.184	.146	.116	.092
30	.742	.552	.412	.308	.231	.174	.131	.099	.075	.057
35	.706	.500	.355	.253	.181	.130	.094	.068	.049	.036
40	.672	.453	.307	.208	.142	.097	.067	.046	.032	.022
45	.639	.410	.264	.171	.111	.073	.048	.031	.021	.014
50	.608	.372	.228	.141	.087	.054	.034	.021	.013	.009

Table A.3 Present-Value Interest Factors for One Dollar Discounted at k Percent for n Periods: $PVIF_{k,n} = \dfrac{1}{(1+k)^n}$ *(continued)*

Period	11%	12%	13%	14%	15%	16%	17%	18%	19%	20%
					Discount (Interest) Rate					
1	.901	.893	.885	.877	.870	.862	.855	.847	.840	.833
2	.812	.797	.783	.769	.756	.743	.731	.718	.706	.694
3	.731	.712	.693	.675	.658	.641	.624	.609	.593	.579
4	.659	.636	.613	.592	.572	.552	.534	.516	.499	.482
5	.593	.567	.543	.519	.497	.476	.456	.437	.419	.402
6	.535	.507	.480	.456	.432	.410	.390	.370	.352	.335
7	.482	.452	.425	.400	.376	.354	.333	.314	.296	.279
8	.434	.404	.376	.351	.327	.305	.285	.266	.249	.233
9	.391	.361	.333	.308	.284	.263	.243	.225	.209	.194
10	.352	.322	.295	.270	.247	.227	.208	.191	.176	.162
11	.317	.287	.261	.237	.215	.195	.178	.162	.148	.135
12	.286	.257	.231	.208	.187	.168	.152	.137	.124	.112
13	.258	.229	.204	.182	.163	.145	.130	.116	.104	.093
14	.232	.205	.181	.160	.141	.125	.111	.099	.088	.078
15	.209	.183	.160	.140	.123	.108	.095	.084	.074	.065
16	.188	.163	.141	.123	.107	.093	.081	.071	.062	.054
17	.170	.146	.125	.108	.093	.080	.069	.060	.052	.045
18	.153	.130	.111	.095	.081	.069	.059	.051	.044	.038
19	.138	.116	.098	.083	.070	.060	.051	.043	.037	.031
20	.124	.104	.087	.073	.061	.051	.043	.037	.031	.026
21	.112	.093	.077	.064	.053	.044	.037	.031	.026	.022
22	.101	.083	.068	.056	.046	.038	.032	.026	.022	.018
23	.091	.074	.060	.049	.040	.033	.027	.022	.018	.015
24	.082	.066	.053	.043	.035	.028	.023	.019	.015	.013
25	.074	.059	.047	.038	.030	.024	.020	.016	.013	.010
30	.044	.033	.026	.020	.015	.012	.009	.007	.005	.004
35	.026	.019	.014	.010	.008	.006	.004	.003	.002	.002
40	.015	.011	.008	.005	.004	.003	.002	.001	.001	.001
45	.009	.006	.004	.003	.002	.001	.001	.001	*	*
50	.005	.003	.002	.001	.001	.001	*	*	*	*

*$PVIF = .000$ when rounded to three decimal places.

Table A.3 Present-Value Interest Factors for One Dollar Discounted at k Percent for n Periods: $PVIF_{k,n} = \dfrac{1}{(1+k)^n}$ (continued)

				Discount (Interest) Rate						
Period	21%	22%	23%	24%	25%	30%	35%	40%	45%	50%
1	.826	.820	.813	.806	.800	.769	.741	.714	.690	.667
2	.683	.672	.661	.650	.640	.592	.549	.510	.476	.444
3	.564	.551	.537	.524	.512	.455	.406	.364	.328	.296
4	.467	.451	.437	.423	.410	.350	.301	.260	.226	.198
5	.386	.370	.355	.341	.328	.269	.223	.186	.156	.132
6	.319	.303	.289	.275	.262	.207	.165	.133	.108	.088
7	.263	.249	.235	.222	.210	.159	.122	.095	.074	.059
8	.218	.204	.191	.179	.168	.123	.091	.068	.051	.039
9	.180	.167	.155	.144	.134	.094	.067	.048	.035	.026
10	.149	.137	.126	.116	.107	.073	.050	.035	.024	.017
11	.123	.112	.103	.094	.086	.056	.037	.025	.017	.012
12	.102	.092	.083	.076	.069	.043	.027	.018	.012	.008
13	.084	.075	.068	.061	.055	.033	.020	.013	.008	.005
14	.069	.062	.055	.049	.044	.025	.015	.009	.006	.003
15	.057	.051	.045	.040	.035	.020	.011	.006	.004	.002
16	.047	.042	.036	.032	.028	.015	.008	.005	.003	.002
17	.039	.034	.030	.026	.023	.012	.006	.003	.002	.001
18	.032	.028	.024	.021	.018	.009	.005	.002	.001	.001
19	.027	.023	.020	.017	.014	.007	.003	.002	.001	*
20	.022	.019	.016	.014	.012	.005	.002	.001	.001	*
21	.018	.015	.013	.011	.009	.004	.002	.001	*	*
22	.015	.013	.011	.009	.007	.003	.001	.001	*	*
23	.012	.010	.009	.007	.006	.002	.001	*	*	*
24	.010	.008	.007	.006	.005	.002	.001	*	*	*
25	.009	.007	.006	.005	.004	.001	.001	*	*	*
30	.003	.003	.002	.002	.001	*	*	*	*	*
35	.001	.001	.001	.001	*	*	*	*	*	*
40	*	*	*	*	*	*	*	*	*	*
45	*	*	*	*	*	*	*	*	*	*
50	*	*	*	*	*	*	*	*	*	*

* PVIF = .000 when rounded to three decimal places.

Table A.4 Present-Value Interest Factors for a One-Dollar Annuity Discounted at k Percent for n Periods: $PVIFA_{k,n} = \sum_{t=1}^{n} \frac{1}{(1+k)^t}$

Period	1%	2%	3%	4%	5%	6%	7%	8%	9%	10%
1	.990	.980	.971	.962	.952	.943	.935	.926	.917	.909
2	1.970	1.942	1.913	1.886	1.859	1.833	1.808	1.783	1.759	1.736
3	2.941	2.884	2.829	2.775	2.723	2.673	2.624	2.577	2.531	2.487
4	3.902	3.808	3.717	3.630	3.546	3.465	3.387	3.312	3.240	3.170
5	4.853	4.713	4.580	4.452	4.329	4.212	4.100	3.993	3.890	3.791
6	5.795	5.601	5.417	5.242	5.076	4.917	4.767	4.623	4.486	4.355
7	6.728	6.472	6.230	6.002	5.786	5.582	5.389	5.206	5.033	4.868
8	7.652	7.326	7.020	6.733	6.463	6.210	5.971	5.747	5.535	5.335
9	8.566	8.162	7.786	7.435	7.108	6.802	6.515	6.247	5.995	5.759
10	9.471	8.983	8.530	8.111	7.722	7.360	7.024	6.710	6.418	6.145
11	10.368	9.787	9.253	8.760	8.306	7.887	7.499	7.139	6.805	6.495
12	11.255	10.575	9.954	9.385	8.863	8.384	7.943	7.536	7.161	6.814
13	12.134	11.348	10.635	9.986	9.394	8.853	8.358	7.904	7.487	7.103
14	13.004	12.106	11.296	10.563	9.899	9.295	8.746	8.244	7.786	7.367
15	13.865	12.849	11.938	11.118	10.380	9.712	9.108	8.560	8.061	7.606
16	14.718	13.578	12.561	11.652	10.838	10.106	9.447	8.851	8.313	7.824
17	15.562	14.292	13.166	12.166	11.274	10.477	9.763	9.122	8.544	8.022
18	16.398	14.992	13.754	12.659	11.690	10.828	10.059	9.372	8.756	8.201
19	17.226	15.679	14.324	13.134	12.085	11.158	10.336	9.604	8.950	8.365
20	18.046	16.352	14.878	13.590	12.462	11.470	10.594	9.818	9.129	8.514
21	18.857	17.011	15.415	14.029	12.821	11.764	10.836	10.017	9.292	8.649
22	19.661	17.658	15.937	14.451	13.163	12.042	11.061	10.201	9.442	8.772
23	20.456	18.292	16.444	14.857	13.489	12.303	11.272	10.371	9.580	8.883
24	21.244	18.914	16.936	15.247	13.799	12.550	11.469	10.529	9.707	8.985
25	22.023	19.524	17.413	15.622	14.094	12.783	11.654	10.675	9.823	9.077
30	25.808	22.397	19.601	17.292	15.373	13.765	12.409	11.258	10.274	9.427
35	29.409	24.999	21.487	18.665	16.374	14.498	12.948	11.655	10.567	9.644
40	32.835	27.356	23.115	19.793	17.159	15.046	13.332	11.925	10.757	9.779
45	36.095	29.490	24.519	20.720	17.774	15.456	13.606	12.108	10.881	9.863
50	39.197	31.424	25.730	21.482	18.256	15.762	13.801	12.234	10.962	9.915

Discount (Interest) Rate

Table A.4 Present-Value Interest Factors for a One-Dollar Annuity Discounted at k Percent for n Periods: $PVIFA_{k,n} = \sum_{t=1}^{n} \dfrac{1}{(1+k)^t}$ *(continued)*

Discount (Interest) Rate

Period	11%	12%	13%	14%	15%	16%	17%	18%	19%	20%
1	.901	.893	.885	.877	.870	.862	.855	.847	.840	.833
2	1.713	1.690	1.668	1.647	1.626	1.605	1.585	1.566	1.547	1.528
3	2.444	2.402	2.361	2.322	2.283	2.246	2.210	2.174	2.140	2.106
4	3.102	3.037	2.974	2.914	2.855	2.798	2.743	2.690	2.639	2.589
5	3.696	3.605	3.517	3.433	3.352	3.274	3.199	3.127	3.058	2.991
6	4.231	4.111	3.998	3.889	3.784	3.685	3.589	3.498	3.410	3.326
7	4.712	4.564	4.423	4.288	4.160	4.039	3.922	3.812	3.706	3.605
8	5.146	4.968	4.799	4.639	4.487	4.344	4.207	4.078	3.954	3.837
9	5.537	5.328	5.132	4.946	4.772	4.607	4.451	4.303	4.163	4.031
10	5.889	5.650	5.426	5.216	5.019	4.833	4.659	4.494	4.339	4.192
11	6.207	5.938	5.687	5.453	5.234	5.029	4.836	4.656	4.487	4.327
12	6.492	6.194	5.918	5.660	5.421	5.197	4.988	4.793	4.611	4.439
13	6.750	6.424	6.122	5.842	5.583	5.342	5.118	4.910	4.715	4.533
14	6.982	6.628	6.303	6.002	5.724	5.468	5.229	5.008	4.802	4.611
15	7.191	6.811	6.462	6.142	5.847	5.575	5.324	5.092	4.876	4.675
16	7.379	6.974	6.604	6.265	5.954	5.669	5.405	5.162	4.938	4.730
17	7.549	7.120	6.729	6.373	6.047	5.749	5.475	5.222	4.990	4.775
18	7.702	7.250	6.840	6.467	6.128	5.818	5.534	5.273	5.033	4.812
19	7.839	7.366	6.938	6.550	6.198	5.877	5.585	5.316	5.070	4.843
20	7.963	7.469	7.025	6.623	6.259	5.929	5.628	5.353	5.101	4.870
21	8.075	7.562	7.102	6.687	6.312	5.973	5.665	5.384	5.127	4.891
22	8.176	7.645	7.170	6.743	6.359	6.011	5.696	5.410	5.149	4.909
23	8.266	7.718	7.230	6.792	6.399	6.044	5.723	5.432	5.167	4.925
24	8.348	7.784	7.283	6.835	6.434	6.073	5.747	5.451	5.182	4.937
25	8.422	7.843	7.330	6.873	6.464	6.097	5.766	5.467	5.195	4.948
30	8.694	8.055	7.496	7.003	6.566	6.177	5.829	5.517	5.235	4.979
35	8.855	8.176	7.586	7.070	6.617	6.215	5.858	5.539	5.251	4.992
40	8.951	8.244	7.634	7.105	6.642	6.233	5.871	5.548	5.258	4.997
45	9.008	8.283	7.661	7.123	6.654	6.242	5.877	5.552	5.261	4.999
50	9.042	8.305	7.675	7.133	6.661	6.246	5.880	5.554	5.262	4.999

Table A.4 Present-Value Interest Factors for a One-Dollar Annuity Discounted at k Percent for n Periods: $PVIFA_{k,n} = \sum\limits_{t=1}^{n} \dfrac{1}{(1+k)^t}$ (continued)

| Period | \multicolumn{10}{c}{Discount (Interest) Rate} |
	21%	22%	23%	24%	25%	30%	35%	40%	45%	50%
1	.826	.820	.813	.806	.800	.769	.741	.714	.690	.667
2	1.509	1.492	1.474	1.457	1.440	1.361	1.289	1.224	1.165	1.111
3	2.074	2.042	2.011	1.981	1.952	1.816	1.696	1.589	1.493	1.407
4	2.540	2.494	2.448	2.404	2.362	2.166	1.997	1.849	1.720	1.605
5	2.926	2.864	2.803	2.745	2.689	2.436	2.220	2.035	1.876	1.737
6	3.245	3.167	3.092	3.020	2.951	2.643	2.385	2.168	1.983	1.824
7	3.508	3.416	3.327	3.242	3.161	2.802	2.508	2.263	2.057	1.883
8	3.726	3.619	3.518	3.421	3.329	2.925	2.598	2.331	2.109	1.922
9	3.905	3.786	3.673	3.566	3.463	3.019	2.665	2.379	2.144	1.948
10	4.054	3.923	3.799	3.682	3.570	3.092	2.715	2.414	2.168	1.965
11	4.177	4.035	3.902	3.776	3.656	3.147	2.752	2.438	2.185	1.977
12	4.278	4.127	3.985	3.851	3.725	3.190	2.779	2.456	2.196	1.985
13	4.362	4.203	4.053	3.912	3.780	3.223	2.799	2.469	2.204	1.990
14	4.432	4.265	4.108	3.962	3.824	3.249	2.814	2.477	2.210	1.993
15	4.489	4.315	4.153	4.001	3.859	3.268	2.825	2.484	2.214	1.995
16	4.536	4.357	4.189	4.033	3.887	3.283	2.834	2.489	2.216	1.997
17	4.576	4.391	4.219	4.059	3.910	3.295	2.840	2.492	2.218	1.998
18	4.608	4.419	4.243	4.080	3.928	3.304	2.844	2.494	2.219	1.999
19	4.635	4.442	4.263	4.097	3.942	3.311	2.848	2.496	2.220	1.999
20	4.657	4.460	4.279	4.110	3.954	3.316	2.850	2.497	2.221	1.999
21	4.675	4.476	4.292	4.121	3.963	3.320	2.852	2.498	2.221	2.000
22	4.690	4.488	4.302	4.130	3.970	3.323	2.853	2.498	2.222	2.000
23	4.703	4.499	4.311	4.137	3.976	3.325	2.854	2.499	2.222	2.000
24	4.713	4.507	4.318	4.143	3.981	3.327	2.855	2.499	2.222	2.000
25	4.721	4.514	4.323	4.147	3.985	3.329	2.856	2.499	2.222	2.000
30	4.746	4.534	4.339	4.160	3.995	3.332	2.857	2.500	2.222	2.000
35	4.756	4.541	4.345	4.164	3.998	3.333	2.857	2.500	2.222	2.000
40	4.760	4.544	4.347	4.166	3.999	3.333	2.857	2.500	2.222	2.000
45	4.761	4.545	4.347	4.166	4.000	3.333	2.857	2.500	2.222	2.000
50	4.762	4.545	4.348	4.167	4.000	3.333	2.857	2.500	2.222	2.000

Index